STATISTICAL HANDBOOK ON RACIAL GROUPS IN THE UNITED STATES

by
Tim B. Heaton
Bruce A. Chadwick
and
Cardell K. Jacobson

Oryx Press
2000

The rare Arabian Oryx is believed to have inspired the myth of the unicorn. This desert antelope became virtually extinct in the early 1960s. At that time, several groups of international conservationists arranged to have nine animals sent to the Phoenix Zoo to be the nucleus of a captive breeding herd. Today, the Oryx population is over 1,000, and over 500 have been returned to the Middle East.

© 2000 by The Oryx Press
4041 North Central at Indian School Road
Phoenix, Arizona 85012-3397

Published simultaneously in Canada
Printed and bound in the United States of America

∞ The paper used in this publication meets the minimum requirements of American National Standard for Information Science—Permanence of Paper for Printed Library Materials, ANSI Z39.48, 1984.

Library of Congress Cataloging-in-Publication Data

Heaton, Tim B.
  Statistical handbook on racial groups in the United States / by Tim B. Heaton, Bruce A. Chadwick, and Cardell K. Jacobson.
    p. cm.
  Includes bibliographical references and index.
  ISBN 1-57356-266-1 (alk. paper)
  1. Ethnology—United States—Statistics. 2. United States—Population—Statistics. I. Chadwick, Bruce, A. II. Jacobson, Cardell K., 1941– III. Title.
  E184.A1 H417 2000
  305.8'00973'021—dc21   00-028477
                                                                 CIP

Contents

List of Tables and Figures

G.   RELIGION AND RELIGIOSITY

H.   CRIME AND DELINQUENCY

Preface

Racial and ethnic diversity has been a salient feature of American society through most of its history. Today, we are a racially conscious society, and one's racial or ethnic membership is a significant part of one's identity. As Hoffman (1994:4) has noted, "Our society is obsessed with race and confused by it." We often treat race as a polar phenomenon; you are either this or that. But by so doing, we ignore the tremendous, even overwhelming, similarities that the various racial and ethnic groups share. Indeed, Hoffman calculates that race accounts for a minuscule one percent (.012) of all human genetic material. In this volume we use common parlance in our designation of racial and ethnic groups. That is, we use the traditional groupings designated by the Census Bureau and other researchers. In so doing, however, we are aware that we are ignoring the overwhelming similarities of the various groups and emphasizing the differences.

Though we use the concepts of race and ethnicity throughout this book, we also recognize that use of the concept "race" has a long, tortured, and distorted history. Johann Blumenbach is generally credited for having created the modern, and pejorative use of the term "race" (Feagin and Feagin, 1996; Gould, 1994). In early Europe the concept "race" had been used to describe what we would characterize today as kinship groups. In the late 18th century, however, Blumenbach assumed that "the most beautiful race of men" were those from the Caucasus mountains of eastern Europe. He also (falsely) assumed that humans were first created in this area. He used the famous taxonomist Linnaeus's four categories, and added a fifth. But he also created a hierarchical classification of the human groups that continued through much of the next two centuries. Unfortunately, the classification system also provided justification for the racial and ethnic oppression that occurred during colonization and the economic expansion of that era. In more recent decades, social scientists have emphasized the cultural aspects of groups, not biological ones.

Since races share almost all of the same genetic material, race is not really a biological phenomenon, but a social one; and race is defined socially, not genetically or biologically. The very concepts of race and ethnic groups are what social scientists refer to as social constructions. Consider the case of someone who has one grandparent who is "Black." Genetically, they would be considered to be "White," but socially, they would probably be considered "Black." The number of intergroup marriages in the United States has increased in recent decades, with an attendant number of people who have multiple-group identities. Indeed, the years 2000 census is the first census that allows individuals to indicate that they consider themselves to be "multiracial."

One irony of allowing people to identify themselves as multiracial is that all "races" are an accumulation of intermarriage between a variety of groups. The continent of Africa "discovered" by Europeans was made up of diverse peoples of different colors, cultures, and what would be considered "races" by our current definitions. A great deal of variety existed among Africans, or "Blacks" who were brought to this country. The same is true of Hispanics, Asians, Whites, and the Native Americans who possessed this land before European invasion. In this sense, pure races do not exist. The groups we observe today are an admixture of other groups.

Nevertheless, the social constructions of race are powerful, and have real consequences. Individuals identify with a group, and with each other. Racial or ethnic identity gives meaning to people's lives. It influences much that we do in life, with whom we associate, even life outcomes. Since we rely on data that have already been collected by the government or other researchers who ask people their racial or ethnic identity, we have used these conventional groupings in compiling this volume.

Demographic trends are reshaping the racial and ethnic mix of the nation. Immigration has by far the largest impact, but differences in family size, mortality, and intergroup marriage also play important roles. As a result of these trends, the Hispanic and Asian populations will more than double their percentages overall in the U.S. population over the next 50 years. The Black population will also increase, but to a smaller degree, and the White, non-Hispanic population will shrink in relative size. Because the racial and ethnic composition of our society is changing, it is all the more important to understand racial and ethnic differences.

This volume documents important differences among groups, but also points to major similarities among them. Examples of racial difference are found in geographic segregation, political representation and participation, military service, beliefs about racial inequality, religious participation and belief, sexual experience among adolescents, contraceptive use, perceptions of health and access to health care, arrest rates, types of classes taken in high school, college enrollment, marriage rates, ties with extended family, and income. Examples of similarity include sex ratios, self-characterization as liberal or conservative, adolescents who have a romantic relationship, opposition to pornography, marital satisfaction, time spent with children, employment status, and the importance of work. While similarities give hope for common ground, the differences underscore the importance of racial categories in defining social arrangements in the United States. Unfortunately, many of the differences indicate that minorities, Blacks and Hispanics in particular, do not enjoy the same quality of life as Whites. Some of the differences can be explained by socioeconomic disadvantage, but differences in history, immigration, geographic distribution, and cultural heritage are also important. Nevertheless, the array of differences and similarities negate any facile conclusions regarding the characterization of any particular group. We hope that the detailed content of this volume will aid in understanding the role of racial identity in American society.

Acknowledgments

The availability of the broad range of information represented in this volume is only possible because of the countless hours of work in government agencies and research institutions. We are greatly indebted to so many who have devoted their careers to providing data that helps us understand the society in which we live. We have relied heavily on and express our thanks to the following sources:

The National Survey of Families and Households. For details see Sweet, J.A., Bumpass, L.L., and Call, V. R. A. (1988). The design and content of the National Survey of Families and Households (Working Paper NSFH-1). Madison: University of Wisconsin, Center for Demography and Ecology.

The National Longitudinal Study of Adolescent Health. The Add Health project is designed by J. Richard Udry (PI) and Peter Bearman, and funded by grant P01-HD31921 from the National Institute of Child Health and Human Development to the Carolina Population Center, University of North Carolina at Chapel Hill, with cooperative funding participation by the National Cancer Institute; the National Institute of Alcohol Abuse and Alcoholism; the National Institute on Deafness and Other Communication Disorders; the National Institute of Drug Abuse; the National Institute of General Medical Sciences; the National Institute of Mental Health; the National Institute of Nursing Research; the Office of AIDS Research, National Institutes of Health (NIH); the Office of Behavioral and Social Science Research, NIH; the Office of the Director, NIH; the Office of Research on Women's Health, NIH; the Office of Population Affairs, Department of Health and Human Services (HHS); the National Center for Health Statistics; Centers for Disease Control and Prevention; the Office of Minority Health, Centers for Disease Control and Prevention, HHS; the Office of Minority Health, Office of the Assistant Secretary for Health, HHS; the Office of the Assistant Secretary for Planning and Evaluation, HHS; and the National Science Foundation. These data are not available from the authors. Persons interested in obtaining data files from the *National Longitudinal Study of Adolescent Health* should contact Jo Jones, Carolina Population Center, 123 West Franklin Street, Chapel Hill, NC 27516-3997 (email: jo_jones@unc.edu).

The National Survey of Family Growth. See Abma, J; Chandra, A; Mosher, W; Peterson L. Fertility, family planning and women's health; New data from the 1995 National Survey of Family Growth, National Center for Health Statistics. Vital Health Stat 23(19). 1997.

The *General Social Survey.* Davis, James Allan and Smith, Tom W.: General Social Surveys, 1972–98. [machine-readable data file]. Principal Investigator, James A. Davis; Director and Co-Principal Investigator, Tom W. Smith; Co-Principal Investigator, Peter V. Marsden, NORC ed. Chicago: National Opinion Research Center, producer, 1998; Storrs, CT: The Roper Center for Public Opinion Research, University of Connecticut, distributor. 1 data file (38,116 logical records) and 1 codebook (1479 pp).

Statistical Abstracts of the United States: 1998. U.S. Bureau of the Census, Washington, DC, 1998.

Gallup Poll Monthly, various months and years.

Current Population Surveys, March 1962–1998 [machine readable data files]/conducted by the Bureau of the Census for the Bureau of Labor Statistics. Washington, DC: Bureau of the Census [producer and distributor], 1962–1998. Santa Monica, CA: Unicon Research Corporation [producer and distributor of CPS Utilities], 1999.

U.S. Department of Education. National Center for Education Statistics. *Digest of Educational Statistics,* 1998, NCES 1999-036, by Thomas D. Snyder. Produc-

tions Manager, Charlene M. Hoffman. Program Analyst, Claire M. Geddes. Washington, DC, 1999.

Unified Crime Reports for the United States, 1999. Washington, DC, Federal Bureau of Investigation.

References

Feagin, Joe R., and Clariece Booher Feagin. 1996. *Racial and Ethnic Relations, fifth ed.* Upper Saddle River, NJ: Prentice Hall.
Gould, Stephen Jay. 1994. "The Geometer of Race." *Discover* 15:65-69.
Hoffman, Paul. 1994. "The Science of Race." *Discover* 15:4.

A. Demographic Context

The racial and ethnic composition of the United States has shifted as a result of immigration and differences in births and deaths. As a result of these demographic trends, a growing percentage of the population will belong to one of the various minority groups. In this section, we present data about size, growth, and projections of minority groups. We also document how demographic structure (age and sex composition) varies across groups. The next section considers geographic distribution, and geographic mobility. Finally, our attention turns to immigration, a major source of growth for some groups. Differences in rates of fertility and mortality are examined in subsequent sections.

A1. SIZE, GROWTH, AND PROJECTIONS

At the dawn of the new millennium, a majority of the population (72%) is White, Non-Hispanic, but this figure is projected to decline to a bare majority in the next 50 years (A1.1). The major gains will be among those of Hispanic origin, which will increase from 11.4 percent of the population in 2000 to about 25 percent in the year 2050. The Asian population will more than double as a percentage of the total population from 3.9 percent to 8.2 percent. Blacks will increase only slightly from 12.2 to 13.6 percent and Native Americans will remain less than 1 percent of the total population (A1.2).

The major source of growth among groups that are declining as a percentage (Non-Hispanic Whites) or are remaining relatively stable (Blacks and Native Americans) is natural increase. Natural increase occurs when births exceed deaths. In contrast, the major source of growth among Asians, Pacific Islanders, and Hispanics is immigration (A1.3).

A2. AGE AND SEX

Demographic structure is defined as the age and sex composition of a population. Each of the major minority groups is, on average, younger than the White, Non-Hispanic majority (A2.1). Detailed breakdown (A2.2) show that there are more children in each of the minority groups than in the White majority. Another way to portray age structure is in terms of dependency ratios, defined as the number of children (under 18) and elderly (65 and over) divided by those aged 18-64. This ratio compares the population that is generally working and economically independent with the population that generally needs care and economic support. The ratio is an indicator of the extent to which age structure places economic burden on the working age population. The overall ratios are similar across groups, but somewhat lower among Asian and Pacific Islanders (A2.3). But the elderly ratio is higher among Whites relative to other groups. Each group is expected to age over the next 25 years.

The population is roughly evenly divided by sex, and this mix is not expected to change greatly over the next 25 years (A2.4). Blacks and Asians have somewhat unbalanced ratios compared to other groups.

A3. GEOGRAPHIC DISTRIBUTION AND MOBILITY

Minority groups are concentrated in different geographic areas (A3.1). While Blacks are concentrated in the South (52%), most other groups are concentrated in the West, which contains 47.6 percent of Native Americans, 55.7 percent of Asians and Pacific Islanders, and 45.2 percent of Hispanics. Concentrations are even more evident in the distribution by states (A3.2). The largest concentrations of Hispanics are found in California, Texas, Florida, New York, and Illinois, each with more than one million. Mexicans are the largest group within the Hispanic category and are concentrated in the Southwest and California. The second largest group, Puerto Ricans, are concentrated in the Northeast, while Cubans are more likely to live in the South. Several states contain more than one million Blacks. One of these is California; the others are either Southern or contain large Northern cities where Blacks migrated to take advantage of industrial growth. Only California has more than one million Asians and Pacific Islanders. With the exceptions of Asian Indians and Pakistanis, Asians are concentrated on the West Coast. Native Americans are concentrated in the Southwest and Oklahoma.

Several of the nation's largest cities now have substantial minority populations (A3.4 and A3.5). The New York metropolitan area has nearly 20 million inhabitants, and 42 percent belong to minority groups. Los Angeles is not far behind in total population, of which 58 percent are racial minorities. Some cities over 100,000 have large majorities that are either Black (e.g., Gary, Indiana which is 80% Black) or Hispanic (eg., Brownsville, Texas with 90% Hispanic). Overall, Blacks and other racial minorities are overrepresented in large central cities and underrepresented in suburbs (A3.6).

A4. IMMIGRATION AND ANCESTRY

The United States is known as a nation of immigrants. High rates of immigration combined with intermarriage and periods of high mortality among the native population have created a nation with largely immigrant heritage. Four major waves of immigration have populated the country (Martin and Midgley, 1999). The first wave arrived from England and Northern Europe before 1820. The second wave came between 1820 and 1860. Many of these immigrants were from Germany, Britain, and Ireland. The third wave arrived between 1880 and 1914, coming from Southern and Eastern Europe. The fourth wave began after 1965 and Asians and Latin Americans predominated in this group (A4.1 through A4.4). Although immigration is affected by economic and political conditions around the globe, U.S. immigration policy plays a major role in the size and composition of immigrant streams. In 1882, for the first time, the federal government prohibited immigrants from a particular country, China. Since then a variety of different restrictions have controlled the flow of people from different countries (Martin and Midgley, 1999). An estimated five million undocumented immigrants are in this country currently (A4.5), with a majority living in border states or New York. The major source of these immigrants is Mexico (A4.6).

Because of these historical changes in immigration, residents of the United States have a very diverse mix of ancestries (A4.7). About 14 percent of the population speaks a language other than English. Spanish is the most common foreign language spoken (A4.8).

Finally, we note that Blacks are less likely to migrate from city to city or across state boundaries than Whites or other racial groups (A4.9.) Other minorities, on the other hand, are more mobile.

REFERENCE:

Martin, Philip and Elizabeth Midgley. 1999. "Immigration to the United States." *Population Bulletin* 54 no. 2.

A1. SIZE, GROWTH, AND PROJECTIONS

A1.1. Resident Population, by Hispanic Origin, Status, and Projections: 1980 to 2050

[In thousands, except as indicated. As of July, except as indicated.These data are consistent with the 1980 and 1990 decennial enumerations and have been modified from the official census counts.]

[Minus sign (-) indicates decrease]

YEAR	Total	Hispanic origin \1	White	Black	American Indian, Eskimo, Aleut	Asian, Pacific Islander
					NOT OF HISPANIC ORIGIN	
1980 (April) \2	226,546	14,609	180,906	26,142	1,326	3,563
1980	227,225	14,869	181,140	26,215	1,336	3,665
1981	229,466	15,560	181,974	26,532	1,377	4,022
1982	231,664	16,240	182,782	26,856	1,420	4,367
1983	233,792	16,935	183,561	27,159	1,466	4,671
1984	235,825	17,640	184,243	27,444	1,512	4,986
1985	237,924	18,368	184,945	27,738	1,558	5,315
1986	240,133	19,154	185,678	28,040	1,606	5,655
1987	242,289	19,946	186,353	28,351	1,654	5,985
1988	244,499	20,786	187,012	28,669	1,703	6,329
1989	246,819	21,648	187,713	29,005	1,755	6,698
1990 (April) \3	248,765	22,372	188,307	29,299	1,796	6,992
1990	249,440	22,575	188,581	29,397	1,802	7,084
1991	252,124	23,432	189,590	29,849	1,829	7,425
1992	255,002	24,361	190,657	30,333	1,856	7,794
1993	257,753	25,334	191,606	30,778	1,882	8,153
1994	260,292	26,302	192,426	31,189	1,906	8,469
1995	262,761	27,274	193,198	31,566	1,929	8,794
1996	265,179	28,305	193,875	31,927	1,952	9,120
1997	267,636	29,348	194,571	32,298	1,976	9,443
PROJECTIONS						
Lowest series:						
1998	268,396	29,115	195,037	32,647	1,999	9,598
1999	269,861	29,757	195,307	32,962	2,020	9,815
2000	271,237	30,393	195,505	33,267	2,041	10,030
2005	276,990	33,527	195,589	34,652	2,145	11,077
2010	281,468	36,652	194,628	35,856	2,243	12,088
2015	285,472	39,927	193,150	36,956	2,337	13,102
2020	288,807	43,287	191,047	37,913	2,424	14,136
2030	291,070	49,834	183,295	39,202	2,573	16,166
2040	287,685	56,104	171,054	39,841	2,695	17,991
2050	282,524	62,230	157,701	40,118	2,793	19,683
Middle series:						
1998	270,002	29,566	195,786	32,789	2,005	9,856
1999	272,330	30,461	196,441	33,180	2,029	10,219
2000	274,634	31,366	197,061	33,568	2,054	10,584
2005	285,981	36,057	199,802	35,485	2,183	12,454
2010	297,716	41,139	202,390	37,466	2,320	14,402
2015	310,134	46,705	205,019	39,512	2,461	16,437
2020	322,742	52,652	207,393	41,538	2,601	18,557
2030	346,899	65,570	209,998	45,448	2,891	22,993
2040	369,980	80,164	209,621	49,379	3,203	27,614
2050	393,931	96,508	207,901	53,555	3,534	32,432
Highest series:						
1998	271,647	30,019	196,521	32,971	2,010	10,127
1999	274,865	31,172	197,556	33,457	2,038	10,642
2000	278,129	32,350	198,594	33,952	2,066	11,166
2005	295,318	38,648	203,949	36,589	2,218	13,914

A1.1. Resident Population, by Hispanic Origin, Status, and Projections: 1980 to 2050 *(continued)*

YEAR	Total	Hispanic origin \1	NOT OF HISPANIC ORIGIN			
			White	Black	American Indian, Eskimo, Aleut	Asian, Pacific Islander
2010	314,571	45,760	209,963	39,572	2,391	16,885
2015	335,597	53,686	216,482	42,800	2,575	20,055
2020	357,702	62,279	223,082	46,183	2,765	23,392
2030	405,089	81,803	235,898	53,604	3,192	30,593
2040	458,444	105,274	248,715	62,132	3,703	38,620
2050	518,903	133,106	262,140	71,863	4,295	47,498
PERCENT DISTRIBUTION						
Lowest series:						
1998	100.0	10.8	72.7	12.2	0.7	3.6
1999	100.0	11.0	72.4	12.2	0.7	3.6
2000	100.0	11.2	72.1	12.3	0.8	3.7
2005	100.0	12.1	70.6	12.5	0.8	4.0
2010	100.0	13.0	69.1	12.7	0.8	4.3
2020	100.0	15.0	66.2	13.1	0.8	4.9
2030	100.0	17.1	63.0	13.5	0.9	5.6
2040	100.0	19.5	59.5	13.8	0.9	6.3
2050	100.0	22.0	55.8	14.2	1.0	7.0
Middle series:						
1998	100.0	11.0	72.5	12.1	0.7	3.7
1999	100.0	11.2	72.1	12.2	0.7	3.8
2000	100.0	11.4	71.8	12.2	0.7	3.9
2005	100.0	12.6	69.9	12.4	0.8	4.4
2010	100.0	13.8	68.0	12.6	0.8	4.8
2020	100.0	16.3	64.3	12.9	0.8	5.7
2030	100.0	18.9	60.5	13.1	0.8	6.6
2040	100.0	21.7	56.7	13.3	0.9	7.5
2050	100.0	24.5	52.8	13.6	0.9	8.2
Highest series:						
1998	100.0	11.1	72.3	12.1	0.7	3.7
1999	100.0	11.3	71.9	12.2	0.7	3.9
2000	100.0	11.6	71.4	12.2	0.7	4.0
2005	100.0	13.1	69.1	12.4	0.8	4.7
2010	100.0	14.5	66.7	12.6	0.8	5.4
2020	100.0	17.4	62.4	12.9	0.8	6.5
2030	100.0	20.2	58.2	13.2	0.8	7.6
2040	100.0	23.0	54.3	13.6	0.8	8.4
2050	100.0	25.7	50.5	13.8	0.8	9.2
PERCENT CHANGE						
(middle series)						
2000-2010	8.4	31.2	2.7	11.6	12.9	36.1
2010-2020	8.4	28.0	2.5	10.9	12.1	28.9
2020-2030	7.5	24.5	1.3	9.4	11.1	23.9
2030-2040	6.7	22.3	-0.2	8.6	10.8	20.1
2040-2050	6.5	20.4	-0.8	8.5	10.3	17.4

Notes:
\1 Persons of Hispanic origin may be of any race.
\2 Total population count has been revised since the 1980 census publications. Numbers by age, race, Hispanic origin, and sex have not been revised.
\3 The April 1, 1990, census count (248,765,170) includes count resolution corrections processed through August 1997, and does not include adjustments for census coverage errors except for adjustments estimated for the 1995 Census Test in Oakland, California; Patterson, New Jersey; and six Louisiana parishes. These adjustments amounted to a total of 55,297 persons.

Source: No. 19, U.S. Bureau of the Census, *Statistical Abstract of the United States: 1998.* Washington, DC, 1999.

A1.2. Projections of Percent of the Population, by Racial and Ethnic Groups, 2000 and 2050

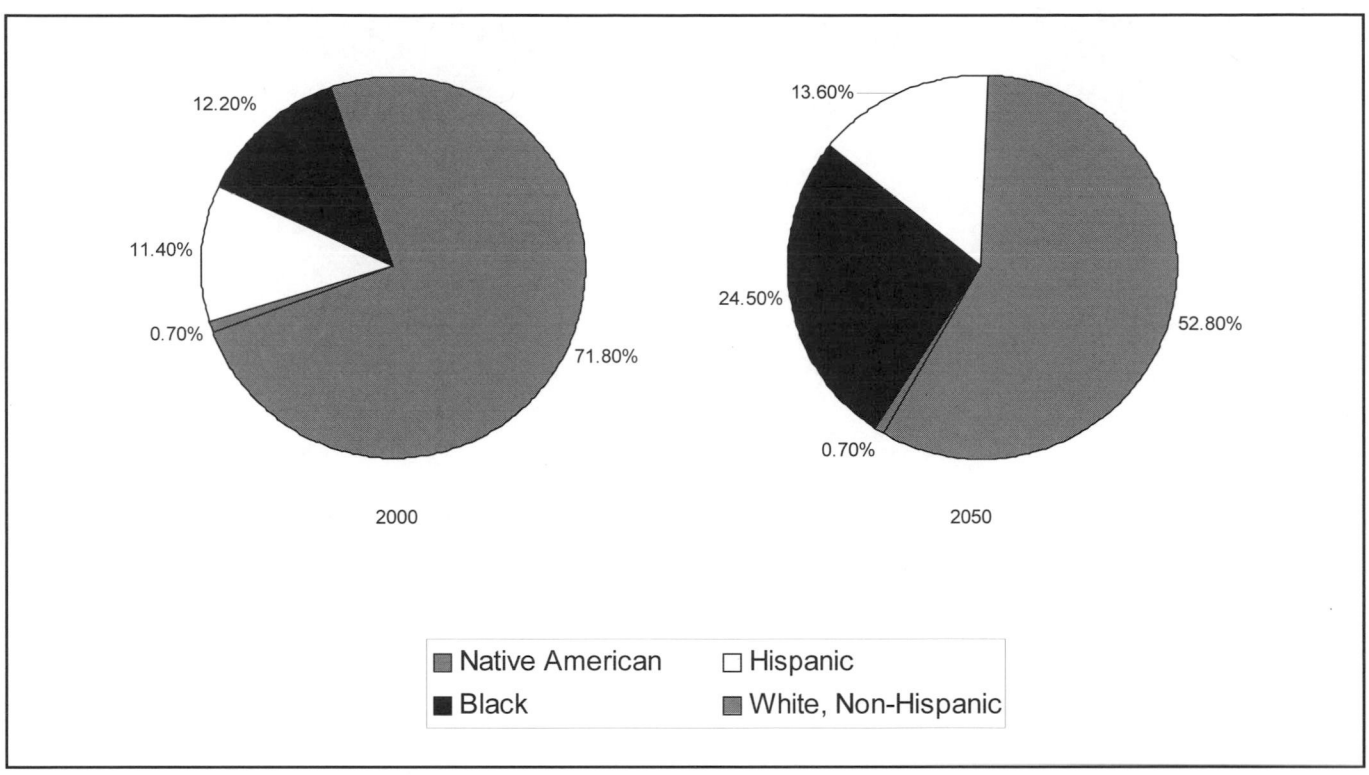

2000

2050

Native American ▢ Hispanic

Black ▢ White, Non-Hispanic

Source: No. 18, U.S. Bureau of the Census, *Statistical Abstract of the United States: 1998.* Washington, DC, 1999.

A1.3. Components of Population Change, by Race and Hispanic Origin, and Projections:1980 to 2050

[The estimates prior to 1990 are consistent with the original census count of 248,709,873. Starting with 1990, the April 1, 1990, census count (248,765,170) includes count resolution corrections processed through August 1997, and does not include adjustments for census coverage errors except for adjustments estimated for the 1995 Census Test in Oakland, California; Patterson, New Jersey; and six Louisiana parishes. These adjustments amounted to a total of 55,297 persons. Minus sign (–) indicates net outmigration.]

YEAR	Population at start of period (1,000)	Net increase \1 Total (1,000)	Net increase \1 Percent \2	Natural increase Births (1,000)	Natural increase Deaths (1,000)	Net migration \3 (1,000)	RATE PER 1,000 MIDYEAR POPULATION Net growth rate \1	Total	Natural increase Birth rate	Natural increase Death rate	Net migration rate \3
WHITE											
1980 \4	194,713	1,270	0.7	2,203	1,277	429	8.6	6.3	15.0	8.7	2.9
1981	195,983	1,408	0.7	2,909	1,731	350	7.2	6.0	14.8	8.8	1.8
1982	197,391	1,395	0.7	2,942	1,729	308	7.0	6.1	14.9	8.7	1.6
1983	198,786	1,325	0.7	2,904	1,766	319	6.6	5.7	14.6	8.9	1.6
1984	200,111	1,308	0.7	2,924	1,782	306	6.5	5.7	14.6	8.9	1.5
1985	201,419	1,378	0.7	2,991	1,819	354	6.8	5.8	14.8	9.0	1.8
1986	202,798	1,347	0.7	2,970	1,831	363	6.6	5.6	14.6	9.0	1.8
1987	204,144	1,355	0.7	2,992	1,843	370	6.6	5.6	14.6	9.0	1.8
1988	205,500	1,375	0.7	3,046	1,877	380	6.4	5.7	14.8	9.1	1.8
1989	206,874	1,502	0.7	3,132	1,854	410	7.2	6.2	15.1	8.9	2.0
1990	208,376	1,673	0.8	3,265	1,860 \4	268	8.0	6.7	15.6	8.9 \4	1.3
1991	210,024	1,930	0.9	3,241	1,869 \4	557	9.1	6.5	15.4	8.9 \4	2.6
1992	211,954	1,931	0.9	3,202	1,874	603	9.1	6.2	15.0	8.8	2.8
1993	213,884	1,730	0.8	3,150	1,951	531	8.1	5.6	14.7	9.1	2.5
1994	215,614	1,664	0.8	3,121	1,960	503	7.7	5.4	14.4	9.1	2.3
1995	217,278	1,634	0.8	3,099	1,987	523	7.5	5.1	14.2	9.1	2.4
1996	218,912	1,665	0.8	3,113	2,001	553	7.6	5.1	14.2	9.1	2.5
1997	220,577	1,630	0.7	3,091	2,015	554	7.4	4.9	14.0	9.1	2.5
Projections:\6											
1998	221,905	1,470	0.7	3,005	2,026	491	6.6	4.4	13.5	9.1	2.2
1999	223,376	1,442	0.6	2,993	2,042	491	6.4	4.3	13.4	9.1	2.2
2000	224,818	1,419	0.6	2,986	2,058	491	6.3	4.1	13.2	9.1	2.2
2005	231,775	1,381	0.6	3,025	2,135	491	5.9	3.8	13.0	9.2	2.1
2010	238,853	1,480	0.6	3,184	2,195	491	6.2	4.1	13.3	9.2	2.0
2015	246,421	1,546	0.6	3,320	2,265	491	6.3	4.2	13.4	9.2	2.0
2020	254,126	1,515	0.6	3,384	2,360	491	5.9	4.0	13.3	9.3	1.9
2025	261,514	1,415	0.5	3,418	2,493	491	5.4	3.5	13.0	9.5	1.9
2030	268,383	1,318	0.5	3,486	2,659	491	4.9	3.1	13.0	9.9	1.8
2040	281,096	1,248	0.4	3,752	2,994	491	4.4	2.7	13.3	10.6	1.7
2050	293,934	1,373	0.5	4,008	3,126	491	4.7	3.0	13.6	10.6	1.7
BLACK											
1980 \4	26,683	289	1.1	445	173	62	14.4	13.5	22.1	8.6	3.1
1981	26,973	367	1.4	588	229	67	13.5	13.2	21.7	8.4	2.5
1982	27,339	364	1.3	593	227	58	13.2	13.3	21.5	8.2	2.1

A1.3. Components of Population Change, by Race and Hispanic Origin, and Projections: 1980 to 2050 (continued)

YEAR	Population at start of period (1,000)	TOTAL (Jan. 1-Dec. 31) Net increase Total (1,000)	Per-cent \2	Natural increase Births (1,000)	Deaths (1,000)	Net migra-tion \3 (1,000)	RATE PER 1,000 MIDYEAR POPULATION Net growth rate \1	Total	Natural increase Birth rate	Death rate	Net migra-tion rate \3
1983	27,703	349	1.3	586	233	57	12.5	12.7	21.0	8.4	2.0
1984	28,053	353	1.3	593	236	57	12.5	12.6	21.0	8.4	2.0
1985	28,406	364	1.3	608	244	61	12.7	12.7	21.3	8.5	2.1
1986	28,769	374	1.3	621	250	65	12.9	12.8	21.5	8.6	2.2
1987	29,144	394	1.4	642	255	69	13.4	13.2	21.9	8.7	2.4
1988	29,538	402	1.4	672	264	56	13.5	13.7	22.6	8.9	1.9
1989	29,939	438	1.5	709	268	58	14.5	14.7	23.5	8.9	1.9
1990	30,377	448	1.5	692	266 \4	22	14.6	13.9	22.6	8.7 \4	0.7
1991	30,837	575	1.9	683	270 \4	162	18.5	13.3	21.9	8.7 \4	5.2
1992	31,413	535	1.7	674	269	131	16.9	12.8	21.3	8.5	4.1
1993	31,948	484	1.5	659	282	107	15.0	11.7	20.5	8.8	3.3
1994	32,432	454	1.4	636	282	100	13.9	10.8	19.5	8.6	3.0
1995	32,885	422	1.3	603	286	105	12.8	9.6	18.2	8.7	3.2
1996	33,307	432	1.3	596	282	118	12.9	9.4	17.8	8.4	3.5
1997	33,739	433	1.3	599	278	112	12.7	9.5	17.6	8.2	3.3
Projections:\6											
1998	34,306	461	1.3	677	307	90	13.3	10.7	19.6	8.9	2.6
1999	34,767	459	1.3	681	313	90	13.1	10.6	19.5	8.9	2.6
2000	35,225	457	1.3	685	319	90	12.9	10.3	19.3	9.0	2.6
2005	37,505	460	1.2	718	348	90	12.2	9.8	19.0	9.2	2.4
2010	39,866	489	1.2	767	369	90	12.2	9.9	19.1	9.2	2.3
2015	42,337	498	1.2	804	396	90	11.7	9.6	18.9	9.3	2.1
2020	44,826	496	1.1	834	429	90	11.0	9.0	18.5	9.5	2.0
2025	47,293	491	1.0	867	466	90	10.3	8.4	18.2	9.8	1.9
2030	49,753	495	1.0	908	503	90	9.9	8.1	18.2	10.1	1.8
2040	54,831	527	1.0	997	560	90	9.6	7.9	18.1	10.2	1.6
2050	60,306	575	1.0	1,087	603	90	9.5	7.9	17.9	10.0	1.5
AMERICAN INDIAN, ESKIMO, ALEUT											
1980 \4	1,420	38	2.7	28	9	1	35.3	21.4	26.2	4.8	0.5
1981	1,459	51	3.5	37	8	0	34.6	20.6	25.1	4.5	0.3
1982	1,510	57	3.8	41	8	0	37.2	22.5	26.9	4.3	0.3
1983	1,567	59	3.8	42	8	0	37.1	21.8	26.0	4.3	0.3
1984	1,626	61	3.8	41	8	0	36.7	20.8	25.0	4.2	0.2
1985	1,687	64	3.8	43	7	0	37.3	20.7	24.8	4.2	0.2
1986	1,751	66	3.8	43	7	0	37.1	19.8	23.9	4.1	0.1
1987	1,817	70	3.9	44	7	0	37.7	19.5	23.6	4.1	0.2

A1.3. Components of Population Change, by Race and Hispanic Origin, and Projections:1980 to 2050 (continued)

| YEAR | Population at start of period (1,000) | TOTAL (Jan. 1-Dec. 31) | | | | | RATE PER 1,000 MIDYEAR POPULATION | | | | |
| | | Net increase \1 | | Natural increase | | Net migra-tion \3 (1,000) | Net growth rate \1 | Net increase \1 | Natural increase | | Net migra-tion rate \3 |
		Total (1,000)	Per-cent \2	Births (1,000)	Deaths (1,000)			Total	Birth rate	Death rate	
AMERICAN INDIAN, ESKIMO, ALEUT											
1988	1,887	75	4.0	46	7	0	38.9	19.7	23.9	4.1	0.1
1989	1,962	82	4.2	49	7	0	41.1	20.6	24.6	4.1	0.1
1990	2,044	36	1.8	42	8 \4	3	17.3	16.0	20.1	4.1 \4	1.3
1991	2,091	37	1.8	39	9 \4	7	17.5	14.3	18.4	4.1 \4	3.2
1992	2,128	38	1.8	39	9	7	17.6	14.2	18.4	4.2	3.4
1993	2,166	36	1.7	39	10	7	16.5	13.3	17.7	4.4	3.2
1994	2,202	34	1.5	38	10	6	15.3	12.7	17.0	4.3	2.6
1995	2,236	33	1.5	37	10	6	14.8	12.1	16.6	4.4	2.7
1996	2,269	35	1.5	38	10	7	15.3	12.3	16.8	4.5	3.0
1997	2,305	36	1.6	39	10	7	15.4	12.4	16.8	4.4	2.9
Projections:\6											
1998	2,321	32	1.4	40	12	4	13.8	12.1	17.2	5.1	1.7
1999	2,353	32	1.4	41	12	4	13.7	12.0	17.2	5.2	1.6
2000	2,386	33	1.4	42	13	4	13.7	12.1	17.3	5.2	1.6
2005	2,554	35	1.4	45	14	4	13.7	12.2	17.7	5.5	1.5
2010	2,735	37	1.4	49	16	4	13.5	12.1	17.8	5.7	1.4
2015	2,923	38	1.3	51	17	4	12.8	11.5	17.4	5.9	1.3
2020	3,111	38	1.2	53	19	4	12.0	10.8	16.9	6.1	1.2
2025	3,300	38	1.2	55	21	4	11.6	10.4	16.7	6.3	1.2
2030	3,495	40	1.1	59	23	4	11.4	10.3	16.7	6.4	1.1
2040	3,910	43	1.1	65	26	4	10.9	9.9	16.6	6.7	1.0
2050	4,349	45	1.0	72	30	4	10.3	9.5	16.4	6.9	0.9
ASIAN, PACIFIC ISLANDER											
1980 \4	3,729	302	8.1	67	8	232	103.4	20.1	22.9	2.9	79.3
1981	4,032	374	9.3	96	12	272	88.6	19.9	22.7	2.7	64.4
1982	4,405	341	7.7	105	13	228	74.3	20.1	22.8	2.7	49.8
1983	4,746	332	7.0	107	14	216	67.7	19.0	21.8	2.8	44.0
1984	5,078	348	6.9	111	15	225	66.3	18.4	21.2	2.8	42.9
1985	5,426	365	6.7	118	16	233	65.1	18.3	21.1	2.9	41.6
1986	5,791	371	6.4	122	17	233	62.0	17.7	20.4	2.8	39.0
1987	6,162	376	6.1	132	18	226	59.2	17.9	20.8	2.8	35.7
1988	6,538	391	6.0	146	19	226	58.2	18.8	21.6	2.8	33.6
1989	6,929	417	6.0	150	21	244	58.4	18.1	21.1	2.9	34.2
1990	7,345	375	5.1	149	21 \4	246	49.6	17.0	19.8	2.7 \4	32.6

A1.3. Components of Population Change, by Race and Hispanic Origin, and Projections: 1980 to 2050 *(continued)*

| YEAR | TOTAL (Jan. 1-Dec. 31) | | | | | | RATE PER 1,000 MIDYEAR POPULATION | | | | |
| | Population at start of period (1,000) | Net increase \1 | | Natural increase | | Net migration \3 (1,000) | Net growth rate \1 | Total | Natural increase | | Net migration rate \3 |
		Total (1,000)	Percent \2	Births (1,000)	Deaths (1,000)				Birth rate	Death rate	
1991	7,736	362	4.7	148	22 \4	236	45.7	15.9	18.7	2.8 \4	29.8
1992	8,098	390	4.8	150	24	263	46.9	15.3	18.1	2.9	31.7
1993	8,488	362	4.3	153	25	235	41.8	14.7	17.6	2.9	27.1
1994	8,850	326	3.7	158	27	195	36.2	14.5	17.5	3.0	21.7
1995	9,176	346	3.8	160	28	214	37.0	14.1	17.1	3.0	22.9
1996	9,522	345	3.6	167	30	207	35.5	14.2	17.3	3.1	21.3
1997	9,866	337	3.4	171	30	196	33.6	14.0	17.0	3.0	19.5
Projections:\6											
1998	10,291	379	3.7	176	32	235	36.2	13.7	16.8	3.1	22.4
1999	10,670	383	3.6	181	34	235	35.2	13.6	16.7	3.1	21.6
2000	11,053	386	3.5	186	36	235	34.3	13.4	16.6	3.2	20.9
2005	13,012	401	3.1	212	46	235	30.4	12.6	16.1	3.5	17.8
2010	15,056	420	2.8	243	58	235	27.5	12.1	15.9	3.8	15.4
2015	17,195	439	2.6	275	71	235	25.2	11.7	15.8	4.1	13.5
2020	19,424	456	2.3	308	87	235	23.2	11.3	15.7	4.4	12.0
2025	21,731	469	2.2	339	105	235	21.4	10.6	15.4	4.8	10.7
2030	24,098	480	2.0	369	125	235	19.7	10.1	15.2	5.1	9.7
2040	28,985	500	1.7	434	169	235	17.1	9.1	14.9	5.8	8.0
2050	34,091	524	1.5	505	216	235	15.3	8.4	14.7	6.3	6.8
HISPANIC ORIGIN \7											
1980 \4	14,609	613	4.2	261	45	339	54.5	19.2	23.2	4.0	30.2
1981	15,222	685	4.5	360	64	306	44.0	19.0	23.1	4.1	19.7
1982	15,907	684	4.3	376	66	282	42.1	19.1	23.2	4.1	17.4
1983	16,591	697	4.2	375	69	290	41.2	18.1	22.1	4.0	17.2
1984	17,288	709	4.1	386	70	284	40.2	17.9	21.9	4.0	16.1
1985	17,997	763	4.2	415	73	302	41.6	18.6	22.6	4.0	16.4
1986	18,760	789	4.2	433	76	302	41.2	18.6	22.6	4.0	15.8
1987	19,550	815	4.2	452	77	299	40.9	18.8	22.7	3.9	15.0
1988	20,365	843	4.1	480	81	289	40.5	19.2	23.1	3.9	13.9
1989	21,207	915	4.3	537	82	291	42.3	21.0	24.8	3.8	13.4
1990	22,122	822	3.7	595	84 \4	311	36.4	22.6	26.4	3.7 \4	13.8
1991	23,005	875	3.8	628	85 \4	333	37.4	23.1	26.8	3.6 \4	14.2
1992	23,881	961	4.0	649	87	399	39.5	23.1	26.6	3.6	16.4
1993	24,842	969	3.9	661	93	402	38.3	22.4	26.1	3.7	15.8
1994	25,812	963	3.7	672	97	387	36.6	21.9	25.6	3.7	14.7
1995	26,774	1,018	3.8	680	103	441	37.3	21.2	24.9	3.8	16.2

A1.3. Components of Population Change, by Race and Hispanic Origin, and Projections: 1980 to 2050 *(continued)*

YEAR	Population at start of period (1,000)	TOTAL (Jan. 1-Dec. 31) Net increase Total (1,000)	Per cent \2	Births (1,000)	Deaths (1,000)	Net migra-tion \3 (1,000)	Net growth rate \1	RATE PER 1,000 MIDYEAR POPULATION Total	Birth rate	Death rate	Net migra-tion rate \3
1996	27,792	1,038	3.7	698	106	446	36.7	20.9	24.7	3.7	15.8
1997	28,831	1,051	3.6	714	109	446	35.8	20.6	24.3	3.7	15.2
Projections:\6											
1998	29,123	890	3.1	654	113	350	30.1	18.3	22.1	3.8	11.8
1999	30,013	900	3.0	668	118	350	29.5	18.0	21.9	3.9	11.5
2000	30,913	910	2.9	683	123	350	29.0	17.9	21.8	3.9	11.2
2005	35,576	971	2.7	769	149	350	26.9	17.2	21.3	4.1	9.7
Projections:\6											
2010	40,611	1,067	2.6	888	171	350	25.9	17.4	21.6	4.2	8.5
2015	46,132	1,154	2.5	1,001	197	350	24.7	17.2	21.4	4.2	7.5
2020	52,044	1,223	2.3	1,099	226	350	23.2	16.6	20.9	4.3	6.6
2025	58,289	1,290	2.2	1,198	258	350	21.9	15.9	20.3	4.4	5.9
2030	64,890	1,369	2.1	1,313	294	350	20.9	15.5	20.0	4.5	5.3
2040	79,393	1,550	2.0	1,580	380	350	19.3	15.0	19.7	4.7	4.4
2050	95,653	1,720	1.8	1,860	490	350	17.8	14.2	19.3	5.1	3.6
WHITE, NON-HISPANIC											
1980 \4	180,906	716	0.4	1,958	1,234	113	5.3	5.3	14.4	9.1	0.8
1981	181,623	802	0.4	2,571	1,671	70	4.4	4.9	14.1	9.2	0.4
1982	182,425	801	0.4	2,590	1,667	55	4.4	5.1	14.2	9.1	0.3
1983	183,226	723	0.4	2,555	1,701	57	3.9	4.7	13.9	9.3	0.3
1984	183,949	700	0.4	2,565	1,716	50	3.8	4.6	13.9	9.3	0.3
1985	184,649	729	0.4	2,607	1,750	82	3.9	4.6	14.1	9.5	0.4
1986	185,378	682	0.4	2,571	1,760	91	3.7	4.4	13.8	9.5	0.5
1987	186,060	673	0.4	2,577	1,771	99	3.6	4.3	13.8	9.5	0.5
1988	186,733	677	0.4	2,606	1,802	119	3.6	4.3	13.9	9.6	0.6
1989	187,410	750	0.4	2,642	1,778	147	4.0	4.6	14.1	9.5	0.8
1990	188,160	927	0.5	2,720	1,782 \4	-11	4.9	5.0	14.4	9.5 \4	-0.1
1991	189,028	1,133	0.6	2,667	1,790 \4	257	6.0	4.6	14.1	9.4 \4	1.4
1992	190,161	1,060	0.6	2,609	1,794	245	5.6	4.3	13.7	9.4	1.3
1993	191,221	851	0.4	2,546	1,865	170	4.4	3.6	13.3	9.7	0.9
1994	192,071	793	0.4	2,508	1,871	156	4.1	3.3	13.0	9.7	0.8
1995	192,864	705	0.4	2,478	1,893	120	3.7	3.0	12.8	9.8	0.6
1996	193,570	717	0.4	2,476	1,903	145	3.7	3.0	12.8	9.8	0.7
1997	194,287	670	0.3	2,437	1,914	147	3.4	2.7	12.5	9.8	0.8

A1.3. Components of Population Change, by Race and Hispanic Origin, and Projections: 1980 to 2050 (continued)

YEAR	Population at start of period (1,000)	Net increase \1 Total (1,000)	Net increase \1 Per-cent \2	Natural increase Births (1,000)	Natural increase Deaths (1,000)	Net migra-tion \3 (1,000)	Net growth rate \1	Total	Natural increase Birth rate	Natural increase Death rate	Net migra-tion rate \3
TOTAL (Jan. 1-Dec. 31)											
Projections:\6											
1998	195,438	675	0.3	2,410	1,922	186	3.4	2.5	12.3	9.8	1.0
1999	196,113	638	0.3	2,385	1,934	186	3.2	2.3	12.1	9.8	0.9
2000	196,751	605	0.3	2,365	1,946	186	3.1	2.1	12.0	9.9	0.9
2005	199,544	514	0.3	2,328	2,000	186	2.6	1.7	11.7	10.0	0.9
2010	202,127	527	0.3	2,380	2,040	186	2.6	1.7	11.8	10.1	0.9
2015	204,760	513	0.3	2,414	2,087	186	2.5	1.6	11.8	10.2	0.9
2020	207,176	421	0.2	2,391	2,156	186	2.0	1.1	11.5	10.4	0.9
2025	208,978	262	0.1	2,336	2,261	186	1.3	0.4	11.2	10.8	0.9
2030	209,943	94	0.0	2,302	2,395	186	0.4	-0.4	11.0	11.4	0.9
2040	209,685	-137	-0.1	2,329	2,653	186	-0.7	-1.6	11.1	12.7	0.9
2050	207,986	-165	-0.1	2,336	2,687	186	-0.8	-1.7	11.2	12.9	0.9
BLACK, NON-HISPANIC											
1980 \4	26,142	253	1.0	434	171	47	12.8	13.3	22.0	8.7	2.4
1981	26,394	319	1.2	573	226	51	12.0	13.1	21.6	8.5	1.9
1982	26,713	309	1.2	577	224	39	11.5	13.1	21.5	8.3	1.5
1983	27,023	292	1.1	569	230	38	10.7	12.5	21.0	8.5	1.4
1984	27,314	293	1.1	575	233	40	10.7	12.5	21.0	8.5	1.5
1985	27,607	297	1.1	588	241	42	10.7	12.5	21.2	8.7	1.5
1986	27,904	302	1.1	600	247	46	10.8	12.6	21.4	8.8	1.6
1987	28,206	318	1.1	618	251	51	11.2	13.0	21.8	8.9	1.8
1988	28,524	320	1.1	647	260	39	11.2	13.5	22.6	9.1	1.3
1989	28,844	346	1.2	680	264	40	11.9	14.4	23.4	9.1	1.4
1990	29,191	397	1.4	659	262 \4	0	13.5	13.5	22.4	8.9 \4	0
1991	29,586	521	1.8	646	265 \4	140	17.5	12.8	21.7	8.9 \4	4.7
1992	30,107	472	1.6	636	265	101	15.6	12.2	21.0	8.7	3.3
1993	30,579	421	1.4	620	277	79	13.7	11.1	20.1	9.0	2.6
1994	31,000	389	1.3	597	277	69	12.5	10.2	19.1	8.9	2.2
1995	31,389	361	1.2	564	281	78	11.4	9.0	17.9	8.9	2.5
1996	31,750	371	1.2	556	276	92	11.6	8.8	17.4	8.7	2.9
1997	32,121	371	1.2	558	272	85	11.5	8.8	17.3	8.4	2.6
Projections:\6											
1998	32,593	392	1.2	636	301	57	12.0	10.2	19.4	9.2	1.7
1999	32,985	389	1.2	638	306	57	11.7	10.0	19.2	9.2	1.7
2000	33,374	387	1.2	641	312	57	11.5	9.8	19.1	9.3	1.7
2005	35,293	385	1.1	667	339	57	10.8	9.2	18.8	9.6	1.6

RATE PER 1,000 MIDYEAR POPULATION

A1.3. Components of Population Change, by Race and Hispanic Origin, and Projections: 1980 to 2050 (continued)

YEAR	Population at start of period (1,000)	TOTAL (Jan. 1-Dec. 31)					RATE PER 1,000 MIDYEAR POPULATION				
		Net increase \1		Natural increase		Net migra-tion \3 (1,000)	Net growth rate \1 Total	Natural increase			Net migra-tion rate \3
		Total (1,000)	Per-cent \2	Births (1,000)	Deaths (1,000)			Total	Birth rate	Death rate	
2010	37,263	406	1.1	708	359	57	10.8	9.3	18.9	9.6	1.5
2015	39,307	409	1.0	735	383	57	10.4	8.9	18.6	9.7	1.4
2020	41,338	400	1.0	757	414	57	9.6	8.2	18.2	10.0	1.4
2025	43,316	390	0.9	781	449	57	9.0	7.7	18.0	10.3	1.3
2030	45,254	387	0.9	812	483	57	8.5	7.3	17.9	10.6	1.3
2040	49,178	403	0.8	879	533	57	8.2	7.0	17.8	10.8	1.2
2050	53,339	434	0.8	944	568	57	8.1	7.0	17.6	10.6	1.1

Notes:

- Represents or rounds to zero.

\1 Prior to 1990, includes "error of closure" (the amount necessary to make the components of change add to the net change between censuses), for which figures are not shown separately. Net change for 1990 excludes "error of closure" for the three months prior to the April 1 census data. Therefore, it may not equal the difference between the populations at the beginning of 1990 and 1991.

\2 Percent of population at beginning of period.

\3 Covers net international migration and movement of Armed Forces, federally affiliated civilian citizens, and their dependents.

\4 Represents data for period April 1, 1980, to December 31, 1980.

\5 Data reflect movement of Armed Forces due to the Gulf War.

\6 Based on middle series of assumptions.

\7 Persons of Hispanic origin may be of any race.

Source: No. 19, U.S. Bureau of the Census, *Statistical Abstract of the United States: 1998.* Washington, DC, 1999.

A1.4. Households—Projections, by Race and Hispanic Origin of Householder: 1998 to 2010

[In thousands. These numbers are based on the 1990 census, as enumerated, with modifications for age and race, and household estimates from 1991 to 1994, and are projected forward using alternative marital status and household-type proportions. Race and Hispanic origin of householders were not tabulated for either series 1 or series 2. Series 3, shown here, reflects the consequences of projected change in both the age/sex structure and race/origin composition of the population. Current patterns of family and householdership are assumed to remain at their 1990 proportions.]

CHARACTERISTIC OF HOUSEHOLDER	1998	1999	2000	2001	2002	2003	2004	2005	2006	2007	2008	2009	2010
Households, total	100,684	101,683	102,734	103,754	104,784	105,814	106,835	107,892	108,963	110,051	111,161	112,271	113,426
White	85,271	85,952	86,676	87,371	88,076	88,783	89,479	90,204	90,942	91,687	92,453	93,211	94,010
Black	11,753	11,948	12,149	12,346	12,545	12,740	12,936	13,137	13,337	13,546	13,754	13,969	14,185
American Indian, Eskimo, Aleutian	727	740	754	769	783	797	812	827	843	858	874	890	906
Asian, Pacific Islander	2,933	3,043	3,155	3,268	3,381	3,494	3,608	3,724	3,842	3,960	4,079	4,201	4,324
Hispanic origin \1	8,195	8,474	8,761	9,051	9,341	9,635	9,931	10,236	10,549	10,865	11,191	11,522	11,866

Notes: \1 Persons of Hispanic origin may be of any race.

Source: No. 20, U.S. Bureau of the Census, *Statistical Abstract of the United States: 1998.* Washington, DC, 1999.

A2. AGE AND SEX

A2.1. Average Age, by Race: March 1999

		Age of Person
Non-Hispanic White	Average	37.07
	Number	**92152**
Non-Hispanic Black	Average	31.58
	Number	**12693**
American Indians/Aleuts/ Eskimos	Average	29.66
	Number	**1508**
Asians and Pacific Islanders	Average	32.24
	Number	**4513**
Hispanics	Average	28.06
	Number	**20751**
All Groups	Average	34.87
	Number	**13161**

Source: U.S. Bureau of the Census, *Current Population Surveys: March 1998.* Washington, DC, 1999.

A2.2. Resident Population, by Age and Hispanic Origin: 1980 to 1997

[In thousands, except percent. As of July, except 1980 and 1990 as of April. These data are consistent with the 1980 and 1990 decennial enumerations and have been modified from the official census counts. Total population count for 1980 has been revised since the 1980 census publications. Numbers by age, race, Hispanic origin, and sex for 1980 have not been corrected. Hispanic persons may be of any race]

YEAR AND SEX	Total, all years	Under 5 years	5 to 9 years	10 to 14 years	15 to 19 years	20 to 24 years	25 to 29 years	30 to 34 years	35 to 39 years	40 to 44 years	45 to 49 years
HISPANIC ORIGIN											
1980	14,609	1,663	1,537	1,475	1,606	1,586	1,376	1,129	854	712	622
1981	15,560	1,726	1,596	1,551	1,647	1,727	1,524	1,252	934	762	649
1982	16,240	1,782	1,655	1,595	1,664	1,829	1,642	1,319	1,006	796	671
1983	16,935	1,842	1,720	1,637	1,676	1,931	1,760	1,396	1,075	836	698
1984	17,640	1,887	1,796	1,671	1,705	2,020	1,874	1,482	1,146	878	727
1985	18,368	1,938	1,874	1,704	1,753	2,083	1,983	1,574	1,229	923	754
1986	19,154	2,022	1,936	1,738	1,827	2,139	2,087	1,675	1,315	978	783
1987	19,946	2,106	2,004	1,793	1,895	2,175	2,173	1,783	1,389	1,055	817
1988	20,786	2,206	2,078	1,854	1,968	2,215	2,253	1,885	1,474	1,130	857
1989	21,648	2,348	2,137	1,926	2,031	2,259	2,308	1,977	1,567	1,209	901
1990 \1	22,372	2,469	2,180	1,991	2,086	2,322	2,340	2,046	1,643	1,277	937
Male	11,398	1,260	1,112	1,018	1,107	1,272	1,248	1,064	836	636	458
Female	10,974	1,208	1,068	973	979	1,051	1,091	983	807	641	479
1991	23,432	2,643	2,240	2,091	2,098	2,359	2,399	2,181	1,770	1,399	1,001
Male	11,970	1,350	1,143	1,071	1,110	1,297	1,289	1,143	907	701	491
Female	11,461	1,293	1,097	1,020	988	1,062	1,110	1,038	863	698	509
1992	24,361	2,814	2,299	2,171	2,154	2,378	2,447	2,277	1,879	1,467	1,088
Male	12,464	1,437	1,174	1,113	1,138	1,310	1,320	1,199	968	739	536
Female	11,898	1,377	1,126	1,058	1,015	1,068	1,127	1,078	911	728	552
1993	25,334	2,962	2,375	2,259	2,221	2,412	2,469	2,383	1,988	1,559	1,157
Male	12,974	1,514	1,213	1,158	1,173	1,327	1,336	1,258	1,029	788	572
Female	12,360	1,448	1,161	1,101	1,048	1,085	1,132	1,125	960	771	585
1994	26,302	3,100	2,471	2,329	2,302	2,433	2,489	2,483	2,095	1,653	1,239
Male	13,483	1,586	1,263	1,194	1,218	1,335	1,353	1,314	1,088	838	614
Female	12,819	1,514	1,208	1,136	1,084	1,098	1,137	1,168	1,007	815	625
1995	27,274	3,205	2,593	2,384	2,387	2,466	2,508	2,559	2,202	1,757	1,327
Male	13,997	1,641	1,326	1,221	1,264	1,350	1,368	1,360	1,148	895	660
Female	13,277	1,564	1,267	1,163	1,123	1,116	1,140	1,199	1,054	862	667
1996	28,305	3,287	2,748	2,448	2,488	2,500	2,542	2,612	2,316	1,865	1,427
Male	14,532	1,684	1,405	1,254	1,318	1,363	1,387	1,392	1,212	952	712
Female	13,773	1,602	1,342	1,194	1,170	1,137	1,155	1,220	1,104	912	715
1997	29,348	3,347	2,928	2,515	2,580	2,571	2,567	2,664	2,415	1,976	1,494
Male	15,074	1,717	1,498	1,289	1,367	1,397	1,400	1,423	1,268	1,013	748
Female	14,274	1,630	1,431	1,226	1,213	1,173	1,167	1,241	1,148	963	746
WHITE, NON-HISPANIC											
1980	180,906	11,842	12,262	13,703	16,166	16,574	15,358	14,091	11,315	9,437	9,104
1981	181,974	12,192	11,618	13,642	15,496	16,688	15,717	14,905	11,563	9,676	8,946

A2.2. Resident Population, by Age and Hispanic Origin: 1980 to 1997 *(continued)*

YEAR AND SEX	Total, all years	Under 5 years	5 to 9 years	10 to 14 years	15 to 19 years	20 to 24 years	25 to 29 years	30 to 34 years	35 to 39 years	40 to 44 years	45 to 49 years
1982	182,782	12,384	11,452	13,410	14,932	16,560	16,006	14,716	12,563	10,007	8,923
1983	183,561	12,562	11,464	13,083	14,393	16,365	16,226	14,886	12,923	10,582	9,044
1984	184,243	12,625	11,602	12,648	13,945	16,141	16,344	15,132	13,446	10,958	9,196
1985	184,945	12,683	11,764	12,206	13,716	15,789	16,381	15,452	13,945	11,292	9,296
1986	185,678	12,679	12,038	11,682	13,686	15,219	16,436	15,701	14,667	11,492	9,490
1987	186,353	12,641	12,225	11,533	13,468	14,662	16,277	15,978	14,495	12,497	9,809
1988	187,012	12,620	12,400	11,570	13,170	14,124	16,041	16,185	14,673	12,872	10,366
1989	187,713	12,675	12,462	11,726	12,754	13,701	15,780	16,292	14,930	13,409	10,730
1990 \1	188,307	12,721	12,516	11,854	12,450	13,524	15,508	16,332	15,162	13,839	10,971
Male	91,748	6,532	6,430	6,094	6,370	6,852	7,790	8,178	7,584	6,897	5,433
Female	96,560	6,189	6,085	5,760	6,080	6,673	7,718	8,154	7,578	6,942	5,538
1991	189,590	12,840	12,566	12,207	11,854	13,458	14,843	16,440	15,573	14,660	11,188
Male	92,413	6,592	6,455	6,275	6,081	6,811	7,446	8,233	7,793	7,316	5,541
Female	97,178	6,248	6,111	5,932	5,774	6,646	7,397	8,207	7,780	7,345	5,648
1992	190,657	12,882	12,550	12,444	11,737	13,281	14,258	16,383	15,900	14,528	12,231
Male	92,997	6,611	6,445	6,396	6,034	6,734	7,149	8,207	7,962	7,251	6,066
Female	97,661	6,271	6,105	6,048	5,703	6,546	7,108	8,176	7,938	7,277	6,165
1993	191,606	12,862	12,555	12,661	11,825	12,974	13,708	16,224	16,184	14,726	12,606
Male	93,498	6,602	6,446	6,507	6,086	6,580	6,868	8,124	8,107	7,351	6,254
Female	98,107	6,261	6,109	6,154	5,739	6,394	6,840	8,100	8,077	7,375	6,352
1994	192,426	12,750	12,660	12,746	12,022	12,572	13,278	16,013	16,357	15,029	13,122
Male	93,937	6,543	6,498	6,550	6,190	6,382	6,645	8,014	8,197	7,504	6,511
Female	98,489	6,207	6,161	6,196	5,832	6,190	6,633	7,999	8,160	7,525	6,610
1995	193,198	12,520	12,776	12,795	12,276	12,165	13,064	15,634	16,491	15,359	13,655
Male	94,363	6,423	6,558	6,574	6,322	6,189	6,534	7,817	8,266	7,671	6,780
Female	98,835	6,097	6,218	6,220	5,954	5,976	6,530	7,817	8,225	7,688	6,876
1996	193,875	12,301	12,857	12,838	12,561	11,717	13,017	15,079	16,577	15,689	14,346
Male	94,738	6,308	6,598	6,595	6,468	5,976	6,505	7,533	8,310	7,838	7,126
Female	99,137	5,993	6,259	6,243	6,092	5,741	6,513	7,546	8,267	7,851	7,219
1997	194,571	12,128	12,900	12,819	12,802	11,609	12,821	14,476	16,513	16,013	14,205
Male	95,127	6,221	6,618	6,584	6,591	5,931	6,405	7,223	8,277	8,003	7,056
Female	99,444	5,907	6,282	6,235	6,211	5,678	6,416	7,253	8,236	8,010	7,149
BLACK, NON-HISPANIC											
1980	26,142	2,399	2,455	2,635	2,944	2,689	2,292	1,865	1,438	1,233	1,127
1981	26,532	2,474	2,375	2,628	2,904	2,733	2,384	2,029	1,469	1,270	1,133
1982	26,856	2,518	2,360	2,622	2,847	2,746	2,473	2,093	1,553	1,313	1,142
1983	27,159	2,557	2,363	2,603	2,784	2,761	2,542	2,161	1,632	1,354	1,165
1984	27,444	2,564	2,409	2,561	2,724	2,763	2,599	2,229	1,740	1,390	1,190
1985	27,738	2,572	2,464	2,528	2,672	2,759	2,634	2,304	1,847	1,428	1,217
1986	28,040	2,588	2,521	2,450	2,676	2,728	2,665	2,371	1,991	1,452	1,241
1987	28,351	2,611	2,559	2,433	2,674	2,675	2,670	2,456	2,060	1,535	1,279
1988	28,669	2,654	2,594	2,436	2,663	2,614	2,674	2,522	2,133	1,616	1,313
1989	29,005	2,739	2,596	2,481	2,623	2,564	2,663	2,573	2,206	1,721	1,342
1990 \1	29,299	2,801	2,599	2,528	2,608	2,530	2,651	2,602	2,267	1,812	1,364
Male	13,822	1,416	1,315	1,276	1,314	1,231	1,255	1,210	1,047	834	621
Female	15,477	1,385	1,285	1,251	1,293	1,299	1,397	1,392	1,219	979	743
1991	29,849	2,882	2,626	2,614	2,539	2,541	2,625	2,644	2,365	1,980	1,398
Male	14,088	1,457	1,329	1,321	1,282	1,238	1,244	1,230	1,095	912	636
Female	15,761	1,425	1,296	1,293	1,257	1,303	1,381	1,414	1,270	1,068	762
1992	30,333	2,929	2,654	2,666	2,537	2,566	2,580	2,668	2,459	2,058	1,484
Male	14,334	1,482	1,344	1,349	1,283	1,258	1,226	1,243	1,143	948	675
Female	15,998	1,448	1,309	1,318	1,254	1,309	1,355	1,425	1,316	1,110	809
1993	30,778	2,951	2,704	2,716	2,556	2,562	2,534	2,684	2,543	2,132	1,566
Male	14,552	1,494	1,370	1,375	1,293	1,257	1,204	1,251	1,184	983	712
Female	16,227	1,457	1,334	1,341	1,262	1,304	1,331	1,433	1,359	1,149	854
1994	31,189	2,921	2,790	2,732	2,615	2,548	2,476	2,690	2,608	2,212	1,670

A2.2. Resident Population, by Age and Hispanic Origin: 1980 to 1997 *(continued)*

YEAR AND SEX	Total, all years	Under 5 years	5 to 9 years	10 to 14 years	15 to 19 years	20 to 24 years	25 to 29 years	30 to 34 years	35 to 39 years	40 to 44 years	45 to 49 years
Male	14,750	1,479	1,414	1,384	1,324	1,252	1,177	1,254	1,215	1,021	760
Female	16,440	1,442	1,376	1,347	1,291	1,296	1,300	1,436	1,393	1,191	910
1995	31,566	2,858	2,861	2,736	2,695	2,520	2,451	2,677	2,661	2,290	1,780
Male	14,932	1,447	1,451	1,388	1,365	1,240	1,166	1,249	1,242	1,058	810
Female	16,633	1,411	1,412	1,349	1,329	1,279	1,285	1,428	1,419	1,232	970
1996	31,927	2,779	2,929	2,762	2,765	2,466	2,463	2,659	2,696	2,371	1,916
Male	15,107	1,408	1,485	1,402	1,402	1,216	1,172	1,242	1,259	1,098	872
Female	16,820	1,371	1,445	1,360	1,363	1,250	1,290	1,417	1,437	1,273	1,044
1997	32,298	2,703	2,976	2,790	2,819	2,466	2,477	2,610	2,716	2,464	1,990
Male	15,288	1,370	1,509	1,417	1,430	1,217	1,181	1,219	1,269	1,145	906
Female	17,011	1,334	1,467	1,374	1,389	1,249	1,296	1,391	1,447	1,319	1,084

AMERICAN INDIAN, ESKIMO, ALEUT, NON-HISPANIC

YEAR AND SEX	Total, all years	Under 5 years	5 to 9 years	10 to 14 years	15 to 19 years	20 to 24 years	25 to 29 years	30 to 34 years	35 to 39 years	40 to 44 years	45 to 49 years
1980	1,326	136	135	145	158	138	116	100	79	66	55
1981	1,377	144	133	148	161	142	120	110	85	70	58
1982	1,420	151	133	150	161	147	122	115	90	75	60
1983	1,466	160	134	153	159	154	125	120	96	79	63
1984	1,512	166	139	154	157	159	131	123	102	84	66
1985	1,558	171	145	154	157	162	137	126	108	90	70
1986	1,606	175	152	154	159	162	141	131	118	94	73
1987	1,654	177	160	155	161	160	146	135	125	100	77
1988	1,703	178	169	158	164	156	153	141	130	107	81
1989	1,755	182	175	164	164	153	158	149	135	112	86
1990 \1	1,796	185	179	170	165	151	160	156	138	117	90
Male	884	94	91	87	85	77	80	75	66	57	44
Female	912	91	88	83	80	74	81	81	71	60	46
1991	1,829	185	181	178	161	155	157	158	142	123	93
Male	900	94	92	91	82	79	79	77	68	60	45
Female	929	91	89	88	79	76	79	81	74	64	48
1992	1,856	184	182	184	160	158	154	159	145	126	99
Male	914	93	93	93	82	81	77	78	70	61	48
Female	942	91	90	91	79	77	77	81	75	65	51
1993	1,882	182	184	191	162	160	151	159	148	129	103
Male	926	92	94	96	82	82	76	78	72	62	50
Female	956	90	90	94	80	78	75	81	76	67	53
1994	1,906	177	187	195	166	160	150	159	150	133	107
Male	938	90	95	98	84	82	76	78	73	64	52
Female	968	88	92	96	82	78	74	81	77	69	55
1995	1,929	171	191	198	172	158	151	157	152	136	111
Male	949	86	97	100	87	81	77	78	74	65	54
Female	980	85	93	98	85	78	74	80	78	71	57
1996	1,952	169	190	200	178	156	155	155	154	139	116
Male	960	85	97	101	90	79	79	77	75	67	56
Female	992	83	93	99	88	77	76	78	79	72	60
1997	1,976	166	190	202	184	155	157	152	155	142	118
Male	972	84	96	102	92	78	81	76	76	69	57
Female	1,003	82	94	99	92	77	76	76	79	74	61

ASIAN, PACIFIC ISLANDER, NON-HISPANIC

YEAR AND SEX	Total, all years	Under 5 years	5 to 9 years	10 to 14 years	15 to 19 years	20 to 24 years	25 to 29 years	30 to 34 years	35 to 39 years	40 to 44 years	45 to 49 years
1980	3,563	308	311	285	294	332	378	376	279	221	182
1981	4,022	356	339	332	333	373	424	435	315	250	200
1982	4,367	393	356	367	357	400	461	470	354	274	215
1983	4,671	426	372	393	375	422	487	504	391	299	232
1984	4,986	453	392	415	400	446	510	537	433	325	250
1985	5,315	478	419	435	430	472	536	570	474	355	269
1986	5,655	498	452	451	464	497	564	600	520	382	290
1987	5,985	517	484	463	499	520	591	632	550	421	312

A2.2. Resident Population, by Age and Hispanic Origin: 1980 to 1997 *(continued)*

YEAR AND SEX	Total, all years	Under 5 years	5 to 9 years	10 to 14 years	15 to 19 years	20 to 24 years	25 to 29 years	30 to 34 years	35 to 39 years	40 to 44 years	45 to 49 years
1988	6,329	538	518	478	531	545	619	659	583	462	336
1989	6,698	564	546	500	560	582	653	685	617	508	362
1990 \1	6,992	586	566	523	582	612	673	701	640	546	385
Male	3,419	299	287	267	301	315	333	337	302	254	185
Female	3,573	287	279	256	281	297	340	363	338	291	199
1991	7,425	637	585	563	579	664	692	729	675	599	421
Male	3,624	326	298	287	298	341	341	353	320	278	201
Female	3,801	311	288	276	281	323	351	376	355	321	220
1992	7,794	679	599	599	582	703	713	751	709	628	461
Male	3,797	348	305	305	298	359	349	364	338	291	219
Female	3,997	331	294	294	284	344	364	387	371	337	243
1993	8,153	712	615	637	590	730	731	778	737	662	503
Male	3,963	365	314	324	301	371	355	377	352	308	237
Female	4,189	347	301	313	289	359	376	401	384	354	267
1994	8,469	745	634	664	602	738	749	796	762	688	548
Male	4,109	382	325	337	307	374	361	385	365	321	256
Female	4,360	363	309	327	296	364	388	411	397	367	292
1995	8,794	772	661	685	623	736	780	811	786	715	591
Male	4,258	395	340	349	317	372	374	391	377	335	274
Female	4,536	377	321	336	307	365	406	420	410	380	316
1996	9,120	789	701	701	652	723	816	824	807	746	634
Male	4,409	403	361	357	331	363	390	395	388	350	294
Female	4,711	386	340	344	322	360	426	429	420	396	340
1997	9,443	806	745	714	683	711	847	839	825	778	662
Male	4,557	410	384	365	346	356	403	400	397	366	307
Female	4,887	396	361	349	337	355	444	439	428	411	355
1995, PERCENT											
Hispanic origin	100.0	11.8	9.5	8.7	8.8	9.0	9.2	9.4	8.1	6.4	4.9
White, non-Hispanic	100.0	6.5	6.6	6.6	6.4	6.3	6.8	8.1	8.5	7.9	7.1
Black, non-Hispanic	100.0	9.1	9.1	8.7	8.5	8.0	7.8	8.5	8.4	7.3	5.6
American Indian, Eskimo, Aleut, non-Hispanic	100.0	8.9	9.9	10.3	8.9	8.2	7.8	8.1	7.9	7.1	5.8
Asian, Pacific Islander, non-Hispanic	100.0	8.8	7.5	7.8	7.1	8.4	8.9	9.2	8.9	8.1	6.7
1996, PERCENT											
Hispanic origin	100.0	11.6	9.7	8.6	8.8	8.8	9.0	9.2	8.2	6.6	5.0
White, non-Hispanic	100.0	6.3	6.6	6.6	6.5	6.0	6.7	7.8	8.6	8.1	7.4
Black, non-Hispanic	100.0	8.7	9.2	8.7	8.7	7.7	7.7	8.3	8.4	7.4	6.0
American Indian, Eskimo, Aleut, non-Hispanic	100.0	8.7	9.7	10.2	9.1	8.0	7.9	7.9	7.9	7.1	5.9

A2.2. Resident Population, by Age and Hispanic Origin: 1980 to 1997 *(continued)*

YEAR AND SEX	Total, all years	Under 5 years	5 to 9 years	10 to 14 years	15 to 19 years	20 to 24 years	25 to 29 years	30 to 34 years	35 to 39 years	40 to 44 years	45 to 49 years
Asian, Pacific Islander, non-Hispanic	100.0	8.7	7.7	7.7	7.1	7.9	8.9	9.0	8.8	8.2	7.0
1997, PERCENT											
Hispanic origin	100.0	11.4	10.0	8.6	8.8	8.8	8.7	9.1	8.2	6.7	5.1
White, non-Hispanic	100.0	6.2	6.6	6.6	6.6	6.0	6.6	7.4	8.5	8.2	7.3
Black, non-Hispanic	100.0	8.4	9.2	8.6	8.7	7.6	7.7	8.1	8.4	7.6	6.2
American Indian, Eskimo, Aleut, non-Hispanic	100.0	8.4	9.6	10.2	9.3	7.8	7.9	7.7	7.8	7.2	6.0
Asian, Pacific Islander, non-Hispanic	100.0	8.5	7.9	7.6	7.2	7.5	9.0	8.9	8.7	8.2	7.0

YEAR AND SEX	50 to 54 years	55 to 59 years	60 to 64 years	65 to 74 years	75 to 84 years	85 years and over	5 to 13 years	14 to 17 years	18 to 24 years
HISPANIC ORIGIN									
1980	564	454	321	457	203	49	2,715	1,251	2,240
1981	598	487	353	481	220	53	2,848	1,258	2,415
1982	610	506	378	496	234	55	2,947	1,262	2,534
1983	618	527	401	513	248	58	3,041	1,279	2,645
1984	626	549	426	532	261	61	3,131	1,324	2,738
1985	639	571	448	556	273	66	3,227	1,382	2,804
1986	653	590	469	582	286	72	3,329	1,435	2,876
1987	674	604	489	614	301	77	3,449	1,478	2,940
1988	701	613	511	646	315	82	3,578	1,505	3,032
1989	730	622	533	684	330	88	3,688	1,535	3,128
1990 \1	750	634	550	715	340	91	3,786	1,575	3,217
Male	361	299	253	312	130	32	1,933	820	1,755
Female	389	335	297	403	209	59	1,853	755	1,463
1991	790	655	578	767	359	102	3,930	1,618	3,242
Male	381	310	267	335	138	36	2,008	841	1,772
Female	408	346	312	431	221	66	1,921	776	1,469
1992	825	679	592	809	373	111	4,054	1,681	3,267
Male	399	321	274	354	143	38	2,073	876	1,786
Female	426	358	318	454	230	72	1,982	805	1,480
1993	874	707	603	856	388	120	4,204	1,741	3,322
Male	423	335	279	377	150	42	2,148	910	1,813
Female	451	372	324	480	239	79	2,054	832	1,509
1994	919	740	614	901	405	129	4,340	1,818	3,377
Male	445	351	284	398	157	44	2,220	950	1,839
Female	473	389	330	503	249	85	2,122	866	1,538
1995	972	766	634	947	428	139	4,499	1,892	3,439
Male	472	364	294	419	167	48	2,300	991	1,870
Female	500	402	340	527	261	92	2,199	901	1,569
1996	1,028	800	652	989	454	150	4,710	1,965	3,509
Male	500	380	302	440	179	51	2,408	1,029	1,903
Female	528	419	350	550	275	99	2,300	937	1,606

A2.2. Resident Population, by Age and Hispanic Origin: 1980 to 1997 *(continued)*

YEAR AND SEX	50 to 54 years	55 to 59 years	60 to 64 years	65 to 74 years	75 to 84 years	85 years and over	5 to 13 years	14 to 17 years	18 to 24 years
1997	1,116	836	677	1,021	481	160	4,941	2,040	3,612
Male	544	398	314	454	192	54	2,529	1,067	1,955
Female	572	438	363	567	289	106	2,413	975	1,656
WHITE, NON-HISPANIC									
1980	9,824	9,963	8,775	13,614	6,863	2,014	23,126	12,313	23,267
1981	9,662	9,844	8,985	13,860	7,070	2,109	22,530	11,707	23,207
1982	9,461	9,716	9,139	14,074	7,253	2,185	22,207	11,202	22,947
1983	9,189	9,677	9,175	14,295	7,442	2,256	21,849	10,904	22,553
1984	8,978	9,540	9,269	14,465	7,632	2,321	21,495	10,854	21,987
1985	8,853	9,386	9,327	14,645	7,828	2,382	21,202	10,899	21,376
1986	8,751	9,262	9,239	14,866	8,028	2,443	21,223	10,746	20,658
1987	8,730	9,074	9,126	15,091	8,235	2,511	21,432	10,377	20,080
1988	8,859	8,816	9,099	15,224	8,431	2,560	21,708	9,891	19,665
1989	9,008	8,614	8,980	15,388	8,632	2,630	21,880	9,431	19,330
1990 \1	9,058	8,548	8,872	15,511	8,767	2,675	22,106	9,225	19,014
Male	4,443	4,129	4,174	6,837	3,275	730	11,360	4,742	9,643
Female	4,615	4,419	4,697	8,674	5,492	1,946	10,745	4,481	9,372
1991	9,294	8,436	8,776	15,622	9,021	2,809	22,418	9,259	18,408
Male	4,562	4,083	4,148	6,908	3,404	765	11,519	4,770	9,333
Female	4,733	4,353	4,628	8,714	5,618	2,044	10,900	4,488	9,074
1992	9,599	8,447	8,607	15,704	9,202	2,906	22,624	9,389	17,999
Male	4,713	4,094	4,080	6,962	3,500	792	11,622	4,840	9,146
Female	4,886	4,353	4,526	8,742	5,702	2,114	11,002	4,549	8,851
1993	10,158	8,576	8,382	15,794	9,364	3,008	22,782	9,529	17,703
Male	4,992	4,161	3,983	7,028	3,590	822	11,701	4,913	9,005
Female	5,166	4,415	4,399	8,767	5,775	2,186	11,081	4,617	8,698
1994	10,515	8,754	8,204	15,782	9,525	3,097	22,856	9,831	17,313
Male	5,168	4,249	3,907	7,044	3,681	851	11,736	5,069	8,815
Female	5,347	4,505	4,296	8,736	5,845	2,246	11,119	4,762	8,498
1995	10,842	8,838	8,138	15,751	9,706	3,187	23,036	10,011	16,965
Male	5,330	4,292	3,880	7,060	3,784	882	11,828	5,161	8,654
Female	5,512	4,546	4,258	8,692	5,922	2,305	11,207	4,850	8,311
1996	11,013	9,031	8,053	15,602	9,928	3,267	23,102	10,231	16,640
Male	5,414	4,389	3,847	7,013	3,908	911	11,860	5,273	8,504
Female	5,599	4,642	4,206	8,590	6,020	2,356	11,242	4,958	8,135
1997	12,030	9,327	8,062	15,369	10,144	3,354	23,141	10,379	16,610
Male	5,923	4,536	3,858	6,930	4,025	947	11,876	5,350	8,499
Female	6,107	4,792	4,204	8,439	6,119	2,407	11,264	5,030	8,111
BLACK, NON-HISPANIC									
1980	1,114	1,024	861	1,327	582	157	4,530	2,331	3,862
1981	1,111	1,033	874	1,346	604	166	4,474	2,262	3,904
1982	1,106	1,038	888	1,360	622	173	4,463	2,196	3,916
1983	1,098	1,040	904	1,373	641	181	4,446	2,141	3,926
1984	1,090	1,038	917	1,382	659	187	4,451	2,106	3,900
1985	1,086	1,036	929	1,394	677	192	4,436	2,135	3,853
1986	1,086	1,033	936	1,407	697	198	4,449	2,139	3,788
1987	1,089	1,029	941	1,421	715	205	4,491	2,121	3,730
1988	1,105	1,021	945	1,436	733	211	4,551	2,082	3,674
1989	1,124	1,011	945	1,453	748	216	4,592	2,011	3,661
1990 \1	1,138	1,009	946	1,465	759	219	4,643	1,977	3,644
Male	512	446	407	601	273	65	2,346	1,003	1,787
Female	626	563	539	864	486	154	2,297	974	1,857

A2.2. Resident Population, by Age and Hispanic Origin: 1980 to 1997 (continued)

YEAR AND SEX	50 to 54 years	55 to 59 years	60 to 64 years	65 to 74 years	75 to 84 years	85 years and over	5 to 13 years	14 to 17 years	18 to 24 years
BLACK, NON-HISPANIC									
1991	1,169	1,015	953	1,495	770	234	4,730	1,989	3,602
Male	525	448	410	616	276	69	2,392	1,010	1,768
Female	644	568	543	879	494	165	2,337	979	1,833
1992	1,212	1,025	954	1,517	778	245	4,810	2,024	3,589
Male	544	451	410	628	280	72	2,435	1,029	1,770
Female	668	574	544	890	499	173	2,375	995	1,820
1993	1,251	1,045	954	1,540	787	254	4,885	2,076	3,576
Male	561	459	411	639	283	74	2,474	1,055	1,767
Female	690	585	543	902	503	180	2,411	1,022	1,809
1994	1,289	1,070	951	1,556	798	262	4,960	2,160	3,565
Male	578	469	409	647	289	76	2,512	1,100	1,763
Female	711	602	542	909	509	186	2,446	1,061	1,802
1995	1,328	1,096	955	1,570	811	272	5,053	2,197	3,565
Male	595	480	410	654	297	79	2,561	1,119	1,764
Female	734	616	545	916	514	193	2,492	1,078	1,799
1996	1,355	1,119	958	1,584	824	280	5,129	2,249	3,544
Male	606	489	411	662	303	81	2,601	1,146	1,757
Female	749	630	548	923	521	199	2,528	1,104	1,787
1997	1,438	1,161	967	1,594	841	287	5,208	2,275	3,568
Male	643	507	414	667	311	84	2,642	1,161	1,771
Female	795	653	553	927	531	203	2,567	1,115	1,797
AMERICAN INDIAN, ESKIMO, ALEUT, NON-HISPANIC									
1980	49	43	32	46	20	6	249	127	199
1981	51	44	35	48	21	6	251	126	207
1982	53	46	37	50	23	6	253	124	214
1983	54	47	39	51	24	7	257	122	222
1984	56	48	41	54	25	7	262	124	225
1985	58	49	43	56	26	7	266	127	224
1986	60	51	44	58	28	8	273	131	224
1987	63	53	45	61	29	8	283	132	222
1988	66	55	46	63	30	8	293	131	221
1989	69	56	47	66	31	8	307	130	220
1990 \1	72	58	48	68	31	9	316	131	217
Male	34	28	23	30	12	3	161	67	112
Female	37	30	26	38	19	6	155	64	106
1991	74	59	49	70	33	10	325	131	218
Male	36	28	23	31	14	3	166	66	112
Female	38	31	26	39	21	6	161	64	107
1992	76	61	50	72	35	11	331	133	220
Male	37	29	23	32	14	4	168	68	112
Female	40	32	27	41	21	7	164	66	108
1993	79	62	51	74	36	12	338	138	221
Male	38	30	24	33	14	4	171	71	113
Female	41	33	27	41	22	8	166	67	109
1994	82	64	51	75	38	13	343	144	222
Male	39	30	24	34	15	4	174	72	113
Female	43	34	27	42	22	9	169	70	109
1995	84	65	53	76	38	14	349	150	221
Male	40	31	25	34	16	5	177	75	113
Female	44	34	28	42	23	10	171	74	109
1996	87	67	54	78	40	16	350	154	221
Male	42	32	25	36	16	5	178	77	111
Female	45	35	29	43	24	11	172	77	109

A2.2. Resident Population, by Age and Hispanic Origin: 1980 to 1997 *(continued)*

YEAR AND SEX	50 to 54 years	55 to 59 years	60 to 64 years	65 to 74 years	75 to 84 years	85 years and over	5 to 13 years	14 to 17 years	18 to 24 years
1997	92	70	55	79	43	17	350	159	222
Male	44	33	26	36	18	6	177	80	112
Female	48	37	29	44	25	12	172	79	111
ASIAN, PACIFIC ISLANDER, NON-HISPANIC									
1980	158	131	98	136	60	14	540	226	455
1981	173	146	113	154	66	15	608	255	512
1982	185	157	125	168	70	16	653	276	550
1983	195	166	137	181	74	17	687	295	580
1984	206	176	149	193	80	18	725	319	611
1985	218	187	160	208	85	20	763	346	644
1986	232	198	171	224	90	21	807	375	682
1987	247	208	182	240	97	23	849	393	722
1988	264	219	191	256	104	24	896	413	763
1989	281	230	201	273	111	26	944	427	818
1990 \1	297	240	210	287	116	27	984	436	863
Male	145	108	90	129	55	11	500	225	445
Female	152	132	120	159	62	16	484	211	418
1991	324	257	226	315	129	31	1,040	442	909
Male	157	118	97	138	59	13	530	228	466
Female	167	140	129	176	69	18	511	215	442
1992	346	275	238	338	139	34	1,086	452	945
Male	167	127	102	148	63	14	553	231	483
Female	179	148	135	190	76	20	533	221	463
1993	370	292	249	362	148	37	1,131	468	972
Male	178	136	108	157	66	15	576	239	494
Female	192	156	141	205	82	22	555	228	478
1994	394	309	259	383	158	41	1,168	490	980
Male	188	146	113	164	70	17	596	250	497
Female	206	163	146	219	90	24	572	240	483
1995	421	327	269	402	171	45	1,207	519	979
Male	200	155	119	171	74	18	618	265	494
Female	220	172	151	231	97	26	589	255	485
1996	448	345	280	419	184	49	1,260	548	970
Male	212	164	125	176	79	20	645	279	487
Female	236	181	155	243	106	29	614	270	482
1997	487	364	295	436	198	54	1,310	576	967
Male	229	172	133	183	85	22	673	293	485
Female	258	191	162	253	114	32	637	284	483
1995, PERCENT									
Hispanic origin	3.6	2.8	2.3	3.5	1.6	0.5	16.5	6.9	12.6
White, non-Hispanic	5.6	4.6	4.2	8.2	5.0	1.6	11.9	5.2	8.8
Black, non-Hispanic	4.2	3.5	3.0	5.0	2.6	0.9	16.0	7.0	11.3
American Indian, Eskimo, Aleut, non-Hispanic	4.4	3.4	2.7	3.9	2.0	0.7	18.1	7.8	11.5
Asian, Pacific Islander, non-Hispanic	4.8	3.7	3.1	4.6	1.9	0.5	13.7	5.9	11.1

A2.2. Resident Population, by Age and Hispanic Origin: 1980 to 1997 *(continued)*

YEAR AND SEX	50 to 54 years	55 to 59 years	60 to 64 years	65 to 74 years	75 to 84 years	85 years and over	5 to 13 years	14 to 17 years	18 to 24 years
1996, PERCENT									
Hispanic origin	3.6	2.8	2.3	3.5	1.6	0.5	16.6	6.9	12.4
White, non-Hispanic	5.7	4.7	4.2	8.0	5.1	1.7	11.9	5.3	8.6
Black, non-Hispanic	4.2	3.5	3.0	5.0	2.6	0.9	16.1	7.0	11.1
American Indian, Eskimo, Aleut, non-Hispanic	4.5	3.4	2.8	4.0	2.0	0.8	17.9	7.9	11.3
Asian, Pacific Islander, non-Hispanic	4.9	3.8	3.1	4.6	2.0	0.5	13.8	6.0	10.6
1997, PERCENT									
Hispanic origin	3.8	2.8	2.3	3.5	1.6	0.5	16.8	7.0	12.3
White, non-Hispanic	6.2	4.8	4.1	7.9	5.2	1.7	11.9	5.3	8.5
Black, non-Hispanic	4.5	3.6	3.0	4.9	2.6	0.9	16.1	7.0	11.0
American Indian, Eskimo, Aleut, non-Hispanic	4.7	3.5	2.8	4.0	2.2	0.9	17.7	8.0	11.2
Asian, Pacific Islander, non-Hispanic	5.2	3.9	3.1	4.6	2.1	0.6	13.9	6.1	10.2

Notes:
\1 The April 1, 1990, census count (248,765,170) includes count resolution corrections processed through August 1997, and does not include adjustments for census coverage errors except for adjustments estimated for the 1995 Census Test in Oakland, CA; Patterson, NJ; and six parishes in Louisiana. These adjustments amounted to a total of 55,297 persons.

Source: No. 23, U.S. Bureau of the Census, *Statistical Abstract of the United States: 1998.* Washington, DC, 1999.

A2.3. Youth and Elderly Dependency Ratios: 1997

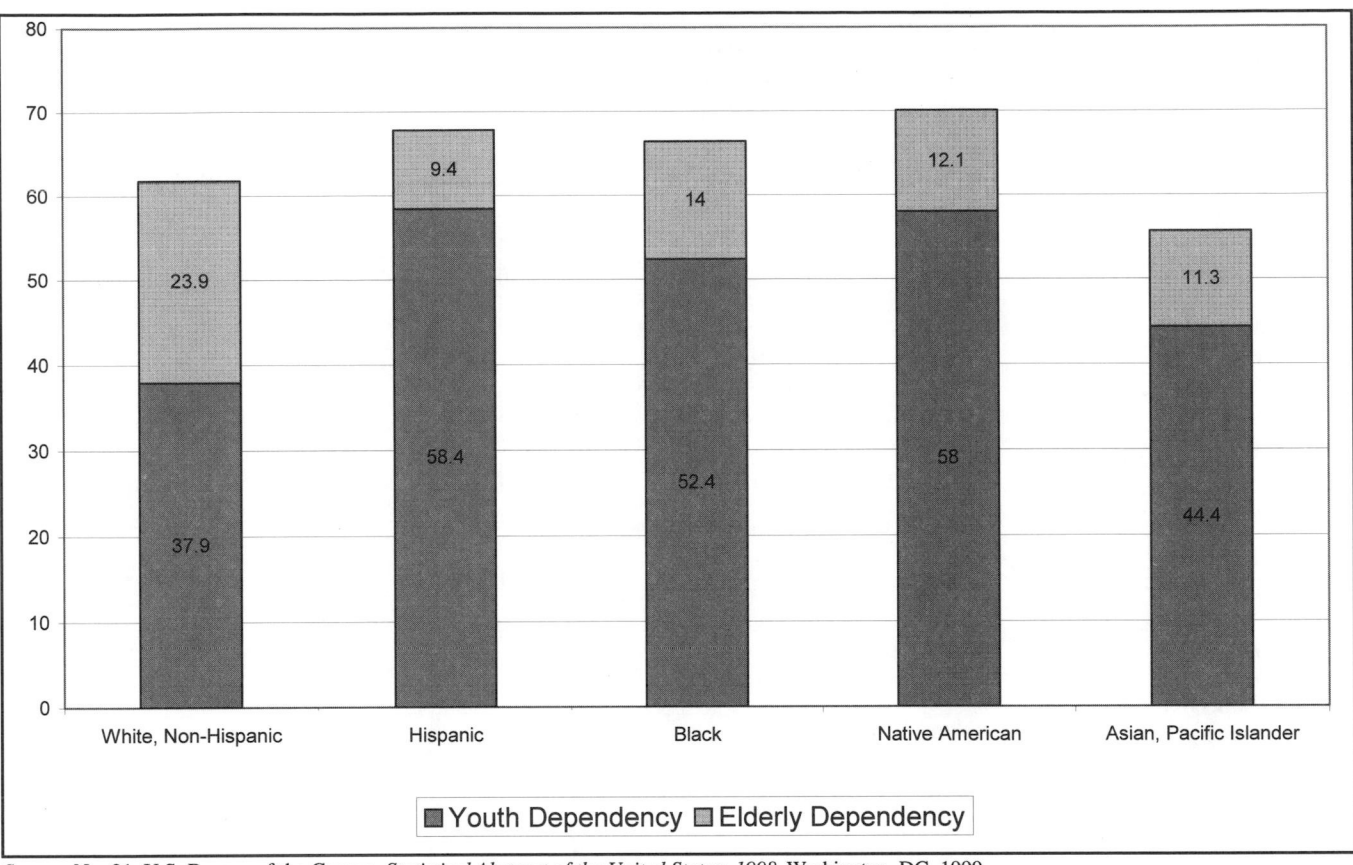

Source: No. 21, U.S. Bureau of the Census, *Statistical Abstract of the United States: 1998.* Washington, DC, 1999.

A2.4. Projections of Hispanic and Non-Hispanic Populations, by Age and Sex: 2000 to 2025

[As of July 1. Resident population. Data are for middle series.]

AGE AND SEX	POPULATION (1,000)				PERCENT DISTRIBUTION			
	2000	2005	2010	2025	2000	2005	2010	2025
Hispanic origin, total \1	**31,366**	**36,057**	**41,139**	**58,930**	**100.0**	**100.0**	**100.0**	**100.0**
Under 5 years old	3,203	3,580	4,080	5,662	10.2	9.9	9.9	9.6
5 to 13 years old	5,651	6,215	6,654	9,479	18.0	17.2	16.2	16.1
14 to 17 years old	2,179	2,672	3,007	3,944	6.9	7.4	7.3	6.7
18 to 24 years old	3,679	4,270	5,101	6,560	11.7	11.8	12.4	11.1
25 to 34 years old	5,181	5,414	6,059	8,748	16.5	15.0	14.7	14.8
35 to 44 years old	4,836	5,421	5,562	7,345	15.4	15.0	13.5	12.5
45 to 54 years old	3,049	3,927	4,833	5,791	9.7	10.9	11.7	9.8
55 to 64 years old	1,717	2,260	2,997	5,272	5.5	6.3	7.3	8.9
65 to 74 years old	1,120	1,308	1,606	3,595	3.6	3.6	3.9	6.1
75 to 84 years old	568	748	896	1,771	1.8	2.1	2.2	3.0
85 years old and over	183	242	345	763	0.6	0.7	0.8	1.3
Male	15,799	18,082	20,557	29,276	50.4	50.1	50.0	49.7
Female	15,566	17,975	20,582	29,654	49.6	49.9	50.0	50.3
Non-Hispanic White, total	**197,061**	**199,802**	**202,390**	**209,117**	**100.0**	**100.0**	**100.0**	**100.0**
Under 5 years old	11,807	11,367	11,445	11,510	6.0	5.7	5.7	5.5
5 to 13 years old	23,125	22,072	21,063	21,396	11.7	11.0	10.4	10.2

A2.4. Projections of Hispanic and Non-Hispanic Populations, by Age and Sex: 2000 to 2025 *(continued)*

AGE AND SEX	POPULATION (1,000)				PERCENT DISTRIBUTION			
	2000	2005	2010	2025	2000	2005	2010	2025
14 to 17 years old	10,444	10,769	10,230	9,622	5.3	5.4	5.1	4.6
18 to 24 years old	17,510	18,443	18,880	16,785	8.9	9.2	9.3	8.0
25 to 34 years old	25,144	23,806	24,631	24,935	12.8	11.9	12.2	11.9
35 to 44 years old	32,382	29,299	25,628	26,278	16.4	14.7	12.7	12.6
45 to 54 years old	28,485	31,024	31,541	23,797	14.5	15.5	15.6	11.4
55 to 64 years old	19,039	23,285	27,137	27,490	9.7	11.7	13.4	13.1
65 to 74 years old	14,825	14,660	16,653	26,504	7.5	7.3	8.2	12.7
75 to 84 years old	10,607	10,868	10,394	15,373	5.4	5.4	5.1	7.4
85 years old and over	3,694	4,209	4,788	5,428	1.9	2.1	2.4	2.6
Male	96,438	97,946	99,381	103,169	48.9	49.0	49.1	49.3
Female	100,624	101,856	103,009	105,948	51.1	51.0	50.9	50.7
Non-Hispanic Black, total	**33,568**	**35,485**	**37,466**	**43,511**	**100.0**	**100.0**	**100.0**	**100.0**
Under 5 years old	2,929	3,016	3,187	3,571	8.7	8.5	8.5	8.2
5 to 13 years old	5,391	5,430	5,531	6,339	16.1	15.3	14.8	14.6
14 to 17 years old	2,285	2,568	2,547	2,831	6.8	7.2	6.8	6.5
18 to 24 years old	3,751	3,975	4,354	4,609	11.2	11.2	11.6	10.6
25 to 34 years old	4,863	4,883	5,111	5,942	14.5	13.8	13.6	13.7
35 to 44 years old	5,347	5,154	4,877	5,521	15.9	14.5	13.0	12.7
45 to 54 years old	3,922	4,654	5,008	4,613	11.7	13.1	13.4	10.6
55 to 64 years old	2,301	2,850	3,601	4,498	6.9	8.0	9.6	10.3
65 to 74 years old	1,608	1,695	1,921	3,634	4.8	4.8	5.1	8.4
75 to 84 years old	862	919	947	1,457	2.6	2.6	2.5	3.3
85 years old and over	310	344	381	496	0.9	1.0	1.0	1.1
Male	15,871	16,760	17,676	20,494	47.3	47.2	47.2	47.1
Female	17,697	18,725	19,790	23,017	52.7	52.8	52.8	52.9
Non-Hispanic American Indian, Eskimo, Aleut, total	**2,054**	**2,183**	**2,320**	**2,744**	**100.0**	**100.0**	**100.0**	**100.0**
Under 5 years old	180	192	206	229	8.8	8.8	8.9	8.4
5 to 13 years old	352	347	364	429	17.1	15.9	15.7	15.6
14 to 17 years old	165	175	166	198	8.0	8.0	7.1	7.2
18 to 24 years old	239	268	282	304	11.6	12.3	12.1	11.1
25 to 34 years old	303	316	349	390	14.7	14.5	15.0	14.2
35 to 44 years old	301	293	290	372	14.7	13.4	12.5	13.6
45 to 54 years old	231	259	272	275	11.2	11.8	11.7	10.0
55 to 64 years old	136	164	195	227	6.6	7.5	8.4	8.3
65 to 74 years old	82	91	106	176	4.0	4.2	4.6	6.4
75 to 84 years old	46	52	57	92	2.2	2.4	2.4	3.4
85 years old and over	21	27	34	52	1.0	1.2	1.4	1.9
Male	1,008	1,070	1,136	1,342	49.1	49.0	48.9	48.9
Female	1,046	1,113	1,184	1,401	50.9	51.0	51.1	51.1
Non-Hispanic Asian, Pacific Islander, total	**10,584**	**12,454**	**14,402**	**20,748**	**100.0**	**100.0**	**100.0**	**100.0**
Under 5 years old	867	973	1,093	1,526	8.2	7.8	7.6	7.4
5 to 13 years old	1,524	1,787	1,993	2,770	14.4	14.4	13.8	13.4
14 to 17 years old	680	803	944	1,277	6.4	6.4	6.6	6.2
18 to 24 years old	1,080	1,311	1,521	2,114	10.2	10.5	10.6	10.2

A2.4. Projections of Hispanic and Non-Hispanic Populations, by Age and Sex: 2000 to 2025 *(continued)*

AGE AND SEX	POPULATION (1,000)				PERCENT DISTRIBUTION			
	2000	2005	2010	2025	2000	2005	2010	2025
25 to 34 years old	1,744	1,887	2,141	3,104	16.5	15.2	14.9	15.0
35 to 44 years old	1,793	1,998	2,165	2,876	16.9	16.0	15.0	13.9
45 to 54 years old	1,344	1,644	1,910	2,415	12.7	13.2	13.3	11.6
55 to 64 years old	770	1,046	1,354	2,055	7.3	8.4	9.4	9.9
65 to 74 years old	500	615	771	1,516	4.7	4.9	5.4	7.3
75 to 84 years old	231	311	387	787	2.2	2.5	2.7	3.8
85 years old and over	51	78	123	308	0.5	0.6	0.9	1.5
Male	5,065	5,928	6,835	9,838	47.9	47.6	47.5	47.4
Female	5,520	6,526	7,567	10,910	52.1	52.4	52.5	52.6

Notes:
\1 Persons of Hispanic origin may be of any race.

Source: No. 21, U.S. Bureau of the Census, *Statistical Abstract of the United States: 1998.* Washington, DC, 1999.

A3. GEOGRAPHIC DISTRIBUTION AND MOBILITY

A3.1. Resident Population, by Region, Race, and Hispanic Origin: 1990

[As of April 1.]

RACE AND HISPANIC ORIGIN	POPULATION (1,000)					PERCENT DISTRIBUTION				
	United States	Northeast	Midwest	South	West	United States	Northeast	Midwest	South	West
Total	248,710	50,809	59,669	85,446	52,786	100.0	20.4	24.0	34.4	21.2
White	199,686	42,069	52,018	65,582	40,017	100.0	21.1	26.0	32.8	20.0
Black	29,986	5,613	5,716	15,829	2,828	100.0	18.7	19.1	52.8	9.4
American Indian, Eskimo, Aleut	1,959	125	338	563	933	100.0	6.4	17.2	28.7	47.6
American Indian	1,878	122	334	557	866	100.0	6.5	17.8	29.7	46.1
Eskimo	57	2	2	3	51	100.0	2.9	3.5	4.9	88.8
Aleut	24	2	2	3	17	100.0	8.1	8.1	11.5	72.3
Asian or Pacific Islander	7,274	1,335	768	1,122	4,048	100.0	18.4	10.6	15.4	55.7
Chinese	1,645	445	133	204	863	100.0	27.0	8.1	12.4	52.4
Filipino	1,407	143	113	159	991	100.0	10.2	8.1	11.3	70.5
Japanese	848	74	63	67	643	100.0	8.8	7.5	7.9	75.9
Asian Indian	815	285	146	196	189	100.0	35.0	17.9	24.0	23.1
Korean	799	182	109	153	355	100.0	22.8	13.7	19.2	44.4
Vietnamese	615	61	52	169	334	100.0	9.8	8.5	27.4	54.3
Laotian	149	16	28	29	76	100.0	10.7	18.6	19.6	51.0
Cambodian	147	30	13	19	85	100.0	20.5	8.8	13.1	57.7
Thai	91	12	13	24	43	100.0	12.9	14.2	26.0	46.8
Hmong	90	2	37	2	50	100.0	1.9	41.3	1.8	55.0
Pakistani	81	28	15	22	17	100.0	34.3	18.9	26.5	20.4
Hawaiian	211	4	6	12	189	100.0	2.0	2.6	5.8	89.6
Samoan	63	2	2	4	55	100.0	2.4	3.6	6.4	87.6
Guamanian	49	4	3	8	34	100.0	7.3	6.4	16.8	69.5
Other Asian or Pacific Islander	263	49	34	54	126	100.0	18.6	12.9	20.5	48.0
Other races	9,805	1,667	829	2,350	4,960	100.0	17.0	8.5	24.0	50.6
Hispanic origin \1	22,354	3,754	1,727	6,767	10,106	100.0	16.8	7.7	30.3	45.2
Mexican	13,496	175	1,153	4,344	7,824	100.0	1.3	8.5	32.2	58.0
Puerto Rican	2,728	1,872	258	406	192	100.0	68.6	9.4	14.9	7.0
Cuban	1,044	184	37	735	88	100.0	17.6	3.5	70.5	8.5
Other Hispanic	5,086	1,524	279	1,282	2,002	100.0	30.0	5.5	25.2	39.4
Not of Hispanic origin	226,356	47,055	57,942	78,679	42,680	100.0	20.8	25.6	34.8	18.9

Notes:
\1 Persons of Hispanic origin may be of any race.

Source: No. 30. U.S. Bureau of the Census, *Statistical Abstract of the United States: 1998.* Washington, DC, 1999.

A3.2. Resident Population, by Race, Hispanic Origin, and State: 1997

[In thousands. As of July 1. These estimates are consistent with data released in PE-64, PE-65, PPL-110, PPL-111, and PPL-112 released July 28, 1998. These estimates are developed using a cohort-component method whereby each component of population change–births, deaths, domestic migration, and international migration is estimated separately for each birth cohort by sex and race.]

STATE	Total	White			RACE			Hispanic origin \1
		Total	Hispanic	Non-Hispanic	Black	American Indian, Eskimo, Aleut	Asian, Pacific Islander	
United States	267,636	221,334	26,763	194,571	33,947	2,322	10,033	29,348
Alabama	4,319	3,156	34	3,122	1,120	15	28	39
Alaska	609	462	19	443	24	97	27	23
Arizona	4,555	4,046	933	3,113	161	255	93	999
Arkansas	2,523	2,086	40	2,046	406	13	18	45
California	32,268	25,788	9,306	16,482	2,397	307	3,777	9,941
Colorado	3,893	3,598	522	3,076	168	36	90	556
Connecticut	3,270	2,886	229	2,657	300	8	76	259
Delaware	732	575	21	554	140	2	14	24
District of Columbia	529	179	31	148	333	2	16	38
Florida	14,654	12,094	1,952	10,141	2,253	55	253	2,106
Georgia	7,486	5,206	181	5,024	2,126	17	137	207
Hawaii	1,187	396	49	347	35	7	749	95
Idaho	1,210	1,174	80	1,094	7	16	13	86
Illinois	11,896	9,671	1,107	8,564	1,815	27	383	1,183
Indiana	5,864	5,313	125	5,188	484	14	53	137
Iowa	2,852	2,753	48	2,704	56	9	36	53
Kansas	2,595	2,375	120	2,255	153	23	44	133
Kentucky	3,908	3,593	26	3,567	283	6	26	30
Louisiana	4,352	2,882	97	2,785	1,396	19	53	113
Maine	1,242	1,222	8	1,214	6	6	9	9
Maryland	5,094	3,487	150	3,337	1,397	15	195	179
Massachusetts	6,118	5,510	284	5,226	384	14	210	359
Michigan	9,774	8,172	225	7,946	1,392	60	151	254
Minnesota	4,686	4,377	70	4,307	133	57	118	81
Mississippi	2,731	1,709	17	1,691	993	10	18	22
Missouri	5,402	4,717	73	4,645	607	21	58	82
Montana	879	816	13	803	3	55	5	15
Nebraska	1,657	1,555	62	1,493	66	15	21	68
Nevada	1,677	1,448	231	1,218	125	30	74	253
New Hampshire	1,173	1,149	15	1,133	8	2	13	17
New Jersey	8,053	6,438	826	5,611	1,170	21	424	959
New Mexico	1,730	1,503	663	840	44	158	24	693
New York	18,137	13,902	1,943	11,958	3,208	74	953	2,570
North Carolina	7,425	5,595	129	5,466	1,643	95	92	149

A3.2. Resident Population, by Race, Hispanic Origin, and State: 1997 (continued)

STATE	Total	White			Black	American Indian, Eskimo, Aleut	Asian, Pacific Islander	Hispanic origin \1
		Total	Hispanic	Non-Hispanic				
North Dakota	641	602	6	596	4	30	5	7
Ohio	11,186	9,763	153	9,610	1,278	22	129	173
Oklahoma	3,317	2,757	102	2,655	257	260	45	122
Oregon	3,243	3,040	174	2,866	58	44	101	190
Pennsylvania	12,020	10,648	254	10,394	1,164	17	191	302
Rhode Island	987	913	49	864	47	5	22	61
South Carolina	3,760	2,588	39	2,550	1,130	9	32	46
South Dakota	738	670	6	664	5	58	4	8
Tennessee	5,368	4,422	49	4,374	884	12	49	57
Texas	19,439	16,448	5,515	10,933	2,374	93	524	5,723
Utah	2,059	1,962	123	1,838	18	29	51	133
Vermont	589	579	5	575	3	2	4	5
Virginia	6,734	5,139	209	4,930	1,344	18	233	239
Washington	5,610	5,003	302	4,701	196	100	311	340
West Virginia	1,816	1,747	9	1,738	58	2	9	10
Wisconsin	5,170	4,761	114	4,646	286	46	77	128
Wyoming	480	461	26	435	4	11	4	28

Notes:
\1 Persons of Hispanic origin may be of any race.

Source: No. 34, U.S. Bureau of the Census, *Statistical Abstract of the United States: 1998.* Washington, DC, 1999.

A3.3. Population Projections, by Race and Hispanic Origin Status—States: 2000 to 2010

[In thousands. As of July 1. The population projections for states, by single year of age, sex, race, and Hispanic origin prepared for July 1, 1995 to 2025 use the cohort-component method. This method requires separate assumptions for each component of population change: births, deaths, internal migration, and international migration. These components are produced and refined using various administrative records and census distributions. State estimates for 1994 are the starting points for these projections and they are consistent with the middle series of the national projections reported in the U.S. Bureau of the Census, Current Population Reports, series P25-1130. The two series of projections are based on different internal migration assumptions: 1) Series A, is the preferred series model and uses state-to-state migration observed from 1975-76 through 1993-94; and 2) Series B, the economic model, uses the Bureau of Economic Analysis employment projections. Persons of Hispanic origin may be of any race]

| | HISPANIC ORIGIN | | | NOT OF HISPANIC ORIGIN | | | | | | | | | | | |
| | | | | WHITE | | | BLACK | | | AMERICAN INDIAN, ESKIMO, ALEUT | | | ASIAN, PACIFIC ISLANDER | | |
STATE	2000	2005	2010	2000	2005	2010	2000	2005	2010	2000	2005	2010	2000	2005	2010
United States	31,366	36,057	41,138	197,062	199,802	202,390	33,569	35,485	37,466	2,055	2,184	2,321	10,585	12,454	14,402
Alabama	37	42	47	3,231	3,355	3,468	1,133	1,179	1,223	18	18	20	32	38	42
Alaska	31	37	41	461	476	487	27	29	31	91	91	91	44	67	94
Arizona	1,071	1,269	1,450	3,254	3,441	3,518	150	168	179	232	245	256	91	109	119
Arkansas	33	40	46	2,155	2,249	2,320	407	421	432	15	16	18	19	21	23
California	10,647	12,268	14,214	15,562	15,123	15,394	2,138	2,158	2,268	170	161	165	4,006	4,731	5,603
Colorado	594	682	770	3,268	3,434	3,505	178	200	216	30	34	37	98	117	132
Connecticut	288	332	386	2,622	2,574	2,561	293	313	338	6	6	6	76	91	109
Delaware	25	29	33	582	596	597	143	154	165	2	2	2	15	17	19
District of Columbia	40	46	55	152	156	163	315	310	322	0	0	0	13	16	19
Florida	2,390	2,845	3,319	10,405	10,764	11,145	2,159	2,349	2,536	39	42	44	239	279	319
Georgia	189	226	252	5,270	5,515	5,671	2,262	2,495	2,702	15	16	16	138	162	181
Hawaii	107	119	132	363	372	383	27	28	29	4	4	5	755	818	891
Idaho	96	121	140	1,211	1,314	1,368	6	7	8	18	21	23	15	17	19
Illinois	1,267	1,450	1,637	8,553	8,487	8,445	1,813	1,853	1,900	18	18	19	399	457	512
Indiana	140	162	179	5,338	5,453	5,509	494	520	540	14	14	15	58	68	74
Iowa	54	61	71	2,737	2,755	2,762	60	67	72	8	9	10	41	50	56
Kansas	138	166	191	2,293	2,337	2,377	167	180	193	23	25	26	48	55	60
Kentucky	32	38	42	3,643	3,727	3,781	285	295	306	6	6	8	27	31	35
Louisiana	119	138	156	2,792	2,803	2,841	1,438	1,509	1,588	18	18	20	58	68	79
Maine	8	10	14	1,230	1,251	1,284	5	5	5	6	6	6	9	11	13
Maryland	214	258	300	3,371	3,368	3,372	1,462	1,577	1,687	14	14	14	213	248	284
Massachusetts	437	524	619	5,182	5,123	5,063	332	361	391	10	10	10	239	294	350
Michigan	261	289	319	7,790	7,767	7,732	1,417	1,466	1,517	55	57	59	157	184	208
Minnesota	95	114	132	4,387	4,480	4,546	152	178	202	61	68	76	135	166	192
Mississippi	21	24	27	1,755	1,804	1,836	1,010	1,047	1,076	8	8	8	19	23	25
Missouri	90	105	121	4,745	4,863	4,953	622	656	689	22	24	26	61	69	76
Montana	20	26	28	861	904	926	3	4	4	59	65	72	7	9	9
Nebraska	61	72	80	1,540	1,572	1,596	70	78	84	14	16	18	21	27	29
Nevada	277	350	403	1,366	1,456	1,445	128	146	156	25	26	26	77	93	101

A3.3. Population Projections, by Race and Hispanic Origin Status—States: 2000 to 2010 (continued)

STATE	HISPANIC ORIGIN			WHITE			BLACK			AMERICAN INDIAN, ESKIMO, ALEUT			ASIAN, PACIFIC ISLANDER		
	2000	2005	2010	2000	2005	2010	2000	2005	2010	2000	2005	2010	2000	2005	2010
New Hampshire	17	20	22	1,184	1,233	1,273	7	8	8	2	2	2	14	17	21
New Jersey	1,044	1,196	1,348	5,558	5,462	5,387	1,104	1,165	1,232	14	15	15	456	556	656
New Mexico	736	821	912	912	958	984	34	36	37	157	174	195	22	25	28
New York	2,805	3,071	3,357	11,640	11,271	11,023	2,668	2,714	2,790	53	54	56	981	1,140	1,304
North Carolina	121	139	154	5,748	6,040	6,233	1,726	1,844	1,943	92	96	99	92	109	124
North Dakota	6	8	10	611	620	625	5	5	5	32	37	43	6	6	7
Ohio	183	206	230	9,672	9,669	9,638	1,306	1,370	1,433	20	22	22	136	161	181
Oklahoma	124	143	167	2,653	2,700	2,769	276	303	332	273	289	309	47	54	61
Oregon	195	237	278	2,990	3,133	3,253	59	66	71	45	49	53	110	129	147
Pennsylvania	334	391	448	10,460	10,398	10,325	1,181	1,228	1,276	16	18	18	210	249	285
Rhode Island	76	92	112	851	838	834	40	44	48	4	5	6	26	33	39
South Carolina	42	50	58	2,624	2,738	2,848	1,152	1,200	1,249	8	8	9	31	36	40
South Dakota	8	9	10	698	721	729	5	5	6	60	66	72	5	6	7
Tennessee	57	67	75	4,607	4,828	4,969	925	993	1,051	12	14	14	55	64	70
Texas	5,875	6,624	7,421	11,273	11,587	11,866	2,406	2,620	2,833	60	63	66	506	593	671
Utah	138	164	185	1,961	2,117	2,219	18	21	23	33	39	43	58	71	81
Vermont	6	6	8	600	619	630	2	4	4	2	2	2	6	7	8
Virginia	269	322	376	5,061	5,175	5,270	1,394	1,500	1,606	16	16	17	257	309	358
Washington	360	437	519	4,881	5,115	5,346	179	191	203	95	103	112	342	410	477
West Virginia	11	15	17	1,758	1,761	1,757	58	58	58	2	2	2	11	13	15
Wisconsin	136	156	173	4,732	4,799	4,833	318	356	390	45	48	51	97	122	143
Wyoming	35	42	48	469	501	529	4	5	6	12	14	17	4	6	7

Source: No. 38, U.S. Bureau of the Census, Statistical Abstract of the United States: 1998. Washington, DC, 1999.

A3.4. Metropolitan Areas—Racial and Hispanic Origin Populations: 1996

[As of July 1. Areas as defined by U.S. Office of Management and Budget, June 30, 1996. Covers 273 metropolitan areas: 17 consolidated metropolitan statistical area (CMSAs) and 245 metropolitan statistical areas (MSAs) located outside of New England as well as 11 New England county metropolitan areas (NECMAs) in New England.]

METROPOLITAN AREA \1	NUMBER					PERCENT OF TOTAL METROPOLITAN POPULATION			
	Total	Black	American Indian, Eskimo, Aleut	Asian and Pacific Islander	Hispanic origin \2	Black	American Indian, Eskimo, Aleut	Asian and Pacific Islander	Hispanic origin \2
New York-Northern New Jersey-Long Island, NY-NJ-CT-PA CMSA/NECMA \1	19,846,588	3,838,950	60,605	1,222,350	3,325,071	19.3	0.3	6.2	16.8
Los Angeles-Riverside-Orange County, CA CMSA	15,495,155	1,305,764	112,525	1,712,608	5,850,261	8.4	0.7	11.1	37.8
Chicago-Gary-Kenosha, IL-IN-WI CMSA	8,599,774	1,655,501	20,132	339,558	1,124,558	19.3	0.2	3.9	13.1
Washington-Baltimore, DC-MD-VA-WV CMSA	7,164,519	1,839,778	22,176	341,941	351,073	25.7	0.3	4.8	4.9
San Francisco-Oakland-San Jose, CA CMSA	6,605,428	572,837	48,800	1,197,820	1,228,470	8.7	0.7	18.1	18.6
Philadelphia-Wilmington-Atlantic City, PA-NJ-DE-MD CMSA	5,973,463	1,159,594	14,129	163,613	278,021	19.4	0.2	2.7	4.7
Boston-Worcester-Lawrence-Lowell-Brockton, MA-NH NECMA	5,796,488	330,651	12,278	195,198	296,811	5.7	0.2	3.4	5.1
Detroit-Ann Arbor-Flint, MI CMSA	5,284,171	1,107,856	22,142	98,265	123,857	21.0	0.4	1.9	2.3
Dallas-Fort Worth, TX CMSA	4,574,561	650,691	26,998	154,375	689,738	14.2	0.6	3.4	15.1
Houston-Galveston-Brazoria, TX CMSA	4,253,428	777,628	15,510	205,608	1,004,935	18.3	0.4	4.8	23.6
Atlanta, GA MSA	3,541,230	913,943	7,872	91,004	105,376	25.8	0.2	2.6	3.0
Miami-Fort Lauderdale, FL CMSA	3,514,403	688,225	8,645	64,399	1,286,005	19.6	0.2	1.8	36.6
Seattle-Tacoma-Bremerton, WA CMSA	3,320,829	164,942	44,791	254,200	132,672	5.0	1.3	7.7	4.0
Cleveland-Akron, OH CMSA	2,913,430	480,887	5,808	36,947	65,136	16.5	0.2	1.3	2.2
Minneapolis-St. Paul, MN-WI MSA	2,765,116	121,612	27,574	94,299	54,151	4.4	1.0	3.4	2.0
Phoenix-Mesa, AZ MSA	2,746,703	109,922	64,877	60,924	536,414	4.0	2.4	2.2	19.5
San Diego, CA MSA	2,655,463	168,703	23,809	272,131	665,624	6.4	0.9	10.2	25.1
St. Louis, MO-IL MSA	2,548,238	448,563	5,061	31,028	33,092	17.6	0.2	1.2	1.3
Pittsburgh, PA MSA	2,379,411	196,828	2,589	22,334	17,171	8.3	0.1	0.9	0.7
Denver-Boulder-Greeley, CO CMSA	2,277,401	119,346	18,752	62,667	319,640	5.2	0.8	2.8	14.0
Tampa-St. Petersburg-Clearwater, FL MSA	2,199,231	224,393	7,374	35,283	189,457	10.2	0.3	1.6	8.6
Portland-Salem, OR-WA CMSA	2,078,357	55,521	21,601	81,669	115,412	2.7	1.0	3.9	5.6
Cincinnati-Hamilton, OH-KY-IN CMSA	1,920,931	221,699	2,814	19,084	12,155	11.5	0.1	1.0	0.6
Kansas City, MO-KS MSA	1,690,343	224,502	8,035	24,339	58,773	13.3	0.5	1.4	3.5
Milwaukee-Racine, WI CMSA	1,642,658	243,475	9,350	26,217	76,109	14.8	0.6	1.6	4.6
Sacramento-Yolo, CA CMSA	1,632,133	114,760	21,535	159,026	234,892	7.0	1.3	9.7	14.4

A3.4. Metropolitan Areas—Racial and Hispanic Origin Populations: 1996 (continued)

METROPOLITAN AREA \1	NUMBER					PERCENT OF TOTAL METROPOLITAN POPULATION			
	Total	Black	American Indian, Eskimo, Aleut	Asian and Pacific Islander	Hispanic origin \2	Black	American Indian, Eskimo, Aleut	Asian and Pacific Islander	Hispanic origin \2
Norfolk-Virginia Beach-Newport News, VA-NC MSA	1,540,252	458,209	5,384	49,181	44,047	29.7	0.3	3.2	2.9
Indianapolis, IN MSA	1,492,297	202,510	3,186	14,930	16,643	13.6	0.2	1.0	1.1
San Antonio, TX MSA	1,490,111	98,585	6,471	24,562	776,796	6.6	0.4	1.6	52.1
Columbus, OH MSA	1,447,646	189,062	3,236	27,950	14,383	13.1	0.2	1.9	1.0
Orlando, FL MSA	1,417,291	195,005	5,155	35,307	149,143	13.8	0.4	2.5	10.5
Charlotte-Gastonia-Rock Hill, NC-SC MSA	1,321,068	269,929	5,176	18,883	20,125	20.4	0.4	1.4	1.5
New Orleans, LA MSA	1,312,890	459,408	4,254	27,967	62,857	35.0	0.3	2.1	4.8
Salt Lake City-Ogden, UT MSA	1,217,842	15,113	10,206	35,945	88,655	1.2	0.8	3.0	7.3
Las Vegas, NV-AZ MSA	1,201,073	108,709	14,103	50,296	169,160	9.1	1.2	4.2	14.1
Buffalo-Niagara Falls, NY MSA	1,175,240	134,100	8,222	14,935	29,876	11.4	0.7	1.3	2.5
Greensboro—Winston-Salem—High Point, NC MSA	1,141,238	223,983	4,260	10,917	14,093	19.6	0.4	1.0	1.2
Nashville, TN MSA	1,117,178	175,915	2,645	15,297	12,725	15.7	0.2	1.4	1.1
Hartford, CT NECMA	1,110,102	104,214	2,305	24,720	89,693	9.4	0.2	2.2	8.1
Rochester, NY MSA	1,088,037	108,210	4,124	19,938	40,358	9.9	0.4	1.8	3.7
Memphis, TN-AR-MS MSA	1,078,151	452,067	2,026	11,745	12,085	41.9	0.2	1.1	1.1
Austin-San Marcos, TX MSA	1,041,330	104,218	4,894	30,881	253,053	10.0	0.5	3.0	24.3
Oklahoma City, OK MSA	1,026,657	111,201	48,330	22,182	46,867	10.8	4.7	2.2	4.6
Raleigh-Durham-Chapel Hill, NC MSA	1,025,253	248,388	3,009	24,478	21,253	24.2	0.3	2.4	2.1
Grand Rapids-Muskegon-Holland, MI MSA	1,015,099	75,801	6,050	12,574	37,319	7.5	0.6	1.2	3.7
Jacksonville, FL MSA	1,008,633	222,712	3,507	25,029	32,847	22.1	0.3	2.5	3.3
West Palm Beach-Boca Raton, FL MSA	992,840	142,583	1,928	14,936	97,297	14.4	0.2	1.5	9.8
Louisville, KY-IN MSA	991,765	128,898	1,590	7,665	7,618	13.0	0.2	0.8	0.8
Dayton-Springfield, OH MSA	950,661	136,092	1,964	11,858	8,667	14.3	0.2	1.2	0.9
Richmond-Petersburg, VA MSA	935,174	279,974	2,937	16,611	13,145	29.9	0.3	1.8	1.4
Providence-Warwick-Pawtucket, RI NECMA	907,479	43,702	4,322	20,129	57,384	4.8	0.5	2.2	6.3
Greenville-Spartanburg-Anderson, SC MSA	896,679	160,801	1,365	7,103	8,639	17.9	0.2	0.8	1.0
Birmingham, AL MSA	894,702	258,937	1,437	4,956	5,606	28.9	0.2	0.6	0.6
Albany-Schenectady-Troy, NY MSA	878,527	44,513	1,699	14,928	18,558	5.1	0.2	1.7	2.1
Honolulu, HI MSA	871,766	32,909	4,317	560,958	63,465	3.8	0.5	64.3	7.3
Fresno, CA MSA	861,753	42,938	11,781	80,559	354,950	5.0	1.4	9.3	41.2
Tucson, AZ MSA	767,873	28,543	26,415	18,003	213,858	3.7	3.4	2.3	27.9
Tulsa, OK MSA	756,493	64,048	50,136	8,127	20,123	8.5	6.6	1.1	2.7
Syracuse, NY MSA	745,691	46,498	4,556	11,064	12,533	6.2	0.6	1.5	1.7
El Paso, TX MSA	684,446	24,681	3,531	9,868	502,780	3.6	0.5	1.4	73.5
Omaha, NE-IA MSA	681,698	57,828	4,057	10,461	29,125	8.5	0.6	1.5	4.3

A3.4. Metropolitan Areas—Racial and Hispanic Origin Populations: 1996 (*continued*)

METROPOLITAN AREA \1	NUMBER					PERCENT OF TOTAL METROPOLITAN POPULATION			
	Total	Black	American Indian, Eskimo, Aleut	Asian and Pacific Islander	Hispanic origin \2	Black	American Indian, Eskimo, Aleut	Asian and Pacific Islander	Hispanic origin \2
Albuquerque, NM MSA	670,092	21,905	38,350	13,053	257,097	3.3	5.7	1.9	38.4
Knoxville, TN MSA	649,277	41,662	1,770	6,946	5,279	6.4	0.3	1.1	0.8
Scranton—Wilkes-Barre—Hazleton, PA MSA	628,073	6,356	458	4,172	4,483	1.0	0.1	0.7	0.7
Bakersfield, CA MSA	622,729	39,650	10,956	27,523	210,503	6.4	1.8	4.4	33.8
Harrisburg-Lebanon-Carlisle, PA MSA	614,755	46,682	901	8,975	13,583	7.6	0.1	1.5	2.2
Allentown-Bethlehem-Easton, PA MSA	614,304	15,386	752	9,221	35,486	2.5	0.1	1.5	5.8
Toledo, OH MSA	611,417	74,503	1,619	7,619	23,966	12.2	0.3	1.2	3.9
Youngstown-Warren, OH MSA	598,582	60,817	985	2,832	9,196	10.2	0.2	0.5	1.5
Springfield, MA NECMA	591,804	45,572	1,188	11,494	57,803	7.7	0.2	1.9	9.8
Baton Rouge, LA MSA	567,388	176,361	1,025	7,574	9,344	31.1	0.2	1.3	1.6
Little Rock-North Little Rock, AR MSA	548,352	114,320	1,813	4,352	8,366	20.8	0.3	0.8	1.5
Stockton-Lodi, CA MSA	533,392	30,746	5,941	81,342	147,994	5.8	1.1	15.2	27.7
Sarasota-Bradenton, FL MSA	528,803	35,912	1,390	4,241	21,662	6.8	0.3	0.8	4.1
Mobile, AL MSA	518,975	145,140	2,452	4,523	6,325	28.0	0.5	0.9	1.2
Wichita, KS MSA	512,965	41,420	5,569	11,751	27,204	8.1	1.1	2.3	5.3
McAllen-Edinburg-Mission, TX MSA	495,594	1,408	1,137	1,932	432,876	0.3	0.2	0.4	87.3
Charleston-North Charleston, SC MSA	495,143	154,031	1,589	7,730	9,254	31.1	0.3	1.6	1.9
Columbia, SC MSA	488,207	147,355	1,046	6,491	7,582	30.2	0.2	1.3	1.6
Fort Wayne, IN MSA	475,299	34,497	1,415	4,123	10,281	7.3	0.3	0.9	2.2
Colorado Springs, CO MSA	472,924	36,338	4,271	15,076	47,691	7.7	0.9	3.2	10.1
Johnson City-Kingsport-Bristol, TN-VA MSA	458,229	10,197	877	1,803	2,642	2.2	0.2	0.4	0.6
Daytona Beach, FL MSA	456,464	47,769	1,396	5,303	23,246	10.5	0.3	1.2	5.1
Melbourne-Titusville-Palm Bay, FL MSA	453,998	41,932	1,967	9,022	18,608	9.2	0.4	2.0	4.1
Augusta-Aiken, GA-SC MSA	453,612	149,234	1,133	9,125	9,416	32.9	0.2	2.0	2.1
Lancaster, PA MSA	450,834	13,505	624	6,803	21,296	3.0	0.1	1.5	4.7
Lansing-East Lansing, MI MSA	447,538	35,215	2,942	11,167	20,487	7.9	0.7	2.5	4.6
Chattanooga, TN-GA MSA	446,096	64,265	1,009	4,127	3,915	14.4	0.2	0.9	0.9
Kalamazoo-Battle Creek, MI MSA	444,428	44,187	2,509	6,034	10,735	9.9	0.6	1.4	2.4
Lexington, KY MSA	441,073	44,606	690	6,206	4,461	10.1	0.2	1.4	1.0
Lakeland-Winter Haven, FL MSA	440,954	67,981	1,624	4,037	23,492	15.4	0.4	0.9	5.3
Des Moines, IA MSA	427,436	17,724	1,190	8,772	10,743	4.1	0.3	2.1	2.5
Jackson, MS MSA	421,068	182,152	397	2,340	2,444	43.3	0.1	0.6	0.6
Modesto, CA MSA	415,786	7,680	5,063	27,354	111,063	1.8	1.2	6.6	26.7
Spokane, WA MSA	404,920	6,534	6,454	9,384	10,692	1.6	1.6	2.3	2.6
Saginaw-Bay City-Midland, MI MSA	403,301	42,618	2,234	3,432	20,676	10.6	0.6	0.9	5.1
Canton-Massillon, OH MSA	402,928	28,229	1,062	2,041	3,555	7.0	0.3	0.5	0.9

A3.4. Metropolitan Areas—Racial and Hispanic Origin Populations: 1996 (continued)

METROPOLITAN AREA \1	NUMBER					PERCENT OF TOTAL METROPOLITAN POPULATION			
	Total	Black	American Indian, Eskimo, Aleut	Asian and Pacific Islander	Hispanic origin \2	Black	American Indian, Eskimo, Aleut	Asian and Pacific Islander	Hispanic origin \2
Madison, WI MSA	395,366	13,864	1,440	12,144	8,119	3.5	0.4	3.1	2.1
Pensacola, FL MSA	385,820	68,004	4,314	9,739	9,445	17.6	1.1	2.5	2.4
Santa Barbara-Santa Maria-Lompoc, CA MSA	385,573	11,669	4,684	22,097	123,677	3.0	1.2	5.7	32.1
Corpus Christi, TX MSA	384,056	15,728	1,791	4,237	217,039	4.1	0.5	1.1	56.5
Fort Myers-Cape Coral, FL MSA	380,001	29,652	1,069	3,280	22,501	7.8	0.3	0.9	5.9
Shreveport-Bossier City, LA MSA	379,596	137,823	1,006	2,791	5,463	36.3	0.3	0.7	1.4
Beaumont-Port Arthur, TX MSA	375,795	92,500	1,033	7,864	19,185	24.6	0.3	2.1	5.1
Boise City, ID MSA	372,587	2,029	2,644	5,541	28,497	0.5	0.7	1.5	7.6
Lafayette, LA MSA	368,635	107,164	612	3,019	5,187	29.1	0.2	0.8	1.4
York, PA MSA	368,332	14,208	535	3,148	7,240	3.9	0.1	0.9	2.0
Davenport-Moline-Rock Island, IA-IL MSA	357,800	21,458	1,044	3,330	18,040	6.0	0.3	0.9	5.0
Rockford, IL MSA	352,369	26,934	892	4,487	15,600	7.6	0.3	1.3	4.4
Reading, PA MSA	352,353	12,597	434	4,479	22,651	3.6	0.1	1.3	6.4
Visalia-Tulare-Porterville, CA MSA	349,922	5,837	6,059	20,140	157,013	1.7	1.7	5.8	44.9
Peoria-Pekin, IL MSA	346,501	27,639	641	3,562	4,901	8.0	0.2	1.0	1.4
Biloxi-Gulfport-Pascagoula, MS MSA	343,184	68,201	1,040	7,735	6,376	19.9	0.3	2.3	1.9
Appleton-Oshkosh-Neenah, WI MSA	340,564	1,519	3,381	5,588	3,293	0.4	1.0	1.6	1.0
Salinas, CA MSA	339,047	20,175	3,572	34,250	135,397	6.0	1.1	10.1	39.9
Huntsville, AL MSA	330,153	65,497	1,718	6,016	5,097	19.8	0.5	1.8	1.5
Provo-Orem, UT MSA	319,694	544	2,413	5,878	12,817	0.2	0.8	1.8	4.0
Huntington-Ashland, WV-KY-OH MSA	316,641	7,085	357	1,115	1,539	2.2	0.1	0.4	0.5
Brownsville-Harlingen-San Benito, TX MSA	315,015	1,250	609	1,214	265,784	0.4	0.2	0.4	84.4
Hickory-Morganton-Lenoir, NC MSA	314,965	24,149	646	2,881	3,273	7.7	0.2	0.9	1.0
Montgomery, AL MSA	314,955	115,694	609	2,257	3,084	36.7	0.2	0.7	1.0
Macon, GA MSA	312,689	118,860	687	3,197	4,784	38.0	0.2	1.0	1.5
Eugene-Springfield, OR MSA	306,862	2,620	3,524	7,257	10,558	0.9	1.1	2.4	3.4
Utica-Rome, NY MSA	302,405	15,459	666	3,062	7,711	5.1	0.2	1.0	2.5
Reno, NV MSA	298,787	7,498	6,453	15,432	36,121	2.5	2.2	5.2	12.1
Killeen-Temple, TX MSA	296,896	58,532	1,953	12,156	44,296	19.7	0.7	4.1	14.9
Springfield, MO MSA	296,345	4,902	1,718	2,376	2,941	1.7	0.6	0.8	1.0
Evansville-Henderson, IN-KY MSA	288,735	17,754	491	1,635	1,784	6.1	0.2	0.6	0.6
Fort Pierce-Port St. Lucie, FL MSA	287,255	41,005	1,048	2,783	16,064	14.3	0.4	1.0	5.6
Fayetteville, NC MSA	284,800	90,947	5,130	8,920	21,567	31.9	1.8	3.1	7.6
Savannah, GA MSA	282,610	103,563	650	3,986	5,047	36.6	0.2	1.4	1.8
Erie, PA MSA	280,570	16,952	506	1,957	4,458	6.0	0.2	0.7	1.6
Columbus, GA-AL MSA	272,273	107,734	916	4,783	11,237	39.6	0.3	1.8	4.1

A3.4. Metropolitan Areas—Racial and Hispanic Origin Populations: 1996 (continued)

METROPOLITAN AREA \1	NUMBER					PERCENT OF TOTAL METROPOLITAN POPULATION			
	Total	Black	American Indian, Eskimo, Aleut	Asian and Pacific Islander	Hispanic origin \2	Black	American Indian, Eskimo, Aleut	Asian and Pacific Islander	Hispanic origin \2
Fayetteville-Springdale-Rogers, AR MSA	260,940	2,404	3,325	2,354	6,932	0.9	1.3	0.9	2.7
Tallahassee, FL MSA	259,380	85,876	789	4,433	8,059	33.1	0.3	1.7	3.1
South Bend, IN MSA	257,740	27,456	896	3,415	6,964	10.7	0.3	1.3	2.7
Charleston, WV MSA	254,575	13,996	285	1,590	1,164	5.5	0.1	0.6	0.5
Binghamton, NY MSA	254,053	5,066	466	5,216	3,439	2.0	0.2	2.1	1.4
Portland, ME NECMA	251,087	1,779	611	2,676	1,979	0.7	0.2	1.1	0.8
New London-Norwich, CT NECMA	250,735	13,281	1,523	5,000	10,317	5.3	0.6	2.0	4.1
Anchorage, AK MSA	250,505	15,635	16,480	14,848	11,860	6.2	6.6	5.9	4.7
Duluth-Superior, MN-WI MSA	239,465	1,586	4,814	1,822	1,517	0.7	2.0	0.8	0.6
Odessa-Midland, TX MSA	239,414	15,773	1,325	2,394	72,759	6.6	0.6	1.0	30.4
Johnstown, PA MSA	239,017	4,530	165	717	1,568	1.9	0.1	0.3	0.7
Lubbock, TX MSA	232,035	19,159	846	3,851	62,248	8.3	0.4	1.7	26.8
Lincoln, NE MSA	231,765	5,558	1,632	5,340	6,973	2.4	0.7	2.3	3.0
Ocala, FL MSA	230,068	33,586	904	1,671	9,139	14.6	0.4	0.7	4.0
San Luis Obispo-Atascadero-Paso Robles, CA MSA	229,437	6,462	2,707	8,464	37,826	2.8	1.2	3.7	16.5
Roanoke, VA MSA	229,105	30,343	280	2,108	1,868	13.2	0.1	0.9	0.8
Fort Collins-Loveland, CO MSA	221,725	1,489	1,489	4,093	16,681	0.7	0.7	1.8	7.5
Yakima, WA MSA	216,234	3,337	12,162	3,913	64,024	1.5	5.6	1.8	29.6
Green Bay, WI MSA	213,072	1,343	4,595	3,688	2,144	0.6	2.2	1.7	1.0
Asheville, NC MSA	210,042	16,371	631	1,303	2,349	7.8	0.3	0.6	1.1
Wilmington, NC MSA	206,738	41,255	933	1,250	2,617	20.0	0.5	0.6	1.3
Longview-Marshall, TX MSA	206,732	44,787	941	1,040	7,406	21.7	0.5	0.5	3.6
Amarillo, TX MSA	206,015	12,066	1,953	5,027	32,994	5.9	0.9	2.4	16.0
Lynchburg, VA MSA	205,559	40,121	384	1,197	1,613	19.5	0.2	0.6	0.8
Springfield, IL MSA	204,130	16,979	362	1,964	1,875	8.3	0.2	1.0	0.9
Barnstable-Yarmouth, MA NECMA	201,970	3,819	1,380	1,556	3,088	1.9	0.7	0.8	1.5
Waco, TX MSA	201,775	33,113	766	2,011	30,142	16.4	0.4	1.0	14.9
Gainesville, FL MSA	196,525	42,940	481	6,941	9,223	21.8	0.2	3.5	4.7
Chico-Paradise, CA MSA	192,507	2,698	3,758	7,208	18,487	1.4	2.0	3.7	9.6
Merced, CA MSA	192,311	9,213	2,119	19,864	73,590	4.8	1.1	10.3	38.3
Fort Smith, AR-OK MSA	191,482	8,092	9,387	5,079	4,314	4.2	4.9	2.7	2.3
Burlington, VT NECMA	190,548	1,667	974	2,691	2,263	0.9	0.5	1.4	1.2
Houma, LA MSA	189,869	30,306	7,040	1,837	3,252	16.0	3.7	1.0	1.7
Naples, FL MSA	188,187	10,671	806	1,153	32,220	5.7	0.4	0.6	17.1
Clarksville-Hopkinsville, TN-KY MSA	186,368	38,783	819	4,233	8,222	20.8	0.4	2.3	4.4
Richland-Kennewick-Pasco, WA MSA	179,949	3,482	1,524	4,822	30,759	1.9	0.8	2.7	17.1

A3.4. Metropolitan Areas—Racial and Hispanic Origin Populations: 1996 (continued)

METROPOLITAN AREA \1	NUMBER					PERCENT OF TOTAL METROPOLITAN POPULATION			
	Total	Black	American Indian, Eskimo, Aleut	Asian and Pacific Islander	Hispanic origin \2	Black	American Indian, Eskimo, Aleut	Asian and Pacific Islander	Hispanic origin \2
Cedar Rapids, IA MSA	179,411	3,891	407	1,926	2,533	2.2	0.2	1.1	1.4
Lake Charles, LA MSA	178,881	44,189	422	835	2,338	24.7	0.2	0.5	1.3
Laredo, TX MSA	176,792	333	373	853	167,728	0.2	0.2	0.5	94.9
Mansfield, OH MSA	175,441	11,960	297	895	1,398	6.8	0.2	0.5	0.8
Lafayette, IN MSA	171,200	3,121	423	6,346	3,464	1.8	0.2	3.7	2.0
Elkhart-Goshen, IN MSA	168,941	8,401	520	1,409	4,082	5.0	0.3	0.8	2.4
Medford-Ashland, OR MSA	168,609	473	2,217	2,027	9,528	0.3	1.3	1.2	5.7
Champaign-Urbana, IL MSA	167,392	17,807	314	9,718	3,652	10.6	0.2	5.8	2.2
Fort Walton Beach, FL MSA	165,873	17,085	1,114	6,248	6,888	10.3	0.7	3.8	4.2
Fargo-Moorhead, ND-MN MSA	165,191	622	1,891	2,160	2,733	0.4	1.1	1.3	1.7
Tyler, TX MSA	165,002	36,192	677	999	11,703	21.9	0.4	0.6	7.1
Topeka, KS MSA	164,938	14,813	1,918	1,635	10,571	9.0	1.2	1.0	6.4
Myrtle Beach, SC MSA	163,856	29,468	396	1,650	1,893	18.0	0.2	1.0	1.2
Las Cruces, NM MSA	163,849	3,081	1,253	1,898	94,444	1.9	0.8	1.2	57.6
Redding, CA MSA	161,740	1,280	4,523	3,844	8,092	0.8	2.8	2.4	5.0
Benton Harbor, MI MSA	161,434	26,814	682	1,920	3,106	16.6	0.4	1.2	1.9
St. Cloud, MN MSA	160,326	683	535	1,456	1,013	0.4	0.3	0.9	0.6
Tuscaloosa, AL MSA	158,779	43,772	237	1,533	1,361	27.6	0.1	1.0	0.9
Sioux Falls, SD MSA	156,598	1,141	2,114	1,173	1,080	0.7	1.3	0.7	0.7
Wheeling, WV-OH MSA	155,808	3,295	132	625	623	2.1	0.1	0.4	0.4
Lima, OH MSA	155,499	13,563	276	971	1,804	8.7	0.2	0.6	1.2
Jackson, MI MSA	154,563	13,024	688	892	2,830	8.4	0.4	0.6	1.8
Bellingham, WA MSA	152,512	891	4,931	3,560	6,057	0.6	3.2	2.3	4.0
Parkersburg-Marietta, WV-OH MSA	151,597	1,695	241	629	536	1.1	0.2	0.4	0.4
Janesville-Beloit, WI MSA	150,584	8,822	434	1,429	2,453	5.9	0.3	0.9	1.6
Terre Haute, IN MSA	149,671	6,446	370	1,512	1,384	4.3	0.2	1.0	0.9
Monroe, LA MSA	147,302	48,547	259	972	1,430	33.0	0.2	0.7	1.0
Joplin, MO MSA	145,716	1,657	2,496	1,034	1,518	1.1	1.7	0.7	1.0
Bangor, ME NECMA	144,989	605	1,195	1,148	877	0.4	0.8	0.8	0.6
Charlottesville, VA MSA	144,815	23,079	166	3,681	1,987	15.9	0.1	2.5	1.4
Panama City, FL MSA	144,637	17,868	1,298	3,714	3,441	12.4	0.9	2.6	2.4
Jacksonville, NC MSA	144,533	28,477	1,044	4,489	11,697	19.7	0.7	3.1	8.1
Rocky Mount, NC MSA	144,157	59,900	369	470	1,388	41.6	0.3	0.3	1.0
Eau Claire, WI MSA	143,245	340	695	3,289	832	0.2	0.5	2.3	0.6
Jamestown, NY MSA	140,800	3,078	629	751	5,215	2.2	0.4	0.5	3.7
Decatur, AL MSA	139,979	16,781	2,107	525	1,111	12.0	1.5	0.4	0.8

A3.4. Metropolitan Areas—Racial and Hispanic Origin Populations: 1996 *(continued)*

METROPOLITAN AREA \1	NUMBER					PERCENT OF TOTAL METROPOLITAN POPULATION			
	Total	Black	American Indian, Eskimo, Aleut	Asian and Pacific Islander	Hispanic origin \2	Black	American Indian, Eskimo, Aleut	Asian and Pacific Islander	Hispanic origin \2
Bloomington-Normal, IL MSA	139,133	6,547	265	2,240	2,362	4.7	0.2	1.6	1.7
Steubenville-Weirton, OH-WV MSA	138,315	5,842	217	504	778	4.2	0.2	0.4	0.6
Santa Fe, NM MSA	137,223	1,219	3,830	1,488	62,068	0.9	2.8	1.1	45.2
Athens, GA MSA	137,204	31,279	259	3,597	3,012	22.8	0.2	2.6	2.2
Yuba City, CA MSA	136,555	4,026	3,327	15,749	23,915	2.9	2.4	11.5	17.5
Wichita Falls, TX MSA	136,311	12,870	1,160	2,752	13,609	9.4	0.9	2.0	10.0
Florence, AL MSA	136,083	17,755	271	371	725	13.0	0.2	0.3	0.5
Pittsfield, MA NECMA	134,788	2,980	259	1,300	1,717	2.2	0.2	1.0	1.3
Dothan, AL MSA	132,945	29,655	476	1,514	2,331	22.3	0.4	1.1	1.8
Bryan-College Station, TX MSA	131,904	15,819	378	6,082	21,706	12.0	0.3	4.6	16.5
State College, PA MSA	131,489	3,366	207	5,617	1,846	2.6	0.2	4.3	1.4
Altoona, PA MSA	131,450	1,244	137	517	563	0.9	0.1	0.4	0.4
Pueblo, CO MSA	131,217	2,853	1,161	1,017	51,218	2.2	0.9	0.8	39.0
Punta Gorda, FL MSA	130,426	5,800	340	1,357	4,428	4.4	0.3	1.0	3.4
Alexandria, LA MSA	126,290	37,755	551	1,130	1,684	29.9	0.4	0.9	1.3
Billings, MT MSA	125,966	704	3,942	724	3,822	0.6	3.1	0.6	3.0
Columbia, MO MSA	125,676	10,788	422	4,536	1,687	8.6	0.3	3.6	1.3
Yuma, AZ MSA	125,142	4,307	2,046	2,275	56,067	3.4	1.6	1.8	44.8
Texarkana, TX-Texarkana, AR MSA	123,919	28,943	591	546	2,272	23.4	0.5	0.4	1.8
Florence, SC MSA	123,365	48,883	162	419	672	39.6	0.1	0.3	0.5
Waterloo-Cedar Falls, IA MSA	122,806	9,086	234	1,301	1,347	7.4	0.2	1.1	1.1
Glens Falls, NY MSA	122,267	2,466	244	577	2,155	2.0	0.2	0.5	1.8
Dover, DE MSA	122,244	25,073	739	2,207	3,686	20.5	0.6	1.8	3.0
Sharon, PA MSA	122,155	6,726	123	539	657	5.5	0.1	0.4	0.5
Abilene, TX MSA	122,130	8,289	599	2,189	21,302	6.8	0.5	1.8	17.4
Wausau, WI MSA	121,791	133	560	3,444	642	0.1	0.5	2.8	0.5
La Crosse, WI-MN MSA	121,544	605	421	3,757	956	0.5	0.3	3.1	0.8
Sioux City, IA-NE MSA	121,108	2,250	2,426	2,292	5,841	1.9	2.0	1.9	4.8
Williamsport, PA MSA	119,083	3,181	226	634	835	2.7	0.2	0.5	0.7
Greenville, NC MSA	119,064	40,835	284	1,181	1,706	34.3	0.2	1.0	1.4
Muncie, IN MSA	118,600	7,885	288	817	1,106	6.6	0.2	0.7	0.9
Flagstaff, AZ-UT MSA	118,011	1,957	33,563	1,321	13,324	1.7	28.4	1.1	11.3
Albany, GA MSA	117,286	56,428	299	760	1,424	48.1	0.3	0.6	1.2
Bloomington, IN MSA	116,176	3,360	270	3,618	1,955	2.9	0.2	3.1	1.7
Decatur, IL MSA	115,416	15,185	150	635	692	13.2	0.1	0.6	0.6

A3.4. Metropolitan Areas—Racial and Hispanic Origin Populations: 1996 (continued)

METROPOLITAN AREA \1	NUMBER					PERCENT OF TOTAL METROPOLITAN POPULATION			
	Total	Black	American Indian, Eskimo, Aleut	Asian and Pacific Islander	Hispanic origin \2	Black	American Indian, Eskimo, Aleut	Asian and Pacific Islander	Hispanic origin \2
Anniston, AL MSA	113,511	21,677	248	1,028	1,588	19.1	0.2	0.5	1.4
Rochester, MN MSA	113,182	1,073	325	4,809	1,412	0.9	0.3	4.2	1.2
Goldsboro, NC MSA	111,581	36,893	332	1,301	2,332	33.1	0.3	1.2	2.1
Lawton, OK MSA	111,171	19,845	5,255	3,827	8,840	17.9	4.7	3.4	8.0
Sheboygan, WI MSA	109,705	733	440	2,896	2,347	0.7	0.4	2.6	2.1
Danville, VA MSA	109,246	37,124	116	401	632	34.0	0.1	0.4	0.6
Grand Junction, CO MSA	108,371	506	826	967	9,992	0.5	0.8	0.9	9.2
Hattiesburg, MS MSA	107,897	28,216	164	800	957	26.2	0.2	0.7	0.9
Sumter, SC MSA	107,161	47,794	203	1,213	1,595	44.6	0.2	1.1	1.5
Grand Forks, ND-MN MSA	103,883	1,736	1,964	1,377	3,009	1.7	1.9	1.3	2.9
San Angelo, TX MSA	102,580	4,548	518	1,448	30,776	4.4	0.5	1.4	30.0
Gadsden, AL MSA	102,129	14,841	238	453	488	14.5	0.2	0.4	0.5
Lewiston-Auburn, ME NECMA	101,754	572	244	685	995	0.6	0.2	0.7	1.0
Iowa City, IA MSA	101,609	2,443	226	5,060	2,326	2.4	0.2	5.0	2.3
Cumberland, MD-WV MSA	100,600	2,592	80	489	545	2.6	0.1	0.5	0.5
Sherman-Denison, TX MSA	100,589	7,399	1,216	642	3,673	7.4	1.2	0.6	3.7
Kokomo, IN MSA	100,579	5,057	253	681	1,567	5.0	0.3	0.7	1.6
Jackson, TN MSA	98,489	29,101	91	407	622	29.5	0.1	0.4	0.6
St. Joseph, MO MSA	97,336	3,007	305	370	2,176	3.1	0.3	0.4	2.2
Elmira, NY MSA	93,282	5,722	222	973	1,693	6.1	0.2	1.0	1.8
Owensboro, KY MSA	90,818	3,920	109	318	398	4.3	0.1	0.4	0.4
Bismarck, ND MSA	90,103	117	2,487	459	589	0.1	2.8	0.5	0.7
Lawrence, KS MSA	89,899	3,898	2,233	3,354	3,066	4.3	2.5	3.7	3.4
Dubuque, IA MSA	88,201	397	97	592	647	0.5	0.1	0.7	0.7
Rapid City, SD MSA	87,145	1,784	6,804	1,279	2,419	2.0	7.8	1.5	2.8
Pine Bluff, AR MSA	83,007	37,956	204	414	733	45.7	0.2	0.5	0.9
Victoria, TX MSA	81,541	5,544	280	392	31,717	6.8	0.3	0.5	38.9
Great Falls, MT MSA	81,087	1,309	3,508	918	1,583	1.6	4.3	1.1	2.0
Cheyenne, WY MSA	79,175	2,438	633	1,135	8,144	3.1	0.8	1.4	10.3
Jonesboro, AR MSA	76,155	4,636	217	551	849	6.1	0.3	0.7	1.1
Pocatello, ID MSA	73,608	823	1,977	924	4,094	1.1	2.7	1.3	5.6
Casper, WY MSA	63,875	523	466	364	2,345	0.8	0.7	0.6	3.7
Enid, OK MSA	57,312	2,101	1,223	705	1,398	3.7	2.1	1.2	2.4

Notes:
\1 Metropolitan areas are shown in rank order of total population.
\2 Persons of Hispanic origin may be of any race.
\3 Includes data for New Haven-Bridgeport-Stamford-Waterbury-Danbury, CT NECMA.

Source: No. 44, U.S. Bureau of the Census, *Statistical Abstract of the United States: 1998.* Washington, DC, 1999.

A3.5. Metropolitan Areas with Large Numbers of Selected Racial Groups and of Hispanic Origin Population: 1996

[As of July 1. For Black, Hispanic origin, and Asian and Pacific Islander populations, areas selected had 100,000 or more of specified group; for American Indian, Eskimo, and Aleut population, areas selected are ten areas with largest number of that group. Areas as defined by U.S. Office of Management and Budget, June 30, 1996. Based on 273 metropolitan areas: 17 consolidated metropolitan statistical areas (CMSAs) and 245 metropolitan statistical areas (MSAs) located outside of New England as well as 11 New England county metropolitan areas (NECMAs) in New England.]

METROPOLITAN AREA	Number of specified group (1,000)	Percent of total metro-area
BLACK		
New York-Northern New Jersey-Long Island, NY-NJ-CT-PA CMSA/NECMA \2	3,839	19.3
Washington-Baltimore, DC-MD-VA-WV CMSA	1,840	25.7
Chicago-Gary-Kenosha, IL-IN-WI CMSA	1,656	19.3
Los Angeles-Riverside-Orange County, CA CMSA	1,306	8.4
Philadelphia-Wilmington-Atlantic City, PA-NJ-DE-MD CMSA	1,160	19.4
Detroit-Ann Arbor-Flint, MI CMSA	1,108	21.0
Atlanta, GA MSA	914	25.8
Houston-Galveston-Brazoria, TX CMSA	778	18.3
Miami-Fort Lauderdale, FL CMSA	688	19.6
Dallas-Fort Worth, TX CMSA	651	14.2
San Francisco-Oakland-San Jose, CA CMSA	573	8.7
Cleveland-Akron, OH CMSA	481	16.5
New Orleans, LA MSA	459	35.0
Norfolk-Virginia Beach-Newport News, VA-NC MSA	458	29.7
Memphis, TN-AR-MS MSA	452	41.9
St. Louis, MO-IL MSA	449	17.6
Boston-Worcester-Lawrence-Lowell-Brockton, MA-NH NECMA	331	5.7
Richmond-Petersburg, VA MSA	280	29.9
Charlotte-Gastonia-Rock Hill, NC-SC MSA	270	20.4
Birmingham, AL MSA	259	28.9
Raleigh-Durham-Chapel Hill, NC MSA	248	24.2
Milwaukee-Racine, WI CMSA	243	14.8
Kansas City, MO-KS MSA	225	13.3
Tampa-St. Petersburg-Clearwater, FL MSA	224	10.2
Greensboro—Winston-Salem—High Point, NC MSA	224	19.6
Jacksonville, FL MSA	223	22.1
Cincinnati-Hamilton, OH-KY-IN CMSA	222	11.5
Indianapolis, IN MSA	203	13.6
Pittsburgh, PA MSA	197	8.3
Orlando, FL MSA	195	13.8
Columbus, OH MSA	189	13.1
Jackson, MS MSA	182	43.3
Baton Rouge, LA MSA	176	31.1
Nashville, TN MSA	176	15.7
San Diego, CA MSA	169	6.4
Seattle-Tacoma-Bremerton, WA CMSA	165	5.0
Greenville-Spartanburg-Anderson, SC MSA	161	17.9
Charleston-North Charleston, SC MSA	154	31.1
Augusta-Aiken, GA-SC MSA	149	32.9
Columbia, SC MSA	147	30.2
Mobile, AL MSA	145	28.0
West Palm Beach-Boca Raton, FL MSA	143	14.4
Shreveport-Bossier City, LA MSA	138	36.3
Dayton-Springfield, OH MSA	136	14.3
Buffalo-Niagara Falls, NY MSA	134	11.4
Louisville, KY-IN MSA	129	13.0
Minneapolis-St. Paul, MN-WI MSA	122	4.4
Denver-Boulder-Greeley, CO CMSA	119	5.2

A3.5. Metropolitan Areas with Large Numbers of Selected Racial Groups and of Hispanic Origin Population: 1996 *(continued)*

METROPOLITAN AREA	Number of specified group (1,000)	Percent of total metro-area
BLACK *(continued)*		
Macon, GA MSA	119	38.0
Montgomery, AL MSA	116	36.7
Sacramento-Yolo, CA CMSA	115	7.0
Little Rock-North Little Rock, AR MSA	114	20.8
Oklahoma City, OK MSA	111	10.8
Phoenix-Mesa, AZ MSA	110	4.0
Las Vegas, NV-AZ MSA	109	9.1
Rochester, NY MSA	108	9.9
Columbus, GA-AL MSA	108	39.6
Lafayette, LA MSA	107	29.1
Austin-San Marcos, TX MSA	104	10.0
Hartford, CT NECMA	104	9.4
Savannah, GA MSA	104	36.6
HISPANIC ORIGIN \1		
Los Angeles-Riverside-Orange County, CA CMSA	5,850	37.8
New York-Northern New Jersey-Long Island, NY-NJ-CT-PA CMSA/NECMA \2	3,325	16.8
Miami-Fort Lauderdale, FL CMSA	1,286	36.6
San Francisco-Oakland-San Jose, CA CMSA	1,228	18.6
Chicago-Gary-Kenosha, IL-IN-WI CMSA	1,125	13.1
Houston-Galveston-Brazoria, TX CMSA	1,005	23.6
San Antonio, TX MSA	777	52.1
Dallas-Fort Worth, TX CMSA	690	15.1
San Diego, CA MSA	666	25.1
Phoenix-Mesa, AZ MSA	536	19.5
El Paso, TX MSA	503	73.5
McAllen-Edinburg-Mission, TX MSA	433	87.3
Fresno, CA MSA	355	41.2
Washington-Baltimore, DC-MD-VA-WV CMSA	351	4.9
Denver-Boulder-Greeley, CO CMSA	320	14.0
Boston-Worcester-Lawrence-Lowell-Brockton, MA-NH NECMA	297	5.1
Philadelphia-Wilmington-Atlantic City, PA-NJ-DE-MD CMSA	278	4.7
Brownsville-Harlingen-San Benito, TX MSA	266	84.4
Albuquerque, NM MSA	257	38.4
Austin-San Marcos, TX MSA	253	24.3
Sacramento-Yolo, CA CMSA	235	14.4
Corpus Christi, TX MSA	217	56.5
Tucson, AZ MSA	214	27.9
Bakersfield, CA MSA	211	33.8
Tampa-St. Petersburg-Clearwater, FL MSA	189	8.6
Las Vegas, NV-AZ MSA	169	14.1
Laredo, TX MSA	168	94.9
Visalia-Tulare-Porterville, CA MSA	157	44.9
Orlando, FL MSA	149	10.5
Stockton-Lodi, CA MSA	148	27.7
Salinas, CA MSA	135	39.9
Seattle-Tacoma-Bremerton, WA CMSA	133	4.0
Detroit-Ann Arbor-Flint, MI CMSA	124	2.3
Santa Barbara-Santa Maria-Lompoc, CA MSA	124	32.1
Portland-Salem, OR-WA CMSA	115	5.6
Modesto, CA MSA	111	26.7
Atlanta, GA MSA	105	3.0
ASIAN AND PACIFIC ISLANDER		
Los Angeles-Riverside-Orange County, CA CMSA	1,713	11.1
New York-Northern New Jersey-Long Island, NY-NJ-CT-PA CMSA/NECMA \2	1,222	6.2

A3.5. Metropolitan Areas with Large Numbers of Selected Racial Groups and of Hispanic Origin Population: 1996 *(continued)*

METROPOLITAN AREA	Number of specified group (1,000)	Percent of total metro-area
San Francisco-Oakland-San Jose, CA CMSA	1,198	18.1
Honolulu, HI MSA	561	64.3
Washington-Baltimore, DC-MD-VA-WV CMSA	342	4.8
Chicago-Gary-Kenosha, IL-IN-WI CMSA	340	3.9
San Diego, CA MSA	272	10.2
Seattle-Tacoma-Bremerton, WA CMSA	254	7.7
Houston-Galveston-Brazoria, TX CMSA	206	4.8
Boston-Worcester-Lawrence-Lowell-Brockton, MA-NH NECMA	195	3.4
Philadelphia-Wilmington-Atlantic City, PA-NJ-DE-MD CMSA	164	2.7
Sacramento-Yolo, CA CMSA	159	9.7
Dallas-Fort Worth, TX CMSA	154	3.4
AMERICAN INDIAN, ESKIMO, ALEUT		
Los Angeles-Riverside-Orange County, CA CMSA	113	0.7
Phoenix-Mesa, AZ MSA	65	2.4
New York-Northern New Jersey-Long Island, NY-NJ-CT-PA CMSA/NECMA \2	61	0.3
Tulsa, OK MSA	50	6.6
San Francisco-Oakland-San Jose, CA CMSA	49	0.7
Oklahoma City, OK MSA	48	4.7
Seattle-Tacoma-Bremerton, WA CMSA	45	1.3
Albuquerque, NM MSA	38	5.7
Flagstaff, AZ-UT MSA	34	28.4
Minneapolis-St. Paul, MN-WI MSA	28	1.0

Notes:
\1 Persons of Hispanic origin may be of any race.
\2 Includes data for New Haven-Bridgeport-Stamford-Waterbury-Danbury, CT NECMA.

Source: No. 45, U.S. Bureau of the Census, *Statistical Abstract of the United States: 1998.* Washington, DC, 1999.

A3.6. Size of Residence

	White	Black	Other	Total
Large Central City (250,000+) SMSA[a]	14.6	32.3	35.1	18.5
Medium Central City (50-250,000) SMSA[a]	15.3	19.8	13.6	15.8
Suburb of Large Central City SMSA[a]	21.6	17.0	23.6	21.1
Suburb of Medium Central City SMSA[a]	16.9	10.3	14.7	15.8
Unincorporated area of Large Central City (division, township,etc.) SMSA[a]	2.9	1.3	1.6	2.5
Unincorporated area of Medium Central City SMSA[a]	2.9	2.8	.5	2.5
Small City (10,000-49,999)	2.6	5.5	4.7	7.9
Town or Village (2,500-9,999)	8.6	2.5	4.2	6.8
Incorporated area less than 2,500 or an unincorporated area of 1,000-2,499)	7.8	8.3	1.0	7.5
Open country within larger civil divisions (township, division)	1.9	.5	1.0	1.7

Notes:
[a] Standard Metropolitan Statistical Area

Source: General Social Survey, 1998.

A4. IMMIGRATION AND ANCESTRY

A4.1. Immigration: 1820 to 1996

[In thousands, except rate. For fiscal years ending in year shown, except as noted; For 1820-1867, alien passengers arriving, 1868-1891 and 1895-1897, immigrants arriving; 1892-1894 and 1898 to the present, immigrants admitted. Rates based on Bureau of the Census estimates as of July 1 for resident population through 1929, and for total population thereafter (excluding Alaska and Hawaii prior to 1959).]

	IMMIGRANTS			IMMIGRANTS			Total
Period	Number	Rate \1	YEAR	Number	Rate \1	Year	population
1820 to 1830 \2	152	1.2	1970	373	1.8		
1831 to 1840 \3	599	3.9	1971	370	1.8		
1841 to 1850 \4	1,713	8.4	1972	385	1.8		
1851 to 1860 \4	2,598	9.3	1973	400	1.9		
1861 to 1870 \5	2,315	6.4	1974	395	1.9		
1871 to 1880	2,812	6.2	1975	386	1.8		
1881 to 1890	5,247	9.2	1976	399	1.9		
1891 to 1900	3,688	5.3	1977	462	2.1		
			1978	601	2.8		
			1979	460	2.1		
			1980	531	2.3		
			1981	597	2.6	1981	229,966
			1982	594	2.6	1982	232,188
			1983	560	2.4	1983	234,307
1901 to 1910	8,795	10.4	1984	544	2.3	1984	236,348
1911 to 1920	5,736	5.7	1985	570	2.4	1985	238,466
1921 to 1930	4,107	3.5	1986	602	2.5	1986	240,651
1931 to 1940	528	0.4	1987	602	2.5	1987	242,804
1941 to 1950	1,035	0.7	1988	643	2.6	1988	245,021
			1989	1,091	4.4	1989	247,342
			1990	1,536	6.1	1990	249,949
			1991	1,827	7.2	1991	252,636
1951 to 1960	2,515	1.5	1992	974	3.8	1992	255,382
1961 to 1970	3,322	1.7	1993	904	3.5	1993	258,089
1971 to 1980	4,493	2.1	1994	804	3.1	1994	260,602
1981 to 1990	7,338	3.1	1995	720	2.7	1995	263,039
1991 to 1996	6,146	4.0	1996	916	3.5	1996	265,453

Notes:

\1 Annual rate per 1,000 U.S. population. Rate computed by dividing sum of annual immigration totals by sum of annual U.S. population totals for same number of years.

\2 Oct. 1, 1819, to Sept. 30, 1830.

\3 Oct. 1, 1830, to Dec. 31, 1840.

\4 Calendar years.

\5 Jan. 1, 1861, to June 30, 1870.

Source: No. 5, U.S. Bureau of the Census, *Statistical Abstract of the United States: 1998.* Washington, DC, 1999.

A4.2. Immigrants Admitted, by Class of Admission: 1980 to 1996

[For fiscal year ending September 30.]

CLASS OF ADMISSION	1980	1983	1984	1985	1986	1987	1988	1989	1990	1991	1992	1993	1994	1995	1996
Immigrants, total	530,639	559,763	543,903	570,009	601,708	601,516	643,025	1,090,924	1,536,483	1,827,167	973,977	904,292	804,416	720,461	915,900
New arrivals	339,355	336,799	344,629	356,365	376,110	86,995	377,885	402,431	435,729	443,107	511,769	536,294	490,429	380,291	421,405
Adjustments	191,284	222,964	199,274	213,544	225,598	214,521	265,140	688,493	1,100,754	1,384,060	462,208	367,998	313,987	340,170	494,495
Preference immigrants, total	264,367	272,131	264,183	266,703	269,556	269,328	259,499	274,833	272,742	275,613	329,321	373,788	335,252	323,458	411,673
Family-sponsored immigrants, total	216,856	213,488	212,324	213,257	212,939	211,809	200,772	217,092	214,550	216,088	213,123	226,776	211,961	238,122	294,174
Unmarried sons/daughters of U.S. citizens and their children (1st preference)	5,668	6,892	7,569	9,319	10,910	11,382	12,107	13,259	15,861	15,385	12,486	12,819	13,181	15,182	20,909
Spouses, unmarried sons/daughters of alien residents, and their children (2nd pref.)	110,269	116,623	112,309	114,997	110,926	110,758	102,777	112,771	107,686	110,126	118,247	128,308	115,000	144,535	182,834
Married sons/daughters of U.S. citizens (3rd preference) \1	10,752	20,948	14,681	18,460	20,702	20,703	21,940	26,975	26,751	27,115	22,195	23,385	22,191	20,876	25,452
Brothers or sisters of U.S. citizens (4th preference) \1	90,167	69,025	77,765	70,481	70,401	68,966	63,948	64,087	64,252	63,462	60,195	62,264	61,589	57,529	64,979
Employment-based immigrants, total	47,511	58,643	51,859	53,446	56,617	57,519	58,727	57,741	58,192	59,525	116,198	147,012	123,291	85,336	117,499
Priority workers (1st preference) \1	(X)	(X)	(X)	(X)	(X)	(X)	(X)	(X)	(X)	(X)	5,456	21,114	21,053	17,339	27,501
Professionals w/ advanced degrees (2nd preference) \1	(X)	(X)	(X)	(X)	(X)	(X)	(X)	(X)	(X)	(X)	58,401	29,468	14,432	10,475	18,462
Skilled workers, professionals, unskilled workers (3rd preference) \1	(X)	(X)	(X)	(X)	(X)	(X)	(X)	(X)	(X)	(X)	47,568	87,689	76,956	50,245	62,756
Special immigrants (4th preference) \1	3,142	3,175	2,338	2,551	2,992	3,646	5,120	4,986	4,463	4,576	4,063	8,158	10,406	6,737	7,844
Employment creation (5th preference) \1	(X)	(X)	(X)	(X)	(X)	(X)	(X)	(X)	(X)	(X)	59	583	444	540	936
Professional or highly skilled immigrants \1 \2	18,583	27,250	24,852	24,905	26,823	26,921	26,680	26,798	26,546	27,748	340	(X)	(X)	(X)	(X)
Professional or highly skilled immigrants \1 \2	(X)	(X)	(X)	(X)	(X)	(X)	(X)	(X)	(X)	(X)	(X)	(X)	(X)	(X)	(X)
Needed skilled or unskilled workers \1 \2	25,786	28,218	24,669	25,990	26,802	26,952	26,927	25,957	27,183	27,201	311	(X)	(X)	(X)	(X)
Immediate relatives	157,743	177,792	183,247	204,368	223,468	218,575	219,340	217,514	231,680	237,103	235,484	255,059	249,764	220,360	300,430
Spouses of U.S. citizens	96,854	112,666	116,596	129,790	137,597	132,452	130,977	125,744	125,426	125,397	128,396	145,843	145,247	123,238	169,760
Children of U.S. citizens	27,207	30,429	32,080	35,592	40,639	40,940	40,863	41,276	46,065	48,130	42,324	46,788	48,147	48,740	63,971
Orphans	5,139	7,127	8,327	9,286	9,945	10,097	9,120	7,948	7,088	9,008	6,536	7,348	8,200	9,384	11,366
Parents of U.S. citizens	33,682	34,697	34,571	38,986	45,232	45,183	47,500	50,494	60,189	63,576	64,764	62,428	56,370	48,382	66,699
Refugees and asylees	88,057	102,685	92,127	95,040	104,383	91,840	81,719	84,288	97,364	139,079	117,037	127,343	121,434	114,664	128,565
Cuban Refugee Act, Nov. 1966	6,021	3,274	3,460	14,288	30,152	26,869	10,993	5,206	5,730	5,486	5,365	6,976	8,316	9,579	20,131
Indochinese Refugee Act, Oct. 1977	22,497	3,122	875	166	136	83	42	40	33	22	29	24	11	10	5
Refugee-Parolee Act, Oct. 1978	46,058	13,409	7,657	3,766	1,720	866	437	381	153	69	82	53	20	22	9
Asylees, Refugee Act of 1980	1,250	2,914	5,607	5,000	5,000	5,000	5,445	5,145	4,937	22,664	10,658	11,804	5,983	7,837	10,037
Refugees, Refugee Act of 1980	(X)	79,965	74,528	71,820	67,375	59,022	64,801	73,516	86,511	110,838	100,902	108,486	107,104	97,169	98,383
Other refugees	12,231	1	1	0	0	0	0	0	0	0	1	0	0	47	0
Other immigrants	20,472	7,155	4,346	3,898	4,301	21,773	82,467	514,289	934,697	1,175,372	292,135	148,102	97,966	61,979	75,232
Children born abroad to resident aliens	3,428	3,356	3,639	3,429	3,450	3,174	2,997	2,740	2,410	2,224	2,116	2,030	1,883	1,894	1,660
Diversity Programs \3	(X)	(X)	(X)	(X)	(X)	3,040	6,029	7,068	29,161	22,070	36,348	33,480	41,056	47,245	58,790
Amerasians (P.L. 100-202) \4	(X)	(X)	(X)	(X)	(X)	(X)	319	8,589	13,059	16,010	17,253	11,116	2,822	939	956
Immigration Reform and Control Act of 1986: legalization adjustments	(X)	(X)	(X)	(X)	(X)	(X)	(X)	478,814	880,372	1,123,162	163,342	24,278	6,022	4,267	4,635
legalization dependents \5	(X)	(X)	(X)	(X)	(X)	(X)	(X)	(X)	(X)	(X)	52,272	55,344	34,074	277	184
Other	17,044	3,799	707	469	851	15,559	73,122	17,078	9,695	11,906	20,804	21,854	12,109	7,357	9,007

Notes:
X Not applicable.
\1 Includes spouses and children.
\2 Category was eliminated in 1992 by the Immigration Act of 1990.
\3 Includes categories of immigrants admitted under three laws intended to diversify immigration: PL. 99-603, PL. 100-658, and PL. 101-649.
\4 Under Public Law 100-202 Amerasians are aliens born in Vietnam between January 1, 1962 and January 1, 1976 who were fathered by U.S. citizens.
\5 Spouses and children of persons granted permanent resident status under provisions of the Immigration Reform and Control Act of 1986.

Source: No. 6, U.S. Bureau of the Census, Statistical Abstract of the United States: 1998. Washington, DC, 1999.

A4.3. Immigrants, by Country of Birth: 1961 to 1996

[In thousands. For fiscal years ending in year shown.]

COUNTRY OF BIRTH	1961-1970, total	1971-1980, total	1981-1990, total	1988	1989	1990	1991	1992	1993	1994	1995	1996
All countries	3,321.7	4,493.3	7,338.1	643.0	1,090.9	1,536.5	1,827.2	974.0	904.3	804.4	720.5	915.9
Europe \1	1,238.6	801.3	705.6	64.8	82.9	112.4	135.2	145.4	158.3	160.9	128.2	147.6
Bulgaria	(NA)	(NA)	(NA)	0.2	0.3	0.4	0.6	1.0	1.0	1.0	1.8	2.1
Czechoslovakia	21.4	10.2	11.5	1.5	1.0	1.4	1.2	1.2	1.0	0.9	1.2	1.4
France	34.3	17.8	23.1	2.5	2.6	2.8	2.5	3.3	2.9	2.7	2.5	3.1
Germany	200.0	66.0	70.1	6.8	6.8	7.5	6.5	9.9	7.3	7.0	6.2	6.7
Greece	90.2	93.7	29.1	2.5	2.5	2.7	2.1	1.9	1.9	1.4	1.3	1.5
Hungary	17.3	11.6	9.8	1.2	1.2	1.7	1.5	1.3	1.1	0.9	0.9	1.2
Ireland	42.4	14.1	32.8	5.1	7.0	10.3	4.8	12.2	13.6	17.3	5.3	1.7
Italy	206.7	130.1	32.9	2.9	2.9	3.3	2.6	2.6	2.5	2.3	2.2	2.5
Netherlands, The	27.8	10.7	11.9	1.2	1.2	1.4	1.3	1.6	1.4	1.2	1.2	1.4
Poland	73.3	43.6	97.4	9.5	15.1	20.5	19.2	25.5	27.8	28.0	13.8	15.8
Portugal	79.3	104.5	40.0	3.2	3.8	4.0	4.5	2.7	2.1	2.2	2.6	3.0
Romania	14.9	17.5	38.9	3.9	4.6	4.6	8.1	6.5	5.6	3.4	4.9	5.8
Soviet Union, former	15.7	43.2	84.0	2.9	11.1	25.5	57.0	43.6	58.6	63.4	54.5	62.8
Armenia	(NA)	(NA)	(NA)	(NA)	(NA)	(NA)	(NA)	6.1	6.3	4.0	2.0	2.4
Azerbaijan	(NA)	(NA)	(NA)	(NA)	(NA)	(NA)	(NA)	1.6	2.9	3.8	1.9	2.0
Belarus	(NA)	(NA)	(NA)	(NA)	(NA)	(NA)	(NA)	3.2	4.7	5.4	3.8	4.3
Moldova	(NA)	(NA)	(NA)	(NA)	(NA)	(NA)	(NA)	1.7	2.6	2.3	1.9	1.8
Russia	(NA)	(NA)	(NA)	(NA)	(NA)	(NA)	(NA)	8.9	12.1	15.2	14.6	19.7
Ukraine	(NA)	(NA)	(NA)	(NA)	(NA)	(NA)	(NA)	14.4	18.3	21.0	17.4	21.1
Uzbekistan	(NA)	(NA)	(NA)	(NA)	(NA)	(NA)	(NA)	1.7	2.7	3.4	3.6	4.7
Other republics	(NA)	(NA)	(NA)	(NA)	(NA)	(NA)	(NA)	1.3	1.6	2.3	2.5	3.3
Unknown republic	(NA)	(NA)	(NA)	(NA)	(NA)	(NA)	(NA)	4.7	7.4	7.0	6.8	3.5
Spain	30.5	30.0	15.8	1.5	1.6	1.9	1.8	1.6	1.4	1.4	1.3	1.7
Sweden	16.7	6.3	10.2	1.2	1.1	1.2	1.1	1.5	1.4	1.1	1.0	1.3
Switzerland	16.3	6.6	7.0	0.8	0.8	0.8	0.7	1.0	1.0	0.9	0.9	1.0
United Kingdom	230.5	123.5	142.1	13.2	14.1	15.9	13.9	20.0	18.8	16.3	12.4	13.6
Yugoslavia	46.2	42.1	19.2	1.9	2.5	2.8	2.7	2.6	2.8	3.4	8.3	11.9
Asia \1	445.3	1,633.8	2,817.4	264.5	312.1	338.6	358.5	357.0	358.0	292.6	267.9	307.8
Afghanistan	0.4	2.0	26.6	(NA)	3.2	3.2	2.9	2.7	3.0	2.3	1.4	1.3
Bangladesh	(NA)	(NA)	15.2	(NA)	(NA)	4.3	10.7	3.7	3.3	3.4	6.1	8.2
Burma	(NA)	(NA)	9.2	(NA)	(NA)	(NA)	0.9	0.8	0.8	0.9	1.2	1.3
Cambodia	1.2	8.4	116.6	9.6	6.1	5.2	3.3	2.6	1.6	1.4	1.5	1.6
China \2	96.7 \2	202.5 \2	388.8	28.7	32.3	31.8	33.0	38.9	65.6	54.0	35.5	41.7
Hong Kong	25.6	47.5	63.0	8.5	9.7	9.4	10.4	10.5	9.2	7.7	7.2	7.8
India	31.2	176.8	261.9	26.3	31.2	30.7	45.1	36.8	40.1	34.9	34.7	44.9
Indonesia	(NA)	(NA)	14.3	(NA)	(NA)	3.5	2.2	2.9	1.8	1.4	1.0	1.1

A4.3. Immigrants, by Country of Birth: 1961 to 1996 (continued)

COUNTRY OF BIRTH	1961-1970, total	1971-1980, total	1981-1990, total	1988	1989	1990	1991	1992	1993	1994	1995	1996
Iran	10.4	46.2	154.8	15.2	21.2	25.0	19.6	13.2	14.8	11.4	9.2	11.1
Israel	12.9	26.6	36.3	3.6	4.2	4.7	4.2	5.1	4.5	3.4	2.5	3.1
Japan	38.5	47.9	43.2	4.5	4.8	5.7	5.0	11.0	6.9	6.1	4.8	6.0
Jordan	14.0	29.6	32.6	3.2	3.9	4.4	4.3	4.0	4.7	4.0	3.6	4.4
Korea	35.8	272.0	338.8	34.7	34.2	32.3	26.5	19.4	18.0	16.0	16.0	18.2
Laos	0.1	22.6	145.6	10.7	12.5	10.4	10.0	8.7	7.3	5.1	3.9	2.8
Lebanon	7.5	33.8	41.6	4.9	5.7	5.6	6.0	5.8	5.5	4.3	3.9	4.4
Malaysia	(NA)	(NA)	11.3	(NA)	(NA)	(NA)	1.9	2.2	2.0	1.5	1.2	1.4
Pakistan	4.9	31.2	61.3	5.4	8.0	9.7	20.4	10.2	8.9	8.7	9.8	12.5
Philippines	101.5	360.2	495.3	50.7	57.0	63.8	63.6	61.0	63.5	53.5	51.0	55.9
Sri Lanka	(NA)	(NA)	(NA)	0.6	0.8	1.0	1.4	1.1	1.1	1.0	1.0	1.3
Syria	4.6	13.3	20.6	2.2	2.7	3.0	2.8	2.9	2.9	2.4	2.4	3.1
Taiwan	(\2)	(\2)	(\2)	9.7	14.0	15.2	13.3	16.3	14.3	10.0	9.4	13.4
Thailand	5.0	44.1	64.4	6.9	9.3	8.9	7.4	7.1	6.7	5.5	5.1	4.3
Turkey	6.8	18.6	20.9	1.6	2.0	2.5	2.5	2.5	2.2	1.8	2.9	3.7
Vietnam	4.6	179.7	401.4	25.0	37.7	48.8	55.3	77.7	59.6	41.3	41.8	42.1
Yemen	(NA)	(NA)	7.1	(NA)	(NA)	(NA)	1.5	2.1	1.8	0.7	1.5	2.2
North America \1	1,351.1	1,645.0	3,125.0	250.0	607.4	957.6	1,211.0	384.0	301.4	272.2	231.5	340.5
Canada	286.7	114.8	119.2	11.8	12.2	16.8	13.5	15.2	17.2	16.1	12.9	15.8
Mexico	443.3	637.2	1,653.3	95.0	405.2	679.1	946.2	213.8	126.6	111.4	89.9	163.6
Caribbean \1	519.5	759.8	892.7	112.4	88.9	115.4	140.1	97.4	99.4	104.8	96.8	116.8
Antigua and Barbuda	(NA)	(NA)	12.9	(NA)	(NA)	(NA)	0.9	0.6	0.6	0.4	0.4	0.4
Bahamas, The	(NA)	(NA)	7.3	(NA)	(NA)	(NA)	1.1	0.6	0.7	0.6	0.6	0.8
Barbados	9.4	20.9	17.4	1.5	1.6	1.7	1.5	1.1	1.2	0.9	0.7	1.0
Cuba	256.8	276.8	159.2	17.6	10.0	10.6	10.3	11.8	13.7	14.7	17.9	26.5
Dominican Republic	94.1	148.0	251.8	27.2	26.7	42.2	41.4	42.0	45.4	51.2	38.5	39.6
Grenada	(NA)	(NA)	10.6	(NA)	(NA)	(NA)	1.0	0.8	0.8	0.6	0.6	0.8
Haiti	37.5	58.7	140.2	34.8	13.7	20.3	47.5	11.0	10.1	13.3	14.0	18.4
Jamaica	71.0	142.0	213.8	21.0	24.5	25.0	23.8	18.9	17.2	14.3	16.4	19.1
Trinidad and Tobago	24.6	61.8	39.5	3.9	5.4	6.7	8.4	7.0	6.6	6.3	5.4	7.3
Central America \1	97.7	132.4	458.7	30.0	101.0	146.2	111.1	57.6	58.2	39.9	31.8	44.3
Belize	(NA)	(NA)	18.1	(NA)	(NA)	3.9	2.4	1.0	1.0	0.8	0.6	0.8
Costa Rica	17.4	12.1	15.5	1.4	2.0	2.8	2.3	1.5	1.4	1.2	1.1	1.5
El Salvador	15.0	34.4	214.6	12.0	57.9	80.2	47.4	26.2	26.8	17.6	11.7	17.9
Guatemala	15.4	25.6	87.9	5.0	19.0	32.3	25.5	10.5	11.9	7.4	6.2	8.8
Honduras	15.5	17.2	49.5	4.3	7.6	12.0	11.5	6.6	7.3	5.3	5.5	5.9
Nicaragua	10.1	13.0	44.1	3.3	8.8	11.6	17.8	8.9	7.1	5.3	4.4	6.9
Panama	18.4	22.7	29.0	2.5	3.5	3.4	4.2	2.8	2.7	2.4	2.2	2.6
South America \1	228.3	284.4	455.9	41.0	58.9	85.8	79.9	55.3	53.9	47.4	45.7	61.8
Argentina	42.1	25.1	25.7	2.4	3.3	5.4	3.9	3.9	2.8	2.3	1.8	2.5

A4.3. Immigrants, by Country of Birth: 1961 to 1996 *(continued)*

COUNTRY OF BIRTH	1961-1970, total	1971-1980, total	1981-1990, total	1988	1989	1990	1991	1992	1993	1994	1995	1996
Bolivia	(NA)	(NA)	12.3	(NA)	(NA)	(NA)	3.0	1.5	1.5	1.4	1.3	1.9
Brazil	20.5	13.7	23.7	2.0	3.3	4.2	8.1	4.8	4.6	4.5	4.6	5.9
Chile	11.5	17.6	23.4	2.1	3.0	4.0	2.8	1.9	1.8	1.6	1.5	1.7
Colombia	70.3	77.6	124.4	10.3	15.2	24.2	19.7	13.2	12.8	10.8	10.8	14.3
Ecuador	37.0	50.2	56.0	4.7	7.5	12.5	10.0	7.3	7.3	5.9	6.4	8.3
Guyana	7.1	47.5	95.4	8.7	10.8	11.4	11.7	9.1	8.4	7.7	7.4	9.5
Peru	18.6	29.1	64.4	5.9	10.2	15.7	16.2	9.9	10.4	9.2	8.1	12.9
Uruguay	(NA)	(NA)	8.3	(NA)	(NA)	(NA)	1.2	0.7	0.6	0.5	0.4	0.5
Venezuela	8.5	7.1	17.9	1.8	2.1	3.1	2.6	2.3	2.7	2.4	2.6	3.5
Africa \1	39.3	91.5	192.3	18.9	25.2	35.9	36.2	27.1	27.8	26.7	42.5	52.9
Egypt	17.2	25.5	31.4	3.0	3.7	4.1	5.6	3.6	3.6	3.4	5.6	6.2
Ethiopia	(NA)	(NA)	27.2	(NA)	(NA)	4.3	5.1	4.6	5.3	3.9	7.0	6.1
Ghana	(NA)	(NA)	14.9	(NA)	(NA)	4.5	3.3	1.9	1.6	1.5	3.2	6.6
Kenya	(NA)	(NA)	7.9	(NA)	(NA)	(NA)	1.2	1.0	1.1	1.0	1.4	1.7
Liberia	(NA)	(NA)	8.1	(NA)	(NA)	(NA)	1.3	1.0	1.1	1.8	1.9	2.2
Morocco	(NA)	(NA)	6.7	(NA)	(NA)	(NA)	1.6	1.3	1.2	1.1	1.7	1.8
Nigeria	1.5	8.8	35.3	3.3	5.2	8.8	7.9	4.6	4.4	4.0	6.8	10.2
Sierra Leone	(NA)	(NA)	5.2	(NA)	(NA)	(NA)	1.0	0.7	0.7	0.7	0.9	1.9
South Africa	4.5	11.5	15.7	(NA)	1.9	2.0	1.9	2.5	2.2	2.1	2.6	3.0
Other countries \3	19.1	37.3	41.9	3.9	4.3	6.3	6.3	5.2	4.9	4.6	4.7	5.3
Australia	9.9	14.3	13.9	1.4	1.5	1.8	1.7	2.2	2.3	2.0	1.8	2.0

Notes:
NA Not available.
\1 Includes countries not shown separately.
\2 Data for Taiwan included with China: Mainland.
\3 Includes New Zealand and unknown countries.

Source: No. 7, U.S. Bureau of the Census, *Statistical Abstract of the United States: 1998.* Washington, DC, 1999.

A4.4. Immigrants Admitted as Permanent Residents Under Refugee Acts, by Country of Birth: 1961 to 1996

[For fiscal years ending in year shown. Covers immigrants who were allowed to enter the United States under 1953 Refugee Relief Act and later acts; Hungarian parolees under July 1958 Act; refugee-escapee parolees under July 1960 Act; conditional entries by refugees under Oct. 1965 Act; Cuban parolees under Nov. 1966 Act; beginning 1978, Indochina refugees under Act of Oct. 1977; beginning 1980, refugee-parolees under the Act of Oct. 1978, and asylees under the Act of March 1980; and beginning 1981 refugees under the Act of March 1980]

COUNTRY OF BIRTH	1961-70, total	1971-80, total	1981-90, total	1989	1990	1991	1992	1993	1994	1995	1996
Total	212,843	539,447	1,013,620	84,288	97,364	139,079	117,037	127,343	121,434	114,664	128,565
Europe \1	55,235	71,858	155,512	18,348	33,111	62,946	42,721	53,195	54,978	46,998	51,977
Albania	1,952	395	353	55	64	75	539	1,198	733	314	154
Austria	233	185	424	26	84	131	90	54	25	15	15
Bulgaria	1,799	1,238	1,197	126	178	311	562	303	138	105	100
Czechoslovakia	5,709	3,646	8,204	640	883	659	319	119	41	38	25
Estonia	16	2	25	0	5	9	155	125	176	83	98
Germany	665	143	851	(NA)	(NA)	214	94	82	84	61	90
Greece	586	478	1,408	185	315	127	28	39	65	50	33
Hungary	4,044	4,358	4,942	588	868	817	229	80	37	28	40
Italy	1,198	346	394	44	86	206	105	32	11	7	17
Latvia	49	16	48	8	6	34	315	493	568	387	359
Lithuania	72	23	37	5	11	75	157	228	214	151	136
Netherlands, The	3,134	8	14	0	4	5	2	7	3	0	0
Poland	3,197	5,882	33,889	3,842	3,903	4,205	1,512	731	334	245	183
Portugal	1,361	21	21	0	2	2	0	4	2	3	1
Romania	7,158	6,812	29,798	3,338	3,186	4,276	4,971	3,654	1,199	592	447
Soviet Union, former \2	871	31,309	72,306	9,264	23,186	51,551	33,504	45,900	50,756	40,120	42,356
Armenia	(NA)	(NA)	(NA)	(NA)	(NA)	(NA)	479	329	342	214	182
Azerbaijan	(NA)	(NA)	(NA)	(NA)	(NA)	(NA)	1,551	2,790	2,668	1,594	1,446
Belarus	(NA)	(NA)	(NA)	(NA)	(NA)	(NA)	3,008	4,480	5,156	3,421	3,480
Moldova	(NA)	(NA)	(NA)	(NA)	(NA)	(NA)	1,588	2,546	2,154	1,597	1,415
Russia	(NA)	(NA)	(NA)	(NA)	(NA)	(NA)	7,122	8,965	10,359	8,176	9,745
Ukraine	(NA)	(NA)	(NA)	(NA)	(NA)	(NA)	13,347	16,977	19,366	14,937	16,636
Uzbekistan	(NA)	(NA)	(NA)	(NA)	(NA)	(NA)	1,550	2,475	3,211	3,258	4,144
Spain	4,114	5,317	736	37	84	96	50	37	55	33	46
Yugoslavia \1	18,299	11,297	324	23	23	66	58	77	506	4,744	7,820
Asia \1	19,895	210,683	712,092	56,751	51,867	49,762	53,422	51,783	45,768	43,314	42,076
Afghanistan	0	542	22,946	2,606	2,144	2,100	2,082	2,233	1,665	616	369
Cambodia	0	7,739	114,064	5,648	4,719	2,550	1,695	808	557	268	210
China \3	5,308	13,760	7,928	500	330	620	884	1,153	774	803	845
Hong Kong	2,128	3,468	1,916	66	30	75	193	90	82	48	47
Indonesia	7,658	222	1,385	77	28	12	13	16	41	62	30
Iran	58	364	46,773	8,167	8,649	8,515	3,093	3,875	2,186	1,245	1,212
Iraq	119	6,851	7,540	191	141	193	365	1,856	4,400	3,848	3,802
Japan	554	56	110	4	1	4	5	3	4	2	0
Korea	1,316	65	120	4	2	1	0	1	3	5	4

A4.4. Immigrants Admitted as Permanent Residents Under Refugee Acts, by Country of Birth: 1961 to 1996 *(continued)*

COUNTRY OF BIRTH	1961-70, total	1971-80, total	1981-90, total	1989	1990	1991	1992	1993	1994	1995	1996
Laos	0	21,690	142,964	12,033	9,824	9,127	8,026	6,547	4,482	3,364	2,155
Lebanon	(NA)	(NA)	1,271	116	118	318	140	204	88	48	77
Malaysia	9	192	1,277	72	59	93	88	37	49	44	15
Pakistan	(NA)	(NA)	666	142	157	166	129	185	181	197	194
Philippines	100	216	3,403	361	290	249	221	122	103	80	80
Syria	383	1,336	2,145	273	393	252	96	115	34	258	208
Thailand	13	1,241	30,259	4,347	4,077	3,603	4,048	3,724	3,076	2,932	1,940
Turkey	1,489	1,193	1,896	175	276	109	16	79	156	58	42
Vietnam	7	150,266	324,453	21,883	20,537	21,543	32,155	30,249	27,318	28,595	29,700
North America \1	132,068	252,633	121,840	6,740	9,910	21,317	15,962	15,926	14,204	16,265	28,070
Cuba	131,557	251,514	113,367	5,245	7,668	7,953	9,919	11,603	11,998	12,355	22,542
El Salvador	1	45	1,383	198	245	1,249	743	811	275	283	262
Guatemala	(NA)	(NA)	(NA)	33	58	296	169	210	131	158	234
Honduras	(NA)	(NA)	(NA)	58	66	133	105	165	81	119	119
Nicaragua	3	36	5,590	1,075	1,694	11,233	4,668	2,892	966	727	766
Panama	(NA)	(NA)	(NA)	22	43	246	243	81	33	38	21
South America \1	123	1,244	1,976	175	264	320	442	461	383	497	922
Chile	4	420	531	19	20	38	16	17	8	10	21
Venezuela	(NA)	(NA)	(NA)	62	87	120	220	135	91	95	150
Africa \1	5,486	2,991	22,149	2,269	2,212	4,731	4,480	5,944	6,078	7,527	5,464
Egypt	5,396	1,473	426	49	69	52	18	35	37	29	66
Ethiopia	2	1,307	18,542	1,784	1,682	3,582	3,268	3,682	2,530	1,802	985
Sudan	(NA)	(NA)	(NA)	97	60	184	369	443	402	935	1,089
Other	36	38	51	5	0	3	10	34	23	63	56

Notes:
NA Not available.
\1 Includes other countries, not shown separately.
\2 Includes other republics and unknown republics, not shown separately.
\3 Includes Taiwan.

Source: No. 9, U.S. Bureau of the Census, *Statistical Abstract of the United States: 1998.* Washington, DC, 1999.

A4.5. Estimated Undocumented Immigrants, by Selected States and Countries of Origin: 1996

[In thousands. As of October. Based on estimates of illegal immigrant population who established residence in the United States before 1982 and did not legalize under the Immigration Reform and Control Act (IRCA) and annual estimates of the number of persons who enter surreptitiously across land borders and non immigrant overstays who established residence here during the 1982 to 1996 period. The estimates for each country were distributed to states by INS based on U.S. residence pattern of each country's total number of applicants for legalization under IRCA.]

STATE OF DESTINATION	Number (1,000)	COUNTRY OF ORIGIN	Number (1,000)
United States, total \1	5,000	Total \1	5,000
California	2,000	Mexico	2,700
Texas	700	El Salvador	335
New York	540	Guatemala	165
Florida	350	Canada	120
Illinois	290	Haiti	105
New Jersey	135	Philippines	95
Arizona	115	Honduras	90
Massachusetts	85	Bahamas, The	70
Virginia	55	Nicaragua	70
Washington	52	Poland	70
Colorado	45	Colombia	65
Maryland	44	Ecuador	55
New Mexico	37	Jamaica	50
Pennsylvania	37	Dominican Republic	50
Michigan	37	Trinidad & Tobago	50
Oregon	33	Pakistan	41
Georgia	32	India	33
District of Columbia	30	Dominica	32
Connecticut	29	Peru	30
Nevada	24	Korea	30

Notes:

NA Not available.

\1 Includes other states and countries not shown separately.

Source: No. 10, U.S. Bureau of the Census, *Statistical Abstract of the United States: 1998.* Washington, DC, 1999.

A4.6. Immigrants Admitted, by Leading Country of Birth and State: 1991 to 1996

[For year ending September 30.]

STATE OR OTHER AREA	FIPS Code	1991 Total \1	Mexico	Philip- pines	Soviet Union	Vietnam	Haiti	El Salvador	India	Dominican Republic
Total \2		1,827,167	946,167	63,596	56,980	55,307	47,527	47,351	45,064	41,405
Alabama	01000	2,706	810	90	40	310	1	9	183	5
Alaska	02000	1,525	328	382	15	43	3	18	17	29
Arizona	04000	40,642	35,279	355	111	806	6	282	210	7
Arkansas	05000	2,559	1,724	84	2	132	3	69	48	-
California	06000	732,735	504,631	32,698	14,409	21,542	129	22,951	10,291	109
Colorado	08000	13,782	9,130	211	582	723	4	81	142	6
Connecticut	09000	12,365	414	370	733	534	687	77	703	204
Delaware	10000	1,937	703	60	67	13	86	11	96	11
District of Columbia	11000	5,510	134	109	25	779	79	1,157	69	128
Florida	12000	141,068	42,928	1,501	759	1,623	30,375	2,064	1,224	2,190
Georgia	13000	23,556	11,668	274	607	1,396	56	509	1,175	41
Hawaii	15000	8,659	192	4,367	8	498	1	15	28	2
Idaho	16000	7,088	6,364	52	60	60	-	35	18	1
Illinois	17000	73,388	39,938	2,924	2,757	967	211	366	3,827	78
Indiana	18000	4,512	1,692	232	220	162	5	25	253	10
Iowa	19000	3,331	1,437	89	81	531	2	24	89	-
Kansas	20000	5,620	3,483	127	185	451	1	87	131	4
Kentucky	21000	1,753	278	100	18	347	7	9	113	2
Louisiana	22000	4,917	946	202	16	708	10	60	251	29
Maine	23000	1,155	98	45	123	112	4	2	25	7
Maryland	24000	17,470	1,331	791	880	697	369	1,514	984	180
Massachusetts	25000	27,020	444	411	3,089	1,961	3,293	530	1,061	1,673
Michigan	26000	16,090	3,547	659	1,019	685	16	37	1,064	44
Minnesota	27000	7,461	780	217	713	732	15	40	226	14
Mississippi	28000	1,254	483	83	-	146	3	-	88	4
Missouri	29000	4,470	757	263	400	709	15	25	218	7
Montana	30000	826	264	46	93	3	-	-	10	-
Nebraska	31000	3,020	1,812	81	75	441	-	25	25	-
Nevada	32000	10,470	7,000	692	30	207	22	280	85	13
New Hampshire	33000	1,421	155	40	45	92	32	7	86	38
New Jersey	34000	56,164	2,981	2,885	1,724	886	2,683	1,149	4,939	3,861
New Mexico	35000	13,519	12,222	88	6	240	7	45	76	2
New York	36000	188,104	4,963	4,045	19,618	2,235	8,906	3,282	9,133	22,190
North Carolina	37000	16,772	11,436	239	54	626	10	392	421	26
North Dakota	38000	565	155	27	13	160	1	-	17	-
Ohio	39000	8,632	1,046	512	880	343	8	33	843	25
Oklahoma	40000	6,403	3,961	132	26	443	6	33	211	2
Oregon	41000	24,575	18,082	305	1,712	908	2	140	124	-
Pennsylvania	42000	20,033	4,477	555	2,516	1,619	164	74	1,361	206
Rhode Island	44000	3,644	117	86	287	54	101	33	73	491
South Carolina	45000	3,836	1,911	202	30	100	5	22	175	14
South Dakota	46000	519	48	30	39	70	-	1	9	-
Tennessee	47000	3,828	1,034	141	180	456	15	31	266	12
Texas	48000	212,600	171,574	1,775	859	5,257	65	8,495	2,601	122
Utah	49000	5,737	2,876	106	246	369	1	61	58	4
Vermont	50000	709	17	11	55	147	3	1	25	3
Virginia	51000	24,942	3,711	1,352	379	1,896	52	2,851	1,194	107
Washington	53000	33,826	22,102	1,563	729	1,889	1	338	386	13
West Virginia	54000	763	201	51	8	51	7	5	71	1
Wisconsin	55000	5,888	1,580	145	452	104	3	30	282	9
Wyoming	56000	566	368	19	4	8	-	-	16	-
U.S. territories and possessions:										
Guam		(NA)	(NA)	(NA)	(NA)	(NA)	(NA)	(NA)	(NA)	(NA)
Northern Mariana Island		(NA)	(NA)	(NA)	(NA)	(NA)	(NA)	(NA)	(NA)	(NA)
Puerto Rico		(NA)	(NA)	(NA)	(NA)	(NA)	(NA)	(NA)	(NA)	(NA)
Virgin Islands		(NA)	(NA)	(NA)	(NA)	(NA)	(NA)	(NA)	(NA)	(NA)
Armed services posts		(NA)	(NA)	(NA)	(NA)	(NA)	(NA)	(NA)	(NA)	(NA)
Other		(NA)	(NA)	(NA)	(NA)	(NA)	(NA)	(NA)	(NA)	(NA)

See footnotes at end ot table.

A4.6. Immigrants Admitted, by Leading Country of Birth and State: 1991 to 1996 *(continued)*

[For year ending September 30.]

STATE OR OTHER AREA	China: Mainland	Korea	Guatemala	1992 Total \1	Mexico	Vietnam	Philip- pines	Soviet Union	Dominican Republic
Total \2	33,025	26,518	25,527	973,977	213,802	77,735	61,022	43,614	41,969
Alabama	56	106	22	2,109	94	347	99	38	1
Alaska	21	150	9	1,165	64	100	368	38	30
Arizona	210	168	597	15,792	10,779	892	420	141	16
Arkansas	16	27	7	1,039	168	157	64	2	0
California	12,265	7,301	13,634	336,663	132,138	33,477	26,846	12,655	108
Colorado	182	240	140	6,553	1,447	909	261	425	9
Connecticut	201	145	168	10,345	121	515	407	618	247
Delaware	54	217	24	1,034	82	69	51	19	14
District of Columbia	125	72	90	4,275	41	751	171	28	113
Florida	495	424	2,477	61,127	2,389	1,844	1,799	447	2,077
Georgia	238	550	218	11,243	1,343	1,796	381	386	44
Hawaii	594	514	1	8,199	99	692	4,001	14	0
Idaho	22	28	43	1,186	380	55	57	53	1
Illinois	1,164	1,162	1,062	43,532	9,861	1,174	2,467	2,379	91
Indiana	135	141	27	3,115	385	161	189	121	6
Iowa	35	125	14	2,228	234	738	112	50	2
Kansas	63	83	23	2,924	452	733	106	126	3
Kentucky	55	86	3	2,119	75	397	124	166	0
Louisiana	108	88	89	4,230	118	1,321	194	35	29
Maine	43	31	4	847	15	103	65	71	2
Maryland	499	1,048	380	15,408	237	1,194	892	1,401	164
Massachusetts	1,150	232	394	22,231	101	2,102	417	1,637	2,076
Michigan	326	482	80	14,268	423	902	555	477	51
Minnesota	188	260	36	6,851	195	1,189	218	436	10
Mississippi	23	15	11	842	46	192	89	7	1
Missouri	139	168	25	4,250	171	1,057	257	206	11
Montana	11	43	1	493	42	15	50	50	0
Nebraska	12	84	18	1,486	316	466	82	30	0
Nevada	140	118	148	5,086	2,128	172	686	26	7
New Hampshire	59	90	6	1,250	15	97	38	36	52
New Jersey	1,020	1,434	649	48,314	537	1,180	4,077	1,273	4,761
New Mexico	37	46	71	3,907	2,543	299	121	31	0
New York	9,667	5,209	1,552	149,399	1,809	2,810	5,484	11,392	25,631
North Carolina	114	258	218	6,425	583	929	279	114	27
North Dakota	6	6	-	513	11	142	41	6	2
Ohio	279	335	34	10,194	187	554	475	1,771	36
Oklahoma	80	116	63	3,147	537	726	150	42	6
Oregon	317	257	327	6,275	846	1,216	307	932	7
Pennsylvania	542	983	102	16,213	259	2,196	510	2,350	200
Rhode Island	64	25	202	2,920	17	65	76	224	528
South Carolina	63	90	52	2,118	141	110	209	29	10
South Dakota	6	27	3	522	13	83	37	80	0
Tennessee	80	107	16	2,995	155	628	154	137	7
Texas	792	1,104	1,737	75,533	39,301	6,669	2,117	480	107
Utah	110	86	65	2,744	425	491	103	105	4
Vermont	15	9	2	668	4	186	14	20	3
Virginia	382	1,093	404	17,739	334	2,339	1,441	316	68
Washington	555	811	220	15,861	1,239	3,179	1,624	2,076	9
West Virginia	24	31	4	723	18	54	49	3	3
Wisconsin	116	129	30	4,261	402	188	165	103	2
Wyoming	9	11	1	281	61	2	27	4	0
U.S. territories and possessions:									
Guam	(NA)	(NA)	(NA)	(NA)	(NA)	(NA)	(NA)	(NA)	(NA)
Northern Mariana Island	(NA)	(NA)	(NA)	(NA)	(NA)	(NA)	(NA)	(NA)	(NA)
Puerto Rico	(NA)	(NA)	(NA)	(NA)	(NA)	(NA)	(NA)	(NA)	(NA)
Virgin Islands	(NA)	(NA)	(NA)	(NA)	(NA)	(NA)	(NA)	(NA)	(NA)
Armed services posts	(NA)	(NA)	(NA)	(NA)	(NA)	(NA)	(NA)	(NA)	(NA)
Other	(NA)	(NA)	(NA)	(NA)	(NA)	(NA)	(NA)	(NA)	(NA)

See footnotes at end ot table.

A4.6. Immigrants Admitted, by Leading Country of Birth and State: 1991 to 1996 (continued)

[For year ending September 30.]

STATE OR OTHER AREA	1993									
	China: Mainland	India	El Salvador	Poland	Total \1	Mexico	China	Philip-pines	Vietnam	Soviet Union
Total \2	38,907	36,755	26,191	25,504	904,292	126,561	65,578	63,457	59,614	58,571
Alabama	99	230	12	10	2,298	67	378	88	226	64
Alaska	13	11	10	45	1,286	48	56	411	16	76
Arizona	290	249	123	61	9,778	4,719	416	345	808	269
Arkansas	30	55	15	1	1,312	115	150	95	129	25
California	11,684	8,254	15,051	767	260,090	63,221	13,700	27,614	25,429	16,886
Colorado	302	169	30	92	6,650	1,688	638	239	651	594
Connecticut	390	532	70	1,180	10,966	136	763	286	454	744
Delaware	63	96	2	8	1,132	53	152	64	13	37
District of Columbia	192	86	640	22	3,608	33	239	123	453	57
Florida	587	975	461	348	61,423	1,832	1,572	1,930	1,384	1,113
Georgia	416	785	121	57	10,213	606	937	369	1,599	515
Hawaii	528	37	5	4	8,528	39	745	4,672	481	20
Idaho	58	26	7	14	1,270	494	132	50	73	81
Illinois	1,220	3,179	263	9,756	46,744	8,911	3,170	2,842	923	2,381
Indiana	175	256	5	101	4,539	486	929	200	182	248
Iowa	54	104	10	15	2,626	186	495	95	661	110
Kansas	112	162	9	14	3,225	560	452	117	616	187
Kentucky	78	131	3	8	2,182	73	334	127	245	164
Louisiana	161	179	27	17	3,725	116	411	165	846	60
Maine	48	15	0	11	838	7	85	53	97	57
Maryland	736	1,150	947	157	16,899	187	1,730	1,007	666	933
Massachusetts	1,440	922	248	543	25,011	99	3,002	425	1,915	2,691
Michigan	618	1,250	15	454	14,913	400	1,574	497	729	1,195
Minnesota	282	257	16	57	7,438	192	911	201	812	942
Mississippi	42	82	0	0	906	31	184	94	90	7
Missouri	241	268	12	44	4,644	182	792	274	810	497
Montana	27	14	1	2	509	12	75	41	7	47
Nebraska	80	50	5	23	1,980	225	252	65	615	157
Nevada	147	91	190	21	4,045	1,049	164	723	121	36
New Hampshire	54	67	1	19	1,263	19	150	49	90	76
New Jersey	1,376	4,058	635	4,339	50,285	462	2,548	4,637	937	1,875
New Mexico	102	58	12	10	3,409	2,010	167	88	229	39
New York	10,986	5,080	2,014	5,565	151,209	1,911	13,958	4,905	1,759	14,345
North Carolina	228	410	45	73	6,892	341	849	290	749	261
North Dakota	31	33	0	1	601	13	59	21	105	106
Ohio	484	843	10	208	10,703	151	1,846	414	481	1,866
Oklahoma	127	220	9	12	2,942	574	317	140	575	23
Oregon	355	176	39	22	7,250	901	676	341	1,070	1,527
Pennsylvania	1,003	1,337	48	517	16,964	220	1,877	549	1,637	2,920
Rhode Island	69	47	32	78	3,168	23	227	86	17	343
South Carolina	80	158	9	27	2,195	66	276	186	136	70
South Dakota	13	13	0	1	543	7	35	38	44	95
Tennessee	94	201	17	28	4,287	125	473	177	457	217
Texas	1,818	2,617	3,586	214	67,380	31,773	3,606	2,031	5,173	808
Utah	197	79	29	29	3,266	297	546	82	395	255
Vermont	25	15	2	5	709	6	83	9	157	45
Virginia	730	1,033	1,300	112	16,451	278	1,133	1,390	1,300	525
Washington	587	357	56	260	17,147	1,108	1,313	1,834	3,080	2,678
West Virginia	59	78	3	6	689	19	113	60	41	8
Wisconsin	199	220	21	133	5,168	356	691	172	116	290
Wyoming	29	7	0	7	263	36	53	13	0	6
U.S. territories and possessions:										
Guam	(NA)	(NA)	(NA)	(NA)	(NA)	(NA)	(NA)	(NA)	(NA)	(NA)
Northern Mariana Island	(NA)	(NA)	(NA)	(NA)	(NA)	(NA)	(NA)	(NA)	(NA)	(NA)
Puerto Rico	(NA)	(NA)	(NA)	(NA)	(NA)	(NA)	(NA)	(NA)	(NA)	(NA)
Virgin Islands	(NA)	(NA)	(NA)	(NA)	(NA)	(NA)	(NA)	(NA)	(NA)	(NA)
Armed services posts	(NA)	(NA)	(NA)	(NA)	(NA)	(NA)	(NA)	(NA)	(NA)	(NA)
Other	(NA)	(NA)	(NA)	(NA)	(NA)	(NA)	(NA)	(NA)	(NA)	(NA)

See footnotes at end ot table.

A4.6. Immigrants Admitted, by Leading Country of Birth and State: 1991 to 1996 *(continued)*

[For year ending September 30.]

STATE OR OTHER AREA	1994									
	Dominican Republic	India	Poland	El Salvador	Total \1	Mexico	Soviet Union	China	Philip-pines	Vietnam
Total \2	45,420	40,121	27,846	26,818	804,416	111,398	63,420	53,985	53,535	41,345
Alabama	2	303	5	14	1,837	95	54	200	83	142
Alaska	18	26	61	5	1,129	45	97	64	330	35
Arizona	9	290	71	102	9,141	4,340	308	653	374	432
Arkansas	0	84	3	25	1,031	142	21	70	85	136
California	126	8,674	888	13,739	208,498	52,088	14,542	17,447	23,942	14,162
Colorado	6	144	101	34	6,825	1,931	730	371	212	508
Connecticut	229	624	1,490	68	9,537	90	659	551	209	277
Delaware	12	129	11	6	984	56	44	142	52	9
District of Columbia	159	46	8	719	3,204	27	87	223	109	243
Florida	2,250	1,138	672	519	58,093	1,885	1,117	871	1,474	1,183
Georgia	51	752	77	62	10,032	665	630	522	288	1,602
Hawaii	2	28	3	4	7,746	47	24	743	4,329	353
Idaho	0	17	8	2	1,559	737	98	94	68	72
Illinois	86	3,991	10,651	267	42,400	7,900	2,970	1,684	2,539	734
Indiana	10	406	104	6	3,725	401	329	375	182	164
Iowa	6	89	26	6	2,163	233	124	237	61	453
Kansas	2	153	14	22	2,902	691	179	236	108	522
Kentucky	4	131	13	5	2,036	60	118	203	78	211
Louisiana	26	160	10	36	3,366	80	35	225	155	650
Maine	13	18	16	5	829	11	47	60	45	39
Maryland	213	1,291	120	1,294	15,937	163	2,144	1,620	752	656
Massachusetts	2,233	907	682	332	22,882	86	2,438	1,995	259	1,366
Michigan	46	1,283	615	11	12,728	413	968	663	456	531
Minnesota	5	236	77	18	7,098	207	762	448	157	806
Mississippi	1	86	11	1	815	34	5	97	66	100
Missouri	7	271	41	12	4,362	195	554	464	243	601
Montana	0	10	2	0	447	10	48	34	25	5
Nebraska	0	58	16	26	1,595	295	156	137	47	377
Nevada	13	88	21	178	4,051	951	58	314	773	117
New Hampshire	69	78	17	4	1,144	8	64	93	47	112
New Jersey	5,176	4,725	3,887	923	44,083	385	1,993	2,174	2,945	564
New Mexico	3	90	9	16	2,936	1,674	60	157	81	89
New York	26,799	5,338	6,517	2,711	144,354	1,310	19,618	11,745	3,878	995
North Carolina	23	526	62	42	6,204	477	245	468	209	855
North Dakota	0	16	6	1	635	11	89	40	20	91
Ohio	23	877	192	11	9,184	134	1,743	872	319	331
Oklahoma	4	178	12	17	2,728	513	34	198	117	527
Oregon	8	161	33	28	6,784	1,472	1,262	421	313	733
Pennsylvania	195	1,397	542	49	15,971	556	2,592	1,621	460	1,040
Rhode Island	581	43	86	24	2,907	24	250	174	54	17
South Carolina	16	198	23	7	2,110	61	51	200	149	171
South Dakota	1	18	8	1	570	13	66	26	19	18
Tennessee	3	332	42	17	3,608	122	166	291	144	354
Texas	103	2,808	174	3,642	56,158	27,015	873	1,932	1,833	4,292
Utah	9	103	27	25	2,951	322	260	291	106	270
Vermont	1	27	4	0	658	3	60	61	15	63
Virginia	80	958	78	1,686	15,342	253	613	971	1,119	1,594
Washington	5	426	179	40	18,180	2,573	3,340	842	1,781	2,607
West Virginia	8	101	1	2	663	10	8	103	56	9
Wisconsin	5	236	129	15	5,328	467	685	407	159	97
Wyoming	2	6	1	0	217	36	0	18	16	0
U.S. territories and possessions:										
Guam	(NA)	(NA)	(NA)	(NA)	(NA)	(NA)	(NA)	(NA)	(NA)	(NA)
Northern Mariana Island	(NA)	(NA)	(NA)	(NA)	(NA)	(NA)	(NA)	(NA)	(NA)	(NA)
Puerto Rico	(NA)	(NA)	(NA)	(NA)	(NA)	(NA)	(NA)	(NA)	(NA)	(NA)
Virgin Islands	(NA)	(NA)	(NA)	(NA)	(NA)	(NA)	(NA)	(NA)	(NA)	(NA)
Armed services posts	(NA)	(NA)	(NA)	(NA)	(NA)	(NA)	(NA)	(NA)	(NA)	(NA)
Other	(NA)	(NA)	(NA)	(NA)	(NA)	(NA)	(NA)	(NA)	(NA)	(NA)

See footnotes at end ot table.

A4.6. Immigrants Admitted, by Leading Country of Birth and State: 1991 to 1996 *(continued)*

[For year ending September 30.]

STATE OR OTHER AREA	Dominican Republic	India	Poland	El Salvador	1995 Total \1	Mexico	Soviet Union, former	Philip- pines	Vietnam	Dominican Republic
Total \2	51,189	34,921	28,048	17,644	720,461	89,932	54,494	50,984	41,752	38,512
Alabama	6	222	10	4	1,900	134	66	85	80	5
Alaska	38	13	35	6	1,049	56	77	268	28	37
Arizona	17	237	69	63	7,700	3,640	215	294	396	15
Arkansas	1	53	7	16	934	167	17	83	123	2
California	120	7,085	598	8,082	166,482	34,416	10,045	22,584	16,755	71
Colorado	3	139	106	20	7,713	2,677	782	151	600	6
Connecticut	249	452	1,459	46	9,240	97	675	208	242	249
Delaware	8	76	16	12	1,051	91	42	48	11	13
District of Columbia	138	63	2	630	3,047	24	99	83	217	98
Florida	2,463	1,033	548	363	62,023	1,922	1,021	1,806	1,194	2,090
Georgia	47	649	156	79	12,381	1,621	678	342	1,658	39
Hawaii	0	37	1	1	7,537	45	16	4,308	332	1
Idaho	1	8	15	14	1,612	841	69	53	90	2
Illinois	119	3,241	11,165	163	33,898	6,500	3,384	2,690	583	102
Indiana	19	365	115	6	3,590	471	203	206	198	12
Iowa	3	135	14	11	2,260	337	94	65	430	0
Kansas	8	126	7	18	2,434	547	165	98	420	3
Kentucky	4	209	15	8	1,857	80	197	90	185	4
Louisiana	57	206	21	23	3,000	91	43	134	386	32
Maine	2	26	17	3	814	20	62	31	60	6
Maryland	233	1,058	117	1,017	15,055	133	1,576	823	722	179
Massachusetts	2,581	805	672	247	20,523	89	2,253	229	1,247	1,970
Michigan	83	1,085	656	14	14,135	507	881	499	541	44
Minnesota	14	183	49	29	8,111	348	800	169	853	11
Mississippi	4	112	0	3	757	26	15	49	32	8
Missouri	6	295	29	18	3,990	270	406	167	449	5
Montana	0	5	2	1	409	11	18	40	2	1
Nebraska	5	62	15	13	1,831	495	119	49	454	2
Nevada	16	68	26	122	4,306	1,127	83	687	98	11
New Hampshire	63	56	10	7	1,186	27	66	44	129	23
New Jersey	5,384	3,782	3,751	578	39,729	375	1,631	2,626	435	4,136
New Mexico	1	96	15	9	2,758	1,655	68	62	92	10
New York	28,250	5,338	6,733	1,983	128,406	848	19,227	3,216	963	21,471
North Carolina	32	426	53	31	5,617	407	241	262	623	27
North Dakota	0	26	1	1	483	12	28	15	15	0
Ohio	33	800	211	19	8,585	212	1,481	300	350	44
Oklahoma	4	194	13	5	2,792	660	42	105	514	2
Oregon	3	161	35	44	4,923	1,166	313	224	695	2
Pennsylvania	369	1,343	535	30	15,065	735	2,585	362	1,028	304
Rhode Island	636	41	114	14	2,609	24	158	50	30	553
South Carolina	4	173	73	3	2,165	122	64	169	162	6
South Dakota	0	13	4	0	495	12	73	13	9	0
Tennessee	9	290	31	11	3,392	88	147	119	354	9
Texas	114	2,254	151	2,499	49,963	22,792	824	1,997	4,251	101
Utah	10	68	22	22	2,831	565	174	59	255	15
Vermont	1	20	6	0	535	6	35	14	17	0
Virginia	70	928	85	1,283	16,319	318	575	1,219	1,236	69
Washington	11	475	128	45	15,862	2,489	2,186	1,381	2,101	15
West Virginia	2	62	8	2	540	7	17	50	5	1
Wisconsin	25	301	124	11	4,919	503	437	144	81	5
Wyoming	0	4	2	0	252	85	13	12	1	0
U.S. territories and possessions:										
Guam	(NA)	(NA)	(NA)	(NA)	(NA)	(NA)	(NA)	(NA)	(NA)	(NA)
Northern Mariana Island	(NA)	(NA)	(NA)	(NA)	(NA)	(NA)	(NA)	(NA)	(NA)	(NA)
Puerto Rico	(NA)	(NA)	(NA)	(NA)	(NA)	(NA)	(NA)	(NA)	(NA)	(NA)
Virgin Islands	(NA)	(NA)	(NA)	(NA)	(NA)	(NA)	(NA)	(NA)	(NA)	(NA)
Armed services posts	(NA)	(NA)	(NA)	(NA)	(NA)	(NA)	(NA)	(NA)	(NA)	(NA)
Other	(NA)	(NA)	(NA)	(NA)	(NA)	(NA)	(NA)	(NA)	(NA)	(NA)

See footnotes at end ot table.

A4.6. Immigrants Admitted, by Leading Country of Birth and State: 1991 to 1996 *(continued)*

[For year ending September 30.]

STATE OR OTHER AREA	China	India	Cuba	Jamaica	Korea	1996 Total \1	Mexico	Philippines	India	Vietnam	China
Total \2	35,463	34,748	17,937	16,398	16,047	915,900	163,572	55,876	44,859	42,067	41,728
Alabama	107	237	4	14	101	1,782	162	74	234	74	112
Alaska	42	9	2	5	95	1,280	111	385	28	24	29
Arizona	270	218	13	9	127	8,900	5,051	316	273	265	251
Arkansas	35	41	5	5	14	1,494	446	96	105	138	45
California	10,256	6,646	428	209	4,789	201,529	64,238	23,438	7,757	13,549	10,864
Colorado	276	177	1	17	203	8,895	3,138	185	203	753	430
Connecticut	304	488	29	930	111	10,874	207	262	681	249	454
Delaware	48	84	3	51	116	1,377	130	60	143	40	66
District of Columbia	117	38	16	97	5	3,784	40	108	60	350	209
Florida	639	1,141	15,112	4,261	311	79,461	3,155	1,796	1,393	977	773
Georgia	362	887	61	213	423	12,608	1,399	252	1,127	1,961	455
Hawaii	480	36	0	4	408	8,436	70	5,208	24	328	555
Idaho	46	29	3	1	11	1,825	839	37	42	88	50
Illinois	986	3,051	96	256	618	42,517	11,715	2,516	3,829	777	1,164
Indiana	221	292	3	21	116	4,692	877	219	364	150	282
Iowa	52	140	1	2	109	3,037	620	95	153	447	106
Kansas	98	148	7	4	43	4,303	1,470	131	166	683	160
Kentucky	84	155	1	10	55	2,019	98	90	162	150	123
Louisiana	171	197	70	13	53	4,092	178	158	336	899	216
Maine	48	27	1	11	5	1,028	14	39	32	69	74
Maryland	633	1,029	34	487	788	20,732	319	942	1,421	633	1,095
Massachusetts	1,287	873	54	437	221	23,085	141	288	1,075	1,452	1,630
Michigan	447	1,247	24	113	266	17,253	828	391	1,745	455	768
Minnesota	212	266	13	27	175	8,977	496	195	376	820	344
Mississippi	75	85	3	7	11	1,073	61	117	122	124	72
Missouri	266	248	23	25	75	5,690	451	261	397	710	326
Montana	20	16	0	0	32	449	15	30	15	0	29
Nebraska	52	47	3	1	57	2,150	893	62	69	236	53
Nevada	148	115	220	12	75	5,874	2,263	806	136	83	166
New Hampshire	58	61	1	9	56	1,512	40	52	90	199	95
New Jersey	1,134	3,958	805	1,294	1,043	63,303	1,125	3,544	6,185	630	2,140
New Mexico	55	85	92	4	33	5,780	4,254	91	123	99	69
New York	11,254	4,859	331	6,884	1,757	154,095	1,553	3,719	5,611	971	11,409
North Carolina	235	423	19	51	250	7,011	661	298	682	582	334
North Dakota	10	28	0	0	6	606	16	19	42	53	10
Ohio	525	806	8	88	181	10,237	320	343	1,122	294	801
Oklahoma	104	268	2	6	57	3,511	931	136	216	580	132
Oregon	371	188	1	8	166	7,554	1,942	338	207	888	434
Pennsylvania	871	1,350	37	437	546	16,938	692	440	1,785	961	1,056
Rhode Island	93	22	3	8	18	3,098	49	65	53	25	102
South Carolina	108	194	2	18	49	2,151	148	166	222	121	141
South Dakota	12	13	0	2	23	519	15	23	20	20	23
Tennessee	135	310	3	13	72	4,343	261	175	384	400	197
Texas	1,002	2,400	131	146	602	83,385	46,403	2,064	3,295	5,793	1,701
Utah	105	74	1	3	64	4,250	1,036	79	134	280	190
Vermont	30	19	0	2	11	654	19	12	19	81	42
Virginia	455	931	36	115	806	21,375	531	1,446	1,208	1,437	743
Washington	776	437	17	10	633	18,833	3,482	1,688	577	2,105	774
West Virginia	29	83	0	11	24	583	18	57	78	2	40
Wisconsin	176	242	9	28	78	3,607	474	112	287	44	215
Wyoming	14	5	0	0	5	280	94	11	10	3	12
U.S. territories and possessions:											
Guam	(NA)	(NA)	(NA)	(NA)	(NA)	2,820	0	2,220	13	14	81
Northern Mariana Island	(NA)	(NA)	(NA)	(NA)	(NA)	176	0	149	0	0	14
Puerto Rico	(NA)	(NA)	(NA)	(NA)	(NA)	8,560	73	7	9	0	66
Virgin Islands	(NA)	(NA)	(NA)	(NA)	(NA)	1,384	3	5	15	1	5
Armed services posts	(NA)	(NA)	(NA)	(NA)	(NA)	109	0	60	4	0	1
Other	(NA)	(NA)	(NA)	(NA)	(NA)	10	7	0	0	0	0

See footnotes at end of table.

A4.6. Immigrants Admitted, by Leading Country of Birth and State: 1991 to 1996 *(continued)*

[For year ending September 30.]

STATE OR OTHER AREA	Dominican Republic	Cuba	Ukraine	Russia	Jamaica	Korea
Total \2	39,604	26,466	21,079	19,668	19,089	18,185
Alabama	2	3	21	42	12	50
Alaska	24	5	14	96	2	109
Arizona	9	8	48	80	6	102
Arkansas	5	0	4	36	6	15
California	83	346	2,630	2,377	250	4,426
Colorado	7	6	216	356	14	220
Connecticut	278	69	197	317	1,053	200
Delaware	9	7	14	23	83	125
District of Columbia	95	3	5	56	104	25
Florida	2,050	22,217	327	380	4,996	262
Georgia	46	57	196	228	209	370
Hawaii	0	1	1	12	3	398
Idaho	0	2	32	26	1	20
Illinois	66	109	1,406	944	229	655
Indiana	15	16	106	125	28	120
Iowa	4	0	17	94	0	122
Kansas	3	8	88	114	15	50
Kentucky	4	16	57	52	9	57
Louisiana	28	79	9	23	14	34
Maine	3	7	13	34	5	6
Maryland	171	26	391	695	623	972
Massachusetts	2,051	64	688	925	497	214
Michigan	52	24	231	434	93	315
Minnesota	10	20	244	342	27	184
Mississippi	2	26	4	19	5	10
Missouri	3	56	91	254	21	129
Montana	0	0	31	24	1	9
Nebraska	2	0	27	37	3	45
Nevada	15	255	21	31	5	86
New Hampshire	38	0	18	67	7	64
New Jersey	5,006	1,593	839	1,133	1,712	2,014
New Mexico	3	179	10	63	5	35
New York	20,579	452	9,185	5,854	7,990	2,429
North Carolina	40	53	60	123	38	278
North Dakota	1	4	2	24	0	7
Ohio	29	19	636	522	112	188
Oklahoma	5	7	7	27	10	69
Oregon	10	27	444	341	28	233
Pennsylvania	296	62	1,026	807	489	553
Rhode Island	560	9	68	60	10	26
South Carolina	2	0	17	41	21	42
South Dakota	2	9	19	10	1	13
Tennessee	3	30	28	101	17	96
Texas	108	258	257	586	164	843
Utah	13	7	47	100	1	66
Vermont	2	0	6	17	2	10
Virginia	50	47	153	491	98	886
Washington	7	9	1,032	940	19	697
West Virginia	0	2	0	10	7	14
Wisconsin	16	10	94	155	28	92
Wyoming	0	2	2	10	0	6
U.S. territories and possessions:						
Guam	0	0	0	0	0	185
Northern Mariana Island	0	0	0	0	0	0
Puerto Rico	7,354	257	0	9	1	1
Virgin Islands	442	0	0	0	14	0
Armed services posts	1	0	0	1	1	8
Other	0	0	0	0	0	0

- Represents zero.
NA Not available.
\1 Includes other countries, not shown separately.
\2 Includes Guam, Puerto Rico, Northern Mariana Islands, Virgin Islands,
and other or unknown areas not shown separately.

Source: No. 11, U.S. Bureau of the Census, *Statistical Abstract of the United States: 1998.* Washington, DC, 1999.

A4.7. Population, by Selected Ancestry Group and Region: 1980 and 1990

[As of April 1. Covers persons who reported single and multiple ancestry groups. Persons who reported a multiple ancestry group may be included in more than one category. Major classifications of ancestry groups do not represent strict geographic or cultural definitions. Ancestry data for 1980 are not entirely comparable with 1990 data. Based on a sample and subject to sampling variability.]

ANCESTRY GROUP	1980 PERCENT DISTRIBUTION BY REGION					1990 NUMBER					1990 PERCENT DISTRIBUTION BY REGION			
	Total (1000)	North-east	Mid-west	South	West	Total	North-east	Mid-west	South	West	North-east	Mid-west	South	West
Austrian	949	(NA)	(NA)	(NA)	(NA)	864,783	329,401	183,307	165,340	186,735	38	21	19	22
British	(X)	(X)	(X)	(X)	(X)	1,119,154	188,052	195,956	440,352	294,794	17	18	39	26
Croatian	253	(NA)	(NA)	(NA)	(NA)	544,270	114,681	236,134	106,302	87,153	21	43	20	16
Czech	1,892	18	49	18	15	1,296,411	129,325	671,371	290,732	204,983	10	52	22	16
Czechoslovakian	(X)	(X)	(X)	(X)	(X)	315,285	72,008	103,162	69,313	70,802	23	33	22	22
Danish	1,518	9	38	10	43	1,634,669	146,046	555,346	194,769	738,508	9	34	12	45
Dutch	6,304	18	35	26	20	6,227,089	1,020,383	2,123,623	1,780,043	1,303,040	16	34	29	21
English	49,598	16	23	40	21	32,651,788	5,873,052	7,293,707	11,375,464	8,109,565	18	22	35	25
European	175	(NA)	(NA)	(NA)	(NA)	466,718	64,179	77,638	144,257	180,644	14	17	31	39
Finnish	616	(NA)	(NA)	(NA)	(NA)	658,870	95,408	310,855	73,761	178,846	14	47	11	27
French \2	12,892	26	27	27	19	10,320,935	2,637,321	2,640,874	2,964,481	2,078,259	26	26	29	20
German	49,224	19	41	22	18	57,947,374	9,928,722	22,477,450	14,630,411	10,910,791	17	39	25	19
Greek	960	(NA)	(NA)	(NA)	(NA)	1,110,373	413,246	255,780	234,530	206,817	37	23	21	19
Hungarian	1,777	39	33	13	14	1,582,302	564,216	504,619	261,688	251,779	36	32	17	16
Irish	40,166	24	26	32	18	38,735,539	9,420,118	9,643,261	12,950,799	6,721,361	24	25	33	17
Italian	12,184	57	16	13	14	14,664,550	7,503,740	2,429,651	2,473,371	2,257,788	51	17	17	15
Latvian	92	(NA)	(NA)	(NA)	(NA)	100,331	32,870	26,830	18,548	22,083	33	27	18	22
Lithuanian	743	(NA)	(NA)	(NA)	(NA)	811,865	352,523	228,210	127,266	103,866	43	28	16	13
Norwegian	3,454	7	55	7	31	3,869,395	241,229	2,000,129	369,485	1,258,552	6	52	10	33
Polish	8,228	41	38	11	10	9,366,106	3,499,502	3,468,832	1,361,537	1,036,235	37	37	15	11
Portuguese	1,024	50	3	6	41	1,153,351	563,801	29,814	90,924	468,812	49	3	8	41
Romanian	315	(NA)	(NA)	(NA)	(NA)	365,544	122,949	96,318	64,601	81,676	34	26	18	22
Russian	2,781	48	17	16	19	2,952,987	1,292,472	473,588	545,671	641,256	44	16	18	22
Scandinavian	475	(NA)	(NA)	(NA)	(NA)	678,880	52,958	221,666	100,981	303,275	8	33	15	45
Scotch-Irish	(X)	(X)	(X)	(X)	(X)	5,617,773	772,250	1,078,883	2,616,155	1,150,485	14	19	47	20
Scottish	10,049	19	23	35	24	5,393,581	1,088,462	1,135,343	1,768,494	1,401,282	20	21	33	26
Serbian	101	(NA)	(NA)	(NA)	(NA)	116,795	26,349	58,782	13,727	17,937	23	50	12	15
Slovak	777	(NA)	(NA)	(NA)	(NA)	1,882,897	759,264	648,461	272,131	203,041	40	34	14	11
Slovene	126	(NA)	(NA)	(NA)	(NA)	124,437	19,697	81,163	10,701	12,876	16	65	9	10
Swedish	4,345	15	43	12	31	4,680,863	669,531	1,858,855	671,099	1,481,378	14	40	14	32
Swiss	982	(NA)	(NA)	(NA)	(NA)	1,045,495	170,618	378,239	181,425	315,213	16	36	17	30
Ukrainian	730	(NA)	(NA)	(NA)	(NA)	740,803	374,282	163,133	104,695	98,693	51	22	14	13
Welsh	1,665	25	27	22	27	2,033,893	446,623	493,214	545,082	548,974	22	24	27	27
Yugoslavian	360	(NA)	(NA)	(NA)	(NA)	257,994	59,941	72,606	30,553	94,894	23	28	12	37
Central & South America \3 and Spain:														
Cuban	(NA)	(NA)	(NA)	(NA)	(NA)	859739	157247	29269	594106	79117	18	3	69	9
Dominican	(NA)	(NA)	(NA)	(NA)	(NA)	505690	436478	6083	53021	10108	86	1	10	2
Hispanic \4	(NA)	(NA)	(NA)	(NA)	(NA)	1113259	149104	61715	347411	555029	13	6	31	50

A4.7. Population, by Selected Ancestry Group and Region: 1980 and 1990 (continued)

ANCESTRY GROUP	1980 Total (1000)	1980 PERCENT DISTRIBUTION BY REGION North-east	Mid-west	South	West	1990 NUMBER Total	North-east	Mid-west	South	West	1990 PERCENT DISTRIBUTION BY REGION North-east	Mid-west	South	West
Mexican	(NA)	(NA)	(NA)	(NA)	(NA)	11,586,983	142,829	1,021,049	3,774,379	6,648,726	1	9	33	57
Puerto Rican	(NA)	(NA)	(NA)	(NA)	(NA)	1,955,323	1,289,858	209,974	293,124	162,367	66	11	15	8
Salvadoran	(NA)	(NA)	(NA)	(NA)	(NA)	499,153	66,537	8,709	114,707	309,200	13	2	23	62
Spanish	(NA)	(NA)	(NA)	(NA)	(NA)	2,024,004	331,319	158,061	614,708	919,916	16	8	30	45
West Indian: \1														
Haitian	90	72	4	21	2	289,521	158,470	7,201	117,261	6,589	55	2	41	2
Jamaican	253	70	6	18	5	435,024	256,637	20,861	133,259	24,267	59	5	31	6
West Indian	(X)	(X)	(X)	(X)	(X)	159,167	104,248	7,132	35,373	12,414	65	4	22	8
North Africa and Southwest Asia:														
Arab	93	19	29	21	30	127,364	25,583	36,498	29,670	35,613	20	29	23	28
Armenian	213	39	14	5	42	308,096	89,331	32,365	23,625	162,775	29	11	8	53
Iranian	123	17	15	26	42	235,521	34,693	22,283	55,109	123,436	15	9	23	52
Lebanese	295	31	27	26	16	394,180	111,321	100,783	108,312	73,764	28	26	27	19
Syrian	107	47	20	18	15	129,606	55,996	24,526	26,162	22,922	43	19	20	18
Subsaharan Africa:														
African	204	33	19	33	1	245,845	71,442	39,542	91,605	43,256	29	16	37	18
Asia:														
Asian Indian	(NA)	(NA)	(NA)	(NA)	(NA)	570,322	180,513	108,383	145,791	135,635	32	19	26	24
Chinese	(NA)	(NA)	(NA)	(NA)	(NA)	1,505,245	374,410	118,844	185,231	826,760	25	8	12	55
Filipino	(NA)	(NA)	(NA)	(NA)	(NA)	1,450,512	149,972	127,070	181,898	991,572	10	9	13	68
Japanese	(NA)	(NA)	(NA)	(NA)	(NA)	1,004,645	89,521	84,897	107,527	722,700	9	8	11	72
Korean	(NA)	(NA)	(NA)	(NA)	(NA)	836,987	180,288	119,455	169,025	368,219	22	14	20	44
Vietnamese	(NA)	(NA)	(NA)	(NA)	(NA)	535,825	50,348	45,010	148,704	291,763	9	8	28	54
North America:														
Acadian/Cajun	(X)	(X)	(X)	(X)	(X)	668,271	9,653	16,484	609,427	32,707	1	2	91	5
Afro-American	(NA)	(NA)	(NA)	(NA)	(NA)	23,777,098	3,658,088	4,875,147	12,936,066	2,307,797	15	21	54	10
American Indian	(NA)	(NA)	(NA)	(NA)	(NA)	8,708,220	754,051	1,907,001	4,086,342	1,960,826	9	22	47	23
American	13,299	(NA)	(NA)	(NA)	(NA)	12,395,999	1,275,211	2,204,709	7,558,114	1,357,965	10	18	61	11
Canadian	456	42	19	15	23	549,990	184,979	100,717	112,858	151,436	34	18	21	28
French Canadian	780	47	23	13	17	2,167,127	973,230	436,548	423,497	333,852	45	20	20	15
Pennsylvania German	(X)	(X)	(X)	(X)	(X)	305,841	164,385	77,033	32,402	32,021	54	25	11	10
United States	(X)	(X)	(X)	(X)	(X)	643,561	101,193	114,282	341,677	86,409	16	18	53	13
White	(NA)	(NA)	(NA)	(NA)	(NA)	1,799,711	121,033	230,641	946,103	501,934	7	13	53	28

Notes:

X Not applicable.
Z Less than .05 percent.
\1 Non-Hispanic groups.
\2 Excludes French Basque.
\3 Hispanic groups.
\4 A general type of response which may encompass several ancestry groups.

Source: No. 58, U.S. Bureau of the Census, Statistical Abstract of the United States: 1998. Washington, DC, 1999.

A4.8. Persons Speaking a Language Other Than English at Home, by Age and Language: 1990

[As of April. Based on a sample and subject to sampling variability]

AGE GROUP AND LANGUAGE SPOKEN AT HOME	Persons who speak language (1,000)	Percent who speak English less than "very well"	LANGUAGE	Persons, 5 years old and over who speak language (1,000)
Persons 5 years old and over	230,446	(X)	Speak only English	198,601
Speak only English	198,601	(X)	Spanish	17,339
Speak other language	31,845	43.9	French	1,702
Speak Spanish or Spanish Creole	17,345	47.9	German	1,547
Speak Asian or Pacific Island language	4,472	54.1	Italian	1,309
Speak other language	10,028	32.4	Chinese	1,249
			Tagalog	843
Persons 5 to 17 years old	45,342	(X)	Polish	723
Speak only English	39,020	(X)	Korean	626
Speak other language	6,323	37.8	Vietnamese	507
Speak Spanish or Spanish Creole	4,168	39.3	Portuguese	430
Speak Asian or Pacific Island language	816	44.2	Japanese	428
Speak other language	1,340	29.2	Greek	388
			Arabic	355
Persons 18 to 64 years old	153,908	(X)	Hindi (Urdu)	331
Speak only English	132,200	(X)	Russian	242
Speak other language	21,708	45.1	Yiddish	213
Speak Spanish or Spanish Creole	12,121	49.6	Thai (Laotian)	206
Speak Asian or Pacific Island language	3,301	54.7	Persian	202
Speak other language	6,286	31.4	French Creole	188
			Armenian	150
Persons 65 years old and over	31,195	(X)	Navaho	149
Speak only English	27,381	(X)	Hungarian	148
Speak other language	3,814	47.2	Hebrew	144
Speak Spanish or Spanish Creole	1,057	62.3	Dutch	143
Speak Asian or Pacific Island language	355	72.0	Mon-Khmer (Cambodian)	127
Speak other language	2,402	36.9	Gujarathi	102

Notes:
X Not applicable.

Source: No. 59, U.S. Bureau of the Census, *Statistical Abstract of the United States: 1998.* Washington, DC, 1999.

A4.9. Geographic Mobility Since Age 16

When you were 16 years old, were you living in this same (city, state?)

	White	Black	Other
Same city	37.6	50.1	33.3
Same state, different city	27.1	20.5	21.7
Different state	35.2	29.4	45
Number	2233	395	189

Source: 1998 General Social Surveys.

B. Education

B1. ENROLLMENT AND GRADUATION

Education is a key to achievement and success in life for a number of reasons. A well-trained, educated workforce is thought to be a necessity in a modern society. Individual and family upward mobility have increasingly become dependent on educational level. This has been particularly true in the latter half of the twentieth century. In addition, education itself is a valued commodity. Thus, it is not surprising that the percentage of the population enrolled in school increased dramatically in the early decades of the twentieth century and the percentages have continued to increase, though less dramatically, in recent decades. The enrollments are not uniform across the various racial and ethnic groups, however.

The differences by groups presented in this chapter reflect a number of factors. Among these are continuing immigration, cultural emphases, history, and social class. Nineteenth-century differences in education levels were more pronounced than those we observe today. At the turn of the last century, immigrants were a much higher percentage of the population than they are today, and while some immigrants sought greater educational opportunities, others first sought employment. Their primary need was to provide for themselves and their families. Blacks living primarily in the South had been excluded from educational opportunities. Thus, the differences observed here reflect continuing changes in the ethnic composition of the United States, the changed educational requirements, the improved opportunities for various groups, changes in the occupational workforce of the United States, location of specific groups in the social structure, and a number of other factors too numerous to mention.

The enrollment rates for those aged 3 to 34 are actually slightly higher for Blacks than for Whites. Hispanics have the lowest enrollment of these three groups. Many of these overall differences are attributable to the differences in preschool enrollment where Blacks have the highest rate and Hispanics are far less likely to be enrolled (see B1.1 and B1.2). The Head Start and preprimary school enrollments are shown in B1.2 and B1.3. The Head Start enrollment pattern also shows Blacks to be the most highly enrolled, with Whites next. Hispanics are the next most likely to be enrolled while Native Americans and Asians seldom have their children enrolled in Head Start. The enrollments for preprimary school show a similar pattern. Enrollment rates for those ages 5 through 15 do not vary much by race or ethnicity. All are in the high 90 percents. Only in the late teenage years do the enrollment rates start to decline. They decline more steeply for Hispanics than for Blacks and more steeply for Blacks than for Whites (B1.1).

The percentage of high school graduates taking courses in mathematics, biology, and chemistry in 1982 and 1994 are presented in B1.4. All of the percentages increase over the 12-year period. The highest enrollment rates in these science and math courses are for the Asian/Pacific Islander group. In several of these math and science courses, Asians have enrollments that are double those of their White counterparts. Many of this group are children of immigrants. The higher enrollments of these immigrant students likely reflect several factors: cultural prescriptions that emphasize achievement, high levels of exposure to these subjects in their homelands, and possibly some selective migration.

At the same time, White students have much higher enrollments than the "Other" ethnic groups in these types of courses. Despite the somewhat lower general enrollments by Hispanics noted in some other courses, their enrollment in these science courses is slightly higher than that of Blacks and Native Americans.

Likewise, the percent of high school seniors who report they are enrolled in college preparatory or academic programs is highest for Asians, then Whites, Blacks, and Hispanics. Native Americans, in part because of lack of opportunity to enroll in such programs, have the lowest rates of enrollments in these kinds of programs (see B1.5). Enrollments in vocational or general programs show a general reverse trend to the rates for college preparatory or academic programs.

The percentage of high school graduates who enrolled in college by race is shown in B1.6. Though this percentage has increased for both Blacks and Whites over the period shown, the percentage of Black high school graduates going on to college in 1996 is what it was for White high school graduates in 1983.

B2. DROPOUTS

The flip side of graduation, of course, is dropping out. The dropout rates for the three major groups, Blacks, Whites, and Hispanics, have all declined over the last 20 years, but the dropout rate during each year has declined the most for Hispanics, then for Blacks, and the least for Whites. In other words, the minority rates are approaching the low White rates (see B2.1). The percentage of status dropouts, those who have ever dropped out, is much higher for Hispanics than for the other two groups. This figure is higher, in part, because of high dropout rates in the past. Additionally, some of this group completed their education in other countries before immigrating here. The completion rates for high school graduation in some of these other countries are much lower than in the United States. And some Hispanic children are encouraged to accept jobs and help with family finances. These higher dropout rates may thus reflect the economic needs and adaptations of working class families who are more likely to be minorities. The data on dropouts are shown in B2.2 and B2.3. The most recent data are in B2.3.

B3. ASPIRATIONS

Educational aspirations usually are measured as those who plan to attend college or get advanced degrees. This is distinguished from actual attainments (discussed in section B4). The number of students saying they plan to attend college is often less than those actually attending. The percentage of high school graduates who plan to attend college in either a 2-year or a 4-year program is shown in B3.1 and B3.2. Asian and Pacific Islanders generally have the highest aspirations, and they are more likely to say they will probably go to college, followed by Whites, Blacks, and Hispanics (B3.3).

B4. ACHIEVEMENTS AND ATTAINMENTS

Of the three largest groups, Whites, Blacks, and Hispanics, Whites are the most likely to have completed four years of high school and most likely to have completed four years of college (B4.1 and B4.2). The disparities decrease for younger cohorts (see B4.4).

Data for Hispanics have been compiled since 1970 and for Asian/Pacific Islanders only since 1990. When Asian/Pacific Islanders are included, they have the highest educational attainment level of all the groups. Some of this education has been obtained elsewhere. The college completion rates of Asian/Pacific Islanders are comparable to that of Whites, while the rates for Blacks and Hispanics are substantially lower (B4.3 and B4.4)

B5. EDUCATIONAL PROFICIENCY

Educational proficiency can be measured in a number of ways. One way is average reading scores. The average reading scores for 1992, 1994, and 1998 are presented in B5.1. Generally, Whites have the highest scores, followed by Asian/Pacific Islanders, and then Hispanics, Blacks, and Native Americans. The scores of the last three groups are roughly equivalent. The percentage of students reading at grade level shows approximately the same pattern (B5.1 and B5.2).

The proficiencies of students, by age or grade level, in a variety of subjects, also exhibit ethnic-racial differences. In reading (B5.2), Blacks and Hispanics are roughly equivalent, but they fall significantly behind Whites. This same pattern can be observed for writing (B5.3), and geography and history (B5.4). Hispanics do slightly better than Blacks on average in math and science, but still fall well below Whites (B5.5 through B5.7).

Math, science, and reading proficiency scores of high school seniors are presented in B5.8 through B5.10. Native Americans/Alaskan Natives have math proficiencies about the same level as Hispanics, but Asian/Pacific Islanders have the highest average math and science proficiency scores. But they are only slightly higher than the average scores of Whites. The average science proficiency scores of Native Americans is higher than that of Hispanics and Blacks, but lower than Whites or Asians. The average reading proficiency scores of all the minority groups are below those of Whites, though those of Asian/Pacific Islanders are the highest of the minorities, followed by Native American/Alaskan Natives, then those of Hispanic origin, and then those of Blacks (B5.10).

The number of students taking Advanced Placement Exams and the number scoring 3 or higher, with 5 being the maximum possible, is another measure of school attainment or proficiency. Table B5.11 presents the number of students taking these exams and the results. White students are far more likely than Black or Hispanic students to take these courses and score well on them. Hispanic students do better than Black students.

Grades received in school and verbal and mathematical scores on the SAT (Scholastic Aptitude Test) are final measures of educational proficiency. Grades received in school are presented in B5.12. Asian students in general have the highest self-reported grades, and Chinese students have the highest of the Asian students. Whites generally have the next highest scores, followed by the other groups. Considerable variations exist by subject, however. On the SAT exams, the Asian students do the best on the math portion, while Whites generally do the best on the verbal portion. Blacks score the lowest on both (B5.13).

All of these educational proficiency scores reflect a variety of conditions: cultural emphases, opportunities to take advanced courses, opportunity to attend good schools, immigration patterns, parental involvement, discrimination, prejudice, etc. We will turn to some of these factors later in the section.

B6. PARENTAL SUPPORT FOR SCHOOLS

Parents support schools in a variety of ways. One way is by reading to young children. The percentage who read to small children is reported in B6.1. White parents are far more likely to read to their children than are minority parents. Minority parents, on the other hand are more likely than White parents to talk to their children about family history or ethnic heritage (see B6.2). Parents engage in more general educational-type activities with their children, and the percentage of parents (by race or ethnicity) who engage in these activities varies greatly. Some of these activities are presented in B6.2. Those parents who attended a school meeting, parent-teacher conference, or class events, or who volunteered at school are presented in B6.3. Generally, White parents are more likely to engage in these kinds of school activities than are minority parents. As we might expect, the achievement levels of the students in section B5 generally reflect the educational levels of the parents (B6.4). The parental education levels of Asian students are generally the highest, and the levels of Hispanics the lowest, although considerable variation exists within these groups.

B7. SCHOOL RELATED ISSUES

Participation in a variety of other activities related to schools also varies considerably by race and ethnic group. For example, Whites are much more likely than Blacks or Hispanics to participate on sports teams or be enrolled in physical education classes (B7.1). Asians, however, tend to be most involved in school clubs, followed by

Native Americans, then Whites, Blacks, and Hispanics. Considerable variation exists within the Asian and Hispanic groups, however (see B7.2).

Likewise, time spent on homework, and conversely, time spent watching television varies by group. Black youth report spending the most time watching television, Whites the least, and Hispanics, Asian/Pacific Islanders, and Native Americans in between (B7.3). Asian/Pacific Islanders report spending the most time on homework, Native Americans the least, and the other groups are intermediate (B7.3).

Much more goes on in schools than education. Hostile remarks, fights, turf battles, drug use, and a host of other activities are reported in conjunction with school attendance. Generally White students report fewer of these "turf" problems than do Black and Hispanic students (see B7.4). Likewise, Black and Hispanic students are more likely than White students to have observed cigarettes and smokeless tobacco used on school property and they generally are more likely to have seen weapons or fights, or to have noticed alcohol, marijuana, and other drugs being offered or sold on school property (B7.5). The percentage of students who report trouble getting along with teachers, paying attention in school, getting homework done, or getting along with other students varies little between groups (B7.6). But minority students generally are more likely than White students to report that other students are prejudiced, and minority students are more likely than White students to disagree that teachers treat students fairly (B7.7). Some of these differences are quite small, however.

Finally, rates of absenteeism, suspension, and expulsion from school are reported in B7.8. White, Native American, and Hispanic students appear to report somewhat higher rates of absenteeism than do the Black and Asian students. On the other hand, Black, Native American, and Hispanic students appear to have the highest suspension and expulsion rates, while White and Asian students have lower rates.

B8. HIGHER EDUCATION ENROLLMENT

Almost 45 percent of high school graduates enroll in college, but Blacks and especially Hispanics and Native Americans/Alaskan Natives are less likely than Whites to pursue a college education. Asians and Pacific Islanders, on the other hand, are more likely than others, including Whites, to enroll in college. The numbers of enrollees and percentages are presented in B8.1. The percentage of minority students in graduate programs and first-year professional programs generally declines from college enrollments. The exception is Asian/Pacific Islanders in first-year professional programs (compare B8.1 and B8.3).

B9. HIGHER EDUCATION GRADUATIONS

The number and percentage of associate degrees granted in 1995–1996 are presented in B9.1. Similar data for bachelor's degrees are presented in B9.2.

The data for advanced degrees, master's degrees, Ph.D.s, and first professional degrees are presented in B9.3, B9.4, and B9.5. Generally, minorities are less likely to complete higher degrees. Two exceptions are evident. First, Asian/Pacific Islanders tend to have higher completion percentages for advanced degrees. Second, the percentage of non-resident alien (foreign) students increases dramatically in graduate programs.

B10. HIGHER EDUCATION FACULTY

As might be expected, the faculty and staff at institutions of higher education reflect the proportions obtaining Ph.D.s. Except for Asian/Pacific Islanders, minorities are generally underrepresented as faculty and staff. Asian/ Pacific Islanders are overrepresented in business, engineering, and the natural sciences. Blacks come close to their average in the population only in the field of education. The percentage of faculty by academic rank is shown in B10.2. Minority faculty tend to be at the lower ranks while Whites are more likely to be the higher ranks. These patterns reflect the more recent entrance of most minority groups into academia.

B1. ENROLLMENT AND GRADUATION

B1.1. Percent of the Population 3–34 Years Old Enrolled in School: October 1997

Age	All Races	White, non-Hispanic	Black, non-Hispanic	Hispanic Origin
total, 3 to 34 years	55.6	55.6	58.6	50.8
3 and 4 years	52.6	54.9	60.0	36.6
5 and 6 years	96.5	96.9	95.7	96.6
7 to 9 years	98.8	98.9	99.2	98.9
10 to 13 years	99.3	99.2	99.4	99.6
14 and 15 years	98.9	98.9	99.2	98.4
16 and 17 years	94.3	95.1	93.5	91.1
18 and 19 years	61.5	64.0	57.8	49.4
20 and 21 years	45.9	49.9	36.0	28.9
22 and 24 years	26.4	27.8	25.7	16.4
25 to 29 years	11.8	12.2	10.6	7.3
30 to 34 years	5.7	5.6	6.5	3.7

Source: U.S. Department of Education. National Center for Education Statistics. Digest for Education Statistics, 1998, NCES, 1999-036, by Thomas D. Snyder. Production Manager, Charlene M. Hoffman. Program Analyst, Claire M. Geddes. Washington, D.C., 1999, p. 16

B1.2. Percentage of Three-Year-Olds Enrolled in Early Childhood Programs, by Race: 1991,1993, 1995

	1991	1993	1995
Total Students	31.4	34.1	37.4
White	33.4	33.7	40.2
Black	31.6	41.9	41.1
Hispanic	19.8	27.2	21.2

Source: National Center for Education Statistics, U.S. Department of Education. The Condition of Education. 1997, Indicator 1, page 48.

B1.3. Head Start—Enrollment

[For fiscal years ending in year shown.]		
YEAR	RACE	Enrollment 1997 (percent)
1989	White	31
1990	Black	36
1991	Hispanic	26
1992	American Indian	4
1993	Asian	3

Source: U.S. Administration for Children and Families. "Head Start 1998 Fact Sheet;" <http://www.acf.dhhs.gov/programs/hsb/facts98.htm>

B1.4. Percentage of High School Graduates Taking Selected Mathematics and Science Courses in High School, by Race/Ethnicity: 1982 and 1994

	White	Black	Hispanic	Asian/ Pacific Islander	American Indian/ Alaskan Native
1982 \1					
Algebra II	36.0	22.0	18.0	45.6	10.8
Trigonometry	13.7	6.0	6.4	26.8	3.0
Analysis/pre-calculus	6.8	2.2	2.8	14.5	1.8
Calculus	5.4	1.3	1.7	12.8	4.0
AP Calculus	1.8	0.3	0.4	5.5	0.1
Biology and chemistry	31.3	19.7	14.2	48.5	21.9
Biology, chemistry, and physics	12.2	4.8	3.9	28.4	7.8
1994					
Algebra II	61.6	43.7	51.0	66.6	39.2
Trigonometry	18.6	13.6	9.8	25.3	6.7
Analysis/pre-calculus	18.2	9.8	13.9	33.9	8.7
Calculus	9.6	3.8	6.0	23.4	3.8
AP Calculus	7.3	2.0	4.6	21.0	2.2
Biology and Chemistry	56.4	42.2	45.1	64.8	39.6
Biology, chemistry, and physics	22.7	13.0	13.4	37.2	8.0

Source: NCES, The 1994 High School Transcript Study Tabulations: Comparative *Data on Credits Earned and Demographics for 1994, 1990, 1987, and 1982 High School Graduates, 1996.*

B1.5. Percent of High School Seniors Who Reported Being in Various High School Programs: 1982 and 1992

	General		College preparatory or academic		Vocational	
	1982	**1992**	**1982**	**1992**	**1982**	**1992**
White	34.8	43.3	40.6	45.7	24.6	11
Black	35.1	48.9	33.3	35.6	31.6	15.4
Hispanic	37.4	56.4	24.9	30.6	37.7	13.1
Asian	27.5	40.3	55.9	50.9	16.6	8.8
American Indian	55.3	60.8	19.1	22.6	25.6	16.7

Source: U.S. Department of Education. National Center for Education Statistics, "High School and Beyond," First Followup survey; and "National Educational Longitudinal Survey," Second Followup survey.

B1.6. College Enrollment of Recent High School Graduates: 1980 to 1996

[For persons 16 to 24 who graduated from high school in the preceeding 12 months. Includes persons receiving GEDs. Based on surveys and subject to sampling error.]

	PERCENT OF HIGH SCHOOL GRADUATES ENROLLED IN COLLEGE \2			
YEAR	Total \1	White	Black	Hispanic \3
1980	49.3	49.9	41.8	52.7
1981	53.9	54.6	42.9	52.1
1982	50.6	52.0	36.5	43.1
1983	52.7	55.0	38.5	54.3
1984	55.2	57.9	40.2	44.3
1985	57.7	59.4	42.3	51.1
1986	53.8	56.0	36.5	44.4
1987	56.8	56.6	51.9	33.5
1988	58.9	60.7	45.0	57.0
1989	59.6	60.4	52.8	55.4
1990	59.9	61.5	46.3	47.3
1991	62.4	64.6	45.6	57.1
1992	61.7	63.4	47.9	54.8
1993	62.6	62.8	55.6	62.5
1994	61.9	63.6	50.9	48.9
1995	61.9	62.6	51.4	53.8
1996	65.0	65.8	55.3	50.5

Notes:
\1 Includes other races, not shown separately.
\2 As of October.
\3 Persons of Hispanic origin may be of any race.

Source: U.S. National Center for Education Statistics. Digest of Education, *Digest of Education Statistics,* annual.

B2. DROPOUTS

B2.1. High School Dropouts, by Race and Hispanic Origin: 1975 to 1996

[In percent]

YEAR	1975	1980	1985	1990	1995	1996
EVENT DROPOUTS \2						
Total \3	**5.8**	**6.0**	**5.2**	**4.0**	**5.4**	**4.7**
White	5.4	5.6	4.8	3.8	5.1	4.5
Black	8.7	8.3	7.7	5.1	6.1	6.3
Hispanic \4	10.9	11.5	9.7	8.0	11.6	8.4
STATUS DROPOUTS \5						
Total \3	**15.6**	**15.6**	**13.9**	**13.6**	**13.9**	**12.8**
White	13.9	14.4	13.5	13.5	13.6	12.5
Black	27.3	23.5	17.6	15.1	14.4	16.0
Hispanic \4	34.9	40.3	31.5	37.3	34.7	34.5

Notes:
\1 Beginning 1987 reflects new editing procedures for cases with missing data on school enrollment.
\2 Percent of students who drop out in a single year without completing high school. For grades 10 to 12.
\3 Includes other races, not shown separately.
\4 Persons of Hispanic origin may be of any race.
\5 Percent of the population who have not completed high school and are not enrolled, regardless of when they dropped out. For persons 18 to 24 years old.

Source: U.S. Bureau of the Census, Current Population Reports, P20-500.

B2.2. Percent of Distribution of the 16–24-Year-Old Population and Percentage Who Were Dropouts: 1995

	Percentage of the population	Dropout rate
Total	100.0	12.0
Born in U.S.	89.4	9.9
Foreign-born	10.6	29.1
White, non-Hispanic	67.9	8.6
Born in U.S.	65.6	8.6
Foreign born	2.3	7.5
Hispanic	13.9	30.0
Born in U.S.	7.9	17.9
Foreign born	5.9	46.2

Source: U.S. Department of Commerce, Bureau of the Census, *Current Population Survey*, October 1995.

B2.3. Percent of High School Dropouts (Status Dropouts) among Persons 16–24 Years Old: October 1997

All races	White, Non-Hispanic	Black, Non-Hispanic	Hispanic Origin
11.0	7.6	13.4	25.3

Source: U.S. Department of Education. National Center for Education Statistics, Digest for Education Statistics, 1998, NCES, 1999-036, by Thomas D. Snyder. Production Manager, Charlene M. Hoffman. Program Analyst, Claire M. Geddes. Washington, D.C., 1999, p. 124.

B3. ASPIRATIONS

B3.1. Percentage of High School Seniors Who Planned to Continue Their Education the Next Year at 4-year Colleges or in Academic Programs at 2-year Colleges: 1972 and 1992

Race/ethnicity	4-year program		2 -year academic program	
	1972	1992	1972	1992
Total	**34**	**54**	**11**	**13**
White	35	55	12	12
Black	32	52	5	11
Hispanic	11	20	11	26
Asian/Pacific Islander	47	65	18	12

Source: National Center For Education Statistics. *Findings from The Condition of Education 1996 Minorities in Higher Education No. 9*, January 1997, p.2

B3.2. Percentage of 1992 High School Seniors Expecting to Complete Various Levels of Education

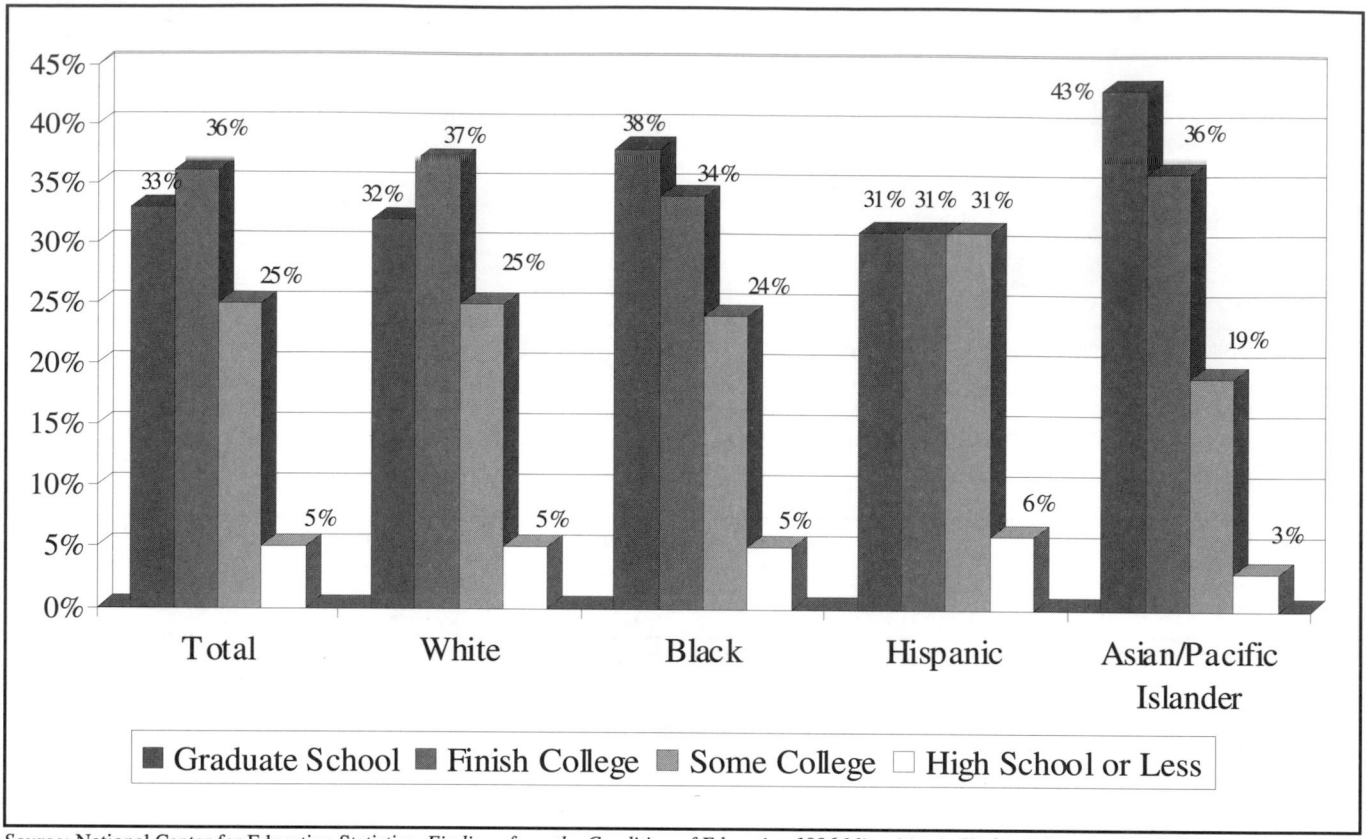

Source: National Center for Education Statistics. *Findings from the Condition of Education 1996 Minorities in Higher Education No. 9.* January 1997, p. 4

B3.3. Educational Expectations

The following are a variety of questions about your educational, employment, financial, and life expectations.

On a scale of 1 to 5, where 1 is low and 5 is high, how much do you want to go to college?

	White	Black	Native American	Asian	Hispanic	Total
1 low	5.1	5.2	2.7	1.7	6.3	5.1
2	3.7	2.8	2.2	1.7	3.5	3.4
3	10.4	9.9	15.4	6.6	14.8	10.8
4	13.7	14.0	17.3	14.6	17.0	14.2
5 high	67.2	68.2	62.4	75.5	58.4	66.5

On a scale of 1 to 5, where 1 is low and 5 is high, how likely is it that you will go to college?

	White	Black	Native American	Asian	Hispanic	Total
1 low	6.8	6.8	6.8	2.8	8.7	6.8
2	5.4	5.1	6.5	3.4	7.5	5.6
3	13.4	16.8	19.5	10.2	21.9	15.0
4	18.3	20.1	22.2	19.7	23.1	19.4
5 high	56.1	51.1	45.1	63.9	38.7	53.2

Source: The National Longitudinal Study of Adolescent Health, 1995.

B4. ACHIEVEMENTS AND ATTAINMENTS

B4.1. Completed 4 Years of High School or More, by Race and Hispanic Origin: 1960 to 1997

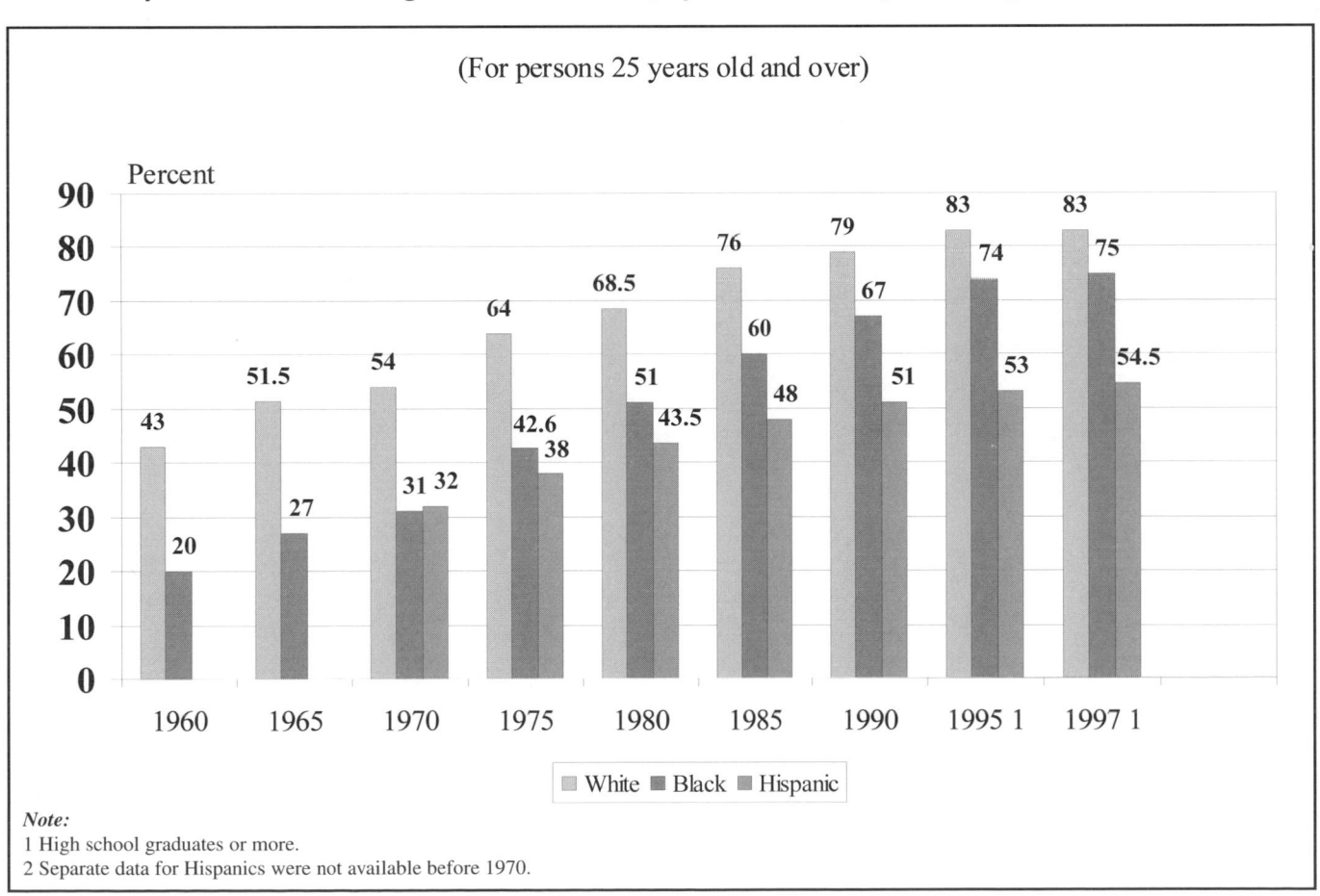

(For persons 25 years old and over)

Note:
1 High school graduates or more.
2 Separate data for Hispanics were not available before 1970.

Source: U.S. Census Bureau, *The Official Statistics,* 1998.

B4.2. Completed 4 Years of College or More, by Race and Hispanic Origin: 1960 to 1997

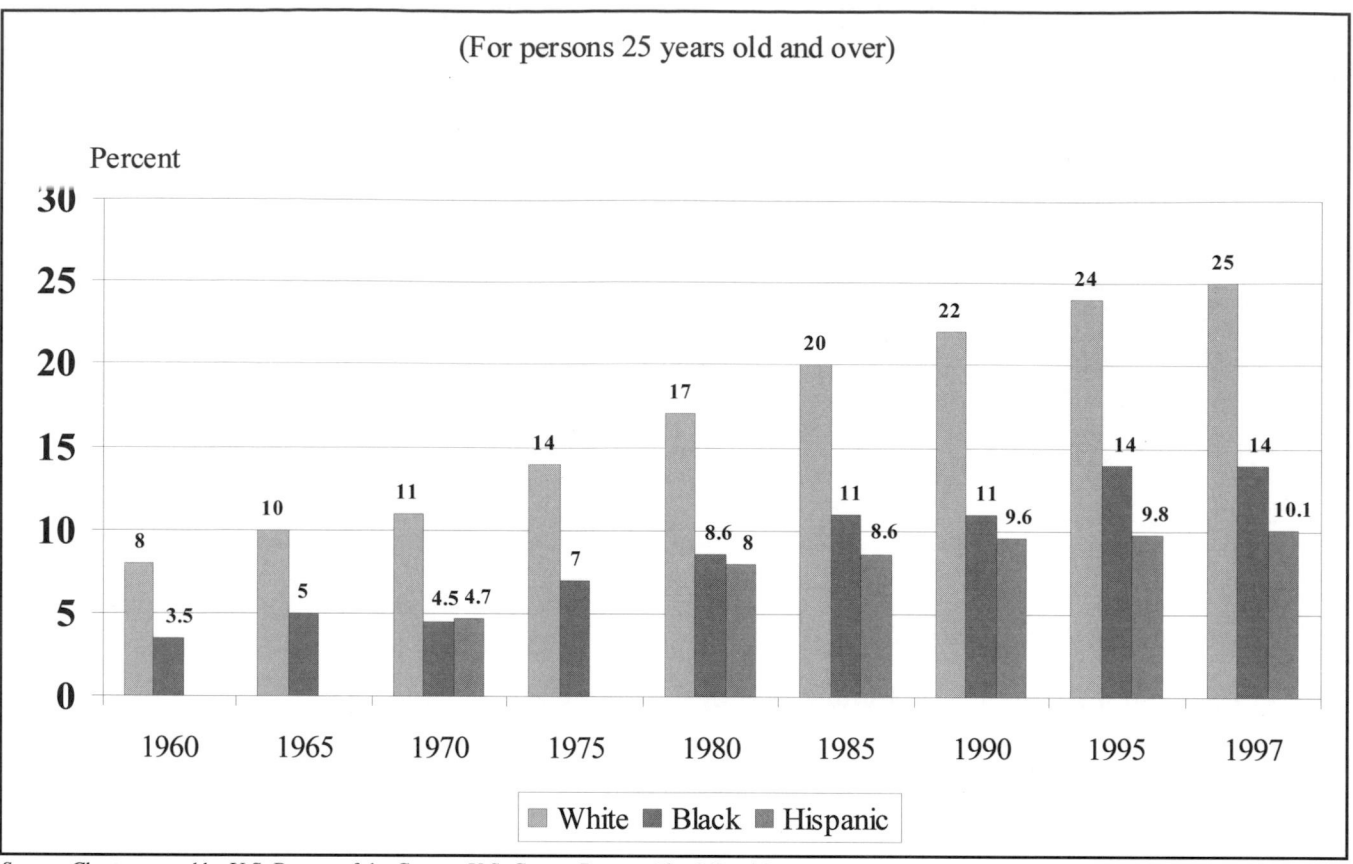

(For persons 25 years old and over)

Percent

White   Black   Hispanic

Source: Chart prepared by U.S. Bureau of the Census. U.S. Census Bureau, *The Official Statistics.*

B4.3. Educational Attainment, by Race and Hispanic Origin: 1960 to 1997

[In percent. For persons 25 years old and over. 1960, 1970, 1980, and 1990 as of April 1 and based on sample data from the censuses of population. Other years as of March and based on the Current Population Survey]

YEAR	Total \1	White	Black	Asian and Pacific Islander	Hispanic \2,3
COMPLETED 4 YEARS OF HIGH SCHOOL OR MORE					
1960	41.1	43.2	20.1	(NA)	(NA)
1965	49.0	51.3	27.2	(NA)	(NA)
1970	52.3	54.5	31.4	(NA)	32.1
1975	62.5	64.5	42.5	(NA)	37.9
1980	66.5	68.8	51.2	(NA)	44.0
1985	73.9	75.5	59.8	(NA)	47.9
1990	77.6	79.1	66.2	80.4	50.8
1991	78.4	79.9	66.7	81.8	51.3
1994 \4	80.9	82.0	72.9	84.8	53.3
1995 \4	81.7	83.0	73.8	(NA)	53.4
1996 \4	81.7	82.8	74.3	83.2	53.1
1997 \4	82.1	83.0	74.9	84.9	54.7
COMPLETED 4 YEARS OF COLLEGE OR MORE					
1960	7.7	8.1	3.1	(NA)	(NA)
1965	9.4	9.9	4.7	(NA)	(NA)
1970	10.7	11.3	4.4	(NA)	4.5
1975	13.9	14.5	6.4	(NA)	(NA)
1980	16.2	17.1	8.4	(NA)	7.6
1985	19.4	20.0	11.1	(NA)	8.5
1990	21.3	22.0	11.3	39.9	9.2
1994 \4	22.2	22.9	12.9	41.2	9.1
1995 \4	23.0	24.0	13.2	(NA)	9.3
1996 \4	23.6	24.3	13.6	41.7	9.3
1997 \4	23.9	24.6	13.3	42.2	10.3

Notes:
NA Not available.
\1 Includes other races, not shown separately.
\2 Persons of Hispanic origin may be of any race.
\3 Includes persons of other Hispanic origin, not shown separately.
\4 Beginning 1992, high school graduates and those with a BA degree or higher.

Source: U.S. Bureau of the Census, U.S. Census of Population, U.S. Summary, PC80-1-C1; and Current Population Reports P20-455, P20-459, P20-462, P20-465RV, P20-475, P20-476, P20-489, P20-493, P20-505; and unpublished data.

B4.4. Years of School Completed by Persons Age 25 and Over and Age 25 to 29: 1997

Percent, by years of school completed.

Age	All Races			White, non-Hispanic			Black, non-Hispanic			Hispanic		
	Less than 5 years of elementary school	High school completion or higher	4 or more years of college	Less than 5 years of elementary school	High school completion or higher	4 or more years of college	Less than 5 years of elementary school	High school completion or higher	4 or more years of college	Less than 5 years of elementary school	High school completion or higher	4 or more years college
25 and over	1.7	82.1	23.9	0.6	86.3	26.2	2	75.3	13.3	9.4	54.7	10.3
25 to 29	0.8	87.4	27.8	0.1	92.9	32.6	0.6	86.9	14.2	4.2	61.8	11

Source: U.S. Department of Education. National Center for Education Statistics, 1998. NCES, 1999-036, by Thomas D. Snyder. Production Manager, Charlene M. Hoffman. Program Analyst, Claire M. Gedes. Washington, D.C., 1999, p. 17.

B5. EDUCATIONAL PROFICIENCY

B5.1. Percentage of Students At or Above Reading Achievement Levels, by Race/Ethnicity: 1992, 1994, and 1998

	1992				1994				1998			
	Below Basic	At or above Basic	At or above Proficient	Advanced	Below Basic	At or above Basic	At or above Proficient	Advanced	Below Basic	At or above Basic	At or above Proficient	Advanced
Grade 4												
White	29	71	35	8	29	71	37	9	27	73	39	10
Black	67	33	8	1	69	31	9	1	64	36	10	1
Hispanic	56	44	16	3	64	36	13	2	60	40	13	2
Asian/Pacific Islander	41	59	25	4	25	75	44	13	31	69	37	12
American Indian	47	53	18	3	52	48	18	3	53	47	14	2
Grade 8												
White	22	78	36	4	22	78	36	4	18*+	82*+	41+	4
Black	55	45	9	0	56	44	9	0	47+	53+	12	0
Hispanic	51	49	14	1	51	49	14	1	46	54	15	1
Asian/Pacific Islander	22	78	39	7	25	75	37	5	18	82	39	4
American Indian	39	61	20	1	37	63	20	1	39	61	18	1
Grade 12												
White	14	86	47	5	19	81	43	5	17	83	47+	7*
Black	39	61	18	1	48	52	13	1	43	57	18	1
Hispanic	34	66	24	2	42	58	20	1	36	64	26	2
Asian/Pacific Islander	22	78	41	5	32	68	31	3	25	75	38	6
American Indian	***	***	***	***	39	61	20	2	35	65	27	3

Notes:
* Indicates that the percentage in 1998 is significantly different from that in 1992. + Indicates that the percentage in 1998 is significantly different from that in 1994.
*** Sample size insufficient to permit a reliable estimate.

Source: U.S. Department of Education. Office of Educational Research and Improvement. National Center for Education Statistics. *The NAEP 1998 Reading Report Card for the Nation.* NCES 1999-459, by P.L. Donahue, K.E. Voelkl, J.R. Campbell, and J. Mazzeo. Washington, D.C.: 1999.

B5.2. Average Reading Proficiency, by Age: 1996

Race/ethnicity	9-year-olds	13-year-olds	17-year-olds
White, non-Hispanic	219.9	267.0	294.4
Black, non-Hispanic	190.0	235.6	265.4
Hispanic	194.1	239.9	264.7

Source: U.S. Department of Education. National Center of Education Statistics. Digest of Education Statistics, 1998 NCES, 1999-036, by Thomas D. Snyder. Production Manager, Charlene M. Hoffman. Program Analyst, Claire M. Geddes. Washington, D.C., 1999, p. 127.

B5.3. Average Writing Performance of 4th, 8th, and 11th Graders: 1996

Race/ethnicity	4th graders	8th graders	11th graders
White	216	271	289
Black	182	242	267
Hispanic	191	246	269

Source: U.S. Department of Education. National Center for Education Statistics. Digest of Education Statistics, 1998, NCES, 1999-036, by Thomas D. Snyder. Production Manager, Charlene M. Hoffman. Program Analyst, Claire M. Geddes. Washington, D.C., 1999. p.133.

B5.4. Average Student Proficiency in Geography and U.S. History, by Race/Ethnicity: 1994

Race	Percentage distribution of 12th graders in geography	Geography Scores			History Scores		
		4th graders	8th graders	12th graders	4th graders	8th graders	12th graders
White	74	218	270	291	215	267	292
Black	12	168	229	258	177	239	265
Hispanic	8	183	239	268	180	243	267

Source: U.S. Department of Education. National Center for Education Statistics. Digest of Education statistics, 1998, NCES, 1999-036, by Thomas D. Snyder. Production Manager, Charlene M. Hoffman. Program Analyst, Claire M. Geddes Washington, D.C., 1999. p. 135.

B5.5. Average Mathematics Proficiency, by Age: 1996

Race/ethnicity	9-year-olds	13-year-olds	17-year-olds
White	237	281	313
Black	212	252	286
Hispanic	215	256	292

Source: U.S. Department of Education. National Center for Education Statistics. Digest of Education Statistics, 1998, NCES, 1999-036, by Thomas D. Snyder. Production Manager, Charlene N. Hoffman. Program Analyst, Claire M. Geddes. Washington, D.C., 1999. p.136.

B5.6. Average Science Proficiency, by Age: 1996

Race/ethnicity	9-year-olds	13-year-olds	17-year-olds
White, non-Hispanic	239	266	307
Black, non-Hispanic	202	226	260
Hispanic	207	232	269

Source: U.S. Department of Education. National Center for Education Statistics. Digest of Education Statistics, 1998, NCES, 1999-036, by Thomas D. Snyder. Production Manager, Charlene M. Hoffman. Program Analyst, Claire M. Geddes. Washington, D.C., 1999. p.144.

B5.7. Percent of Students At or Above Selected Science Proficiency Levels, by Age: 1996

	9-year-olds				13-year-olds				17-year-olds			
	Know everyday science facts	Understand simple scientific principles	Apply general scientific information	Analyze scientific procedures and data	Understand simple scientific principles	Apply general scientific information	Analyze scientific procedures and data	Integrate specialized scientific information	Understand simple scientific principles	Apply general scientific information	Analyze scientific procedures and data	Integrate specialized scientific information
White, non-Hispanic	98.6	83.8	39.6	5.9	97.0	68.5	15.9	0.6	99.3	91.2	58.5	13.8
Black, non-Hispanic	91.0	52.2	10.6	0.3	75.9	25.5	1.9	0.0	93.0	59.8	17.7	0.8
Hispanic	92.6	57.8	13.1	0.4	81.0	30.9	3.2	0.0	94.1	67.6	23.9	3.0

Source: U.S. Department of Education. National Center for Education Statistics. Digest of Education Statistics, 1998, NCES. 1999-036, by Thomas D. Snyder. Production Manager, Charlene M. Hoffman. Program Analyst, Claire M. Geddes. Washington, D.C., 1999. p.142.

B5.8. Average Mathematics Proficiency of Seniors: 1992

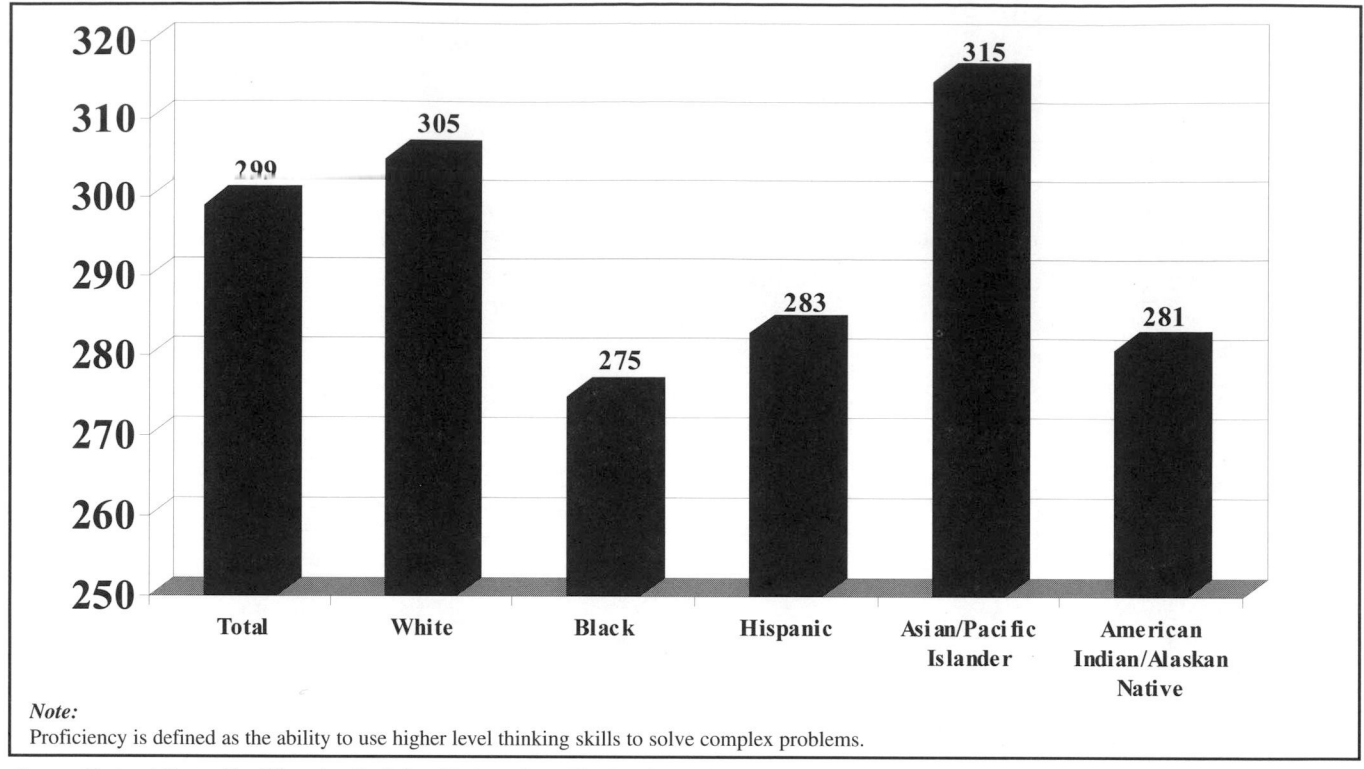

Note:
Proficiency is defined as the ability to use higher level thinking skills to solve complex problems.

Source: National Center For Education Statistics. *Findings from The Condition of Education 1996 Minorities in Higher Education No. 9.* January 1997, p. 10

B5.9. Average Science Proficiency of Seniors: 1990

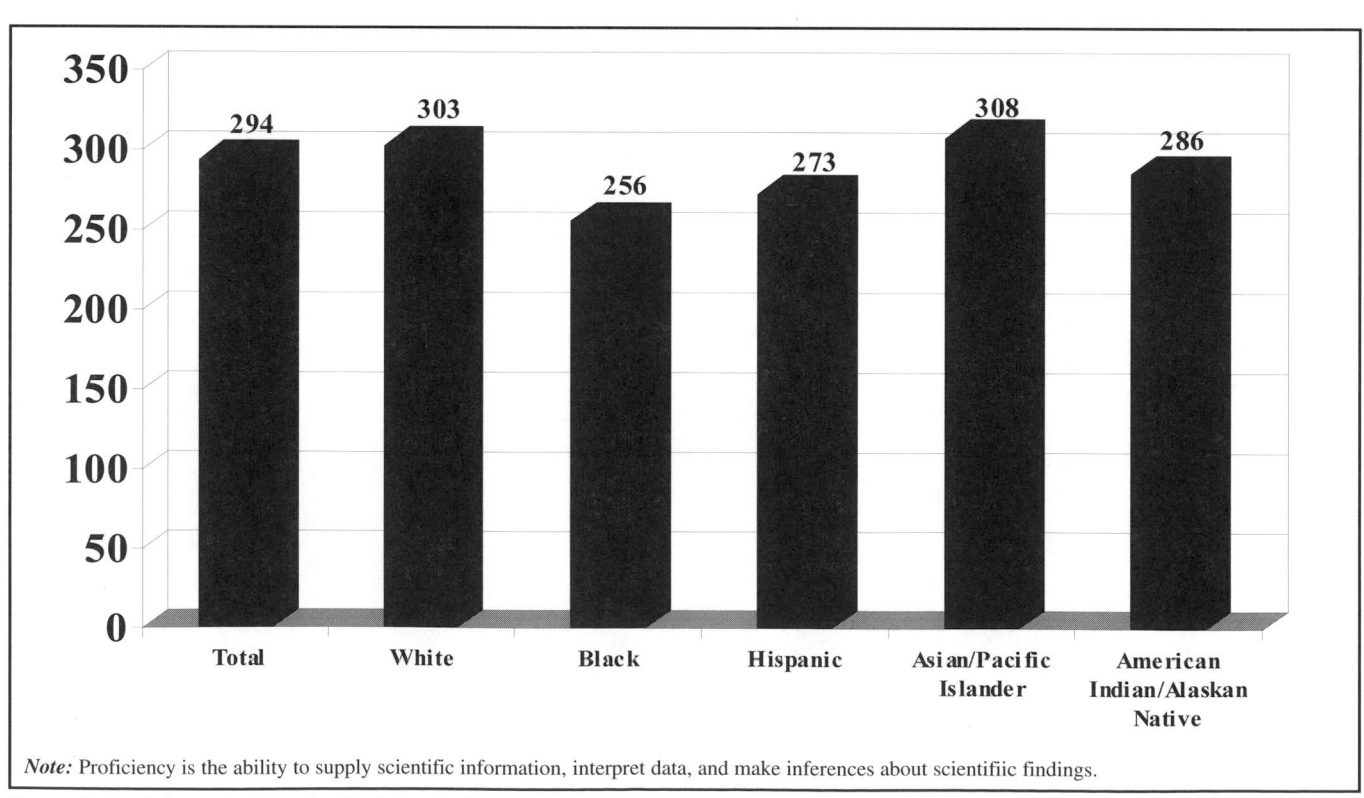

Note: Proficiency is the ability to supply scientific information, interpret data, and make inferences about scientifiic findings.

Source: National Center for Education Statistics. *Findings from The Condition of Education 1996 Minorities in Higher Education No. 9.* January 1997, p. 10.

B5.10. Average Reading Proficiency of Seniors: 1994

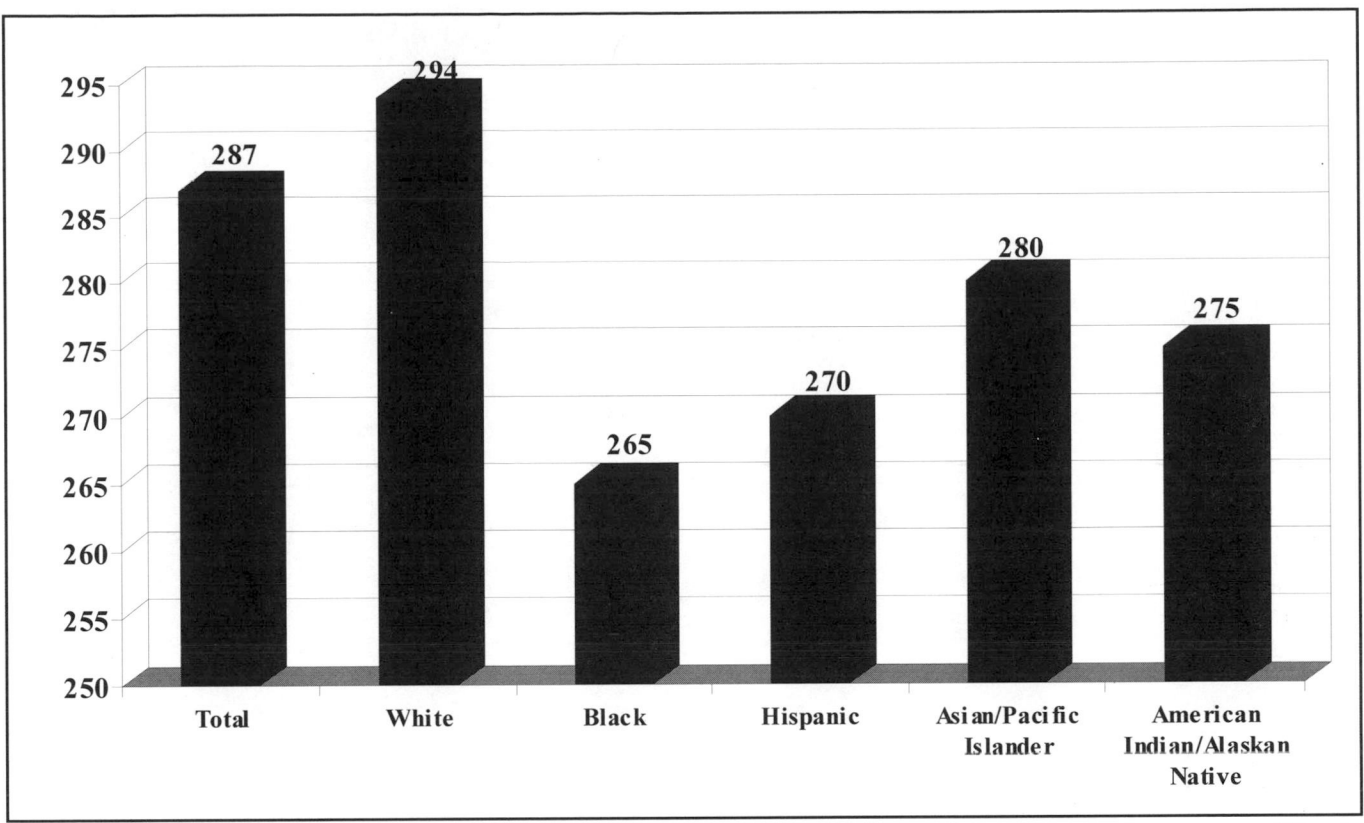

Source: National Center for Education Statistics. *Findings from The Condition of Education 1996 Minorities in Higher Education No. 9.* January 1997, p. 8.

B5.11. Students Taking Advanced Placement Examinations, 1990 to 1995 and Exams Taken, 1996

| | | RACE/ETHNICITY | | |
ITEM	Total \1	White \2	Black \2	Hispanic
STUDENTS TAKING EXAMS \3				
1990	48	48	13	32
1991	53	54	15	32
1992	57	58	14	37
1993	62	61	16	40
1994	60	60	14	34
1995	66	65	18	42
EXAMINATIONS TAKEN				
Total, 1996 \4	824,329	535,055	31,554	59,752
Social studies	262,388	176,126	9,993	14,200
Foreign language	67,019	29,970	1,811	21,419
Calculus	122,852	80,805	4,042	3,320
Computer science	11,065	6,910	363	467
Science	137,511	86,810	4,769	5,622
With scores of 3 or higher, 1996 \4 \5	523,321	344,026	11,078	36,454
Social studies	159,173	109,750	3,530	6,189
Foreign language	47,846	18,132	890	19,374
Calculus	78,185	52,370	1,316	2,437
Computer science	6,231	4,042	85	187
Science	85,126	54,375	1,531	2,396

Notes:
\1 Includes other races, not shown separately.
\2 Non-Hispanic.
\3 Rates per 1,000 11th- and 12th-grade student. Includes a small
number of college students who took exams, about 2 percent of all candidates in 1995.
\4 Includes other exams, not shown separately.
\5 A score of 3 or higher usually receives college credit.

Source: 1984-1995, U.S. National Center for Education Statistics, The Condition of Education, 1997; 1996, The College Entrance Examination Board, New York, NY, The National School Grade Distribution Report, annual, (copyright).

B5.12. Adolescents' Grades in School, 1995

| | Average Grade In | | | |
Race/Ethnicity	English/ Language Arts	Math	History/ Social Studies	Science
White	2.92	2.85	2.96	2.93
Black	2.59	2.53	2.93	2.9
Asian	3.03	3.03	3.06	3.06
Chinese	3.13	3.33	3.21	3.29
Filipino	3.02	2.88	2.99	2.99
Japanese	3.02	3.01	3.1	3.2
Asian Indian	2.91	2.79	2.86	2.89
Korean	3.06	3.17	3.21	3.07
Vietnamese	3.11	3.22	3.06	3
American Indian	2.71	2.64	2.68	2.73
Hispanic	2.66	2.56	2.66	2.66
Mexican	2.74	2.64	2.66	2.69
Chicano/Chicana	2.56	2.55	2.62	2.64
Cuban	2.62	2.42	2.7	2.77
Puerto Rican	2.68	2.57	2.58	2.58
Central/South America	2.6	2.45	2.62	2.62
Total	2.84	2.77	2.88	2.85

Source: Longitudinal Study of Adolescent Health, 1995.

B5.13. Scholastic Assessment Test Score Averages: 1997

	SAT-Verbal	
All Students		505
White		526
Black		434
Hispanic or Latino		466
Mexican American		451
Puerto Rican		454
Asian American		496
American Indian		475
Other		512
	SAT-Mathematical	
All Students		511
White		526
Black		423
Hispanic or Latino		468
Mexican American		458
Puerto Rican		447
Asian American		560
American Indian		475
Other		514

Source: U.S. Department of Education. National Center for Education Statistics. Digest of Education Statistics, 1998, NCES, 1999-036, by Thomas D. Snyder. Production Manager, Charlene M. Hoffman. Program Analyst, Claire M. Geddes. Washington, D.C., 1999. p. 146

B6. PARENTAL SUPPORT FOR SCHOOLS

B6.1. Percentage of 3–5 Year-Olds Who Were Read to Every Day in the Last Week by a Family Member: 1996

Race/ethnicity	
White, non-Hispanic	64
Black, non-Hispanic	44
Hispanic	39

Source: U.S. Department of Education. National Center for Education Statistics. Digest of Education Statistics, 1998, NCES, 1999-036, by Thomas D. Snyder. Production Manager, Charlene M. Hoffman. Program Analyst, Claire M. Geddes. Washington, D.C., 1999. p.154.

B6.2. Percent of Elementary and Secondary School Children Whose Parents Are Involved in Education-related Activities, by Race/Ethnicity: 1996

	Visited a library	Went to a play, concert, or other live show	Visited an art gallery, museum or historical site	Visited a zoo or aquarium	Talked about family history or ethnic heritage	Attended an event sponsored by a community religious, or ethnic group	Decided time for bed on school nights	Decided amount of time child is allowed to watch television	Selected television programs child is allowed to watch	Told a story	Worked on art or craft	Played a game or sport together	Built or made project or fixed something	Worked on household chores
Race/ethnicity of child														
White, non-Hispanic	51.7	32.2	21.0	13.3	52.1	54.9	97.7	77.3	93.4	71.1	68.5	92.4	68.1	97.4
Black, non-Hispanic	43.9	38.1	22.2	21.6	69.5	54.6	97.3	88.5	90.8	66.9	63.5	92.5	59.6	97.0
Hispanic	38.9	26.6	19.6	19.3	58.4	44.3	95.1	83.5	88	70.0	63.3	54.7	56.9	91.8
Other, non-Hispanic	52.3	33.2	24.3	18.3	64.8	49.6	95.5	78.6	89.0	73.8	68.5	90.8	61.9	94.9

Source: U.S. Department of Education. National Center for Education Statistics. Digest of Education Statistics, 1998, NCES 1999-036, by Thomas D. Snyder. Production Manager, Charlene M. Hoffman. Program Analyst, Claire M. Geddes Washington, D.C., 1999, p. 30.

B6.3. Percent of Elementary and Secondary School Children Whose Parents Report They Are Involved in School Activities: 1996

Race/ethnicity of child	Attended a general school meeting	Attended parent-teacher conference	Attended a class event	Volunteered at school
White, non-Hispanic	78.5	71.2	70.9	44.5
Black, non-Hispanic	71.9	68.0	56.0	29.5
Hispanic	72.7	70.7	54.8	27.7
Other, non-Hispanic	72.6	71.4	63.4	36.2

Source: U.S Department of Education. National Center for education Statistics. Digest of Education Statistics, 1998, NCES 1999-036, by Thomas D. Snyder. Production Manager, Charlene M. Hoffman. Program Analyst, Claire M. Geddes. Washington, D.C., 1999, p. 30.

B6.4. Parents' Education

Race/ethnicity	Mother			Father		
	Less than high school	High school	College	Less than high school	High school	College
White	10.1	48.3	41.6	10.7	43.4	45.8
Black	10.7	45.3	43.9	11.1	45.5	43.4
Asian	12.1	31.8	56.2	9.4	27.5	63.1
Chinese	12.9	28.8	58.3	9.6	27.0	63.4
Filipino	10.0	25.8	64.2	8.7	24.7	66.6
Japanese	3.4	33.5	63.1	4.5	25.4	70.1
Asian Indian	12.5	27.5	60.0	10.0	21.2	68.9
Korean	11.0	41.0	47.9	3.8	32.8	63.3
Vietnamese	30.2	35.6	34.3	25.6	28.7	45.7
American Indian	17.5	45.3	37.2	18.8	44.4	36.8
Hispanic	30.8	41.0	28.3	31.7	37.8	30.6
Mexican	42.5	36.3	21.2	43.2	33.9	22.9
Chicano/Chicana	44.7	35.9	19.5	44.6	35.1	20.3
Cuban	23.9	38.0	38.1	29.6	34.6	35.8
Puerto Rican	22.5	48.9	28.7	25.8	41.8	32.5
Central/South America	20.8	45.4	33.7	19.3	40.8	39.9
Total	12.6	46.4	41.6	12.9	42.5	44.6

Source: The Longitudinal Study of Adolescent Health,1995.

B7. SCHOOL RELATED ISSUES

B7.1. High School Students Engaged in Organized Physical Activity: 1995

[In percent. For students in grades 9 to 12. Based on school-based survey and subject to sampling error; for details see source.]

| | PARTICIPATION ON SPORTS TEAM | | ENROLLMENT IN PHYSICAL EDUCATION CLASS | | |
CHARACTERISTIC	Run by school	Run by other organization	Total	Exercised 20 minutes or more per class	Attended daily
All students	50.3	36.9	59.6	69.7	25.4
White, non-Hispanic	53.9	39.1	62.9	71.3	21.7
Black, non-Hispanic	45.0	32.4	50.2	59.0	33.8
Hispanic	37.8	32.0	51.0	68.5	33.1

Source: U.S. National Center for Chronic Disease Prevention and Health Promotion, Physical Activity and Health: A Report of the Surgeon General, 1996.

B7.2. School Club Membership

Race/ethnicity	Average Number of School Club Memberships
White	2.34
Black	2.21
Asian	2.93
Chinese	3.18
Filipino	2.87
Japanese	2.67
Asian Indian	2.86
Korean	2.88
Vietnamese	2.87
American Indian	2.50
Hispanic	2.01
Mexican	1.74
Chicano/Chicana	2.20
Cuban	2.50
Puerto Rican	2.38
Central/South America	1.90
Total	2.25

Source: The Longitudinal Study of Adolescent Health, 1995.

B7.3. Percentage Distribution of 4th-graders in Public Schools by Time Spent on Homework and Television Viewing Each Day: 1996

Race/ethnicity	Time spent on homework each day					Amount of television watched each day			
	Don't have	Don't do	Half hour or less	One hour	More than one hour	Six hours or more	Four to five hours	Two to three hours	One hour or less
White	12.6	2.5	39	30.7	15.1	13.3	19.9	40.5	26.3
Black	7.4	5.2	43.5	24.5	19.4	42.1	19	22.1	16.8
Hispanic	7.8	3.8	42.3	28.1	18.1	21.5	18.2	33.8	26.6
Asian/Pacific Islander	4.8	1.7	41.5	28.8	23.1	18.9	18.8	29.2	33.1
American Indian	14.4	3	44.7	24.2	13.6	25.1	16.2	29.1	29.6

Source: U.S. Department of Education. National Center for Education Statistics. Digest of Education Statistics, 1998, NCES, 1999-036, by Thomas D. Snyder. Production Manager, Charlene M. Hoffman. Program Analyst, Claire M. Geddes Washington, D.C., 1999. p. 132.

B7.4. Percent of Students (Grades 7 to 12) Who Feel that Certain Problems Are Very Serious: 1996

Race/ethnicity	Tight groups of friends that do not talk to one another	Hostile or threatening remarks between groups of students	Threats or destructive acts, other than physical fights	Turf battles between different groups of students	Physical fights between members of different groups of friends	Gang violence
White	9	22	21	16	22	19
African American	12	36	33	32	37	40
Hispanic	13	33	32	33	34	41

Source: U.S. Department of Education. National Center for Education. Digest of Education Statistics, 1998, NCES, 1999-036, by Thomas D. Snyder. Production Manager, Charlene M. Hoffman. Program Analyst, Clarie M. Geddes. Washington, D.C., 1999, p. 158.

B7.5. Percentage of Students in Grades 9 through 12 Who Reported Experience with Drugs or Violence on School Property: 1997

Type of violence or drug-related behavior	Total	White	Black	Hispanic
Feel too unsafe to go to school	4.0	2.4	6.8	7.2
Carried a weapon on school property	8.5	7.8	9.2	10.4
Threatened or injured with a weapon on school property	7.4	6.2	9.9	9.0
In a physical fight on school property	14.8	13.3	20.7	19.0
Property stolen or deliberately damaged on school property	32.9	32.6	34.0	32.1
Cigarette use on school property	14.6	15.8	8.8	11.9
Smokeless tobacco use on school property	5.1	6.5	1.4	3.3
Alcohol use on school property	5.6	4.8	5.6	8.2
Marijuana use on school property	7.0	5.8	9.1	10.4
Offered, sold, or given an illegal drug on school property	31.7	31.0	25.4	41.1

Source: U.S. Department of Education. National Center for Education Statistics. Digest of Education Statistics, 1998, NCES, 1999-036, by Thomas D. Snyder. Production Manager, Charlene M. Hoffman. Program Analyst, Claire M. Geddes. Washington, D.C., 1999, p. 157.

B7.6. Adolescent Troubles in School This Year: 1995

	How Often Have You Had Trouble:			
Race/ethnicity	Getting along with teachers	Paying attention in school	Getting your homework done	Getting along with other students
White	1.15	1.77	1.69	1.46
Black	1.44	1.96	1.98	1.88
Asian	1.29	1.90	1.93	1.62
Chinese	1.05	1.73	1.71	1.35
Filipino	1.34	1.93	2.05	1.73
Japanese	1.32	1.74	1.77	1.38
Asian Indian	1.42	1.91	1.96	1.75
Korean	1.14	1.90	1.96	1.58
Vietnamese	1.43	2.18	2.16	1.77
American Indian	1.44	1.96	1.91	1.79
Hispanic	1.39	1.93	1.99	1.83
Mexican	1.30	1.88	1.90	1.72
Chicano/Chicana	1.39	1.93	1.93	1.81
Cuban	1.34	1.77	1.84	1.66
Puerto Rican	1.46	1.93	2.02	1.94
Central/South America	1.44	2.01	2.10	1.99
Total	1.23	1.82	1.78	1.58

Scale: 0 = never, 1 = just a few times, 2 = about once a week, 3 = almost every day 4 = every day

Source: The Longitudinal Study of Adolescent Health, 1995.

B7.7. Adolescent Ratings of Student Prejudice and Teacher Fairness

Race/ethnicity	Students Are Prejudiced	Teachers Treat Students Fairly
White	2.66	2.58
Black	3.03	2.73
Asian	2.88	2.57
Chinese	2.89	2.52
Filipino	3.00	2.53
Japanese	2.81	2.62
Asian Indian	2.86	2.49
Korean	2.69	2.64
Vietnamese	2.75	2.53
American Indian	2.72	2.80
Hispanic	2.84	2.64
Mexican	2.82	2.62
Chicano/Chicana	2.87	2.82
Cuban	2.87	2.63
Puerto Rican	2.89	2.71
Central/South America	2.83	2.58
Total	2.76	2.60

Scale: 1 = strongly agree, 2 = agree, 3 = neither agree nor disagree, 4 = disagree, 5 = strongly disagree

Source: The Longitudinal Study of Adolescent Health, 1995.

B7.8. Absenteeism, Suspension, and Expulsion

How many times {have you been/were you} absent from school for a full day with an excuse—for example, because you were sick or out of town?

	White	Black	Native American	Asian	Hispanic	Total
Never	10.8	15.0	7.3	21.4	12.7	12.0
1 or 2 times	29.5	35.3	33.4	36.5	31.9	31.1
3 to 10 times	46.4	40.7	43.5	34.2	43.4	44.6
More than 10 times	13.2	9.1	15.8	7.9	12.1	12.3

{Have you received/did you receive} an out-of-school suspension from school?

	White	Black	Native American	Asian	Hispanic	Total
Yes	8.8	21.1	16.4	6.6	11.4	11.2

{Have you been/were you} expelled from school?

	White	Black	Native American	Asian	Hispanic	Total
Yes	.8	3.2	1.8	1.3	3.1	1.4

Source: The Longitudinal Study of Adolescent Health, 1995.

B8. HIGHER EDUCATION ENROLLMENT

B8.1. Total Fall Enrollment in Instututions of Higher Education and Degree-granting Institutions: 1996

Total	In Thousands	Percentage distribution
Total	14,300.3	100.0
White, non-Hispanic	10,226.0	73.9
Total minority	3,609.3	26.1
Black, non-Hispanic	1,499.4	10.8
Hispanic	1,152.2	8.3
Asian or Pacific Islander	823.6	6.0
American Indian/Alaskan Native	134.0	1.0
Nonresident alien	464.9	N/A
4-year		
Total	8,802.8	100.0
White, non-Hispanic	6,483.2	76.9
Total minority	1,946.2	23.1
Black, non-Hispanic	870.2	10.3
Hispanic	508.1	6.0
Asian or Pacific Islander	500.7	5.9
American Indian/Alaskan Native	67.2	0.8
Nonresident alien	373.5	N/A
2-year		
Total	5,497.4	100.0
White, non-Hispanic	3,742.8	69.2
Total minority	1,663.1	30.8
Black, non-Hispanic	629.3	11.6
Hispanic	644.2	11.9
Asian or Pacific Islander	322.9	6.0
American Indian/Alaskan Native	66.7	1.2
Nonresident alien	91.5	N/A

Source: U.S. Department of Education. National Center for Education Statistics. Digest of Education Statistics, 1998, NCES, 1999-036, by Thomas D. Snyder. Production Manager, Charlene M. Hoffman. Program Analyst, Claire M. Geddes. Washington, D.C., 1999, p. 228.

B8.2. Percentage of All Hispanic and White (Non-Hispanic) Students in 2-year Versus 4-year Colleges: 1976 to 1995

	1976	1980	1990	1991	1992	1993	1994	1995
4-year								
White	66.1	63.8	63.1	61.8	62.0	62.6	63.0	63.2
Hispanic	45.2	45.9	45.8	44.2	42.9	43.7	44.3	44.4
2-year								
White	33.9	36.2	36.9	38.2	38.0	37.4	37.0	36.8
Hispanic	54.8	54.1	54.2	55.8	57.1	56.3	55.7	55.6

Source: U.S. Department of Education. National Center for Education Statistics. Higher Education General Survey.

.B8.3. Graduate School and First-year Professional Enrollment in Institutions of Higher Education: 1996

Graduate	In Thousands	Percentage distribution
Total	1,743.1	100.0
White, non-Hispanic	1,273.9	81.7
Total minority	286.0	18.3
Black, non-Hispanic	125.5	8.0
Hispanic	72.7	4.7
Asian or Pacific Islander	79.0	5.1
American Indian/Alaskan Native	8.9	0.6
First-Year Professional		
Total	297.7	100.0
White, non-Hispanic	221.2	76.2
Total minority	68.9	23.8
Black, non-Hispanic	21.4	7.4
Hispanic	14	4.8
Asian or Pacific Islander	31.4	10.8
American Indian/Alaskan Native	2.2	0.7
Nonresident alien	7.7	N/A

Source: U.S. Department of Education. National Center for Education Statistics. Digest of Education Statistics, 1998, NCES, 1999-036 by Thomas D. Snyder. Production Manager, Charlene M. Hoffman. Program Analyst, Claire M. Geddes. Washington, D.C., 1999, pp. 229-230.

B9. HIGHER EDUCATION GRADUATIONS

B9.1. Associate Degrees Conferred by Institutions of Higher Education, by Racial/Ethnic Group: 1995–96

| | Number of degrees conferred | | | | | | | Percentage distribution of degrees conferred | | | | | | |
Total	White, non-Hispanic	Black, non-Hispanic	Hispanic	Asian/Pacific Islander	American Indian/Alaskan Native	Non-resident alien	Total	White, non-Hispanic	Black, non-Hispanic	Hispanic	Asian/Pacific Islander	American Indian/Alaskan Native	Non-resident alien
553,625	425,028	51,672	38,163	23,091	5,556	10,115	100.0	76.8	9.3	6.9	4.2	1.0	1.8

Source: U.S. Department of Education. National Center for Education Statistics. *Digest of Education Statistics, 1998,* NCES, 1999-036, by Thomas D. Snyder. Production Manager, Charlene M. Hoffman. Program Analyst, Claire M. Geddes. Washington, D.C., 1999, p.311.

B9.2. Bachelor's Degrees Conferred by Institutions of Higher Education, by Racial/Ethnic Group: 1995–96

| | Number of degrees conferred | | | | | | | Percentage distribution of degrees conferred | | | | | | |
Total	White, non-Hispanic	Black, non-Hispanic	Hispanic	Asian/Pacific Islander	American Indian/Alaskan Native	Non-resident alien	Total	White, non-Hispanic	Black, non-Hispanic	Hispanic	Asian/Pacific Islander	American Indian/Alaskan Native	Non-resident alien
1,163,036	904,709	91,166	58,288	64,359	6,970	37,544	100.0	77.8	7.8	5.0	5.5	0.6	3.2

Source: U.S. Department of Education. National Center for Education Statistics. *Digest of Education Statistics, 1998,* NCES, 1999-036, by Thomas D. Snyder. Production Manager, Charlene M. Hoffman. Program Analyst, Claire M. Geddes. Washington, D.C., 1999, p.311.

B9.3. Master's Degrees Conferred by Institutions of Higher Education, by Racial/Ethnic Group: 1995–96

| | Number of degrees conferred | | | | | | | Percentage distribution of degrees conferred | | | | | |
Total	White, non-Hispanic	Black, non-Hispanic	Hispanic	Asian/ Pacific Islander	American Indian/ Alaskan Native	Non-resident alien	Total	White, non-Hispanic	Black, non-Hispanic	Hispanic	Asian/ Pacific Islander	American Indian/ Alaskan Native	Non-resident alien
405,521	297,558	25,801	14,412	18,161	1,778	47,811	100.0	73.4	6.4	3.6	4.5	0.4	11.8

Source: U.S. Department of Education. National Center for Education Statistics. Digest of Education Statistics, 1998, NCES, 1999-036, by Thomas D. Snyder. Production Manager, Charlene M. Hoffman. Program Analyst, Claire M. Geddes. Washington, D.C., 1999, p.311.

B9.4. Doctoral Degrees Conferred by Institutions of Higher Education, by Racial/Ethnic Group: 1995–96

| | Number of degrees conferred | | | | | | | Percentage distribution of degrees conferred | | | | | |
Total	White, non-Hispanic	Black, non-Hispanic	Hispanic	Asian/ Pacific Islander	American Indian/ Alaskan Native	Non-resident alien	Total	White, non-Hispanic	Black, non-Hispanic	Hispanic	Asian/ Pacific Islander	American Indian/ Alaskan Native	Non-resident alien
44,645	27,756	1,636	999	2,646	158	11,450	100.0	62.2	3.7	2.2	5.9	0.4	25.6

Source: U.S. Department of Education. National Center for Education Statistics. Digest of Education Statistics, 1998, NCES, 1999-036, by Thomas D. Snyder. Production Manager, Charlene M. Hoffman. Program Analyst, Claire M. Geddes. Washington, D.C., 1999, p.311.

B9.5. First Professional Degrees Conferred by Institutions of Higher Education, by Racial/Ethnic Group: 1995–96

	Number of degrees conferred							Percentage distribution of degrees conferred						
Total	White, non-Hispanic	Black, non-Hispanic	Hispanic	Asian/ Pacific Islander	American Indian/ Alaskan Native	Non-resident alien	Total	White, non-Hispanic	Black, non-Hispanic	Hispanic	Asian/ Pacific Islander	American Indian/ Alaskan Native	Non-resident alien
76,641	59,456	5,016	3,476	6,617	463	1,613	100.0	77.6	6.5	4.5	8.6	0.6	2.1

Source: U.S. Department of Education. National Center for Education Statistics. Digest of Education Statistics, 1998, NCES, 1999-036, by Thomas D. Snyder. Production Manager, Charlene M. Hoffman. Program Analyst, Claire M. Geddes. Washington, D.C., 1999, p.311.

B10. HIGHER EDUCATION FACULTY

B10.1. Full-time and Part-time Instructional Faculty and Staff in Institutions of Higher Education, by Field: Fall 1992

Race/ethnicity	Number in thousands	All Fields	Agriculture and home economics	Business	Education	Engineering	Fine arts	Health	Humanities	Natural Sciences	Social Sciences	Other and not reported
White, non-Hispanic	457	86.5	90.8	88.5	84.7	76.6	88.6	85.9	88.1	85.8	87.3	88.1
Black, non-Hispanic	27	5.2	3.9	4.1	9.4	2.8	5.8	5.6	4.2	3.6	6.2	6.0
Hispanic	14	2.6	1.8	1.6	3.3	3.1	2.5	2.3	4.1	1.9	2.8	2.5
Asian/Pacific Islander	28	5.2	2.9	4.8	1.6	16.8	2.7	6.0	3.2	8.3	3.3	2.9
American Indian/Alaskan Native	3	0.5	0.7	1.0	1.0	0.7	0.5	0.2	0.5	0.3	0.5	0.4

Source: U.S Department of Education. National Center for Education Statistics. Digest of Education Statistics, 1998 NCES, 1999-036, by Thomas D. Snyder. Production Manager, Charlene M. Hoffman. Program Analyst, Claire M. Geddes. Washington, D.C., 1999, p. 262.

B10.2. Full-time Instructional Faculty in Institutions of Higher Education, by Academic Rank: Fall 1995

Academic Rank	Total	White, non-Hispanic	Minority		Black, non-Hispanic	Hispanic	Asian or Pacific Islander	American Indian/Alaskan	Non-resident alien	Race/ethnicity unknown
			Number	Percent						
Total	**550,822**	**468,518**	**69,505**	**12.9**	**26,835**	**12,942**	**27,572**	**2,156**	**10,853**	**1,964**
Professors	159,333	142,819	15,254	9.6	4,768	2,470	7,643	373	975	285
Associate professors	125,082	108,953	14,710	11.9	5,634	2,607	6,119	350	1,179	240
Assistant professors	129,682	104,037	20,725	16.6	8,011	3,736	8,459	519	4,311	609
Instructors	66,708	55,211	10,223	15.6	4,857	2,530	2,323	513	848	426
Lecturers	12,874	10,533	1,838	14.9	798	429	557	54	426	77
Other Faculty	57,143	46,965	6,755	12.6	2,767	1,170	2,471	347	3,114	309

Source: U.S Department of Education. National Center for Education Statistics. Digest of Education Statistics, 1998, NCES, 1999-036, by Thomas D. Snyder. Production Manager, Charlene M. Hoffman. Program Analyst, Claire M. Geddes Washington, D.C., 1999, p. 254.

C. Economics and Employment

C1. EMPLOYMENT AND JOB CHARACTERISTICS

Employment status does not vary a great deal across racial and ethnic groups (C1.1). Unemployment rates are somewhat higher for minority groups other than Asians, however, indicating some disadvantage in the labor force (C1.2). Labor force participation rates have remained fairly stable since 1990 and are projected to remain so through 2006 (C1.3).

Whites are a little more likely to be self-employed than other groups, but the difference is not large (C1.4, C1.5). Whites are also more likely to do job-related work at home, to have flexible schedules, and to hold more than one job (C1.6, C1.7, C1.8).

Blacks and Hispanics are not evenly distributed across occupations and industries (C1.9, C1.10, C1.11). For example, Blacks are overrepresented among dietitians, social workers, postal clerks, and service workers. Hispanics are overrepresented in real estate, certain types of clerical work, service work, textile work, and farm work. Overall, Whites have higher occupational status and work more hours than other groups (C1.12).

The unemployment rate, calculated as those without a job but looking for one divided by the total labor force, shows greater disadvantage among minorities. In 1997, Hispanics were 1.8 times more likely to be unemployed than Whites and Blacks were 2.4 times more likely to be unemployed. Whites are less likely to have experienced unemployment in the last 10 years (C1.13), but more likely to have been without a job and not looking for work (C1.14).

Blacks and "Other" races are somewhat more likely to be supervised on the job, and less likely to be supervisors (C1.15). Union membership is also a little more common among racial minorities (C1.16).

C2. INCOME

Racial differences in income in the United States are dramatic. Whether measured at the household or family level, incomes of Blacks, Native Americans, and Hispanics are only about two-thirds as high as income for Whites. In contrast, income for Asians is noticeably higher than White income (C2.1). Since 1970, real incomes have risen only modestly for Whites, only slightly for Blacks, and have declined for Hispanics (C2.2). Corresponding to their lower average incomes, minority groups are overrepresented in low income groups and underrepresented in high income groups (C2.3). Even within categories of education, income is higher for Whites than for Hispanics (C2.7).

Wages are the major source of income for most people and the most common type of payment is based on a hourly wage (C2.8). Minorities are more likely to work for hourly wages than are Whites. Other sources of income also show some variability by race (C2.9).

C3. POVERTY

The poverty threshold for a family of four was $16,036 in 1997. Fourteen percent of the population was poor in 1997. Poverty rates for Blacks, Native Americans, and Hispanics are more than double the rate for Whites (C3.1). Poverty is less common than in 1960, but has remained fairly stable in the 1980s and 1990s (C3.2). The rates are higher for children of all races (C3.3), as well as the less educated (C3.4), and those in single parent families (C3.5). Poverty is often a short-term experience, but spells of poverty are longer for minority groups (C3.6).

Several programs have been implemented to assist low-income families and individuals. Corresponding to their lower income, Blacks, Native Americans, and Hispanics are more likely to participate in such programs (C3.7, C3.8).

C4. ATTITUDES ABOUT EMPLOYMENT AND ECONOMIC ISSUES

A majority of people in the United States say they are either working class or middle class. Blacks and other minorities are more likely to say working class or lower class than are Whites (C4.1), and are less satisfied with their financial situation (C4.2). Blacks and other racial minorities are, however, optimistic about economic improvement when they compare themselves with their parents or guess how their children will do (C4.3).

Most people think that hard work is more important than luck for getting ahead, and there is little difference between Blacks, Whites, and others in this regard (C4.4). There is also general agreement about how pay should be determined, with job performance as a high priority (C4.5). But Blacks place more emphasis on family responsibilities and qualifications than do other groups. Non-Whites are also more likely to favor raising the minimum wage (C4.6), and to believe that the government should be involved in economic policy (C4.7).

A majority of people believe that there is more to their job than just making money, but work is not viewed as their most important activity (C4.8). Job security is rated as more important than income, opportunity for advancement, interesting work, helping others, independence, or flexible hours (C4.9). Unfortunately, many people do not believe their job offers the characteristics they desire (compare C4.9 and C4.10). In particular, Blacks and other minorities rate their jobs as low on security when compared with Whites. Most people agree that they work hard for the firm and are proud to work

there, but Whites appear to have more job security (C4.11). Overall, Whites report higher job satisfaction than Blacks and other minorities, but each group would continue working even if they didn't need the money (4.12).

Many workers have days when they come home tired and feel stress on the job, but most jobs are not physically demanding or dangerous. Blacks and other minorities are somewhat more likely to report coming home exhausted while Whites are a little more likely to report stress (C4.13). A majority of workers report good relationships between workers and management and among co-workers (C4.14). Blacks, however, are more likely to say they would like to work more hours and earn more money (C4.15). Blacks also report greater concern over losing their jobs (C4.16).

C5. RETIREMENT AND CONSUMPTION

Non-Whites are less likely to depend on personal savings as a source of retirement income. Instead, they place relatively more emphasis on pensions, social security, and investments (C5.1). Correspondingly, non-whites have saved less money in preparation for retirement (C5.2).

Corresponding to their lower incomes, Blacks and Hispanics spend less money than the average (C5.3). This includes lower expenditures for entertainment (C5.4). Although there is some variation across groups, participation in activities such as movies, sporting events, and amusement parks show that each group participates in these types of leisure activities (C5.5). Finally, Blacks and Hispanics are somewhat less likely than Whites to participate in volunteer work (C5.6).

C1. EMPLOYMENT AND JOB CHARACTERISTICS

C1.1. Employment Status Last Week, by Race: March 1998

		Non-Hispanic Whites	Non-Hispanic Blacks	American Indians/Aleuts/ Eskimos	Asians and Pacific Islanders	Hispanics	Total
Work full or part time	%	61.1%	54.7%	55.6%	62.7%	58.7%	60.2%
	N	44439	4939	584	2159	8430	60551
With job, but not at work last week	%	2.3%	1.9%	2.9%	1.8%	1.9%	2.2%
	N	1664	171	31	62	278	2206
Unemployed	%	2.1%	5.2%	5.4%	2.5%	3.9%	2.7%
	N	1528	472	57	86	555	2698
Laid Off	%	.6%	.6%	1.3%	.4%	.9%	.6%
	N	423	55	14	14	134	640
Not in Labor Force	%	33.9%	37.5%	34.7%	32.5%	34.6%	34.3%
	N	24667	3388	365	1120	4967	34507
	Total	72721	9025	1051	3441	14364	100602

Source: Current Population Surveys, March 1998 [Machine readable data files] conducted by the Bureau of the Census for the Bureau of Labor Statistics. Washington: Bureau of Census [producer and distributor]. Santa Monica, CA: Unicon Research Corporation [producer and distributor of CPS Utilities], 1999.

C1.2. Percent Unemployed, by Race: March 1998

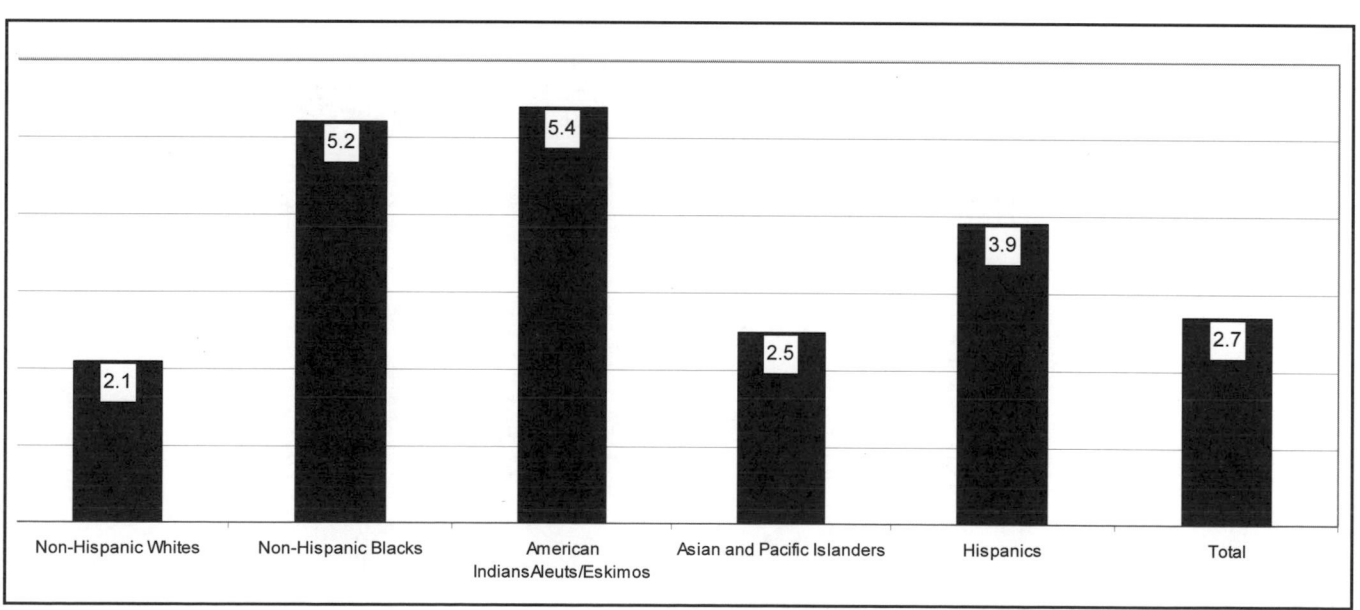

Source: Current Population Surveys, March 1998. See also C1.1.

C1.3. Civilian Labor Force and Participation Rates, with Projections: 1980 to 2006

[For civilian noninstitutional population 16 years old and over. Annual averages of monthly figures. Rates are based on annual average civilian noninstitutional population of each specified group and represent proportion of each specified group in the civilian labor force. Based on Current Population Survey; see text, Section 1, Population, and Appendix III]

RACE, SEX, AND AGE	CIVILIAN LABOR FORCE (millions)						PARTICIPATION RATE (percent)						
	1980	1990 \1	1995	1996	1997 \1	2006, proj.	1980	1985	1990 \1	1995	1996	1997 \1	2006, proj.
Total \2	106.9	125.8	132.3	133.9	136.3	148.8	63.8	64.8	66.5	66.6	66.8	67.1	67.6
White	93.6	107.4	112.0	113.1	114.7	123.6	64.1	65.0	66.9	67.1	67.2	67.5	68.1
Male	54.5	59.6	61.1	61.8	62.6	66.0	78.2	77.0	77.1	75.7	75.8	75.9	74.3
Female	39.1	47.8	50.8	51.3	52.1	57.6	51.2	54.1	57.4	59.0	59.1	59.5	62.0
Black	10.9	13.7	14.8	15.1	15.5	17.2	61.0	62.9	64.0	63.7	64.1	64.7	64.9
Male	5.6	6.8	7.2	7.3	7.4	8.0	70.3	70.8	71.0	69.0	68.7	68.3	69.6
Female	5.3	6.9	7.6	7.9	8.2	9.2	53.1	56.5	58.3	59.5	60.4	61.7	61.3
Hispanic \3	6.1	10.7	12.3	12.8	13.8	17.4	64.0	64.6	67.4	65.8	66.5	67.9	67.4
Male	3.8	6.5	7.4	7.6	8.3	10.2	81.4	80.3	81.4	79.1	79.6	80.1	77.1
Female	2.3	4.2	4.9	5.1	5.5	7.2	47.4	49.3	53.1	52.6	53.4	55.1	57.2
Male	61.5	69.0	71.4	72.1	73.3	78.2	77.4	76.3	76.4	75.0	74.9	75.0	73.6
16 to 19 years	5.0	4.1	4.0	4.0	4.1	4.6	60.5	56.8	55.7	54.8	53.2	52.3	52.5
16 and 17 years	2.1	1.5	1.7	1.7	1.7	1.8	50.1	45.1	43.5	44.0	42.1	41.4	40.9
18 and 19 years	2.9	2.6	2.4	2.4	2.4	2.7	71.3	68.9	67.1	66.3	65.3	63.9	64.6
20 to 24 years	8.6	7.9	7.3	7.1	7.2	8.3	85.9	85.0	84.4	83.1	82.5	82.5	76.5
25 to 34 years	17.0	19.9	18.7	18.4	18.1	16.5	95.2	94.7	94.1	93.0	93.2	93.0	92.3
35 to 44 years	11.8	17.5	19.2	19.6	20.1	18.5	95.5	95.0	94.3	92.3	92.4	92.6	90.6
45 to 54 years	9.9	11.1	13.4	14.0	14.6	18.0	91.2	91.0	90.7	88.8	89.1	89.5	87.5
55 to 64 years	7.2	6.6	6.5	6.7	7.0	9.9	72.1	67.9	67.8	66.0	67.0	67.6	70.2
65 years and over	1.9	2.0	2.2	2.2	2.3	2.6	19.0	15.8	16.3	16.8	16.9	17.1	17.8
Female	45.5	56.8	60.9	61.9	63.0	70.6	51.5	54.5	57.5	58.9	59.3	59.8	61.4
16 to 19 years	4.4	3.7	3.7	3.8	3.8	4.4	52.9	52.1	51.6	52.2	51.3	51.0	51.1
16 and 17 years	1.8	1.4	1.6	1.6	1.6	1.8	43.6	42.1	41.7	43.1	42.9	41.0	42.8
18 and 19 years	2.6	2.3	2.2	2.2	2.3	2.5	61.9	61.7	60.3	61.5	59.9	61.2	59.5
20 to 24 years	7.3	6.8	6.3	6.3	6.3	7.2	68.9	71.8	71.3	70.3	71.3	72.7	71.8
25 to 34 years	12.3	16.1	15.5	15.4	15.3	14.4	65.5	70.9	73.5	74.9	75.2	76.0	77.6
35 to 44 years	8.6	14.7	16.6	17.0	17.3	17.0	65.5	71.8	76.4	77.2	77.5	77.7	80.2
45 to 54 years	7.0	9.1	11.8	12.4	13.0	17.2	59.9	64.4	71.2	74.4	75.4	76.0	79.9
55 to 64 years	4.7	4.9	5.4	5.5	5.7	8.8	41.3	42.0	45.2	49.2	49.6	50.9	55.8
65 years and over	1.2	1.5	1.6	1.6	1.6	1.7	8.1	7.3	8.6	8.8	8.6	8.6	8.7

Notes:
NA Not available.
\1 See footnote 2, Table 644.
\2 Beginning 1975, includes other races, not shown separately.
\3 Persons of Hispanic origin may be of any race.

Source: U.S. Bureau of Labor Statistics, Employment and Earnings, monthly, January issues; Monthly Labor Review, November 1997; and unpublished data.

C1.4. Self Employment, by Race

		White	Black	Other
Male	Self-employed	16%	12.7%	12.3%
	(n)	**156**	**17**	**10**
	Someone else	84%	87.3%	87.7%
	(n)	**819**	**117**	**71**
	Total	100%	100%	100%
	(n)	**975**	**134**	**81**
Female	Self-employed	10.5%	6.2%	5.7%
	(n)	**121**	**14**	**5**
	Someone else	89.5%	93.8%	94.3%
	(n)	**1029**	**213**	**83**
	Total	100%	100%	100%
	(n)	**1150**	**227**	**88**

Source: General Social Survey, 1998.

C1.5. Self-Employed Persons With Home-Based Businesses: 1997

[As of May. For persons at work 16 years and over in nonagriculture industries in home-based businesses as part of their primary job. Based on the Current Population Survey.]

CHARACTERISTIC	PERCENT DISTRIBUTION BY HOURS WORKED AT HOME			MEAN HOURS	
	Less than 8 hours	8 hours or more		Worked at home	Total at work on primary job
		Total	35 hours or more		
Total	30.4	69.6	29.3	23.0	37.3
RACE AND HISPANIC ORIGIN					
White	30.5	69.5	29.0	22.9	36.9
Black	29.2	70.8	47.0	29.1	42.7
Hispanic origin \1	27.8	72.2	31.3	23.8	35.9

Notes:
\1 Persons of Hispanic origin may be of any race.

Source: U.S. Bureau of Labor Statistics, News, USDL 98-93, March 11, 1998.

C1.6. Persons Doing Job-Related Work at Home: 1991 and 1997

[As of May. For persons at work 16 years and over in nonagriculture industries doing job-related work at home as part of their primary job. Based on the Current Population Survey.]

CHARACTERISTIC	Total \1 (1,000)	Rate \2	PERCENT DISTRIBUTION				MEAN HOURS WORKED			
			Wage and salary workers			Self-employed \3	Persons paid to work at home		Persons not paid to work at home	
			Paid	Unpaid	Total	Home based business	Total hours worked \4	Worked at home	Total hours worked \4	Worked at home
Total, 1991	19,967	18.3	9.4	60.9	27.8	(NA)	(NA)	8.0	(NA)	6.0
Total, 1997	21,478	17.8	17.0	51.5	30.1	19.2	40.8	14.9	46.5	8.9
RACE AND HISPANIC ORIGIN										
White	19,646	19.2	17.0	50.7	30.9	19.7	40.7	14.7	46.8	8.8
Black	1,117	8.5	16.6	64.8	16.2	12.1	43.9	17.0	43.8	10.5
Hispanic origin \5	830	7.2	17.5	53.9	27.8	18.8	38.8	18.2	47.0	9.2

Notes:
\B Base figure too small to meet statistical standards for reliability of a derived figure.
NA Not available.
\1 Includes persons who worked 15 hours or more in an unpaid capacity in a family business.
\2 Persons working at home as a percent of the total at work. 1997 excludes persons not responding to the questions on working at home.
\3 Includes incorporated and unincorporated self-employed.
\4 On primary job.
\5 Persons of Hispanic origin may be of any race.

Source: U.S. Bureau of Labor Statistics, News, USDL 98-93, March 11, 1998.

C1.7. Persons on Flexible Schedules: 1997

[As of May. For full-time wage and salary workers 16 years old and over. Data relate to the primary job. Based on the Current Population Survey.]

ITEM	TOTAL With flexible schedules			MALE With flexible schedules			FEMALE With flexible schedules		
	Total \1	Number	Percent	Total \1	Number	Percent	Total \1	Number	Percent
Total	90,549	25,031	27.6	52,073	14,952	28.7	38,476	10,079	26.2
RACE AND HISPANIC ORIGIN									
White	75,683	21,698	28.7	44,495	13,186	29.6	31,188	8,512	27.3
Black	10,884	2,191	20.1	5,323	1,068	20.1	5,561	1,123	20.2
Hispanic origin \2	9,635	1,769	18.4	6,283	1,147	18.3	3,352	622	18.5
MARITAL STATUS									
Never married	21,721	5,523	25.4	12,746	3,180	24.9	8,975	2,343	26.1
Married, spouse present	53,369	15,358	28.8	32,756	10,077	30.8	20,613	5,281	25.6
Other marital status	15,459	4,150	26.8	6,571	1,695	25.8	8,888	2,456	27.6

Notes:
B Percent not shown where base is less than 75,000.
\1 Includes persons who did not provide information on flexible schedules.
\2 Persons of Hispanic origin may be of any race.

Source: U.S. Bureau of Labor Statistics, News, USDL98-119, March 26, 1998.

C1.8. Multiple Jobholders: 1994–1997

[Annual average of monthly figures. For the civilian noninstitutional population 16 years old and over. Multiple jobholders are employed persons who, either 1) had jobs as wage or salary workers with two employers or more; 2) were self-employed and also held a wage and salary job; or 3) were unpaid family workers on their primary jobs but also held wage and salary job. Based on the Current Population Survey.]

	1994						1995						1996						1997					
	TOTAL		MALE		FEMALE		TOTAL		MALE		FEMALE		TOTAL		MALE		FEMALE		TOTAL		MALE		FEMALE	
Total \1	7,260	5.9	3,924	5.9	3,336	5.9	7,693	6.2	4,139	6.1	3,554	6.2	7,832	6.2	4,192	6.1	3,640	6.2	7,955	6.1	4,237	6.1	3,718	6.2
Race and Hispanic origin:																								
White	6,392	6.1	3,462	6.0	2,930	6.1	6,764	6.4	3,650	6.3	3,114	6.4	6,867	6.4	3,686	6.3	3,181	6.5	6,909	6.3	3,693	6.2	3,216	6.4
Black	630	4.9	337	5.4	293	4.4	688	5.2	362	5.6	326	4.8	705	5.2	376	5.8	329	4.6	758	5.4	388	5.9	370	5.0
Hispanic origin \1	394	3.7	243	3.7	151	3.6	430	3.9	252	3.8	178	4.0	442	3.8	254	3.6	188	4.1	494	3.9	305	3.9	190	3.8

Notes:
\1 Persons of Hispanic origin may be of any race.

Source: U.S. Bureau of Labor Statistics, Employment and Earnings, monthly, January 1995, 1996, 1997, and 1998 issues.

C1.9. Employed Civilians, by Occupation, Sex, Race, and Hispanic Origin: 1983 and 1997

[For civilian noninstitutional population 16 years old and over. Annual average of monthly figures. Based on Current Population Survey. Persons of Hispanic origin may be of any race.] Annual average of monthly figures. Based on Current Population Survey;

OCCUPATION	Total employed (1,000)	1983 Percent of total			Total employed (1,000)	1997 Percent of total		
		Female	Black	Hispanic		Female	Black	Hispanic
Total	100,834	43.7	9.3	5.3	129,558	46.2	10.8	9.8
Managerial and professional specialty	23,592	40.9	5.6	2.6	37,686	48.9	7.3	5.0
Executive, administrative, and managerial \2	10,772	32.4	4.7	2.8	18,440	44.3	6.9	5.4
Officials and administrators, public	417	38.5	8.3	3.8	606	49.5	11.9	5.6
Financial managers	357	38.6	3.5	3.1	688	49.3	5.6	5.1
Personnel and labor relations managers	106	43.9	4.9	2.6	108	63.4	7.5	2.9
Purchasing managers	82	23.6	5.1	1.4	114	40.9	6.4	4.6
Managers, marketing, advertising and public relations	396	21.8	2.7	1.7	711	34.6	3.7	4.8
Administrators, education and related fields	415	41.4	11.3	2.4	733	61.3	10.7	5.8
Managers, medicine and health	91	57.0	5.0	2.0	701	76.8	7.4	4.3
Managers, properties and real estate	305	42.8	5.5	5.2	535	49.4	7.1	10.3
Management-related occupations \2	2,966	40.3	5.8	3.5	4,604	57.7	8.4	5.1
Accountants and auditors	1,105	38.7	5.5	3.3	1,625	56.6	7.9	5.0
Professional specialty \2	12,820	48.1	6.4	2.5	19,245	53.3	7.8	4.5
Architects	103	12.7	1.6	1.5	169	17.9	1.7	5.1
Engineers \2	1,572	5.8	2.7	2.2	2,036	9.6	3.9	3.8
Aerospace engineers	80	6.9	1.5	2.1	87	4.7	1.3	2.2
Chemical engineers	67	6.1	3.0	1.4	92	17.3	7.4	1.1
Civil engineers	211	4.0	1.9	3.2	248	7.7	2.2	4.2
Electrical and electronic	450	6.1	3.4	3.1	652	9.2	5.5	3.8
Industrial engineers	210	11.0	3.3	2.4	258	16.4	4.1	5.6
Mechanical	259	2.8	3.2	1.1	352	5.9	2.5	3.2
Mathematical and computer scientists \2	463	29.6	5.4	2.6	1,494	30.4	7.5	3.1
Computer systems analysts, scientists	276	27.8	6.2	2.7	1,236	28.6	7.7	3.1
Operations and systems researchers and analysts	142	31.3	4.9	2.2	201	40.5	7.0	3.3
Natural scientists \2	357	20.5	2.6	2.1	529	31.0	5.1	2.2
Chemists, except biochemists	98	23.3	4.3	1.2	144	25.5	5.5	4.2
Geologists and geodesists	65	18.0	1.1	2.6	59	17.9	-	1.4
Biological and life scientists	55	40.8	2.4	1.8	106	44.7	5.7	0.9
Medical scientists	(\3)	(\3)	(\3)	(\3)	77	46.9	9.6	1.1
Health diagnosing occupations \2	735	13.3	2.7	3.3	1,027	25.2	3.6	4.0
Physicians	519	15.8	3.2	4.5	724	26.2	4.2	4.8
Dentists	126	6.7	2.4	1.0	138	17.3	2.6	1.1
Health assessment and treating occupations	1,900	85.8	7.1	2.2	2,886	86.5	8.4	3.3
Registered nurses	1,372	95.8	6.7	1.8	2,065	93.5	8.3	2.9
Pharmacists	158	26.7	3.8	2.6	200	45.9	4.1	2.6
Dietitians	71	90.8	21.0	3.7	101	88.7	28.5	6.0
Therapists \2	247	76.3	7.6	2.7	455	75.4	6.6	4.0
Respiratory therapists	69	69.4	6.5	3.7	85	59.4	7.7	2.0
Physical therapists	55	77.0	9.7	1.5	110	64.0	5.0	4.1
Speech therapists	51	90.5	1.5	-	102	95.0	3.6	3.7
Physicians' assistants	51	36.3	7.7	4.4	65	63.2	5.5	8.7
Teachers, college and university	606	36.3	4.4	1.8	869	42.7	6.5	3.4
Teachers, except college and university \2	3,365	70.9	9.1	2.7	4,798	75.7	10.2	5.4
Prekindergarten and kindergarten	299	98.2	11.8	3.4	574	97.8	13.2	9.7
Elementary school	1,350	83.3	11.1	3.1	1,872	83.9	10.9	5.4
Secondary school	1,209	51.8	7.2	2.3	1,173	58.4	8.3	4.0
Special education	81	82.2	10.2	2.3	384	82.9	10.8	3.2
Counselors, educational and vocational	184	53.1	13.9	3.2	248	66.2	12.4	4.1
Librarians, archivists, and curators	213	84.4	7.8	1.6	217	77.1	6.3	4.7
Librarians	193	87.3	7.9	1.8	188	80.5	6.5	5.4
Social scientists and urban planners \2	261	46.8	7.1	2.1	441	54.9	8.1	4.5

C1.9. Employed Civilians, by Occupation, Sex, Race, and Hispanic Origin: 1983 and 1997 *(continued)*

OCCUPATION	Total em- ployed (1,000)	1983 Percent of total Fe- male	Black	His- panic	Total em- ployed (1,000)	1997 Percent of total Fe- male	Black	His- panic
Economists	98	37.9	6.3	2.7	135	52.2	6.6	3.7
Psychologists	135	57.1	8.6	1.1	256	59.3	9.2	4.5
Social, recreation, and religious workers \2	831	43.1	12.1	3.8	1,357	54.8	17.2	6.9
Social workers	407	64.3	18.2	6.3	781	69.3	21.7	8.7
Recreation workers	65	71.9	15.7	2.0	126	70.8	13.4	4.9
Clergy	293	5.6	4.9	1.4	350	13.6	12.4	5.0
Lawyers and judges	651	15.8	2.7	1.0	925	26.7	2.8	3.8
Lawyers	612	15.3	2.6	0.9	885	26.6	2.7	3.8
Writers, artists, entertainers, and athletes \2	1,544	42.7	4.8	2.9	2,234	49.3	5.0	5.8
Authors	62	46.7	2.1	0.9	137	53.6	1.7	2.1
Technical writers	(\3)	(\3)	(\3)	(\3)	61	51.1	3.9	3.7
Designers	393	52.7	3.1	2.7	658	58.5	2.9	6.6
Musicians and composers	155	28.0	7.9	4.4	155	36.6	10.5	9.3
Actors and directors	60	30.8	6.6	3.4	136	38.2	7.3	5.1
Painters, sculptors, craft-artists, and artist printmakers	186	47.4	2.1	2.3	251	45.8	3.0	5.6
Photographers	113	20.7	4.0	3.4	132	29.2	6.6	5.3
Editors and reporters	204	48.4	2.9	2.1	257	51.2	4.8	1.7
Public relations specialists	157	50.1	6.2	1.9	148	65.7	7.4	6.7
Announcers	(\3)	(\3)	(\3)	(\3)	61	14.2	9.2	9.9
Athletes	58	17.6	9.4	1.7	92	27.0	7.1	5.5
Technical, sales, and administrative support	31,265	64.6	7.6	4.3	38,309	64.1	10.5	7.9
Technicians and related support	3,053	48.2	8.2	3.1	4,214	51.9	9.7	6.1
Health technologists and technicians \2	1,111	84.3	12.7	3.1	1,693	80.2	13.0	6.3
Clinical laboratory technologists and technicians	255	76.2	10.5	2.9	388	75.9	16.1	7.4
Dental hygienists	66	98.6	1.6	-	107	98.2	1.5	2.3
Health record technologists and technicians	(\3)	(\3)	(\3)	(\3)	(\3)	(\3)	(\3)	(\3)
Radiologic technicians	101	71.7	8.6	4.5	148	69.5	7.5	1.6
Licensed practical nurses	443	97.0	17.7	3.1	408	94.1	15.4	5.6
Engineering and related technologists and technicians \2	822	18.4	6.1	3.5	960	18.6	7.4	6.7
Electrical and electronic technicians	260	12.5	8.2	4.6	391	14.2	7.4	6.8
Drafting occupations	273	17.5	5.5	2.3	222	16.7	3.9	4.6
Surveying and mapping technicians	(\3)	(\3)	(\3)	(\3)	76	10.2	5.1	5.3
Science technicians \2	202	29.1	6.6	2.8	287	39.5	9.4	8.3
Biological technicians	52	37.7	2.9	2.0	106	57.2	11.2	6.0
Chemical technicians	82	26.9	9.5	3.5	85	22.8	10.4	3.7
Technicians, except health, engineering, and science \2	917	35.3	5.0	2.7	1,275	42.2	7.1	4.8
Airplane pilots and navigators	69	2.1	-	1.6	120	1.2	1.8	2.4
Computer programmers	443	32.5	4.4	2.1	626	30.0	5.9	4.5
Legal assistants	128	74.0	4.3	3.6	346	83.9	9.8	5.8
Sales occupations	11,818	47.5	4.7	3.7	15,734	50.2	8.1	7.6
Supervisors and proprietors	2,958	28.4	3.6	3.4	4,635	38.4	4.8	6.8
Sales representatives, finance and business services \2	1,853	37.2	2.7	2.2	2,613	44.0	6.9	4.5
Insurance sales	551	25.1	3.8	2.5	594	42.8	7.7	4.7
Real estate sales	570	48.9	1.3	1.5	781	50.0	4.6	5.1
Securities and financial services sales	212	23.6	3.1	1.1	429	31.2	5.5	2.6
Advertising and related sales	124	47.9	4.5	3.3	173	56.6	10.0	4.2
Sales representatives, commodities, except retail	1,442	15.1	2.1	2.2	1,507	24.9	3.0	5.0
Sales workers, retail and personal services	5,511	69.7	6.7	4.8	6,887	65.7	11.9	10.0
Cashiers	2,009	84.4	10.1	5.4	3,007	78.4	15.6	12.1
Sales-related occupations	54	58.7	2.8	1.3	91	73.5	5.0	4.6
Administrative support, including clerical	16,395	79.9	9.6	5.0	18,361	78.8	12.8	8.6
Supervisors	676	53.4	9.3	5.0	685	59.8	14.4	6.1
Computer equipment operators	605	63.9	12.5	6.0	392	58.5	15.4	7.0

C1.9. Employed Civilians, by Occupation, Sex, Race, and Hispanic Origin: 1983 and 1997 *(continued)*

OCCUPATION	Total em-ployed (1,000)	1983 Percent of total			Total em-ployed (1,000)	1997 Percent of total		
		Fe-male	Black	His-panic		Fe-male	Black	His-panic
Computer operators	597	63.7	12.1	6.0	385	58.4	15.0	7.1
Secretaries, stenographers, and typists \2	4,861	98.2	7.3	4.5	3,692	97.9	9.8	6.9
Secretaries	3,891	99.0	5.8	4.0	3,033	98.6	8.7	6.4
Typists	906	95.6	13.8	6.4	555	94.4	17.0	9.7
Information clerks	1,174	88.9	8.5	5.5	1,993	88.4	11.3	9.5
Receptionists	602	96.8	7.5	6.6	1,005	96.5	8.8	9.7
Records processing occupations, except financial \2	866	82.4	13.9	4.8	935	80.5	15.3	9.5
Order clerks	188	78.1	10.6	4.4	231	74.1	15.9	11.0
Personnel clerks, except payroll and time keeping	64	91.1	14.9	4.6	69	85.0	18.5	13.2
Library clerks	147	81.9	15.4	2.5	155	76.3	13.2	6.6
File clerks	287	83.5	16.7	6.1	295	84.7	15.5	11.7
Records clerks	157	82.8	11.6	5.6	175	82.6	15.0	5.1
Financial records processing \2	2,457	89.4	4.6	3.7	2,196	92.2	7.1	6.4
Bookkeepers, accounting, and auditing clerks	1,970	91.0	4.3	3.3	1,735	92.3	6.3	5.9
Payroll and time keeping clerks	192	82.2	5.9	5.0	155	92.7	10.2	10.4
Billing clerks	146	88.4	6.2	3.9	161	93.8	12.2	6.0
Cost and rate clerks	96	75.6	5.9	5.3	(\3)	(\3)	(\3)	(\3)
Billing, posting, and calculating machine operators	(\3)	(\3)	(\3)	(\3)	98	91.6	8.2	10.1
Duplicating, mail and other office machine operators	68	62.6	16.0	6.1	77	59.4	18.4	12.3
Communications equipment operators	256	89.1	17.0	4.4	185	81.5	21.6	9.7
Telephone operators	244	90.4	17.0	4.3	173	83.5	21.5	8.4
Mail and message distributing occupations	799	31.6	18.1	4.5	977	38.0	20.8	9.5
Postal clerks, except mail carriers	248	36.7	26.2	5.2	320	45.1	27.9	7.0
Mail carrier, postal service	259	17.1	12.5	2.7	314	30.7	15.8	9.3
Mail clerks, except postal service	170	50.0	15.8	5.9	181	51.7	24.2	12.7
Messengers	122	26.2	16.7	5.2	161	22.7	12.4	11.3
Material recording, scheduling, and distributing \2 \4	1,562	37.5	10.9	6.6	1,953	44.2	14.8	11.4
Dispatchers	157	45.7	11.4	4.3	233	51.3	14.7	9.0
Production coordinators	182	44.0	6.1	2.2	263	54.1	5.3	4.3
Traffic, shipping, and receiving clerks	421	22.6	9.1	11.1	638	30.5	17.2	15.2
Stock and inventory clerks	532	38.7	13.3	5.5	454	41.1	16.9	12.8
Weighers, measurers, and checkers	79	47.2	16.9	5.8	53	56.2	11.9	10.9
Expediters	112	57.5	8.4	4.3	245	69.4	14.0	10.1
Adjusters and investigators	675	69.9	11.1	5.1	1,701	74.4	14.0	8.9
Insurance adjusters, examiners, and investigators	199	65.0	11.5	3.3	434	72.5	11.1	8.5
Investigators and adjusters, except insurance	301	70.1	11.3	4.8	983	74.8	14.4	8.6
Eligibility clerks, social welfare	69	88.7	12.9	9.4	112	86.9	15.1	13.6
Bill and account collectors	106	66.4	8.5	6.5	172	68.6	18.3	8.4
Miscellaneous administrative support \2	2,397	85.2	12.5	5.9	3,576	83.4	14.6	9.4
General office clerks	648	80.6	12.7	5.2	818	80.6	12.7	9.8
Bank tellers	480	91.0	7.5	4.3	446	90.1	9.8	9.0
Data entry keyers	311	93.6	18.6	5.6	664	81.9	18.3	9.8
Statistical clerks	96	75.7	7.5	3.4	89	89.0	22.9	3.2
Teachers' aides	348	93.7	17.8	12.6	623	93.1	15.2	12.6
Service occupations	13,857	60.1	16.6	6.8	17,537	59.4	17.6	14.6
Private household \2	980	96.1	27.8	8.5	795	95.4	16.2	26.6
Child care workers	408	96.9	7.9	3.6	260	96.8	11.8	17.4
Cleaners and servants	512	95.8	42.4	11.8	512	94.9	17.8	31.3
Protective service	1,672	12.8	13.6	4.6	2,300	17.9	18.7	8.8
Supervisors, protective service	127	4.7	7.7	3.1	181	12.5	16.5	8.5
Supervisors, police and detectives	58	4.2	9.3	1.2	108	17.4	14.8	6.0
Firefighting and fire prevention	189	1.0	6.7	4.1	233	3.4	11.9	5.7
Firefighting occupations	170	1.0	7.3	3.8	218	3.1	12.4	4.6
Police and detectives	645	9.4	13.1	4.0	1,005	16.4	18.1	7.6

C1.9. Employed Civilians, by Occupation, Sex, Race, and Hispanic Origin: 1983 and 1997 *(continued)*

OCCUPATION	Total em-ployed (1,000)	1983 Percent of total Fe-male	Black	His-panic	Total em-ployed (1,000)	1997 Percent of total Fe-male	Black	His-panic
Police and detectives, public service	412	5.7	9.5	4.4	579	11.8	13.4	9.1
Sheriffs, bailiffs, and other law enforcement officers	87	13.2	11.5	4.0	142	22.2	18.6	7.2
Correctional institution officers	146	17.8	24.0	2.8	284	22.9	27.4	4.9
Guards	711	20.6	17.0	5.6	881	24.4	21.6	11.0
Guards and police, except public service	602	13.0	18.9	6.2	738	18.2	23.7	11.6
Service except private household and protective	11,205	64.0	16.0	6.9	14,442	64.0	17.5	14.9
Food preparation and service occupations \2	4,860	63.3	10.5	6.8	5,999	56.8	11.6	16.4
Bartenders	338	48.4	2.7	4.4	310	57.2	2.0	6.3
Waiters and waitresses	1,357	87.8	4.1	3.6	1,375	77.8	4.7	10.2
Cooks	1,452	50.0	15.8	6.5	2,126	41.8	16.7	20.4
Food counter, fountain, and related occupations	326	76.0	9.1	6.7	322	69.4	12.4	8.5
Kitchen workers, food preparation	138	77.0	13.7	8.1	278	72.6	9.8	14.2
Waiters' and waitresses' assistants	364	38.8	12.6	14.2	536	48.5	9.9	18.4
Health service occupations	1,739	89.2	23.5	4.8	2,447	88.2	30.8	9.2
Dental assistants	154	98.1	6.1	5.7	231	96.7	6.1	11.5
Health aides, except nursing	316	86.8	16.5	4.8	341	76.0	27.6	6.2
Nursing aides, orderlies, and attendants	1,269	88.7	27.3	4.7	1,875	89.4	34.5	9.5
Cleaning and building service occupations \2	2,736	38.8	24.4	9.2	3,108	43.2	21.5	21.3
Maids and housemen	531	81.2	32.3	10.1	643	80.1	27.1	24.8
Janitors and cleaners	2,031	28.6	22.6	8.9	2,226	34.0	19.9	21.0
Personal service occupations \2	1,870	79.2	11.1	6.0	2,888	80.9	14.3	9.6
Barbers	92	12.9	8.4	12.1	79	22.8	36.6	7.8
Hairdressers and cosmetologists	622	88.7	7.0	5.7	748	90.3	10.2	8.7
Attendants, amusement and recreation facilities	131	40.2	7.1	4.3	206	34.8	13.8	7.8
Public transportation attendants	63	74.3	11.3	5.9	115	82.7	10.5	6.2
Welfare service aides	77	92.5	24.2	10.5	95	86.2	25.8	11.3
Family child care providers	(NA)	(NA)	(NA)	(NA)	513	98.2	11.0	11.2
Early childhood teachers' assistants	(NA)	(NA)	(NA)	(NA)	432	95.6	17.2	10.8
Precision production, craft, and repair	12,328	8.1	6.8	6.2	14,124	8.9	8.1	12.1
Mechanics and repairers	4,158	3.0	6.8	5.3	4,675	3.9	7.9	10.2
Mechanics and repairers, except supervisors \2	3,906	2.8	7.0	5.5	4,428	3.7	8.0	10.6
Vehicle and mobile equipment mechanics/repairers \2	1,683	0.8	6.9	6.0	1,898	1.3	7.0	12.0
Automobile mechanics	800	0.5	7.8	6.0	905	1.5	7.8	13.2
Aircraft engine mechanics	95	2.5	4.0	7.6	135	2.9	8.4	10.2
Electrical and electronic equipment repairers \2	674	7.4	7.3	4.5	726	9.5	10.7	9.8
Data processing equipment repairers	98	9.3	6.1	4.5	190	13.3	7.1	8.5
Telephone installers and repairers	247	9.9	7.8	3.7	197	13.1	12.2	6.4
Construction trades	4,289	1.8	6.6	6.0	5,378	2.4	7.1	13.7
Construction trades, except supervisors	3,784	1.9	7.1	6.1	4,685	2.4	7.4	14.6
Carpenters	1,160	1.4	5.0	5.0	1,335	1.6	6.6	12.9
Extractive occupations	196	2.3	3.3	6.0	145	1.3	8.6	14.2
Precision production occupations	3,685	21.5	7.3	7.4	3,926	24.1	9.7	12.2
Operators, fabricators, and laborers	16,091	26.6	14.0	8.3	18,399	24.7	15.1	15.4
Machine operators, assemblers, and inspectors \2	7,744	42.1	14.0	9.4	7,962	37.7	14.8	17.9
Textile, apparel, and furnishings machine operators \2	1,414	82.1	18.7	12.5	1,083	72.1	18.8	28.0
Textile sewing machine operators	806	94.0	15.5	14.5	607	82.0	16.0	33.8
Pressing machine operators	141	66.4	27.1	14.2	102	70.6	22.4	44.1
Fabricators, assemblers, and hand working occupations	1,715	33.7	11.3	8.7	2,113	34.3	14.1	14.1
Production inspectors, testers, samplers, and weighers	794	53.8	13.0	7.7	787	47.6	12.9	16.9
Transportation and material moving occupations	4,201	7.8	13.0	5.9	5,389	9.6	15.2	11.0
Motor vehicle operators	2,978	9.2	13.5	6.0	4,089	11.3	15.3	10.9
Truck drivers	2,195	3.1	12.3	5.7	3,075	5.7	13.4	11.1
Transportation occupations, except motor vehicles	212	2.4	6.7	3.0	174	3.3	11.3	2.6
Material moving equipment operators	1,011	4.8	12.9	6.3	1,125	4.5	15.4	12.7

C1.9. Employed Civilians, by Occupation, Sex, Race, and Hispanic Origin: 1983 and 1997 *(continued)*

OCCUPATION	Total employed (1,000)	1983 Percent of total Female	Black	Hispanic	Total employed (1,000)	1997 Percent of total Female	Black	Hispanic
Industrial truck and tractor operators	369	5.6	19.6	8.2	526	7.2	19.4	17.9
Handlers, equipment cleaners, helpers, and laborers \2	4,147	16.8	15.1	8.6	5,048	20.3	15.5	16.3
Freight, stock, and material handlers	1,488	15.4	15.3	7.1	1,930	24.5	16.0	12.9
Laborers, except construction	1,024	19.4	16.0	8.6	1,323	21.3	16.1	15.6
Farming, forestry, and fishing	3,700	16.0	7.5	8.2	3,503	19.3	4.5	20.6
Farm operators and managers	1,450	12.1	1.3	0.7	1,317	23.1	1.2	2.4
Other agricultural and related occupations	2,072	19.9	11.7	14.0	2,030	17.9	6.6	33.6
Farm workers	1,149	24.8	11.6	15.9	796	19.0	4.8	41.3
Forestry and logging occupations	126	1.4	12.8	2.1	108	5.1	6.7	6.8
Fishers, hunters, and trappers	53	4.5	1.8	2.5	(\3)	(\3)	(\3)	(\3)

Notes:
- Represents or rounds to zero.
NA Not available.
\1 See footnote 2, Table 644.
\2 Includes other occupations, not shown separately.
\3 Level of total employment below 50,000.
\4 Includes clerks.

Source: U.S. Bureau of Labor Statistics, Employment and Earnings, monthy, January issues; and unpublished data. <http://stats.bls.gov/newsrels.htm>

C1.10. Occupations of the Employed, by Selected Characteristics: 1997

[In thousands. Annual averages of monthly figures. For civilian noninstitutional population 25 to 64 years old. Based on Current Population Survey.]

SEX, RACE, AND EDUCATIONAL ATTAINMENT	Total employed	Managerial/ professional	Tech./ sales/ administrative	Service \1	Precision production \2	Operators/ fabricators \3	Farming, forestry, fishing
Male, total \4	57,507	17,574	11,029	4,816	11,273	10,816	2,000
Less than a high school diploma	6,724	364	461	902	1,841	2,495	661
High school graduates, no college	18,492	2,131	3,034	1,832	5,334	5,422	739
Less than a bachelor's degree	14,977	3,547	3,857	1,500	3,346	2,346	379
College graduates	17,314	11,533	3,676	581	751	551	222
White	49,360	15,601	9,519	3,639	10,018	8,756	1,828
Less than a high school diploma	5,628	318	396	671	1,615	2,046	582
High school graduates, no college	15,756	1,923	2,602	1,328	4,779	4,450	674
Less than a bachelor's degree	12,797	3,167	3,289	1,161	2,980	1,838	363
College graduates	15,178	10,193	3,232	478	645	420	210
Black	5,531	1,017	952	883	895	1,666	116
Less than a high school diploma	818	31	40	157	165	366	58
High school graduates, no college	2,141	148	301	404	434	807	47
Less than a bachelor's degree	1,608	267	418	260	245	411	7
College graduates	963	571	192	62	52	81	4
Female, total \5	49,250	16,872	19,431	7,538	1,107	3,778	524
Less than a high school diploma	4,022	231	843	1,585	202	1,047	115
High school graduates, no college	16,444	2,396	7,816	3,558	540	1,932	202
Less than a bachelor's degree	14,556	4,225	7,384	1,888	267	652	139
College graduates	14,229	10,020	3,388	507	98	148	69
White	40,917	14,612	16,462	5,649	878	2,818	497
Less than a high school diploma	3,108	189	699	1,153	168	794	106
High school graduates, no college	13,675	2,134	6,841	2,642	428	1,439	190
Less than a bachelor's degree	12,047	3,662	6,111	1,451	208	481	133
College graduates	12,087	8,628	2,810	403	75	104	67

C1.10. Occupations of the Employed, by Selected Characteristics: 1997 *(continued)*

SEX, RACE, AND EDUCATIONAL ATTAINMENT	Total employed	Managerial/ profes- sional	Tech./ sales/ adminis- trative	Service \1	Precision produc- tion \2	Operators/ fabrica- tors \3	Farming, forestry, fishing
Black	6,102	1,518	2,207	1,534	141	687	16
Less than a high school diploma	661	32	108	351	16	147	6
High school graduates, no college	2,192	201	751	771	76	387	7
Less than a bachelor's degree	2,017	448	1,034	362	39	133	2
College graduates	1,233	837	314	51	10	20	1

Notes:
\1 Includes private household workers.
\2 Includes craft and repair.
\3 Includes laborers.
\4 Includes other races, not shown separately.

Source: U.S. Bureau of Labor Statistics, unpublished data.

C1.11. Employment, by Industry: 1970 to 1997

[In thousands, except percent. Data from 1985 to 1990, and also beginning 1995, not strictly comparable with other years due to changes in industrial classification.]

INDUSTRY	1970	1980	1990	1995	Total	Percent		
						Female	Black	Hispanic\2
Total employed	**78,678**	**99,303**	**118,793**	**124,900**	**129,558**	**46.2**	**10.8**	**9.8**
Agriculture	3,463	3,364	3,223	3,440	3,399	24.9	3.4	19.4
Mining	516	979	724	627	634	14.4	4.2	9.4
Construction	4,818	6,215	7,764	7,668	8,302	9.4	6.8	11.8
Manufacturing	20,746	21,942	21,346	20,493	20,835	32.1	10.4	11.2
Transportation, communication, and other public utilities	5,320	6,525	8,168	8,709	9,182	28.8	14.9	8.6
Wholesale and retail trade	15,008	20,191	24,622	26,071	26,777	47.3	8.9	11.1
Wholesale trade	2,672	3,920	4,669	4,986	4,907	29.6	6.3	10.7
Retail trade	12,336	16,270	19,953	21,086	21,869	51.2	9.4	11.2
Finance, insurance, real estate	3,945	5,993	8,051	7,983	8,297	58.4	9.7	7.2
Services \3	20,385	28,752	39,267	43,953	46,393	62.0	12.1	8.5
Business and repair services \3	1,403	3,848	7,485	7,526	8,450	37.2	11.6	11.0
Advertising	147	191	277	267	298	53.5	5.8	5.4
Services to dwellings and buildings	(NA)	370	827	829	829	48.5	15.3	23.4
Personnel supply services	(NA)	235	710	853	1,018	62.6	21.1	10.5
Computer and data processing	(NA)	221	805	1,136	1,535	31.0	6.5	4.4
Detective/protective services	(NA)	213	378	506	555	20.3	23.6	11.8
Automobile services	600	952	1,457	1,459	1,635	14.5	9.6	15.4
Personal services \3	4,276	3,839	4,733	4,375	4,404	68.9	13.6	16.8
Private households	1,782	1,257	1,036	971	921	90.9	17.6	25.6
Hotels and lodging places	979	1,149	1,818	1,495	1,549	53.4	14.5	19.0
Entertainment and recreation	717	1,047	1,526	2,238	2,465	44.5	9.0	9.1
Professional and related services \3	12,904	19,853	25,351	29,661	30,935	69.4	12.3	6.6
Hospitals	2,843	4,036	4,700	4,961	5,130	76.3	16.2	6.3
Health services, except hospitals	1,628	3,345	4,673	5,967	6,395	79.1	14.4	7.3
Elementary, secondary schools	6,126	5,550	5,994	6,653	6,866	75.4	12.2	7.2
Colleges and universities	(\4)	2,108	2,637	2,768	2,759	52.0	10.0	5.7
Social services	828	1,590	2,239	2,979	3,182	81.6	17.1	9.0
Legal services	429	776	1,215	1,335	1,398	56.1	5.6	5.8
Public administration \5	4,476	5,342	5,627	5,957	5,738	44.5	16.5	6.5

Notes:
NA Not available.
\2 Persons of Hispanic origin may be of any race.
\3 Includes industries not shown separately.
\4 Included with elementarly/secondary schools.
\5 Includes workers involved in uniquely governmental activities, e.g., judicial and legislative.

Source: U.S. Bureau of Labor Statistics, Employment and Earnings, monthly, January issues; and unpublished data

C1.12. Hours Worked and Occupational Status, by Race

Race	Sex	Mean hours worked last week	Occupational Prestige
White	Male	45.6	45.3
	(n)	**734**	**982**
	Female	38.6	44.7
	(n)	**728**	**1157**
	Total	42.1	44.9
	(n)	**1462**	**2139**
Black	Male	43.5	38.8
	(n)	**106**	**138**
	Female	38.6	41.2
	(n)	**155**	**229**
	Total	40.57	40.3
	(n)	**261**	**367**
Other	Male	45	40.7
	(n)	**67**	**82**
	Female	36	41.7
	(n)	**66**	**90**
	Total	40.7	41.2
	(n)	**133**	**172**

Source: General Social Survey, 1998.

C1.13. Unemployment in Last 10 Years

At any time during the last ten years, have you been unemployed and looking for work for as long as a month?			
	White	**Black**	**Other**
Yes	28.7%	37.8%	37.2%
No	71.3	62.2	62.8
Don't know	.1	—	—
(N)	**1490**	**278**	**1897**

Source: General Social Survey, 1998.

C1.14. Experience Out of the Labor Force

Since your first full-time job, has there ever been a time when you've been without a job and not looking for a job?			
	White	**Black**	**Other**
Yes	38.1%	29.7%	34.4%
No	61.9	70.3	65.6
(N)	**1068**	**185**	**96**

Source: General Social Survey, 1998.

C1.15. Job Supervision

Do you (does your spouse) have a supervisor on (your/his/her) job to whom you are (he/she/is) directly responsible?	White	Black	Other
Yes	80.2%	86.9%	88%
No	19.6	12.5	12
Don't know	.2	.6	
(N)	1107	176	92
In your job, do you supervise anyone who is directly responsible to you?			
Yes	43.3	34.3	37.1
No	56.1	65.1	62.9
Don't know	.6	.6	
(N)	1091	172	89

Source: General Social Survey, 1998.

C1.16. Union Membership

Do you or your spouse belong to a labor union?	White	Black	Other
I belong	9.6%	12%	10.2%
Spouse belongs	4.4	3.6	3.9
Spouse and I belong	2.5	2.9	1.6
Neither belongs	83.5	0.7	84.3
Don't know	—	.7	—
(N)	1494	275	127

Source: General Social Survey, 1998.

C2. INCOME

C2.1. Total Household Income from Various Sources, by Race: March 1988

		Total household income	Individual (income)
NonHispanic White	Average	$60527.48	$21395.07
	Number	92152	92152
NonHispanic Black	Average	$37155.22	$12475.90
	Number	12693	12693
American Indians/Aleuts/Eskimos	Average	$40254.37	$12451.85
	Number	1508	1508
Asians and Pacific Islanders	Average	$66573.10	$18600.89
	Number	4513	4513
Hispanics	Average	$39056.48	$10874.10
	Number	20751	20751
All Groups	Average	$54863.34	$18677.89
	Number	131617	131617

Source: Current Population Surveys, March 1998 [Machine readable data files] conducted by the Bureau of the Census for the Bureau of Labor Statistics. Washington, D.C.: Bureau of Census [producer and distributor]. Santa Monica, CA: Unicon Research Corporation [producer and distributor of CPS Utilities], 1999.

C2.2. Money Income of Families—Median Income, by Race and Hispanic Origin, in Current and Constant (1996) Dollars: 1970 to 1996

[Constant dollars based on CPI-U-X1 deflator. Families as of March of following year. Beginning with 1980, based on householder concept and restricted to primary families. Based on Current Population Survey]

YEAR	NUMBER (1,000)						MEDIAN INCOME IN CURRENT DOLLARS						MEDIAN INCOME IN CONSTANT (1996) DOLLARS						
	All families \1	White	Black \2	Asian, Pacific Islander	His-panic \3	White, not Hispanic	All families \1	White	Black \2	Asian, Pacific Islander	His-panic \3	White, not Hispanic	All families \1	White	Black \2	Asian, Pacific Islander	His-panic \3	White, not Hispanic	CPI-U-X1 (1982-84=100)
1970	52,227	46,535	4,928	(NA)	(NA)	(NA)	9,867	10,236	6,279	(NA)	(NA)	(NA)	37,485	38,887	23,854	(NA)	(NA)	(NA)	41.3
1980	60,309	52,710	6,317	(NA)	3,235	49,584	21,023	21,904	12,674	(NA)	14,716	22,336	40,079	41,759	24,162	(NA)	28,055	42,584	82.3
1981	61,019	53,269	6,413	(NA)	3,305	50,066	22,388	23,517	13,266	(NA)	16,401	24,052	38,986	40,952	23,101	(NA)	28,561	41,884	90.1
1982	61,393	53,407	6,530	(NA)	3,369	50,123	23,433	24,603	13,598	(NA)	16,227	25,174	38,459	40,379	22,317	(NA)	26,632	41,316	95.6
1983	61,997	53,934	6,675	(NA)	3,567	50,208	24,580	25,757	14,506	(NA)	16,956	26,508	38,721	40,575	22,851	(NA)	26,711	41,758	99.6
1984	62,706	54,400	6,778	(NA)	3,939	50,563	26,433	27,686	15,431	(NA)	18,832	28,452	39,917	41,809	23,302	(NA)	28,438	42,966	103.9
1985	63,558	54,991	6,921	(NA)	4,206	50,912	27,735	29,152	16,786	(NA)	19,027	30,057	40,443	42,509	24,477	(NA)	27,745	43,828	107.6
1986	64,491	55,676	7,096	(NA)	4,403	51,426	29,458	30,809	17,604	(NA)	19,995	31,669	42,171	44,105	25,201	(NA)	28,624	45,336	109.6
1987	65,204	56,086	7,202	(NA)	4,576	51,702	30,970	32,385	18,406	(NA)	20,300	33,509	42,775	44,729	25,422	(NA)	28,038	46,281	113.6
1988	65,837	56,492	7,409	1,481	4,823	51,850	32,191	33,915	19,329	36,560	21,769	35,116	42,695	44,981	25,636	48,489	28,872	46,574	118.3
1989	66,090	56,590	7,470	1,531	4,840	51,955	34,213	35,975	20,209	40,351	23,446	37,062	43,290	45,520	25,571	51,057	29,667	46,895	124.0
1990	66,322	56,803	7,471	1,536	4,981	52,038	35,353	36,915	21,423	42,246	23,431	38,239	42,440	44,315	25,717	50,715	28,128	45,904	130.7
1991	67,173	57,224	7,716	1,624	5,177	52,287	35,939	37,783	21,548	40,974	23,895	39,241	41,401	43,525	24,823	47,201	27,527	45,205	136.2
1992	68,216	57,669	7,982	1,760	5,733	52,302	36,573	38,670	21,103	42,255	23,555	40,334	40,900	43,245	23,600	47,255	26,342	45,106	140.3
1993	68,506	57,881	7,993	1,737	5,946	52,470	36,959	39,300	21,542	44,456	23,654	41,110	40,131	42,672	23,391	48,271	25,684	44,638	144.5
1994	69,313	58,444	8,093	1,589	6,202	53,029	38,782	40,884	24,698	46,122	24,318	42,549	41,059	43,284	26,148	48,830	25,746	45,047	148.2
1995	69,597	58,872	8,055	2,125	6,287	52,861	40,611	42,646	25,970	46,356	24,570	45,018	41,810	43,905	26,737	47,725	25,296	46,347	152.4
1996	70,241	58,934	8,455	2,247	6,631	52,625	42,300	44,756	26,522	49,105	26,179	47,023	42,300	44,756	26,522	49,105	26,179	47,023	156.9

Notes:

NA Not available.

\1 Includes other races not shown separately.

\2 Prior to 1967 data are for Black and Other Races.

\3 Persons of Hispanic origin may be of any race.

\4 Based on 1940 census population controls.

\5 Implementation of expanded income questions to show wage and salary, farm self-employment, nonfarm self-employment, and all other nonearned income separately.

\6 Implementation of 1950 census population controls.

\7 Implementation of first hot deck procedure to impute missing income entries (all income data imputed if any missing).

\8 Implementation of 1960 census population controls.

Source: U.S. Bureau of the Census, Current Population Reports, P60, No. 197.

C2.3. Money Income of Households—Percent Distribution, by Income Level, Race, and Hispanic Origin, in Constant (1996) Dollars: 1970 to 1996

[Constant dollars based on CPI-U-X1 deflator. Households as of March of following year. Based on Current Population Survey.]

YEAR	Number of households (1,000)	Under $10,000 Total	Under $5,000	$5,000-$9,999	$10,000-$14,999	$15,000-$24,999	$25,000-$34,999	$35,000-$49,999	$50,000-$74,999	$75,000 and over Total	$75,000-$99,999	$100,000 and over	Median income (dollars)	Mean income (dollars)
ALL HOUSEHOLDS \1														
1970	64,778	13.7	4.9	8.8	7.7	15.6	16.4	21.3	16.8	8.5	5.3	3.2	34,181	37,994
1975	72,867	13.0	3.3	9.7	8.8	16.2	15.6	19.4	17.8	9.2	5.7	3.5	32,943	38,468
1980	82,368	12.9	3.3	9.6	8.2	16.4	14.3	19.1	17.9	11.2	6.8	4.4	33,763	40,155
1985	88,458	12.7	3.7	9.0	8.3	15.6	14.2	17.8	17.8	13.5	7.7	5.8	34,439	42,383
1990	94,312	12.0	3.6	8.4	7.9	15.0	14.1	17.8	17.9	15.2	8.0	7.2	35,945	44,901
1994	98,990	12.6	3.8	8.8	8.7	15.8	14.1	16.3	16.9	15.5	7.8	7.7	34,158	45,665
1995	99,627	11.8	3.5	8.3	8.5	15.6	13.9	16.9	17.4	15.7	8.0	7.7	35,082	46,265
1996	101,018	11.8	3.4	8.4	8.6	15.4	13.7	16.3	18.0	16.4	8.2	8.2	35,492	47,123
WHITE														
1970	57,575	12.5	4.4	8.1	7.2	14.9	16.5	22.0	17.7	9.0	5.6	3.4	34,560	39,324
1975	64,392	11.6	2.9	8.7	8.4	15.9	15.5	20.0	18.8	9.9	6.1	3.8	34,451	39,889
1980	71,872	11.3	2.7	8.6	7.7	16.0	14.5	19.7	18.9	12.1	7.3	4.8	35,620	41,776
1985	76,576	11.1	3.1	8.0	7.8	15.2	14.3	18.4	18.6	14.5	8.2	6.3	36,320	44,123
1990	80,968	10.2	2.8	7.4	7.6	14.8	14.3	18.3	18.8	16.2	8.5	7.7	37,492	46,712
1994	83,737	10.8	3.0	7.8	8.4	15.5	14.2	16.8	17.7	16.5	8.3	8.2	36,026	47,678
1995	84,511	10.2	2.8	7.4	8.2	15.4	14.0	17.3	18.1	16.8	8.5	8.3	36,822	48,109
1996	85,059	10.0	2.6	7.4	8.2	15.1	13.7	16.7	18.8	17.4	8.5	8.9	37,161	48,994
BLACK														
1970	6,180	25.0	9.8	15.2	12.1	21.5	15.2	14.5	8.7	2.8	2.1	0.7	21,035	25,685
1975	7,489	25.4	6.9	18.5	13.3	19.0	16.0	14.1	9.4	2.8	2.1	0.7	20,682	25,816
1980	8,847	25.9	7.9	18.0	12.9	19.8	13.2	14.4	10.0	3.8	2.8	1.0	20,521	26,633
1985	9,797	25.8	8.4	17.4	11.9	19.1	13.1	13.9	11.0	5.2	3.6	1.6	21,609	28,194
1990	10,671	26.3	9.7	16.6	11.1	17.0	13.3	14.5	11.2	6.5	4.2	2.3	22,420	29,788
1994	11,655	25.2	8.6	16.6	11.1	18.3	13.4	13.1	11.7	7.2	4.0	3.2	22,261	30,977
1995	11,577	23.5	8.2	15.3	11.3	18.5	13.7	14.7	11.5	6.7	4.3	2.4	23,054	31,298
1996	12,109	23.1	8.2	14.9	11.6	17.7	13.9	14.0	12.4	7.4	4.7	2.7	23,482	32,460
HISPANIC \2														
1975	2,948	16.8	4.5	12.3	11.7	22.1	17.5	18.1	10.3	3.5	2.3	1.2	24,749	29,381
1980	3,906	16.7	5.0	11.7	10.7	21.2	16.2	16.9	12.8	5.5	3.6	1.9	26,025	31,788
1985	5,213	17.9	5.3	12.6	12.0	19.5	15.2	16.4	12.3	6.6	4.6	2.0	25,467	31,822
1990	6,220	16.7	5.3	11.4	11.6	18.6	15.8	17.0	12.8	7.5	4.5	3.0	26,806	33,579
1994	7,735	19.2	5.7	13.5	12.1	19.1	15.2	15.0	11.8	7.6	4.3	3.3	24,796	33,436
1995	7,939	19.2	5.8	13.4	12.3	21.0	15.2	14.0	11.8	6.5	3.8	2.7	23,535	32,122
1996	8,225	17.2	5.1	12.1	11.9	21.0	15.0	15.0	12.3	7.7	4.2	3.5	24,906	34,005

Notes:
\1 Includes other races not shown separately. 2/ Persons of Hispanic origin may be of any race. Income data for Hispanic origin households are not available prior to 1972.

Source: U.S. Bureau of the Census. Current Population Reports, P60-197.

C2.4. Money Income of Households—Median Income, by Race and Hispanic Origin, in Current and Constant (1996) Dollars: 1970 to 1996

[Constant dollars based on CPI-U-X1 deflator. Households as of March of following year. Based on Current Population Survey]

	MEDIAN INCOME IN CURRENT DOLLARS						MEDIAN INCOME IN CONSTANT (1996) DOLLARS					
YEAR	All house-holds\1	White	Black	Asian, Pacific Islander	His-panic\2	White, not Hispanic	All house-holds\1	White	Black	Asian, Pacific Islander	His-panic\2	White, not Hispanic
1970..........	8,734	9,097	5,537	(NA)	(NA)	(NA)	33,181	34,560	21,035	(NA)	(NA)	(NA)
1980..........	17,710	18,684	10,764	(NA)	13,651	19,015	33,763	35,620	20,521	(NA)	26,025	36,251
1981..........	19,074	20,153	11,309	(NA)	15,300	20,444	33,215	35,094	19,693	(NA)	26,643	35,601
1982..........	20,171	21,117	11,968	(NA)	15,178	21,471	33,105	34,657	19,642	(NA)	24,910	35,238
1983..........	20,885	21,902	12,429	(NA)	15,906	(NA)	32,900	34,502	19,579	(NA)	25,057	(NA)
1984 6/........	22,415	23,647	13,471	(NA)	16,992	24,138	33,849	35,709	20,343	(NA)	25,660	36,451
1985 5/........	23,618	24,908	14,819	(NA)	17,465	25,468	34,439	36,320	21,609	(NA)	25,467	37,137
1986..........	24,897	26,175	15,080	(NA)	18,352	26,770	35,642	37,471	21,588	(NA)	26,272	38,323
1987 4/........	26,061	27,458	15,672	(NA)	19,336	28,213	35,994	37,924	21,646	(NA)	26,706	38,967
1988..........	27,225	28,781	16,407	32,267	20,359	29,574	36,108	38,172	21,760	42,795	27,002	39,224
1989..........	28,906	30,406	18,083	36,102	21,921	31,060	36,575	38,473	22,881	45,681	27,737	39,301
1990..........	29,943	31,231	18,676	38,450	22,330	31,945	35,945	37,492	22,420	46,158	26,806	38,349
1991..........	30,126	31,569	18,807	36,449	22,691	32,323	34,705	36,367	21,665	41,989	26,140	37,236
1992 3/.........	30,636	32,209	18,755	37,801	22,597	33,290	34,261	36,020	20,974	42,274	25,271	37,229
1993 2/.........	31,241	32,960	19,533	38,347	22,886	34,173	33,922	35,788	21,209	41,638	24,850	37,105
1994..........	32,264	34,028	21,027	40,482	23,421	35,126	34,158	36,026	22,261	42,858	24,796	37,188
1995..........	34,076	35,766	22,393	40,614	22,860	37,178	35,082	36,822	23,054	41,813	23,535	38,276
1996..........	35,492	37,161	23,482	43,276	24,906	(NA)	35,492	37,161	23,482	43,276	24,906	38,787

Notes:
NA Not Available.
\1 Includes other races not shown separately.
\2 Persons of Hispanic origin may be of any race.
\3 Beginning 1983, data based on revised Hispanic population controls and not directly comparable with prior years.
\4 Beginning 1987, data based on revised processing procedures and not directly comparable with prior years.
\5 Based on 1990 census population controls

Source: U.S. Bureau of the Census, Current Population Reports, P60-197, Money Income in the United States: 1996; and Internet site <http://www.census.gov/hhes/income/h:stinc/inchdet.html> (accessed 25 March 1998)

C2.5. Median Income of Persons with Income, in Constant (1996) Dollars, by Sex, Race, and Hispanic Origin: 1980 to 1996

[Age as of March of following year. Persons 15 years old and over. Constant dollars, based on CPI-U-X1 deflator.]

ITEM	MALE 1980	MALE 1990	MALE 1995	MALE 1996	FEMALE 1980	FEMALE 1990	FEMALE 1995	FEMALE 1996
NUMBER WITH INCOME (1,000)								
All races	**78,661**	**88,220**	**92,066**	**93,439**	**80,826**	**92,245**	**96,007**	**96,558**
White	69,420	76,480	79,022	80,041	70,573	78,566	80,608	80,741
Black	7,387	8,820	9,339	9,410	8,596	10,687	11,607	11,817
Asian and Pacific Islander	(NA)	2,235	3,095	3,277	(NA)	2,333	3,025	3,226
Hispanic \1	3,996	6,767	8,577	9,305	3,617	5,903	7,478	7,744
White, not Hispanic origin	65,564	69,987	70,754	71,084	67,084	72,939	73,506	73,445
MEDIAN INCOME IN CONSTANT (1996) DOLLARS (dol.)								
All races	**23,888**	**24,361**	**23,228**	**23,834**	**9,380**	**12,089**	**12,488**	**12,815**
White	25,409	25,414	24,601	24,949	9,431	12,385	12,680	12,961
Black	15,269	15,448	16,479	16,491	8,731	9,997	11,285	11,772
Asian and Pacific Islander	(NA)	23,282	22,816	23,374	(NA)	13,308	13,242	14,634
Hispanic \1	18,414	16,170	15,278	15,437	8,398	9,042	9,192	9,484
White, not Hispanic origin	26,082	26,360	26,233	26,290	9,494	12,702	13,185	13,514

Notes:
NA Not Available.
\1 Persons of Hispanic origin may be of any race.

Source: U.S. Bureau of the Census, Current Population Reports, P60-197. Internet site <http://www.census.gov/hhes/income/histinc/index.html\> (accessed 25 March 1998).

C2.6. Per Capita Money Income in Current and Constant (1996) Dollars, by Race and Hispanic Origin: 1970 to 1996

[In dollars. Constant dollars based on CPI-U-X1. As of March of Following Year]

| YEAR | CURRENT DOLLARS | | | | | CONSTANT (1996) DOLLARS | | | | |
	All races \1	White	Black	Asian, Pacific Islander	His-panic\2	All races \1	White	Black	Asian, Pacific Islander	His-panic\2
1970	3,177	3,354	1,869	(NA)	(NA)	12,070	12,742	7,100	(NA)	(NA)
1980	7,787	8,233	4,804	(NA)	4,865	14,845	15,696	9,159	(NA)	9,275
1985 \3	11,013	11,671	6,840	(NA)	6,613	16,059	17,018	9,974	(NA)	9,643
1986	11,670	12,352	7,207	(NA)	7,000	16,706	17,683	10,317	(NA)	10,021
1987 \4	12,391	13,143	7,645	(NA)	7,653	17,114	18,153	10,559	(NA)	10,570
1988	13,123	13,896	8,271	(NA)	7,956	17,405	18,430	10,970	(NA)	10,552
1989	14,056	14,896	8,747	(NA)	8,390	17,785	18,848	11,068	(NA)	10,616
1990	14,387	15,265	9,017	(NA)	8,424	17,271	18,325	10,825	(NA)	10,113
1991	14,617	15,510	9,170	(NA)	8,662	16,839	17,867	10,564	(NA)	9,978
1992 \5	14,847	15,785	9,239	(NA)	8,591	16,604	17,653	10,332	(NA)	9,607
1993	15,777	16,800	9,863	15,691	8,830	17,131	18,242	10,709	17,037	9,588
1994	16,555	17,611	10,650	16,902	9,435	17,527	18,645	11,275	17,894	9,989
1995	17,227	18,304	10,982	16,567	9,300	17,736	18,844	11,306	17,056	9,575
1996	18,136	19,181	11,899	17,921	10,048	18,136	19,181	11,899	17,921	10,048

Notes:
NA Not Available
\1 Includes other races not shown separately.
\2 Persons of Hispanic origin may be of any race.
\3 Beginning 1985, data based on revised Hispanic population controls.
\4 Beginning 1987, data based on revised processing procedures and not directly comparable with prior years.
\5 Based on 1990 population controls.

Source: US Bureau of the Census, Current Population Reports, P60-197; and Internet site <http://www.census.gov/hhes/income/histinc/index.html> (accessed 25 March 1998).

C2.7. Median Annual Earnings (in 1997 Constant Dollars) of Full-time, Year-round Wage and Salary Workers Ages 25–34, by Sex, Race, and Highest Educational Level: 1994 to 96

	Men		Women	
	White	**Hispanic**	**White**	**Hispanic**
Grades 9–11	$21,513	$16,510	$15,532	$13,699
High school diploma	26,446	21,118	19,323	17,708
Some college	29,272	25,361	23,141	21,412
Bachelor's degree	38,813	34,400	31,085	29,090

Source: U.S. Department of Commerce, Bureau of the Census, March *Current Population Surveys.*

C2.8. Type of Pay

As of last week, did your main job pay an hourly wage, daily wage, weekly wage, monthly salary, annual salary, or other pay rate, irrespective of the time between payrolls and the use of bonuses or profit-sharing?

	White	**Black**	**Other**
Hourly wage	45.4	61.4	54.6
Daily wage	1.5	.5	—
Weekly wage	8.8	9.2	13.4
Monthly salary	11.3	7.6	15.5
Annual salary	18.5	11.4	7.2
Other pay rate	14.5	9.8	9.3
(N)	**1066**	**184**	**97**

Source: General Social Survey, 1998.

C2.9. Average Household Income from Various Sources, by Race: March 1998

		Alimony Payments	Child Support	Dividend Payments	Disability Benefits	EDUC Asst Benefits	Financial Assistance
Non Hispanic White	Average	$41.03	$266.31	$1094.64	$158.07	$308.36	$78.44
	Number	92152	92152	92152	92152	92152	92152
Non Hispanic Black	Average	$1.80	$215.61	$181.60	$180.89	$352.48	$41.47
	Number	12693	12693	12693	12693	12693	12693
American Indians/Aleuts/Eskimos	Average	$8.75	$163.57	$328.05	$68.60	$427.79	$26.81
	Number	1508	1508	1508	1508	1508	1508
Asians and Pacific Islanders	Average	$5.58	$102.24	$926.39	$51.28	$523.69	$303.93
	Number	4513	4513	4513	4513	4513	4513
Hispanics	Average	$16.15	$178.19	$267.06	$102.34	$206.75	$63.00
	Number	20751	20751	20751	20751	20751	20751
All Groups	Average	$31.74	$240.71	$861.55	$146.80	$305.25	$79.58
	Number	131617	131617	131617	131617	131617	131617

		Farm Self Employed	Interest	Other Income	Public Asst/Welfare	Retirement	Rent
Non Hispanic White	Average	$371.50	$2059.48	$139.74	$74.71	$1668.89	$639.25
	Number	92152	92152	92152	92152	92152	92152
Non Hispanic Black	Average	$10.80	$440	$140.07	$486.61	$1004.55	$112.49
	Number	12693	12693	12693	12693	12693	12693
American Indians/Aleuts/Eskimos	Average	$13.18	$452.09	$401.95	$446.88	$1101.55	$172.00
	Number	1508	1508	1508	1508	1508	1508
Asians and Pacific Islanders	Average	$115.68	$1459.22	$173.05	$329.36	$1183.50	$436.90
	Number	4513	4513	4513	4513	4513	4513
Hispanics	Average	$63.50	$417.67	$82.80	$434.91	$408.74	$150.01
	Number	20751	20751	20751	20751	20751	20751
All Groups	Average	$275.28	$1605.45	$134.94	$184.22	$1383.00	$499.02
	Number	131617	131617	131617	131617	131617	131617

C2.9. Average Household Income from Various Sources, by Race: March 1998 *(continued)*

		Workers Comp	Wage & Salary	Total Family Income	Income Other Than Earnings	Adjusted Personal Gross Income	Age of Person
Non Hispanic White	Average	$130.48	$46200.25	$57259.69	$9591.44	$17187.20	37.07
	Number	92152	92152	92152	92152	92152	92512
Non Hispanic Black	Average	$114.51	$29857.31	$33721.93	$5818.12	$10622.11	31.58
	Number	12693	12693	12693	12693	12693	12693
American Indians/Aleuts/Eskimos	Average	$94.79	$32051.05	$35722.22	$5874.32	$10421.21	29.66
	Number	1508	1508	1508	1508	1508	1508
Asians and Pacific Islanders	Average	$71.22	$54703.43	$60834.17	$7072.61	$15016.19	32.24
	Number	4513	4513	4513	4513	4513	4513
Hispanics	Average	$111.65	$33188.95	$35278.92	$3912.14	$9404.61	28.06
	Number	20751	20751	20751	20751	20751	20751
All Groups	Average	$123.53	$42702.22	$51400.01	$8203.18	$15175.09	34.87
	Number	131617	131617	131617	131617	131617	13161

Source: Current Population Surveys, March 1998 [Machine readable data files] conducted by the Bureau of the Census for the Bureau of Labor Statistics. Washington, D.C.: Bureau of Census [producer and distributor]. Santa Monica, CA: Unicon Research Corporation [producer and distributor of CPS Utilities], 1999.

C3. POVERTY

C3.1. Percentage Living below Poverty Level, by Race: March 1998

	NonHispanic Whites	NonHispanic Blacks	American Indians/ Aleuts/Eskimos	Asians and Pacific Islanders	Hispanics	Total
%	9.0%	26.8%	28.6%	13.5%	27.5%	14.0%
N	8317	3401	431	607	5711	18467
Total	92152	122693	1508	4513	20751	131617

Source: Current Population Surveys, March 1998 [Machine readable data files] conducted by the Bureau of the Census for the Bureau of Labor Statistics. Washington, D.C.: Bureau of Census [producer and distributor]. Santa Monica, CA: Unicon Research Corporation [producer and distributor of CPS.]

C3.2. Persons below Poverty Level and below 125 Percent of Poverty Level: 1960 to 1996

[Persons as of March of the following year. Based on Current Population Survey]

YEAR	ALL PERSONS (1,000)					NUMBER BELOW POVERTY LEVEL					PERCENT BELOW POVERTY LEVEL					PERCENT OF POVERTY LEVEL		125 PERCENT OF POVERTY LEVEL		CUTOFFS FOR NONFARM FAMILY OF 4\3	
	All races\1	White	Black	Asian and Pacific Islander	His-panic\2	All races\1	White	Black	Asian and Pacific Islander	His-panic\2	All races\1	White	Black	Asian and Pacific Islander	His-panic\2	Number (1,000)	Percent of total population	Number (mil.)	Percent of total population	At poverty level	At 125 percent of poverty level
1960	179,503	158,863	(NA)	(NA)	(NA)	39,851	28,309	(NA)	(NA)	(NA)	22.2	17.8	(NA)	(NA)	(NA)	54,560	30.4	14,709	8.2	3,022	3,778
1970	202,183	177,376	22,515	(NA)	(NA)	25,420	17,484	7,548	(NA)	(NA)	12.6	9.9	33.5	(NA)	(NA)	35,624	17.6	10,204	5.0	3,968	4,960
1975	210,864	183,164	24,089	(NA)	11,117	25,877	17,770	7,545	(NA)	2,991	12.3	9.7	31.3	(NA)	23.0	37,182	17.6	11,305	5.4	5,500	6,875
1976	212,303	184,165	24,399	(NA)	11,269	24,975	16,713	7,595	(NA)	2,783	11.8	9.1	31.1	(NA)	26.9	35,509	16.7	10,534	5.0	5,815	7,269
1977	213,867	185,254	24,710	(NA)	12,046	24,720	16,416	7,726	(NA)	2,700	11.6	8.9	31.3	(NA)	24.7	35,659	16.7	10,939	5.1	6,191	7,739
1978	215,556	186,450	24,956	(NA)	12,079	24,497	16,259	7,625	(NA)	2,607	11.4	8.7	30.6	(NA)	22.4	34,155	15.8	9,658	4.5	6,662	8,328
1979 \4	222,903	191,742	25,944	(NA)	13,371	26,072	17,214	8,050	(NA)	2,921	11.7	9.0	31.0	(NA)	21.6	36,616	16.4	10,544	4.7	7,412	9,265
1980	225,027	192,912	26,408	(NA)	13,600	29,272	19,699	8,579	(NA)	3,491	13.0	10.2	32.5	(NA)	21.8	40,658	18.1	11,386	5.1	8,414	10,518
1981	227,157	194,504	26,834	(NA)	14,021	31,822	21,553	9,173	(NA)	3,713	14.0	11.1	34.2	(NA)	25.7	43,748	19.3	11,926	5.3	9,287	11,609
1982	229,412	195,919	27,216	(NA)	14,385	34,398	23,517	9,697	(NA)	4,301	15.0	12.0	35.6	(NA)	26.5	46,520	20.3	12,122	5.3	9,862	12,328
1983 \5	231,700	197,496	27,678	(NA)	16,544	35,303	23,984	9,882	(NA)	4,633	15.2	12.1	35.7	(NA)	29.9	47,150	20.3	11,847	5.1	10,178	12,723
1984	233,816	198,941	28,087	(NA)	16,916	33,700	22,955	9,490	(NA)	4,806	14.4	11.5	33.8	(NA)	28.0	45,288	19.4	11,588	5.0	10,609	13,261
1985	236,594	200,918	28,485	(NA)	18,075	33,064	22,860	8,926	(NA)	5,236	14.0	11.4	31.3	(NA)	28.4	44,166	18.7	11,102	4.7	10,989	13,736
1986	238,554	202,282	28,871	(NA)	18,758	32,370	22,183	8,983	(NA)	5,117	13.6	11.0	31.1	(NA)	29.0	43,486	18.2	11,116	4.7	11,203	14,004
1987 \6	240,982	203,605	29,362	6,322	19,395	32,221	21,195	9,520	1,021	5,422	13.4	10.4	32.4	16.1	27.3	43,032	17.9	10,811	4.5	11,611	14,514
1988	243,530	205,235	29,849	6,447	20,064	31,745	20,715	9,356	1,117	5,357	13.0	10.1	31.3	17.3	28.0	42,551	17.5	10,806	4.4	12,092	15,115
1989	245,992	206,853	30,332	6,673	20,746	31,528	20,785	9,302	939	5,430	12.8	10.0	30.7	14.1	26.7	42,653	17.3	11,125	4.5	12,674	15,843
1990	248,644	208,611	30,806	7,014	21,405	33,585	22,326	9,837	858	6,006	13.5	10.7	31.9	12.2	26.2	44,837	18.0	11,252	4.5	13,359	16,699
1991	251,179	210,121	31,312	7,192	22,068	35,708	23,747	10,242	996	6,339	14.2	11.3	32.7	13.8	28.1	47,527	18.9	11,819	4.7	13,924	17,405
1992 \7	256,549	213,060	32,411	7,779	25,646	38,014	25,259	10,827	985	7,592	14.8	11.9	33.4	12.7	29.6	50,592	19.7	12,578	4.9	14,335	17,919
1993	259,278	214,899	32,910	7,434	26,559	39,265	26,226	10,877	1,134	8,126	15.1	12.2	33.1	15.3	30.6	51,801	20.0	12,536	4.8	14,763	18,454
1994	261,616	216,460	33,353	6,654	27,442	38,059	25,379	10,196	974	8,416	14.5	11.7	30.6	14.6	30.7	50,401	19.3	12,342	4.7	15,141	18,926
1995	263,733	218,028	33,740	9,644	28,344	36,425	24,423	9,872	1,411	8,574	13.8	11.2	29.3	14.6	30.3	48,761	18.5	12,336	4.7	15,569	19,461
1996	266,218	219,656	34,110	10,054	29,614	36,529	24,650	9,694	1,454	8,697	13.7	11.2	28.4	14.5	29.4	49,310	18.5	12,781	4.8	16,036	20,045

Notes:
NA Not available.
\1 Includes other races not shown separately.
\2 Persons of Hispanic origin may be of any race.
\3 Beginning 1981, income cutoffs for nonfarm families are applied to all families, both farm and nonfarm.
\4 Population controls based on 1980 census; see text, sections 1 and 14.
\5 Beginning 1983, data based on revised Hispanic population controls and not directly comparable with prior years.
\6 Beginning 1987, data based on revised processing procedures and not directly comparable with prior years.
\7 Beginning 1992, based on 1990 population controls.

Source: U.S. Bureau of the Census, Current Population Reports, Poverty in the United States: 1997, series P60-201; and <http://www.census.gov/hhes/poverty/histpov/perindex.html>

C3.3. Children below Poverty Level, by Race and Hispanic Origin: 1970 to 1996

[Persons as of March of the following year. Covers only related children in families under 18 years old. Based on the Current Population Survey.]

YEAR	NUMBER (1,000)				NUMBER BELOW POVERTY LEVEL (1,000)				PERCENT BELOW POVERTY LEVEL			
	All races\1	White	Black	His-panic\2	All races\1	White	Black	His-panic\2	All races\1	White	Black	His-panic\2
1970	68,815	58,472	9,448	(NA)	10,235	6,138	3,922	(NA)	14.9	10.5	41.5	(NA)
1980	62,168	51,002	9,287	5,211	11,114	6,817	3,906	1,718	17.9	13.4	42.1	33.0
1981	61,756	50,553	9,291	5,291	12,068	7,429	4,170	1,874	19.5	14.7	44.9	35.4
1982	61,565	50,305	9,269	5,436	13,139	8,282	4,388	2,117	21.3	16.5	47.3	38.9
1983 \3	61,578	50,183	9,245	5,977	13,427	8,534	4,273	2,251	21.8	17.0	46.2	37.7
1984	61,681	50,192	9,356	5,982	12,929	8,086	4,320	2,317	21.0	16.1	46.2	38.7
1985	62,019	50,358	9,405	6,346	12,483	7,838	4,057	2,512	20.1	15.6	43.1	39.6
1986	62,009	50,356	9,467	6,511	12,257	7,714	4,037	2,413	19.8	15.3	42.7	37.1
1987 \4	62,423	50,360	9,546	6,692	12,275	7,398	4,234	2,606	19.7	14.7	44.4	38.9
1988	62,906	50,590	9,681	6,908	11,935	7,095	4,148	2,576	19.0	14.0	42.8	37.3
1989	63,225	50,704	9,847	7,040	12,001	7,164	4,257	2,496	19.0	14.1	43.2	35.5
1990	63,908	51,028	9,980	7,300	12,715	7,696	4,412	2,750	19.9	15.1	44.2	37.7
1991	64,800	51,627	10,178	7,473	13,658	8,316	4,637	2,977	21.1	16.1	45.6	39.8
1992	65,691	52,122	10,471	7,589	13,876	8,333	4,850	2,946	21.1	16.0	46.3	38.8
1992 \5	67,256	53,110	10,823	8,829	14,521	8,752	5,015	3,440	21.6	16.5	46.3	39.0
1993	68,040	53,614	10,969	9,188	14,961	9,123	5,030	3,666	22.0	17.0	45.9	39.9
1994	68,819	54,221	11,044	9,621	14,610	8,826	4,787	3,956	21.2	16.3	43.3	41.1
1995	69,425	54,532	11,198	10,011	13,999	8,474	4,644	3,938	20.2	15.5	41.5	39.3
1996	69,411	54,599	11,155	10,255	13,764	8,488	4,411	4,090	19.8	15.5	39.5	39.9

Notes:
NA Not available.
\1 Includes other races not shown separately.
\2 Persons of Hispanic origin may be of any race.
\3 Beginning 1983, data based on revised Hispanic population controls and not directly comparable with prior years.
\4 Beginning 1987, data based on revised processing procedures and not directly comparable with prior years.
\5 Beginning 1992, based on 1990 population controls.

Source: U.S. Bureau of the Census, Current Population Reports, Poverty in the United States: 1997 series P60-201; and <http://www.census.gov/hhes/poverty/histpov/perindex.html>

C3.4. Families below Poverty Level, by Selected Characteristics: 1996

[Families as of March 1997. Based on Current Population Survey.]

CHARACTERISTIC	NUMBER BELOW POVERTY LEVEL (1,000)				PERCENT BELOW POVERTY LEVEL			
	All races\1	White	Black	His-panic\2	All races\1	White	Black	His-panic\2
Total	7,708	5,059	2,206	1,748	11.0	8.6	26.1	26.4
Age of householder:								
15 to 24 years old	970	600	338	227	33.7	27.8	55.7	43.6
25 to 34 years old	2,293	1,467	701	543	16.7	13.2	35.4	28.5
35 to 44 years old	2,080	1,381	572	549	10.9	8.8	23.5	28.5
45 to 54 years old	974	653	245	203	6.8	5.3	15.5	18.9
55 to 64 years old	690	463	179	126	7.7	6.0	20.0	19.0
65 years old and over	664	474	158	87	6.0	4.8	17.2	16.7
Northeast	1,393	879	441	348	10.4	7.7	28.3	32.0
Midwest	1,382	976	378	124	8.4	6.7	25.1	25.1
South	3,136	1,765	1,264	533	12.3	8.7	26.9	23.6
West	1,797	1,440	123	744	12.0	11.3	17.9	26.6
Education of householder: \3								
No high school diploma	2,819	1,902	762	1,024	24.4	20.7	39.9	37.5
High school diploma, no college	2,231	1,422	700	291	10.2	7.7	25.1	18.4
Some college, less than Bachelor's degree	1,246	821	348	154	7.3	5.7	16.2	13.4
Bachelor's degree or more	404	294	45	39	2.4	2.0	4.6	6.2
Work experience of householder:								
Total \4	7,037	4,580	2,046	1,657	11.9	9.4	27.2	27.1
Worked during year	3,886	2,671	1,026	943	7.6	6.2	17.2	19.2
Year-round, full-time	1,202	875	275	398	3.1	2.6	6.6	11.4
Not year-round, full-time	2,684	1,796	751	545	22.1	18.4	41.2	38.3
Did not work	3,151	1,909	1,020	714	39.6	32.0	65.5	59.8

Notes:
X Not applicable.
\1 Includes other races not shown separately.
\2 Hispanic persons may be of any race.
\3 Householder 25 years old and over.
\4 Persons 16 years old and over.

Source: U.S. Bureau of the Census, Current Population Reports, series P60-189, P60-194, and P60-198; and earlier reports. <http://www.census.gov/hhes/www/poverty.html>.

C3.5. Persons below Poverty Level, by Race and Family Status: 1979 to 1996

[Persons as of March of following year. Based on Current Population Survey.]

RACE AND FAMILY STATUS	NUMBER BELOW POVERTY LEVEL (mil.)					PERCENT BELOW POVERTY LEVEL				
	1979 \1	1990	1994	1995	1996	1979 \1	1990	1994	1995	1996
All persons \2	26.1	33.6	38.1	36.4	36.5	11.7	13.5	14.5	13.8	13.7
In families	20.0	25.2	29.0	27.5	27.4	10.2	12.0	13.1	12.3	12.2
Householder	5.5	7.1	8.1	7.5	7.7	9.2	10.7	11.6	10.8	11.0
Related children under 18 years	10.0	12.7	14.6	14.0	13.8	16.0	19.9	21.2	20.2	19.8
Unrelated individuals	5.7	7.4	8.3	8.2	8.5	21.9	20.7	21.5	20.9	20.8
Male	2.0	2.9	3.3	3.4	3.3	16.9	16.9	17.8	18.0	17.0
Female	3.8	4.6	5.0	4.9	5.1	26.0	24.0	24.9	23.5	24.2
White \2	17.2	22.3	25.4	24.4	24.7	9.0	10.7	11.7	11.2	11.2
In families	12.5	15.9	18.5	17.6	17.6	7.4	9.0	10.1	9.6	9.6
Householder	3.6	4.6	5.3	5.0	5.1	6.9	8.1	9.1	8.5	8.6
Related children under 18 years	5.9	7.7	8.8	8.5	8.5	11.4	15.1	16.3	15.5	15.5
Unrelated individuals	4.5	5.7	6.3	6.3	6.5	19.7	18.6	19.3	19.0	18.9
Black \2	8.1	9.8	10.2	9.9	9.7	31.0	31.9	30.6	29.3	28.4
In families	6.8	8.2	8.4	8.2	8.0	30.0	31.0	29.6	28.5	27.6
Householder	1.7	2.2	2.2	2.1	2.2	27.8	29.3	27.3	26.4	26.1
Related children under 18 years	3.7	4.4	4.8	4.6	4.4	40.8	44.2	43.3	41.5	39.5
Unrelated individuals	1.2	1.5	1.6	1.6	1.6	37.3	35.1	34.8	32.6	32.2
In families with female householder, no spouse present	9.4	12.6	14.4	14.2	13.8	34.9	37.2	38.6	36.5	35.8
Householder	2.6	3.8	4.2	4.1	4.2	30.4	33.4	34.6	32.4	32.6
Related children under 18 years	5.6	7.4	8.4	8.4	8.0	48.6	53.4	52.9	50.3	49.3

Notes:
\1 Population controls based on 1980 census; see text Section 14.
\2 Includes other races and members of unrelated subfamilies not shown separately.

Source: U.S. Bureau of the Census, Current Population Reports, Poverty in the United States: 1996, series P60-198; and <http://www.census.gov/hhes/poverty/histpov/perindex.html>.

C3.6. Monthly Measures of Poverty Status, by Selected Characteristics, by Age, Region, Educational Attainment, and Disability Status: 1993–94

[In thousands, except percent. Covers two-year calendar period. Based on Survey of Income and Program Participation.]

CHARACTERISTIC	PERSONS POOR IN AN AVERAGE MONTH OF 1994		PERSONS POOR 2 OR MORE MONTHS IN 1994		PERSONS POOR ALL 24 MONTHS OF 1993-94		Median duration of poverty spells (months)
	Number (1,000)	Percent	Number (1,000)	Percent	Number (1,000)	Percent	
Total \1	**40,009**	**15.4**	**54,800**	**21.4**	**13,105**	**5.3**	**4.5**
Under 18 years old	17,169	24.5	22,529	32.4	6,489	9.4	5.3
18 to 64 years old	19,652	12.3	28,317	18.1	5,156	3.4	4.0
65 years old and over	3,188	10.2	3,954	13.5	1,459	5.4	6.7
White	27,543	12.7	38,861	18.3	7,793	3.8	4.2
Black	10,304	31.2	13,059	40.2	4,461	14.1	6.8
Hispanic origin \2	8,555	31.4	10,940	41.8	3,262	13.5	5.0
Region: \3							
Northeast	7,303	14.1	9,892	19.3	2,822	5.5	4.4
Midwest	8,740	13.2	12,069	18.4	2,571	4.0	3.9
South	14,701	16.8	20,044	23.3	5,085	6.1	5.6
West	9,265	16.8	12,795	24.3	2,628	5.2	4.4
Educational attainment: \4							
Less than 4 years of high school	9,507	24.8	12,221	33.0	3,736	10.5	6.4
High school graduate, no college	8,263	11.6	11,973	17.3	2,120	3.1	4.0
One or more years of college	5,071	6.3	8,077	10.1	759	1.0	3.7
Disability status: \5							
With a work disability	7,059	21.6	8,991	29.8	2,519	8.6	5.8
With no work disability	15,539	10.5	23,445	15.9	3,444	2.4	4.0

Notes:
\1 Includes other characteristics not shown separately.
\2 Persons of Hispanic origin may be of any race.
\3 For composton of regions, see table 27.
\4 Persons 18 years old and over.
\5 Persons 15 to 69 years old.

Source: U.S. Bureau of the Census, Current Population Reports, P70-42 (revised after publication) and P70-45; and unpublished data from the Survey of Income and Program Participation. <http://www.census.gov/hhes/www/poverty.html>.

C3.7. Persons Participating in Selected Means-Tested Government Assistance Programs, by Selected Characteristics: 1993

[In percent, except as indicated. Average monthly participation. Covers noninstitutional population. Persons are considered participants in aid to families with dependent children (AFDC), general assistance, and food stamp programs if they are the primary recipients or if they are covered under another person's allotment. Persons receiving supplemental security income (SSI) payments are considered to be participants in an assistance program as are persons covered by medicaid or living in public or subsidized rental housing. Based on the Survey of Income and Program Population.]

YEAR AND SELECTED CHARACTERISTIC	Major means-tested assistance programs \1	AFDC or General Assistance	SSI stamps	Food assistance	Medicaid	Housing
NUMBER OF RECIPIENTS (1,000)	35,968	12,790	4,987	22,553	26,453	10,759
PERCENT OF POPULATION PARTICIPATING						
Total	14.0	5.0	1.9	8.7	10.3	4.2
Under 18 years old	23.7	11.4	0	16.9	19.5	6.6
18 to 64 years old	10.0	3.0	2.0	6.1	6.6	3.0
65 years old and over	12.0	0.2	5.9	3.9	8.1	4.8
White	10.6	3.1	1.5	6.2	7.7	2.7
White, non-Hispanic	8.7	2.4	1.4	4.9	6.2	2.3
Black	35.5	16.4	4.7	25.4	27.0	13.7
Hispanic origin \2	28.9	10.9	2.9	18.9	21.6	7.9
Poverty status: \3						
Below the poverty level	57.3	26.8	6.6	45.7	44.9	18.0
At or above the poverty level	6.5	1.2	1.1	2.4	4.3	1.8
Family status:						
In married-couple families	7.7	1.7	0.9	4.3	5.2	1.6
In families with female householder, no spouse present	42.9	23.9	3.6	32.6	34.8	14.4
Unrelated individuals	12.8	0.8	5.2	4.9	8.1	5.7

Notes:
- Represents or rounds to zero.
\1 Covers AFDC, general assistance, SSI, food stamps, medicaid, and housing assistance.
\2 Persons of Hispanic origin may be of any race.
\3 For explanation of poverty level, see text, Section 14.

Source: U.S. Bureau of the Census, Current Population Reports, P70-58 and earlier reports. <http://www.census.gov/hhes/www/progpart9293.html>.

C3.8. Percentage of Households Receiving Food Stamps, Energy Assistance, and Free/Low-price Lunch, by Race: March 1998

	NonHispanic Whites	NonHispanic Blacks	American Indians Aleuts/Eskimos	Asians and Pacific Islanders	Hispanics	Total
Percentage of Households Receiving Food Stamps						
%	5.3%	21.3%	24.2%	6.6%	17.4%	9.0%
N	4840	2707	365	296	3610	11818
Total	92152	12693	1508	4513	17141	131617
Percentage of Households Receiving Energy Assistance						
%	2.1%	5.9%	11.5%	1.0%	2.8%	2.6%
N	1899	755	174	46	587	3461
Total	92152	12643	1508	4513	20751	131617
Percentage of Households in Which Children Receive Free/Low price Lunch						
%	26.2%	66.6%	71.2%	30.5%	70.0%	42.3%
N	6598	3544	473	445	6858	17978
Total	25158	5321	664	1458	9796	42397

Source: Current Population Surveys, March 1998 [Machine readable data files] conducted by the Bureau of the Census for the Bureau of Labor Statistics. Washington: Bureau of Census [producer and distributor]. Santa Monica, CA: Unicon Research Corporation [producer and distributor of CPS Utilities], 1999.

C4. ATTITUDES ABOUT EMPLOYMENT AND ECONOMIC ISSUES

C4.1. Subjective Class Identification

If you were asked to use one of four names for your social class, which would you say you belong in: the lower class, the working class, the middle class, or the upper class?

	White (percent)	Black (percent)	Other (percent)
Lower class	4.3	9.5	9.4
Working class	42.3	56.3	53.4
Middle class	49.4	31.3	34
Upper class	3.8	3	2.6
Don't know	.1	.5	
(N)	**2230**	**400**	**191**

Source: General Social Survey, 1998.

C4.2. Satisfaction with Financial Situation

We are interested in how people are getting along financially these days. So far as you and your family are concerned, would you say that you are pretty well satisfied with your present financial situation, more or less satisfied, or not satisfied at all?

	White	Black	Other
Satisfied	32.6%	18.8%	23.0%
More or less	44.8	42.3	43.5
Not at all satisfied	22.3	39	33.5
Don't know	.2	—	—
(N)	**2238**	**400**	**191**

During the last few years, has your financial situation been getting better, worse, or has it stayed the same?

	White	Black	Other
Better	46.6%	35.7%	41.8%
Worse	15.1	16.1	22.2
Stayed same	37.9	47.2	35.4
Don't know	.4	1	.5
(N)	**2236**	**398**	**189**

Compared with American families in general, would you say your family income is far below average, below average, average, above average, or far above average?

	White	Black	Other
Far below average	5.2%	8.5%	8.9%
Below average	20.8	32.1	24.1
Average	46.6	46.9	48.7
Above average	23.7	9.3	14.1
Far above average	2.3	2.3	1.6
Don't know	1.3	1	2.6
(N)	**2237**	**399**	**191**

Source: General Social Survey, 1998.

C4.3. Relative Standard of Living

Compared to your parents when they were the age you are now, do you think your own standard of living now is much better, somewhat better, about the same, somewhat worse, or much worse than theirs was?

	White	Black	Other
Much better	32.9%	30%	37.7%
Somewhat better	30.6	32.1	30.8
About the same	21.8	18.6	22.3
Somewhat worse	10.5	12.5	4.6
Much worse	2.8	4.3	2.3
Don't know	1.4	2.5	2.3
(N)	**1500**	**280**	**130**

When your children are at the age you are now, do you think their standard of living will be much better, somewhat better, about the same, somewhat worse, or much worse than yours is now?

	White	Black	Other
Much better	18%	33.6%	40%
Somewhat better	31.9	35	25.4
About the same	21.6	9.6	13.1
Somewhat worse	9.8	7.1	4.6
Much worse	3	3.2	4.6
No children (Volunteered)	11.8	6.8	6.2
Don't know	3.9	4.6	6.2
(N)	**1496**	**280**	**130**

Source: General Social Survey, 1998.

C4.4. Opinion of How People Get Ahead

Some people say that people get ahead by their own hard work; others say that lucky breaks or help from other people are more important. Which do you think is most important?

	White	Black	Other
Hard work	67.0%	64.4%	66.9%
Both equally	22.6	20.5	21.8
Luck or help	9.7	14	11.3
Don't know	.7	1.1	—
(N)	**1484**	**264**	**124**

Source: General Social Survey, 1998.

C4.5. How Should Pay Be Determined?

In deciding on pay for two people doing the same kind of work, how important should _____ be?

	White	Black	Other	Total
How well the person does the job?				
Essential	50.3%	40.2%	53.6%	49.1%
Very important	42.9	53.0	37.7	44.0
Fairly important	6.4	5.5	7.2	6.3
Not very important	0.2	0.6	1.4	0.3
Not important at all	0.2	0.6	–	0.3
(N)	**940**	**164**	**69**	**1173**
The person's family responsibilities?				
Essential	6.9%	8.0%	7.4%	7.1%
Very important	19.2	36.2	23.5	21.8
Fairly important	24.8	18.4	41.2	24.9
Not very important	29.5	20.9	26.5	28.1
Not important at all	19.6	16.6	1.5	18.1
(N)	**923**	**163**	**68**	**1154**
The person's education and formal qualifications?				
Essential	16.5%	26.7%	22.1%	18.2%
Very important	39.0	49.1	51.5	41.1
Fairly important	31.3	17.6	22.1	28.9
Not very important	9.2	5.5	4.4	8.4
Not important at all	3.9	1.2	–	3.3
(N)	**941**	**165**	**68**	**1174**
How long the person has been with the firm?				
Essential	11.4%	14.0%	17.9%	12.2%
Very important	33.8	45.7	43.3	36.0
Fairly important	37.5	24.4	28.4	35.1
Not very important	13.0	10.4	9.0	12.4
Not important at all	4.3	5.5	1.5	4.3
(N)	**926**	**164**	**67**	**1160**

Source: General Social Survey, 1998.

C4.6. Percent of Whites and Non-Whites Who Favor Raising the Minimum Wage

	Favor	Oppose	No Opinion	Number of Interviews
Race				
White	76%	22%	2%	862
Non-white	88%	12%	0%	134

Source: The Gallup Poll Monthly, February 1995, p. 15.

C4.7. Attitudes toward Government Economic Policies

Some people think the government should do everything possible to improve the standard of living of all poor Americans; they are Point 1. Other people think it is not the government's responsibility, and that each person should take care of himself; they are Point 5. Where would you place yourself on this scale?

	White	Black	Other
Government action	9.5%	27.2%	16.3%
2	12	16.1	12.4
Agree with both	43.6	39.1	43.4
4	18.4	9	12.4
People help themselves	13.5	4.7	11.6
Don't know	3.1	3.9	3.9
(N)	**1497**	**279**	**129**

Some people think that the government in Washington is trying to do too many things that should be left to individuals and private businesses. Others disagree and think that the government should do even more to solve our country's problems. Where would you place yourself on this scale?

	White	Black	Other
Government do more	8.2%	20.8%	16.2%
2	10.5	18.3	17.7
Agree with both	39.2	38.7	40.8
4	20.7	5.7	10
Government does too much	16.5	9.3	6.9
Don't know	4.9	7.2	8.5
(N)	**1499**	**279**	**130**

In general, some people think that it is the responsibility of the government in Washington to see to it that people have help in paying for doctors and hospital bills. Others think that these matters are not the responsibility of the federal government and that people should take care of these things themselves. Where would you place yourself on this scale?

	White	Black	Other
Government should help	22.1%	37.3%	30%
2	22.3	21.9	22.3
Agree with both	33.4	28	24.6
4	10.8	4.7	7.7
People help themselves	8.8	5	9.2
Don't know	2.6	3.2	6.2
(N)	**1496**	**279**	**130**

Some people think that (Blacks/Negroes/African-Americans) have been discriminated against for so long that the government has a special obligation to help improve their living standards. Others believe that the government should not be giving special treatment to (Blacks/Negroes/African-Americans).

	White	Black	Other
Government help blacks	4.2%	20.1%	3.8%
2	9	17.6	8.5
Agree with both	28.7	39.6	39.2
4	23.9	7.2	16.2
No special treatment	30.9	12.2	23.1
Don't know	3.3	3.2	9.2
(N)	**1496**	**278**	**130**

Source: General Social Survey, 1998

C4.8. Attitudes toward Your Job

A job is just a way of earning money—no more.	White	Black	Other
Strongly agree	5.2%	10.4%	13.4%
Agree	15.3	31.9	20.9
Neither	16.7	16	23.9
Disagree	43.6	34.4	28.4
Strongly disagree	19.2	7.4	13.4
(N)	**936**	**163**	**67**
I would enjoy having a paying job even if I did not need that money.			
Strongly agree	8.4%	14.4%	14.7%
Agree	49.9	52.1	48.5
Neither	16.6	12	17.6
Disagree	18.1	16.2	16.2
Strongly disagree	6.9	5.4	2.9
(N)	**927**	**167**	**68**
Work is a person's most important activity.			
Strongly agree	6.4%	15.1%	10.1%
Agree	19.6	30.1	39.1
Neither	19.4	18.7	14.5
Disagree	38.1	28.3	27.5
Strongly disagree	16.5	7.8	8.7
(N)	**950**	**166**	**69**

Source: General Social Survey, 1998.

C4.9. Importance of Job Characteristics

On the following list there are various aspects of jobs. Please circle one number to show how important you personally consider it is in a job.	White	Black	Other
Job security?			
Very important	57.7%	61.8%	52.9%
Important	36.8	34.5	38.6
Neither	3.6	1.8	7.1
Not important	1.2	1.8	1.4
Not important at all	.6	—	—
(N)	**934**	**165**	**70**
High income?			
Very important	19.7%	38%	36.2%
Important	58.5	47.2	47.8
Neither	16.9	8.6	13
Not important	4.4	5.5	2.9
Not important at all	.4	.6	—
(N)	**933**	**163**	**69**
Good opportunities for advancement?			
Very important	32.9%	52.8%	54.4%
Important	54.5	40.4	39.7
Neither	9.5	5.6	2.9
Not important	2.8	1.2	2.9
Not important at all	.3	—	—
(N)	**928**	**161**	**68**
An interesting job?			
Very important	51.4%	48.8%	52.2%
Important	44.8	42.7	39.1
Neither	2.5	5.5	7.2
Not important	1.2	2.4	1.4
Not important at all	.2	.6	—
(N)	**934**	**164**	**69**

C4.9. Importance of Job Characteristics *(continued)*

	White	Black	Other
A job that allows someone to work independently?			
Very important	28.1%	33.1%	29%
Important	51.2	47.6	47.8
Neither	17.2	16.3	17.4
Not important	2.9	2.4	5.8
Not important at all	.5	.6	—
(N)	**925**	**166**	**69**
A job that allows someone to help other people?			
Very important	28.1%	38%	32.4%
Important	51.8	46.6	50
Neither	16.5	12.3	14.7
Not important	3	3.1	2.9
Not important at all	.6	—	—
(N)	**934**	**16.**	**68**
A job that is useful to society?			
Very important	29.7%	39%	32.4%
Important	49.1	41.5	39.7
Neither	17.4	16.5	26.5
Not important	3	3	1.5
Not important at all	.8	—	—
(N)	**930**	**164**	**68**
A job with flexible working hours?			
Very important	16.5%	21.3%	14.5%
Important	37.6	39	43.5
Neither	33.8	30.5	33.3
Not important	10.7	8.5	7.2
Not important at all	1.5	.6	1.4
(N)	**924**	**164**	**69**

Source: General Social Survey, 1998.

C4.10. Rating of Job Characteristics

For each statement about you main job below, please circle one code to show how much you agree or disagree that it applies to your job.

	White	Black	Other
My job is secure.			
Strongly agree	25.9%	18.2%	12%
Agree	46.9	40	46
Neither agree nor disagree	15.1	13.6	24
Disagree	9.2	24.5	16
Strongly disagree	2.9	3.6	2
(N)	**661**	**110**	**50**
My income is high.			
Strongly agree	5%	3.6%	6%
Agree	20.2	17.1	18
Neither agree nor disagree	30.3	24.3	40
Disagree	36.2	40.5	26
Strongly disagree	8.3	14.4	10
(N)	**663**	**111**	**50**
My opportunities for advancement are high.			
Strongly agree	6.4%	8.1%	6%
Agree	23.1	28.8	34
Neither agree nor disagree	33.2	18.9	38
Disagree	29.7	34.2	16
Strongly disagree	7.6	9.9	6
(N)	**659**	**111**	**50**

C4.10. Rating of Job Characteristics *(continued)*

	White	Black	Other
My job is interesting.			
Strongly agree	24.1%	15.2%	21.6%
Agree	51.9	47.3	51
Neither agree nor disagree	14.9	17	19.6
Disagree	5.7	16.1	7.8
Strongly disagree	3.3	4.5	—
(N)	**663**	**112**	**51**
I can work independently.			
Strongly agree	29.1%	23.4%	33.3%
Agree	52.3	52.3	51
Neither agree nor disagree	9.9	9.9	11.8
Disagree	6.6	12.6	3.9
Strongly disagree	2.1	1.8	—
(N)	**664**	**111**	**51**
In my job I can help other people.			
Strongly agree	31.5%	25.9%	31.4%
Agree	48.5	56.3	49
Neither agree nor disagree	13.3	8	11.8
Disagree	5.3	8.9	7.8
Strongly disagree	1.5	.9	—
(N)	**664**	**112**	**51**
My job is useful to society.			
Strongly agree	29.1%	27.3%	19.6%
Agree	40.8	47.3	52.9
Neither agree nor disagree	20.3	15.5	25.5
Disagree	8	7.3	2
Strongly disagree	1.7	2.7	—
(N)	**659**	**110**	**51**

Source: General Social Survey, 1998.

C4.11. Attitudes toward Place of Employment

To what extent do you agree or disagree with each of the following statements?	White	Black	Other	Total
I am willing to work harder than I have to in order to help the firm or organization I work for succeed.				
Strongly agree	23.9%	24.3%	14.3%	23.4%
Agree	54.3	49.5	51.0	53.4
Neither agree nor disagree	16.9	12.6	34.7	17.4
Disagree	4.6	11.7	–	5.3
Strongly disagree	0.3	1.8	–	0.5
(N)	**652**	**111**	**49**	**812**
I am proud to be working for my firm or organization.				
Strongly agree	25.2%	18.9%	14.3%	23.7%
Agree	51.5	51.4	51.0	51.4
Neither agree nor disagree	18.9	22.5	34.7	20.3
Disagree	3.8	6.3	–	3.9
Strongly disagree	0.6	0.9	–	0.6
(N)	**651**	**111**	**49**	**811**
Given the chance, I would change my present type of work for something different.				
Strongly agree	12.3%	21.8%	14.3%	13.7%
Agree	24.6	30.9	32.7	25.9
Neither agree nor disagree	23.2	20.9	28.6	23.2
Disagree	27.5	23.6	18.4	26.4
Strongly disagree	12.4	2.7	6.1	10.7
(N)	**651**	**110**	**49**	**810**

C4.11. Attitudes toward Place of Employment *(continued)*

	White	Black	Other	Total
I would turn down another job that offered quite a bit more pay in order to stay with this organization.				
Strongly agree	6.5%	3.6%	–%	5.7%
Agree	16.6	11.8	8.3	15.4
Neither agree nor disagree	25.1	21.8	37.5	25.4
Disagree	35.6	38.2	41.7	36.4
Strongly disagree	16.2	24.5	12.5	17.2
(N)	**634**	**110**	**48**	**792**
I am proud of the type of work I do.				
Strongly agree	32.7%	20.9%	28.0%	30.8%
Agree	47.5	47.3	38.0	46.9
Neither agree nor disagree	15.7	20.0	34.0	17.4
Disagree	2.6	8.2	–	3.2
Strongly disagree	1.5	3.6	–	1.7
(N)	**661**	**110**	**50**	**821**
All in all, how likely is it that you will try to find a job with another firm or organization within the next 12 months?				
Very likely	12.9%	20.0%	20.4%	14.3%
Likely	16.0	20.9	16.3	16.7
Unlikely	24.2	31.8	20.4	25.0
Very unlikely	47.0	27.3	42.9	44.0
(N)	**645**	**110**	**49**	**804**

Source: General Social Survey, 1998.

C4.12. Job Satisfaction

On the whole, how satisfied are you with the work you do—would you say you are very satisfied, moderately satisfied, a little dissatisfied, or very dissatisfied?			
	White	Black	Other
Very satisfied	51.2%	33.8%	41.7%
Moderately satisfied	36.5	44.3	45.4
A little dissatisfied	9.4	13.8	9.2
Very dissatisfied	2.7	7.4	3.1
Don't know	.2	.6	.6
(N)	**1735**	**325**	**163**
If you were to get enough money to live as comfortably as you would like for the rest of your life, would you continue to work or would you stop working?			
Continue working	69.3%	62.6%	72.8%
Stop working	29.5	34.1	27.2
Don't know	1.2	3.3	—
(N)	**1029**	**182**	**92**

Source: General Social Survey, 1998.

C4.13. Working Conditions

How often . . .

Do you come home from work exhausted?

	White	Black	Other
Always	6.9%	15.0%	10.0%
Often	34.4	28.3	26.0
Sometimes	48.4	47.8	44.0
Hardly ever	8.7	6.2	12.0
Never	1.5	2.7	8.0
(N)	**665**	**113**	**50**

Do you have to do hard physical work?

	White	Black	Other
Always	8.0%	10.8%	15.7%
Often	13.4	12.6	5.9
Sometimes	23.6	27.9	33.3
Hardly ever	25.0	26.1	15.7
Never	30.1	22.5	29.4
(N)	**665**	**111**	**51**

Do you find your work stressful?

	White	Black	Other
Always	11.2%	9.9%	5.9%
Often	28.9	21.6	23.5
Sometimes	44.5	53.2	43.1
Hardly ever	11.2	8.1	13.7
Never	4	7.2	13.7
(N)	**667**	**111**	**51**

Do you work in dangerous conditions?

	White	Black	Other
Always	6.0%	6.3%	8.0%
Often	6.2	7.2	12.0
Sometimes	16.1	23.4	20.0
Hardly ever	29.1	20.7	20.0
Never	42.6	42.3	40.0
(N)	**664**	**111**	**50**

Source: General Social Survey, 1998.

C4.14. Relationships in the Workplace

In general, how would you describe relations in your workplace...

	White	Black	Other	Total
Between management and employees?				
Very good	27.9%	25.4%	28.6%	27.6%
Quite good	42.7	42.1	46.9	42.9
Neither good nor bad	21.8	22.8	24.5	22.1
Quite bad	5.3	7.0	–	5.2
Very bad	2.3	2.6	–	2.2
(N)	**642**	**114**	**49**	**805**
Between co-workers/colleagues?				
Very good	32.3%	34.3%	38.8%	33.0%
Quite good	50.9	46.3	36.7	49.4
Neither good nor bad	14.8	15.7	24.5	15.5
Quite bad	1.7	1.9	–	1.6
Very bad	0.3	1.9	–	0.5
(N)	**635**	**108**	**49**	**792**

Source: General Social Survey, 1998.

C4.15. Preference for Hours and Money

Think of the number of hours you work and the money you earn in your main job, including regular overtime. If you had only one of these three choices, which of the following would you prefer?

	White	Black	Other
More hours and money	29.1%	51.5%	35.7%
Same and same	59.1	45.5	61.9
Fewer and less	11.8	3	2.4
(N)	**618**	**101**	**42**

Source: General Social Survey, 1998.

C4.16. Possibility of Job Loss and Re-employment

Thinking about the next 12 months, how likely do you think it is that you will lose your job or be laid off—very likely, fairly likely, not too likely, or not at all likely?

	White	Black	Other
Very likely	2.6%	9.1%	5.7%
Fairly likely	4.2	4.9	3.4
Not too likely	25.7	27.4	28.4
Not likely	66.1	54.9	62.5
Don't know	1.4	3.7	
(N)	**1000**	**164**	**88**

About how easy would it be for you to find a job with another employer with approximately the same income and fringe benefits you now have? Would you say very easy, somewhat easy, or not easy at all?

	White	Black	Other
Very easy	30.6%	25.6%	33%
Somewhat easy	34.3	37.2	38.6
Not easy	33.2	32.3	27.3
Don't know	1.9	4.9	1.1
(N)	**997**	**164**	**88**

Source: General Social Survey, 1998.

C5. RETIREMENT AND CONSUMPTION

C5.1. Anticipated Sources of Retirement Income, by Race: 1995

Race	Major	Minor	None
		Personal Savings	
White	46%	36%	18%
Non-White	38%	33%	27%
		401k et al	
White	35%	24%	41%
Non-White	41%	15%	41%
		Company Pension	
White	30%	23%	46%
Non-White	46%	28%	24%
		Social Security	
White	28%	53%	18%
Non-White	36%	34%	28%
		Part-time Work	
White	19%	53%	26%
Non-White	23%	44%	31%
		Inheritance	
White	7%	31%	62%
Non-White	7%	20%	72%
		Number of Interviews	
White		489	
Non-White		75	

Source: The Gallup Poll Monthly, May, 1995, pp. 20-21.

C5.2. How Much Money Saved Last Year for Retirement, Including Savings Plans, IRAs, and 401Ks, in Percent, by Race

Race	Nothing/ Zero	Less than $1,000	$1,000- $2,000	$2,001- 5,000	$5,001- 10,000	Over $10,000	No. of Interviews
White	30	2	11	16	12	13	489
Non-white	40	3	11	15	10	9	75

Source: The Gallup Poll Monthly, May 1995, p. 19.

C5.3. **Average Annual Expenditures of All Consumer Units, by Race, Hispanic Origin, and Age of Householder: 1995**

[In dollars. Based on Consumer Expenditure Survey. Data are averages for the noninstitutional population. Expenditures reported here are out-of-pocket.]

ITEM	All consumer units	Black	Hispanic	AGE Under 25 years	25-34 years	35-44 years	45-54 years	55-64 years	65 yrs. and over
Expenditures, total	$32,277	$23,750	$26,794	$18,429	$31,488	$38,425	$42,181	$32,604	$22,265
Food	4,505	3,446	4,678	2,690	4,470	5,367	5,469	4,539	3,388
Food at home	2,803	2,442	3,370	1,407	2,759	3,345	3,223	2,832	2,367
Cereals and bakery products	441	371	454	227	422	539	501	425	385
Cereals and cereal products	165	163	203	95	172	208	183	151	130
Bakery products	276	208	251	133	251	331	318	274	255
Meats, poultry, fish, and eggs	752	866	1,097	331	724	900	899	807	610
Beef	228	221	331	108	217	273	274	253	175
Pork	156	207	229	61	159	181	184	169	127
Other meats	104	107	121	52	99	129	114	111	86
Poultry	138	172	205	66	132	170	169	127	113
Fish and seafood	97	120	148	27	90	111	125	114	81
Eggs	30	39	62	16	28	36	32	33	28
Dairy products	297	209	347	155	301	352	338	293	248
Fresh milk and cream	123	92	179	66	135	147	134	121	98
Other dairy products	174	117	168	89	167	206	204	171	150
Fruits and vegetables	457	388	593	213	433	509	513	496	437
Fresh fruits	144	117	202	61	137	157	157	153	151
Fresh vegetables	137	108	185	57	122	148	166	157	132
Processed fruits	96	94	117	55	96	110	100	102	87
Processed vegetables	80	69	89	40	78	94	90	84	67
Other food at home	856	609	879	482	878	1,044	973	811	687
Nonalcoholic beverages	240	184	258	155	246	289	283	230	182
Food away from home	1,702	1,004	1,309	1,283	1,711	2,022	2,246	1,707	1,021
Alcoholic beverages	277	157	197	277	299	314	348	253	171
Housing	10,465	8,144	9,223	5,908	10,541	12,631	12,894	10,291	7,590
Shelter	5,932	4,502	5,572	3,625	6,162	7,552	7,560	5,358	3,668
Owned dwellings	3,754	1,922	2,354	485	3,104	5,066	5,576	3,799	2,401
Mortgage interest and charges	2,107	1,097	1,521	306	2,211	3,385	3,201	1,719	511
Property taxes	932	425	466	86	546	986	1,414	1,117	973
Maintenance, repair, insurance, other	716	400	367	93	347	695	961	963	917
Rented dwellings	1,786	2,433	3,102	2,985	2,873	2,102	1,334	986	931
Other lodging	392	147	115	155	185	384	650	572	335
Utilities, fuels, and public services	2,193	2,206	1,958	1,159	1,989	2,388	2,628	2,442	1,982
Natural gas	268	315	223	95	222	279	314	322	284
Electricity	870	840	693	436	762	962	1,034	984	801
Fuel oil and other fuels	87	48	19	17	49	86	92	105	129
Telephone	708	781	796	541	745	778	859	723	517

C5.3. Average Annual Expenditures of All Consumer Units, by Race, Hispanic Origin, and Age of Householder: 1995 (continued)

ITEM	All consumer units	Black	Hispanic	AGE Under 25	25-34	35-44	45-54	55-64	65 yrs.
Water and other public services	260	222	226	69	211	284	329	308	251
Household operations	508	318	316	199	701	604	445	574	466
Personal services	258	226	211	155	559	378	115	65	127
Other household expenses	250	92	104	44	141	226	330	309	339
Housekeeping supplies	430	255	387	135	360	490	501	514	423
Household furnishings and equipment	1,403	862	991	790	1,329	1,597	1,760	1,603	1,051
Household textiles	100	46	59	24	83	112	158	126	67
Furniture	327	319	278	271	391	434	397	279	143
Floor coverings	177	34	122	38	85	142	165	167	366
Major appliances	155	170	118	93	137	171	189	176	132
Small appliances, misc. housewares	85	41	50	63	71	85	101	143	58
Miscellaneous household equipment	557	252	364	301	561	653	750	712	284
Apparel and services	1,704	1,765	1,719	1,206	1,904	2,079	2,090	1,833	876
Men and boys	425	366	422	279	511	536	519	431	191
Women and girls	660	655	507	383	611	774	868	830	407
Children under 2 years old	81	92	158	95	154	106	59	45	18
Footwear	278	405	334	230	334	380	311	207	145
Other apparel products and services	259	247	298	219	294	284	333	320	115
Transportation	6,016	4,515	5,145	4,033	6,188	7,488	8,017	5,726	3,377
Vehicle purchases (net outlay)	2,639	2,077	2,497	1,913	2,846	3,643	3,516	2,208	1,166
Cars and trucks, new	1,194	927	861	555	1,273	1,730	1,332	1,118	680
Cars and trucks, used	1,411	1,111	1,636	1,322	1,531	1,873	2,129	953	485
Gasoline and motor oil	1,006	713	891	701	1,014	1,182	1,324	1,063	604
Other vehicle expenses	2,016	1,453	1,438	1,236	2,029	2,289	2,725	2,142	1,285
Vehicle finance charges	261	245	172	179	347	322	361	223	78
Maintenance and repairs	653	507	477	379	579	720	923	709	474
Vehicle insurance	713	503	528	455	668	781	930	792	531
Rent, lease, licenses, other	390	198	261	222	435	465	510	419	201
Public transportation	355	273	319	184	299	374	452	413	323
Health care	1,732	1,059	1,055	465	1,096	1,609	1,850	1,509	2,647
Entertainment	1,612	925	1,060	1,081	1,682	1,951	2,138	1,577	929
Personal care products and services	403	370	369	243	387	450	517	407	326
Reading	163	75	74	71	134	173	199	188	161
Education	471	256	293	667	335	436	1,028	566	155
Tobacco products and smoking supplies	269	176	142	245	270	310	347	314	139
Miscellaneous	766	456	526	347	687	815	1,018	548	603
Cash contributions	925	564	378	114	455	908	1,463	1,043	1,101
Personal insurance and pensions	2,967	1,842	1,936	1,081	3,040	3,894	4,803	3,211	802
Life and other personal insurance	374	345	190	69	251	440	563	555	245
Pensions and Social Security	2,593	1,498	1,746	1,012	2,788	3,453	4,240	2,656	558
Personal taxes	3,055	1,484	1,640	1,075	3,299	3,794	4,916	3,128	1,083

Source: U.S. Bureau of Labor Statistics, Consumer Expenditures in 1995; and unpublished data.

C5.4. Expenditures per Consumer Unit for Entertainment and Reading: 1985 to 1995

[Data are annual averages. In dollars, except as indicated. Based on Consumer Expenditure Survey.]

YEAR AND CHARACTERISTIC	ENTERTAINMENT AND READING		ENTERTAINMENT				Reading
	Total	Percent of total expenditures	Total	Fees and admissions	Television radios, and sound equipment	Other equipment and services \1	
1985	1,311	5.6	1,170	320	371	479	141
1986	1,289	5.4	1,149	308	371	470	140
1987	1,335	5.5	1,193	323	379	491	142
1988	1,479	5.7	1,329	353	416	560	150
1989	1,581	5.7	1,424	377	429	618	157
1990	1,575	5.6	1,422	371	454	597	153
1991	1,635	5.5	1,472	378	468	627	163
1992	1,662	5.6	1,500	379	492	629	162
1993	1,792	5.8	1,626	414	590	621	166
1994	1,732	5.5	1,567	439	533	595	165
1995	1,775	5.5	1,612	433	542	637	163
Age of reference person:							
Under 25 years old	1,152	6.3	1,081	225	456	400	71
25 to 34 years old	1,816	5.8	1,682	394	580	708	134
35 to 44 years old	2,124	5.5	1,951	531	657	763	173
45 to 54 years old	2,337	5.5	2,138	585	664	889	199
55 to 64 years old	1,765	5.4	1,577	418	492	666	188
65 to 74 years old	1,336	5.3	1,156	377	397	382	180
75 years old and over	790	4.3	652	223	260	170	138
Origin of reference person							
Hispanic	1,134	4.2	1,060	231	459	369	74
Non-Hispanic	1,829	5.6	1,659	450	549	660	170
Black	1,008	4.3	935	147	516	273	73
Other	1,929	5.7	1,747	487	553	708	182
Region of residence							
Northeast	1,730	5.2	1,544	429	520	595	186
Midwest	1,772	5.5	1,602	419	572	612	170
South	1,594	5.3	1,459	373	514	572	135
West	2,116	6.0	1,939	552	570	816	177
Size of consumer unit							
One person	1,112	5.7	992	265	367	360	120
Two or more persons	2,035	5.5	1,856	499	611	747	179
Two persons	1,854	5.6	1,667	459	516	693	187
Three persons	2,010	5.3	1,834	452	618	764	176
Four persons	2,376	5.6	2,187	650	739	797	189
Five persons or more	2,132	5.1	1,986	476	701	809	146

Notes:

\1 Other equipment and services includes pets, toys, and playground equipment; sports, exercise, and photographic equipment; and recreational vehicles.

Source: U.S. Bureau of Labor Statistics, Consumer Expenditure Survey, annual.

C5.5. Participation in Various Leisure Activities: 1997

[In percent, except as indicated. Covers activities engaged in at least once in the prior 12 months.]

ITEM	Adult population (mil.)	ATTENDANCE AT			PARTICIPATION IN						
		Movies	Sports events	Amusement park	Exercise program	Playing sports	Outdoor activities \1	Charity work	Home improvement/repair	Gardening	Computer hobbies
Total	**195.6**	**66**	**41**	**57**	**76**	**45**	**44**	**43**	**66**	**65**	**40**
Sex: Male	94.2	66	49	58	75	56	51	40	71	57	44
Female	101.4	65	34	57	77	35	38	46	61	73	37
Race: Hispanic	19.1	59	35	66	69	35	34	31	61	59	25
White	146.1	68	44	56	78	48	50	45	70	69	43
African American	22.1	60	35	55	74	34	17	44	51	54	37
American Indian	3.0	65	34	59	83	49	51	34	58	64	37
Asian	5.3	76	29	58	70	48	46	41	58	52	62
Age: 18 to 24 years old	23.7	88	51	76	85	67	54	35	57	46	68
25 to 34 years old	40.1	79	51	70	82	63	53	41	63	60	51
35 to 44 years old	45.3	73	46	68	79	52	55	50	76	71	47
45 to 54 years old	33.7	65	42	53	77	40	45	46	75	71	40
55 to 64 years old	20.9	46	33	40	69	19	33	44	71	69	23
65 to 74 years old	19.6	38	21	29	65	23	24	40	55	75	11
75 years old and over	12.3	28	16	18	56	13	14	40	44	65	7
Education: Grade school	13.7	14	13	34	46	13	21	20	40	60	1
Some high school	26.9	52	25	54	66	30	32	31	59	58	19
High school graduate	62.0	62	38	58	74	41	43	36	65	66	35
Some college	50.3	78	48	64	81	54	50	50	71	66	52
College graduate	25.2	82	59	61	87	61	55	55	76	70	63
Graduate school	17.4	81	55	53	88	57	56	67	73	71	59
Income: $10,000 or less	15.0	37	15	39	55	19	23	32	42	57	19
$10,001 to $20,000	26.5	46	26	51	69	27	31	34	53	59	22
$20,001 to $30,000	29.4	56	28	55	72	40	38	37	61	64	30
$30,001 to $40,000	32.1	71	42	64	77	46	47	47	68	65	40
$40,001 to $50,000	25.9	73	51	67	80	51	52	42	75	70	47
$50,001 to $75,000	35.0	82	54	65	86	60	58	50	80	70	54
$75,001 to $100,000	16.2	81	66	64	86	61	52	51	79	72	64
Over $100,000	15.5	87	65	56	90	66	58	59	81	70	69

Source: U.S. National Endowment for the Art, 1997 Survey of Public Participation in the Arts Research Division Note #70, July 1998.

C5.6. Percent of Adult Population Doing Volunteer Work: 1995

[Volunteers are persons who worked in some way to help others for no monetary pay during the previous year. Based on a sample survey of 2,719 persons 18 years old and over conducted during the spring of the following year and subject to sampling variability; see source.]

AGE, SEX, RACE AND HISPANIC ORIGIN	Percent of population volunteering activity	Average hours volunteered per week
1995, total	48.8	4.2
18-24 years old	38.4	2.8
25-34 years old	50.8	4.3
35-44 years old	55.0	4.3
45-54 years old	55.3	4.5
55-64 years old	47.9	4.8
65-74 years old	44.7	4.1
75 years old and over	33.7	4.4
Male	45.1	4.2
Female	52.2	4.2
White	51.9	4.2
Black	35.3	4.5
Hispanic	40.4	4.3

EDUCATIONAL ATTAINMENT AND HOUSEHOLD INCOME	Percent of population volunteering	Average hours volunteered per week
Elementary school	18.7	(B)
Some high school	26.1	3.3
High school graduate	43.1	4.0
Technical, trade, or business school	51.2	4.4
Some college	56.3	3.9
College graduate	70.7	4.8
Under $10,000	34.7	3.6
$10,000-$19,999	34.3	3.2
$20,000-$29,999	45.2	3.7
$30,000-$39,999	46.0	3.7
$40,000-$49,999	52.7	5.8
$50,000-$59,999	64.1	5.1
$60,000-$74,999	56.4	4.4
$75,000-$99,999	64.8	4.0
$100,000 or more	69.4	4.4

TYPE OF ACTIVITY	Percent of population involved in
Arts, culture, humanities	6.2
Education	17.5
Environment	7.1
Health	13.2
Human services	12.7
Informal	20.3
International, foreign	1.6
Political organizations	3.8
Private, community foundations	2.7
Public and societal benefit	6.7
Recreation - adults	7.3
Religion	25.8
Work-related organizations	7.9
Youth development	15.4

Notes:
B Base figure too small to meet statistical standards for reliability.
\1 Hispanic persons may be of any race.

Source: Hodgkinson, Virginia, Murray Weitzman, and the Gallup Organization, Inc., *Giving and Volunteering in the United States:* 1992, 1994 and 1996 Editions. (Copyright and published by INDEPENDENT SECTOR, Washington, D.C., fall 1992, 1994, and 1996.)

D. Health, Well-Being, and Lifestyles

Health involves the identification of disease and other health problems which sets a person or group apart from others. The one exception to these relative comparisons is the finality of death. Death rates, life expectancy, and longevity are absolute measures of health. Sometimes, health is measured by asking individuals to compare their physical well-being with that of their neighbors or other groups.

Important to understanding the health of individuals and racial and ethnic groups is their access to health care, both preventive and corrective. Insurance coverage is critical for individuals and families to obtain adequate health care. Mental or emotional health seems to be increasing in importance in American society. Concern about depression and other emotional problems receive great attention today. Insurance companies and state mental health agencies are coming under pressure to expand the availability of mental health care.

Life satisfaction is both a source and a consequence of good health. Obviously, good health contributes to life satisfaction or general happiness. At the same time, a positive outlook on life has been found to be related to health. Finally, leisure and recreational activities have been discovered to foster health and well-being.

The link between social class and health is significant, as those in the upper classes enjoy conditions and opportunities that contribute to good health throughout the life course. Mothers in the higher socioeconomic classes are more likely than others to have good prenatal care which increases the probability of a healthy child. Children in families with higher socioeconomic status also enjoy a diet conducive to good health and live in a home and neighborhood with fewer risks of injury. They are assured of preventive health care such as immunization against childhood diseases. When illness or injury befall those with higher socioeconomic status, they have greater access to medical care from physicians and other

health care providers. As those in the upper classes, regardless of their race or ethnicity, grow older, they receive more and better treatment for the chronic diseases associated with age. Racial and ethnic groups are over-represented among families living in poverty, and they tend to have shorter life expectancy and poorer health. Part of the difference in health and longevity in general may be the consequence of the differential life styles among racial and ethnic groups; it is nearly impossible to separate the effects of race and social class in describing the health of Americans.

D1. LIFE EXPECTANCY AND DEATH RATES

Members of different racial and ethnic groups have somewhat different life expectancies as can be seen in D1.10. For example, in 1995, a newborn White male could expect to live 73.4 years, while a newborn Black male could expect only 65.2 years. The age-adjusted death rate for Blacks in 1996 was 7.4 per 1,000 as compared to 4.7 among Whites (see D1.1 and D1.2).

The number of deaths by selected causes for 1992 through 1995 for Blacks and Whites are presented in D1.3, and the death rates from the same causes are shown in D1.4. Both White men and women have higher rates of death from heart disease and cancer than Black men and women. On the other hand, Black men and women have higher rates of death due to diabetes mellitus and Black men have higher rates of death from accidents, suicide, and homicide.

D2. HEALTH AND HEALTH RISKS

Perceptions of health for several racial and ethnic groups are shown in D2.1. As can be seen, Whites have the most positive perceptions of their health, followed by Native Americans, Asian/Pacific Islanders, and Hispanics. Blacks reported the most negative perceptions of their health. Similar findings are contained in D2.2.

Perceptions of health among teenagers vary. Black teenagers have more positive views of their health than do White teens (see D2.3). Health risk behaviors—including obesity, smoking, and lack of immunization—tend to occur more often among minority populations as compared with the White majority (see D2.4 through D2.7).

D3. HEALTH CARE

Not surprisingly, Whites, who generally report a higher socioeconomic status, receive health care, both preventive and corrective, more frequently than do other groups. More Whites than minorities have the financial means or insurance to pay for health care. The higher rates of physical examinations and routine dental examinations for the White majority are shown in D3.1 and D3.2, while D3.4 demonstrates that White women receive prenatal health care more often than minority women. Native Americans have reasonably good rates of such health care because of the efforts of the Indian Health Care Service. Minority group members tend to have higher rates of examinations for sexually transmitted diseases or for AIDS (see D3.3).

Whites' greater health insurance coverage and minorities' reliance on Medicare and Medicaid are revealed in D3.5 through D3.9. The lack of insurance deprives many minority children and adults of needed health care. Blacks and Native Americans are the groups with the highest percentages for retiring or leaving jobs because of health problems (see D3.10). On the other hand, Asian/Pacific Islanders and Hispanics reported the lowest rates of early retirement because of health problems. Whites are in the middle.

D4. ATTITUDES ABOUT HEALTH CARE

Attitudes and opinions about the treatment doctors deliver to patients are presented in D4.1 to D4.3. A general trend appears in these tables. Considerable concern is expressed about the care given by doctors in American society. For example, more than half of the "Other" and White respondents agree that doctors are not as thorough as they should be.

Health care near the end of life, especially for the elderly, is of interest in society. Concerns about economic and emotional burdens associated with terminal illness as well as controlling pain and trusting family or doctor to make decisions about medical treatment under such circumstances were raised by a significant number of respondents in D4.4. Considerable support for euthanasia is reported in D4.5 as 70 percent of the White responders, 66 percent of the "Others," and 51 percent of the Black respondents approve of ending a patient's life under certain conditions. If the patient has an "incurable" disease or medical problem and if a board of directors appointed by court agrees that the patient cannot be cured, than a majority of respondents approved of ending the patient's life.

D5. MENTAL AND EMOTIONAL HEALTH CARE

Research has documented that minorities have higher rates of mental or emotional problems than do Whites. Even though minorities have high incidences of emotional illness, they have lower rates of treatment. Both of these findings are probably influenced by minorities of lower socioeconomic status. Whites have more access to treatment for emotional illness, and significantly more Whites than minorities report they have been treated by a psychiatrist (D5.1). As a general rule, minorities report higher rates of symptoms associated with mental or emotional illness in D5.4. Information about the self-concept or self-esteem of adults is presented in D5.6. Blacks have the strongest feelings of self-esteem. On the other hand, Black adolescents in 1995 reported lower feelings of self-esteem or self-image as compared with Whites and "Other" minorities (D5.7).

D6. LIFE SATISFACTION AND GENERAL HAPPINESS

Information about life satisfaction and happiness is presented in D6.1. This table clearly reveals that Whites are the happiest, followed by "Other" minorities, with Blacks being the least content. Whites have the highest overall feelings of happiness as well as satisfaction with specific aspects of life. The other table in this section describes general feelings about how "others treat you" and what the future holds.

D7. LEISURE, RECREATIONAL, AND CULTURAL ACTIVITIES

Whites, compared with other groups, indicate that they would like to spend less time at work and more time with family and friends in recreation (see D7.1). At the same time, D7.2 and D7.3 show that Whites more often participate in leisure time activities such as visits to movie theaters, museums, or art galleries. More Whites read the newspaper every day compared with Blacks and "Others." Finally, in 1998, Blacks reported more time spent in activities in volunteer organizations than other groups.

D1. LIFE EXPECTANCY AND DEATH RATES

D1.1. Deaths and Death Rates, by Sex and Race: 1970 to 1996

[Rates are per 1,000 population for specified groups. Excludes fetal deaths. The standard population for this table is the total population of the United States enumerated in 1940.]

SEX AND RACE	1970	1975	1980	1981	1982	1983	1984	1985	1986	1987	1988	1989	1990	1991	1992	1993	1994	1995	1996
Deaths \1 (1,000)	1,921	1,893	1,990	1,978	1,975	2,019	2,039	2,086	2,105	2,123	2,168	2,150	2,148	2,170	2,176	2,269	2,279	2,312	2,322
Male \1 (1,000)	1,078	1,051	1,075	1,064	1,056	1,072	1,077	1,098	1,104	1,108	1,126	1,114	1,113	1,122	1,122	1,162	1,163	1,173	1,169
Female \1 (1,000)	843	842	915	914	918	947	963	989	1,001	1,015	1,042	1,036	1,035	1,048	1,053	1,107	1,116	1,139	1,154
White (1,000)	1,682	1,660	1,739	1,731	1,729	1,766	1,782	1,819	1,831	1,843	1,877	1,854	1,853	1,869	1,874	1,951	1,960	1,987	2,001
Male (1,000)	942	918	934	925	919	932	935	950	953	953	965	951	951	956	957	988	989	997	997
Female (1,000)	740	743	805	806	810	834	847	869	879	890	911	903	902	912	917	963	971	990	1,004
Black (1,000)	226	218	233	229	227	233	236	244	250	255	264	268	266	270	269	282	282	286	282
Male (1,000)	128	124	130	127	126	128	129	134	137	140	144	146	145	147	147	154	153	154	149
Female (1,000)	98	94	103	101	101	105	107	111	113	115	120	121	120	122	123	129	129	132	132
Death rates \1	9.5	8.8	8.8	8.6	8.5	8.6	8.6	8.8	8.8	8.8	8.8	8.7	8.6	8.6	8.5	8.8	8.8	8.8	8.8
Male \1	10.9	10.0	9.8	9.5	9.4	9.4	9.4	9.5	9.4	9.4	9.5	9.3	9.2	9.1	9.0	9.2	9.2	9.1	9.0
Female \1	8.1	7.6	7.9	7.8	7.7	7.9	7.9	8.1	8.1	8.2	8.3	8.2	8.1	8.1	8.1	8.4	8.4	8.5	8.5
White	9.5	8.9	8.9	8.8	8.7	8.9	8.9	9.0	9.0	9.0	9.1	8.9	8.9	8.9	8.8	9.1	9.1	9.1	9.1
Male	10.9	10.0	9.8	9.7	9.5	9.6	9.6	9.6	9.6	9.5	9.6	9.4	9.3	9.3	9.2	9.4	9.3	9.3	9.2
Female	8.1	7.8	8.1	8.0	8.0	8.2	8.2	8.4	8.4	8.5	8.7	8.5	8.5	8.5	8.4	8.8	8.8	8.9	9.0
Black	10.0	8.8	8.8	8.4	8.2	8.4	8.4	8.5	8.6	8.7	8.9	8.9	8.8	8.6	8.5	8.8	8.6	8.6	8.4
Male	11.9	10.6	10.3	9.9	9.7	9.7	9.7	9.9	10.0	10.1	10.3	10.3	10.1	10.0	9.8	10.1	9.9	9.8	9.4
Female	8.3	7.3	7.3	7.1	7.0	7.2	7.2	7.3	7.4	7.5	7.6	7.6	7.5	7.4	7.4	7.6	7.5	7.6	7.5
Age-adjusted death rates \1	7.1	6.3	5.9	5.7	5.5	5.5	5.5	5.5	5.4	5.4	5.4	5.3	5.2	5.1	5.0	5.1	5.1	5.0	4.9
Male \1	9.3	8.4	7.8	7.5	7.3	7.3	7.2	7.2	7.2	7.1	7.1	6.9	6.8	6.7	6.6	6.6	6.5	6.5	6.3
Female \1	5.3	4.6	4.3	4.2	4.1	4.1	4.1	4.1	4.1	4.0	4.1	4.0	3.9	3.9	3.8	3.9	3.9	3.9	3.8
White	6.8	6.0	5.6	5.4	5.3	5.3	5.3	5.2	5.2	5.1	5.1	5.0	4.9	4.9	4.8	4.9	4.8	4.8	4.7
Male	8.9	8.0	7.5	7.2	7.1	7.0	6.9	6.9	6.8	6.7	6.7	6.5	6.4	6.3	6.2	6.3	6.2	6.1	5.9
Female	5.0	4.4	4.1	4.0	3.9	3.9	3.9	3.9	3.9	3.8	3.9	3.8	3.7	3.7	3.6	3.7	3.6	3.6	3.6
Black	10.4	8.9	8.4	8.0	7.8	7.9	7.9	7.9	8.0	8.0	8.1	8.1	7.9	7.8	7.7	7.9	7.7	7.7	7.4
Male	13.2	11.6	11.1	10.7	10.4	10.4	10.4	10.5	10.6	10.6	10.8	10.8	10.8	10.6	10.5	10.5	10.3	10.2	9.7
Female	8.1	6.7	6.3	6.0	5.9	6.0	5.9	5.9	5.9	5.9	6.0	5.9	5.8	5.8	5.7	5.8	5.7	5.7	5.6

Notes:
\1 Includes other races not shown separately.

Source: U.S. National Center for Health Statistics, Vital Statistics of the United States, annual; and Monthly Vital Statistics Report.

D1.2. Death Rates, by Age, Sex, and Race: 1970 to 1996

[Number of deaths per 100,000 population in specified group. Excludes deaths of nonresidents of the U.S. (except as noted) and fetal deaths. The standard population for this table is the total population of the U.S. enumerated in 1940.]

SEX, YEAR, AND RACE	All ages \1	Under 1 year	1-4 years	5-14 years	15-24 years	25-34 years	35-44 years	45-54 years	55-64 years	65-74 years	75-84 years	85 years and over
MALE \2												
1970	1,090	2,410	93	51	189	215	403	959	2,283	4,874	10,010	17,822
1980	977	1,429	73	37	172	196	299	767	1,815	4,105	8,817	18,801
1985	949	1,220	59	32	139	180	279	672	1,711	3,856	8,502	18,614
1986	945	1,174	58	32	149	195	289	656	1,670	3,787	8,360	18,351
1987	939	1,150	58	32	143	195	292	648	1,649	3,717	8,241	18,212
1988	945	1,145	57	31	147	200	302	633	1,635	3,682	8,237	18,711
1989	926	1,133	55	31	142	204	308	622	1,596	3,558	7,957	18,019
1990	918	1,083	52	29	147	204	310	610	1,553	3,492	7,889	18,057
1991	912	1,024	52	29	148	204	312	605	1,525	3,439	7,689	17,801
1992	902	957	48	27	142	202	319	592	1,482	3,374	7,483	17,740
1993	924	946	50	27	146	209	329	596	1,480	3,395	7,653	18,257
1994	915	899	47	27	146	209	333	599	1,444	3,332	7,441	17,972
1995	914	844	45	27	141	205	333	599	1,417	3,285	7,377	17,979
1996	900	821	43	26	132	180	301	577	1,397	3,248	7,271	17,580
White												
1970	1,087	2,113	84	48	171	177	344	883	2,203	4,810	10,099	18,552
1980	983	1,230	66	35	167	171	257	699	1,729	4,036	8,830	19,097
1985	964	1,057	53	30	134	159	243	612	1,626	3,771	8,486	18,980
1988	958	964	52	29	136	173	260	569	1,547	3,588	8,197	19,021
1989	937	941	48	28	129	177	263	556	1,504	3,455	7,913	18,242
1990	931	896	46	26	131	176	268	549	1,467	3,398	7,845	18,268
1991	926	861	46	27	128	176	269	545	1,444	3,350	7,642	18,021
1992	917	781	43	25	122	176	277	533	1,399	3,287	7,441	17,956
1993	939	773	43	25	123	181	283	534	1,395	3,307	7,597	18,443
1994	932	740	41	24	124	180	287	536	1,365	3,247	7,386	18,196
1995	932	718	39	25	122	178	288	535	1,331	3,199	7,321	18,153
1996	923	683	37	24	115	156	263	519	1,314	3,176	7,230	17,903
Black												
1970	1,187	4,299	151	67	321	560	957	1,778	3,257	5,803	9,455	12,222
1980	1,034	2,587	111	47	209	407	690	1,480	2,873	5,131	9,232	16,099
1985	989	2,220	90	42	174	352	630	1,293	2,780	5,172	9,262	15,774
1988	1,026	2,190	92	44	222	417	707	1,297	2,713	5,148	9,455	16,643
1989	1,027	2,172	90	44	235	426	718	1,312	2,700	5,130	9,163	16,752
1990	1,008	2,112	86	41	252	431	700	1,261	2,618	4,946	9,130	16,955
1991	999	1,957	88	42	278	426	702	1,257	2,534	4,851	9,013	16,664
1992	978	1,958	78	41	269	413	697	1,223	2,494	4,747	8,745	16,717
1993	1,006	1,922	86	41	289	429	730	1,266	2,518	4,791	9,013	17,033
1994	988	1,797	84	42	278	434	732	1,268	2,423	4,654	8,830	16,267
1995	981	1,591	78	40	249	417	721	1,273	2,438	4,611	8,779	16,729
1996	940	1,698	73	39	235	363	632	1,190	2,397	4,423	8,588	16,017

D1.2. Death Rates, by Age, Sex, and Race: 1970 to 1996 *(continued)*

SEX, YEAR, AND RACE	All ages \1	Under 1 year	1-4 years	5-14 years	15-24 years	25-34 years	35-44 years	45-54 years	55-64 years	65-74 years	75-84 years	85 years and over
FEMALE \2												
1970	808	1,864	75	32	68	102	231	517	1,099	2,580	6,678	15,518
1980	785	1,142	55	24	58	76	159	413	934	2,145	5,440	14,747
1985	809	951	45	21	50	69	139	375	926	2,097	5,162	14,554
1986	812	923	46	20	52	72	140	368	914	2,096	5,088	14,494
1987	817	919	46	19	51	75	139	364	909	2,069	5,045	14,514
1988	831	921	46	21	52	75	140	355	916	2,064	5,091	14,851
1989	819	917	46	21	51	76	139	345	894	2,020	4,967	14,395
1990	812	856	41	19	49	74	138	343	879	1,991	4,883	14,274
1991	811	804	43	18	50	74	139	339	873	1,977	4,801	14,067
1992	807	771	39	18	47	74	141	326	855	1,971	4,731	13,901
1993	839	759	40	19	49	76	144	330	861	2,001	4,899	14,417
1994	838	736	38	18	48	78	146	330	842	1,990	4,871	14,265
1995	847	690	36	18	48	78	150	328	841	1,986	4,883	14,492
1996	852	673	34	18	46	75	146	325	831	1,989	4,879	14,441
White												
1970	813	1,615	66	30	62	84	193	463	1,015	2,471	6,699	15,980
1980	806	963	49	23	56	65	138	373	876	2,067	5,402	14,980
1985	840	799	40	20	48	59	122	342	869	2,027	5,112	14,745
1988	865	754	41	19	49	63	120	320	859	1,996	5,040	15,019
1989	852	740	39	19	48	63	119	311	838	1,949	4,911	14,526
1990	847	690	36	18	46	62	117	309	823	1,924	4,839	14,401
1991	848	659	38	17	47	62	117	306	822	1,909	4,753	14,188
1992	844	619	33	16	44	61	117	294	799	1,909	4,696	14,016
1993	879	618	34	17	44	63	120	297	811	1,938	4,845	14,558
1994	880	605	32	16	44	64	122	297	792	1,930	4,822	14,416
1995	891	572	31	17	44	64	126	294	788	1,925	4,831	14,639
1996	899	557	28	16	43	63	123	292	784	1,930	4,840	14,647
Black												
1970	829	3,369	129	44	112	231	533	1,044	1,986	3,861	6,692	10,707
1980	733	2,124	84	31	71	150	324	768	1,561	3,057	6,212	12,367
1985	734	1,821	71	29	60	138	277	668	1,533	2,968	6,078	12,703
1988	765	1,834	71	31	69	158	305	655	1,513	2,948	5,991	13,461
1989	763	1,840	73	29	68	161	299	641	1,478	2,936	5,930	13,509
1990	748	1,736	68	28	69	160	299	639	1,453	2,866	5,688	13,310
1991	745	1,581	71	26	73	159	304	633	1,400	2,854	5,707	13,259
1992	736	1,610	69	26	68	159	314	621	1,405	2,797	5,483	13,264
1993	760	1,543	72	30	73	165	317	632	1,364	2,857	5,887	13,351
1994	753	1,453	70	27	72	168	327	629	1,342	2,816	5,779	13,166
1995	759	1,342	63	27	70	167	328	619	1,350	2,824	5,840	13,472
1996	752	1,407	63	26	67	155	317	611	1,311	2,790	5,766	13,315

Notes:
\1 Includes unknown age.
\2 Includes other races not shown separately.

Source: U.S. National Center for Health Statistics, Vital Statistics of the United States, annual; and Monthly Vital Statistics Report; and unpublished data.

D1.3. Death Rates, by Selected Causes, by Race and Age: 1992 to 1995

[In thousands. Excludes deaths of nonresidents of the U.S. Deaths classified according to ninth revision of International Classification of Diseases.]

AGE, SEX, AND RACE	Total \1	Heart disease	Cancer	Accidents and adverse effects	Cerebro-vascular diseases	Chronic obstructive pulmonary diseases \2	Pneu-monia, flu	Suicide	Chronic liver disease, cirrhosis	Diabetes mellitus	Homicide & legal inter-vention
1992											
ALL RACES \3											
Both sexes, total \4	2,175.6	717.7	520.6	86.8	143.8	91.9	75.7	30.5	25.3	50.1	25.5
Under 1 year old	34.6	0.7	1.0	0.8	0.2	(Z)	0.6	(Z)	(Z)	(Z)	0.3
1 to 4 years old	6.8	0.3	0.5	2.5	0.1	0.1	0.2	(Z)	(Z)	(Z)	0.4
5 to 14 years old	8.2	0.3	1.1	3.4	0.1	0.1	0.1	0.3	(Z)	(Z)	0.6
15 to 24 years old	34.5	1.0	1.8	13.7	0.2	0.2	0.2	4.7	(Z)	0.1	8.0
25 to 34 years old	58.5	3.4	5.3	13.8	0.8	0.3	0.7	6.2	0.8	0.7	7.3
35 to 44 years old	91.3	12.7	16.9	12.0	2.6	0.7	1.4	6.0	3.6	1.6	4.5
45 to 54 years old	125.0	31.4	41.2	7.5	4.8	2.3*	1.6	4.0	4.6	3.2	2.0
55 to 64 years old	241.0	72.5	91.6	6.4	9.7	10.1	3.1	5.8	7.1	1.0	
65 to 74 years old	477.9	156.5	161.2	8.2	25.0	28.7	10.2	3.0	6.3	14.0	0.7
75 to 84 years old	609.9	226.7	142.6	10.2	49.4	34.5	24.0	2.4	3.4	15.0	0.4
85 years old and over	487.4	212.0	58.2	8.3	51.0	15.0	33.3	0.7	0.8	8.3	0.1
Male, total \4	1,122.3	357.5	274.8	57.9	56.6	50.5	35.5	24.5	16.5	21.7	20.1
Under 1 year old	19.5	0.4	0.1	0.5	0.1	(Z)	0.4	(Z)	(Z)	(Z)	0.2
1 to 4 years old	3.8	0.2	0.3	1.5	(Z)	(Z)	0.1	(Z)	(Z)	(Z)	0.2
5 to 14 years old	5.1	0.2	0.6	2.3	(Z)	0.1	0.1	0.2	(Z)	(Z)	0.4
15 to 24 years old	26.2	0.6	1.1	10.3	0.1	0.1	0.1	4.0	(Z)	0.1	6.9
25 to 34 years old	42.9	2.3	2.6	10.7	0.4	0.2	0.4	5.1	0.5	0.4	5.8
35 to 44 years old	63.0	9.5	7.5	9.2	1.4	0.4	0.9	4.7	2.7	1.0	3.5
45 to 54 years old	79.3	23.3	20.6	5.5	2.6	1.2	1.1	3.0	3.3	1.8	1.6
55 to 64 years old	146.9	50.0	50.9	4.4	5.3	5.6	2.1	2.4	4.0	3.6	0.8
65 to 74 years old	274.2	95.8	90.3	5.0	12.7	16.2	6.0	2.4	3.8	6.4	0.4
75 to 84 years old	299.9	110.4	75.5	5.2	20.4	19.2	12.4	2.0	1.8	6.0	0.2
85 years old and over	161.2	65.1	25.5	3.1	13.6	7.6	11.9	0.6	0.3	2.4	0.1
Female, total \4	1,053.3	360.2	245.7	28.9	87.1	41.5	40.3	6.0	8.8	28.4	5.4
Under 1 year old	15.1	0.3	(Z)	0.4	0.1	(Z)	0.2	(Z)	(Z)	(Z)	0.1
1 to 4 years old	3.0	0.1	0.2	1.0	(Z)	(Z)	0.1	(Z)	(Z)	(Z)	0.2
5 to 14 years old	3.1	0.1	0.5	1.1	(Z)	(Z)	0.1	0.1	(Z)	(Z)	0.2
15 to 24 years old	8.3	0.3	0.7	3.4	0.1	0.1	0.1	0.6	(Z)	0.1	1.1
25 to 34 years old	15.6	1.1	2.7	3.1	0.4	0.1	0.2	1.1	0.3	0.3	1.5
35 to 44 years old	28.3	3.2	9.4	2.8	1.2	0.3	0.5	1.3	0.9	0.6	1.0
45 to 54 years old	45.8	8.1	20.6	2.0	2.2	1.1	0.6	1.0	1.2	1.4	0.4
55 to 64 years old	94.1	22.6	40.7	2.0	4.4	4.5	1.3	0.7	1.8	3.6	0.2
65 to 74 years old	203.8	60.7	71.0	3.2	12.3	12.5	4.2	0.6	2.4	7.6	0.2
75 to 84 years old	310.0	116.4	67.2	4.9	29.0	15.3	11.5	0.4	1.6	9.0	0.2
85 years old and over	326.2	147.0	32.7	5.2	37.3	7.5	21.4	0.1	0.5	5.8	0.1
WHITE											
Both sexes, total \4	1,873.8	633.5	454.5	72.4	124.4	85.2	67.5	27.6	21.3	40.4	12.5
Under 1 year old	22.2	0.5	0.1	0.5	0.1	(Z)	0.4	(Z)	(Z)	(Z)	0.2
1 to 4 years old	4.7	0.2	0.4	1.8	(Z)	(Z)	0.1	(Z)	(Z)	(Z)	0.2
5 to 14 years old	5.9	0.2	0.9	2.5	0.1	0.1	0.1	0.3	(Z)	(Z)	0.3
15 to 24 years old	24.3	0.6	1.5	11.5	0.1	0.1	0.2	3.9	(Z)	0.1	3.2
25 to 34 years old	41.5	2.3	4.2	11.3	0.5	0.2	0.4	5.4	0.5	0.5	3.4
35 to 44 years old	66.0	9.1	13.3	9.6	1.6	0.5	0.8	5.4	2.7	1.2	2.4
45 to 54 years old	97.1	24.4	33.6	6.0	3.3	1.9	1.2	3.7	3.6	2.3	1.2
55 to 64 years old	198.0	59.4	77.4	5.2	7.1	9.0	2.7	3.0	4.9	5.2	0.7
65 to 74 years old	414.9	135.8	141.8	7.1	20.5	26.6	8.7	2.9	5.6	11.2	0.4
75 to 84 years old	549.7	204.8	128.6	9.2	44.0	32.6	21.8	2.3	3.2	12.8	0.3
85 years old and over	448.9	196.2	52.8	7.7	47.1	14.2	31.0	0.7	0.7	7.2	0.1
BLACK											
Both sexes, total \4	269.2	75.6	58.4	11.8	17.0	5.9	7.1	2.1	3.3	8.7	12.3
Under 1 year old	11.3	0.2	(Z)	0.3	0.1	(Z)	0.2	(Z)	(Z)	(Z)	0.1
1 to 4 years old	1.8	0.1	0.1	0.6	(Z)	(Z)	0.1	(Z)	(Z)	(Z)	0.2
5 to 14 years old	1.9	0.1	0.2	0.7	(Z)	(Z)	(Z)	(Z)	(Z)	(Z)	0.3

D1.3. Death Rates, by Selected Causes, by Race and Age: 1992 to 1995 *(continued)*

AGE, SEX, AND RACE	Total \1	Heart disease	Cancer	Accidents and adverse effects	Cerebro-vascular diseases	Chronic obstructive pulmonary diseases \2	Pneu-monia, flu	Suicide	Chronic liver disease, cirrhosis	Diabetes mellitus	Homicide & legal inter-vention
15 to 24 years old	9.0	0.3	0.3	1.7	(Z)	0.1	0.1	0.5	(Z)	(Z)	4.6
25 to 34 years old	15.4	1.1	0.9	2.0	0.2	0.1	0.2	0.6	0.2	0.2	3.8
35 to 44 years old	23.2	3.3	3.1	2.1	0.9	0.2	0.5	0.5	0.8	0.4	1.9
45 to 54 years old	25.0	6.4	6.7	1.2	1.4	0.4	0.4	0.2	0.8	0.8	0.7
55 to 64 years old	38.4	12.0	12.6	1.0	2.3	0.9	0.7	0.1	0.8	1.7	0.3
65 to 74 years old	56.1	18.7	17.3	0.9	3.9	1.8	1.3	0.1	0.6	2.5	0.2
75 to 84 years old	53.1	19.4	12.5	0.9	4.8	1.6	1.8	0.1	0.2	2.1	0.1
85 years old and over	33.9	14.0	4.8	0.5	3.4	0.7	1.8	(Z)	(Z)	1.0	(Z)
1993											
ALL RACES \3											
Both sexes, total \4	2,268.6	743.5	529.9	90.5	150.1	101.1	82.8	31.1	25.2	53.9	26.0
Under 1 year old	33.5	0.7	0.1	0.9	0.2	0.1	0.5	(Z)	(Z)	(Z)	0.3
1 to 4 years old	7.1	0.3	0.5	2.6	(Z)	0.1	0.2	(Z)	(Z)	(Z)	0.5
5 to 14 years old	8.7	0.3	1.1	3.5	0.1	0.1	0.1	0.3	(Z)	(Z)	0.7
15 to 24 years old	35.5	1.0	1.7	14.0	0.2	0.2	0.3	4.8	(Z)	0.1	8.4
25 to 34 years old	59.6	3.5	5.1	14.0	0.8	0.3	0.7	6.3	0.7	0.6	7.3
35 to 44 years old	96.0	13.1	16.8	13.3	2.5	0.7	1.6	6.2	3.8	1.7	4.5
45 to 54 years old	131.8	32.7	42.4	8.0	5.1	2.5	1.9	4.2	4.7	3.4	2.1
55 to 64 years old	241.6	72.0	90.7	6.4	9.6	10.7	3.7	3.1	5.6	7.5	1.0
65 to 74 years old	487.8	158.1	163.3	8.1	25.3	31.3	10.8	3.0	6.1	15.0	0.7
75 to 84 years old	638.0	234.0	146.5	10.7	51.4	38.3	25.9	2.4	3.5	16.3	0.4
85 years old and over	528.4	227.6	61.7	9.0	54.9	16.9	37.2	0.8	0.7	9.2	0.1
Male, total \4	1,161.8	367.5	279.4	60.1	59.0	54.4	38.0	25.0	16.3	23.4	20.3
Under 1 year old	19.0	0.4	0.1	0.5	0.1	(Z)	0.3	0	(Z)	(Z)	0.2
1 to 4 years old	4.0	0.2	0.3	1.5	(Z)	(Z)	0.1	0	(Z)	(Z)	0.3
5 to 14 years old	5.2	0.1	0.6	2.2	(Z)	0.1	0.1	0.2	(Z)	(Z)	0.4
15 to 24 years old	26.9	0.6	1.0	10.6	0.1	0.1	0.1	4.1	(Z)	0.1	7.2
25 to 34 years old	43.7	2.4	2.5	10.9	0.4	0.1	0.4	5.2	0.5	0.3	5.7
35 to 44 years old	66.4	9.6	7.7	10.2	1.4	0.4	1.0	4.8	2.7	1.0	3.5
45 to 54 years old	83.4	24.2	21.1	5.9	2.7	1.3	1.2	3.1	3.5	1.9	1.6
55 to 64 years old	146.9	49.6	50.4	4.4	5.2	5.8	2.2	2.4	3.8	3.8	0.7
65 to 74 years old	279.6	96.8	91.7	4.9	13.0	17.2	6.4	2.4	3.7	7.0	0.4
75 to 84 years old	313.6	114.3	77.2	5.5	21.5	21.0	13.2	2.0	1.7	6.6	0.2
85 years old and over	172.8	69.4	26.8	3.5	14.6	8.4	12.9	0.6	0.3	2.7	0.1
Female, total \4	1,106.8	376.0	250.5	30.4	91.1	46.7	44.8	6.1	8.9	30.5	5.7
Under 1 year old	14.5	0.3	(Z)	0.4	0.1	(Z)	0.2	0	(Z)	0	0.2
1 to 4 years old	3.1	0.1	0.2	1.0	(Z)	(Z)	0.1	0	(Z)	(Z)	0.2
5 to 14 years old	3.5	0.2	0.5	1.2	(Z)	0.1	0.1	0.1	(Z)	(Z)	0.2
15 to 24 years old	8.6	0.4	0.7	3.4	0.1	0.1	0.1	0.7	(Z)	0.1	1.2
25 to 34 years old	16.0	1.2	2.6	3.1	0.4	0.2	0.3	1.1	0.2	0.3	1.6
35 to 44 years old	29.6	3.5	9.1	3.1	1.2	0.4	0.5	1.3	1.0	0.7	1.1
45 to 54 years old	48.4	8.5	21.3	2.1	2.3	1.2	0.7	1.0	1.3	1.5	0.5
55 to 64 years old	94.7	22.5	40.3	2.0	4.4	4.9	1.5	0.7	1.8	3.7	0.2
65 to 74 years old	208.2	61.3	71.6	3.3	12.3	14.1	4.4	0.6	2.4	8.0	0.3
75 to 84 years old	324.5	119.8	69.3	5.2	29.9	17.3	12.6	0.4	1.7	9.7	0.2
85 years old and over	355.7	158.2	34.9	5.5	40.3	8.5	24.3	0.1	0.4	6.5	0.1
WHITE											
Both sexes, total \4	1,951.4	655.4	461.9	75.2	130.0	93.6	73.7	28.0	21.3	43.5	12.3
Under 1 year old	21.5	0.4	0.1	0.6	0.2	(Z)	0.3	0	(Z)	(Z)	0.2
1 to 4 years old	4.8	0.2	0.4	1.8	(Z)	(Z)	0.1	0	(Z)	(Z)	0.2
5 to 14 years old	6.3	0.2	0.9	2.5	0.1	0.1	0.1	0.3	(Z)	(Z)	0.3
15 to 24 years old	24.5	0.6	1.4	11.6	0.2	0.1	0.2	4.0	(Z)	0.1	3.1
25 to 34 years old	42.0	2.4	4.0	11.5	0.5	0.2	0.5	5.4	0.5	0.4	3.3
35 to 44 years old	68.8	9.4	13.2	10.5	1.6	0.5	1.0	5.6	2.8	1.2	2.3
45 to 54 years old	101.9	25.3	34.4	6.5	3.4	2.0	1.4	3.9	3.7	2.5	1.3
55 to 64 years old	198.2	58.6	76.7	5.3	7.1	9.5	2.9	2.9	4.8	5.5	0.6
65 to 74 years old	422.8	136.6	143.3	7.0	20.8	29.0	9.2	2.9	5.5	11.9	0.5
75 to 84 years old	574.0	211.1	131.7	9.7	45.6	36.2	23.4	2.3	3.3	13.8	0.3
85 years old and over	486.2	210.4	55.8	8.3	50.6	16.0	34.7	0.8	0.7	8.0	0.1
BLACK											
Both sexes, total \4	282.2	79.0	59.9	12.7	17.6	6.4	7.7	2.3	3.2	9.4	12.9
Under 1 year old	10.9	0.2	(Z)	0.3	(Z)	(Z)	0.2	0	(Z)	0	0.1
1 to 4 years old	2.0	0.1	0.1	0.7	(Z)	(Z)	0.1	0	(Z)	(Z)	0.2

D1.3. Death Rates, by Selected Causes, by Race and Age: 1992 to 1995 *(continued)*

AGE, SEX, AND RACE	Total \1	Heart disease	Cancer	Accidents and adverse effects	Cerebro-vascular diseases	Chronic obstructive pulmonary diseases \2	Pneu-monia, flu	Suicide	Chronic liver disease, cirrhosis	Diabetes mellitus	Homicide & legal inter-vention
5 to 14 years old	2.0	0.1	0.2	0.8	(Z)	0.1	(Z)	(Z)	(Z)	(Z)	0.3
15 to 24 years old	9.7	0.3	0.3	1.9	(Z)	0.1	0.1	0.6	(Z)	(Z)	5.1
25 to 34 years old	15.9	1.1	0.9	2.1	0.2	0.1	0.2	0.6	0.1	0.2	3.8
35 to 44 years old	24.9	3.5	3.0	2.4	0.8	0.3	0.5	0.4	0.8	0.5	2.1
45 to 54 years old	26.9	6.7	7.0	1.3	1.5	0.4	0.5	0.2	0.8	0.9	0.7
55 to 64 years old	38.6	12.2	12.3	1.0	2.3	1.0	0.7	0.1	0.7	1.7	0.3
65 to 74 years old	57.9	19.4	17.8	1.0	4.0	1.9	1.4	0.1	0.5	2.8	0.2
75 to 84 years old	56.3	20.3	13.1	0.8	5.0	1.8	2.1	0.1	0.2	2.3	0.1
85 years old and over	37.0	15.2	5.2	0.6	3.7	0.7	2.0	(Z)	(Z)	1.1	(Z)
1994											
ALL RACES \3											
Both sexes, total \4	2,279.0	732.4	534.3	91.4	153.3	101.6	80.2	31.1	25.4	56.7	24.9
1 to 4 years old	6.8	0.3	0.5	2.5	0.1	0.4	0.2	0	(Z)	(Z)	0.5
5 to 14 years old	8.5	0.3	1.1	3.5	0.1	0.1	0.1	0.3	(Z)	(Z)	0.6
15 to 24 years old	35.2	1.0	1.7	13.9	0.2	0.2	0.2	5.0	(Z)	0.1	8.1
25 to 44 years old	158.8	16.8	21.9	27.0	3.5	1.1	2.2	12.7	4.4	2.5	11.4
45 to 64 years old	375.0	103.0	132.8	15.2	14.9	13.0	5.5	7.1	10.6	11.5	0
65 years old and over	1,662.6	610.3	376.2	28.3	134.3	87.0	72.8	6.0	10.3	42.6	0
Male, total \4	1,162.7	361.3	280.5	60.5	60.2	53.7	37.3	25.2	16.5	24.8	19.7
1 to 4 years old	3.8	0.1	0.3	1.5	0	0	0.1	0	0	0	0.3
5 to 14 years old	5.2	0.2	0.6	2.3	0	0.1	0.1	0.2	0	0	0.4
15 to 24 years old	26.8	0.6	1.1	10.4	0.1	0.1	0.1	4.3	0	0	7.0
25 to 44 years old	111.9	11.9	10.1	20.7	1.8	0	1.3	10.3	3.2	1.5	9.0
45 to 64 years old	231.6	72.6	71.2	10.8	8.2	6.9	3.4	5.4	7.5	6.0	0
65 years old and over	765.3	275.4	197.2	14.2	49.9	45.9	32.0	0	0	17.2	0
Female, total \4	1,116.2	371.1	253.8	30.9	93.1	47.9	44.1	6.0	8.9	31.9	5.2
1 to 4 years old	3.0	0.1	0.2	1.0	0	0	0.1	0	0	0	0.2
5 to 14 years old	3.3	0.2	0.4	1.2	0	(Z)	(Z)	0	0	0	0.2
15 to 24 years old	8.5	0.4	0.7	3.5	0	0.1	0.1	0.7	0	0	1.1
25 to 44 years old	46.9	4.9	11.8	6.3	1.7	0	0.8	2.5	1.3	1.0	2.4
45 to 64 years old	143.4	30.3	61.7	4.4	6.8	6.1	2.1	1.7	3.1	5.5	0
65 years old and over	897.3	334.9	179.0	14.2	84.4	41.1	40.7	0	0	25.4	0
WHITE											
Both sexes, total \4	1,959.9	646.1	465.8	75.9	132.5	94.1	72.6	28.0	21.5	45.7	12.0
1 to 4 years old	4.6	0.2	0.4	1.7	0	0	0.1	0	0	0	0.3
5 to 14 years old	6.1	0.2	0.8	2.6	0	0.1	0.1	0.3	0	0	0.3
15 to 24 years old	24.5	0.6	1.4	11.5	0.1	0.1	0.2	4.1	0	0	3.1
25 to 44 years old	112.5	11.8	17.2	21.8	2.2	0	1.4	11.2	3.4	1.8	5.5
45 to 64 years old	300.5	82.7	110.8	12.2	10.6	11.4	4.2	6.7	8.6	8.4	0
65 years old and over	1,490.8	550.1	335.1	25.4	119.4	81.7	66.3	0	0	35.4	0
White males, total \4	988.8	318.5	243.0	49.8	51.0	49.2	32.7	22.6	14.0	20.4	0
1 to 4 years old	2.6	0.1	0.2	1.1	0	0	0.1	0	0	0	0.1
5 to 14 years old	3.7	0.1	0.5	1.7	0	0	0	0.2	0	0	0.2
15 to 24 years old	18.3	0.4	0.9	8.6	0.1	0.1	0.1	3.6	0	0	2.6
25 to 44 years old	80.7	8.8	8.0	16.9	1.2	0	0.9	9.0	2.5	1.1	4.3
45 to 64 years old	187.0	60.0	59.0	8.6	5.8	6.1	2.5	5.1	6.2	4.6	0
65 years old and over	684.6	248.8	174.4	12.5	43.8	42.7	28.9	0	0	14.7	0
White females, total \4	971.1	327.5	222.8	26.1	81.5	44.8	39.9	0	0	25.3	0
1 to 4 years old	2.0	0.1	0.2	0.7	0	0	0.1	0	0	0	0.1
5 to 14 years old	2.4	0.1	0.4	0.9	0	0	0	0.1	0	0	0.1
15 to 24 years old	6.2	0.2	0.5	2.9	0.1	0	0.1	0.5	0	0	0.6
25 to 44 years old	31.8	3.0	9.2	4.9	1.0	0	0.5	2.2	0.9	0.7	1.3
45 to 64 years old	113.5	22.6	51.8	3.6	4.8	5.4	1.7	1.6	2.4	3.8	0
65 years old and over	806.2	301.2	160.7	12.9	75.5	39.1	37.5	0	0	20.7	0
BLACK											
Both sexes, total \4	282.4	76.9	59.9	12.8	18.0	6.5	7.5	2.3	3.2	9.8	0
1 to 4 years old	1.9	0.1	0.1	0.7	0	0	0	0	0	0	0
5 to 14 years old	2.0	0.1	0.2	0.8	0	0	0	0	0	0	0
5 to 14 years old	2.0	0.1	0.2	0.8	0	0	0	0	0	0	0

D1.3. Death Rates, by Selected Causes, by Race and Age: 1992 to 1995 *(continued)*

AGE, SEX, AND RACE	Total \1	Heart disease	Cancer	Accidents and adverse effects	Cerebro-vascular diseases	Chronic obstructive pulmonary diseases \2	Pneu-monia, flu	Suicide	Chronic liver disease, cirrhosis	Diabetes mellitus	Homicide & legal inter-vention
15 to 24 years old	9.4	0.3	0.3	1.8	0	0.1	0	0.6	0	0	0
25 to 44 years old	42.0	4.6	4.0	4.3	1.2	0	0.7	1.1	0.8	0.6	0
45 to 64 years old	66.2	18.3	19.3	2.5	3.9	1.4	1.2	0	1.6	2.7	0
65 years old and over	150.6	53.3	36.2	2.4	12.8	4.5	5.3	0	4.5	6.4	0
Black males, total \4	153.0	37.2	32.9	8.8	7.8	3.9	3.9	0	0	3.8	10.1
1 to 4 years old	1.1	0.1	0	0.4	0	0	0	0	0	0	0
5 to 14 years old	1.2	0	0.1	0.5	0	0	0	0	0	0	0.2
15 to 24 years old	7.5	0.2	0.1	1.4	0	0.1	0	0.6	0	(z)	4.3
25 to 44 years old	28.4	2.8	1.7	3.2	0.6	0	0.4	0.9	0.5	0.4	4.5
45 to 64 years old	39.8	11.2	10.8	1.8	2.1	0.8	0.8	0	1.1	1.3	0.8
65 years old and over	69.4	22.8	20.0	1.3	5.0	2.7	2.5	0	0	2.2	0
Black females, total \4	18466.6	39.6	27.1	3.9	10.2	2.7	3.6	0	0	0	0
1 to 4 years old	0.9	0.1	0	0.3	0	0	0	0	0	0	0.1
5 to 14 years old	0.8	0	0.1	0.3	0	0	0	0	0	0	0.1
15 to 24 years old	2.0	0.1	0.1	0.4	0	0	0	0.1	0	0	0.5
25 to 44 years old	13.7	1.7	2.2	1.1	0.6	0.2	0.3	0	0.3	0.3	1.1
45 to 64 years old	26.5	7.1	8.5	0.7	1.7	0.7	0.4	0	0.5	1.5	0
65 years old and over	81.2	30.5	16.1	1.1	7.8	1.7	2.7	0	0	4.2	0
1995											
ALL RACES \3											
Both sexes, total \4	2,312.1	737.6	538.5	93.3	158.0	102.9	82.9	31.3	25.2	59.3	22.9
Under 1 years old	29.6	0.7	0.1	0.8	0.2	(Z)	0.5	(X)	(Z)	-	0.3
1 to 4 years old	6.4	0.3	0.5	2.3	0.1	(Z)	0.2	(X)	(Z)	(Z)	0.5
5 to 9 years old	3.8	0.1	0.5	1.6	(Z)	(Z)	0.1	(Z)	(Z)	(Z)	0.2
10 to 14 years old	4.8	0.2	0.5	1.9	(Z)	0.1	0.1	0.3	(Z)	(Z)	0.4
15 to 19 years old	15.1	0.4	0.7	6.6	0.1	0.1	0.1	1.9	(Z)	(Z)	3.3
20 to 24 years old	19.2	0.6	1.0	7.2	0.1	0.1	0.1	2.9	(Z)	0.1	4.0
25 to 29 years old	22.7	1.1	1.6	6.4	0.2	0.1	0.2	2.9	0.1	0.2	3.2
30 to 34 years old	35.1	2.4	3.3	7.1	0.5	0.2	0.4	3.4	0.5	0.4	2.9
35 to 39 years old	46.5	4.9	6.3	7.5	1.1	0.3	0.7	3.3	1.3	0.8	2.3
40 to 44 years old	55.8	8.7	10.8	6.7	1.7	0.5	0.8	3.1	2.4	1.1	1.8
45 to 49 years old	65.6	14.2	18.0	5.3	2.4	0.9	1.0	2.6	2.7	1.6	1.2
50 to 54 years old	77.4	20.3	26.2	4.0	3.0	1.8	1.1	2.0	2.6	2.4	0.8
55 to 59 years old	96.6	27.0	36.1	3.3	3.9	3.4	1.3	1.4	2.5	3.4	0.6
60 to 64 years old	138.9	41.2	51.8	3.4	5.8	6.5	2.1	1.4	2.9	4.8	0.4
65 to 69 years old	204.3	62.2	73.6	3.8	9.6	12.2	3.8	1.4	3.0	7.1	0.3
70 to 74 years old	276.5	87.8	89.2	4.6	16.1	18.0	6.9	1.5	2.9	9.1	0.3
75 to 79 years old	315.5	106.8	83.7	5.3	23.1	20.5	10.7	1.3	2.1	9.4	0.2
80 to 84 years old	336.7	123.3	68.4	5.7	30.6	18.7	15.3	1.0	1.3	8.7	0.1
85 years old and over	561.3	235.3	66.2	9.7	59.4	19.1	37.6	0.8	0.8	10.1	0.1
Male, total \4	1,173.0	362.7	281.6	61.4	61.6	53.9	37.8	25.4	16.5	26.1	17.7
Under 1 year old	16.6	0.3	(Z)	0.4	0.1	(Z)	0.3	(X)	(Z)	-	0.2
1 to 4 years old	3.6	0.1	0.3	1.4	(Z)	(Z)	0.1	(X)	(Z)	(Z)	0.3
5 to 9 years old	2.2	0.1	0.3	1.0	(Z)	(Z)	(Z)	(Z)	(Z)	(Z)	0.1
10 to 14 years old	3.0	0.1	0.3	1.3	(Z)	0.1	(Z)	0.3	(Z)	(Z)	0.3
15 to 19 years old	11.1	0.3	0.4	4.6	(Z)	0.1	0.1	1.6	(Z)	(Z)	2.8
20 to 24 years old	14.7	0.4	0.6	5.7	0.1	0.1	0.7	2.5	(Z)	0.1	3.4
25 to 29 years old	16.6	0.7	0.8	4.9	0.1	0.1	0.1	2.4	0.1	0.1	2.6
30 to 34 years old	25.3	1.7	1.5	5.4	0.3	0.1	0.3	2.8	0.3	0.2	2.2
35 to 39 years old	32.3	3.5	2.7	5.7	0.6	0.2	0.4	2.6	0.9	0.4	1.7
40 to 44 years old	37.8	6.5	5.0	5.1	0.9	0.2	0.5	2.4	1.8	0.6	1.4
45 to 49 years old	42.6	10.7	8.5	4.0	1.4	0.5	0.7	2.0	2.0	1.0	0.9
50 to 54 years old	48.3	14.9	13.3	2.9	1.6	0.9	0.7	1.5	1.9	1.3	0.6
55 to 59 years old	58.8	19.0	19.3	2.3	2.2	1.8	0.8	1.1	1.7	1.8	0.4
60 to 64 years old	83.4	27.7	29.0	2.3	3.2	3.5	1.3	1.1	1.9	2.4	0.3
65 to 69 years old	119.4	39.7	41.4	2.4	5.0	6.6	2.2	1.1	1.9	3.4	0.2
70 to 74 years old	154.6	52.3	49.5	2.6	8.0	9.8	4.0	1.3	1.8	4.1	0.1
75 to 79 years old	164.4	57.1	44.9	2.9	10.5	11.1	5.8	1.1	1.1	4.2	0.1
80 to 84 years old	155.0	56.1	34.9	2.8	11.9	9.8	7.4	0.8	0.6	3.4	0.1

D1.3. Death Rates, by Selected Causes, by Race and Age: 1992 to 1995 *(continued)*

AGE, SEX, AND RACE	Total \1	Heart disease	Cancer	Accidents and adverse effects	Cerebro-vascular diseases	Chronic obstructive pulmonary diseases \2	Pneumonia, flu	Suicide	Chronic liver disease, cirrhosis	Diabetes mellitus	Homicide & legal inter-vention
85 years old and over	182.8	71.6	28.9	3.7	15.6	9.1	13.1	0.6	0.4	2.9	(Z)
Female, total \4	1,139.2	374.8	256.8	31.9	96.4	49.0	45.1	5.9	8.7	33.1	5.2
Under 1 year old	13.0	0.3	(Z)	0.4	0.1	(Z)	0.2	(X)	(Z)	-	0.1
1 to 4 years old	2.8	0.1	0.2	0.9	(Z)	(Z)	0.1	(X)	(Z)	(Z)	0.2
5 to 9 years old	1.6	0.1	0.2	0.6	(Z)	(Z)	(Z)	-	-	(Z)	0.1
10 to 14 years old	1.8	0.1	0.2	0.7	(Z)	(Z)	(Z)	0.1	(Z)	(Z)	0.1
15 to 19 years old	4.0	0.1	0.3	2.0	(Z)	0.1	(Z)	0.3	(Z)	(Z)	0.5
20 to 24 years old	4.4	0.2	0.4	1.5	0.1	0.1	0.1	0.4	(Z)	(Z)	0.5
25 to 29 years old	6.1	0.4	0.8	1.4	0.1	0.1	0.1	0.4	(Z)	0.1	0.6
30 to 34 years old	9.8	0.7	1.7	1.7	0.3	0.1	0.2	0.6	0.1	0.2	0.7
35 to 39 years old	14.1	1.4	3.6	1.8	0.5	0.2	0.2	0.7	0.4	0.3	0.6
40 to 44 years old	18.0	2.2	5.8	1.6	0.8	0.3	0.3	0.7	0.6	0.4	0.5
45 to 49 years old	23.0	3.5	9.5	1.3	1.1	0.5	0.3	0.6	0.7	0.7	0.3
50 to 54 years old	29.1	5.4	12.9	1.1	1.4	0.9	0.4	0.5	0.7	1.0	0.2
55 to 59 years old	37.8	8.0	16.8	1.0	1.8	1.7	0.5	0.3	0.8	1.6	0.1
60 to 64 years old	55.4	13.5	22.9	1.2	2.6	3.0	0.8	0.3	0.9	2.4	0.1
65 to 69 years old	84.9	22.5	32.2	1.4	4.6	5.5	1.5	0.3	1.1	3.7	0.1
70 to 74 years old	122.0	35.6	39.8	2.0	8.1	8.1	2.9	0.3	1.1	5.0	0.1
75 to 79 years old	151.1	49.7	38.8	2.4	12.6	9.4	4.9	0.2	1.0	5.2	0.1
80 to 84 years old	181.6	67.2	33.6	2.9	18.6	8.9	7.8	0.2	0.7	5.3	0.1
85 years old and over	378.4	163.7	37.3	6.0	43.7	10.0	24.5	0.1	0.5	7.1	0.1
WHITE											
Both sexes, total \4	1,987.4	649.1	468.9	77.7	136.5	95.1	73.6	28.2	21.4	47.5	11.4
Under 1 year old	19.5	0.5	0.1	0.5	0.2	(Z)	0.3	(X)	(Z)	-	0.2
1 to 4 years old	4.4	0.2	0.4	1.6	(Z)	(Z)	0.1	(X)	(Z)	(Z)	0.2
5 to 9 years old	2.7	0.1	0.4	1.2	(Z)	(Z)	(Z)	(Z)	(Z)	(Z)	0.1
10 to 14 years old	3.5	0.1	0.4	1.5	(Z)	0.1	(Z)	0.3	(Z)	(Z)	0.2
15 to 19 years old	10.9	0.3	0.5	5.6	(Z)	0.1	0.1	1.6	(Z)	(Z)	1.4
20 to 24 years old	13.3	0.4	0.7	6.0	0.1	0.1	0.1	2.4	(Z)	0.1	1.6
25 to 29 years old	15.7	0.7	1.3	5.2	0.1	0.1	0.1	2.4	0.1	0.1	1.5
30 to 34 years old	24.9	1.6	2.5	5.8	0.4	0.1	0.3	3.0	0.4	0.3	1.4
35 to 39 years old	33.1	3.5	5.0	6.0	0.7	0.2	0.4	3.0	1.0	0.5	1.2
40 to 44 years old	40.1	6.4	8.5	5.3	1.0	0.4	0.5	2.9	1.9	0.8	1.0
45 to 49 years old	49.3	10.7	14.5	4.2	1.6	0.7	0.7	2.4	2.1	1.2	0.7
50 to 54 years old	60.5	15.9	21.4	3.3	2.1	1.5	0.8	1.8	2.1	1.7	0.5
55 to 59 years old	77.3	21.5	30.1	2.7	2.7	3.0	1.0	1.3	2.0	2.4	0.3
60 to 64 years old	114.3	33.8	43.7	2.8	4.4	5.9	1.7	1.3	2.5	3.5	0.3
65 to 69 years old	174.0	52.7	64.0	3.2	7.6	11.2	3.1	1.3	2.7	5.5	0.2
70 to 74 years old	241.3	76.3	78.8	4.0	13.5	16.7	6.0	1.4	2.7	7.3	0.2
75 to 79 years old	281.8	95.3	75.1	4.7	20.1	19.3	9.6	1.3	2.0	7.9	0.1
80 to 84 years old	304.6	112.0	61.7	5.1	27.5	17.7	13.9	1.0	1.2	7.4	0.1
85 years old and over	515.9	217.3	59.8	9.0	54.5	18.1	34.9	0.8	0.8	8.7	0.1
White males, total \4	997.3	318.8	244.0	50.7	52.0	49.3	32.9	22.9	14.1	21.4	8.3
Under 1 year old	11.1	0.2	(Z)	0.3	0.1	(Z)	0.2	(X)	(Z)	-	0.1
1 to 4 years old	2.5	0.1	0.2	1.0	(Z)	(Z)	(Z)	(X)	(Z)	(Z)	0.1
5 to 9 years old	1.6	0.1	0.2	0.7	(Z)	(Z)	(Z)	(Z)	(Z)	(Z)	0.1
10 to 14 years old	2.2	0.1	0.2	1.0	(Z)	(Z)	(Z)	0.2	(Z)	(Z)	0.2
15 to 19 years old	7.8	0.2	0.3	3.8	(Z)	(Z)	(Z)	1.4	(Z)	(Z)	1.1
20 to 24 years old	10.2	0.2	0.5	4.7	(Z)	(Z)	0.1	2.1	(Z)	(Z)	1.3
25 to 29 years old	11.7	0.4	0.7	4.0	0.1	(Z)	0.1	2.1	0.1	0.1	1.1
30 to 34 years old	18.3	1.2	1.2	4.4	0.2	0.1	0.2	2.4	0.3	0.2	1.1
35 to 39 years old	23.5	2.6	2.2	4.6	0.4	0.1	0.3	2.4	0.7	0.3	0.9
40 to 44 years old	27.6	4.9	3.9	4.0	0.6	0.1	0.3	2.2	1.4	0.5	0.8
45 to 49 years old	32.2	8.4	6.9	3.1	0.9	0.3	0.4	1.8	1.6	0.7	0.5
50 to 54 years old	37.9	12.1	10.8	2.4	1.1	0.7	0.5	1.4	1.5	1.0	0.3
55 to 59 years old	47.4	15.6	16.0	1.9	1.5	1.5	0.6	1.1	1.4	1.3	0.2
60 to 64 years old	69.4	23.3	24.4	1.9	2.4	3.1	1.0	1.0	1.7	1.8	0.2
65 to 69 years old	102.6	34.3	35.9	2.0	4.0	6.0	1.8	1.1	1.7	2.8	0.2
70 to 74 years old	135.9	46.2	43.5	2.3	6.7	9.0	3.5	1.2	1.6	3.5	0.1
75 to 79 years old	147.5	51.6	40.1	2.5	9.1	10.4	5.2	1.1	1.1	3.6	0.1
80 to 84 years old	140.9	51.5	31.3	2.5	10.7	9.2	6.7	0.8	0.6	3.0	(Z)
85 years old and over	166.8	65.8	25.8	3.4	14.2	8.5	12.0	0.6	0.3	2.6	(Z)

D1.3. Death Rates, by Selected Causes, by Race and Age: 1992 to 1995 *(continued)*

AGE, SEX, AND RACE	Total \1	Heart disease	Cancer	Accidents and adverse effects	Cerebro-vascular diseases	Chronic obstructive pulmonary diseases \2	Pneu-monia, flu	Suicide	Chronic liver disease, cirrhosis	Diabetes mellitus	Homicide & legal inter-vention
White females, total \4	990.2	330.3	224.9	27.1	84.4	45.8	40.7	5.3	7.3	26.1	3.0
Under 1 year old	8.4	0.2	(Z)	0.2	0.1	(Z)	0.1	(X)	(Z)	-	0.1
1 to 4 years old	1.9	0.1	0.1	0.7	(Z)	(Z)	(Z)	(X)	(Z)	-	0.1
5 to 9 years old	1.1	(Z)	0.2	0.4	(Z)	(Z)	(Z)	-	-	(Z)	(Z)
10 to 14 years old	1.3	(Z)	0.2	0.5	(Z)	(Z)	(Z)	0.1	(Z)	(Z)	0.1
15 to 19 years old	3.1	0.1	0.2	1.7	(Z)	(Z)	(Z)	0.2	(Z)	(Z)	0.3
20 to 24 years old	3.1	0.1	0.3	1.3	(Z)	(Z)	(Z)	0.3	(Z)	(Z)	0.3
25 to 29 years old	4.1	0.3	0.6	1.1	0.1	(Z)	0.6	0.4	(Z)	0.1	0.3
30 to 34 years old	6.6	0.5	1.3	1.3	0.2	0.1	0.1	0.5	0.1	0.1	0.4
35 to 39 years old	9.7	0.9	2.8	1.4	0.3	0.1	0.2	0.6	0.3	0.2	0.3
40 to 44 years old	12.5	1.4	4.6	1.3	0.4	0.2	0.2	0.6	0.4	0.3	0.3
45 to 49 years old	17.1	2.3	7.7	1.0	0.7	0.4	0.2	0.6	0.5	0.5	0.2
50 to 54 years old	22.6	3.8	10.7	0.9	1.0	0.8	0.3	0.4	0.5	0.7	0.1
55 to 59 years old	29.9	6.0	14.1	0.8	1.3	1.5	0.4	0.3	0.6	1.1	0.1
60 to 64 years old	44.9	10.5	19.4	1.0	1.9	2.7	0.7	0.3	0.8	1.7	0.1
65 to 69 years old	71.4	18.3	28.1	1.2	3.6	5.2	1.3	0.3	1.0	2.7	0.1
70 to 74 years old	105.4	30.0	35.3	1.8	6.8	7.7	2.5	0.3	1.1	3.9	0.1
75 to 79 years old	134.3	43.8	35.0	2.2	11.0	8.9	4.4	0.2	1.0	4.2	0.1
80 to 84 years old	163.7	60.5	30.4	2.6	16.8	8.5	7.2	0.2	0.6	4.4	0.1
85 years old and over	349.7	151.5	34.1	5.6	40.3	9.6	22.9	0.1	0.4	6.2	(Z)
BLACK											
Both sexes, total \4	286.4	78.6	60.6	12.7	18.5	6.7	7.8	2.2	3.1	10.4	10.8
Under 1 year old	9.1	0.2	(Z)	0.2	0.1	(Z)	0.2	(X)	(Z)	-	0.1
1 to 4 years old	1.7	0.1	0.1	0.5	(Z)	(Z)	0.1	(X)	(Z)	(Z)	0.2
5 to 9 years old	0.9	(Z)	0.1	0.4	(Z)	(Z)	(Z)	(Z)	-	(Z)	0.1
10 to 14 years old	1.1	0.1	0.1	0.4	(Z)	0.1	(Z)	(Z)	(Z)	(Z)	0.2
15 to 19 years old	3.7	0.1	0.1	0.8	(Z)	0.1	(Z)	0.2	(Z)	(Z)	1.8
20 to 24 years old	5.0	0.2	0.2	0.9	(Z)	0.1	(Z)	0.3	(Z)	(Z)	2.3
25 to 29 years old	6.2	0.3	0.3	0.9	0.1	0.1	0.1	0.3	(Z)	0.1	1.7
30 to 34 years old	9.2	0.7	0.6	1.0	0.1	0.1	0.1	0.3	0.1	0.1	1.4
35 to 39 years old	12.2	1.3	1.1	1.2	0.4	0.1	0.2	0.3	0.2	0.2	1.1
40 to 44 years old	14.3	2.2	2.0	1.2	0.6	0.2	0.2	0.2	0.4	0.3	0.7
45 to 49 years old	14.7	3.2	3.0	0.9	0.7	0.2	0.3	0.1	0.5	0.4	0.4
50 to 54 years old	14.9	4.0	4.1	0.6	0.8	0.3	0.3	0.1	0.4	0.6	0.2
55 to 59 years old	17.1	4.9	5.2	0.5	1.0	0.4	0.3	0.1	0.4	0.8	0.2
60 to 64 years old	21.7	6.7	7.1	0.5	1.2	0.6	0.4	0.1	0.3	1.1	0.1
65 to 69 years old	26.8	8.6	8.5	0.5	1.8	0.9	0.6	0.1	0.3	1.4	0.1
70 to 74 years old	30.9	10.2	9.2	0.5	2.3	1.1	0.8	0.1	0.2	1.6	0.1
75 to 79 years old	29.4	10.1	7.5	0.5	2.5	1.0	0.9	(Z)	0.1	1.3	0.1
80 to 84 years old	27.8	9.9	5.9	0.4	2.7	0.8	1.1	(Z)	0.1	1.2	(Z)
85 years old and over	39.5	15.7	5.5	0.6	4.2	0.9	2.2	(Z)	(Z)	1.2	(Z)
Black males, total \4	154.2	38.4	32.9	8.8	8.0	3.9	4.0	0.4	2.0	4.1	8.8
Under 1 year old	5.0	0.1	(Z)	0.1	(Z)	(Z)	0.1	(X)	(Z)	-	0.1
1 to 4 years old	1.0	0.1	(Z)	0.3	(Z)	(Z)	(Z)	(X)	(Z)	-	0.1
5 to 9 years old	0.5	(Z)	(Z)	0.2	(Z)	(Z)	(Z)	(Z)	-	(Z)	(Z)
10 to 14 years old	0.7	(Z)	(Z)	0.3	(Z)	(Z)	(Z)	(Z)	-	(Z)	0.1
15 to 19 years old	2.9	0.1	0.1	0.6	(Z)	(Z)	(Z)	0.2	(Z)	(Z)	1.6
20 to 24 years old	3.9	0.1	0.1	0.7	(Z)	(Z)	(Z)	0.3	(Z)	(Z)	2.0
25 to 29 years old	4.4	0.2	0.1	0.7	(Z)	(Z)	(Z)	0.3	(Z)	(Z)	1.4
30 to 34 years old	6.3	0.5	0.3	0.8	0.1	(Z)	0.1	0.3	(Z)	0.1	1.1
35 to 39 years old	8.1	0.8	0.5	0.9	0.2	0.1	0.1	0.2	0.2	0.1	0.8
40 to 44 years old	9.3	1.4	0.9	0.9	0.3	0.1	0.2	0.2	0.3	0.1	0.6
45 to 49 years old	9.4	2.1	1.4	0.7	0.4	0.1	0.2	0.1	0.3	0.2	0.4
50 to 54 years old	9.3	2.6	2.2	0.4	0.5	0.1	0.2	0.1	0.3	0.3	0.2
55 to 59 years old	10.1	3.1	2.9	0.4	0.6	0.2	0.2	0.1	0.3	0.4	0.1
60 to 64 years old	12.5	3.9	4.1	0.4	0.7	0.4	0.2	(Z)	0.2	0.5	0.1
65 to 69 years old	14.9	4.8	4.9	0.3	0.9	0.5	0.3	(Z)	0.2	0.6	0.1
70 to 74 years old	16.2	5.2	5.3	0.3	1.1	0.7	0.5	0.1	0.1	0.6	0.1
75 to 79 years old	14.5	4.8	4.2	0.3	1.1	0.6	0.5	(Z)	(Z)	0.5	(Z)
80 to 84 years old	12.0	3.9	3.1	0.2	1.0	0.5	0.6	(Z)	(Z)	0.4	(Z)
85 years old and over	13.3	4.7	2.6	0.2	1.1	0.5	0.8	(Z)	(Z)	0.3	(Z)
Black females, total \4	132.2	40.3	27.7	3.9	10.5	2.8	3.8	0.4	1.1	6.3	1.9
Under 1 year old	4.1	0.1	(Z)	0.1	(Z)	(Z)	0.1	(X)	(Z)	-	0.1

D1.3. Death Rates, by Selected Causes, by Race and Age: 1992 to 1995 (continued)

AGE, SEX, AND RACE	Total \1	Heart disease	Cancer	Accidents and adverse effects	Cerebro-vascular diseases	Chronic obstructive pulmonary diseases \2	Pneu-monia, flu	Suicide	Chronic liver disease, cirrhosis	Diabetes mellitus	Homicide & legal inter-vention
1 to 4 years old	0.8	(Z)	(Z)	0.2	(Z)	(Z)	(Z)	(X)	-	(Z)	0.1
5 to 9 years old	0.4	(Z)	(Z)	0.1	(Z)	(Z)	(Z)				(Z)
10 to 14 years old	0.4	(Z)	(Z)	0.1	(Z)	(Z)	(Z)	(Z)	(Z)	(Z)	(Z)
15 to 19 years old	0.8	0.1	(Z)	0.2	(Z)	(Z)	(Z)	(Z)	(Z)	(Z)	0.2
20 to 24 years old	1.1	0.1	0.1	0.2	(Z)	(Z)	(Z)	(Z)	(Z)	(Z)	0.2
25 to 29 years old	1.8	0.1	0.1	0.2	(Z)	(Z)	(Z)	(Z)	(Z)	(Z)	0.3
30 to 34 years old	2.9	0.2	0.4	0.3	0.1	(Z)	(Z)	0.1	(Z)	(Z)	0.3
35 to 39 years old	4.1	0.5	0.7	0.3	0.2	0.1	0.1	(Z)	0.1	0.1	0.3
40 to 44 years old	4.9	0.8	1.1	0.3	0.3	0.1	0.1	(Z)	0.1	0.1	0.2
45 to 49 years old	5.3	1.1	1.5	0.2	0.3	0.1	0.1	(Z)	0.1	0.2	0.1
50 to 54 years old	5.7	1.4	1.9	0.2	0.3	0.1	0.1	(Z)	0.1	0.3	(Z)
55 to 59 years old	7.0	1.9	2.3	0.1	0.5	0.2	0.1	(Z)	0.1	0.5	(Z)
60 to 64 years old	9.2	2.8	3.0	0.2	0.6	0.2	0.2	(Z)	0.1	0.7	(Z)
65 to 69 years old	11.9	3.8	3.6	0.2	0.9	0.3	0.2	(Z)	0.1	0.8	(Z)
70 to 74 years old	14.7	5.0	3.9	0.2	1.2	0.4	0.4	(Z)	0.1	1.0	(Z)
75 to 79 years old	14.9	5.4	3.3	0.2	1.4	0.4	0.4	(Z)	0.1	0.9	(Z)
80 to 84 years old	15.8	6.0	2.8	0.2	1.6	0.3	0.6	(Z)	(Z)	0.8	(Z)
85 years old and over	26.3	10.9	2.9	0.3	3.1	0.4	1.4	(Z)	(Z)	0.9	(Z)

Notes:
- Represents zero. X Not applicable. Z Fewer than 50.
\1 Includes other causes, not shown separately.
\2 Includes allied conditions.
\3 Includes other races, not shown separately.
\4 Includes those deaths with age not stated.

Source: U.S. National Center for Health Statistics, Vital Statistics of the United States, annual.

D1.4. Death Rates, by Leading Causes, by Race and Age: 1970 to 1995

[Deaths per 100,000 population in specified group. Excludes deaths of nonresidents of the United States, except as noted. The standard population for this table is the total population of the United States enumerated in 1940. Beginning 1979, deaths classified according to ninth revision of International Classification of Diseases; for earlier years, classified according to revision in use at that time.]

YEAR, RACE, AND AGE	Heart disease	Cancer	Accidents and adverse effects	Cerebro-vascular diseases	Chronic obstructive pulmonary diseases \1	Pneu-monia, flu	Suicide	Chronic liver disease, cirrhosis	Diabetes mellitus	Homicide & legal inter-vention
All races, both sexes: \2										
1970	253.6	129.9	53.7	66.3	(NA)	22.1	11.8	14.7	14.1	9.1
1980	336.0	183.9	46.7	75.1	24.7	24.1	11.9	13.5	15.4	10.7
1981	328.5	183.9	43.9	71.3	25.6	23.4	12.0	12.8	15.1	10.3
1982	326.2	187.3	40.6	68.1	25.8	21.1	12.2	12.0	14.9	9.7
1983	329.5	189.5	39.6	66.6	28.3	23.9	12.1	11.7	15.5	8.6
1984	324.4	192.3	39.4	65.4	29.3	25.0	12.4	11.6	15.2	8.4
1985	324.1	194.0	39.3	64.3	31.4	28.4	12.4	11.3	15.5	8.4
1986	318.8	195.5	39.7	62.3	31.9	29.1	12.9	10.9	15.5	9.0
1987	313.8	196.8	39.2	61.8	32.3	28.6	12.7	10.8	15.9	8.7
1988	312.9	198.4	39.7	61.6	33.9	31.8	12.4	10.8	16.5	9.0
1989	297.3	201.0	38.5	59.0	34.2	31.0	12.2	10.8	19.0	9.3
1990	289.5	203.2	37.0	57.9	34.9	32.0	12.4	10.4	19.2	10.0
1991	285.9	204.1	35.4	56.9	35.9	30.9	12.2	10.1	19.4	10.5
1992	281.4	204.1	34.0	56.4	36.0	29.7	12.0	9.9	19.6	10.0
1993	288.4	205.6	35.1	58.2	39.2	32.1	12.1	9.8	20.9	10.1
1994	281.3	205.2	35.1	58.9	39.0	31.3	12.0	9.8	21.8	(NA)
1995	280.7	204.9	35.5	60.1	39.2	31.6	11.9	9.6	22.6	(NA)
1 to 4 years old	1.8	3.3	15.9	(NA)	(NA)	1.1	(NA)	(NA)	(NA)	3.0
5 to 14 years old	0.9	2.8	9.3	(NA)	0.3	0.3	0.9	(NA)	(NA)	1.5
15 to 24 years old	2.8	4.8	38.7	0.5	0.6	0.6	13.8	(NA)	(NA)	22.6
25 to 44 years old	20.2	26.4	32.5	4.2	(NA)	2.6	15.3	5.3	3.0	13.8
45 to 64 years old	202.3	261.0	29.9	29.3	25.6	10.8	14.0	20.8	22.5	(NA)

D1.4. Death Rates, by Leading Causes, by Race and Age: 1970 to 1995 *(continued)*

YEAR, RACE, AND AGE	Heart disease	Cancer	Accidents and adverse effects	Cerebro-vascular diseases	Chronic obstructive pulmonary diseases \1	Pneu-monia, flu	Suicide	Chronic liver disease, cirrhosis	Diabetes mellitus	Homicide & legal inter-vention
1981	359.2	204.4	63.6	59.6	35.7	24.3	18.7	16.9	12.7	16.7
1982	354.0	207.7	58.4	56.7	35.3	22.5	19.2	15.9	12.6	15.4
1983	354.4	209.8	56.2	55.3	37.9	24.6	19.2	15.4	12.9	13.7
1984	346.3	211.7	55.9	53.8	38.4	25.7	19.8	15.3	13.0	13.1
1985	344.1	213.4	55.4	52.5	40.3	28.7	20.0	14.9	13.2	13.0
1986	334.5	214.4	56.1	50.6	40.3	29.3	20.7	14.4	13.2	14.2
1987	326.6	215.9	54.9	50.1	39.9	28.5	20.6	14.5	13.8	13.4
1988	323.6	216.7	55.3	50.2	41.1	30.9	20.2	14.4	14.3	14.0
1989	306.1	218.9	53.1	47.7	40.1	29.7	20.0	14.4	16.4	14.7
1990	297.6	221.3	51.1	46.8	40.8	30.4	20.4	13.7	16.7	16.2
1991	292.6	221.5	48.6	46.1	41.1	29.4	20.1	13.2	17.2	16.9
1992	287.2	220.8	46.5	45.5	40.5	28.5	19.6	13.2	17.4	16.2
1993	292.1	222.1	47.8	46.9	43.2	30.2	19.9	12.9	18.6	16.1
1994	284.3	220.7	47.6	47.4	42.3	29.4	19.8	(NA)	19.5	15.5
1995	282.7	219.5	47.9	48.0	42.0	29.4	19.8	(NA)	20.4	13.8
1 to 4 years old	1.8	3.5	18.7	(NA)	(NA)	1.2	(NA)	(NA)	(NA)	3.3
5 to 14 years old	0.9	3.1	12.0	(NA)	0.4	0.3	1.2	(NA)	(NA)	1.9
15 to 24 years old	3.4	5.8	56.8	0.5	0.8	0.6	23.4	(NA)	(NA)	38.3
25 to 44 years old	28.8	24.4	50.2	4.5	(NA)	3.2	24.8	7.7	3.6	21.7
45 to 64 years old	295.5	289.6	43.9	33.3	28.2	13.7	22.1	30.5	24.4	(NA)
65 years old and over	2,043.6	1,463.6	105.0	370.4	341.0	237.6	(NA)	(NA)	127.6	(NA)
All races, females:										
1970	175.2	108.8	28.2	60.8	(NA)	16.7	6.8	9.8	14.4	3.7
1980	305.1	163.6	27.1	86.1	15.0	23.2	5.5	9.3	17.6	4.5
1981	299.5	164.6	25.3	82.3	16.2	22.6	5.8	8.8	17.3	4.3
1982	299.8	167.9	23.8	78.8	16.9	19.8	5.6	8.2	17.1	4.2
1983	306.1	170.3	23.8	77.2	19.2	23.2	5.4	8.1	18.0	3.9
1984	303.8	173.9	23.8	76.5	20.7	24.3	5.4	8.1	17.3	3.9
1985	305.2	175.7	24.0	75.5	23.0	28.2	5.2	7.8	17.8	4.0
1986	303.9	177.5	24.1	73.4	23.9	28.9	5.4	7.6	17.7	4.2
1987	301.7	178.8	24.3	73.0	25.2	28.7	5.2	7.4	17.9	4.2
1988	302.8	181.0	24.9	72.4	27.0	32.6	5.0	7.3	18.7	4.2
1989	289.0	184.0	24.6	69.7	28.6	32.3	4.8	7.4	21.4	4.1
1990	281.8	186.0	23.6	68.6	29.2	33.4	4.8	7.2	21.5	4.2
1991	279.5	187.5	22.9	67.2	31.1	32.2	4.7	7.1	21.6	4.4
1992	275.8	188.2	22.1	66.7	31.8	30.8	4.6	6.7	21.7	4.1
1993	284.9	189.8	23.0	69.0	35.4	34.0	4.6	6.8	23.1	4.3
1994	278.5	190.5	23.2	69.8	35.9	33.1	(NA)	(NA)	24.0	(NA)
1995	278.8	191.0	23.7	71.7	36.4	33.6	(NA)	(NA)	24.6	(NA)
1 to 4 years old	1.8	3.0	12.9	(NA)	(NA)	1.0	(NA)	(NA)	(NA)	2.7
5 to 14 years old	0.8	2.4	6.6	(NA)	0.2	0.2	0.5	(NA)	(NA)	1.2
15 to 24 years old	2.1	3.9	19.8	(NA)	0.5	0.6	3.7	(NA)	(NA)	6.2
25 to 44 years old	11.7	28.3	15.1	4.0	(NA)	2.0	5.9	3.0	2.4	5.8
45 to 64 years old	115.3	234.4	16.7	25.7	23.1	8.1	6.4	11.7	20.8	(NA)
65 years old and over	1,701.7	909.2	72.0	429.0	208.8	207.0	(NA)	(NA)	129.1	(NA)
White, both sexes:										
1970	249.1	127.8	51.0	61.8	(NA)	19.8	12.4	13.4	12.9	4.7
1980	350.8	189.0	46.3	76.3	26.9	24.8	12.7	13.0	14.8	7.0
1981	344.5	189.5	44.0	72.6	28.0	24.4	12.9	12.4	14.6	6.6
1982	342.8	193.2	40.6	69.5	28.2	22.0	13.2	11.8	14.6	6.3
1983	345.9	195.6	39.4	68.0	30.9	25.1	13.1	11.5	15.0	5.6
1984	341.0	198.6	39.5	67.0	32.0	26.2	13.5	11.4	14.7	5.5
1985	340.6	200.8	39.1	65.8	34.4	29.9	13.4	11.0	15.0	5.5
1986	334.9	202.7	39.5	63.9	35.0	30.6	14.0	10.8	14.9	5.7
1987	330.0	204.4	39.0	63.5	35.5	30.2	13.8	10.6	15.3	5.4
1988	329.2	206.2	39.3	63.1	37.2	33.8	13.5	10.6	15.9	5.4
1989	312.6	209.2	38.1	60.5	37.5	32.7	13.2	10.7	18.3	5.4
1990	305.4	211.6	36.9	59.7	38.4	33.9	13.5	10.3	18.5	5.8
1991	301.9	213.1	35.3	58.7	39.8	32.8	13.3	10.1	18.8	6.1
1992	297.5	213.5	34.0	58.4	40.0	31.7	13.0	10.0	19.0	5.9
1993	305.1	215.1	35.0	60.5	43.6	34.3	13.1	9.9	20.2	5.7
1994	298.5	215.2	35.1	61.2	43.5	33.5	12.9	9.9	21.1	(NA)

D1.4. Death Rates, by Leading Causes, by Race and Age: 1970 to 1995 *(continued)*

YEAR, RACE, AND AGE	Heart disease	Cancer	Accidents and adverse effects	Cerebro-vascular diseases	Chronic obstructive pulmonary diseases \1	Pneu-monia, flu	Suicide	Chronic liver disease, cirrhosis	Diabetes mellitus	Homicide & legal inter-vention
1995	297.6	215.0	35.7	62.6	43.6	33.8	12.9	9.8	21.8	(NA)
1 to 4 years old	1.4	3.3	13.9	(NA)	(NA)	0.9	(NA)	(NA)	(NA)	2.1
5 to 14 years old	0.8	2.8	8.5	(NA)	0.2	0.2	0.9	(NA)	(NA)	1.0
15 to 24 years old	2.2	4.9	40.1	0.5	0.5	0.6	14.2	(NA)	(NA)	10.9
25 to 44 years old	17.2	25.1	31.7	3.2	(NA)	2.0	16.3	5.0	2.6	8.1
45 to 64 years old	188.7	252.8	27.9	24.1	26.0	9.6	15.2	19.7	19.2	(NA)
65 years old and over	1,848.9	6,126.3	85.4	401.3	274.7	223.0	(NA)	(NA)	118.8	(NA)
White males:										
1970	347.6	154.3	76.2	68.8	(NA)	26.0	18.2	18.8	12.7	7.3
1980	384.0	208.7	66.3	63.3	37.9	25.1	19.9	17.3	12.8	10.9
1981	375.8	207.9	63.1	59.4	38.6	24.5	20.0	16.5	12.6	10.4
1982	371.0	211.7	57.9	56.7	38.3	22.9	20.7	15.8	12.5	9.6
1983	371.0	213.8	55.6	55.5	41.1	25.1	20.7	15.2	12.7	8.6
1984	362.9	215.8	55.4	53.9	41.6	26.2	21.3	15.1	12.7	8.3
1985	360.3	218.1	54.6	52.7	43.7	29.4	21.6	14.5	12.9	8.2
1986	350.2	219.8	55.2	50.7	43.6	30.1	22.4	14.2	12.9	8.6
1987	341.8	221.6	53.9	50.2	43.3	29.3	22.2	14.2	13.5	8.0
1988	338.9	222.8	54.0	50.3	44.5	32.0	21.8	14.3	13.9	7.9
1989	320.5	224.9	51.9	47.8	43.4	30.4	21.5	14.2	16.0	8.2
1990	312.7	227.7	50.3	47.0	44.3	31.4	22.0	13.6	16.5	9.0
1991	307.6	228.9	47.7	46.3	44.9	30.6	21.7	13.4	16.9	9.3
1992	302.4	228.6	45.9	46.1	44.4	29.7	21.2	13.3	17.2	9.1
1993	307.6	229.8	47.0	47.7	47.3	31.5	21.4	13.1	18.3	8.6
1994	300.1	228.9	46.9	48.1	46.4	30.8	21.3	13.2	19.2	(NA)
1995	297.9	228.1	47.4	48.6	46.1	30.8	21.4	13.2	20.0	(NA)
1 to 4 years old	1.4	3.7	16.5	0.4	(NA)	1.0	(NA)	(NA)	(NA)	2.3
5 to 14 years old	0.8	3.1	10.9	(NA)	0.3	0.2	1.3	(NA)	(NA)	1.1
15 to 24 years old	2.8	5.9	58.3	0.5	0.5	0.6	24.1	(NA)	(NA)	17.4
25 to 44 years old	25.4	23.2	48.8	3.4	(NA)	2.5	26.1	7.4	3.2	12.3
45 to 64 years old	280.8	275.7	40.4	27.1	28.3	11.9	23.8	28.8	21.4	(NA)
65 years old and over	2,051.4	1,437.8	103.4	361.4	351.8	237.9	(NA)	(NA)	120.9	(NA)
White females:										
1970	167.8	107.6	27.2	56.2	(NA)	15.0	1.2	8.7	12.8	2.2
1980	319.2	170.3	27.2	88.8	16.4	24.6	5.9	8.8	16.8	3.2
1981	314.7	172.0	25.7	85.1	17.9	24.2	6.2	8.5	16.6	3.1
1982	315.9	175.6	24.1	81.7	18.6	21.1	6.1	8.0	16.6	3.1
1983	321.9	178.2	24.0	79.9	21.3	25.0	5.9	7.9	17.3	2.8
1984	320.2	182.2	24.3	79.4	22.9	26.1	6.0	7.9	16.6	2.9
1985	321.8	184.4	24.3	78.4	25.5	30.4	5.6	7.6	17.0	2.9
1986	320.4	186.4	24.5	76.5	26.7	31.2	5.9	7.5	16.8	3.0
1987	318.7	187.9	24.7	76.2	28.1	31.1	5.8	7.3	17.0	3.0
1988	319.9	190.5	25.3	75.4	30.2	35.4	5.5	7.2	17.7	2.9
1989	305.1	194.2	24.9	72.6	31.9	34.9	5.3	7.4	20.5	2.8
1990	298.4	196.1	24.0	71.8	32.8	36.3	5.3	7.1	20.5	2.8
1991	296.5	198.0	23.4	70.5	35.0	35.0	5.2	7.1	20.6	3.0
1992	292.9	199.0	22.6	70.3	35.8	33.6	5.1	6.8	20.7	2.8
1993	302.8	200.9	23.5	72.8	40.0	37.0	5.0	6.9	22.1	3.0
1994	296.8	201.9	23.6	73.9	40.6	36.2	(NA)	(NA)	22.9	(NA)
1995	297.4	202.4	24.4	76.0	41.2	36.6	(NA)	(NA)	23.5	(NA)
1 to 4 years old	1.4	2.9	11.2	(NA)	(NA)	0.9	(NA)	(NA)	(NA)	1.9
5 to 14 years old	0.8	2.5	6.0	0.2	(NA)	0.2	0.5	(NA)	(NA)	0.8
15 to 24 years old	1.6	3.9	21.0	0.4	(NA)	0.5	3.8	(NA)	(NA)	3.9
25 to 44 years old	8.9	27.0	14.3	2.9	(NA)	1.5	6.5	2.6	2.0	3.7
45 to 64 years old	100.9	231.0	15.9	21.4	23.9	7.4	7.0	10.9	17.1	(NA)
65 years old and over	1,709.5	911.9	73.1	428.7	221.6	212.7	(NA)	(NA)	117.4	(NA)
Black, both sexes:										
1970	307.6	156.7	74.4	114.5	(NA)	40.4	6.1	24.8	26.5	46.1
1980	274.0	169.1	50.6	75.6	12.7	21.2	6.0	18.0	20.8	38.6
1981	264.2	168.9	45.4	71.6	13.0	19.4	6.1	16.0	20.1	37.4
1982	259.8	172.0	42.5	68.0	13.2	17.4	6.0	14.0	19.0	34.4
1983	269.2	175.0	42.6	66.6	14.6	18.8	5.8	13.9	20.8	30.5
1984	264.8	178.2	41.4	65.1	15.2	20.1	6.2	13.8	20.6	29.2
1985	268.4	178.2	42.7	64.2	16.3	22.2	6.3	14.2	21.4	29.0
1986	268.6	179.6	43.5	62.0	16.8	23.1	6.5	12.9	21.8	32.8
1987	265.1	180.8	43.6	61.1	17.2	22.4	6.7	13.4	22.2	32.4
1988	267.4	181.6	45.4	62.2	18.4	24.2	6.8	13.1	23.5	35.0
1989	256.9	184.3	44.5	59.6	18.8	25.2	7.1	12.8	26.4	36.4

D1.4. Death Rates, by Leading Causes, by Race and Age: 1970 to 1995 *(continued)*

YEAR, RACE, AND AGE	Heart disease	Cancer	Accidents and adverse effects	Cerebro-vascular diseases	Chronic obstructive pulmonary diseases \1	Pneu-monia, flu	Suicide	Chronic liver disease, cirrhosis	Diabetes mellitus	Homicide & legal inter-vention
1990	246.4	187.2	40.7	57.1	18.6	24.8	6.9	12.3	26.6	39.8
1991	243.9	185.9	40.0	55.7	18.7	23.7	6.7	11.1	27.3	41.6
1992	238.8	184.5	37.3	53.8	18.5	22.3	6.8	10.5	27.3	38.9
1993	245.5	186.1	39.5	54.6	20.0	24.0	7.0	10.0	29.1	40.2
1994	235.2	183.5	39.1	55.2	19.9	22.9	(NA)	(NA)	30.1	37.4
1995	237.3	182.9	38.5	55.9	20.1	23.5	(NA)	(NA)	31.4	32.5
1 to 4 years old	4.2	3.3	26.3	(NA)	(NA)	1.9	(NA)	(NA)	(NA)	7.4
5 to 14 years old	1.3	2.9	13.8	(NA)	1.1	0.4	0.7	(NA)	(NA)	4.3
15 to 24 years old	5.7	4.8	23.4	(NA)	1.7	(NA)	11.6	(NA)	(NA)	88.1
25 to 44 years old	43.5	37.6	41.3	11.6	(NA)	6.8	10.5	7.8	6.0	53.0
45 to 64 years old	353.4	373.2	47.9	74.5	27.8	22.7	(NA)	31.8	52.8	18.5
65 years old and over	1,988.3	1,349.2	89.0	478.4	167.3	196.7	(NA)	(NA)	240.1	(NA)
Black males:										
1970	375.9	198.0	119.5	122.5	(NA)	53.8	9.9	33.1	21.2	82.1
1980	301.0	205.5	77.1	73.1	19.3	26.9	10.3	24.0	16.0	66.6
1981	290.0	206.4	70.3	68.3	19.8	25.0	10.3	21.4	15.0	64.8
1982	284.0	209.4	65.0	64.7	19.1	22.2	10.2	18.5	14.4	59.5
1983	290.9	212.2	63.7	61.8	21.4	24.2	10.0	18.4	16.1	51.8
1984	285.2	216.4	63.0	60.7	21.9	25.0	10.7	18.4	16.2	49.2
1985	288.6	214.9	64.8	59.2	23.4	27.1	11.0	19.4	16.5	49.0
1986	285.5	214.5	66.0	58.0	24.1	28.0	11.2	17.6	16.8	55.8
1987	280.7	215.8	66.0	56.6	23.9	27.4	11.8	18.6	17.2	54.2
1988	281.6	215.7	68.4	57.6	25.9	28.8	11.7	17.6	18.8	59.1
1989	268.8	220.6	66.7	54.3	25.2	29.2	12.4	17.7	21.5	62.3
1990	256.8	221.9	60.7	53.1	25.2	28.9	12.0	16.6	21.1	69.2
1991	253.9	217.5	59.8	52.1	24.5	26.7	12.1	14.5	22.1	72.0
1992	246.9	214.4	54.9	49.5	23.8	25.5	12.0	14.5	21.8	67.5
1993	251.4	216.8	58.3	49.8	25.7	26.6	12.5	13.8	23.9	69.7
1994	240.4	212.1	57.0	50.5	24.9	25.2	(NA)	(NA)	24.7	65.1
1995	244.2	209.1	56.2	51.0	24.9	25.6	(NA)	(NA)	26.1	56.3
1 to 4 years old	3.9	3.2	30.8	(NA)	(NA)	2.1	(NA)	(NA)	(NA)	8.4
5 to 14 years old	1.5	3.3	18.0	(NA)	1.3	(S)	1.1	(NA)	(NA)	5.6
15 to 24 years old	6.8	5.4	52.6	(NA)	2.1	(NA)	20.6	(NA)	1.0	157.6
25 to 44 years old	57.6	35.4	65.3	12.3	(NA)	8.5	18.9	10.7	7.1	90.9
45 to 64 years old	484.7	468.2	78.4	92.1	34.1	32.9	(NA)	49.0	54.9	33.4
65 years old and over	2,203.6	1,933.5	126.4	485.2	264.5	244.6	(NA)	(NA)	211.1	(NA)
Black females:										
1970	251.7	123.5	35.3	107.9	(NA)	29.2	2.9	17.8	30.9	15.0
1980	249.7	136.5	26.9	77.9	6.8	16.1	2.2	12.6	25.2	13.5
1981	241.2	135.2	23.0	74.5	6.8	14.5	2.4	11.2	24.7	12.8
1982	238.1	138.5	22.3	70.9	7.9	13.2	2.2	9.9	23.1	12.0
1983	249.7	141.6	23.8	70.9	8.5	13.9	2.1	9.9	25.0	11.4
1984	246.4	143.9	22.1	69.1	9.2	15.7	2.2	9.7	24.5	11.3
1985	250.3	145.2	22.9	68.6	10.0	17.8	2.1	9.6	25.7	11.1
1986	253.4	148.3	23.3	65.6	10.2	18.8	2.3	8.8	26.2	12.2
1987	251.1	149.5	23.4	65.1	11.2	17.9	2.1	8.7	26.6	12.7
1988	254.6	150.9	24.8	66.3	11.7	20.1	2.4	9.1	27.7	13.3
1989	246.2	151.8	24.6	64.5	13.1	21.5	2.4	8.4	30.7	13.1
1990	237.0	156.1	22.8	60.7	12.6	21.2	2.3	8.5	31.5	13.5
1991	235.0	157.4	22.2	59.0	13.4	20.9	1.9	8.1	32.0	14.2
1992	231.6	157.6	21.5	57.8	13.7	19.5	2.0	6.8	32.3	13.1
1993	240.2	158.4	22.5	58.8	14.9	21.7	2.1	6.7	33.9	13.6
1994	230.6	157.6	22.9	59.3	15.4	20.8	(NA)	(NA)	35.0	(NA)
1995	231.3	159.1	22.5	60.4	15.8	21.7	(NA)	(NA)	36.1	(NA)
1 to 4 years old	4.4	3.4	21.7	(NA)	(NA)	1.8	(NA)	(NA)	(NA)	6.4
5 to 14 years old	1.2	2.5	9.5	(NA)	0.8	(NA)	(S)	(NA)	(NA)	3.0
15 to 24 years old	4.7	4.2	15.0	(NA)	1.2	(NA)	2.7	(NA)	(NA)	18.7
25 to 44 years old	31.0	39.6	9.7	11.0	3.5	5.3	(NA)	5.3	5.0	19.5
45 to 64 years old	247.8	296.8	23.3	60.3	22.7	14.5	(NA)	18.0	51.2	(NA)
65 years old and over	1,852.6	981.0	65.5	474.1	106.0	166.5	(NA)	(NA)	258.4	(NA)

Notes: NA Not available.
S Figure does not meet publication standards.
\1 Includes allied conditions.
\2 Includes other races not shown separately.

Source: U.S. National Center for Health Statistics, Monthly Vital Statistics Report and Vital Statistics of the United States, annual.

D1.5. Estimated Deaths of Persons with Acquired Immunodeficiency Syndrome (AIDS), by Race and Ethnicity: 1991 to 1996

[Estimates are adjusted for delays in reporting of deaths. Total estimates of less than 1,000, 1,000 to 2,499, 2,500 to 4,999, and 5,000 or more are rounded to the nearest 10, 25, 50, and 100, respectively. Annual estimates are through the most recent year for which reliable estimates are available. Because there is uncertainty in the estimates of deaths of persons with AIDS, changes over time in the estimates of deaths of persons with AIDS should not be computed from these rounded estimates.]

CHARACTERISTIC	1991	1992	1993	1994	1995	1996
Total	36,600	41,100	44,600	49,400	50,700	39,200
RACE/ETHNICITY						
White, not Hispanic	18,900	20,400	21,400	22,300	21,800	14,700
Black, not Hispanic	11,100	13,300	15,200	17,800	19,100	16,700
Hispanic	6,200	7,100	7,600	8,700	9,100	7,300
Asian/Pacific Islander	250	270	300	400	360	290
American Indian/Alaska Native	90	80	130	140	180	100

Source: Centers for Disease Control and Prevention, HIV/AIDS Surveillance Report, 1996; 8 no.1.

D1.6. Infant, Maternal, and Neonatal Mortality Rates and Fetal Mortality Ratio, by Race: 1960 to 1996

[Deaths per 1,000 live births, except as noted. Excludes deaths of nonresidents of U.S. Beginning 1980, race for live births tabulated according to race of mother, for infant and neonatal mortality rates. Beginning 1989, race for live births tabulated according to race of mother, for maternal mortality rates and mortality rates.]

ITEM	1960	1970	1975	1978	1979	1980	1981	1982	1983	1984	1985	1986	1987	1988	1989	1990	1991	1992	1993	1994	1995	1996
Infant deaths \1	26.0	20.0	16.1	13.8	13.1	12.6	11.9	11.5	11.2	10.8	10.6	10.4	10.1	10.0	9.8	9.2	8.9	8.5	8.4	8.0	7.6	7.2
White	22.9	17.8	14.2	12.0	11.4	10.9	10.3	9.9	9.6	9.3	9.2	8.8	8.5	8.4	8.1	7.6	7.3	6.9	6.8	6.6	6.3	6.0
Black and other	43.2	30.9	24.2	21.1	19.8	20.2	18.8	18.3	17.8	17.1	16.8	16.7	16.5	16.1	16.3	15.5	15.1	14.4	14.1	13.5	(NA)	(NA)
Black	44.3	32.6	26.2	23.1	21.8	22.2	20.8	20.5	20.0	19.2	19.0	18.9	18.8	18.5	18.6	18.0	17.6	16.8	16.5	15.8	15.1	14.2
Maternal deaths \2	37.1	21.5	12.8	9.6	9.6	9.2	8.5	7.9	8.0	7.8	7.8	7.2	6.6	8.4	7.9	8.2	7.9	7.8	7.5	8.3	7.1	(NA)
White	26.0	14.4	9.1	6.4	6.4	6.7	6.3	5.8	5.9	5.4	5.2	4.9	5.1	5.9	5.6	5.4	5.8	5.0	4.8	6.2	4.2	(NA)
Black and other	97.9	55.9	29.0	23.0	22.7	19.8	17.3	16.4	16.3	16.9	18.1	16.0	12.0	17.4	16.5	19.1	15.6	18.2	17.6	16.2	18.5	(NA)
Black	103.6	59.8	31.3	25.0	25.1	21.5	20.4	18.2	18.3	19.7	20.4	18.8	14.2	19.5	18.4	22.4	18.3	20.8	20.5	18.5	22.1	(NA)
Fetal deaths \3	16.1	14.2	10.7	9.7	9.4	9.2	9.0	8.9	8.5	8.2	7.9	7.7	7.7	7.5	7.5	7.5	7.3	7.4	(NA)	(NA)	(NA)	(NA)
White	14.1	12.4	9.5	8.5	8.4	8.2	8.0	7.9	7.5	7.4	7.0	6.8	6.7	6.4	6.4	6.4	6.2	6.3	(NA)	(NA)	(NA)	(NA)
Black and other	26.8	22.6	16.0	14.7	13.8	13.4	12.8	12.7	12.4	11.5	11.3	11.2	11.5	11.4	11.7	11.9	11.4	11.7	(NA)	(NA)	(NA)	(NA)
Neonatal deaths \4	18.7	15.1	11.6	9.5	8.9	8.5	8.0	7.7	7.3	7.0	7.0	6.7	6.5	6.3	6.2	5.8	5.6	5.4	5.3	5.1	4.9	4.7
White	17.2	13.8	10.4	8.4	7.9	7.4	7.0	6.7	6.3	6.1	6.0	5.7	5.4	5.3	5.1	4.8	4.5	4.3	4.3	4.2	4.1	3.9
Black and other	26.9	21.4	16.8	14.0	12.9	13.2	12.5	12.0	11.4	10.9	11.0	10.8	10.7	10.3	10.3	9.9	9.5	9.2	9.0	8.6	(NA)	(NA)
Black	27.8	22.8	18.3	15.5	14.3	14.6	14.0	13.6	12.9	12.3	12.6	12.3	12.3	12.1	11.9	11.6	11.2	10.8	10.7	10.2	9.8	9.2

Notes:

NA Not available.

\1 Represents deaths of infants under 1 year old, exclusive of fetal deaths.

\2 Per 100,000 live births from deliveries and complications of pregnancy, childbirth, and the puerperium. Beginning 1979, deaths are classified according to the ninth revision of the International Classification of Diseases; earlier years classified according to the revision in use at the time.

\3 Beginning 1970, includes only those deaths with stated or presumed period of gestation of 20 weeks or more; for prior years, includes gestational age not stated.

\4 Represents deaths of infants under 28 days old, exclusive of fetal deaths.

Source: U.S. National Center for Health Statistics, Vital Statistics of the United States, annual; and Monthly Vital Statistics Report.

D1.7. Deaths and Death Rates for Injury by Firearms, by Race and Sex: 1980 to 1995

[Age-adjusted rates per 100,000]

YEAR	ALL RACES			White			ALL OTHER Total			Black		
	Both sexes	Male	Female	Both sexes	Male	Female	Both sexes	Male	Female	Both sexes	Male	Female
NUMBER												
1980	33,780	28,322	5,458	24,849	20,714	4,135	8,931	7,608	1,323	8,505	7,265	1,240
1985	31,566	26,382	5,184	24,507	20,389	4,118	7,059	5,993	1,066	6,565	5,584	981
1990	37,155	31,736	5,419	26,299	22,249	4,050	10,856	9,487	1,369	10,175	8,922	1,253
1993	39,595	33,711	5,884	26,948	22,608	4,268	12,647	11,031	1,616	11,763	10,310	1,453
1994	38,505	33,021	5,484	26,403	22,408	3,995	12,102	10,613	1,489	11,223	9,880	1,343
1995	35,957	30,724	5,233	25,438	21,510	3,928	10,519	9,214	1,305	9,643	8,494	1,149
RATE \1												
1980	14.8	25.3	4.8	12.4	21.1	4.2	29.1	53.0	8.1	33.5	61.8	9.1
1985	12.7	21.8	4.2	11.4	19.4	3.9	19.7	35.4	5.7	23.2	42.2	6.5
1990	14.6	25.4	4.2	11.9	20.5	3.7	26.9	48.9	6.5	33.4	61.5	7.8
1993	15.6	26.9	4.6	12.2	20.7	3.9	30.1	54.4	7.3	37.6	68.8	8.8
1994	15.1	26.2	4.2	11.9	20.4	3.6	28.4	51.6	6.6	35.5	65.1	8.0
1995	13.9	24.1	4.0	11.3	19.3	3.5	24.4	44.4	5.7	30.3	55.6	6.8

Notes:
\1 Age-adjusted death rate. For method of computation see source.

Source: U.S. National Center for Health Statistics, Monthly Vital Statistics Reports.

D1.8. Deaths and Death Rates for Drug-Induced Causes, by Race and Sex: 1980 to 1995

[Age-adjusted rates per 100,000]

YEAR	ALL RACES			White			ALL OTHER Total			Black		
	Both sexes	Male	Female	Both sexes	Male	Female	Both sexes	Male	Female	Both sexes	Male	Female
NUMBER												
1980	6,900	3,771	3,129	5,814	3,088	2,726	1,086	683	403	1,006	648	358
1985	8,663	5,342	3,321	6,946	4,172	2,774	1,717	1,170	547	1,600	1,107	493
1990	9,463	5,897	3,566	7,603	4,646	2,957	1,860	1,251	609	1,703	1,155	548
1993	13,275	9,052	4,223	10,394	7,005	3,389	2,881	2,047	834	2,688	1,924	764
1994	13,923	9,491	4,432	10,895	7,339	3,556	3,028	2,152	876	2,780	1,995	785
1995	14,218	9,909	4,309	11,173	7,730	3,443	3,045	2,179	866	2,800	2,011	789
RATE \1												
1980	3.0	3.4	2.6	2.9	3.2	2.6	3.7	4.9	2.5	4.1	5.8	2.7
1985	3.5	4.5	2.6	3.3	4.0	2.5	4.9	7.2	2.9	5.9	8.9	3.3
1990	3.6	4.6	2.6	3.3	4.2	2.5	4.6	6.7	2.8	5.7	8.4	3.4
1993	4.8	6.8	3.0	4.5	6.2	2.8	6.6	10.0	3.6	8.3	13.0	4.4
1994	5.0	7.0	3.0	4.7	6.5	2.9	6.8	10.5	3.7	8.6	13.4	4.4
1995	5.1	7.3	3.0	4.8	6.8	2.8	6.7	10.4	3.5	8.5	13.3	4.4

Notes:
\1 Age-adjusted death rate. For method of computation see source.

Source: U.S. National Center for Health Statistics, Monthly Vital Statistics Reports.

D1.9. Deaths and Death Rates for Alcohol-Induced Causes, by Race and Sex: 1980 to 1995

[Age-adjusted rates per 100,000]

YEAR	ALL RACES			White			ALL OTHER Total			Black		
	Both sexes	Male	Female	Both sexes	Male	Female	Both sexes	Male	Female	Both sexes	Male	Female
NUMBER												
1980	19,765	14,447	5,318	14,815	10,936	3,879	4,950	3,511	1,439	4,451	3,170	1,281
1985	17,741	13,216	4,525	13,216	9,922	3,294	4,525	3,294	1,231	4,114	3,030	1,084
1990	19,757	14,842	4,915	14,904	11,334	3,570	4,853	3,508	1,345	4,337	3,172	1,165
1993	19,557	14,873	4,684	15,293	11,716	3,577	4,264	3,157	1,107	3,663	2,759	904
1994	20,163	15,293	4,870	15,853	12,154	3,699	4,310	3,139	1,171	3,648	2,700	948
1995	20,231	15,443	4,788	15,991	12,338	3,653	4,240	3,105	1,135	3,538	2,614	924
RATE \1												
1980	8.4	13.0	4.3	6.9	10.8	3.5	18.8	29.5	10.0	20.4	32.4	10.6
1985	7.0	11.0	3.4	5.8	9.2	2.8	14.6	23.5	7.2	16.8	27.7	8.0
1990	7.2	11.4	3.4	6.2	9.9	2.8	13.6	22.0	6.8	16.1	26.6	7.7
1993	6.7	10.8	3.0	6.1	9.7	2.7	10.8	17.8	5.0	12.5	21.3	5.5
1994	6.8	10.9	3.1	6.2	9.9	2.7	10.6	17.3	5.2	12.2	20.4	5.6
1995	6.7	10.8	3.0	6.2	9.9	2.7	10.1	16.7	4.8	11.5	19.4	5.3

Notes:
\1 Age-adjusted death rate. For method of computation see source.

Source: U.S. National Center for Health Statistics, Monthly Vital Statistics Reports.

D1.10. Expectation of Life and Expected Deaths, by Race, Sex, and Age: 1995

AGE IN 1990 (years)	EXPECTATION OF LIFE IN YEARS	White		Black		EXPECTED DEATHS PER 1,000 ALIVE AT SPECIFIED AGE \1	White		Black	
	Total	Male	Female	Male	Female	Total	Male	Female	Male	Female
At birth	75.8	73.4	79.6	65.2	73.9	7.57	6.98	5.55	16.22	13.74
1	75.4	72.9	79.0	65.3	73.9	0.58	0.57	0.44	1.10	0.82
2	74.4	72.0	78.1	64.3	73.0	0.43	0.41	0.33	0.79	0.66
3	73.4	71.0	77.1	63.4	72.0	0.33	0.31	0.26	0.60	0.53
4	72.5	70.0	76.1	62.4	71.0	0.27	0.26	0.21	0.49	0.42
5	71.5	69.1	75.1	61.5	70.1	0.23	0.23	0.18	0.43	0.34
6	70.5	68.1	74.1	60.5	69.1	0.21	0.22	0.16	0.40	0.28
7	69.5	67.1	73.1	59.5	68.1	0.20	0.21	0.15	0.36	0.24
8	68.5	66.1	72.2	58.5	67.1	0.18	0.19	0.14	0.31	0.21
9	67.5	65.1	71.2	57.5	66.1	0.16	0.17	0.13	0.25	0.21
10	66.6	64.1	70.2	56.6	65.2	0.15	0.15	0.12	0.20	0.21
11	65.6	63.1	69.2	55.6	64.2	0.16	0.16	0.13	0.20	0.23
12	64.6	62.1	68.2	54.6	63.2	0.21	0.22	0.16	0.32	0.26
13	63.6	61.2	67.2	53.6	62.2	0.31	0.35	0.21	0.59	0.31
14	62.6	60.2	66.2	52.6	61.2	0.45	0.54	0.28	0.95	0.36
15	61.6	59.2	65.2	51.7	60.2	0.61	0.74	0.35	1.37	0.43
16	60.7	58.3	64.3	50.8	59.3	0.75	0.94	0.42	1.77	0.50
17	59.7	57.3	63.3	49.8	58.3	0.87	1.09	0.47	2.11	0.57
18	58.8	56.4	62.3	48.9	57.3	0.94	1.20	0.48	2.36	0.62
19	57.8	55.4	61.3	48.1	56.4	0.98	1.26	0.47	2.54	0.67
20	56.9	54.5	60.4	47.2	55.4	1.01	1.32	0.45	2.72	0.72
21	55.9	53.6	59.4	46.3	54.4	1.05	1.38	0.44	2.91	0.77
22	55.0	52.7	58.4	45.4	53.5	1.08	1.42	0.43	3.07	0.84
23	54.1	51.7	57.4	44.6	52.5	1.10	1.43	0.44	3.17	0.92
24	53.1	50.8	56.5	43.7	51.6	1.11	1.43	0.46	3.25	1.02
25	52.2	49.9	55.5	42.9	50.6	1.12	1.42	0.48	3.30	1.12
26	51.2	48.9	54.5	42.0	49.7	1.13	1.41	0.50	3.37	1.23
27	50.3	48.0	53.6	41.1	48.7	1.17	1.44	0.53	3.49	1.34
28	49.3	47.1	52.6	40.3	47.8	1.23	1.53	0.56	3.69	1.45
29	48.4	46.2	51.6	39.4	46.9	1.32	1.65	0.60	3.94	1.57
30	47.5	45.2	50.6	38.6	46.0	1.42	1.79	0.64	4.21	1.70
31	46.5	44.3	49.7	37.7	45.0	1.51	1.92	0.68	4.49	1.83
32	45.6	43.4	48.7	36.9	44.1	1.61	2.04	0.73	4.76	1.97
33	44.7	42.5	47.7	36.1	43.2	1.70	2.14	0.79	5.02	2.12

D1.10. Expectation of Life and Expected Deaths, by Race, Sex, and Age: 1995 *(continued)*

AGE IN 1990 (years)	EXPECTATION OF LIFE IN YEARS					EXPECTED DEATHS PER 1,000 ALIVE AT SPECIFIED AGE \1				
	Total	White		Black		Total	White		Black	
		Male	Female	Male	Female		Male	Female	Male	Female
34	43.8	41.6	46.8	35.3	42.3	1.79	2.23	0.85	5.28	2.27
35	42.8	40.7	45.8	34.5	41.4	1.89	2.32	0.92	5.55	2.43
36	41.9	39.8	44.9	33.6	40.5	1.99	2.42	0.99	5.84	2.60
37	41.0	38.8	43.9	32.8	39.6	2.10	2.53	1.06	6.18	2.78
38	40.1	37.9	42.9	32.0	38.7	2.22	2.66	1.13	6.56	2.97
39	39.2	37.0	42.0	31.2	37.8	2.34	2.79	1.20	6.99	3.18
40	38.3	36.1	41.0	30.5	36.9	2.47	2.94	1.28	7.45	3.40
41	37.3	35.3	40.1	29.7	36.1	2.62	3.10	1.37	7.92	3.63
42	36.4	34.4	39.2	28.9	35.2	2.76	3.27	1.47	8.40	3.86
43	35.5	33.5	38.2	28.2	34.3	2.92	3.43	1.59	8.88	4.10
44	34.6	32.6	37.3	27.4	33.5	3.07	3.60	1.72	9.37	4.34
45	33.8	31.7	36.3	26.7	32.6	3.25	3.80	1.87	9.88	4.60
46	32.9	30.8	35.4	25.9	31.7	3.46	4.02	2.04	10.43	4.89
47	32.0	29.9	34.5	25.2	30.9	3.70	4.30	2.24	11.02	5.21
48	31.1	29.1	33.5	24.5	30.1	4.00	4.64	2.47	11.67	5.56
49	30.2	28.2	32.6	23.7	29.2	4.35	5.04	2.75	12.38	5.95
50	29.3	27.3	31.7	23.0	28.4	4.74	5.49	3.05	13.15	6.37
51	28.5	26.5	30.8	22.3	27.6	5.16	5.99	3.39	13.97	6.84
52	27.6	25.6	29.9	21.6	26.8	5.62	6.52	3.75	14.82	7.35
53	26.8	24.8	29.0	21.0	26.0	6.11	7.10	4.12	15.68	7.93
54	25.9	24.0	28.1	20.3	25.2	6.64	7.73	4.52	16.58	8.58
55	25.1	23.2	27.3	19.6	24.4	7.21	8.41	4.96	17.48	9.26
56	24.3	22.4	26.4	19.0	23.6	7.84	9.17	5.44	18.48	9.99
57	23.5	21.6	25.5	18.3	22.8	8.58	10.07	5.99	19.73	10.82
58	22.7	20.8	24.7	17.7	22.1	9.45	11.14	6.62	21.32	11.78
59	21.9	20.0	23.9	17.0	21.3	10.42	12.36	7.33	23.17	12.83
60	21.1	19.3	23.0	16.4	20.6	11.50	13.70	8.11	25.29	14.01
61	20.4	18.5	22.2	15.9	19.9	12.62	15.11	8.93	27.45	15.24
62	19.6	17.8	21.4	15.3	19.2	13.77	16.59	9.79	29.36	16.40
63	18.9	17.1	20.6	14.7	18.5	14.92	18.12	10.67	30.84	17.44
64	18.2	16.4	19.8	14.2	17.8	16.11	19.73	11.59	32.02	18.42
65	17.4	15.7	19.1	13.6	17.1	17.35	21.43	12.57	32.99	19.34
70	14.1	12.5	15.4	11.0	13.9	26.18	32.69	19.52	48.22	29.73
75	11.0	9.7	12.0	8.8	11.1	39.26	49.26	30.73	65.70	41.08
80	8.3	7.2	8.9	6.8	8.4	60.15	75.57	49.53	89.94	59.43
85 and over	6.0	5.2	6.3	5.1	6.2	1,000.0	1,000.0	1,000.0	1,000.0	1,000.0

Notes:

\1 Based on the proportion of the cohort who are alive at the beginning of an indicated age interval who will die before reaching the end of that interval. For example, out of every 1,000 people alive and exactly 50 years old at the beginning of the period, between 4 and 5 (4.76) will die before reaching their 51st birthdays.

Source: U.S. National Center for Health Statistics, Vital Statistics of the United States, annual; and unpublished data.

D2. HEALTH AND HEALTH RISKS

D2.1. Self-Reported Health Condition, by Race and Ethnicity: March 1998

		Non Hispanic Whites	Non Hispanic Blacks	American Indians/ Aleuts/Eskimos	Asians and Pacific Islanders	Hispanics	Total
Excellent	%	36.6%	26.9%	31.8%	30.8%	30.4%	34.1%
	N	**33721**	**3419**	**479**	**1388**	**6398**	**45305**
Very Good	%	30.9%	27.0%	27.5%	33.3%	30.8%	30.6%
	N	**28502**	**3432**	**415**	**1504**	**6384**	**40237**
Good	%	21.7%	29.9%	26.5%	27.5%	27.9%	23.7%
	N	**20030**	**3792**	**400**	**1241**	**5784**	**31247**
Fair	%	7.4%	11.4%	9.8%	6.2%	7.7%	7.8%
	N	**6802**	**1447**	**148**	**278**	**1603**	**10278**
Poor	%	3.4%	4.8%	4.4%	2.3%	3.3%	3.5%
	N	**3097**	**603**	**66**	**102**	**682**	**4550**
	Total	92152	12693	1508	4513	20751	131617

Source: Current Population Surveys, March 1998 [Machine readable data files] conducted by the Bureau of the Census for the Bureau of Labor Statistics. Washington, D.C.: Bureau of Census [producer and distributor]. Santa Monica, CA: Unicon Research Corporation [producer and distributor of CPS].

D2.2. Adolescents' Self-Reported General Health, by Race: 1995

1. Because of a physical, learning, or emotional condition you have had for at least a year, do you have any limitations attending school or in your ability to do regular work?

	White	Black	Native American	Asian	Hispanic	Total
Yes	4.6	5.9	8.9	5.1	7.6	5.3

2. Has there been any time over the past year when you thought you should get medical care?

	White	Black	Native American	Asian	Hispanic	Total
Yes	16.6	23.2	26.4	21.4	21.5	18.7

3. How do you think of yourself in terms of weight?

	White	Black	Native American	Asian	Hispanic	Total
Very underweight	1.0	1.1	2.2	1.0	2.4	1.2
Slightly underweight	14.1	13.9	12.4	19.8	15.5	14.4
About the right weight	54.3	57.8	50.4	51.3	48.2	53.9
Slightly overweight	26.8	23.5	30.5	27.1	30.3	26.9
Very overweight	3.6	3.6	4.6	.8	3.5	3.5

4. Are you trying to lose weight, gain weight, or stay the same weight

	White	Black	Native American	Asian	Hispanic	Total
Lose weight	32.0	30.1	35.7	30.9	38.3	32.2
Gain weight	15.0	27.1	16.5	22.2	20.3	17.9
Stay the same weight	37.0	32.4	34.9	34.8	27.3	34.9
Not trying to do anything about weight	16.0	10.4	13.0	12.2	14.1	14.7

Source: The National Longitudinal Study of Adolescent Health, 1995.

D2.3. Adolescents' Self-Rating of Their Health, by Race and Ethnicity: 1995

Race/Ethniciy	How is Your Health? (a)	Physical Symptoms (b)	Limited Activities (c)
White	2.10	1.20	.32
Black	2.06	1.10	.33
Asian	2.16	1.15	.36
Chinese	2.07	1.15	.33
Filipino	2.17	1.18	.36
Japanese	2.10	1.09	.32
Asian Indian	2.04	1.12	.36
Korean	2.18	1.14	.28
Vietnamese	2.30	1.05	.42
American Indian	2.23	1.31	.41
Hispanic	2.17	1.09	.35
Mexican	2.22	1.05	.32
Chicano/Chicana	2.36	1.21	.50
Cuban	2.12	1.06	.36
Puerto Rican	2.21	1.22	.38
Central/South America	2.06	1.03	.33
Total	2.10	1.16	.31

Notes:
a. Scale: 1 = excellent, 2 = very good, 3 = good, 4 = fair, 5 = poor
b. Average reported times in the last month students (1) felt really sick, (2) woke up feeling tired, (3) were dizzy, (4) had chest pain, (5) had a headache, (6) had muscle aches or pains, (7) had a stomachache, (8) had a poor appetite, (9) had trouble sleeping, (10) felt depressed, (11) were moody, (12) cried a lot, (13) were afraid of things.
Scale: 0 = never, 1 = rarely, 2 = occasionally, 3 = often, 4 = every day
c. Activities limited because of health or emotional problems include: (1) missing school, (2) missing a social or recreational activity, (3) walking, (4) running, (5) bending or lifting, (6) using hands or fingers.
Scale: 0 = never, 1 = just a few times, 2 = about once a week, 3 = almost every day, 4 = every day.

Source: National Longitudinal Study of Adolescent Health, 1995.

D2.4. Adolescents' Self-Reported Probability of Life Chances, by Race and Ethnicity: 1995

Race/Ethniciy	Live to 35	Marry by 25	Be killed by 21	Get HIV or AIDS	Graduate from college	Have middle-class income by 30
White	6.75	4.54	1.43	1.01	6.29	5.21
Black	6.27	3.58	1.33	0.97	6.40	4.86
Asian	6.43	4.17	1.47	1.20	6.55	4.92
Chinese	6.70	3.90	1.45	1.32	6.68	5.22
Filipino	6.69	4.36	1.47	1.18	6.61	4.85
Japanese	6.60	4.03	1.53	1.28	6.60	5.01
Asian Indian	6.33	4.38	1.39	0.93	6.47	5.03
Korean	6.42	4.17	1.30	1.02	6.93	5.13
Vietnamese	5.74	4.08	1.39	1.35	6.33	4.13
American Indian	6.34	4.26	1.62	1.12	6.01	4.86
Hispanic	6.17	4.24	1.48	1.08	5.84	4.61
Mexican	6.11	4.25	1.51	1.02	5.58	4.53
Chicano/Chicana	5.77	4.09	2.05	1.39	4.89	4.40
Cuban	6.26	4.72	1.54	1.25	6.06	4.94
Puerto Rican	6.58	4.36	1.34	1.07	5.95	4.92
Central/South America	6.12	4.07	1.40	1.08	6.15	4.66
Total	6.59	4.31	1.42	1.00	6.27	5.08

Notes:
Scale: 0 = no chance, 2 = some chance, 4 = about 50-50, 6 = pretty likely, 8 = it will happen

Source: National Longitudinal Study of Adolescent Health, 1995.

D2.5. Percent of Population Overweight, by Age, Sex, and Race: 1976 to 1994

[In percent. Overweight is defined for men as body mass index greater than or equal to 27.8 kilograms/meter squared, and for women as body mass index greater than or equal to 27.3 kilograms/meter squared. These points were used because they represent the sex-specific 85th percentiles for persons 20-29 years of age in the 1976-80 National Health and Nutrition Examination Survey (NHANES). Data are based on physical examinations of a sample of the civilian noninstitutional population in the NHANES.]

SEX, AGE, AND RACE	1976-80	1988-94
Persons 20 to 74 years old, \1	**25.4**	**34.8**
Male	24.0	33.7
Female \2	26.5	35.9
White male	24.2	34.3
White female \2	24.4	33.9
Black male	25.7	34.0
Black female \2	44.3	53.0
MALE		
20 to 34 years old	17.3	25.4
35 to 44 years old	28.9	34.9
45 to 54 years old	31.0	37.7
55 to 64 years old	28.1	43.7
65 to 74 years old	25.2	42.9
75 years old and over	(NA)	27.7
FEMALE \2		
20 to 34 years old	16.8	25.6
35 to 44 years old	27.0	36.8
45 to 54 years old	32.5	45.4
55 to 64 years old	37.0	48.2
65 to 74 years old	38.4	42.3
75 years old and over	(NA)	35.1

Notes:
NA Not available.
\1 Age-adjusted. Includes other races not shown separately.
\2 Excludes pregnant women.

Source: U.S. National Center for Health Statistics, Health United States, 1996–7.

D2.6. Current Cigarette Smoking, by Race and Age: 1979 to 1995

[In percent. Prior to 1992, a current smoker is a person who has smoked at least 100 cigarettes and who now smokes. Beginning 1992, definition includes persons who smoke only "some days." Excludes unknown smoking status. Based on the National Health Interview Survey.]

SEX, RACE, AND AGE	1979	1985	1990	1991	1992	1993	1994	1995
Total smokers, 18 years old and over	33.3	30.1	25.5	25.6	26.5	25.0	25.5	24.7
Male, total	37.5	32.6	28.4	28.1	28.6	27.7	28.2	27.0
18 to 24 years	35.0	28.0	26.6	23.5	28.0	28.8	29.8	27.8
25 to 34 years	43.9	38.2	31.6	32.8	32.8	30.2	31.4	(NA)
35 to 44 years	41.8	37.6	34.5	33.1	32.9	32.0	33.2	(NA)
45 to 64 years	39.3	33.4	29.3	29.3	28.6	29.2	28.3	27.1
65 years and over	20.9	19.6	14.6	15.1	16.1	13.5	13.2	14.3
White, total	36.8	31.7	28.0	27.4	28.2	27.0	27.7	(NA)
18 to 24 years	34.3	28.4	27.4	25.1	30.0	30.4	31.8	(NA)
25 to 34 years	43.6	37.3	31.6	32.1	33.5	29.9	32.5	(NA)
35 to 44 years	41.3	36.6	33.5	32.1	30.9	31.2	32.0	(NA)
45 to 64 years	38.3	32.1	28.7	28.0	28.1	27.8	26.9	(NA)
65 years and over	20.5	18.9	13.7	13.7	14.9	12.5	11.9	(NA)
Black, total	44.1	39.9	32.5	35.0	32.2	32.7	33.7	(NA)
18 to 24 years	40.2	27.2	21.3	15.0	16.2	19.9	18.7	(NA)
25 to 34 years	47.5	45.6	33.8	39.4	29.5	30.7	29.8	(NA)
35 to 44 years	48.6	45.0	42.0	44.4	47.5	36.9	44.5	(NA)
45 to 64 years	50.0	46.1	36.7	42.0	35.4	42.4	41.2	(NA)
65 years and over	26.2	27.7	21.5	24.3	28.3	27.9	25.6	(NA)
Female, total	29.9	27.9	22.8	23.5	24.6	22.5	23.1	22.6
18 to 24 years	33.8	30.4	22.5	22.4	24.9	22.9	25.2	21.8
25 to 34 years	33.7	32.0	28.2	28.4	30.1	27.3	28.8	(NA)
35 to 44 years	37.0	31.5	24.8	27.6	27.3	27.4	26.8	(NA)
45 to 64 years	30.7	29.9	24.8	24.6	26.1	23.0	22.8	24.0
65 years and over	13.2	13.5	11.5	12.0	12.4	10.5	11.1	11.5
White, total	30.1	27.7	23.4	23.7	25.1	23.1	23.7	(NA)
18 to 24 years	34.5	31.8	25.4	25.1	28.5	26.8	28.5	(NA)
25 to 34 years	34.1	32.0	28.5	28.4	31.5	28.4	30.2	(NA)
35 to 44 years	37.2	31.0	25.0	27.0	27.6	27.3	27.1	(NA)
45 to 64 years	30.6	29.7	25.4	25.3	25.8	23.4	23.2	(NA)
65 years and over	13.8	13.3	11.5	12.1	12.6	10.5	11.1	(NA)
Black, total	31.1	31.0	21.2	24.4	24.2	20.8	21.7	(NA)
18 to 24 years	31.8	23.7	10.0	11.8	10.3	8.2	11.8	(NA)
25 to 34 years	35.2	36.2	29.1	32.4	26.9	24.7	24.8	(NA)
35 to 44 years	37.7	40.2	25.5	35.3	32.4	31.5	28.2	(NA)
45 to 64 years	34.2	33.4	22.6	23.4	30.9	21.3	23.5	(NA)
65 years and over	8.5	14.5	11.1	9.6	11.1	10.2	13.6	(NA)

Notes:
NA Not available.

Source: U.S. National Center for Health Statistics, Health United States, 1996-97 and Injury Chartbook, 1997, and U.S. Centers for Disease Control and Prevention, Morbidity and Mortality Weekly Report, Vol. 46, no. 51, December 26, 1997.

D2.7. Children Immunized Against Specified Diseases, by Race and Ethnicity: 1994 to 1996

[In percent. Covers civilian noninstitutionalized population ages 19 months to 35 months. Based on estimates from the National Immunization Survey. The health care providers of the children are contacted to verify and/or complete vaccination information. Results are based on race/ethnic status of the child]

VACCINATION	1994	1995	1996 Total	White non-Hispanic	Hispanic	Black non-Hispanic	American Indian/ Alaskan Native	Asian/ Pacific Islander
Diphtheria-tetanus-pertussis (DPT)/ diphtheria-tetanus:								
3+ doses	94	95	95	96	93	93	93	96
4+ doses	76	79	81	83	77	79	83	84
Polio: 3+ doses	83	88	91	92	89	90	89	90
Hib \1: 3+ doses	86	92	92	93	89	90	90	92
Measles containing vaccine (MCV)	89	90	91	92	88	89	87	94
Hepatitis B: 3+ doses	37	68	82	82	80	82	78	84
4+ DPT/3+ polio/1+ MCV	74	76	78	80	73	76	81	81
4+ DPT/3+ polio/1+ MCV/3+ hiB	69	74	77	79	71	74	80	78

Notes:
\1 Haemophilus B.

Source: U.S. Centers for Disease Control and Prevention, Atlanta, GA, Morbidity and Mortality Weekly Report, Vol. 46, No. 41, October 17, 1997; and unpublished data.

D2.8. Acute Conditions, by Race and Ethnicity and Income, 1995

[Covers civilian noninstitutional population. Estimates include only acute conditions which were medically attended or caused at least 1 day of restricted activity. Based on National Health Interview Survey.]

CHARACTERISTIC	NUMBER OF CONDITIONS (mil.)					RATE PER 100 POPULATION				
	Infective and parasitic	Respiratory		Digestive System	Injuries	Infective and parasitic	Respiratory		Digestive System	Injuries
		Common cold	Influenza				Common cold	Influenza		
Male	23.8	28.4	49.8	7.2	34.7	18.6	22.3	39.0	5.7	27.2
Female	28.8	32.1	58.3	8.6	29.9	21.5	23.9	43.4	6.4	22.3
White	46.0	47.8	95.5	12.3	56.7	21.2	22.0	44.0	5.7	26.1
Black	5.8	8.8	8.7	3.1	5.9	17.6	26.9	26.5	9.6	18.1
FAMILY INCOME										
Under $10,000	4.7	6.5	10.3	2.4	6.3	21.6	30.1	47.7	11.2	29.1
$10,000 to $19,999	8.2	8.3	15.0	2.4	9.2	21.6	21.8	39.7	6.4	24.3
$20,000 to $34,999	9.9	14.2	22.7	2.8	14.2	18.2	26.0	41.6	5.1	26.0
$35,000 or more	23.7	22.0	47.9	5.8	25.9	22.2	20.6	44.8	5.4	24.3

Notes:
NA Not available.
\1 Includes other races and unknown income not shown separately.

Source: U.S. National Center for Health Statistics, Vital and Health Statistics, Series 10, No. 193, and earlier reports; and unpublished data.

D2.9. Adolescents Who Have Thought about Suicide, by Race: 1995

During the past 12 months, did you ever seriously think about committing suicide?						
	White	**Black**	**Native-American**	**Asian**	**Hispanic**	**Total**
No	88.1	91.4	86.5	87.7	88.8	88.6
Yes	11.6	8.6	13.5	12.3	11.2	11.4
Have any of your friends tried to kill themselves during the past 12 months?						
No	83.2	89.4	81.8	86.3	82.5	84.2
Yes	16.8	10.6	18.2	13.7	17.5	15.8

Source: The Longitudinal Study of Adolescent Health, 1995.

D3. HEALTH CARE

D3.1. Adolescents' Access to Health Services, by Race: 1995

In the past year, have you had a routine physical examination?						
	White	**Black**	**Native-American**	**Asian**	**Hispanic**	**Total**
Yes	66.5	65.0	72.2	48.9	54.1	64.4
In the past year, have you had a dental examination by a dentist or hygienist?						
Yes	76.0	55.0	63.1	65.2	56.3	69.5
In the past year, have you received psychological or emotional counseling?						
Yes	10.7	6.5	12.4	7.1	9.7	9.9
In the past year, have you received family planning counseling or services?						
Yes	4.1	4.7	5.7	4.9	4.9	4.4
In the past year, have you received testing or treatment for a sexually transmitted disease or AIDS?						
Yes	4.0	8.5	5.9	3.5	7.0	5.2

Source: The National Longitudinal Study of Adolescent Health, 1995.

D3.2. Number of Women 15–44 Years of Age, Percent Who Received At Least One Medical Service in the 12 Months Prior to Interview from a Medical Care Provider, and Percent Reporting the Specified Method of Payment, by Selected Characteristics: United States, 1995

					Method of payment		
Characteristic	**Number in thousands**	**At least 1 medical service**[1]	**Medicaid at all**	**Insurance alone**	**Own income alone**	**Own income and insurance**	**Other public assistance or free**[2]
					Percent		
All women[3]	60,201	70.6	9.2	24.1	21.2	17.4	3.0
Race and Hispanic origin							
Hispanic	6,702	67.5	17.5	21.6	18.9	8.6	5.0
Non-Hispanic white	42,522	70.8	5.5	24.0	22.9	20.6	2.4
Non-Hispanic black	8,210	76.3	22.6	26.9	16.9	10.0	4.2

Notes:
*Figure does not meet standard of reliability or precision.
[1]Medical services include Pap smear; pelvic exam; prenatal care; postpartum care; HIV test; testing or treatment for other sexually transmitted diseases; testing or treatment for vaginal, urinary or pelvic infection; abortion; or pregnancy test.
[2]Respondents spontaneously mentioned another form of public assistance or that the service was free.
[3]Includes women of other race and origin groups not shown separately.
NOTE: Percents may not add to total who received "at least 1 medical service" because women may have received more than 1 service and used more than 1 payment method.

Source: National Survey of Family Growth, 1995.

D3.3. Number of Women 15–44 Years of Age and Percent Who Received the Specified Medical Services from a Medical Care Provider in the 12 Months Prior to Interview, by Selected Characteristics: United States, 1995

Characteristic	Number in thousands	Pregnancy test	Pap smear	Pelvic exam	HIV test[1]	Other STD[2] test or treatment	Test or treatment for infection[3]
					Percent		
All women	60,201	16.0	61.9	61.3	17.3	7.6	21.0
Race and Hispanic origin							
Hispanic	6,702	19.8	52.2	52.6	21.9	7.2	20.4
Non-Hispanic white	42,522	14.8	63.2	63.2	14.5	7.1	20.9
Non-Hispanic black	8,210	19.8	67.6	63.0	28.7	11.4	24.8
Non-Hispanic other	2,767	14.3	47.7	47.7	14.7	*	13.6

Notes:
*Figure does not meet standard of reliability or precision.
[1]Excludes HIV (human immunodeficiency virus) tests done as part of blood donation.
[2]STD is sexually transmitted disease.
NOTE: Percents do not add to 100 because women could report more than 1 medical service in the 12 months prior to interview.

Source: National Survey of Family Growth, 1995.

D3.4. Prenatal Care, by Race: 1985 to 1995

CHARACTERISTIC	1985	1990	1991	1992	1993	1994	1995
Percent of mothers beginning prenatal care 1st trimester	76.2	74.2	76.2	77.7	78.9	80.2	81.3
White	79.4	77.7	79.5	80.8	81.8	82.8	83.6
Black	61.8	60.7	61.9	63.9	66.0	68.3	70.4
American Indian, Eskimo, Aleut	60.3	57.9	59.9	62.1	63.4	65.2	66.7
Asian and Pacific Islander \1	75.0	(NA)	(NA)	76.6	77.6	79.7	79.9
Filipino	77.2	77.1	77.1	78.7	79.3	81.3	80.9
Chinese	82.4	81.3	82.3	83.8	84.6	86.2	85.7
Japanese	85.8	87.0	87.7	88.2	87.2	89.2	89.7
Hawaiian	(NA)	65.8	68.1	69.9	70.6	77.0	75.9
Hispanic origin \2	61.2	60.2	61.0	64.2	66.6	68.9	70.8
Mexican	59.9	57.8	58.7	62.1	64.8	67.3	69.1
Puerto Rican	58.3	63.5	65.0	67.8	70.0	71.7	74.0
Cuban	82.5	84.8	85.4	86.8	88.9	90.1	89.2
Central and South American	60.6	61.5	63.4	66.8	68.7	71.2	73.2
Percent of mothers beginning prenatal care 3d trimester or no care	5.7	6.0	5.8	5.2	4.8	4.4	4.2
White	4.7	4.9	4.7	4.2	3.9	3.6	3.5
Black	10.0	10.9	10.7	9.9	9.0	8.2	7.6
American Indian, Eskimo, Aleut	11.5	12.9	12.2	11.0	10.3	9.8	9.5
Asian and Pacific Islander \1	6.1	(NA)	(NA)	4.9	4.6	4.1	4.3
Filipino	4.6	4.5	5.0	4.3	4.0	3.6	4.1
Chinese	4.2	3.4	3.4	2.9	2.9	2.7	3.0
Japanese	2.6	2.9	2.5	2.4	2.8	1.9	2.3
Hawaiian	(NA)	8.7	7.5	7.0	6.7	4.7	5.1
Hispanic origin \2	12.5	12.0	11.0	9.5	8.8	7.6	7.4
Mexican	12.9	13.2	12.2	10.5	9.7	8.3	8.1
Puerto Rican	15.5	10.6	9.1	8.0	7.1	6.5	5.5
Cuban	3.7	2.8	2.4	2.1	1.8	1.6	2.1
Central and South American	12.5	10.9	9.5	7.9	7.3	6.5	6.1
Percent of births with low birth weight \3	6.8	7.0	7.1	7.1	7.2	7.3	7.3
White	5.6	5.7	5.8	5.8	6.0	6.1	6.2
Black	12.4	13.3	13.6	13.3	13.3	13.2	13.1
American Indian, Eskimo, Aleut	5.9	6.1	6.2	6.2	6.4	6.4	6.6
Asian and Pacific Islander \1	6.1	(NA)	(NA)	6.6	6.6	6.8	6.9
Filipino	6.9	7.3	7.3	7.4	7.0	7.8	7.8
Chinese	5.0	4.7	5.1	5.0	4.9	4.8	5.3

D3.4. Prenatal Care, by Race: 1985 to 1995 *(continued)*

CHARACTERISTIC	1985	1990	1991	1992	1993	1994	1995
Japanese	5.9	6.2	5.9	7.0	6.5	6.9	7.3
Hawaiian	6.4	7.2	6.7	6.9	6.8	7.2	6.8
Hispanic origin \2	6.2	6.1	6.1	6.1	6.2	6.2	6.3
Mexican	5.8	5.5	5.6	5.6	5.8	5.8	5.8
Puerto Rican	8.7	9.0	9.4	9.2	9.2	9.1	9.4
Cuban	6.0	5.7	5.6	6.1	6.2	6.3	6.5
Central and South American	5.7	5.8	5.9	5.8	5.9	6.0	6.2

Notes:
NA Not available.
\1 Includes other races not shown separately.
\2 Hispanic persons may be of any race. Includes other types, not shown separately.
\3 Births less than 2,500 grams (5 lb.-8 oz.).

Source: U.S. National Center for Health Statistics, Vital Statistics of the United States, annual; Monthly Vital Statistics Report; and unpublished data.

D3.5. Percentage of Households Covered by Group Health, by Race: March 1998

	Non-Hispanic Whites	Non-Hispanic Blacks	American Indians/ Aleuts/Eskimos	Asians and Pacific Islanders	Hispanics	Total
%	65.5%	48.9%	41.4%	61.0%	42.6%	59.9%
N	60441	6201	625	2753	8838	78858
Total	92152	12693	1508	4513	20751	131617

Source: Current Population Surveys, March 1998 [Machine readable data files] conducted by the Bureau of the Census for the Bureau of Labor Statistics. Washington, D.C.: Bureau of Census [producer and distributor]. Santa Monica, CA: Unicon Research Corporation [producer and distributor of CPS Utilities], 1999.

D3.6. Number of Unmarried Women 15–44 Years of Age and Percent Reporting the Specified Sources of Coverage for Health Insurance, by Selected Characteristics: United States, 1995

Characteristic	Number in thousands	Woman's Not covered	CHAMPUS/ employer	Self- Parents	Other Medicaid	CHAMPVA[1]	paid	source[2]
				Percent				
All women	30,528	14.1	33.9	25.1	22.8	1.9	3.6	4.4
Hispanic	3,524	20.7	28.1	17.2	33.5	0.8	1.0	2.7
Non-Hispanic white	19,445	13.2	36.1	29.7	14.7	1.8	4.5	2.5
Non-Hispanic black	6,141	12.7	31.3	14.0	42.7	2.5	2.1	5.1
Non-Hispanic other	1,418	16.4	28.3	29.9	21.4	2.3	3.2	7.0

Notes:
[1]CHAMPUS is the civilian health and medical program of the uniformed services; CHAMPVA is the Veterans Administration civilian health and medical program.
[2]Other sources include school, partner's insurance, former husband's insurance, and other sources not shown separately.
NOTE: Percents do not add to 100 because respondents could report more than one source of coverage.

Source: National Survey of Family Growth, 1995.

D3.7. Percentage of Homes in which Child is Covered by Medicare/Medicaid, by Race: March 1998

	Non-Hispanic Whites	Non-Hispanic Blacks	American Indians/ Aleuts/Eskimos	Asians and Pacific Islanders	Hispanic	Total
%	14.8%	39.1%	34.3%	16.8%	32.5%	21.7%
N	2828	1415	156	178	2065	6642
Total	19114	3615	455	1061	6331	30596

Source: Current Population Surveys, March 1998 [Machine readable data files] conducted by the Bureau of the Census for the Bureau of Labor Statistics. Washington, D.C.: Bureau of Census [producer and distributor]. Santa Monica, CA: Unicon Research Corporation [producer and distributor of CPS Utilities], 1999.

D3.8. Percentage of Households Covered by Medicaid, by Race: March 1998

	Non-Hispanic Whites	Non-Hispanic Blacks	American Indians/ Aleuts/Eskimos	Asians and Pacific Islanders	Hispanic	Total
%	6.8%	22.4%	20.6%	9.2%	18.5%	10.4%
N	6231	2839	311	414	3839	13634
Total	92152	12693	1508	4513	20751	131617

Source: Current Population Surveys, March 1998 [Machine readable data files] conducted by the Bureau of the Census for the Bureau of Labor Statistics. Washington, D.C.: Bureau of Census [producer and distributor]. Santa Monica, CA: Unicon Research Corporation [producer and distributor of CPS Utilities], 1999.

D3.9. Percentage of Households Covered by Medicare, by Race: March 1998

	Non-Hispanic Whites	Non-Hispanic Blacks	American Indians/ Aleuts/Eskimos	Asians and Pacific Islanders	Hispanic	Total
%	15.2%	11.6%	8.6%	7.5%	6.5%	13.1%
N	13976	1472	130	340	1351	17269
Total	92152	12693	1508	4513	20751	131617

Source: Current Population Surveys, March 1998 [Machine readable data files] conducted by the Bureau of the Census for the Bureau of Labor Statistics. Washington, D.C.: Bureau of Census [producer and distributor]. Santa Monica, CA: Unicon Research Corporation [producer and distributor of CPS Utilities], 1999.

D3.10. Percent Retired or Left Job for Health Reasons, by Race: March 1998

	Non-Hispanic Whites	Non-Hispanic Blacks	American Indians/ Aleuts/Eskimos	Asians and Pacific Islanders	Hispanic	Total
%	4.0%	5.8%	5.1%	1.6%	2.7%	3.9%
N	2902	529	54	55	394	3934
Total	73038	9078	1053	3452	14400	101021

Source: Current Population Surveys, March 1998 [Machine readable data files] conducted by the Bureau of the Census for the Bureau of Labor Statistics. Washington, D.C.: Bureau of Census [producer and distributor]. Santa Monica, CA: Unicon Research Corporation [producer and distributor of CPS Utilities], 1999.

D3.11. Nursing Home Residents 65 Years Old and Over, by Race and Ethnicity: 1995

[Covers nursing and related care homes in the conterminous United States that had three or more beds, were staffed for use by residents, and routinely provided nursing and personal care services. Excludes places providing only room and board and places serving specific health problems. Based on the 1995 National Nursing Home Survey, a two-stage survey sample of nursing homes and their residents. Subject to sampling variability.]

CHARACTERISTIC \1	Number (1,000)	Percent distribution
Total \2	1,385	100.0
White	1,240	89.5
Black	118	8.5
Hispanic	32	2.3
Non-Hispanic	1,276	92.1

Notes:
\1 At time of admission.
\2 Includes other and/or unknown, not shown separately.

Source: U.S. National Center for Health Statistics, Advance Data, No. 289, July 2, 1997.

D3.12. Home Health and Hospice Care Patients, by Race: 1996

ITEM	CURRENT PATIENTS \1			DISCHARGES \2		
	Total	Home health care	Hospice care	Total	Home health care	Hospice care
Total (1,000)	2,486.8	2,427.5	59.4	8,168.9	7,775.7	393.2
PERCENT DISTRIBUTION						
Race:						
White	65.5	65.1	83.7	63.5	62.8	78.9
Black	12.0	12.0	8.3	7.6	7.4	11.2
Other or unknown	22.5	22.9	8.0	28.9	29.8	9.9

Source: U.S. National Center for Health Statistics, Vital and Health Statistics, Advance Data, Nos. 259, 272, 274, and 297.

D4. ATTITUDES ABOUT HEALTH CARE

D4.1. Attitudes toward Doctors, by Race: 1998

Think about the medical care you are now receiving. If you have not received any medical care, choose the answer that you would expect to receive if you had to seek care today.

	White	Black	Other	Total
Doctors are not as thorough as they should be.				
Strongly agree	9.5%	8.8%	9.5%	9.4%
Agree	41.8	39.7	48.8	41.9
Uncertain	13.3	19.1	11.9	14.0
Disagree	31.7	30.4	26.2	31.2
Strongly disagree	3.8	2.1	3.6	3.5
(N)	**1085**	**194**	**84**	**1363**
Doctors always do their best to keep the patient from worrying.				
Strongly agree	4.1%	2.5%	5.9%	4.0%
Agree	45.1	61.9	51.8	47.9
Uncertain	20.6	15.7	21.2	20.0
Disagree	27.4	17.3	18.8	25.4
Strongly disagree	2.8	2.5	2.4	2.7
(N)	**1085**	**197**	**85**	**1367**
Doctors sometimes take unnecessary risks in treating their patients.				
Strongly agree	3.7%	3.6%	7.5%	3.9%
Agree	29.5	38.1	28.8	30.7
Uncertain	24.4	27.3	31.3	25.2
Disagree	38.7	25.3	27.5	36.0
Strongly disagree	3.8	5.7	5.0	4.1
(N)	**1058**	**194**	**80**	**1332**
I would trust my doctor.				
Completely	29.2%	26.1%	16.3%	29.0%
A great deal	29.8	25.6	31.4	29.9
Somewhat	31.5	34.7	37.2	33.1
Only a little	6.3	9	9.3	7.2
Not at all	3.2	4.5	5.8	4.7
(N)	**1080**	**199**	**86**	**1365**
I believe that the doctors will be able to control my pain.				
Strongly agree	9.4%	7.9%	5.3%	9.1%
Agree	56.4	48.7	38.2	56.1
Not agree/disagree	17.9	19.6	28.9	24.0
Disagree	12.8	16.9	23.7	13.9
Strongly disagree	3.4	6.9	3.9	4.2
(N)	**1053**	**189**	**76**	**1318**

Source: General Social Survey, 1998.

D4.2. Attitudes about Care Given by Doctors, by Race: 1998

Think about the medical care you are now receiving. If you have not received any medical care, choose the answer that you would expect to receive if you had to seek care today.

	White	Black	Other	Total
Doctors are very careful to check everything when examining their patients.				
Strongly agree	2.8%	1.0%	8.2%	2.9%
Agree	30.3	34.2	40.0	31.5
Uncertain	20.6	20.7	21.2	20.7
Disagree	41.9	38.9	29.4	40.7
Strongly disagree	4.3	5.2	1.2	4.3
(N)	**1085**	**193**	**85**	**1363**
Doctors always treat their patients with respect.				
Strongly agree	5.5%	6.7%	11.8%	6.1%
Agree	43.9	51.3	48.2	45.2
Uncertain	13.8	14.9	16.5	14.1
Disagree	32.7	24.1	21.2	30.7
Strongly disagree	4.1	3.1	2.4	3.8
(N)	**1086**	**195**	**85**	**1366**
I hardly ever see the same doctor when I go for medical care.				
Strongly agree	2.9%	2.6%	4.7%	3.0%
Agree	14.6	20.8	21.2	15.9
Uncertain	3.9	3.6	11.8	4.4
Disagree	58.1	60.9	49.4	58.0
Strongly disagree	20.5	12.0	12.9	18.8
(N)	**1070**	**192**	**85**	**1347**
Doctors always avoid unnecessary expenses.				
Strongly agree	2.5%	1.6%	3.8%	2.5%
Agree	20.7	20.7	16.3	20.5
Uncertain	20.4	20.2	30.0	20.9
Disagree	48.6	45.2	47.5	48.0
Strongly disagree	7.8	12.2	2.5	8.1
(N)	**1071**	**188**	**80**	**1339**
Doctors cause people to worry a lot because they do not explain medical problems to patients.				
Strongly agree	6.4%	9.2%	3.5%	6.6%
Agree	35.3	33.3	25.9	34.4
Uncertain	15.8	14.9	22.4	16.0
Disagree	37.9	39.0	42.4	38.3
Strongly disagree	4.7	3.6	5.9	4.6
(N)	**1085**	**195**	**85**	**1365**

Source: General Social Survey, 1998.

D4.3. Attitudes toward Health Care, by Race: 1998

Think about the medical care you are now receiving. If you have not received any medical care, choose the answer that you would expect to receive if you had to seek care today.

	White	Black	Other	Total
The medical problems I've had in the past are ignored when I seek care for a new medical problem.				
Strongly agree	2.7%	3.1%	2.4%	2.7%
Agree	15.0	16.8	19.5	15.5
Uncertain	14.8	14.7	18.3	15.0
Disagree	59.3	61.3	52.4	59.3
Strongly disagree	8.1	4.2	7.3	7.5
(N)	**1053**	**191**	**82**	**1326**
Doctors never recommend surgery (an operation) unless there is no other way to solve the problem.				
Strongly agree	3.0%	6.3%	7.6%	3.7%
Agree	40.2	37.7	48.1	40.3
Uncertain	19.0	23.0	26.6	20.1
Disagree	34.2	28.3	16.5	32.3
Strongly disagree	3.5	4.7	1.3	3.5
(N)	**1066**	**191**	**79**	**1336**
My doctor is willing to refer me to a specialist when needed.				
Strongly agree	15.1%	10.5%	16.0%	14.5%
Agree	72.1	74.7	63.0	71.9
Uncertain	7.6	6.8	16.0	8.0
Disagree	4.8	7.4	3.7	5.1
Strongly disagree	0.4	0.5	1.2	0.4
(N)	**1072**	**190**	**81**	**1343**
I worry that my doctor is being prevented from telling me the full range of options for my treatment.				
Strongly agree	3.4%	3.2%	3.8%	3.4%
Agree	19.3	15.9	21.3	19.0
Uncertain	16.4	21.7	25.0	17.7
Disagree	52.2	53.4	37.5	51.5
Strongly disagree	8.7	5.8	12.5	8.5
(N)	**1071**	**189**	**80**	**1340**
I worry that I will be denied the treatment or services I need.				
Strongly agree	4.3%	4.1%	6.2%	4.3%
Agree	19.8	16.9	17.3	19.2
Uncertain	13.1	12.8	22.2	13.6
Disagree	53.6	61.0	44.4	54.1
Strongly disagree	9.3	5.1	9.9	8.7
(N)	**1081**	**195**	**81**	**1357**
I worry that my doctor will put cost considerations above the care I need.				
Strongly agree	3.5%	4.7%	2.5%	3.6%
Agree	20.0	19.7	32.1	20.6
Uncertain	14.0	17.1	19.8	14.8
Disagree	53.4	52.8	37.0	52.4
Strongly disagree	9.1	5.7	8.6	8.6
(N)	**1082**	**193**	**81**	**1356**
I doubt that my doctor really cares about me as a person.				
Strongly agree	1.7%	1.6%	4.8%	1.8%
Agree	14.7	12.0	20.2	14.7
Uncertain	14.1	18.2	25.0	15.4
Disagree	56.3	58.9	45.2	56.0
Strongly disagree	13.2	9.4	4.8	12.1
(N)	**1078**	**192**	**84**	**1354**
I trust my doctor's judgements about my medical care.				
Strongly agree	12.9%	8.7%	8.3%	12.0%
Agree	68.5	71.9	72.6	69.2
Uncertain	11.2	11.7	15.5	11.5
Disagree	6.3	6.1	2.4	6.0
Strongly disagree	1.2	1.5	1.2	1.2
(N)	**1084**	**196**	**84**	**1364**

D4.3. Attitudes toward Health Care, by Race: 1998 *(continued)*

	White	Black	Other	Total
I feel my doctor does not do everything he/she should for my medical care.				
Strongly agree	1.6%	2.6%	4.8%	1.9%
Agree	17.6	17.1	28.6	18.2
Uncertain	14.6	17.1	16.7	15.1
Disagree	56.1	56.0	41.7	55.2
Strongly disagree	10.1	7.3	8.3	9.6
(N)	**1076**	**193**	**84**	**1353**
I trust my doctor to put my medical needs above all other considerations when treating my medical problems.				
Strongly agree	10.2%	7.8%	13.6%	10.0%
Agree	64.5	64.1	56.8	63.9
Uncertain	15.1	15.6	16.0	15.2
Disagree	9.5	10.9	13.6	10.0
Strongly disagree	0.7	1.6	—	0.8
(N)	**1072**	**192**	**81**	**1345**
My doctor is a real expert in taking care of medical problems like mine.				
Strongly agree	9.0%	8.2%	9.8%	9.0%
Agree	52.6	54.9	42.7	52.3
Uncertain	26.0	26.6	42.7	27.1
Disagree	11.4	7.6	4.9	10.5
Strongly disagree	1.0	2.7	—	1.1
(N)	**1051**	**184**	**82**	**1317**
I trust my doctor to tell me if a mistake was made about my treatment.				
Strongly agree	7.3%	7.4%	13.6%	7.7%
Agree	56.0	50.5	45.7	54.6
Uncertain	15.5	17.9	24.7	16.4
Disagree	16.5	18.9	13.6	16.7
Strongly disagree	4.7	5.3	2.5	4.7
(N)	**1062**	**190**	**81**	**1333**
I worry that if I run out of money or health insurance I will get second class health care.				
Strongly agree	14.9%	18.6%	17.1%	16.3%
Agree	41.1	41.8	43.9	42.0
Uncertain	13.3	13.4	12.2	13.1
Disagree	26.5	20.6	20.7	25.9
Strongly disagree	4.2	5.7	6.1	5.2
(N)	**1063**	**194**	**82**	**1339**

Source: General Social Survey, 1998.

D4.4. Concerns about Terminal Illness, by Race: 1998

Now, I would like to talk about concerns you may have when considering what may happen at the end of your life. Please tell me how much you agree or disagree with each of these statements:

	White	Black	Other
I worry about the economic burden that a terminal illness might cause my family.			
Strongly agree	22.9%	19.7%	21.2%
Agree	40.6	34.3	34.1
Not agree/disagree	10.5	12.1	11.8
Disagree	19.9	25.3	23.5
Strongly disagree	6.1	8.6	9.4
(N)	**1081**	**198**	**85**
My religious community would be very helpful if I were terminally ill.			
Strongly agree	17.6%	20.4%	18.3%
Agree	38.5	43.5	35.4
Not agree/disagree	15.4	11.8	20.7
Disagree	17.4	16.7	19.5
Strongly disagree	11.1	7.5	6.1
(N)	**1039**	**186**	**82**
I worry about the emotional burden that my family might face making decisions for me at the end of life.			
Strongly agree	21.2%	18.7%	21.2%
Agree	41.8	40.9	42.4
Not agree/disagree	8.7	9.3	7.1
Disagree	22.6	24.9	22.4
Strongly disagree	5.7	6.2	7.1
(N)	**1079**	**193**	**85**
I believe that the doctors will be able to control my pain.			
Strongly agree	9.4%	7.9%	5.3%
Agree	56.4	48.7	38.2
Not agree/disagree	17.9	19.6	28.9
Disagree	12.8	16.9	23.7
Strongly disagree	3.4	6.9	3.9
(N)	**1053**	**189**	**76**

People sometimes are incapable of making decisions about their care and medical treatment at the end of life. If you were incapable, how much trust would you put in the following people to do what was best for you?

	White	Black	Other
I would trust my family.			
Completely	75.3%	68.7%	75.6%
A great deal	17.6	17.9	16.3
Somewhat	5	8.5	5.8
Only a little	1.1	1.5	2.3
Not at all	.9	3.5	0
(N)	**1091**	**201**	**86**
I would trust my doctor.			
Completely	29.2%	26.1%	16.3%
A great deal	29.8	25.6	31.4
Somewhat	31.5	34.7	37.2
Only a little	6.3	9	9.3
Not at all	3.2	4.5	5.8
(N)	**1080**	**199**	**86**
I would trust the courts.			
Completely	3.6%	5.2%	3.5%
A great deal	4	5.2	3.5
Somewhat	27	29.5	32.9
Only a little	22.8	16.1	12.9
Not at all	42.7	44	47.1
(N)	**1063**	**193**	**85**

Source: General Social Survey, 1998.

D4.5. Opinions about Allowing Incurable Patients to Die, by Race: 1998

Would you approve of ending a patient's life if a board of doctors appointed by the court agreed that the patient could not be cured?			
	White	**Black**	**Other**
Yes	70.4%	51.2%	66.4%
No	23.8	44.1	26.6
Don't know	5.7	4.7	7
(N)	**1482**	**254**	**128**

Source: General Social Survey, 1998.

D5. MENTAL AND EMOTIONAL HEALTH CARE

D5.1. Experience with Psychiatrist, by Race: 1998

Have you or has anyone else you know ever seen a psychiatrist, psychologist, or counselor?			
	White	**Black**	**Other**
Yes	63.4%	40.9%	45.3%
No	36.6	59.1	54.7
(N)	**1085**	**198**	**86**

Source: General Social Survey, 1998.

D5.2. Beliefs about Psychiatric Medicine, by Race: 1998

Please tell me how much you agree or disagree with the following statements about medicines prescribed by doctors to help people who are having problems with their emotions, nerves, or their mental health:			
	White	**Black**	**Other**
Psychiatric medicine is harmful to the body.			
Strongly agree	5%	10%	9.2%
Agree	19.5	26.3	27.6
Not agree/disagree	27	25	32.9
Disagree	36.2	35	28.9
Strongly disagree	12.3	3.8	1.3
(N)	**976**	**160**	**76**
If symptoms are no longer present, people should stop taking these medications.			
Strongly agree	14.6%	17.5%	26.8%
Agree	34.8	46.2	39
Not agree/disagree	11.9	7.6	12.2
Disagree	29.5	24	20.7
Strongly disagree	9.2	4.7	1.2
(N)	**1009**	**171**	**82**
Taking these medications interferes with daily activities.			
Strongly agree	7.2%	9.9%	17.1%
Agree	30.9	44.1	36.8
Not agree/disagree	25.9	23	30.3
Disagree	30	21.7	13.2
Strongly disagree	6	1.2	2.6
(N)	**967**	**161**	**76**
Taking these medications helps people deal with day-to-day stresses.			
Strongly agree	12.5%	10%	16.7%
Agree	66.7	70	51.3
Not agree/disagree	14.7	15.3	17.9
Disagree	4.8	3.5	14.1
Strongly disagree	1.3	1.2	—
(N)	**1031**	**170**	**78**

D5.2. Beliefs about Psychiatric Medicine, by Race: 1998 *(continued)*

	White	Black	Other
Taking these medications makes things easier in relations with family and friends.			
Strongly agree	10.7%	7.5%	9.5%
Agree	60.7	54.4	44.6
Not agree/disagree	18.6	20	27
Disagree	8.1	17.5	17.6
Strongly disagree	1.9	.6	1.4
(N)	**1003**	**160**	**74**
These medications help people control their symptoms.			
Strongly agree	13.4%	9.8%	11.8%
Agree	71.5	70.7	67.1
Not agree/disagree	11.1	10.9	13.2
Disagree	3.4	8	7.9
Strongly disagree	.6	.6	—
(N)	**1025**	**174**	**76**
Taking medication helps people feel better about themselves.			
Strongly agree	9.5%	7.2%	4%
Agree	54	45.5	38.7
Not agree/disagree	23.6	18	24
Disagree	11.1	25.1	30.7
Strongly disagree	1.8	4.2	2.7
(N)	**1009**	**167**	**75**

Source: General Social Survey, 1998.

D5.3. Reasons to Take Psychiatric Medicine, by Race: 1998

How likely would you be to take doctor-prescribed psychiatric medication in the following situations?			
	White	**Black**	**Other**
. . . Because you were having trouble in your personal life.			
Very likely	9.4%	6.3%	4.7%
Somewhat likely	15.7	14.6	11.8
Mixed	11.6	14.6	11.8
Somewhat unlikely	19.6	16.1	15.3
Very unlikely	43.6	52.1	55.3
(N)	**1061**	**192**	**85**
. . . Because you didn't know how to cope anymore with the stresses of life.			
Very likely	13.8%	6.2%	10.8%
Somewhat likely	24.3	26.4	15.7
Mixed	13.8	11.4	13.3
Somewhat unlikely	18.4	16.6	16.9
Very unlikely	29.7	39.4	43.4
(N)	**1062**	**193**	**83**
. . . Because you were feeling depressed, tired, were having trouble sleeping and concentrating, and felt worthless.			
Very likely	16.3%	12%	16.9%
Somewhat likely	26.9	20.4	20.5
Mixed	14.1	9.9	10.8
Somewhat unlikely	16.9	19.4	13.3
Very unlikely	25.8	38.2	38.6
(N)	**1060**	**191**	**83**
. . . For no apparent reason, you were having periods of intense fear in which you were trembling, sweating, feeling dizzy, and feared losing control or going crazy.			
Very likely	27.8%	20%	24.4%
Somewhat likely	30.6	27.4	20.7
Mixed	14.6	8.4	14.6
Somewhat unlikely	9.7	12.1	12.2
Very unlikely	17.4	32.1	28
(N)	**1054**	**190**	**82**

Source: General Social Survey, 1998.

D5.4. Indicators of Depression, by Race: 1998

In the past 30 days, about how often did you feel:

	White	Black	Other
So sad nothing could cheer you up?			
All of the time	1.2%	2.6%	2.9%
Most of the time	4.2	5.1	9.7
Some of the time	16.1	20.5	19.4
Little of time	27.7	33.3	32
None of the time	50.7	38.5	35.9
(N)	**1132**	**195**	**103**
Nervous?			
All of the time	3%	3.1%	3.8%
Most of the time	6.5	4.1	10.6
Some of the time	27.9	24.5	26
Little of time	33.8	25.5	30.8
None of the time	28.8	42.9	28.8
(N)	**1129**	**196**	**104**
Restless or fidgety?			
All of the time	3.7%	3.6%	3%
Most of the time	9.6	7.7	8.9
Some of the time	28.9	25.6	35.6
Little of time	31.7	25.6	35.6
None of the time	26.1	37.4	29.7
(N)	**1128**	**195**	**101**
Hopeless?			
All of the time	1.3%	1.5%	—%
Most of the time	2.8	2.6	6.8
Some of the time	8.6	8.8	13.6
Little of time	13	13.4	21.4
None of the time	74.4	73.7	58.3
(N)	**1127**	**194**	**103**
That everything was an effort?			
All of the time	2.5%	14.8%	7.8%
Most of the time	7.8	9.7	13.7
Some of the time	22.4	21.9	28.4
Little of time	32.7	19.9	25.5
None of the time	34.5	33.7	24.5
(N)	**1124**	**196**	**102**
Worthless?			
All of the time	1.3%	2.1%	—%
Most of the time	2.8	1	2.9
Some of the time	6.5	8.2	13.6
Little of time	11.4	9.8	13.6
None of the time	77.9	78.9	69.9
(N)	**1127**	**194**	**103**

Source: General Social Survey, 1998.

D5.5. Attitudes toward Psychiatric Medication for Children, by Race: 1998

How likely would you be to give doctor prescribed psychiatric medication to your child or a child you were responsible for in the following situations:

	White	**Black**	**Other**
. . . Because s/he is hostile, often loses his/her temper, often argues with adults, actively defies authority and seems spiteful or vindictive?			
Very likely	12.3%	14%	10.4%
Somewhat likely	22.3	15.6	19.5
Mixed	17	15.6	14.3
Somewhat unlikely	16.8	11.3	18.2
Very unlikely	31.7	43.5	37.7
(N)	**1036**	**186**	**77**
. . . Because s/he is not paying attention at school, does not follow through with school work and chores, has difficulty organizing activities, is easily distracted, talks excessively, and seems to run around or fidget constantly?			
Very likely	9.9%	9.1%	7.7%
Somewhat likely	20.5	13.4	16.7
Mixed	17.9	13.4	15.4
Somewhat unlikely	20.5	17.6	17.9
Very unlikely	31.3	46.5	42.3
(N)	**1036**	**187**	**78**
. . . Because s/he was talking about killing him or herself?			
Very likely	36.5%	29.9%	25.6%
Somewhat likely	22	20.3	17.9
Mixed	17.8	14.4	17.9
Somewhat unlikely	7	8	14.1
Very unlikely	16.7	27.3	24.4
(N)	**1036**	**187**	**78**

Source: General Social Survey, 1998.

D5.6. Feelings of Self Esteem, by Race: 1998

You have a lot of good qualities.

	White	Black	Native American	Asian	Hispanic	Total
Strongly agree	40.6	48.8	36.7	29.9	33.9	40.6
Agree	53.2	46.9	54.1	58.5	52.9	52.4
Neither agree nor disagree	5.3	3.0	8.4	11.5	12.3	6.1
Disagree	0.7	1.0	–	–	0.7	0.7
Strongly disagree	.01	.02	–	–	–	.01

You have a lot to be proud of.

	White	Black	Native American	Asian	Hispanic	Total
Strongly agree	45.0	53.0	40.5	36.3	41.1	45.3
Agree	47.0	41.5	47.6	48.1	47.2	46.2
Neither agree nor disagree	6.6	4.3	10.8	12.8	9.0	6.9
Disagree	1.2	1.0	1.1	2.4	2.6	1.4
Strongly disagree	0.2	0.2	–	–	–	0.2

You like yourself just the way you are.

	White	Black	Native American	Asian	Hispanic	Total
Strongly agree	34.8	47.9	30.8	30.5	35.1	36.7
Agree	44.5	37.3	47.0	48.4	42.1	43.2
Neither agree nor disagree	13.2	8.6	15.1	15.9	14.6	12.8
Disagree	6.6	5.4	5.9	4.7	6.7	6.4
Strongly disagree	0.9	0.8	1.1	–	1.5	0.9

You feel like you are doing everything just about right.

	White	Black	Native American	Asian	Hispanic	Total
Strongly agree	23.1	27.0	18.4	17.3	20.7	23.1
Agree	51.2	49.6	53.4	51.0	47.5	50.5
Neither agree nor disagree	18.1	15.8	17.6	23.2	22.1	18.5
Disagree	6.8	6.9	9.8	7.9	9.0	7.2
Strongly disagree	0.8	0.7	–	–	0.7	0.8

You feel socially accepted.

	White	Black	Native American	Asian	Hispanic	Total
Strongly agree	33.2	39.3	27.8	24.0	30.1	33.3
Agree	54.7	49.9	54.1	60.6	54.8	54.1
Neither agree nor disagree	9.2	8.1	14.3	12.4	11.9	9.6
Disagree	2.3	2.3	2.7	2.8	2.9	2.5
Strongly disagree	0.6	0.4	1.1	–	0.4	0.6

You feel loved and wanted.

	White	Black	Native American	Asian	Hispanic	Total
Strongly agree	44.8	50.8	41.2	31.6	41.0	44.6
Agree	48.1	42.3	50.7	51.0	44.7	47.0
Neither agree nor disagree	5.6	5.3	6.0	14.1	12.0	6.7
Disagree	1.3	1.3	1.6	3.3	2.1	1.4
Strongly disagree	0.2	0.3	–	–	0.2	0.2

Source: General Social Survey, 1998.

D5.7. Adolescent Reports of Self Image and Social Acceptance, by Race and Ethnicity, 1995

Race/Ethnicity	Negative Self Image (a, c)	Social Unacceptance (b, c)
White	2.08	2.28
Black	1.89	2.30
Asian	2.15	2.37
Chinese	2.20	2.43
Filipino	2.15	2.32
Japanese	2.13	2.28
Asian Indian	2.04	2.30
Korean	2.23	2.50
Vietnamese	2.14	2.39
American Indian	2.09	2.42
Hispanic	2.03	2.29
Mexican	2.06	2.27
Chicano/Chicana	2.17	2.42
Cuban	1.98	2.24
Puerto Rican	2.05	2.36
Central/South America	1.96	2.25
Total	2.05	2.29

Notes:
a. Items include: (1) I have a lot of energy, (2) I am well coordinated, (3) I am physically fit, (4) I have a lot of good qualities, (5) I have a lot to be proud of, (6) I like myself just the way I am, (7) I feel like I am doing everything just right.
b. Items include (1) I feel close to people at this school, (2) I feel like part of this school, (3) I am happy at this school, (4) I feel socially accepted, (5) I feel loved and wanted.
c. Scale: 1 = strongly agree, 2 = agree, 3 = neither agree nor disagree, 4 = disagree, 5 = strongly disagree

Source: National Longitudinal Study of Adolescent Health, 1995

D6. LIFE SATISFACTION AND GENERAL HAPPINESS

D6.1. General Happiness, by Race: 1998

Taken all together, how would you say things are these days—would you say that you are very happy, pretty happy, or not too happy?

	White	Black	Other
Very happy	33.7%	22%	28.5%
Pretty happy	56.1	57.8	52.7
Not too happy	10.2	20.2	17.7
Don't know			1.1
(N)	**2226**	**396**	**186**

Source: General Social Survey, 1998.

D6.2. Beliefs about Human Nature, by Race: 1998.

Would you say that most of the time people try to be helpful, or that they are mostly just looking out for themselves?

	White	Black	Other
Helpful	50%	38.6%	40.8%
Look out for self	40.4	52.9	46.9
Depends	9.2	8.6	10.8
Don't know	.3	—	1.5
(N)	**1499**	**280**	**130**

Do you think most people would try to take advantage of you if they got a chance, or would they try to be fair?

	White	Black	Other
Take advantage	33.6%	56.8%	48.1%
Fair	57.4	33.6	32.6
Depends	7.9	9.6	17.1
Don't know	1.1	—	2.3
(N)	**1499**	**280**	**129**

Do you think most people can be trusted?

	White	Black	Other
Can trust	42.4%	17.4%	23.4%
Cannot trust	51.6	77.4	66.5
Depends	5.6	5.3	10.1
Don't know	.4	—	—
(N)	**1855**	**340**	**158**

Source: General Social Survey, 1998.

D7. LEISURE, RECREATIONAL, AND CULTURAL ACTIVITIES

D7.1. Preferences for Time Allocation, by Race: 1998

Suppose you could change the way you spend your time, spending more on some things and less on others. Which of these things on the following list would you like to spend more time on, which would you like to spend less time on, and which would you like to spend the same amount of time as now?

	White	Black	Other
Time in a paid job?			
Spend much more	8%	30.4%	21.7%
Spend a bit more	16.3	14.4	21.7
Spend same	39	31.2	40
Spend a bit less	23.9	16.8	11.7
Spend much less	12.7	7.2	5
(N)	**735**	**125**	**60**
Time doing household work?			
Spend much more	3.8%	10.8%	7.2%
Spend a bit more	20.1	18.4	26.1
Spend same	33.3	35.4	30.4
Spend a bit less	23.2	14.6	13
Spend much less	19.7	20.9	23.2
(N)	**926**	**158**	**69**
Time with your family?			
Spend much more	42%	40.1%	44.9%
Spend a bit more	38.6	37.7	34.8
Spend same	17.8	21	17.4
Spend a bit less	.6	—	1.4
Spend much less	1	1.2	1.4
(N)	**938**	**162**	**69**

D7.1. Preferences for Time Allocation, by Race: 1998 *(continued)*

	White	Black	Other
Time with your friends?			
Spend much more	20.8%	13.3%	17.9%
Spend a bit more	46.9	38	47.8
Spend same	29.9	36.1	31.3
Spend a bit less	1.9	6.3	1.5
Spend much less	.4	6.3	1.5
(N)	**946**	**158**	**67**
Time in leisure activities?			
Spend much more	32.4%	27.8%	18.8%
Spend a bit more	41.7	40.5	52.2
Spend same	23	23.4	24.6
Spend a bit less	2	5.1	1.4
Spend much less	.9	3.2	2.9
(N)	**939**	**158**	**69**

Source: General Social Survey, 1998.

D7.2. Leisure or Cultural Activities, by Race: 1998

Have you visited an art museum or gallery within the past twelve months?

	White	Black	Other	Total
Yes	38.9%	24.0%	37.5%	36.8%
No	61.1	76.0	62.5	63.2
(N)	**1134**	**196**	**104**	**1434**

Have you made art or craft objects such as pottery, woodworking, quilts, or paintings within the past twelve months?

	White	Black	Other	Total
Yes	41.3%	21.9%	31.7%	37.9%
No	58.7	78.1	68.3	62.1
(N)	**1134**	**196**	**104**	**1434**

Have you attended a live ballet or dance performance, not including school performances within the past twelve months?

	White	Black	Other	Total
Yes	20.4%	13.8%	24.0%	19.7%
No	79.6	86.2	76.0	80.3
(N)	**1134**	**196**	**104**	**1434**

Have you attended a classical music or opera performance, not including school performances, within the past twelve months?

	White	Black	Other	Total
Yes	18.7%	9.2%	12.5%	16.9%
No	81.3	90.8	87.5	83.1
(N)	**1135**	**196**	**104**	**1435**

Have you taken part in a music, dance, or theatrical performance within the past twelve months?

	White	Black	Other	Total
Yes	10.9%	8.7%	11.7%	10.6%
No	89.1	91.3	88.3	89.4
(N)	**1133**	**196**	**103**	**1432**

Have you gone to see a movie at a movie theater within the past twelve months?

	White	Black	Other	Total
Yes	67.8%	58.2%	67.3%	66.4%
No	32.2	41.8	32.7	33.6
(N)	**1133**	**196**	**104**	**1433**

Have you played a musical instrument, like a piano, guitar, or violin, within the past twelve months?

	White	Black	Other	Total
Yes	25.4%	14.3%	21.2%	23.5%
No	74.6	85.7	78.8	76.5
(N)	**1132**	**196**	**104**	**1432**

Source: General Social Survey, 1998.

D7.3. Time Reading Newspaper, by Race: 1998

How often do you read the newspaper—every day, a few times a week, once a week, less than once a week, or never?

	White	Black	Other
Every day	45.7 %	34.1%	30.5%
Few times a week	21.2	28.6	25
Once a week	15.1	15.7	22.7
Less than once a week	10.3	11.4	15.6
Never	7.7	10.2	6.3
(N)	**1487**	**255**	**128**

Source: General Social Survey, 1998.

D7.4. Participation in Voluntary Associations, by Race: 1998

Have you done any voluntary activity in the past 12 months in any of the following areas?

	White	Black	Other
Political activities (helping political parties, political movements, election campaigns, etc.)			
No	89.8%	92%	88.5%
Yes, 1-2 times	7.3	4	3.4
Yes, 3-5 times	1.5	2	4.6
Yes, 6/more times	1.4	2	3.4
(N)	**988**	**150**	**87**
Charitable activities (helping the sick, elderly, poor, etc.)			
No	62.1%	52.3%	67%
Yes, 1-2 times	20.9	19.9	17
Yes, 3-5 times	9.2	13.2	9.1
Yes, 6/more times	7.8	14.6	6.8
(N)	**988**	**151**	**88**
Religious and church-related activities (helping churches and religious groups)			
No	66.4%	46.7%	70.1%
Yes, 1-2 times	15.2	17.8	16.1
Yes, 3-5 times	6.1	13.2	5.7
Yes, 6/more times	12.4	22.4	8
(N)	**987**	**152**	**87**
Any other kinds of voluntary activities			
No	62%	59.5%	62.1%
Yes, 1-2 times	17.7	20.9	18.4
Yes, 3-5 times	8.4	9.8	12.6
Yes, 6/more times	11.9	9.8	6.9
(N)	**984**	**153**	**87**

Source: General Social Survey, 1998.

D7.5. Daily Activities of Adolescents, by Race: 1995

During the past week, how many times did you:

1. work around the house, such as cleaning, cooking, doing laundry, doing yardwork, or caring for a pet?

	White	Black	Native American	Asian	Hispanic	Total
Not at all	2.9%	2.9%	3.2%	1.6%	5.0%	3.1%
1 or 2 times	24.4	24.8	18.1	25.2	28.4	24.9
3 or 4 times	35.3	34.5	33.4	35.6	32.6	34.9
5 or more times	37.4	37.8	45.3	37.6	34.0	37.2

2. do hobbies, such as collecting baseball cards, playing a musical instrument, reading, or doing arts and crafts?

	White	Black	Native American	Asian	Hispanic	Total
Not at all	16.5	23.4	15.6	11.6	21.3	17.9
1 or 2 times	33.6	37.1	34.2	36.6	37.1	34.7
3 or 4 times	23.1	21.4	24.0	26.6	22.8	22.9
5 or more times	26.8	18.1	26.1	25.2	18.8	24.5

3. watch television or videos, or play video games?

	White	Black	Native American	Asian	Hispanic	Total
Not at all	3.4	2.7	5.4	4.5	3.9	3.5
1 or 2 times	21.0	15.1	20.5	17.9	19.6	19.8
3 or 4 times	25.6	22.5	22.1	29.7	26.9	25.3
5 or more times	50.0	59.7	52.0	47.9	49.6	51.4

4. go roller-blading, roller-skating, skate-boarding, or bicycling?

	White	Black	Native American	Asian	Hispanic	Total
Not at all	60.0	71.2	63.9	61.7	61.6	62.1
1 or 2 times	22.6	19.9	21.6	21.8	26.0	22.6
3 or 4 times	9.6	6.1	7.0	12.2	8.5	8.9
5 or more times	7.8	2.8	7.5	4.3	3.9	6.4

5. play an active sport, such as baseball, softball, basketball, soccer, swimming, or football?

	White	Black	Native American	Asian	Hispanic	Total
Not at all	26.6	31.8	27.0	25.1	31.4	28.0
1 or 2 times	28.1	27.4	25.3	33.2	27.4	27.9
3 or 4 times	19.4	17.8	18.1	15.9	18.4	18.8
5 or more times	25.9	23.1	29.6	25.9	22.7	25.3

6. exercise, such as jogging, walking, doing karate, jumping rope, doing gymnastics or dancing?

	White	Black	Native American	Asian	Hispanic	Total
Not at all	16.3	15.6	11.9	14.3	15.2	15.8
1 or 2 times	31.9	31.9	35.0	36.9	34.4	32.3
3 or 4 times	25.7	26.9	23.7	26.5	24.9	25.9
5 or more times	26.1	25.6	29.4	22.4	31.1	26.0

7. just hang out with friends?

	White	Black	Native American	Asian	Hispanic	Total
Not at all	5.3	9.4	9.9	7.3	9.7	6.7
1 or 2 times	21.6	24.6	19.9	25.0	26.8	22.8
3 or 4 times	29.4	26.3	27.7	32.7	26.7	28.8
5 or more times	43.7	39.7	42.5	35.0	36.7	41.8

Source: The National Longitudinal Study of Adolescent Health, 1995.

E. Family

The material in this section reports different patterns of family life among racial and ethnic groups. The powerful social forces surrounding race and ethnicity ripple throughout family life. A word of caution is in order before examining the facts and figures describing racial and ethnic families. Social class exerts a very powerful impact on American families and families living in a slum function much differently than families living in an upper-middle class suburb. Thus, some of the differences noted between Black, Hispanic, Asian, and White families are the consequence of over-representation of racial and ethnic families in the lower social classes.

E1. MARRIAGE AND FERTILITY

Minority individuals, especially Blacks, do not marry as often as Whites. As can be seen in E1.1, more than 60 percent of White women over the age of 18 years were married in 1997 as compared with 40 percent of Black women. Nearly as many Hispanic as White women, 59 percent, were married. More than 90 percent of White women eventually marry at least once as compared with 70 percent of Black women. Similar differences in marriage rates appear for men.

A higher proportion of Black women are the head of a single-parent household as compared with other women (E1.3). Nearly half of Black households, 47 percent, are headed by single women as compared with 24 percent of Hispanic households and 14 percent of White households. The percent of single-parent families headed by men is similar among the different racial and ethnic groups. Seven percent of Black and Hispanic households are headed by single men while five percent of White and Asian households are of this type.

The numbers of children born to women between the age of 15 and 44 in different racial and ethnic groups are presented in E1.6. Hispanic women reported the most children, an average of 1.57 children, while White women

had the fewest births, 1.16. Black women were in between, with 1.43 children. The numbers are lower than two because many women have yet to bear children and others have not completed their families. When additional children *expected to be born* were added, fertility increased to 2.66 for Hispanic women, 2.29 for Black women, and 2.11 for White women.

E2. MARITAL HAPPINESS

Husbands and wives among the different racial and ethnic groups report fairly high marital happiness or satisfaction. The several tables in this section report overall marital happiness as well as satisfaction with different aspects of family life. The levels of happiness indicated by White, Black, and Hispanic husbands and wives are very similar. Hispanic couples generally report a bit more happiness and satisfaction than Black couples and White couples.

E3. FAMILY ROLES

The division of family roles is presented in E3.1 and E3.2, which report the number of hours wives and husbands spend doing various household chores each week. Hispanic wives devote the most time to household chores followed by Black wives and then White wives. Hispanic husbands do not help around the house as much as Black husbands, and White husbands help the least. Wives spend more time doing household chores than their husbands, and the differences would be much greater if child care activities were included in the calculation of time devoted to family activities. Minority individuals, both men and women, report more support than do Whites for traditional division of labor, with men being the providers and women the keepers of the home as well as the ones nurturing young children.

E4. DIVORCE

Blacks report a slightly higher divorce rate than Whites and Hispanics (see E4.1). Twelve percent of Black women over the age of 18 were divorced in 1997 as compared with 11 percent of White women and nine percent of Hispanic women. Lack of love and limited understanding were identified by divorced persons as the most important factors leading to divorce regardless of race or ethnicity (see E4.4). As can be seen in E4.5, divorce is generally not sought by the husband and wife equally. In only one fourth of the divorces did husband and wife both desire it, while in nearly half of the divorces—46 percent—one spouse wanted a divorce while the other did not.

Information about parental custody of children, visiting of children with non-custodial parents, and who makes decisions affecting the children is presented in E4.6 through E4.10. Overall, parents seem to deal with children following divorce in similar ways, regardless of racial/ethnic background.

E5. FAMILY ACTIVITIES

Time spent with children doing a variety of activities is also quite similar regardless of race of ethnicity (see E5.1 through E5.5). Parents report they spend considerable time eating meals as a family, helping children with school work, participating in leisure activities, and just talking. Monitoring children's activities and disciplining them when appropriate also seems to be done about the same by parents from different racial and ethnic groups (see E5.6 through E5.8). Hispanic parents appear to be the most demonstrative; more than 90 percent reported they gave their child at least one hug or kiss during the past week. Fewer Black parents—83 percent—indicated they had done so. Finally, significantly more Black parents indicated they spank their children than did parents in other racial and ethnic groups (see E5.24).

E6. CHILD CARE ARRANGEMENTS

There is some variation in how White, Black, and Hispanic families obtain child care. Overall, child care is provided about equally by day care centers, grandparents, and non-relative babysitters for all of the groups. Both Hispanic and White mothers get more help with child care from the fathers of their children than do Black mothers (see E6.3).

E7. EXTENDED FAMILY

Blacks reported greater contact, both phoning and writing, and visiting with an aged mother than either Whites or Hispanics (see E7.1). Also, more Black adults reported they both received help from and gave assistance to aged parents than did White or Hispanic adults (see E7.3 and E7.4). On the other hand, more Hispanic families than White or Black families have an elderly parent living with them (see E7.5). Overall, there is considerable contact or association among members of extended families.

E1. MARRIAGE AND FERTILITY

E.1.1. Marital Status of the Population, by Sex, Race, and Hispanic Origin: 1980 to 1997

[In millions, except percent. As of March. Persons 18 years and over. Excludes members of the Armed Forces except those living off post or with their families on post. Based on Current Population Survey.]

MARITAL STATUS, RACE, AND HISPANIC ORIGIN	TOTAL				MALE				FEMALE			
	1980	1990	1995	1997	1980	1990	1995	1997	1980	1990	1995	1997
Total \1	**159.5**	**181.8**	**191.6**	**195.6**	**75.7**	**86.9**	**92.0**	**94.2**	**83.8**	**95.0**	**99.6**	**101.4**
Never married	32.3	40.4	43.9	45.9	18.0	22.4	24.6	25.4	14.3	17.9	19.3	20.5
Married	104.6	112.6	116.7	116.6	51.8	55.8	57.7	57.9	52.8	56.7	58.9	58.7
Widowed	12.7	13.8	13.4	13.7	2.0	2.3	2.3	2.7	10.8	11.5	11.1	11.1
Divorced	9.9	15.1	17.6	19.3	3.9	6.3	7.4	8.2	6.0	8.8	10.3	11.1
Percent of total	**100.0**	**100.0**	**100.0**	**100.0**	**100.0**	**100.0**	**100.0**	**100.0**	**100.0**	**100.0**	**100.0**	**100.0**
Never married	20.3	22.2	22.9	23.5	23.8	25.8	26.8	27.0	17.1	18.9	19.4	20.2
Married	65.5	61.9	60.9	59.7	68.4	64.3	62.7	61.5	63.0	59.7	59.2	57.9
Widowed	8.0	7.6	7.0	7.0	2.6	2.7	2.5	2.9	12.8	12.1	11.1	10.9
Divorced	6.2	8.3	9.2	9.9	5.2	7.2	8.0	8.7	7.1	9.3	10.3	11.0
White, total	**139.5**	**155.5**	**161.3**	**164.1**	**66.7**	**74.8**	**78.1**	**79.8**	**72.8**	**80.6**	**83.2**	**84.3**
Never married	26.4	31.6	33.2	34.5	15.0	18.0	19.2	19.7	11.4	13.6	14.0	14.7
Married	93.8	99.5	102.0	101.8	46.7	49.5	50.6	50.8	47.1	49.9	51.3	50.9
Widowed	10.9	11.7	11.3	11.7	1.6	1.9	1.9	2.3	9.3	9.8	9.4	9.4
Divorced	8.3	12.6	14.8	16.1	3.4	5.4	6.3	6.9	5.0	7.3	8.4	9.2
Percent of total	**100.0**	**100.0**	**100.0**	**100.0**	**100.0**	**100.0**	**100.0**	**100.0**	**100.0**	**100.0**	**100.0**	**100.0**
Never married	18.9	20.3	20.6	21.0	22.5	24.1	24.6	24.7	15.7	16.9	16.9	17.5
Married	67.2	64.0	63.2	62.1	70.0	66.2	64.9	63.8	64.7	61.9	61.7	60.4
Widowed	7.8	7.5	7.0	7.1	2.5	2.6	2.5	2.8	12.8	12.2	11.3	11.2
Divorced	6.0	8.1	9.1	9.8	5.0	7.2	8.1	8.7	6.8	9.0	10.1	10.9
Black, total	**16.6**	**20.3**	**22.1**	**22.8**	**7.4**	**9.1**	**9.9**	**10.2**	**9.2**	**11.2**	**12.2**	**12.6**
Never married	5.1	7.1	8.5	8.9	2.5	3.5	4.1	4.2	2.5	3.6	4.4	4.7
Married	8.5	9.3	9.6	9.7	4.1	4.5	4.6	4.6	4.5	4.8	4.9	5.0
Widowed	1.6	1.7	1.7	1.6	0.3	0.3	0.3	0.3	1.3	1.4	1.4	1.3
Divorced	1.4	2.1	2.4	2.6	0.5	0.8	0.8	1.0	0.9	1.3	1.5	1.6
Percent of total	**100.0**	**100.0**	**100.0**	**100.0**	**100.0**	**100.0**	**100.0**	**100.0**	**100.0**	**100.0**	**100.0**	**100.0**
Never married	30.5	35.1	38.4	39.1	34.3	38.4	41.7	41.5	27.4	32.5	35.8	37.2
Married	51.4	45.8	43.2	42.4	54.6	49.2	46.7	45.3	48.7	43.0	40.4	40.0
Widowed	9.8	8.5	7.6	7.2	4.2	3.7	3.1	3.3	14.3	12.4	11.3	10.4
Divorced	8.4	10.6	10.7	11.3	7.0	8.8	8.5	9.9	9.5	12.0	12.5	12.4
Hispanic, \2 total	**7.9**	**13.6**	**17.6**	**19.1**	**3.8**	**6.7**	**8.8**	**9.7**	**4.1**	**6.8**	**8.8**	**9.4**
Never married	1.9	3.7	5.0	5.8	1.0	2.2	3.0	3.5	0.9	1.5	2.1	2.3
Married	5.2	8.4	10.4	11.1	2.5	4.1	5.1	5.5	2.6	4.3	5.3	5.6
Widowed	0.4	0.5	0.7	0.7	0.1	0.1	0.2	0.1	0.3	0.4	0.6	0.6
Divorced	0.5	1.0	1.4	1.4	0.2	0.4	0.6	0.6	0.3	0.6	0.8	0.9
Percent of total	**100.0**	**100.0**	**100.0**	**100.0**	**100.0**	**100.0**	**100.0**	**100.0**	**100.0**	**100.0**	**100.0**	**100.0**
Never married	24.1	27.2	28.6	30.6	27.3	32.1	33.8	35.7	21.1	22.5	23.5	25.2
Married	65.6	61.7	59.3	58.1	67.1	60.9	57.9	56.9	64.3	62.4	60.7	59.3
Widowed	4.4	4.0	4.2	3.8	1.6	1.5	1.8	1.5	7.1	6.5	6.6	6.1
Divorced	5.8	7.0	7.9	7.6	4.0	5.5	6.6	5.8	7.6	8.5	9.2	9.3

Notes:
\1 Includes persons of other races, not shown separately.
\2 Hispanic persons may be of any race.

Source: US Bureau of the Census, Current Population Reports, P20-506, and earlier reports.; and unpublished data.

E1.2. Marital Status, by Race: March 1998

		NonHispanic Whites	NonHispanic Blacks	American Indians/ Aleuts/Eskimos	Asians and Pacific Islanders	Hispanics	Total
Married, spouse present	%	45.6%	23.9%	28.2%	42.1%	35.5%	41.6%
	N	42036	3039	426	1899	7369	54763
Married/armed forces, spouse present	%	.3%	.3%	.3%	.4%	.2%	.3%
	N	270	33	4	18	34	359
Married, spouse absent	%	.6%	1.1%	1.2%	2.3%	1.5%	.9%
	N	557	138	18	106	321	1140
Widowed	%	5.5%	5.8%	4.5%	3.2%	2.4%	5.0%
	N	5083	736	68	143	507	6537
Divorced	%	7.4%	7.9%	8.8%	3.6%	4.8%	7.0%
	N	6852	1009	132	161	995	9149
Separated	%	1.3%	3.5%	2.0%	1.0%	2.7%	1.7%
	N	1178	440	30	46	555	2249
Never married	%	39.3%	57.5%	55.0%	47.4%	52.9%	43.6%
	N	36176	4298	830	2140	10976	57420
	Total	92152	12693	1508	4513	20751	131617

Source: Current Population Surveys, March 1998 [Machine readable data files] conducted by the Bureau of the Census for the Bureau of Labor Statistics. Washington: Bureau of Census [producer and distributor]. Santa Monica, CA: Unicon Research Corporation [producer and distributor of CPS Utilities], 1999.

E1.3. Family and Nonfamily Households, by Race, Hispanic Origin, and Type: 1980 to 1997

[As of March, except as noted. Based on Current Population Survey, except as noted.]

RACE, HISPANIC ORIGIN AND TYPE	NUMBER (1,000)					PERCENT DISTRIBUTION				
	1980	1985	1990	1995	1997	1980	1985	1990	1995	1997
TOTAL HOUSEHOLDS										
Total \1	80,776	86,789	93,347	98,990	101,018	100	100	100	100	100
White	70,766	75,328	80,163	83,737	85,059	88	87	86	85	84
Black	8,586	9,480	10,486	11,655	12,109	11	11	11	12	12
Hispanic \2	3,684	4,883	5,933	7,735	8,225	5	6	6	8	8
FAMILY HOUSEHOLDS										
White, total	52,243	54,400	56,590	58,437	58,934	100	100	100	100	100
Married couple	44,751	45,643	46,981	47,899	47,650	86	84	83	82	81
Male householder \3	1,441	1,816	2,303	2,507	2,944	3	3	4	4	5
Female householder \3	6,052	6,941	7,306	8,031	8,339	12	13	13	14	14
Black, total	6,184	6,778	7,470	8,093	8,455	100	100	100	100	100
Married couple	3,433	3,469	3,750	3,842	3,851	56	51	50	47	46
Male householder \3	256	344	446	536	657	4	5	6	7	8
Female householder \3	2,495	2,964	3,275	3,716	3,947	40	44	44	46	47
Asian or Pacific Islander, total \4	818	(NA)	1,531	1,588	2,246	100	(NA)	100	100	100
Married couple	691	(NA)	1,256	1,290	1,763	84	(NA)	82	81	78
Male householder \3	39	(NA)	86	98	186	5	(NA)	6	6	8
Female householder \3	88	(NA)	188	200	297	11	(NA)	12	13	13
Hispanic, total \2	3,029	3,939	4,840	6,200	6,631	100	100	100	100	100
Married couple	2,282	2,824	3,395	4,235	4,520	75	72	70	68	68
Male householder \3	138	210	329	479	494	5	5	7	8	7
Female householder \3	610	905	1,116	1,485	1,617	20	23	23	24	24
NONFAMILY HOUSEHOLDS										
White, total	18,522	20,928	23,573	25,300	26,125	100	100	100	100	100
Male householder	7,499	8,608	9,951	11,093	11,481	40	41	42	44	44
Female householder	11,023	12,320	13,622	14,207	14,644	60	59	58	56	56
Black, total	2,402	2,703	3,015	3,562	3,654	100	100	100	100	100
Male householder	1,146	1,244	1,313	1,653	1,669	48	46	44	46	46
Female householder	1,256	1,459	1,702	1,909	1,985	52	54	56	54	54
Hispanic, total \2	654	944	1,093	1,535	1,593	100	100	100	100	100
Male householder	365	509	587	790	854	56	54	54	51	54
Female householder	289	435	506	745	740	44	46	46	49	46

Notes:
NA Not available.
\1 Includes other races not shown separately.
\2 Hispanic persons may be of any race. 1970 data as of April.
\3 No spouse present.
\4 1980 data as of April and are from 1980 Census of Population. When comparing 1995 estimates of number of households with other years, caution should be used.

Source: US Bureau of the Census, Current Population Reports, P20-509, and earlier reports; and unpublished data

E1.4. Number of Family Members Under 18, by Race: March 1998

Number of Family Members		NonHispanic Whites	NonHispanic Blacks	American Indians/ Aleuts/ Eskimos	Asians and Pacific Islanders	Hispanics	Total
0	%	48.7%	37.1%	35.1%	39.3%	28.1%	43.9%
	N	44887	4707	530	1773	5830	57727
1	%	17.3%	20.3%	19.1%	21.9%	20.6%	18.3%
	N	15970	2583	288	989	4267	24097
2	%	20.0%	22.1%	19.2%	22.7%	24.7%	21.0%
	N	18420	2808	289	1024	5118	27659
3	%	9.9%	12.2%	14.9%	9.5%	15.8%	11.1%
	N	9079	1545	224	430	3279	14557
4	%	2.8%	4.6%	8.3%	3.5%	7.1%	3.7%
	N	2572	578	125	156	1479	4910
5	%	.9%	2.1%	3.1%	1.8%	2.3%	1.3%
	N	799	261	45	79	487	1671
6+	%	.5%	1.7%	.5%	1.4%	1.4%	.8%
	N	425	211	7	62	291	1006
	%	100.0	100.0	100.0	100.0	100.0	100.0
Total		92152	12693	1508	4513	20751	131617

Source: Current Population Surveys, March 1998 [Machine readable data files] conducted by the Bureau of the Census for the Bureau of Labor Statistics. Washington, D.C.: Bureau of Census [producer and distributor]. Santa Monica, CA: Unicon Research Corporation [producer and distributor of CPS Utilities], 1999.

E1.5. Children Under 18 Years Old, by Presence of Parents: 1970 to 1997

[As of March. Excludes persons under 18 years old who maintained households or family groups. Based on Current Population Survey; includes members of Armed Forces living off post or with their families on post, but excludes all other members of Armed Forces.]

| RACE, HISPANIC ORIGIN, AND YEAR | Number (1,000) | Both parents | PERCENT LIVING WITH | | | | | | Father only | Neither parent |
| | | | Mother only | | | | | | | |
			Total	Divorced	Married, spouse absent	Never married	Widowed			
ALL RACES \1										
1970	69,162	85	11	3	5	1	2		1	3
1980	63,427	77	18	8	6	3	2		2	4
1985	62,475	74	21	9	5	6	2		3	3
1987	62,932	73	21	9	5	6	1		3	3
1988	63,179	73	21	8	5	7	1		3	3
1989	63,637	73	22	8	5	7	1		3	3
1990	64,137	73	22	8	5	7	2		3	3
1991	65,093	72	22	8	6	8	1		3	3
1992	65,965	71	23	8	6	8	1		3	3
1993	66,893	71	23	9	6	8	1		3	3
1994	69,508	69	23	8	6	9	1		3	4
1995	70,254	69	23	9	6	8	1		4	4
1996	70,908	68	24	9	6	9	1		4	4
1997	70,983	68	24	8	5	9	1		4	4
WHITE										
1970	58,790	90	8	3	3	(Z)	2		1	2
1980	52,242	83	14	7	4	1	2		2	2
1985	50,836	80	16	8	4	2	1		2	2
1987	51,112	79	16	8	4	3	1		3	2
1988	51,030	79	16	8	4	3	1		3	2
1989	51,134	80	16	8	4	3	1		3	2
1990	51,390	79	16	8	4	3	1		3	2
1991	51,918	79	17	8	5	3	1		3	2
1992	52,493	77	18	8	5	4	1		3	2
1993	53,075	77	17	8	4	4	1		3	2
1994	54,795	76	18	8	4	4	1		3	3
1995	55,327	76	18	8	5	4	1		3	3
1996	55,714	75	18	8	5	5	1		4	3
1997	55,869	75	18	8	4	5	1		4	3
BLACK										
1970	9,422	59	30	5	16	4	4		2	10
1980	9,375	42	44	11	16	13	4		2	12
1985	9,479	40	51	11	12	25	3		3	7
1987	9,612	40	50	10	12	26	3		3	7
1988	9,699	39	51	8	12	28	3		3	7
1989	9,835	38	51	10	12	27	2		3	8
1990	10,018	38	51	10	12	27	2		4	8
1991	10,209	36	54	10	11	31	2		4	7
1992	10,427	36	54	10	12	31	1		3	7
1993	10,660	36	54	10	12	31	1		3	7
1994	11,177	33	53	10	12	30	1		4	10
1995	11,301	33	52	11	11	29	2		4	11
1996	11,434	33	53	9	11	31	2		4	9
1997	11,369	35	52	9	11	31	1		5	8
HISPANIC \2										
1970\3	4,006	78	(NA)	(NA)	(NA)	(NA)	(NA)		(NA)	(NA)
1980	5,459	75	20	6	8	4	2		2	4
1985	6,057	68	27	7	11	7	2		2	3

E1.5. Children Under 18 Years Old, by Presence of Parents: 1970 to 1997 (continued)

RACE, HISPANIC ORIGIN, AND YEAR	Number (1,000)	Both parents	PERCENT LIVING WITH							
			Mother only					Father only	Neither parent
			Total	Divorced	Married, spouse absent	Never married	Widowed		
HISPANIC (continued)										
1987	6,647	66	28	8	9	9	2	3	4
1988	6,786	66	27	8	9	9	2	3	4
1989	6,973	67	28	8	10	9	1	3	3
1990	7,174	67	27	7	10	8	2	3	3
1991	7,462	66	27	7	10	9	2	3	4
1992	7,619	65	28	8	9	10	1	4	3
1993	7,776	65	28	7	8	11	1	4	4
1994	9,496	63	28	6	9	11	2	4	5
1995	9,843	63	28	8	9	10	1	4	4
1996	10,251	62	29	7	9	11	1	4	5
1997	10,526	64	27	7	7	12	1	4	5

Notes:
NA Not available.
Z Less than 0.5 percent.
\1 Includes other races not shown separately.
\2 Hispanic persons may be of any race.
\3 All persons under 18 years old.

Source: U.S. Bureau of the Census, Current Population Reports, P20-506, and earlier reports; and unpublished data.

E1.6. Number of Children Ever Born to Women 15–44 Years of Age, Additional Births Expected, and Total Births Expected, by Race and Hispanic Origin: 1995

Characteristic	Number in thousands	Children ever born Mean	Additional births expected	Total births expected
All women	60,201	1.242	0.973	2.214
Race and Hispanic origin				
Hispanic	6,702	1.569	1.093	2.663
Non-Hispanic white	42,522	1.163	0.951	2.114
Non-Hispanic black	8,210	1.425	0.867	2.292
Non-Hispanic other	2,766	1.123	0.316	2.440

Source: National Survey of Family Growth, 1995.

E1.7. Percent of Women 18–44 Years of Age Who Are Seeking to Adopt a Child, and Percent Who Have Taken Specified Steps toward Adoption, by Race and Hispanic Origin: 1995

Characteristic	Number in thousands	Currently seeking to adopt	Steps toward adoption	
			Applied to an agency	Got a lawyer
			Percent	
All women /1	54,748	0.9	0.2	0.0
Race and Hispanic origin				
Hispanic	6,015	1.2	0.4	-
Non-Hispanic white	38,987	0.7	0.1	0.1
Non-Hispanic black	7,357	1.8	0.2	0.0
Non-Hispanic other	2,390	1.8	0.3	0.3

Notes:
- Quantity zero.
0.0 Quantity more than zero but less than 0.05.
/1Includes women with missing information on adoption or infertility services.

Source: National Survey of Family Growth, 1995.

E1.8. Percent of Women 15–44 Years of Age Who Have Ever Cohabited, Are Currently Cohabiting, Have Ever Married, or Have Ever Married or Cohabited, by Race and Hispanic Origin: 1995

Characteristic	Number in thousands	Ever cohabited	Currently cohabiting	Ever married	Ever married or cohabited
				Percent	
All women	60,201	41.1	7.0	62.3	72.5
Race and Hispanic origin					
Hispanic	6,702	36.7	8.2	61.4	71.8
Non-Hispanic white	42,522	42.6	7.0	66.4	75.3
Non-Hispanic black	8,210	40.1	6.9	43.1	60.3
Non-Hispanic other	2,767	31.7	4.6	68.5	66.8

Source: National Survey of Family Growth, 1995.

E1.9. Number of Women 15–44 Years of Age, and Percent Distribution Who Have Cohabited Relative to First Marriage, by Race and Hispanic Origin: 1995

Characteristic	Number in thousands	Total	Never cohabited	Never married	Ever cohabited	
					Before first marriage	After first marriage
All women	60,201	100.0%	58.9%	10.2%	23.6%	7.3%
Race and Hispanic origin						
Hispanic	6,702	100.0	63.3	10.4	19.2	7.1
Non-Hispanic white	42,522	100.0	57.4	8.9	25.6	8.1
Non-Hispanic black	8,210	100.0	59.9	17.3	17.9	5.0
Non-Hispanic other	2,767	100.0	68.3	8.3	19.8	3.6

Note:
Percents may not add to 100 due to rounding.

Source: National Survey of Family Growth, 1995.

E1.10. Number of Women 15–44 Years of Age Who Have Ever Cohabited and Percent Distribution by Status of First Cohabitation, by Race and Hispanic Origin: 1995

Characteristic	Number in thousands	Total	Intact cohabitation	Dissolved cohabitation	Intact marriage	Dissolved marriage
All women	24,737	100.0%	9.8%	32.8%	36.5%	20.8%
Race and Hispanic origin						
Hispanic	2,460	100.0	13.2	33.2	35.3	18.3
Non-Hispanic white	18,104	100.0	9.5	29.8	39.3	21.4
Non-Hispanic black	3,295	100.0	9.8	49.1	22.8	18.3
Non-Hispanic other	878	100.0	6.8	32.8	35.0	25.3

Note:
Percent may not add to 100 due to rounding.

Source: National Survey of Family Growth, 1995.

E1.11. Married Couples of Same or Mixed Race and Origin: 1970 to 1997

[In thousands. As of March, except as noted. Persons 15 years old and over. Persons of Hispanic origin may be of any race. Except as noted, based on Current Population Survey and includes members of Armed Forces living off post or with their families on post, but excludes all other members of Armed Forces.]

RACE AND ORIGIN OF SPOUSES	1970 \1	1980	1990	1992	1993	1994	1995	1996	1997
Married couples, total	44,598	49,714	53,256	53,512	54,199	54,251	54,937	54,664	54,666
RACE									
Same race couples	43,922	48,264	50,889	50,873	51,437	51,204	51,733	51,616	51,489
White/White	40,578	44,910	47,202	47,358	47,782	47,606	48,030	48,056	47,791
Black/Black	3,344	3,354	3,687	3,515	3,655	3,598	3,703	3,560	3,698
Interracial couples	310	651	964	1,161	1,195	1,283	1,392	1,260	1,264
Black/White	65	167	211	246	242	296	328	337	311
Black husband/White wife	41	122	150	163	182	196	206	220	201
White husband/Black wife	24	45	61	83	60	100	122	117	110
White/other race \2	233	450	720	883	920	909	988	884	896
Black/other race \2	12	34	33	32	33	78	76	39	57
All other couples \2	366	799	1,401	1,478	1,567	1,764	1,811	1,789	1,912
HISPANIC ORIGIN									
Hispanic/Hispanic	1,368	1,906	3,085	3,297	3,419	3,755	3,857	3,888	4,034
Hispanic/other origin (not Hispanic)	584	891	1,193	1,155	1,206	1,283	1,434	1,464	1,662
All other couples (not of Hispanic origin)	42,645	46,917	48,979	49,060	49,573	49,212	49,646	49,312	48,970

Notes:
\1 As of April and based on Census of Population.
\2 Excluding White and Black.

Source: U.S. Bureau of the Census, Current Population Reports, P20-509; and unpublished data.

E2. MARITAL HAPPINESS

E2.1. Happiness in Marriage, by Race

Taking things all together, how would you describe your marriage? Would you say your marriage is very happy, pretty happy, or not too happy?

	Race		
Happiness	White	Black	Other
Very happy	66.1%	47.1%	57.5%
Pretty happy	31.6	47.1	37
Not too happy	2.3	5.8	5.5
Don't know	.1	—	—
(N)	1144	121	73

Source: General Social Survey, 1998.

E2.2. Happiness with Aspects of Marriage, by Race, 1994

	Aspects of Marriage								
	Overall Relationship	Understanding From Spouse	Love and Affection	Time with Spouse	Demands from Spouse	Sexual Relationship	Way Spouse Spends Money	Housework Spouse Does	Spouse as Parent
Total	*6.0	5.5	5.8	5.2	5.4	5.3	5.5	5.6	6.1
Race of Respondent									
Black	5.8	5.5	5.6	5.2	5.1	5.3	5.1	5.3	6.0
White	6.0	5.5	5.8	5.2	5.4	5.3	5.5	5.6	6.1
Hispanic	6.0	5.7	5.9	5.5	5.2	5.5	5.4	5.6	6.2
Other	5.9	5.7	5.9	5.3	5.3	5.7	5.7	5.5	5.9

Note:
*Mean score or on a scale from 1 for very unhappy to 7 for very happy.

Source: National Survey of Families and Households, 1994.

E2.3. Assessments of Various Aspects of Family Life by Married Individuals, by Race, 1994

	Percent Who "Agree"				
	Our Family Has Fun Together	Things Are Tense and Stressful in Our Family	Family Members Show Concern and Love for Each Other	Family Members Feel Distant and Apart From Each Other	Our Family Works Well Together As a Team
Total	89	14	92	7	76
Race of Respondent					
Black	91	11	92	9	82
White	88	13	92	6	73
Hispanic	91	17	90	14	82
Other	91	8	95	8	85

Source: National Survey of Families and Households,, 1994.

E2.4. Disagreement on Selected Topics among Married Couples, by Race, 1994

	Household Tasks	Money	Spending Time Together	Sex	In-laws	Children
Total	*2.0	2.1	2.0	1.8	1.5	2.1
Race of Respondent						
Black	2.3	2.4	2.3	2.0	1.6	2.2
White	2.0	2.0	1.9	1.7	1.5	2.1
Hispanic	2.2	2.3	2.3	2.0	1.6	2.1
Other	2.1	1.9	1.9	1.7	1.5	2.1

Note:
* Mean on scale: 1=never, 2=once a month, 3=several times a month, 4=about once a week, 5= several times a week, 6=almost every day

Source: National Survey of Families and Households, 1994.

E2.5. How Married Couples Deal with Disagreements, by Race, 1994

Question: When you have a serious disagreement with your husband/wife, how often do you:

	Keep Opinions to Self	Discuss Disagreements Calmly	Argue Heatedly or Shout	End up Hitting or Throwing Things
Total	*2.5	3.3	2.1	1.1
Race of Respondent				
Black	2.6	3.4	2.1	1.1
White	2.5	3.4	2.1	1.1
Hispanic	2.4	3.3	2.1	1.1
Other	2.4	3.5	2.2	1.2

Note:
* Means on scale: 1=never, 2=seldom, 3=sometimes, 4=often, 5=always

Source: National Survey of Families and Households, 1994..

E3. FAMILY ROLES

E3.1. Average Hours per Week Wives Spend Doing Household Tasks, by Race, 1994

	Hours per Week								
	Preparing Meals	Washing Dishes	Cleaning House	Outdoor Tasks	Shopping	Washing Ironing	Paying Bills	Auto Maintenance	Driving
Total	6.2	5.9	7.3	2.2	3.3	4.3	2.0	.3	1.6
Race of Respondent									
Black	9.3	6.2	7.6	1.7	4.2	4.5	2.6	.4	2.0
White	8.8	5.8	7.1	2.3	3.1	4.2	1.8	.2	1.5
Hispanic	11.0	7.4	8.8	2.1	4.1	4.9	2.5	.4	2.2
Other	8.7	6.1	6.9	1.8	3.2	3.7	1.8	.3	2.2

Source: National Survey of Families and Households, 1994.

E3.2. Average Hours per Week Husbands Spend Doing Household Tasks, by Race, 1994

	Hours per Week								
	Preparing Meals	Washing Dishes	Cleaning House	Outdoor Tasks	Shop-ping	Washing Ironing	Paying Bills	Auto Maintenance	Driving
Total	3.0	2.4	2.2	4.8	1.8	1.1	1.5	1.6	1.7
Race of Respondent	4.1	3.0	3.2	4.3	2.2	1.7	2.0	2.3	2.1
Black	2.9	2.3	2.0	4.8	1.7	1.0	1.5	1.4	1.1
White	3.0	2.3	2.2	4.5	2.3	1.3	1.7	2.8	2.4
Hispanic	3.4	2.5	2.3	4.1	1.6	1.2	1.7	1.5	1.9
Other									

Source: National Survey of Families and Households, 1994.

E3.3. Attitudes toward Women's Roles, by Race, 1994

	Percent who agree that				
	mother working doesn't hurt child	better for man to work, woman to tend home	women should help husband's career first	preschool kids suffer if mother works	women should work
Total	67	38	21	46	83
Race of Respondent					
White	65	39	21	49	84
Black	78	35	18	30	76
Other	63	45	25	50	85

Source: National Survey of Families and Households, 1994.

E4. DIVORCE

E4.1. Marriage Experience for Women, by Age and Race: 1975 to 1990

[In percent. As of June. Based on Current Population Survey.]

MARITAL STATUS AND AGE	ALL RACES				WHITE				BLACK				HISPANIC ORIGIN \1		
	1975	1980	1985	1990	1975	1980	1985	1990	1975	1980	1985	1990	1980	1985	1990
DIVORCED AFTER FIRST MARRIAGE															
20 to 24 years old	11.2	14.2	13.9	12.5	11.3	14.7	14.4	12.8	10.6	10.5	11.0	9.6	9.4	11.0	6.8
25 to 29 years old	17.1	20.7	21.0	19.2	17.7	21.0	21.5	19.8	15.3	20.2	18.2	17.8	13.9	14.8	13.5
30 to 34 years old	19.8	26.2	29.3	28.1	20.0	25.8	29.0	28.6	20.5	31.4	34.4	26.6	21.1	19.2	19.9
35 to 39 years old	21.5	27.2	32.0	34.1	21.2	26.7	32.0	34.6	22.7	32.9	34.6	35.8	21.9	26.3	29.7
40 to 44 years old	20.5	26.1	32.1	35.8	19.7	25.5	32.0	35.2	27.4	33.7	36.9	45.1	19.7	22.8	26.6
45 to 49 years old	21.0	23.1	29.0	35.2	20.3	22.7	28.4	35.5	26.9	29.0	36.0	39.8	23.9	24.3	24.6
50 to 54 years old	18.0	21.8	25.7	29.5	16.8	21.0	24.6	28.5	29.7	29.0	33.7	39.2	22.5	21.8	22.9
REMARRIED AFTER DIVORCE															
20 to 24 years old	47.9	45.5	44.3	38.1	50.1	47.0	46.0	39.3	(B)	(B)	(B)	(B)	(B)	(B)	(B)
25 to 29 years old	60.2	53.4	55.3	51.8	62.0	56.4	58.3	52.8	43.1	27.9	25.4	44.4	(B)	50.5	49.5
30 to 34 years old	64.4	60.9	61.4	59.6	67.5	63.3	64.3	61.4	41.8	42.0	41.1	42.0	58.3	44.9	45.9
35 to 39 years old	69.5	64.9	63.0	65.0	70.9	66.9	64.9	66.5	62.6	50.6	44.8	54.0	45.2	57.1	51.2
40 to 44 years old	69.7	67.4	64.7	67.1	71.9	68.6	67.5	69.5	57.1	58.4	45.4	50.3	(B)	50.6	53.9
45 to 49 years old	69.6	69.2	67.9	65.9	70.7	70.4	69.6	67.2	61.7	62.7	54.6	55.0	(B)	78.9	51.0
50 to 54 years old	73.5	72.0	68.2	63.0	73.4	72.6	68.4	65.4	73.7	72.7	64.3	50.2	(B)	(B)	62.2

Notes:
B Base is less than 75,000.
NA Not available.
\1 Persons of Hispanic origin may be of any race.

Source: U.S. Bureau of the Census, Current Population Reports, P23-180.

E4.2. First Marriage Dissolution and Years until Remarriage for Women, by Race and Hispanic Origin: 1988

[For women 15 to 44 years old. Based on 1988 National Survey of Family Growth. Marriage dissolution includes death of spouse, separation because of marital discord, and divorce]

ITEM	Number (1,000)	YEARS UNTIL REMARRIAGE (cumulative percent)					
		All	1	2	3	4	5
ALL RACES \1							
Year of dissolution of first marriage:							
All years	11,577	56.8	20.6	32.8	40.7	46.2	49.7
1980-84	3,504	47.5	16.3	28.1	36.4\2	41.1 \2	45.4
1975-79	3,235	65.3	21.9	36.0	44.7	52.7	55.4
1970-74	1,887	83.2	24.9	38.6	47.9	56.4	61.2
1965-69	1,013	89.9	32.6	48.7	60.2	65.0	72.8
WHITE							
Year of dissolution of first marriage:							
All years	10,103	59.9	21.9	35.2	43.5	49.4	53.0
1980-84	3,030	51.4	18.2	31.1	40.3\2	45.2\2	49.8
1975-79	2,839	69.5	23.2	38.5	46.9	55.6	58.4
1970-74	1,622	87.5	24.9	39.8	49.8	59.3	64.3
1965-69	893	91.0	34.7	52.3	64.9	69.3	76.9
BLACK							
Year of dissolution of first marriage:							
All years	1,166	34.0	10.9	16.5	19.6	22.7	25.0
1980-84	380	19.7 \3	4.7 \3	10.6 \3	12.9 \2	14.8 \2	14.8
1975-79	301	32.3 \3	11.4 \3	15.6	18.5	22.2	24.9
1970-74	227	59.0	22.3	29.4	35.3	38.7	42.3
1965-69	98	81.2 \3	20.9 \3	27.3 \3	31.3	40.8	52.1
Hispanic, \4 all years	942	44.7	12.5	16.6	22.7	27.8	29.9

Notes:
\1 Includes other races.
\2 The percent having remarried is biased downward because the women had not completed the indicated number of years since dissolution of first marriage at the time of the survey.
\3 Figure does not meet standard of reliability or precision.
\4 Hispanic persons may be of any race.

Source: National Center for Health Statistics, Advance Data from Vital and Health Statistics, No. 194. http://www.cdc.gov/nchswww/nchshome.htm

E4.3. Relationship with Spouse before Separation: Respondents Who Experienced a Marital Separation in the Last Six Years, by Race and Hispanic Origin, 1994

Question: How much does each of these statements describe your relationship in the months before you separated (rated on a 7-point scale where 1=not at all true and 7=very true).

	Relationship was boring	Relationship was stressful	I didn't love him/her anymore	He/she didn't love me anymore
Total (percent)	4.4	2.4	2.7	2.6
Race of Respondent				
Black	4.4	2.8	2.7	2.8
White	4.5	2.3	2.6	2.5
Hispanic	3.9	3.1	3.4	2.8

Source: National Survey of Families and Households, 1994.

E4.4. Aspects of Marriage before Separation: Respondents Who Experienced a Marital Separation in the Last Six Years, by Race and Hispanic Origin, 1994

	Understanding from Spouse	Love and Affection	Time with Spouse	Demands Spouse Placed on You	Sexual Relationship	Way Spouse Spent Money	Work You and Spouse Did Around the House	Your Spouse as Parent
Questions: In the months before you separated, how happy were you with:								
Total	2.2	2.4	2.7	2.6	2.6	2.7	3.1	3.7
Race of Respondent								
Black	2.6	2.8	2.7	2.8	3.2	2.7	3.1	3.8
White	2.1	2.3	2.6	2.5	2.5	2.7	3.0	3.7
Hispanic	2.9	3.1	3.4	2.8	3.3	3.0	3.4	3.9

Notes:
(rated on a 7-point scale where 1=very unhappy and 7=very happy)

Source: National Survey of Families and Households.

E4.5. Who Wanted the Divorce: Respondents Who Experienced a Marital Separation in the Last Six Years, by Race and Hispanic Origin, 1994

	I did . . partner did not	I did . . . more than partner	Both of Us	Partner wanted it more	Partner did . . . I did not
Total (percent)	26	18	23	13	20
Race of Respondent					
Black	29	18	21	8	24
White	26	18	23	14	20
Hispanic	28	13	26	15	20

Source: National Survey of Families and Households.

E4.6. Parental Contact with Child Living With Other Parent, by Race and Hispanic Origin, 1994

Question: About how often did child talk on telephone or receive a letter from (his/her) (mother/father) during the last 12 months since (he/she) and child stopped living together?

	N	*Talk on Phone*			*See Parent in Person*			*Stay Overnight*
		Once a a year	Several times a a year	About weekly	Once a year	Several times a a year	About weekly	Yes
Total	(687)	35%	32%	33%	36%	36%	28%	65%
Race of Respondent								
White	(399)	32%	33%	35%	35%	40%	25%	74%
Black	(190)	33%	35%	32%	35%	35%	30%	51%
Hispanic	(89)	51%	20%	29%	47%	24%	29%	52%

Source: National Survey of Families and Households.

E4.7. Frequency Child Stays with Non-Resident Father, 1995

Questions about biological father who is not living with you at this time
In the last 12 months, about how often have you stayed overnight with him?

	White	Black	Native-American	Asian	Hispanic	Total
Not at all	47.4	61.6	61.0	48.1	63.5	53.3
Once or twice	13.9	11.6	8.5	9.9	6.9	12.3
Several times	14.8	12.4	17.8	14.8	12.6	14.0
About once a month	8.2	5.7	3.4	16.0	4.7	7.2
About once a week	6.5	2.7	5.9	2.5	7.3	5.5
More than once a week	9.2	6.2	3.4	8.6	5.1	7.8

Source: The National Longitudinal Study of Adolescent Health.

E4.8. Non-Resident Biological Father, 1995

Questions about biological father who is not living with you at this time
Do you know anything about your biological father?

	White	Black	Native-American	Asian	Hispanic	Total
No	15.6	20.2	16.6	25.6	28.3	18.8
Yes	84.4	79.8	83.4	74.4	71.7	81.2

In the last 12 months, about how often have you talked to him in person or on the telephone, or received a letter from him?

	White	Black	Native-American	Asian	Hispanic	Total
Not at all	14.2	14.8	16.8	20.0	23.6	15.5
Once or twice	14.7	17.1	28.6	13.8	19.7	21.2
Several times	19.3	26.3	16.8	13.8	19.7	21.2
About once a month	10.4	7.8	5.9	15.0	10.4	9.7
About once a week	16.9	10.6	16.8	17.5	11.6	14.6
More than once a week	24.5	23.4	15.1	20.0	22.2	23.6

Source: The National Longitudinal Study of Adolescent Health.

E4.9. Influence Divorced or Separated Parents Have on Major Decisions about Children, by Race and Hispanic Origin, 1994

Question: How much influence does child's (mother/father) have in making major decision about such things as education, religion, and health care?

	Pretty much	A great deal	N	None	A little	Some
Total	(666)	59%	12%	13%	7%	10%
Race of Respondent						
White	(385)	59%	13%	14%	7%	7%
Black	(185)	58%	10%	11%	8%	12%
Hispanic	(87)	55%	12%	15%	5%	14%

Source: National Survey of Families and Households.

E4.10. Problems with Child Arrangements for Divorced or Separated Parents, by Race and Hispanic Origin, 1994

I'm going to read a list of things that sometimes happen with arrangements for children to spend time with the other parent. How often, if ever, did child's (mother/father) NOT show up for a visit, make last-minute changes, and YOU make last-minute changes?

	N	*NOT Show Up* Never/ Seldom	Some times	Very often/ Always	*Make Changes* Never/ Seldom	Some times	often/ Always	*YOU Make Changes* Never/ Seldom	Some times	Very often/ Always
Total	(424)	67%	17%	16%	56%	21%	23%	87%	11%	3%
Race of Respondent										
White	(258)	71%	16%	13%	50%	24%	26%	87%	10%	3%
Black	(117)	63%	17%	20%	64%	16%	20%	86%	12%	2%
Hispanic	(45)	56%	27%	17%	67%	16%	17%	84%	12%	5%

Source: National Survey of Families and Households.

E5. FAMILY ACTIVITIES

E5.1. Hours per Week Parents Spend with 5–17-Year-Old Child in Various Activities, by Race and Hispanic Origin, 1994

	N	Alone with child	Checking homework	Helping with homework	Talking about school work	Talking about things learned in school
Total	1966	5.7 hrs	3.9 hrs	2.4 hrs	4.1 hrs	3.9 hrs
Race of Respondent						
Black	(1502)	5.6 hrs	3.9 hrs	2.4 hrs	4.2 hrs	4.9 hrs
White	(247)	6.2 hrs	4.2 hrs	2.8 hrs	3.9 hrs	3.9 hrs
Hispanic	(178)	6.3 hrs	3.8 hrs	2.4 hrs	4.2 hrs	4.0 hrs
Other	(37)	5.9 hrs	2.8 hrs	2.2 hrs	3.9 hrs	3.7 hrs

Source: National Survey of Families and Households.

E5.2. Time Parents Spent with Children in Various Activities, by Race and Hispanic Origin, 1994

	Activity				
	Leisure Activities Away from Home	At Home Working or Playing Together	Having Private Talks	Helping with Reading or Homework	Watching Television or Videos
Total (percent)	*3.4	4.1	4.0	4.3	4.8
Race of Respondent					
Black	3.3	4.0	4.1	4.5	4.9
White	3.5	4.1	4.0	4.3	4.7
Hispanic	3.4	4.1	3.9	4.3	4.9
Other	3.1	3.5	4.0	4.1	4.7

Notes:
*1=never or rarely, 2=once a month or less, 3=several times a month, 4=about once a week, 5= several times a week, 6=almost every day

Source: National Survey of Families and Households.

E5.3. Frequency that Parents Reported They Spend with Children Age 5–17 Years in Leisure Activities and Family Meals, by Race and Hispanic Origin, 1994

Question: Over the past 3 months, about how often have you spent time with child in leisure activities, working on something together or just having private talks? Had a meal together with him or her?

	(N)	Leisure Activities			Meal Together		
		Never/Once a month	About once a week	About every day	Never/Once a month	About once a week	About every day
Total	(1283)	38%	40%	22%	44%	34%	22%
Race of Respondent							
White	(1025)	36%	42%	22%	41%	37%	22%
Black	(144)	43%	38%	19%	50%	29%	21%
Hispanic	(97)	47%	20%	33%	61%	10%	29%

Source: National Survey of Families and Households.

E5.4. Activities with Mother, Reported by Teenage Child, by Race and Hispanic Origin, 1996

Questions about various aspects of their relationship with their parents (or parental figures in the household). Which of the things listed on this card have you done with {MOM NAME} in the past four weeks?

	White	Black	Native American	Asian	Hispanic	Total
Shopping	68.7%	67.2%	65.9%	68.9%	68.5%	68.4%
Played a sport	8.0	6.0	9.0	4.1	7.1	7.4
Religious service or church-related event	35.9	45.0	21.3	36.9	36.0	36.9
Talked about someone you're dating, or a party you went to	52.6	44.1	46.6	32.5	45.7	49.4
Movie, play, museum, or concert, or sports event	23.5	21.9	24.1	20.9	19.3	22.7
Talked about a personal problem you were having	41.5	43.7	42.4	33.5	39.7	41.3
Had a serious argument about your behavior	33.1	30.1	37.6	30.2	31.9	32.5
Talked about your school work or grades	68.3	63.5	63.7	62.5	63.3	66.6
Worked on a project for school	15.7	12.9	18.1	10.2	11.3	14.5
Talked about other things you're doing in school	62.1	57.9	58.7	56.3	55.2	60.3
No activity	2.6	3.4	1.7	4.3	2.1	2.7

Source: The National Longitudinal Study of Adolescent Health.

E5.5. Activities with Father, Reported by Teenage Child, by Race and Hispanic Origin, 1996

Questions about various aspects of their relationship with their parents (or parental figures in the household).
Which of the things listed on this card have you done with {DAD NAME} in the past four weeks?

	White	Black	Native-American	Asian	Hispanic	Total
Shopping	23.7%	25.4%	28.3%	28.0%	25.5%	24.4%
Playcd a sport	28.8	21.3	24.8	18.1	24.5	27.1
Religious service or church-related event	28.7	33.4	21.5	30.2	26.7	28.7
Talked about someone you're dating, or a party you went to	31.2	24.2	27.0	16.1	24.2	29.0
Movie, play, museum, or concert, or sports event	24.2	14.0	19.0	15.4	18.4	22.1
Talked about a personal problem you were having	19.8	21.7	25.7	19.6	19.4	20.1
Had a serious argument about your behavior	25.4	21.2	31.5	21.9	24.9	24.9
Talked about your school work or grades	56.3	50.5	51.9	61.0	47.6	54.8
Worked on a project for school	12.7	9.0	17.1	13.4	10.3	12.3
Talked about other things you're doing in school	51.3	43.5	44.6	49.6	45.2	49.7
No Activity	8.4	14.9	10.0	9.6	12.3	9.6

Source: The National Longitudinal Study of Adolescent Health.

E5.6. Supervision of Teenage Child(ren), by Race and Hispanic Origin, 1996

Questions about the woman who functions as a mother in the respondents' household; she could be the biological mother, stepmother, foster mother or adoptive mother; or perhaps a grandmother or aunt.
How often is she at home when you leave for school?

	White	Black	Native American	Asian	Hispanic	Total
Always	59.6%	57.8%	63.2%	50.3%	59.0%	58.9%
Most of the time	13.0	11.5	12.9	15.1	11.0	12.6
Some of the time	7.2	9.6	7.9	8.9	8.5	7.8
Almost never	5.4	4.1	3.5	7.8	5.6	5.3
Never	9.9	12.0	7.4	12.5	10.6	10.3
She takes me to school	4.9	5.0	5.0	5.4	5.3	5.0
Total	100%	100%	100%	100%	100%	100%

Source: The National Longitudinal Study of Adolescent Health.

E5.7. Supervision of Teenage Child(ren), by Race and Hispanic Origin, 1996

Questions about the woman who functions as a mother in the respondents' household; she could be the biological mother, stepmother, foster mother or adoptive mother; or perhaps a grandmother or aunt.
How often is she at home when you return from school?

	White	Black	Native American	Asian	Hispanic	Total
Always	22.4%	33.4%	31.5%	23.5%	40.3%	26.7%
Most of the time	23.6	18.9	22.1	19.8	18.5	22.0
Some of the time	16.5	18.8	16.2	21.3	15.1	16.9
Almost never	12.9	9.5	14.1	14.0	9.1	11.9
Never	21.4	17.0	13.5	18.8	14.2	19.5
She brings me home from school	3.1	2.5	2.6	2.6	2.8	3.0
Total	100%	100%	100%	100%	100%	100%

Source: The National Longitudinal Study of Adolescent Health.

E5.8. Supervision of Teenage Child(ren), by Race and Hispanic Origin, 1996

Questions about the woman who functions as a mother in the respondents' household; she could be the biological mother, stepmother, foster mother, or adoptive mother; or perhaps a grandmother or aunt.
How often is she at home when you go to bed?

	White	Black	Native American	Asian	Hispanic	Total
Always	74.2%	78.6%	66.7%	74.1%	85.3%	76.0%
Most of the time	19.4	11.4	21.6	14.9	8.4	16.7
Some of the time	4.4	5.7	6.7	5.4	2.7	4.5
Almost never	0.9	1.3	2.0	2.6	1.4	1.1
Never	1.2	3.0	2.9	3.0	2.1	1.7
Total	100%	100%	100%	100%	100%	100%

Source: The National Longitudinal Study of Adolescent Health.

E5.9. Closeness to Parents, by Race and Hispanic Origin, 1996

Questions about various aspects of their relationship with their parents (or parental figures in the household).
How close do you feel to {MOM NAME}?

	White	Black	Native American	Asian	Hispanic	Total
Not close at all	0.9%	0.7%	1.7%	1.5%	0.9%	0.9%
Not very close	1.9	1.3	1.2	5.2	2.1	1.9
Somewhat close	10.2	9.6	11.7	15.8	8.6	10.2
Quite close	34.5	21.6	33.5	32.8	25.7	31.3
Extremely close	52.5	66.9	51.9	44.7	62.6	55.7
Total	100%	100%	100%	100%	99.9%	100%

How much do you think she cares about you?

	White	Black	Native American	Asian	Hispanic	Total
Not at all	0.3%	0.1%	0.1%	0.4%	0.2%	0.3%
Very little	2.2	3.7	1.7	3.7	3.7	2.7
Somewhat	1.8	1.5	1.7	3.4	1.4	1.8
Quite a bit	9.2	7.4	10.5	9.7	8.0	8.9
Very much	86.4	87.3	86.0	82.8	86.6	86.4
Total	99.9%	100%	100%	100%	99.9%	100.1%

Source: The National Longitudinal Study of Adolescent Health.

E5.10. Closeness to Parents, by Race and Hispanic Origin, 1996

Questions about various aspects of their relationship with their parents (or parental figures in the household).
How close do you feel to {DAD NAME}?

	White	Black	Native American	Asian	Hispanic	Total
Not close at all	2.1%	3.4%	4.8%	2.5%	2.6%	2.4%
Not very close	4.7	4.8	5.6	6.8	2.9	4.6
Somewhat close	18.3	20.5	15.9	21.1	20.2	18.8
Quite close	35.6	30.1	33.3	33.2	32.6	34.5
Extremely close	39.3	41.2	40.4	36.4	41.7	39.7
Total	100%	100%	100%	100%	100%	100%

How much do you think he cares about you?

	White	Black	Native American	Asian	Hispanic	Total
Not at all	0.3%	0.1%	0.1%	0.4%	0.2%	0.3%
Not at all	0.3%	0.9%	1.5%	0.8%	0.2%	0.4%
Very little	2.6	4.9	0.7	2.3	3.8	2.9
Somewhat	4.5	5.0	7.8	3.8	4.0	4.5
Quite a bit	15.7	19.1	14.8	16.4	15.0	15.9
Very much	76.9	70.1	75.2	76.8	77.1	76.3
Total	100%	100%	100%	100%	100%	100%

Source: The National Longitudinal Study of Adolescent Health.

E5.11. Parental Regulation, by Race and Hispanic Origin, 1996

Questions about various aspects of their relationship with their parents (or parental figures in the household).
Do your parents let you make your own decisions about. . .

	White	Black	Native American	Asian	Hispanic	Total
The time you must be home on weekend nights?	38.4%	38.6%	41.2%	41.5%	38.5%	38.6%
The people you hang around with?	89.0	83.8	84.3	80.2	80.0	86.6
What you wear?	93.4	89.6	91.2	84.8	87.6	91.8
How much television you watch?	87.2	85.3	87.1	70.2	78.1	85.1
Which television programs you watch?	81.5	79.4	86.8	74.8	77.6	80.6
What time you go to bed on week nights?	69.6	70.2	71.7	66.6	61.6	68.8
What you eat?	85.6	83.6	87.1	78.3	80.8	84.5

Source: The National Longitudinal Study of Adolescent Health.

E5.12. Frequency Parents Talk to 5–17-Year-Old Child about Things That Worry or Excite the Child, by Race and Hispanic Origin, 1994

	N	Talk about things that worry			Talk about things that excite		
		Almost never	Two/three times per month	Several times per week	Almost never	Two/three times per month	Several times per week
Total	(2601)	20%	47%	33%	62%	16%	22%
Race of respondent							
White	(1970)	21	25	54	65	17	18
Black	(319)	41	31	28	59	17	24
Hispanic	(262)	36	20	44	61	17	22
Other	(47)	30	40	30	70	11	19

Source: National Survey of Families and Households.

E5.13. Frequency Parents Kiss or Hug Their Children, 1994

Some families are very physical in expressing affection and others are not physical. During the past week, have you given (child) a hug or a kiss to express your affection?

	N	Gave hug or kiss (% yes)	Average number of times
Total	(1989)	91%	11
Race of Respondent			
White	(1520)	92%	12
Black	(249)	83%	8
Hispanic	(165)	91%	11
Other	(36)	81%	10

Source: National Survey of Families and Households.

E5.14. Parents' Perception of Characteristics of 5–17-Year-Old Children

Sometimes, for one reason or another, some children are particularly difficult to raise. Would you describe (child) as particularly difficult (easy) to raise? Have long-lasting physical condition, has long-lasting mental or emotional problem, seen a therapist or doctor for any emotional or behavioral problem?

	N	Difficult to raise	Easy to raise	Has physical handicap	Has emotional problem	Seen therapist
Total	(3442)	20%	62%	3.9%	7.1%	15%
Race of Respondent						
White	(2556)	21%	59%	3.7%	7.8%	16%
Black	(464)	17%	66%	6.5%	5.6%	11%
Hispanic	(362)	20%	72%	2.1%	5.0%	11%
Other	(54)	13%	75%	4.9%	2.3%	7%

Source: National Survey of Families and Households.

E5.15. Parents' Report of Values Important for Children

If you had to choose, which thing on this list would you pick as the most important for a child to learn to prepare him or her for life? To obey?

	White	Black	Other
Most important	16.8%	30.4%	17.8%
2nd important	11.4	18.3	14
3rd important	16.9	17.2	17.8
4th important	38.3	26	33.3
Least important	16.5	8.1	17.1
(N)	**1478**	**273**	**129**
To be well-liked or popular?			
Most important	.8%	1.8%	1.6%
2nd important	1.8	3.7	3.9
3rd important	3.2	3.3	7.0
4th important	18.5	11.7	19.4
Least important	75.7	79.5	68.2
(N)	**1478**	**273**	**129**
To think for himself or herself?			
Most important	52.5%	37.4%	38.8%
2nd important	18	20.5	17.1
3rd important	12.2	21.6	16.3
4th important	12.9	16.1	17.8
Least important	4.5	4.4	10.1
(N)	**1478**	**273**	**129**
To work hard?			
Most important	15.6%	22.3%	26.4%
2nd important	37.1	33.7	38.8
3rd important	33.9	25.3	21.7
4th important	12.2	14.7	13.2
Least important	1.2	4.0	0.0
(N)	**1478**	**273**	**129**
To help others when they need help?			
Most important	14.3%	8.1%	15.5%
2nd important	31.7	23.8	26.4
3rd important	33.8	32.6	37.2
4th important	18.1	31.5	16.3
Least important	2.2	4	4.7
(N)	**1478**	**273**	**129**

Source: General Social Survey, 1998.

E5.16. Adolescents' Perceptions of Parents' Attitudes, 1996

Regardless of whether you have done these things or not, how would your mother feel about each of the following things? How would she feel about your having sex at this time in your life?

	White	Black	Native American	Asian	Hispanic	Total
Strongly disapprove	53.3%	40.8%	40.9%	64.2%	49.5%	51.0%
Disapprove	25.9	26.0	25.8	21.6	24.8	25.6
Neither approve or disapprove	18.5	26.0	26.4	12.0	21.8	19.9
Approve	1.9	5.9	6.4	1.7	2.9	2.7
Strongly approve	.5	1.4	.6	.4	1.0	.7

How would she feel about your having sexual intercourse with someone who was special to you and whom you knew well–like a steady boyfriend/girlfriend?

	White	Black	Native American	Asian	Hispanic	Total
Strongly disapprove	42.6%	32.1%	33.1%	55.2%	37.3%	40.6%
Disapprove	25.9	22.1	25.0	21.1	25.3	25.1
Neither approve or disapprove	22.8	28.8	27.3	18.0	25.5	23.9
Approve	7.6	14.4	11.6	4.8	9.7	8.9
Strongly approve	1.2	2.6	2.9	.9	2.1	1.5

How would she feel about your using birth control at this time in your life?

	White	Black	Native American	Asian	Hispanic	Total
Strongly disapprove	27.1%	19.0%	15.2%	39.4%	26.9%	26.0%
Disapprove	12.9	11.9	12.0	15.6	15.5	13.2
Neither approve or disapprove	19.9	18.8	24.3	23.3	21.5	20.1
Approve	19.9	26.7	20.8	10.6	18.7	20.5
Strongly approve	20.2	23.6	27.8	11.0	17.5	20.2

Regardless of whether you have done these things or not, how would your father feel about each of the following things? How would he feel about your having sex at this time in your life?

	White	Black	Native American	Asian	Hispanic	Total
Strongly disapprove	55.6%	43.4%	46.8%	65.6%	54.0%	54.5%
Disapprove	22.2	20.6	21.9	15.2	19.7	21.4
Neither approve or disapprove	18.5	27.1	25.3	15.7	20.7	19.6
Approve	3.1	6.5	5.2	3.0	4.3	3.6
Strongly approve	.6	2.3	.7	.5	1.2	.8

How would he feel about your having sexual intercourse with someone who was special to you and whom you knew well–like a girlfriend/boyfriend?

	White	Black	Native American	Asian	Hispanic	Total
Strongly disapprove	48.9%	38.8%	41.1%	57.5%	48.3%	48.1%
Disapprove	22.6	19.4	22.2	17.6	18.3	21.6
Neither approve or disapprove	21.5	27.7	26.3	19.1	22.7	22.2
Approve	5.8	11.5	8.5	4.6	8.8	6.7
Strongly approve	1.2	2.5	1.9	1.3	1.9	1.4

How would he feel about your using birth control at this time in your life?

	White	Black	Native American	Asian	Hispanic	Total
Strongly disapprove	31.4%	22.0%	25.3%	41.4%	35.2%	31.2%
Disapprove	13.5	14.8	11.9	12.9	13.9	13.6
Neither approve or disapprove	22.5	22.6	25.7	26.7	21.5	22.7
Approve	16.0	22.2	13.8	10.0	15.2	16.2
Strongly approve	16.5	18.3	23.4	9.0	14.2	16.2

Regardless of whether you have ever had a child, would you consider having a child in the future as an unmarried person?

	White	Black	Native American	Asian	Hispanic	Total
No	79.4%	66.2%	73.2%	81.8%	74.0%	76.6%
Yes	20.6	33.8	26.8	18.2	26.0	23.4

Source: The National Longitudinal Study of Adolescent Health, 1996.

E5.17. Parents' Disagreement about Dress and Friends with 5–17-Year-Old Children, 1994

In the last 3 months, how often have you and child had open disagreements about each of the following: how he/she dresses, boyfriend/girlfriend, or friends?

	N	Dress			Boyfriend/Girlfriend			Friends		
		Never/Rarely	Once a month or less	Once a week or less	Never/Rarely	Once a month or less	Once a week or less	Never/Rarely	Once a month or less	Once a week or less
Total	2597	73%	18%	9%	92%	5%	3%	91%	7%	2%
Race of Respondent										
White	1967	74%	18%	8%	94%	4%	2%	92%	6%	2%
Black	317	65%	22%	13%	90%	6%	4%	88%	8%	4%
Hispanic	263	77%	12%	11%	87%	9%	4%	83%	11%	6%

Source: National Survey of Families and Households.

E5.18. Parents' Disagreement with 5–17-Year-Old Children about Sex, Smoking, Drinking, and Drugs, 1994

In the past 3 months, how often have you and child had open disagreements about each of the following: sexual behavior, smoking, drinking, and drug use?

| | N | **Sexual Behavior** | | | **Smoking, Drinking, and Drug Use** | | |
		Never/ Rarely	Once a month or less	More than once a month	Never/ Rarely	Once a month or less	More than once a month
Total	(1078)	97%	2%	1%	97%	2%	1%
Race of Respondent							
White	(766)	97%	2%	1%	97%	3%	0%
Black	(146)	97%	2%	1%	99%	0%	1%
Hispanic	(129)	97%	0%	3%	96%	4%	1%

Source: National Survey of Families and Households.

E5.19. Parents' Disagreement with 5–17-Year-Old Children about Money and Staying Out Late, 1996

In the past 3 months, how often have you and child had open disagreements about each of the following: money? staying out late?

| | N | **Money** | | | **Staying Out Late** | | |
		Never/ Rarely	Once a month or less	More than once a month	Never/ Rarely	Once a month or less	More than once a month
Total	(2590)	85%	11%	4%	90%	8%	3%
Race of Respondent							
White	(1965)	86%	11%	3%	90%	7%	3%
Black	(317)	81%	11%	8%	93%	5%	3%
Hispanic	(261)	82%	13%	5%	86%	11%	3%

Source: National Survey of Families and Households.

E5.20. Parents' Disagreement with 5–17-Year-Old Children about Helping Around the House, School, and Getting Along with Family, 1994

In the past 3 months, how often have you and child had open disagreements about each of the following: helping around the house, school, and getting along wi h family members?

	N	Helping around Home			School			Getting along with Family		
		Never/Rarely	Once a month or less	Once a week or more	Never/Rarely	Once a month or less	Once a week or more	Never/Rarely	Once a month or less	Once a week or more
Total	(2596)	47%	35%	18%	78%	15%	7%	55%	25%	20%
Race of Respondent										
White	(1966)	46%	37%	17%	77%	13%	10%	50%	28%	22%
Black	(316)	51%	27%	22%	79%	15%	6%	69%	15%	16%
Hispanic	(262)	53%	26%	21%	81%	12%	7%	69%	12%	19%

Source: National Survey of Families and Households.

E5.21. How Parents Deal with Disagreements with 5–17-Year-Old Children, 1994

There are various ways parents deal with serious disagreements with their sons and daughters. How often do you handle disagreements with child by: refusing to talk about it? letting child have own way? discussing calmly? arguing heatedly or shouting?

	N	Refuse to Talk			Let Have Own Way			Calm Discussion			Argue and Shout		
		Never/ Seldom	Some- times	Often always	Never/ Seldom	Some- times	Often always	Never/ Seldom	Some- times	Often always	Never/ Seldom	Some- times	Often always
Total	(1127)	80%	4%	16%	72%	14%	14%	29%	39%	32%	90%	7%	3%
Race of Respondent													
White	(906)	81%	4%	15%	71%	15%	14%	28%	41%	31%	91%	6%	3%
Black	(130)	74%	3%	23%	74%	13%	13%	38%	26%	36%	85%	9%	6%
Hispanic	(86)	81%	5%	14%	75%	12%	13%	31%	28%	41%	84%	13%	3%

Source: National Survey of Families and Households.

E5.22. Parents' Perception of School Problems of 5–17-Year-Old Children, 1994

Has child ever dropped out of school? Ever repeated a grade? Been suspended or expelled? Skipped school, refused to go to school last year? Been asked to meet with teacher or principal during last year?

	N	Dropped out	Repeated a grade	Suspended/ Expelled	Skipped school/ Wouldn't go	Meet with teacher or principal
Total	(3442)	2.4%	17.0%	10.0%	4.7%	9.7%
Race of Respondent						
White	(2856)	2.3%	14.0%	7.5%	8.5%	13.0%
Black	(464)	2.8%	28.3%	21.7%	9.0%	26.3%
Hispanic	(364)	2.7%	21.5%	12.2%	8.7%	20.0%
Other	(54)	1.6%	8.2%	10.8%	16.2%	8.8%

Source: National Survey of Families and Households.

E5.23. How Parents Discipline a 5–17-Year-Old Child When They Do Something Especially Bad, 1994

When (child) does something especially bad, how often do you talk to, yell at, take away privileges from, or spank him/her for what he/she did wrong?

	N	Talk to			Yell at			Take away privileges			Spank		
		Less than half the time	About half the time	More than half the time	Less than half the time	About half the time	More than half the time	Less than half the time	About half the time	More than half the time	Less than half the time	About half the time	More than half the time
Total	1991	3%	6%	91%	44%	24%	32%	44%	24%	72%	79%	10%	11%
Race of Respondent													
White	1520	2%	5%	93%	44%	23%	33%	46%	23%	31%	95%	4%	1%
Black	248	2%	8%	92%	41%	25%	34%	36%	24%	40%	84%	9%	7%
Hispanic	180	6%	9%	85%	41%	27%	32%	41%	31%	23%	94%	5%	1%
Other	37	5%	16%	79%	40%	27%	33%	57%	24%	29%	100%	0%	0%

Source: National Survey of Families and Households.

E5.24. Frequency Parents Spank or Hit Children, 1994

Sometimes children behave well and sometimes they don't. In the last week, have you had to spank or hit (child) when she/he behaved badly?

	N	Child 5–17 years spanked or hit	Average number of times
Total	(1989)	10%	2
Race of Respondent			
White	(1520)	9%	2
Black	(248)	15%	2
Other	(36)	6%	2
Hispanic	(181)	8%	2

Source: National Survey of Families and Households.

E5.25. Child 5–17 Years of Age Allowed To Be Home Alone, 1994

Is child allowed to be at home alone in the afternoon after school, between 3 and 6 pm? At night? Overnight if you went on a trip?

	N	*After School* Yes	Some-times	No	*At Night* Yes	Some-times	No	*Overnight* Yes	Some-times	No
Total	(1989)	43%	52%	6%	22%	74%	4%	6%	94%	1%
Race of Respondent										
White	(1521)	44%	51%	5%	24%	72%	5%	5%	94%	1%
Black	(249)	35%	60%	5%	12%	84%	4%	4%	96%	1%
Hispanic	(181)	37%	53%	11%	20%	79%	1%	7%	93%	0%
Other	(36)	64%	30%	6%	38%	62%	0%	19%	78%	3%

Source: National Survey of Families and Households.

E5.26. Frequency of Friends Visiting in Home of 5–17-Year-Old Child and How Many of the Friends the Child's Parent Knows, 1994

	N	Frequency friends come to home Once a month	Several times a month	Several times a week	Child's friends known by parents All or most	About half	Few or more
Total							
Race of Respondent	(1518)	37%	30%	33%	68%	30%	2%
White	(247)	23%	38%	39%	81%	18%	1%
Black	(181)	37%	28%	35%	66%	30%	4%
Hispanic	(36)	44%	30%	26%	78%	20%	0%
Other							

Source: National Survey of Families and Households.

E5.27. Payment of Allowance to Children 5–17 Years Old, 1994

Does your child receive an allowance? Does this allowance pay for work regularly done around the house? Is he/she paid for extra jobs around the house?

	N	Paid allowance	Paid for work	Paid for extra work
Total	(1984)	50%	64%	42%
Race of Respondent				
White	(1519)	48%	66%	45%
Black	(249)	64%	58%	38%
Hispanic	(177)	50%	56%	29%

Source: National Survey of Families and Households.

E6. CHILD CARE ARRANGEMENTS

E6.1. Women Who Took Maternity Leave for Most Recent Birth, 1995

Characteristic of the mother	Number in thousands	Total	Not employed	Took maternity leave	Did not take leave		
					Not needed	Not offered	Other reasons
All women	34,958	100.0	48.0	37.3	2.3	0.9	11.6
Race and Hispanic origin							
Hispanic	4,372	100.0	57.8	28.9	1.1	0.8	11.4
Non-Hispanic white	24,009	100.0	44.7	39.6	3.0	0.9	12.0
Non-Hispanic black	5,149	100.0	53.5	34.5	0.4	1.1	10.6
Non-Hispanic other	1,428	100.0	53.7	34.8	1.5	0.6	9.4

Note:
Percents may not add to 100 due to rounding.

Source: National Survey of Family Growth, 1995.

E6.2. Primary Child Care Arrangements Used for Preschoolers by Families with Employed Mothers: Fall 1993

Characteristics	Number of children	Care in child's home by				Care in another home by			Organized facilities		Mother cares for child[1]	Other[2]
		Father	Grand-parent	Other relative	Non-relative	Grand-parent	Other relative	Non-relative	Day-care center	Nursery/pre-school		
All Preschoolers	9,937	1,585	649	328	492	996	543	1,645	1,823	1,149	616	111
Race and Hispanic Origin:												
White, not Hispanic	7,295	1,252	389	141	370	699	299	1,294	1,461	807	529	54
Black, not Hispanic	1,161	101	123	82	17	106	135	164	188	191	33	22
Hispanic origin	1,078	161	86	85	76	158	88	136	110	119	34	26
Other	403	71	50	21	30	33	21	51	64	31	21	9

Notes:
- Rounds to or represents zero.
1 Includes mothers working at home or away from home.
2 Includes preschoolers in kindergarten and school-based activities.

Source: The National Survey of Family Growth, 1995.

E6.3. Child Care Arrangements for Working Women, 1995

Characteristic	Number in thousands	Other parent or stepparent	Grandparent or other relative	Non-relative	Day care center or preschool	Brother or sister	Child cares for self	School (regular hours)	Other arrangement1
All women	7,493	16.5	22.4	13.3	14.8	13.6	5.9	14.2	9.1
Race and Hispanic origin									
Hispanic	735	18.0	32.6	13.5	8.7	10.4	1.8	10.0	10.8
Non-Hispanic white	5,277	18.0	18.9	14.4	16.3	14.9	6.4	14.3	0.0
Non-Hispanic black	1,189	9.9	27.9	9.1	11.1	10.3	6.0	19.2	8.5
Non-Hispanic other	294	13.4	37.2	9.5	18.6	12.1	5.7	2.9	2.6

Notes:
1Other arrangements include before- or after-school care program, respondent while she was working, and other arrangements not shown separately. Percents may add to more than 100 because some women reported more than one type of child care arrangement.

Source: The National Survey of Family Growth, 1995.

E6.4. Number of Women 15–44 Years of Age Who Were Working the Week Prior to Interview and Have At Least One Child under 13 Years of Age, and Mean Amount Paid per Week for Child Care, by Number of Children and Selected Characteristics: United States, 1995

Characteristic	Number in thousands			Percent with no payment for child care	Mean amount paid (in dollars) per week for child care[1]		
	One child	Two children	Three or more children		One child	Two children	Three or more children
All women[2]	8,691	5,932	2,084	50.7	58	80	82
Race and Hispanic origin							
Hispanic	884	622	335	49.4	49	69	73
Non-Hispanic white	6,233	4,361	1,395	60.1	59	82	85
Non-Hispanic black	1,250	720	277	52.5	54	66	67

Notes:
[1]Limited to women who reported any payment for child care. Mean amount paid refers to mean of the "typical" weekly payment for child care.
[2]Includes women with missing information on child care payment, and women of other race and origin groups not shown separately.

Source: National Survey of Family Growth, 1995.

E6.5. Number of Women 15–44 Years of Age Who Were Working Most of the Time the Week Prior to Interview and Have At Least One Child under Five Years of Age, and Percent Using the Specified Child Care Arrangement in the Four Weeks Prior to Interview for Their Youngest Child, by Selected Characteristics: United States, 1995

Characteristic	Number in thousands	Other parent or stepparent	Grandparent or other relative	Nonrelative	Day care center or preschool	Other arrangement[1]
					Percent	
All women	6,332	13.5	32.0	30.5	28.7	4.7
Race and Hispanic origin						
Hispanic	842	15.4	37.3	27.8	16.8	6.6
Non-Hispanic white	4,322	13.3	28.6	34.7	30.4	4.5
Non-Hispanic black	914	10.2	36.3	19.7	36.6	2.5
Non-Hispanic other	254	21.3	66.5	7.8	11.8	8.5

Notes:
[1]Other arrangements include child's sibling; child cares for self; school (regular hours); before- or after-school care/program; respondent while she was working; and other arrangements not shown separately.
Percents may add to more than 100 because some women reported more than one type of child care arrangement.

Source: National Survey of Family Growth, 1995.

E6.6. Number of Women 15–44 Years of Age Who Were Not Working the Week Prior to Interview and Have At Least One Child under Five Years of Age, and Percent Regularly Using the Specified Child Care Arrangement in the Four Weeks Prior to Interview for Their Youngest Child, by Selected Characteristics: United States, 1995

Characteristic	Number in thousands	Grandparent or other relative	Nonrelative	Day care center or preschool	None	Other arrangement[1]
				Percent		
All women	7,138	6.1	5.3	7.6	80.0	3.7
Race and Hispanic origin						
Hispanic	1,225	3.8	2.7	3.1	88.4	2.3
Non-Hispanic white	4,480	5.9	6.5	7.9	79.0	4.0
Non-Hispanic black	1,073	7.8	4.4	12.8	72.6	2.9
Non-Hispanic other	359	10.9	2.9	3.8	83.7	7.0

Notes:
[1]Other arrangements include child's brother/sister; child cares for self, school (regular hours); before- or after-school care/program; respondent while she was working; other parent or stepparent and other arrangements not shown separately.
Percents may not add to 100 because some women reported more than one type of child care arrangement.

Source: National Survey of Family Growth, 1995.

E7. EXTENDED FAMILY

E7.1. Frequency Adult Respondents Have Contact with Their Aged Mothers, 1994

During the past 12 months, about how often did you see (phone or write) your mother?

		Visit mother			Phone or write mother		
		Never/once a year	Several times a year	Once a week or more	Never/once a year	Several times a year	Once a week or more
Total	(5513)	14%	43%	43%	7%	31%	62%
Race of Respondent							
White	(4467)	13%	45%	42%	6%	31%	63%
Black	(523)	11%	35%	54%	6%	23%	71%
Hispanic	(436)	25%	36%	39%	12%	34%	54%
Other	(83)	33%	27%	40%	6%	39%	55%

Source: National Survey of Families and Households.

E7.2. Respondents' Reported Relationships with Aged Parents, 1994

Taking all these together, how would you describe your relationship with your mother (father)?

	Relationships with Mother (N=6004)	Relationships with Father (N=4331)
Total	8.1[a]	7.4[a]
Race of Respondent		
White	8.0	7.4
Black	8.7	7.1
Hispanic	8.2	7.2
Other	8.0	7.6

Note:
[a] mean varying between "0" equals "really bad" to "10" equals "absolutely perfect."

Source: National Survey of Families and Households.

E7.3. Percent of Respondents Who Gave Help to Aged Parents during the Past Month, 1994

Have you GIVEN help with _____ to your parents DURING THE LAST MONTH?

	Shopping, transportation, running errands (N=7323)	Housework, yard, car repairs (N=7323)	Advice, encouragement, moral, or emotional support (N=7306)
Total	34%	29%	64%
Race of Respondent			
White	32	29	66
Black	45	36	62
Hispanic	39	28	57
Other	37	29	69

Source: National Survey of Families and Households.

E7.4. Percent of Adults Who Received Help from Aged Parents during the Past Month, 1994

DURING THE LAST MONTH, have you RECEIVED help from your parents?	Shopping, errands, transportation (N=7323)	Advice, encouragement, moral or emotional support (N=7321)	Child care while you worked (N=28613)	Child care other than when working (N=3630)
Total	17%	56%	29%	30%
Race of Respondent				
White	16	55	29	31
Black	23	63	36	35
Hispanic	17	64	22	19
Other	19	55	39	26

Source: National Survey of Families and Households.

E7.5. Residence of Aged Parents, 1994

Do/Does your parents/mother/father live in:	N	House, Apartment	Home of child/relation	Adult care/old folks home	Nursing home	Someplace close	Total
Total							
Race of Respondent							
White	(4466)	93%	3%	1%	3%	0%	100%
Black	(528)	90%	7%	0%	2%	1%	100%
Hispanic	(441)	88%	10%	0%	1%	1%	100%
Other	(83)	86%	10%	0%	4%	0%	100%

Source: National Survey of Families and Households.

E7.6. Should Aged Parents Live with Their Children, 1998

As you know, many older people share a home with their grown children. Do you think this is generally a good idea or a bad idea?

	White	Black	Other
A good idea	43%	47.3%	59.2%
A bad idea	35.8	33.3	23.1
Depends	20	17.9	16.9
Don't know	1.2	1.4	.8
(N)	**1496**	**279**	**130**

Source: General Social Survey, 1998.

E7.7. Assistance Given to Adult Children, 1994

Next we are interested in help and support that you may have given to your child age 19 and older. During the last month have you given: Help with shopping/transportation? Advice, encouragement, moral or emotional support? Child care while parents work? Child care part time other than when working? About how many hours would you say you support helping your children?

	Shopping Transportation	Advice, Encouragement, Emotional Support	Child Care Working	Child Care Not Working	Number hours?
Total	17	74	27	32	5.6
Race of Respondent					
White	17	74	27	32	5.6
Black	16	72	26	28	7.5
Hispanic	19	78	32	28	8.5

Source: National Survey of Families and Households.

E7.8. Assistance Received from Adult Children, 1994

Next we are interested in the help and support that you may have received from your children age 19 and older. During the past month have you received help from your children with: Shopping/transportation? Housework or yard work? Advice, encouragement, moral or emotional support? In an average week about how many hours do your children spend helping you?

	Shopping Transportation	Housework Yard Work	Encouragement, Emotional Support	Hours of Help Received
Total	28	29	50	3.9
Race of Respondent				
White	26	27	49	3.3
Black	39	36	51	6.2
Hispanic	40	35	55	5.7

Source: National Survey of Families and Households.

E7.9. Grandparents' Interaction with Grandchildren, 1994

The next question is about grandchildren. How many grandchildren do you have? On a scale of 1 to 10, how would you describe your closeness with your grandchildren? Have you ever had primary responsibility for caring for a grandchild?

	Number of Grandchildren	Closeness to Grandchildren 0 = not close, 10=very close	Primary Responsibility % Yes
Total	5.3	8.7	11
Race of Respondent			
White	5.1	8.6	9
Black	5.7	9.1	23
Hispanic	7.0	8.8	14

Source: National Survey of Families and Households.

F. Sex, Fertility, and Contraception

F1. ROMANCE AND SEXUAL EXPERIENCE

Adolescents express some ambivalence toward romance. While few say they are not at all interested, only about one-fifth say they are very much interested in having a romantic relationship. Slightly over half (56%) say they have had a romantic relationship in the last 18 months. Asians are a little less likely to have been in a romantic relationship, but otherwise there are not great differences across racial groups (F.1).

A large percentage of women aged 14–44 say they have had sexual intercourse after menarche, and most never-married women say they have. Among adolescents, Blacks are the most likely to be sexually experienced, followed by Hispanics, with Non-Hispanic Whites being the least likely to have had sexual intercourse (F1.2). The average age at first intercourse in 17.8, but younger for Blacks and older for Hispanics and other races (F1.3). Less than 20 percent or women report having first intercourse after or the same month as marriage. Only 8 percent of Blacks have first intercourse before or the same month as marriage, compared to around 40 percent for Hispanics and the "Other" category (F1.4).

Teens who initiate sexual activity before age 16 generally have older partners. This is especially true among Hispanics. Age differences are less dramatic if women wait until after age 16 but there are still substantial age disparities in some cases (F1.5). When asked their relationship to their first voluntary sexual partner, the most common response is that they were going steady, especially for Whites and Blacks. Over a fourth of Hispanics and other races are married to their first sexual partner. (F1.6).

About a third of women aged 15–44 say they have not had any sexual partners in the last year, and another 47 percent say they've only had one partner. Only 3 percent report having four or more partners. Hispanics and the "Other" category report having fewer partners (F1.7). If asked about lifetime experience, then women report a larger number of partners. About 28 percent say they have had more than five partners. Consistent with patterns noted above, the sexual behavior of Hispanics and the "Other" group is more conservative (F1.8). The frequency of sexual intercourse is quite variable. About 40 percent say they average one to three times per week (F1.9). A nontrivial percentage report they have paid for sex, and an even greater percent say they have had sex with someone other than their spouse while they were married (F1.10).

One fifth of women aged 14–44 have been forced to have sexual intercourse. The percentage is even higher among Black women (F1.11). About eight percent of these women say their first sexual intercourse was not voluntary. The percentage having nonvoluntary first intercourse is even higher when intercourse occurred before age 16 (F1.12).

Adolescents have various motivations to avoid or pursue sexual relationships. Most do not think their friends would respect them more, but this is less true for Blacks than for other groups. About 37 percent say they would feel guilty, more than two thirds say their mothers would be upset, 41 percent say it would give them a great deal of pleasure, but most do not think it would make them more attractive to the opposite sex. Most do not think that sex would decrease their loneliness, but a majority say it would be embarrassing to them and their family. Most do not think they would have to quit school. About a third think sex could lead to marriage to the wrong person and a clear majority think sex would force them to grow up (F1.13).

About 95 percent of men and more than 96 percent of women report having exclusively heterosexual relationships. The frequency of same-sex relationships does not vary significantly by race (F1.14).

Public opinion opposes sexual activity among younger teens aged 14–16, but attitudes regarding nonmarital sex among older people are more varied. Blacks are more opposed to nonmarital sex than other groups. A large majority say that extramarital sex is always or almost always wrong. About sixty percent say that same-sex relationships are always or almost always wrong (F1.15).

Nearly 15 percent of women age 15–44 are at risk of infection from HIV because they had sex with a man who had had sex with another woman around the same time. HIV-risk behaviors are higher for Blacks and other races than for Hispanics or Whites (F1.17).

F2. FERTILITY

More than one-third of women aged 14–44 are not able to have children, generally because of sterilization. Sterilization is less common among the "Other" race category than among Blacks, Whites, or Hispanics (F2.1).

Birth rates have remained relatively stable since 1980. Women are now averaging about two children each, just enough to maintain replacement fertility. Fertility rates are somewhat higher for Blacks, Hispanics, and Native Americans than for Whites and Asians (F2.2, F2.3, and F2.4). These rates are not expected to change much in the next 10 years (F2.4). The pattern for pregnancies parallels that for births: pregnancy rates are higher for Blacks and Hispanics (F2.5).

Timing and intendedness of childbearing varies across racial groups. Seventeen percent of all women report having a birth before marriage, and an additional eight percent have a child within eight months of marriage. Premarital birth rates are highest among Blacks, comparatively high among Hispanics, and lower among Whites and other races (F2.6). Twenty-eight percent of women aged 15–44 have had an unintended birth, but most of these births are mistimed rather than unwanted (F2.7 and F2.8). A majority of Hispanics and Whites report being quite happy about their pregnancy, but Blacks are less likely to express such happiness (F2.9). The rate of induced abortion is 17.9 for Whites, 36.2 for Hispanics, and 65.9 for Blacks (F2.10). About one fifth of married women have not had any children (F2.11).

The conditions under which children are born also vary by race. Minority babies are more likely to experience a variety of risk factors including having a teenage mother, having an unmarried mother, not receiving prenatal care, and having a low birth weight (F2.12 to F2.15). White mothers are more likely to smoke than Black mothers, but the reverse is the case for drinking (F2.15 and F2.16). More than half of mothers breastfeed their babies, but the percentage is only one-fourth among Black mothers (F2.17).

F3. CONTRACEPTION AND ABORTION

More than half of women aged 15–44 say they used contraception at first intercourse, but the rate was much lower for Hispanic women (36%) than for Whites (64%) or Blacks (60%). Condoms were the most popular method for all groups, followed by the pill (F3.1 and F3.2). Female sterilization has become the most widely used method among Blacks and Hispanics, but the pill is a close second (F3.3).

About a third of women who have had sex in the last year use condoms for disease prevention, but another third never do. Condom use for disease prevention is more common among Blacks and among those who have had more than one partner in the last year (F3.4).

About 60 percent of school-aged adolescents have had contact with another person's genitals and 42 percent have had sexual intercourse. These forms of sexual behavior are least common among Asians and most common among Blacks. Seventy percent of these adolescents say they used some form of birth control at first intercourse, and 68 percent used birth control the most recent time they had sex. Contraceptive use is highest among adolescent Whites and Blacks and lowest among adolescent Asians, Hispanics, and Native Americans (F3.5).

Adolescents have diverse attitudes toward birth control. They generally do not think it is too much of a hassle, is too expensive, or that it takes too much planning. They do think it interferes with sexual enjoyment and that it is easy to obtain. There do not appear to be strong moral objections to the use of birth control. There are not great racial differences in adolescent attitudes toward birth control (F3.6). A majority of adults believe that birth control should be available to teenagers and a large majority (more than 80%) support sex education in the schools. Again, there are not great differences across racial groups in these attitudes.

After peaking in the early 1980s, abortion rates have declined somewhat. Abortion rates are much higher for Blacks than for Whites (F3.7). A substantial majority of the population supports legal abortion in cases where the baby has a serious defect, the mother's health is seriously endangered by the pregnancy, or the pregnancy resulted from rape. In other cases, the population is more divided. Blacks are more opposed to abortion than are Whites or other races (F3.9).

About 58 percent of women aged 15–24 have received family planning services. The rate is higher among sexually experienced women. Most of these women obtain birth control. Hispanics are a little less likely to have received such services (F3.10). About 15 percent of these women have sought services for infertility (F3.11). A majority of women receive some form of sex education before the age of 18. Birth control methods, sexually transmitted diseases, safe sex, and how to say "no" are common topics. Hispanics and other races are less likely to have had sex education than Blacks or Whites (F3.12).

F1. ROMANCE AND SEXUAL EXPERIENCE

F1.1 Adolescent Romantic Relationships

How much would you like to have a romantic relationship in the next year?

	White	Black	Native American	Asian	Hispanic	Total
Not at all	6.1	9	3.3	8.6	9.3	7
Very little	10.4	14.5	10.6	15.7	15.4	11.9
Somewhat	38.1	37.7	41.2	34.7	32.1	37.2
Quite a bit	24.4	19.6	22.8	23.1	24.1	23.5
Very much	21	19.2	22.2	18	19.1	20.4

In the last 18 months have you had a romantic relationship with anyone?

	White	Black	Native American	Asian	Hispanic	Total
No	41.5	48.1	41.6	56.5	47.1	43.7
Yes	58.5	51.9	58.4	43.5	52.9	56.3

Source: The National Longitudinal Study of Adolescent Health, 1996.

F1.2 Number of Women 15–44 Years of Age and Percent Who Have Ever Had Sexual Intercourse after Menarche for All Women and Never-married Women, by Age at Interview and by Age and Race and Hispanic Origin for Teenagers: United States, 1995.

Age and Race and Hispanic Origin	All women		Never-married women	
	Number in Thousands	Percent	Number in thousands	Percent
All women:	60,201	89.3	22,679	71.5
Age at interview and Race and Hispanic origin				
15-19 years:				
Hispanic	1,150	55.0	1,078	52.0
Non-Hispanic white	5,962	49.5	5,693	47.1
Non-Hispanic black	1,392	59.5	1,351	58.3
15-17 years:				
Hispanic	688	50.0	673	48.8
Non-Hispanic white	3,534	34.9	3,485	33.9
Non-Hispanic black	853	48.2	853	48.2
18-19 years:				
Hispanic	462	62.5	405	57.2
Non-Hispanic white	2,428	70.7	2,208	67.8
Non-Hispanic black	538	77.4	498	75.5

Notes:
*Includes women of other race and origin groups not shown separately.

Source: National Survey of Family Growth, 1995.

F1.3. Number of Women 20–44 Years of Age and Cumulative Percent Who Have Ever Had Sexual Intercourse after Menarche and before Reaching Selected Ages: United States, 1995

Characteristic	Number in thousands	15	Exact age in years 18 % had sexual intercourse	20	Mean age at first intercourse
All women	51,240	9.2	52.3	75	17.8
Race and Hispanic origin					
Hispanic	5,553	7.6	42.2	66.7	18.4
Non-Hispanic white	36,560	8.3	52.8	76	17.7
Non-Hispanic black	6,818	16.1	66.9	85.6	16.8
Non-Hispanic other	2,309	8.1	28.4	48.1	20

Note:
*Mean ages are based only on women who ever had intercourse after menarche.

Source: National Survey of Family Growth, 1995.

F1.4. Number of Ever-married Women 15–44 Years of Age and Percent Distribution by Timing of First Sexual Intercourse after Menarche in Relation to First Marriage, According to Selected Characteristics: United States, 1995

Characteristic	Number in thousands	Total	First intercourse after or same month as marriage	Before Marriage Less than 12 months	12 to 35 months	36 to 59 months	60 months or more
All women	37,521	100	17.8	11.5	20.6	17.6	32.5
Race and Hispanic Origin							
Hispanic	4,116	100	37.7	14.9	15.3	11.1	20.9
Non-Hispanic white	28,250	100	14.6	11.4	22.2	19	32.8
Non-Hispanic black	3,536	100	8.1	9.3	17.4	18.1	47.2
Non-Hispanic other	1,619	100	44.4	9.8	13.8	8.2	23.8

Note:
Percents may not add to 100 due to rounding.

Source: National Survey of Family Growth, 1995.

F1.5. Number of Women 15–44 Years of Age Who Have Ever Had Voluntary Sexual Intercourse and Percent Distribution by Age of First Voluntary Partner, According to Age at First Intercourse and Race and Hispanic Origin: United States, 1995.

Age at first intercourse and race and Hispanic origin	Number in thousands	Total	Age of first voluntary partner in years					
			under 16	16-17	18-19	20-22	23-24	25 and over
All women *	53,614	100	5.8	23.4	26.3	22.3	8.4	13.9
Race and Hispanic origin and age at first intercourse								
Hispanic	5,887	100	4.7	17.9	21.1	25.8	10.3	20.3
Under 16 years	1,305	100	17.3	37.3	22.3	14.4	2.9	6.1
16 -19 years	2,960	100	1.4	18.3	28.4	30	9.4	12.6
20 years and over	1,622	100	-	1	6.7	27.8	18.2	46.2
Non-Hispanic white	38,110	100	5.3	24	27.2	22.8	8.6	12.2
Under 16 years	8,411	100	21.2	45.9	20.8	6.6	2	3.5
16 -19 years	22,166	100	1.1	23.5	37.1	24.7	6.9	6.7
20 years and over	7,534	100	-	0.7	5.4	35.3	20.7	38.1
Non-Hispanic black	7,462	100	9.7	27.5	28.9	18.2	5.4	10.3
Under 16 years	2,684	100	26	41.1	21.6	5.7	1.7	4
16 -19 years	3,946	100	0.5	23.8	39.1	24.2	5.2	7.2
20 years and over	832	100	0.2	0.3	3.9	31	18.7	46

Notes:
*Includes women of other races and origin groups not shown separately.
-Quantity zero.
0.0 Includes women of other race and origin groups not shown separately.
Percents may not add to 100 due to rounding.

Source: National Survey of Family Growth, 1995.

F1.6. Number of Women 15–44 Years of Age Who Have Ever Had Voluntary Sexual Intercourse and Percent Distribution by Type of Relationship with Partner at First Voluntary Intercourse, According to Selected Characteristics: United States, 1995

Characteristic	Number in thousands	Total	Just met	Just friends	Went out once in a while	Going steady	Engaged	Married	Other[1]
					Percent distribution				
All women	53,614	100.0	2.5	9.4	8.3	61.0	6.2	12.2	0.4
Race and Hispanic origin									
Hispanic	5,887	100.0	2.0	8.0	7.1	49.2	7.9	25.2	0.6
Non-Hispanic white	7,462	100.0	2.6	8.3	8.6	62.9	6.4	10.8	0.5
Non-Hispanic black	38,110	100.0	1.9	16.2	8.7	65.8	3.6	3.5	0.3
Non-Hispanic other	2,154	100.0	3.8	9.3	6.2	43.1	5.8	31.5	0.3

Notes:
[1]Other includes living together, family member, and other relationship types not shown separately.
Percents may not add to I00 due to rounding.

Source: National Survey of Family Growth, 1995.

F1.7. Number of Unmarried Women 15–44 Years of Age and Percent Distribution by Number of Male Sexual Partners in the 12 Months Prior to Interview, According to Selected Characteristics, Based on Responses from Interviewer-administered Questionnaire: United States, 1995

Characteristic	Number in thousands	Total	Number of partners in last 12 months				
			0	1	2	3	4 or more
			Percent distribution				
All women	30,528	100.0	34.5	47.0	11.2	4.1	3.3
Race and Hispanic origin							
Hispanic	3,524	100.0	41.2	45.7	6.9	2.5	3.6
Non-Hispanic white	19,445	100.0	35.1	46.5	11.1	3.9	3.4
Non-Hispanic black	6,141	100.0	23.7	52.5	14.7	6.0	3.1
Non-Hispanic other	1,418	100.0	56.1	32.6	7.0	2.4	1.9

Note:
Percents may not add to 100 due to rounding.

Source: National Survey of Family Growth, 1995.

F1.8. Number of Women 15–44 Years of Age and Percent Distribution by Number of Male Sexual Partners in Lifetime, According to Selected Characteristics, Based on Responses from Self-administered Questionnaire: United States, 1995

Characteristic	Number in thousands	Total	Number of partners in lifetime							
			0[1]	1	2	3	4	5	6-9	10 or more
			Percent distribution							
All women	60,201	100.0	10.5	23.5	12.3	9.6	8.4	8.1	12.1	15.5
Race and Hispanic origin										
Hispanic	6,702	100.0	12.1	37.1	15.8	8.9	5.1	5.7	6.9	8.5
Non-Hispanic white	42,522	100.0	10.1	22.4	11.7	9.6	8.6	8.0	13.2	16.4
Non-Hispanic black	8,210	100.0	8.3	14.2	12.1	11.4	11.6	11.6	12.1	18.8
Non-Hispanic other	2,767	100.0	19.8	35.9	14.8	5.7	4.0	4.9	7.2	7.8

[1]*Notes:*
Never had intercourse, or never had voluntary intercourse if first intercourse was not voluntary.
Percents may not add to 100 due to rounding.

Source: National Survey of Family Growth, 1995.

F1.9. Frequency of Sex

About how often did you have sex during the last 12 months?			
	White	**Black**	**Other**
Once or twice	7.4%	9.9%	10.7%
Once a month	13.1	8.6	7.5
2-3 times a month	16.8	16.9	11.3
Weekly	19.7	20.1	15.1
2-3 per week	20.7	17.2	30.8
4+ per week	5.8	5.1	5.7
Not at all	16.4	22.3	18.9
(N)	**1712**	**314**	**159**

Source: General Social Survey, 1998.

F1.10. Types of Sexual Experience

Thinking about the time since your 18th birthday, have you ever had sex with a person you paid or who paid you for sex?

	White	Black	Other
Yes	7.2%	11%	6.5%
No	92.8	89	93.5
(N)	1878	317	155

Have you ever had sex with someone other than your husband or wife while you were married?

	White	Black	Other
Yes	13.7%	14.6%	8.9%
No	64.8	49.5	52.2
Never married	21.5	35.8	38.9
(N)	1914	321	157

Source: General Social Survey, 1995.

F1.11. Number of Women 15–44 Years of Age and Percent Ever Forced to Have Sexual Intercourse, by Age at First Forced Intercourse and Selected Characteristics: United States, 1995

Characteristic	Number in thousands	Ever forced	Age at first forced intercourse[1]			
			Under 15	15-17	18-19	20 and over
				Percent		
All women	60,201	20.4	5.8	6.0	2.9	5.3
Race and Hispanic origin						
Hispanic	6,702	18.7	5.3	6.1	2.5	4.1
Non-Hispanic white	42,522	19.8	5.2	5.8	3.0	5.3
Non-Hispanic black	8,210	25.7	8.8	7.3	2.9	6.4
Non-Hispanic other	2,767	19.4	6.9	4.1	3.5	4.5

Notes:

[1]"Ever forced" means that the woman either responded "yes" to the question asking if she had ever been forced to have intercourse (in the self-administered portion of the interview), or reported her first intercourse as "rape" or "not voluntary" (in the interviewer-administered portion). "Age at first forced intercourse" is based on the self-administered questionnaire unless the only forced intercourse was her first intercourse. For these cases, information is from the interviewer-administered questionnaire.

Percents may not add to total who were "ever forced" because the total includes respondents with missing information on "age at first forced intercourse."

Source: The National Survey of Family Growth, 1995.

F1.12. Number of Women 15–44 Years of Age Who Have Ever Had Sexual Intercourse and Percent Whose First Intercourse Was Not Voluntary, by Selected Characteristics: United States, 1995

Characteristic	Number in thousands	Percent whose first intercourse was not voluntary[1]
All women[2]	53,793	7.8
Race and Hispanic origin and age at first intercourse		
Hispanic	5,907	9.4
Under 16 years	1,456	18.1
16-19 years	2,894	7.4
20 years and over	1,558	5.0
Non-Hispanic white	38,212	7.0
Under 16 years	9,219	15.3
16-19 years	21,628	5.0
20 years and over	7,364	2.6
Non-Hispanic black	7,484	9.1
Under 16 years	2,835	15.0
16-19 years	3,852	5.5
20 years and over	796	5.1

Notes:
[1]Includes first intercourse reported as "rape" or "not voluntary."
[2]Includes women of other race and origin groups not shown separately.

Source: National Survey of Family Growth, 1995.

F1.13. Adolescent Motivations to Engage in Sex

If you had sexual intercourse...
...your friends would respect you more.

	White	Black	Native American	Asian	Hispanic	Total
						Percent
Strongly agree	1.8	4.3	1.4	2.3	3.4	2.4
Agree	5.5	12.9	4.7	7.5	7.6	7.0
Neither agree nor disagree	32.3	32.8	33.1	31.8	31.4	32.3
Disagree	32.7	34.0	36.5	28.0	36.1	33.3
Strongly disagree	27.7	16.0	24.3	30.0	21.4	25.1
...your partner would lose respect for you.						
Strongly agree	6.1	5.2	4.1	4.4	6.7	6.0
Agree	9.4	8.5	13.3	14.9	13.8	10.0
Neither agree nor disagree	35.4	27.5	32.3	40.1	29.8	33.6
Disagree	32.7	41.3	33.4	25.4	33.8	34.0
Strongly disagree	16.5	17.5	16.9	15.1	15.8	16.4
...afterward you would feel guilty.						
Strongly agree	18.4	11.8	16.6	22.3	16.2	17.2
Agree	19.2	17.8	18.8	24.4	21.5	19.4
Neither agree nor disagree	29.2	27.1	27.3	30.0	25.9	28.5
Disagree	23.7	32.7	28.5	17.0	26.0	25.4
Strongly disagree	9.5	10.5	8.8	6.3	10.3	9.6
...it would upset your mother.						
Strongly agree	47.7	36.8	45.3	59.5	44.3	46.0
Agree	26.0	22.9	20.9	18.7	22.4	24.8
Neither agree nor disagree	16.5	21.9	18.5	15.1	19.9	17.7
Disagree	7.6	13.7	10.9	3.8	9.7	8.7
Strongly disagree	2.2	4.7	4.4	2.9	3.7	2.8

F1.13. Adolescent Motivations to Engage in Sex *(continued)*

	White	Black	Native American	Asian	Hispanic	Total
			Percemt			
...it would give you a great deal of pleasure						
Strongly agree	12.1	14.6	13.3	8.2	12.4	12.4
Agree	29.7	27.0	27.8	24.3	26.8	28.8
Neither agree nor disagree	40.8	33.8	40.2	48.6	39.8	39.7
Disagree	10.1	17.2	11.3	9.5	13.3	11.6
Strongly disagree	7.2	7.5	7.4	9.3	7.7	7.4
If R is male: ...it would make you more attractive to women.						
If R is female: ...it would make you more attractive to men.						
Strongly agree	2.5	5.1	1.4	.6	3.3	2.9
Agree	5.4	9.8	5.6	7.0	7.3	6.3
Neither agree nor disagree	38.1	33.0	37.8	43.3	34.4	37.1
Disagree	32.3	31.0	38.9	28.1	32.6	32.1
Strongly disagree	21.8	21.0	16.4	20.9	22.4	21.6
...you would feel less lonely.						
Strongly agree	2.3	4.1	2.5	2.3	3.8	2.8
Agree	9.2	12.8	10.6	12.6	12.3	10.3
Neither agree nor disagree	34.8	29.8	39.8	38.7	34.9	34.4
Disagree	32.5	34.2	33.1	29.8	30.4	32.3
Strongly disagree	21.2	19.1	13.9	16.6	18.6	20.2
If R is male: if you got someone pregnant...						
If R is female: if you got pregnant......it would be embarrassing for your family.						
Strongly agree	38.1	23.1	30.1	57.1	30.6	35.3
Agree	26.2	18.2	25.4	24.4	23.5	24.5
Neither agree nor disagree	19.9	20.1	23.2	11.9	19.3	19.7
Disagree	11.6	26.9	17.1	4.8	19.1	14.8
Strongly disagree	4.2	11.7	4.1	1.9	7.5	5.7
...it would be embarrassing for you.						
Strongly agree	42.7	26.2	34.9	56.8	29.7	38.8
Agree	25.1	19.6	16.5	20.3	21.8	23.3
Neither agree nor disagree	14.9	14.3	23.6	14.4	18.8	15.6
Disagree	11.8	26.9	16.5	5.8	20.6	15.2
Strongly disagree	5.6	13.0	8.5	2.7	9.0	7.1
...you would have to quit school.						
Strongly agree	8.4	4.8	5.5	20.0	9.9	8.3
Agree	13.0	9.6	12.4	17.7	15.3	12.9
Neither agree nor disagree	23.8	13.5	22.6	27.8	19.9	21.8
Disagree	36.8	43.7	31.7	25.5	36.3	37.3
Strongly disagree	18.0	28.5	27.8	9.0	18.6	19.7
...you might marry the wrong person, just to get married.						
Strongly agree	12.7	7.5	10.8	22.3	12.8	12.2
Agree	23.9	12.5	20.7	26.3	22.7	21.9
Neither agree nor disagree	23.2	17.6	26.0	28.2	22.1	22.4
Disagree	24.3	37.9	27.9	14.8	28.3	26.7
Strongly disagree	15.9	24.5	14.6	8.4	14.1	16.8
...you would be forced to grow up.						
Strongly agree	38.6	26.9	32.8	40.9	32.0	35.8
Agree	38.2	33.9	37.7	36.9	36.2	37.2
Neither agree nor disagree	12.1	13.6	13.8	14.7	15.0	12.8
Disagree	8.1	17.8	8.8	6.5	13.0	10.2
Strongly disagree	3.0	7.8	6.9	1.0	3.7	3.9

Source: National Longitudinal Study of Adolescent Health, 1996.

F1.14. Gender of Sex Partners in the Last Year

		White	Black	Other
Male	Exclusively male	3.4%	4.4%	5%
	Both male and female	1	2.2	—
	Exclusively female	95.6	93.3	95
	(N)	**706**	**90**	**60**
Female	Exclusively male	96.5%	96.1%	100%
	Both male and female	.8	1.3	—
	Exclusively female	2.7	2.6	—
	(N)	**796**	**152**	**71**

Source: General Social Survey, 1998.

F1.15. Attitudes toward Nonmarital Sex

There's been a lot of discussion about the way morals and attitudes about sex are changing in this country. If a man and woman have sex relations before marriage, do you think it is always wrong, almost always wrong, wrong only sometimes, or not wrong at all?

	White	Black	Other
Always wrong	24.3%	34.5%	21.1%
Almost always wrong	8.2	9.8	14.8
Sometimes wrong	21.1	16.1	18.8
Not wrong at all	42.8	37.3	41.4
Don't know	3.6	2.4	3.9
(N)	**1486**	**255**	**128**

What if they are in their early teens, say 14 to 16 years old? In that case, do you think sex relations before marriage are always wrong, almost always wrong, wrong only sometimes, or not wrong at all?

	White	Black	Other
Always wrong	70.3%	73.2%	68%
Almost always wrong	15.9	15.7	18
Sometimes wrong	8.5	7.5	8.6
Not wrong at all	3.4	3.1	3.9
Don't know	1.8	.4	1.6
(N)	**1486**	**254**	**128**

What is your opinion about a married person having sexual relations with someone other than the marriage partner—is it always wrong, almost always wrong, wrong only sometimes, or not wrong at all?

	White	Black	Other
Always wrong	78.6%	75%	79%
Almost always wrong	12.3	12.9	11.3
Sometimes wrong	5.7	6.4	4
Not wrong at all	2	3.8	3.2
Don't know	1.4	1.9	2.4
(N)	**1489**	**264**	**124**

What about sexual relations between two adults of the same sex?

	White	Black	Other
Always wrong	52.7%	64.6%	50.8%
Almost always wrong	5.1	6.5	5.6
Sometimes wrong	7	4.9	3.2
Not wrong at all	28.9	17.5	31.5
Don't know	6.3	6.5	8.9
(N)	**1487**	**263**	**124**

Source: General Social Survey, 1998.

F1.16. Attitudes toward Extramarital Sex and Homosexual Relationships

	White	Black	Other	Total
What about a married person having sexual relations with someone other than his or her husband or wife, is it? . . .				
Always wrong	78.8%	84.7%	86.8%	80.0%
Almost always wrong	14.3	8.9	6.6	13.1
Wrong only sometimes	6.2	4.5	3.3	5.8
Not wrong at all	0.7	1.9	3.3	1.0
(N)	**1004**	**157**	**91**	**1252**
And what about sexual relations between two adults of the same sex, is it...				
Always wrong	60.0%	79.6%	59.3%	62.4%
Almost always wrong	6.1	2.8	4.7	5.6
Wrong only sometimes	8.1	3.5	5.8	7.4
Not wrong at all	25.7	14.1	30.2	24.6
(N)	**921**	**142**	**86**	**1149**

Source: General Social Survey, 1998.

F1.17. Number of Women 15–44 Years of Age and Percent Reporting the Specified HIV-Risk Behaviors in the 12 Months Prior to Interview, by Selected Characteristics: United States, 1995

| | | | | Partner behavior[1] | |
Characteristic	Number in thousands	Respondent injected drugs without prescription in last year	Had sex with other men since 1980	Injected drugs without prescription since 1980	Had sex with other women around same time as sex with respondent
			Percent		
All women[2]	60,201	1.2	2.0	2.5	14.3
Unmarried women	30,528	1.8	2.4	4.3	28.4
Race and Hispanic origin:					
Hispanic	3,524	1.2	3.0	3.9	28.6
Non-Hispanic white	19,445	1.7	1.9	4.6	25.2
Non-Hispanic black	6,141	2.6	2.0	3.3	35.2
Non-Hispanic other	1,418	1.0	11.8	8.1	38.8

Notes:

[1] Partner behavior questions were inapplicable if respondent reported zero partners in the last 12 months, based on both interviewer-administered and self-administered (Audio CASI) questions. Audio CASI is audio computer-assisted self-interviewing. The partner behavior questions asked only about partners that the respondent had intercourse with in the 12 months prior to interview.

[2] Includes women with missing information on specific HIV risk behaviors, number of partners in last 12 months, or consistency of condom use.

HIV is human immunodeficiency virus, the virus that causes acquired immunodeficiency syndrome (AIDS).

Source: National Survey of Family Growth, 1995.

F2. FERTILITY

F2.1. Number of Women 15–44 Years of Age and Percent Distribution by Fecundity Status, According to Selected Characteristics: United States, 1995

| Characteristic | Number in thousands | Total | Surgically sterile | | Impaired fecundity | Fecund |
| | | | Contraceptive | Noncontraceptive | | |
				Percent distribution		
All women	60,201	100.0	24.2	3.1	10.2	62.5
Race and Hispanic origin						
Hispanic	6,702	100.0	22.9	2.3	10.8	64.0
Non-Hispanic white	42,522	100.0	24.7	3.2	10.0	62.2
Non-Hispanic black	8,210	100.0	25.5	3.7	10.1	60.7
Non-Hispanic other	2,767	100.0	15.6	2.3	13.1	69.1

Note:
Percents may not add to 100 due to rounding.

Source: National Survey of Family Growth, 1995.

F2.2. Births and Birth Rates: 1960 to 1996

[Births in thousands and by race of child, except as indicated. Beginning 1970, excludes births to nonresidents of the United States. For population bases used to derive these data.

ITEM	1960	1965	1970	1975	1980	1981	1982	1983
Live births \1	4,258	3,760	3,731	3,144	3,612	3,629	3,681	3,639
White	3,601	3,124	3,091	2,552	2,936	2,948	2,985	2,946
Black	602	581	572	512	568	566	569	563
American Indian	(NA)	(NA)	26	(NA)	29	30	32	33
Asian or Pacific Islander	(NA)	(NA)	(NA)	(NA)	74	85	93	96
Male	2,180	1,927	1,915	1,613	1,853	1,860	1,886	1,866
Female	2,078	1,833	1,816	1,531	1,760	1,769	1,795	1,773
Males per 100 females	105	105	106	105	105	105	105	105
Age of mother:								
Under 20 years old	594	599	656	595	562	537	524	499
20 to 24 years old	1,427	1,337	1,419	1,094	1,226	1,212	1,206	1,160
25 to 29 years old	1,093	926	995	937	1,108	1,128	1,152	1,148
30 to 34 years old	688	529	428	376	550	581	605	625
35 to 39 years old	360	283	180	115	141	146	168	180
40 years old or more	97	86	53	28	24	25	26	27
Age of father:								
Under 20 years old	123	140	189	159	137	129	125	116
20 to 24 years old	990	964	1,015	779	803	785	768	722
25 to 29 years old	1,193	1,011	1,085	979	1,082	1,083	1,093	1,070
30 to 34 years old	875	681	599	537	739	768	780	782
35 to 39 years old	516	415	298	213	275	286	319	335
40 years old or more	363	302	214	135	139	141	149	153
Age not stated	197	248	330	342	437	437	447	461
Birth rate per 1,000								
population	23.7	19.4	18.4	14.6	15.9	15.8	15.9	15.6
White	22.7	18.3	17.4	13.6	15.1	14.8	14.8	14.8
Black	31.9	27.7	25.3	20.7	21.3	20.2	20.1	20.2
American Indian	(NA)	(NA)	(NA)	(NA)	20.7	20.6	20.1	20.6
Asian or Pacific Islander	(NA)	(NA)	(NA)	(NA)	19.9	19.5	18.8	19.5
Male	24.7	20.3	19.4	15.4	16.8	16.7	16.7	16.4
Female	22.8	18.6	17.4	13.8	15.1	15.0	15.1	14.8

F2.2. Births and Birth Rates: 1960 to 1996 *(continued)*

ITEM	1960	1965	1970	1975	1980	1981	1982	1983
Plural birth ratio \2	20.4	20.1	(NA)	19.2	19.3	19.7	19.9	20.3
White	19.3	19.0	(NA)	18.5	18.5	18.8	19.2	19.6
Black	(NA)	(NA)	(NA)	23.1	24.1	24.7	24.1	24.5
Fertility rate per 1,000								
women \3	118.0	96.6	87.9	66.0	68.4	67.4	67.3	65.8
White \3	113.2	91.4	84.1	62.5	64.8	63.9	63.9	63.4
Black \3	153.5	133.2	115.4	87.9	84.7	85.4	84.1	78.7
American Indian \3	(NA)	(NA)	(NA)	(NA)	82.7	(NA)	(NA)	81.8
Asian or Pacific Islander \3	(NA)	(NA)	(NA)	(NA)	73.2	(NA)	(NA)	71.7
Age of mother:								
10 to 14 years old	0.8	0.8	1.2	1.3	1.1	1.1	1.1	1.1
15 to 19 years old	89.1	70.5	68.3	55.6	53.0	52.2	52.4	51.4
20 to 24 years old	258.1	195.3	167.8	113.0	115.1	112.2	111.6	107.8
25 to 29 years old	197.4	161.6	145.1	108.2	112.9	112.0	112.2	108.5
30 to 34 years old	112.7	94.4	73.3	52.3	61.9	61.4	64.1	64.9
35 to 39 years old	56.2	46.2	31.7	19.5	19.8	20.0	21.2	22.0
40 to 44 years old	15.5	12.8	8.1	4.6	3.9	3.8	3.9	3.9
45 to 49 years old	0.9	0.8	0.5	0.3	0.2	0.2	0.2	0.2

ITEM	1984	1985	1986	1987	1988	1989	1990
Live births \1	3,669	3,761	3,757	3,809	3,910	4,041	4,158
White	2,967	3,038	3,019	3,044	3,102	3,192	3,290
Black	568	582	593	611	639	673	684
American Indian	33	34	34	35	37	39	39
Asian or Pacific Islander	99	105	108	117	129	133	142
Male	1,879	1,928	1,925	1,951	2,002	2,069	2,129
Female	1,790	1,833	1,832	1,858	1,907	1,971	2,029
Males per 100 females	105	105	105	105	105	105	105
Age of mother:							
Under 20 years old	480	478	472	473	489	518	533
20 to 24 years old	1,142	1,141	1,102	1,076	1,067	1,078	1,094
25 to 29 years old	1,166	1,201	1,200	1,216	1,239	1,263	1,277
30 to 34 years old	658	696	721	761	804	842	886
35 to 39 years old	196	214	230	248	270	294	318
40 years old or more	28	29	31	36	41	46	50
Age of father:							
Under 20 years old	109	108	105	105	111	120	129
20 to 24 years old	696	685	651	627	617	613	628
25 to 29 years old	1,067	1,081	1,059	1,053	1,055	1,056	1,060
30 to 34 years old	806	837	845	872	904	922	955
35 to 39 years old	356	381	398	413	431	451	474
40 years old or more	160	167	174	191	205	221	231
Age not stated	475	502	524	549	585	659	681
Birth rate per 1,000							
population	15.6	15.8	15.6	15.7	16.0	16.4	16.7
White	14.8	15.0	14.8	14.9	15.0	15.4	15.8
Black	20.1	20.4	20.5	20.8	21.5	22.3	22.4
American Indian	20.1	19.8	19.2	19.1	19.3	19.7	18.9
Asian or Pacific Islander	18.8	18.7	18.0	18.4	19.2	18.7	19.0
Male	16.4	16.7	16.5	16.5	16.8	17.2	17.6
Female	14.8	15.0	14.9	14.9	15.2	15.6	15.9
Plural birth ratio \2	20.3	21.0	21.6	22.0	22.4	23.0	23.3
White	19.8	20.4	21.2	21.6	22.0	22.5	22.9
Black	24.2	25.3	24.9	25.4	25.8	26.9	27.0
Fertility rate per 1,000							
women \3	65.4	66.2	65.4	65.7	67.2	69.2	70.9
White \3	63.2	64.1	63.1	63.3	64.5	66.4	68.3
Black \3	78.2	78.8	78.9	80.1	82.6	86.2	86.8

F2.2. Births and Birth Rates: 1960 to 1996 *(continued)*

ITEM	1984	1985	1986	1987	1988	1989	1990
American Indian \3	79.8	78.6	75.9	75.6	76.8	79.0	76.2
Asian or Pacific Islander \3	69.2	68.4	66.0	67.1	70.2	68.2	69.6
Age of mother:							
10 to 14 years old	1.2	1.2	1.3	1.3	1.3	1.4	1.4
15 to 19 years old	50.6	51.0	50.2	50.6	53.0	57.3	59.9
20 to 24 years old	106.8	108.3	107.4	107.9	110.2	113.8	116.5
25 to 29 years old	108.7	111.0	109.8	111.6	114.4	117.6	120.2
30 to 34 years old	67.0	69.1	70.1	72.1	74.8	77.4	80.8
35 to 39 years old	22.9	24.0	24.4	26.3	28.1	29.9	31.7
40 to 44 years old	3.9	4.0	4.1	4.4	4.8	5.2	5.5
45 to 49 years old	0.2	0.2	0.2	0.2	0.2	0.2	0.2

ITEM	1991	1992	1993	1994	1995	1996
Live births \1	4,111	4,065	4,000	3,953	3,900	3,915
White	3,241	3,202	3,126	3,121	2,753	3,113
Black	683	674	695	636	394	596
American Indian	39	39	39	38	26	38
Asian or Pacific Islander	145	150	153	158	135	167
Male	2,102	2,082	2,049	2,023	1,996	(NA)
Female	2,009	1,983	1,951	1,930	1,903	(NA)
Males per 100 females	105	105	105	105	105	(NA)
Age of mother:						
Under 20 years old	532	518	514	518	512	506
20 to 24 years old	1,090	1,070	1,038	1,001	966	951
25 to 29 years old	1,220	1,179	1,129	1,089	1,064	1,078
30 to 34 years old	885	895	901	906	905	904
35 to 39 years old	331	345	357	372	384	401
40 years old or more	54	58	61	66	70	75
Age of father:						
Under 20 years old	130	129	132	138	(NA)	(NA)
20 to 24 years old	625	621	608	601	(NA)	(NA)
25 to 29 years old	1,007	969	923	890	(NA)	(NA)
30 to 34 years old	940	940	932	930	(NA)	(NA)
35 to 39 years old	478	488	498	508	(NA)	(NA)
40 years old or more	236	242	246	254	(NA)	(NA)
Age not stated	696	677	661	631	(NA)	(NA)
Birth rate per 1,000						
population	16.3	15.9	15.5	15.2	14.8	14.8
White	15.4	15.0	14.7	14.4	14.2	(NA)
Black	21.9	21.3	20.5	19.5	18.2	(NA)
American Indian	18.3	18.4	17.8	17.1	16.6	(NA)
Asian or Pacific Islander	18.2	18.0	17.7	17.5	17.3	(NA)
Male	17.1	16.7	(NA)	(NA)	(NA)	(NA)
Female	15.6	15.2	(NA)	(NA)	(NA)	(NA)
Plural birth ratio \2	23.9	24.4	25.2	25.7	26.1	(NA)
White	23.4	24.0	24.9	25.5	26.0	(NA)
Black	27.8	28.2	28.7	29.4	28.8	(NA)
Fertility rate per 1,000						
women \3	69.6	68.9	67.6	66.7	65.6	65.7
White \3	67.0	66.5	65.4	64.9	64.4	64.7
Black \3	85.2	83.2	80.5	76.9	72.3	70.8
American Indian \3	75.1	75.4	73.4	70.9	69.1	69.8
Asian or Pacific Islander \3	67.6	67.2	66.7	66.8	66.4	66.6
Age of mother:						
10 to 14 years old	1.4	1.4	1.4	1.4	1.3	1.2
15 to 19 years old	62.1	60.7	59.6	58.9	56.8	54.7
20 to 24 years old	115.7	114.6	112.6	111.1	109.8	111.1
25 to 29 years old	118.2	117.4	115.5	113.9	111.2	113.9
30 to 34 years old	79.5	80.2	80.8	81.5	82.5	84.5

F2.2. Births and Birth Rates: 1960 to 1996 *(continued)*

ITEM	1991	1992	1993	1994	1995	1996
35 to 39 years old	32.0	32.5	32.9	33.7	34.3	35.4
40 to 44 years old	5.5	5.9	6.1	6.4	6.6	6.8
45 to 49 years old	0.2	0.3	0.3	0.3	0.3	0.3

Notes:
NA Not available.
\1 Includes other races not shown separately.
\2 Number of multiple births per 1,000 live births.
\3 Per 1,000 women, 15 to 44 years old in specified group. The rate for age of mother 45 to 49 years old computed by relating births to mothers 45 years old and over to women 45 to 49 years old.

Source: U.S. National Center for Health Statistics; Vital Statistics of the United States, annual; Monthly Vital Statistics Report, and unpublished data.

F2.3. Total Fertility Rate and Intrinsic Rate of Natural Increase: 1960 to 1996

[Based on race of child and registered births only, thru 1979. Beginning 1980, based on race of mother. Beginning 1970, excludes births to nonresidents of United States. The total fertility rate is the number of births that 1,000 women would have in their lifetime if, at each year of age, they experienced the birth rates occurring in the specified year. A total fertility rate of 2,110 represents "replacement level" fertility for the total population under current mortality conditions (assuming no net immigration). The intrinsic rate of natural increase is the rate that would eventually prevail if a population were to experience, at each year of age, the birth rates and death rates occurring in the specified year and if those rates remained unchanged over a long period of time. Minus sign (-) indicates decrease.]

ANNUAL AVERAGE AND YEAR	TOTAL FERTILITY RATE			INTRINSIC RATE OF NATURAL INCREASE		
	Total	White	Black and other	Total	White	Black and other
1960-64	3,449	3,326	4,326	18.6	17.1	27.7
1965-69	2,622	2,512	3,362	8.2	6.4	18.6
1970-74	2,094	1,997	2,680	-0.7	-2.5	9.1
1975-79	1,774	1,685	2,270	-6.6	-8.5	3.0
1980-84	1,819	1,731	2,262	-5.4	-7.3	3.0
1985-88	1,870	1,769	2,339	-4.2	-6.3	4.3
1970	2,480	2,385	3,067	6.0	4.5	14.4
1971	2,267	2,161	2,920	2.6	0.8	12.6
1972	2,010	1,907	2,628	-2.0	-3.9	8.6
1973	1,879	1,783	2,443	-4.5	-6.5	5.7
1974	1,835	1,749	2,339	-5.4	-7.2	4.0
1975	1,774	1,686	2,276	-6.7	-8.6	3.0
1976	1,738	1,652	2,223	-7.4	-9.3	2.1
1977	1,790	1,703	2,279	-6.2	-8.1	3.2
1978	1,760	1,668	2,265	-6.8	-8.8	2.9
1979	1,808	1,716	2,310	-5.7	-7.7	3.8
1980	1,840	1,773	2,177	-5.1	-7.0	4.0
1981	1,812	1,748	2,118	-5.6	-7.4	3.0
1982	1,828	1,767	2,107	-5.2	-7.0	3.0
1983	1,799	1,741	2,066	-5.8	-7.5	2.2
1984	1,807	1,749	2,071	-5.6	-7.3	2.1
1985	1,844	1,787	2,109	-4.8	-6.5	2.7
1986	1,838	1,776	2,136	-4.9	-6.7	2.8
1987	1,872	1,805	2,198	-4.1	-6.1	4.0
1988	1,934	1,857	2,298	-2.9	-5.1	5.7
1989	2,014	1,931	2,433	-1.4	-3.6	7.4
1990	2,081	2,003	2,480	-0.1	-2.3	8.3
1991	2,073	1,996	2,480	-0.2	-2.4	8.2
1992	2,065	1,994	2,442	-0.4	-2.5	7.5
1993	2,046	1,982	2,385	-0.7	-1.9	3.7
1994	2,036	1,985	2,300	(NA)	(NA)	(NA)
1995	2,019	1,989	2,175	(NA)	(NA)	(NA)
1996	2,040	2,019	2,149	(NA)	(NA)	(NA)

Notes:
NA Not available.

Source: U.S. National Center for Health Statistics; Vital Statistics of the United States, annual; Monthly Vital Statistics Report, and unpublished data.

F2.4. Fertility Rates, by Race and Age Group: 1993 to 1997, and Projections

[The total fertility rate is the number of births that 1,000 women would have in their lifetime if, at each year of age, they experienced the birth rates occurring in the specified year. Birth rates represent live births per 1,000 women in age group indicated. Projections are based on middle fertility assumptions.]

AGE GROUP	1993	1994	1995	1996	1997	2000	2010
Fertility rate, all races	2,074	2,079	2,055	2,059	2,063	2,072	2,108
Birth rates:							
10 to 14 years old	1.4	1.4	1.4	1.4	1.4	1.4	1.6
15 to 19 years old	60.5	60.0	59.4	59.4	59.6	60.6	63.6
20 to 24 years old	117.6	118.0	115.4	115.7	115.9	116.2	118.2
25 to 29 years old	118.6	118.8	117.8	117.9	118.1	118.3	119.5
30 to 34 years old	80.1	80.1	78.9	78.8	78.8	79.5	81.0
35 to 39 years old	31.6	31.6	31.6	31.6	31.6	31.6	32.1
40 to 44 years old	5.4	5.4	5.6	5.6	5.6	5.6	5.9
45 to 49 years old	0.2	0.3	0.3	0.3	0.3	0.3	0.3
Fertility rate, White	1,973	1,976	1,984	1,988	1,992	2,004	2,046
Birth rates:							
10 to 14 years old	0.7	0.7	0.8	0.8	0.8	0.8	0.9
15 to 19 years old	50.4	50.0	50.7	50.7	50.9	52.2	56.0
20 to 24 years old	109.6	110.0	108.9	109.2	109.5	109.8	112.6
25 to 29 years old	117.9	118.0	118.7	118.8	119.0	119.4	120.7
30 to 34 years old	80.2	80.2	80.0	79.9	79.8	80.6	82.0
35 to 39 years old	31.0	31.0	31.5	31.5	31.5	31.4	31.7
40 to 44 years old	5.1	5.2	5.4	5.4	5.4	5.4	5.6
45 to 49 years old	0.2	0.2	0.2	0.2	0.2	0.2	0.2
Fertility rate, Black	2,470	2,470	2,427	2,428	2,428	2,431	2,438
Birth rates:							
10 to 14 years old	4.8	4.9	4.8	4.8	4.8	4.6	4.8
15 to 19 years old	114.4	113.3	109.6	109.7	110.1	111.1	111.5
20 to 24 years old	161.0	160.9	157.4	157.4	157.7	158.3	158.7
25 to 29 years old	112.9	112.8	112.0	112.4	112.6	112.1	113.1
30 to 34 years old	67.8	67.8	66.6	66.6	66.5	66.7	67.8
35 to 39 years old	28.1	28.0	27.8	27.8	27.7	27.7	27.7
40 to 44 years old	5.4	5.3	5.4	5.4	5.4	5.4	5.3
45 to 49 years old	0.3	0.3	0.3	0.3	0.3	0.3	0.2
Fertility rate, American Indian, Eskimo, Aleut	2,778	2,779	2,151	2,152	2,153	2,154	2,159
Birth rates:							
10 to 14 years old	2.0	2.0	1.7	1.7	1.7	1.7	1.7
15 to 19 years old	103.9	102.9	78.7	78.2	78.4	80.1	81.8
20 to 24 years old	188.7	188.6	143.3	143.3	143.4	143.6	143.7
25 to 29 years old	141.4	141.4	108.3	108.7	108.8	108.2	109.0
30 to 34 years old	78.2	78.1	61.7	61.7	61.7	62.1	62.9
35 to 39 years old	34.0	34.0	27.4	27.4	27.4	27.3	27.4
40 to 44 years old	7.2	7.2	6.0	6.0	6.0	6.0	6.0
45 to 49 years old	0.4	0.4	0.3	0.3	0.3	0.3	0.3
Fertility rate, Asian and Pacific Islanders	2,514	2,513	1,953	1,952	1,952	1,952	1,954
Birth rates:							
10 to 14 years old	0.8	0.8	0.8	0.9	0.9	0.9	0.8
15 to 19 years old	33.7	33.4	28.5	28.2	28.1	28.6	28.7
20 to 24 years old	99.7	100.1	80.3	80.3	80.0	79.2	79.5
25 to 29 years old	160.8	160.7	121.6	121.5	121.6	122.1	121.7
30 to 34 years old	134.3	134.2	100.9	100.8	100.7	101.1	101.1
35 to 39 years old	61.4	61.2	47.9	48.0	47.9	47.8	47.3
40 to 44 years old	12.7	12.7	10.4	10.4	10.4	10.3	10.3
45 to 49 years old	1.3	1.3	1.0	1.0	1.0	1.0	1.0
Fertility rate, Hispanic	2,900	2,900	2,977	2,977	2,977	2,977	2,977
Birth rates:							
10 to 14 years old	2.3	2.3	2.6	2.6	2.6	2.6	2.6
15 to 19 years old	99.6	99.5	103.7	103.7	103.7	103.7	103.7
20 to 24 years old	180.5	180.5	184.1	184.1	184.7	184.1	184.1
25 to 29 years old	149.8	149.7	152.4	152.4	152.4	152.4	152.4
30 to 34 years old	95.8	95.7	96.7	96.7	96.7	96.7	96.7
35 to 39 years old	43.1	43.0	45.3	45.3	45.3	45.3	45.3
40 to 44 years old	9.2	9.2	10.8	10.8	10.8	10.8	10.8
45 to 49 years old	0.6	0.6	0.6	0.6	0.6	0.6	0.6

Note:
\1 Persons of Hispanic origin may be of any race.

Source: U.S. Bureau of the Census, P6, Population Reports, P25-1130.

F2.5. Number of Women 15–44 Years of Age and Percent Distribution by Number of Pregnancies, According to Selected Characteristics: United States, 1995

Characteristic	Number in thousands	Number of pregnancies[1]					
		Total	None	1	2	3	4 or more
				Percent distribution			
All women	60,201	100.0	33.4	16.4	20.3	14.2	15.7
Race and Hispanic origin							
Hispanic	6,702	100.0	26.8	16.6	19.1	15.2	22.2
Non-Hispanic white	42,522	100.0	34.9	16.2	21.0	14.1	13.7
Non-Hispanic black	8,210	100.0	28.1	17.8	18.1	14.8	21.2
Non-Hispanic other	2,767	100.0	41.2	15.2	17.7	11.2	14.8

Notes:
[1]Based on interviewer-administered portion of the survey.
Percents may not add to 100 due to rounding.

Source: National Survey of Family Growth, 1995.

F2.6. Number of Women 15–44 Years of Age and Percent Distribution by Timing of First Birth in Relation to First Marriage, According to Selected Characteristics: United States, 1995

Characteristic	Number in thousands	Total	Timing of first birth in relation to first marriage				
			Before marriage	0-7 months after	8-47 months after	48 or more months after	No births
					Percent distribution		
All women	60,201	100.0	16.9	8.0	24.7	9.4	41.9
Race and Hispanic origin							
Hispanic	6,702	100.0	21.6	9.2	30.5	3.9	34.8
Non-Hispanic white	42,522	100.0	9.7	8.4	26.5	11.9	43.5
Non-Hispanic black	8,210	100.0	44.7	6.0	9.7	2.3	37.3
Non-Hispanic other	2,767	100.0	11.6	5.9	27.3	6.8	48.4

Note:
Percents may not add to 100 due to rounding.

Source: National Survey of Family Growth, 1995.

F2.7. Number of Women 15–44 Years of Age and Percent Who Ever Had an Unintended Birth, by Selected Characteristics: United States, 1995

Characteristic	Number in thousands	Percent who ever had an unintended birth
All women	60,201	28.4
Race and Hispanic origin		
Hispanic	6,702	34.2
Non-Hispanic white	42,522	25.0
Non-Hispanic black	8,210	42.3
Non-Hispanic other	2,767	24.4

Source: National Survey of Family Growth, 1995.

F2.8. Unintended Birth, Whether Mistimed or Unwanted, by Women 15–44 Years of Age: 1995

| | | WOMEN WHO HAD AN UNINTENDED BIRTH | | |
| | | | First birth unintended | |
CHARACTERISTICS	Number of women, total	Number (1,000)	Percent mistimed	Percent unwanted
Total	60,201	17,077	80.4	19.6
AGE AT BIRTH				
Under 20 years	8,961	7,666	83.4	16.6
20-24 years	9,041	5,674	84.7	15.3
25-29 years	9,693	2,440	73.6	26.4
30-44 years	11,065	1,292	56.8	43.2
BIRTH ORDER				
First birth	(NA)	12,540	84.9	15.1
Second birth	(NA)	2,926	77.5	22.5
Third or higher birth	(NA)	1,611	51.1	48.9
POVERTY LEVEL				
0-149 percent	10,072	5,386	75.5	24.5
0-99 percent	5,992	3,417	73.2	26.8
150-299 percent	14,932	5,606	80.9	19.1
300 percent or more	22,736	4,912	84.3	15.7
RACE AND HISPANIC ORIGIN AND AGE AT BIRTH				
Hispanic	6,702	2,293	74.8	25.2
Non-Hispanic white	42,522	10,641	84.4	15.6
Non-Hispanic black	8,210	3,469	72.9	27.1
Non-Hispanic other	2,767	674	74.8	25.2

Source: U.S. National Center for Health Statistics, Abma, J.; Chandra, A.; Mosher, W.; Peterson, L.; Piccinino, L. Fertility, Family Planning, and Women's Health. New data from the 1995 National Survey of Family Growth, Vital Health Stat. 23(19), 1997.

F2.9. Number of Pregnancies in 1991–95 to Women 15–44 Years of Age at Interview, Percent Distribution by Value on the Scale of How Happy She Was to Be Pregnant, and Mean Scale Value, According to Selected Characteristics: United States, 1995

Characteristic	Number in thousands	Total	Scale value				Mean scale value
			1-3	4-6	6-7	8-10	
			Percent distribution				
All pregnancies[1]	25,666	100.0	18.8	11.6	8.0	61.6	7.3
Race and Hispanic origin and wantedness							
Hispanic	3,924	100.0	18.3	11.4	7.1	63.2	7.4
Intended	2,333	100.0	2.6	5.2	4.4	87.9	9.2
Mistimed	856	100.0	28.6	17.9	12.8	40.7	5.9
Unwanted	732	100.0	56.5	23.5	9.0	11.1	3.6
Non-Hispanic white	16,626	100.0	15.2	10.3	7.5	67.0	7.7
Intended	10,982	100.0	1.6	3.0	4.6	90.8	9.4
Mistimed	3,898	100.0	31.6	26.0	16.5	25.9	5.2
Unwanted	1,683	100.0	66.1	21.6	5.1	7.2	3.0
Non-Hispanic black	3,944	100.0	32.8	19.0	10.9	37.4	5.6
Intended	1,602	100.0	3.8	11.0	12.3	72.9	8.5
Mistimed	1,278	100.0	35.2	30.3	14.1	20.4	4.8
Unwanted	1,032	100.0	75.7	17.1	3.9	3.3	2.3

Notes:
[1]Includes pregnancies with wantedness status reported as "don't know" and pregnancies to women of other race and origin groups not shown separately.
[2]Based on "traditional" version (comparable to Cycle 4 and previous cycles) of wantedness status.

Source: National Survey of Family Growth, 1995.

F2.10. Pregnancies by Outcome, Age of Woman, and Race: 1991

[Live births: source of data is statistics of registered births published annually by National Center for Health Statistics (NCHS). Induced abortions: derived from published reports by the Alan Guttmacher Institute. Fetal losses: based on the National Survey of Family Growth conducted by NCHS].

ITEM	Total	Under 15 years	15-19 years	20-24 years	25-29 years	30-34 years	35-39 years	40 years and over
PREGNANCIES								
Non-Hispanic:								
White, pregnancies	3,964	8	489	1,007	1,145	884	368	63
Live births	2,635	3	250	637	834	640	235	36
Induced abortions	774	4	164	264	163	106	58	16
Fetal losses	556	1	75	107	148	138	76	11
Black, pregnancies	1,344	14	272	439	320	202	81	15
Live births	673	6	149	216	160	98	37	6
Induced abortions	507	7	101	178	119	67	29	7
Fetal losses	164	1	22	45	41	37	15	3
Hispanic:								
Pregnancies	965	5	177	306	250	149	64	14
Live births	623	2	105	199	170	100	39	8
Induced abortions	208	1	40	73	50	28	13	4
Fetal losses	134	1	32	33	30	22	12	2
RATE PER 1,000 WOMEN								
Non-Hispanic:								
White, pregnancies	91.8	1.3	84.7	151.4	154.7	107.6	47.3	8.6
Live births	61.0	0.5	43.4	95.7	112.7	77.9	30.2	4.8
Induced abortions	17.9	0.7	28.4	39.6	22.0	12.9	7.4	2.2
Fetal losses	12.9	0.2	13.0	16.0	20.0	16.8	9.7	1.6
Black, pregnancies	174.8	11.0	216.7	337.2	232.3	142.7	63.9	14.4
Live births	87.6	4.9	118.9	166.1	116.3	69.3	28.9	5.7
Induced abortions	65.9	5.1	80.5	136.4	86.3	47.1	23.0	6.2
Fetal losses	21.3	0.9	17.2	34.7	29.7	26.3	12.1	2.4
Hispanic:								
Pregnancies	167.4	4.8	180.2	285.6	224.3	143.9	74.8	19.8
Live births	108.1	2.4	106.7	186.3	152.8	96.1	44.9	11.1
Induced abortions	36.2	1.4	40.4	68.1	44.4	27.1	15.5	5.2
Fetal losses	23.2	1.0	33.1	31.2	27.1	20.7	14.4	3.6
PERCENT DISTRIBUTION								
Non-Hispanic:								
White, pregnancies	100.0	100.0	100.0	100.0	100.0	100.0	100.0	100.0
Live births	66.5	35.4	51.2	63.2	72.9	72.4	63.8	56.3
Induced abortions	19.5	50.3	33.5	26.2	14.2	12.0	15.6	25.5
Fetal losses	14.0	14.3	15.3	10.6	12.9	15.6	20.5	18.1
Black, pregnancies	100.0	100.0	100.0	100.0	100.0	100.0	100.0	100.0
Live births	50.1	45.0	54.9	49.2	50.1	48.6	45.2	40.0
Induced abortions	37.7	46.7	37.2	40.5	37.1	33.0	36.0	43.3
Fetal losses	12.2	8.2	8.0	10.3	12.8	18.4	18.9	16.7
Hispanic:								
Pregnancies	100.0	100.0	100.0	100.0	100.0	100.0	100.0	100.0
Live births	64.6	50.5	59.2	65.2	68.1	66.8	60.0	56.0
Induced abortions	21.6	29.1	22.4	23.8	19.8	18.8	20.7	26.0
Fetal losses	13.8	20.4	18.4	10.9	12.1	14.4	19.3	18.0

Source: U.S. National Center for Health Statistics, Monthly Vital Statistics Report 43, no. 12.

F2.11. Childless Women, and Children Ever Born, by Race, Age, and Marital Status: 1994 and 1995

[As of June. Covers civilian noninstitutional population. Since the number of women who had a birth during the 12-month period was tabulated and not the actual numbers of births, some small underestimation of fertility for this period may exist due to the omission of: (1) Multiple births, (2) Two or more live births spaced within the 12-month period (the woman is counted only once), (3) Women who had births in the period and who did not survive to the survey date, (4) Women who were in institutions and therefore not in the survey.]

CHARACTERISTIC	Total number of women (1,000)	WOMEN BY NUMBER OF CHILDREN EVER BORN (percent)				CHILDREN EVER BORN	
		Total	None	One	Two or more	Total number (1,000)	Per 1,000 women
1994							
ALL RACES \1							
Women ever married	37,355	100	19.1	22.5	58.5	65,954	1,766
15 to 19 years old	393	100	49.2	43.5	7.2	230	584
20 to 24 years old	3,189	100	37.4	36.4	26.2	3,120	978
25 to 29 years old	6,283	100	28.9	29.0	42.2	8,420	1,340
30 to 34 years old	8,898	100	17.5	22.8	59.7	15,912	1,788
35 to 39 years old	9,584	100	13.3	17.0	69.7	19,408	2,025
40 to 44 years old	9,009	100	12.1	17.6	70.3	18,863	2,094
Women never married	22,733	100	79.8	10.3	9.9	8,690	382
15 to 19 years old	8,405	100	93.5	5.2	1.3	683	81
20 to 24 years old	6,121	100	79.8	12.9	7.4	1,930	315
25 to 29 years old	3,502	100	70.0	13.0	17.1	2,121	606
30 to 34 years old	2,233	100	61.4	14.1	24.4	1,924	862
35 to 39 years old	1,509	100	59.9	15.5	24.5	1,302	863
40 to 44 years old	963	100	68.4	12.6	18.9	730	758
WHITE							
Women ever married	31,863	100	19.6	22.4	58.0	55,152	1,731
15 to 19 years old	346	100	46.4	46.9	6.7	210	607
20 to 24 years old	2,762	100	37.7	36.5	25.9	2,667	966
25 to 29 years old	5,367	100	29.5	28.5	42.1	7,072	1,318
30 to 34 years old	7,643	100	18.0	22.7	59.3	13,350	1,747
35 to 39 years old	8,155	100	13.9	17.0	69.1	16,229	1,990
40 to 44 years old	7,591	100	12.5	17.1	70.4	15,624	2,058
Women never married	16,668	100	87.1	7.9	5.0	3,523	211
15 to 19 years old	6,560	100	95.4	3.8	0.8	377	57
20 to 24 years old	4,589	100	85.4	10.6	4.0	935	204
25 to 29 years old	2,481	100	79.6	10.6	9.7	886	357
30 to 34 years old	1,453	100	76.6	10.3	13.1	649	447
35 to 39 years old	927	100	76.6	11.2	12.2	401	433
40 to 44 years old	659	100	81.9	8.3	9.8	275	418
BLACK							
Women ever married	3,669	100	13.6	24.8	61.7	7,496	2,043
15 to 19 years old	22	100	(B)	(B)	(B)	13	(B)
20 to 24 years old	261	100	26.8	41.1	32.1	319	1,222
25 to 29 years old	618	100	22.2	31.5	46.3	956	1,548
30 to 34 years old	829	100	13.4	25.1	61.4	1,757	2,120
35 to 39 years old	948	100	7.7	18.3	73.9	2,141	2,259
40 to 44 years old	991	100	9.4	22.3	68.3	2,310	2,330
Women never married	4,855	100	53.8	19.4	26.8	4,743	977
15 to 19 years old	1,395	100	85.1	11.7	3.2	259	186
20 to 24 years old	1,154	100	55.2	23.3	21.5	921	798
25 to 29 years old	818	100	40.2	21.1	38.8	1,109	1,354
30 to 34 years old	695	100	30.0	21.7	48.4	1,189	1,712
35 to 39 years old	530	100	31.0	23.7	45.4	821	1,551
40 to 44 years old	263	100	32.5	24.0	43.5	443	1,685

F2.11. Childless Women, and Children Ever Born, by Race, Age, and Marital Status: 1994 and 1995 *(continued)*

CHARACTERISTIC	Total number of women (1,000)	WOMEN BY NUMBER OF CHILDREN EVER BORN (percent)				CHILDREN EVER BORN	
		Total	None	One	Two or more	Total number (1,000)	Per 1,000 women
1995							
ALL RACES \1							
Women ever married	37,378	100	19.0	22.3	58.7	65,948	1,764
15 to 19 years old	319	100	43.9	45.5	10.6	218	684
20 to 24 years old	3,036	100	36.7	34.4	28.9	3,096	1,020
25 to 29 years old	6,105	100	28.8	29.2	42.0	8,112	1,329
30 to 34 years old	9,006	100	18.7	23.0	58.4	15,634	1,736
35 to 39 years old	9,660	100	13.2	16.9	69.8	19,578	2,027
40 to 44 years old	9,252	100	12.3	17.9	69.8	19,310	2,087
Women never married	22,846	100	79.1	10.8	10.2	8,886	389
15 to 19 years old	8,701	100	92.4	6.3	1.3	826	95
20 to 24 years old	6,018	100	78.3	12.6	9.1	2,106	350
25 to 29 years old	3,564	100	69.6	13.4	17.0	2,181	612
30 to 34 years old	2,050	100	61.7	14.9	23.4	1,684	821
35 to 39 years old	1,523	100	60.5	15.4	24.1	1,315	863
40 to 44 years old	992	100	65.9	14.6	19.5	775	782
WHITE							
Women ever married	31,819	100	19.6	22.3	58.1	55,113	1,732
15 to 19 years old	269	100	40.1	48.6	11.3	197	732
20 to 24 years old	2,651	100	37.5	34.3	28.3	2,636	994
25 to 29 years old	5,243	100	29.7	29.6	40.7	6,758	1,289
30 to 34 years old	7,652	100	19.3	22.8	58.1	12,958	1,693
35 to 39 years old	8,233	100	13.6	16.6	69.9	16,519	2,006
40 to 44 years old	7,771	100	12.5	17.9	69.6	16,045	2,065
Women never married	16,784	100	87.0	8.0	5.0	3,597	214
15 to 19 years old	6,806	100	94.6	4.5	0.9	456	67
20 to 24 years old	4,516	100	84.1	10.2	6.7	1,075	238
25 to 29 years old	2,517	100	80.5	10.6	8.8	872	346
30 to 34 years old	1,306	100	77.0	9.9	13.0	605	463
35 to 39 years old	946	100	81.3	10.9	7.8	312	329
40 to 44 years old	693	100	80.4	11.8	7.9	277	400
BLACK							
Women ever married	3,746	100	14.1	22.8	63.1	7,417	1,980
15 to 19 years old	23	(B)	(B)	(B)	(B)	13	(B)
20 to 24 years old	235	100	29.4	36.7	33.9	297	1,263
25 to 29 years old	568	100	16.4	29.1	54.9	951	1,676
30 to 34 years old	888	100	13.9	24.3	61.7	1,841	2,073
35 to 39 years old	986	100	10.7	18.0	71.4	2,079	2,109
40 to 44 years old	1,046	100	11.7	19.4	69.0	2,236	2,137
Women never married	4,872	100	52.1	20.6	27.4	4,773	980
15 to 19 years old	1,439	100	82.9	14.6	2.5	302	210
20 to 24 years old	1,160	100	54.7	22.3	23.0	933	804
25 to 29 years old	851	100	37.4	22.2	40.4	1,166	1,370
30 to 34 years old	641	100	30.9	26.0	43.1	974	1,519
35 to 39 years old	521	100	22.9	23.1	54.0	953	1,831
40 to 44 years old	260	100	28.8	22.5	48.8	444	1,711

Notes:
B Base figure too small to meet statistical standards for reliability.
\1 Includes other races not shown separately.

Source: U.S. Bureau of the Census, Current Population Reports, P20-482.

F2.12. Births, by Race and Type of Hispanic Origin, According to Selected Characteristics: 1985 to 1996

[Represents registered births. Excludes births to nonresidents of the U.S. Data are based on Hispanic-origin of mother and beginning 1990, race of mother. Prior to 1990, data are for race of child and are not comparable. Hispanic-origin data are available from only 23 States and the District of Columbia in 1985 and 1987, 30 States and DC in 1988, 47 States and DC in 1989, and 48 States and DC in 1990. However, in 1985 and 1987 approximately 90 percent of all births to Hispanic mothers occur to residents of the 23 States, in 1988 95% occur to residents of the 30 States; in 1989 99% occur to residents of the 47 States; in 1990 this percent is approximately 99.6.]

RACE AND HISPANIC ORIGIN	1985	1987	1988	1989	1990	1991	1992	1993	1994	1995	1996
Number of births, 1,000	3,761	3,809	3,910	4,041	4,158	4,111	4,065	4,000	3,953	3,900	3,915
White	2,991	2,992	3,046	3,132	3,290	3,241	3,202	3,150	3,121	3,099	3,113
Black	608	642	672	709	684	683	674	659	636	603	596
American Indian, Eskimo, Aleut	43	44	46	49	39	39	39	39	38	37	38
Asian and Pacific Islander \2	116	129	142	147	142	145	150	153	158	160	167
Filipino	21	24	25	26	26	26	29	30	30	31	(NA)
Chinese	18	19	23	23	23	22	25	26	27	27	(NA)
Japanese	10	10	10	11	9	9	9	9	9	9	(NA)
Hawaiian	7	7	8	8	6	6	6	6	6	6	(NA)
Other	(NA)	(NA)	(NA)	(NA)	(NA)	(NA)	(NA)	(NA)	85	88	(NA)
Hispanic origin \3	373	406	450	532	595	623	643	654	665	680	698
Mexican	243	251	271	327	386	411	432	444	455	470	(NA)
Puerto Rican	35	38	46	56	59	60	60	58	57	55	(NA)
Cuban	10	10	10	11	11	11	11	12	12	12	(NA)
Central and South American	41	50	58	72	83	87	89	92	93	95	(NA)
Other and unknown Hispanic	(NA)	(NA)	(NA)	(NA)	(NA)	(NA)	(NA)	(NA)	48	48	(NA)
Births to teenage mothers, percent of total	12.7	12.4	12.5	12.8	12.8	12.9	12.7	12.8	13.1	13.1	12.9
White	10.8	10.4	10.5	10.7	10.9	11.0	10.9	11.0	11.3	11.5	11.3
Black	23.0	22.6	22.7	23.1	23.1	23.1	22.7	22.7	23.2	23.1	22.9
American Indian, Eskimo, Aleut	19.1	18.9	18.4	18.8	19.5	20.3	20.0	20.3	21.0	21.4	(NA)
Asian and Pacific Islander \2	5.5	5.5	5.7	6.1	5.7	5.8	5.6	5.7	5.7	5.6	(NA)
Filipino	5.8	6.0	6.2	6.4	6.1	6.1	5.6	5.8	6.0	6.2	(NA)
Chinese	1.1	1.1	1.1	1.2	1.2	1.1	1.0	1.0	1.0	0.9	(NA)
Japanese	2.9	2.7	2.8	2.9	2.9	2.7	2.6	2.7	2.8	2.5	(NA)
Hawaiian	15.9	15.4	15.4	16.4	18.4	18.1	18.4	18.5	19.6	19.1	(NA)
Other	(NA)	(NA)	(NA)	(NA)	(NA)	(NA)	(NA)	(NA)	6.4	6.3	(NA)
Hispanic origin \3	16.5	16.3	16.4	16.7	16.8	17.2	17.1	17.4	17.8	17.9	17.4
Mexican	17.5	17.3	17.3	17.4	17.7	18.1	18.0	18.2	18.6	18.8	(NA)
Puerto Rican	20.9	20.5	21.4	21.9	21.7	21.7	21.4	22.3	23.2	23.5	(NA)
Cuban	7.1	6.2	6.1	7.0	7.7	7.1	7.1	6.8	7.3	7.7	(NA)
Central and South American	8.2	8.0	8.1	8.6	9.0	9.4	9.6	10.0	10.4	10.6	(NA)
Other and unknown Hispanic	(NA)	(NA)	(NA)	(NA)	(NA)	(NA)	(NA)	(NA)	20.8	20.1	(NA)
Births to unmarried mothers, percent of total	22.0	24.5	25.7	27.1	26.6	28.0	30.1	31.0	32.6	32.2	32.4
White	14.5	16.7	17.7	19.0	16.9	18.0	22.6	23.6	25.4	25.3	25.7
Black	60.1	62.2	63.5	64.5	66.7	68.2	68.1	68.7	70.4	69.9	69.8
American Indian, Eskimo, Aleut	40.7	44.9	45.6	(NA)	53.6	55.3	55.3	55.8	57.0	57.2	(NA)
Asian and Pacific Islander \2	10.1	11.5	12.0	(NA)	(NA)	(NA)	14.7	15.7	16.2	16.3	(NA)
Filipino	12.1	13.4	14.5	(NA)	15.9	16.8	16.8	17.7	18.5	19.5	(NA)
Chinese	3.7	4.9	4.3	(NA)	5.0	5.5	6.1	6.7	7.2	7.9	(NA)
Japanese	7.9	8.0	8.6	(NA)	9.6	9.8	9.8	10.0	11.2	10.8	(NA)
Hawaiian	(NA)	35.0	35.9	(NA)	45.0	45.0	45.7	47.8	48.6	49.0	(NA)
Other	(NA)	(NA)	(NA)	(NA)	(NA)	(NA)	(NA)	(NA)	16.4	16.2	(NA)
Hispanic origin \3	29.5	32.6	34.0	35.5	36.7	38.5	39.1	40.0	43.1	40.8	40.9
Mexican	25.7	28.9	30.6	31.7	33.3	35.3	36.3	37.0	40.8	38.1	(NA)
Puerto Rican	51.1	53.0	53.3	55.2	55.9	57.5	57.5	59.4	60.2	60.0	(NA)
Cuban	16.1	16.1	16.3	17.5	18.2	19.5	20.2	21.0	22.9	23.8	(NA)
Central and South American	34.9	37.1	36.4	38.9	41.2	43.1	43.9	45.2	45.9	44.1	(NA)
Other and unknown Hispanic	(NA)	(NA)	(NA)	(NA)	(NA)	(NA)	(NA)	(NA)	43.5	44.0	(NA)
Percent of mothers beginning prenatal care during first trimester	76.2	74.4	75.9	75.5	74.2	76.2	77.7	78.9	80.2	81.3	81.8
White	79.4	77.9	79.4	79.0	77.7	79.5	80.8	81.8	82.8	83.6	83.9
Black	61.8	59.3	61.1	60.4	60.7	61.9	63.9	66.0	68.3	70.4	71.3
American Indian, Eskimo, Aleut	60.3	(NA)	(NA)	60.5	57.9	59.9	62.1	63.4	65.2	66.7	(NA)
Asian and Pacific Islander \2	75.0	(NA)	(NA)	75.6	(NA)	(NA)	76.6	77.6	79.7	79.9	(NA)

F2.12. Births, by Race and Type of Hispanic Origin, According to Selected Characteristics: 1985 to 1996 (continued)

RACE AND HISPANIC ORIGIN	1985	1987	1988	1989	1990	1991	1992	1993	1994	1995	1996
Filipino	77.2	(NA)	(NA)	78.0	77.1	77.1	78.7	79.3	81.3	80.9	(NA)
Chinese	82.4	(NA)	(NA)	81.9	81.3	82.3	83.8	84.6	86.2	85.7	(NA)
Japanese	85.8	(NA)	(NA)	86.7	87.0	87.7	88.2	87.2	89.2	89.7	(NA)
Hawaiian	(NA)	(NA)	(NA)	69.7	65.8	68.1	69.9	70.6	77.0	75.9	(NA)
Other	(NA)	(NA)	(NA)	(NA)	(NA)	(NA)	(NA)	(NA)	76.2	77.0	(NA)
Hispanic origin \3	61.2	61.0	61.3	59.5	60.2	61.0	64.2	66.6	68.9	70.8	71.9
Mexican	59.9	60.0	58.3	56.7	57.8	58.7	62.1	64.8	67.3	69.1	(NA)
Puerto Rican	58.3	57.4	63.2	62.7	63.5	65.0	67.8	70.0	71.7	74.0	(NA)
Cuban	82.5	83.1	83.4	83.2	84.8	85.4	86.8	88.9	90.1	89.2	(NA)
Central and South American	60.6	59.1	62.8	60.8	61.5	63.4	66.8	68.7	71.2	73.2	(NA)
Other and unknown Hispanic	(NA)	(NA)	(NA)	(NA)	(NA)	(NA)	(NA)	(NA)	72.1	74.3	(NA)
Percent of mothers beginning prenatal care during third trimester	(NA)	6.0	6.1	6.4	6.0	5.8	5.2	4.8	4.4	4.2	4.1
White	(NA)	4.9	5.0	5.2	4.9	4.7	4.2	3.9	3.6	3.5	3.4
Black	(NA)	10.7	10.9	11.7	10.9	10.7	9.9	9.0	8.2	7.6	7.4
American Indian, Eskimo, Aleut	(NA)	(NA)	(NA)	11.9	12.9	12.2	11.0	10.3	9.8	9.5	(NA)
Asian and Pacific Islander \2	(NA)	(NA)	(NA)	5.8	(NA)	(NA)	4.9	4.6	4.1	4.3	(NA)
Filipino	(NA)	(NA)	(NA)	4.6	4.5	5.0	4.3	4.0	3.6	4.1	(NA)
Chinese	(NA)	(NA)	(NA)	3.5	3.4	3.4	2.9	2.9	2.7	3.0	(NA)
Japanese	(NA)	(NA)	(NA)	2.6	2.9	2.5	2.4	2.8	1.9	2.3	(NA)
Hawaiian	(NA)	(NA)	(NA)	7.6	8.7	7.5	7.0	6.7	4.7	5.1	(NA)
Other	(NA)	(NA)	(NA)	(NA)	(NA)	(NA)	(NA)	(NA)	4.8	5.0	(NA)
Hispanic origin \3	(NA)	12.7	12.1	13.0	12.0	11.0	9.5	8.8	7.6	7.4	6.8
Mexican	(NA)	13.0	13.9	14.6	13.2	12.2	10.5	9.7	8.3	8.1	(NA)
Puerto Rican	(NA)	17.1	10.2	11.3	10.6	9.1	8.0	7.1	6.5	5.5	(NA)
Cuban	(NA)	3.9	3.6	4.0	2.8	2.4	2.1	1.8	1.6	2.1	(NA)
Central and South American	(NA)	13.5	9.9	11.9	10.9	9.5	7.9	7.3	6.5	6.1	(NA)
Other and unknown Hispanic	(NA)	(NA)	(NA)	(NA)	(NA)	(NA)	(NA)	(NA)	6.2	6.0	(NA)
Percent of births with low birth weight	6.8	6.9	6.9	7.0	7.0	7.1	7.1	7.2	7.3	7.3	7.4
White	5.6	5.7	5.6	5.7	5.7	5.8	5.8	6.0	6.1	6.2	6.3
Black	12.4	12.7	13.0	13.2	13.3	13.6	13.3	13.3	13.2	13.1	13.0
American Indian, Eskimo, Aleut	5.9	6.2	6.1	6.4	6.1	6.2	6.2	6.4	6.4	6.6	(NA)
Asian and Pacific Islander \2	6.1	6.4	6.3	6.9	(NA)	(NA)	6.6	6.6	6.8	6.9	(NA)
Filipino	6.9	7.3	7.1	7.3	7.3	7.3	7.4	7.0	7.8	7.8	(NA)
Chinese	5.0	5.0	4.7	5.0	4.7	5.1	5.0	4.9	4.8	5.3	(NA)
Japanese	5.9	6.3	6.2	6.4	6.2	5.9	7.0	6.5	6.9	7.3	(NA)
Hawaiian	6.4	6.6	6.8	7.2	7.2	6.7	6.9	6.8	7.2	6.8	(NA)
Other	(NA)	(NA)	(NA)	(NA)	(NA)	(NA)	(NA)	(NA)	7.1	7.1	(NA)
Hispanic origin \3	6.2	6.2	6.2	6.2	6.1	6.1	6.1	6.2	6.2	6.3	6.3
Mexican	5.8	5.7	5.6	5.6	5.5	5.6	5.6	5.8	5.8	5.8	(NA)
Puerto Rican	8.7	9.3	9.4	9.5	9.0	9.4	9.2	9.2	9.1	9.4	(NA)
Cuban	6.0	5.9	5.9	5.8	5.7	5.6	6.1	6.2	6.3	6.5	(NA)
Central and South American	5.7	5.7	5.6	5.8	5.8	5.9	5.8	5.9	6.0	6.2	(NA)
Other and unknown Hispanic	(NA)	(NA)	(NA)	(NA)	(NA)	(NA)	(NA)	(NA)	7.5	7.5	(NA)

Notes:
NA Not available.
\1 Births less than 2,500 grams (5 lb.-8 oz.).
\2 Includes other races not shown separately.
\3 Hispanic persons may be of any race. Includes other types not shown separately.

Source: U.S. National Center for Health Statistics, Vital Statistics of the United States, annual; Monthly Vital Statistics Report; and unpublished data.

F2.13. Births to Teens and Unmarried Mothers, and Prenatal Care: 1985 to 1996

[Represents registered births. Excludes births to nonresidents of the United States. Data are based on race of mother]

CHARACTERISTIC	1985	1987	1988	1989	1990	1991	1992	1993	1994	1995	1996
Percent of births to teenage mothers	12.7	12.4	12.5	12.8	12.8	12.9	12.7	12.8	13.1	13.1	12.9
White	10.8	10.4	10.5	10.7	10.9	11.0	10.9	11.0	11.3	11.5	11.3
Black	23.0	22.6	22.7	23.1	23.1	23.1	22.7	22.7	23.2	23.1	22.9
American Indian, Eskimo, Aleut	19.1	18.9	18.4	18.8	19.5	20.3	20.0	20.3	21.0	21.4	(NA)
Asian and Pacific Islander \1	5.5	5.5	5.7	6.1	5.7	5.8	5.6	5.7	5.7	5.6	(NA)
Filipino	5.8	6.0	6.2	6.4	6.1	6.1	5.6	5.8	6.0	6.2	(NA)
Chinese	1.1	1.1	1.1	1.2	1.2	1.1	1.0	1.0	1.0	0.9	(NA)
Japanese	2.9	2.7	2.8	2.9	2.9	2.7	2.6	2.7	2.8	2.5	(NA)
Hawaiian	15.9	15.4	15.4	16.4	18.4	18.1	18.4	18.5	19.6	19.1	(NA)
Other	(NA)	(NA)	(NA)	(NA)	(NA)	(NA)	(NA)	6.5	6.4	6.3	(NA)
Hispanic origin \2	16.5	16.3	16.4	16.7	16.8	17.2	17.1	17.4	17.8	17.9	17.4
Mexican	17.5	17.3	17.3	17.4	17.7	18.1	18.0	18.2	18.6	18.8	(NA)
Puerto Rican	20.9	20.5	21.4	21.9	21.7	21.7	21.4	22.3	23.2	23.5	(NA)
Cuban	7.1	6.2	6.1	7.0	7.7	7.1	7.1	6.8	7.3	7.7	(NA)
Central and South American	8.2	8.0	8.1	8.6	9.0	9.4	9.6	9.9	10.4	10.6	(NA)
Other and unknown Hispanic	(NA)	(NA)	(NA)	(NA)	(NA)	(NA)	(NA)	21.0	20.8	20.1	(NA)
Percent births to unmarried mothers	22.0	24.5	25.7	27.1	26.6	28.0	30.1	31.0	32.6	32.2	32.4
White	14.5	16.7	17.7	19.0	16.9	18.0	22.6	23.6	25.4	25.3	25.7
Black	60.1	62.2	63.5	64.5	66.7	68.2	68.1	68.7	70.4	69.9	69.8
American Indian, Eskimo, Aleut	40.7	44.9	45.6	(NA)	53.6	55.3	55.3	55.8	57.0	57.2	(NA)
Asian and Pacific Islander \1	10.1	11.5	12.0	(NA)	(NA)	(NA)	14.7	15.7	16.2	16.3	(NA)
Filipino	12.1	13.4	14.5	(NA)	15.9	16.8	16.8	17.7	18.5	19.5	(NA)
Chinese	3.7	4.9	4.3	(NA)	5.0	5.5	6.1	6.7	7.2	7.9	(NA)
Japanese	7.9	8.0	8.6	(NA)	9.6	9.8	9.8	10.0	11.2	10.8	(NA)
Hawaiian	(NA)	35.0	35.9	(NA)	45.0	45.0	45.7	47.8	48.6	49.0	(NA)
Other	(NA)	(NA)	(NA)	(NA)	(NA)	(NA)	(NA)	16.1	16.4	16.2	(NA)
Hispanic origin \2	29.5	32.6	34.0	35.5	36.7	38.5	39.1	40.0	43.1	40.8	40.9
Mexican	25.7	28.9	30.6	31.7	33.3	35.3	36.3	37.0	40.8	38.1	(NA)
Puerto Rican	51.1	53.0	53.3	55.2	55.9	57.5	57.5	59.4	60.2	60.0	(NA)
Cuban	16.1	16.1	16.3	17.5	18.2	19.5	20.2	21.0	22.9	23.8	(NA)
Central and South American	34.9	37.1	36.4	38.9	41.2	43.1	43.9	45.2	45.9	44.1	(NA)
Other and unknown Hispanic	(NA)	(NA)	(NA)	(NA)	(NA)	(NA)	(NA)	38.7	43.5	44.0	(NA)
Percent of mothers beginning prenatal care 1st trimester	76.2	74.4	75.9	75.5	74.2	76.2	77.7	78.9	80.2	81.3	81.8
White	79.4	77.9	79.4	79.0	77.7	79.5	80.8	81.8	82.8	83.6	83.9
Black	61.8	59.3	61.1	60.4	60.7	61.9	63.9	66.0	68.3	70.4	71.3
American Indian, Eskimo, Aleut	60.3	(NA)	(NA)	60.5	57.9	59.9	62.1	63.4	65.2	66.7	(NA)
Asian and Pacific Islander \1	75.0	(NA)	(NA)	75.6	(NA)	(NA)	76.6	77.6	79.7	79.9	(NA)
Filipino	77.2	(NA)	(NA)	78.0	77.1	77.1	78.7	79.3	81.3	80.9	(NA)
Chinese	82.4	(NA)	(NA)	81.9	81.3	82.3	83.8	84.6	86.2	85.7	(NA)
Japanese	85.8	(NA)	(NA)	86.7	87.0	87.7	88.2	87.2	89.2	89.7	(NA)
Hawaiian	(NA)	(NA)	(NA)	69.7	65.8	68.1	69.9	70.6	77.0	75.9	(NA)
Other	(NA)	(NA)	(NA)	(NA)	(NA)	(NA)	(NA)	74.4	76.2	77.0	(NA)
Hispanic origin \2	61.2	61.0	61.3	59.5	60.2	61.0	64.2	66.6	68.9	70.8	71.9
Mexican	59.9	60.0	58.3	56.7	57.8	58.7	62.1	64.8	67.3	69.1	(NA)
Puerto Rican	58.3	57.4	63.2	62.7	63.5	65.0	67.8	70.0	71.7	74.0	(NA)
Cuban	82.5	83.1	83.4	83.2	84.8	85.4	86.8	88.9	90.1	89.2	(NA)
Central and South American	60.6	59.1	62.8	60.8	61.5	63.4	66.8	68.7	71.2	73.2	(NA)
Other and unknown Hispanic	(NA)	(NA)	(NA)	(NA)	(NA)	(NA)	(NA)	70.0	72.1	74.3	(NA)
Percent of mothers beginning prenatal care 3d trimester or no care	5.7	6.0	6.1	6.4	6.0	5.8	5.2	4.8	4.4	4.2	4.1
White	4.7	4.9	5.0	5.2	4.9	4.7	4.2	3.9	3.6	3.5	3.4
Black	10.0	10.7	10.9	11.7	10.9	10.7	9.9	9.0	8.2	7.6	7.4
American Indian, Eskimo, Aleut	11.5	(NA)	(NA)	11.9	12.9	12.2	11.0	10.3	9.8	9.5	(NA)
Asian and Pacific Islander \1	6.1	(NA)	(NA)	5.8	(NA)	(NA)	4.9	4.6	4.1	4.3	(NA)
Filipino	4.6	(NA)	(NA)	4.6	4.5	5.0	4.3	4.0	3.6	4.1	(NA)
Chinese	4.2	(NA)	(NA)	3.5	3.4	3.4	2.9	2.9	2.7	3.0	(NA)
Japanese	2.6	(NA)	(NA)	2.6	2.9	2.5	2.4	2.8	1.9	2.3	(NA)
Hawaiian	(NA)	(NA)	(NA)	7.6	8.7	7.5	7.0	6.7	4.7	5.1	(NA)
Other	(NA)	(NA)	(NA)	(NA)	(NA)	(NA)	(NA)	5.4	4.8	5.0	(NA)
Hispanic origin \2	12.5	12.7	12.1	13.0	12.0	11.0	9.5	8.8	7.6	7.4	6.8
Mexican	12.9	13.0	13.9	14.6	13.2	12.2	10.5	9.7	8.3	8.1	(NA)
Puerto Rican	15.5	17.1	10.2	11.3	10.6	9.1	8.0	7.1	6.5	5.5	(NA)
Cuban	3.7	3.9	3.6	4.0	2.8	2.4	2.1	1.8	1.6	2.1	(NA)

F2.13. Births to Teens and Unmarried Mothers, and Prenatal Care: 1985 to 1996 *(continued)*

CHARACTERISTIC	1985	1987	1988	1989	1990	1991	1992	1993	1994	1995	1996
Central and South American	12.5	13.5	9.9	11.9	10.9	9.5	7.9	7.3	6.5	6.1	(NA)
Other and unknown Hispanic	(NA)	(NA)	(NA)	(NA)	(NA)	(NA)	(NA)	7.0	6.2	6.0	(NA)
Percent of births with low birth weight \3	6.8	6.9	6.9	7.0	7.0	7.1	7.1	7.2	7.3	7.3	7.4
White	5.6	5.7	5.6	5.7	5.7	5.8	5.8	6.0	6.1	6.2	6.3
Black	12.4	12.7	13.0	13.2	13.3	13.6	13.3	13.3	13.2	13.1	13.0
American Indian, Eskimo, Aleut	5.9	6.2	6.1	6.4	6.1	6.2	6.2	6.4	6.4	6.6	(NA)
Asian and Pacific Islander \1	6.1	6.4	6.3	6.9	(NA)	(NA)	6.6	6.6	6.8	6.9	(NA)
Filipino	6.9	7.3	7.1	7.3	7.3	7.3	7.4	7.0	7.8	7.8	(NA)
Chinese	5.0	5.0	4.7	5.0	4.7	5.1	5.0	4.9	4.8	5.3	(NA)
Japanese	5.9	6.3	6.2	6.4	6.2	5.9	7.0	6.5	6.9	7.3	(NA)
Hawaiian	6.4	6.6	6.8	7.2	7.2	6.7	6.9	6.8	7.2	6.8	(NA)
Other	(NA)	(NA)	(NA)	(NA)	(NA)	(NA)	(NA)	6.9	7.1	7.1	(NA)
Hispanic origin \2	6.2	6.2	6.2	6.2	6.1	6.1	6.1	6.2	6.2	6.3	6.3
Mexican	5.8	5.7	5.6	5.6	5.5	5.6	5.6	5.8	5.8	5.8	(NA)
Puerto Rican	8.7	9.3	9.4	9.5	9.0	9.4	9.2	9.2	9.1	9.4	(NA)
Cuban	6.0	5.9	5.9	5.8	5.7	5.6	6.1	6.2	6.3	6.5	(NA)
Central and South American	5.7	5.7	5.6	5.8	5.8	5.9	5.8	5.9	6.0	6.2	(NA)
Other and unknown Hispanic	(NA)	(NA)	(NA)	(NA)	(NA)	(NA)	(NA)	7.5	7.5	7.5	(NA)

Notes:
NA Not available.
\1 Includes other races not shown separately.
\2 Hispanic persons may be of any race. Includes other types, not shown separately.
\3 Births less than 2,500 grams (5 lb.-8 oz.).

Source: U.S. National Center for Health Statistics, Vital Statistics of the United States, annual; Monthly Vital Statistics Report; and unpublished data.

F2.14. Teenagers—Births and Birth Rates, by Race and Age: 1970 to 1996

[Birth rates per 1,000 women in specified group.]

RACE AND AGE	1970	1971	1972	1973	1974	1975
NUMBER OF BIRTHS						
All races, total \1	**644,708**	**627,942**	**616,280**	**604,096**	**595,449**	**582,238**
15-17 years	223,590	226,298	236,641	238,403	234,177	227,270
18-19 years	421,118	401,644	379,639	365,693	361,272	354,968
White	**463,608**	**446,726**	**433,986**	**424,833**	**420,152**	**410,129**
15-17 years	143,646	143,806	150,897	153,416	152,257	148,344
18-19 years	319,962	302,920	283,089	271,417	267,895	261,785
Black	**171,826**	**171,684**	**172,349**	**168,773**	**164,430**	**161,044**
15-17 years	76,882	79,238	82,217	81,158	77,947	74,946
18-19 years	94,944	92,446	90,132	87,615	86,483	86,098
BIRTH RATE						
All races, total \1	**68.3**	**64.5**	**61.7**	**59.3**	**57.5**	**55.6**
15-17 years	38.8	38.2	39.0	38.5	37.3	36.1
18-19 years	114.7	105.3	96.9	91.2	88.7	85.0
White	**57.4**	**53.6**	**51.0**	**49.0**	**47.9**	**46.4**
15-17 years	29.2	28.5	29.3	29.2	28.7	28.0
18-19 years	101.5	92.3	84.3	79.3	77.3	74.0
Black	**140.7**	**134.5**	**129.8**	**123.1**	**116.5**	**111.8**
15-17 years	101.4	99.4	99.5	96.0	90.0	85.6
18-19 years	204.9	192.6	179.5	166.6	158.7	152.4
HISPANIC-ORIGIN						
15-19 years						
Non-Hispanic white	(NA)	(NA)	(NA)	(NA)	(NA)	(NA)
Black	(NA)	(NA)	(NA)	(NA)	(NA)	(NA)
Hispanic \2	(NA)	(NA)	(NA)	(NA)	(NA)	(NA)

F2.14. Teenagers—Births and Birth Rates, by Race and Age: 1970 to 1996 *(continued)*

RACE AND AGE	1970	1971	1972	1973	1974	1975
18-19 years						
Hispanic \2	(NA)	(NA)	(NA)	(NA)	(NA)	(NA)
Non-Hispanic white	(NA)	(NA)	(NA)	(NA)	(NA)	(NA)
Black	(NA)	(NA)	(NA)	(NA)	(NA)	(NA)
RACE AND AGE	**1976**	**1977**	**1978**	**1979**	**1980**	**1981**
NUMBER OF BIRTHS						
All races, total \1	**558,744**	**559,154**	**543,407**	**549,472**	**552,161**	**527,392**
15-17 years	215,493	213,788	202,661	200,137	198,222	187,397
18-19 years	343,251	345,366	340,746	349,335	353,939	339,995
White	**393,275**	**392,183**	**380,060**	**383,807**	**393,564**	**375,432**
15-17 years	139,901	138,223	130,957	127,970	129,341	122,561
18-19 years	253,374	253,960	249,103	255,837	264,223	252,871
Black	**153,936**	**155,190**	**151,001**	**152,805**	**147,378**	**140,344**
15-17 years	71,429	71,182	67,317	67,728	65,069	60,944
18-19 years	82,507	84,008	83,684	85,077	82,309	79,400
BIRTH RATE						
All races, total \1	**52.8**	**52.8**	**51.5**	**52.3**	**53.0**	**52.2**
15-17 years	34.1	33.9	32.2	32.3	32.5	32.0
18-19 years	80.5	80.9	79.8	81.3	82.1	80.0
White	**44.1**	**44.1**	**42.9**	**43.7**	**45.4**	**44.9**
15-17 years	26.3	26.1	24.9	24.7	25.5	25.4
18-19 years	70.2	70.5	69.4	71.0	73.2	71.5
Black	**104.9**	**104.7**	**100.9**	**101.7**	**97.8**	**94.5**
15-17 years	80.3	79.6	75.0	75.7	72.5	69.3
18-19 years	142.5	142.9	139.7	140.4	135.1	131.0
HISPANIC-ORIGIN						
15-19 years						
Non-Hispanic white	(NA)	(NA)	(NA)	(NA)	(NA)	(NA)
Black	(NA)	(NA)	(NA)	(NA)	(NA)	(NA)
Hispanic \2	(NA)	(NA)	(NA)	(NA)	(NA)	(NA)
18-19 years						
Hispanic \2	(NA)	(NA)	(NA)	(NA)	(NA)	(NA)
Non-Hispanic white	(NA)	(NA)	(NA)	(NA)	(NA)	(NA)
Black	(NA)	(NA)	(NA)	(NA)	(NA)	(NA)
RACE AND AGE	**1982**	**1983**	**1984**	**1985**	**1986**	**1987**
NUMBER OF BIRTHS						
All races, total \1	**513,758**	**489,286**	**469,582**	**467,485**	**461,905**	**462,312**
15-17 years	181,162	172,673	166,744	167,789	168,572	172,591
18-19 years	332,596	316,613	302,938	299,696	293,333	289,721
White	**363,742**	**343,199**	**326,301**	**324,590**	**317,970**	**315,464**
15-17 years	117,644	111,163	106,782	107,993	107,177	108,592
18-19 years	246,098	232,036	219,519	216,597	210,793	206,872
Black	**137,456**	**133,953**	**131,497**	**130,857**	**131,594**	**134,050**
15-17 years	59,362	57,332	55,932	55,656	57,003	59,361
18-19 years	78,094	76,621	75,565	75,201	74,591	74,689
BIRTH RATE						
All races, total \1	**52.4**	**51.4**	**50.6**	**51.0**	**50.2**	**50.6**
15-17 years	32.3	31.8	31.0	31.0	30.5	31.7
18-19 years	79.4	77.4	77.4	79.6	79.6	78.5
White	**45.0**	**43.9**	**42.9**	**43.3**	**42.3**	**42.5**
15-17 years	25.5	25.0	24.3	24.4	23.8	24.6

F2.14. Teenagers—Births and Birth Rates, by Race and Age: 1970 to 1996 *(continued)*

RACE AND AGE	1982	1983	1984	1985	1986	1987
18-19 years	70.8	68.8	68.4	70.4	70.1	68.9
Black	**94.3**	**93.9**	**94.1**	**95.4**	**95.8**	**97.6**
15-17 years	69.7	69.6	69.2	69.3	69.3	72.1
18-19 years	128.9	127.1	128.1	132.4	135.1	135.8
HISPANIC-ORIGIN						
15-19 years						
Non-Hispanic white	(NA)	(NA)	(NA)	(NA)	(NA)	(NA)
Black	(NA)	(NA)	(NA)	(NA)	(NA)	(NA)
Hispanic \2	(NA)	(NA)	(NA)	(NA)	(NA)	(NA)
18-19 years						
Hispanic \2	(NA)	(NA)	(NA)	(NA)	(NA)	(NA)
Non-Hispanic white	(NA)	(NA)	(NA)	(NA)	(NA)	(NA)
Black	(NA)	(NA)	(NA)	(NA)	(NA)	(NA)

RACE AND AGE	1988	1989	1990	1991	1992	1993	1994	1995	1996
NUMBER OF BIRTHS									
All races, total \1	478,353	506,503	521,826	519,577	505,415	501,093	505,488	(NA)	(NA)
15-17 years	176,624	181,044	183,327	188,226	187,549	190,535	195,169	(NA)	(NA)
18-19 years	301,729	325,459	338,499	331,351	317,866	310,558	310,319	(NA)	(NA)
White	323,830	340,472	354,482	352,359	342,739	341,817	348,081	(NA)	(NA)
15-17 years	109,739	111,736	114,934	118,809	118,786	121,309	126,388	(NA)	(NA)
18-19 years	214,091	228,736	239,548	233,550	223,953	220,508	221,693	(NA)	(NA)
Black	140,608	150,699	151,613	150,956	146,800	143,153	140,968	(NA)	(NA)
15-17 years	61,856	63,832	62,881	63,571	63,002	63,156	62,563	(NA)	(NA)
18-19 years	78,752	86,867	88,732	87,385	83,798	79,997	78,405	(NA)	(NA)
BIRTH RATE									
All races, total \1	**53.0**	**57.3**	**59.9**	**62.1**	**60.7**	**59.6**	**58.9**	**56.8**	**54.7**
15-17 years	33.6	36.4	37.5	38.7	37.8	37.8	37.6	36.0	34.0
18-19 years	79.9	84.2	88.6	94.4	94.5	92.1	91.5	89.1	86.5
White	**44.4**	**47.9**	**50.8**	**52.8**	**51.8**	**51.1**	**51.1**	**50.1**	**48.4**
15-17 years	26.0	28.1	29.5	30.7	30.1	30.3	30.7	30.0	28.6
18-19 years	69.6	72.9	78.0	83.5	83.8	82.1	82.1	81.2	78.8
Black	**102.7**	**111.5**	**112.8**	**115.5**	**112.4**	**108.6**	**104.5**	**96.1**	**91.7**
15-17 years	75.7	81.9	82.3	84.1	81.3	79.8	76.3	69.7	64.9
18-19 years	142.7	151.9	152.9	158.6	157.9	151.9	148.3	137.1	133.0
HISPANIC-ORIGIN									
15-19 years									
Hispanic \2	(NA)	(NA)	100.3	106.7	107.1	106.8	107.7	106.7	101.6
Non-Hispanic white	(NA)	(NA)	42.5	43.4	41.7	40.7	40.4	39.3	(NA)
Black	(NA)	(NA)	112.8	115.5	112.4	108.6	104.5	99.3	(NA)
Hispanic \2	(NA)	(NA)	65.9	70.6	71.4	71.7	74.0	72.9	68.9
Non-Hispanic white	(NA)	(NA)	23.2	23.6	22.7	22.7	22.8	22.0	(NA)
Black	(NA)	(NA)	82.3	84.1	81.3	79.8	76.3	72.1	(NA)
18-19 years									
Hispanic \2	(NA)	(NA)	147.7	158.5	159.7	159.1	158.0	157.9	150.7
Non-Hispanic white	(NA)	(NA)	67.4	67.7	69.8	67.7	67.4	66.1	(NA)
Black	(NA)	(NA)	152.9	158.6	157.9	151.9	148.3	141.9	(NA)

Notes:
NA Not available.
\1 Includes races other than white and black.
\2 Persons of Hispanic origin may be of any race.

Source: U.S. National Center for Health Statistics, Monthly Vital Statistics Report . 45, no. 5, Supplement.

F2.15. Percent Low Birthweight, by Smoking Status, Age, and Race of Mother: 1993 to 1995

[Low birthweight is defined as weight of less than 2,500 grams (5 lb. 8 oz.). Excludes California, Indiana, New York, and South Dakota, which did not require reporting of tobacco use during pregnancy.]

AGE OF MOTHER

SMOKING STATUS AND RACE OF MOTHER	All ages	Under 15 years	15-19 Total	15-17 years	18-19 years	20-24 years	25-29 years	30-34 years	35-39 years	40-49 years
1993: All races \1	7.4	13.8	9.6	10.5	9.0	7.5	6.5	6.8	8.0	9.0
Smoker	11.8	14.7	10.8	11.4	10.5	10.4	11.5	13.6	16.1	17.8
Nonsmoker	6.6	13.8	9.3	10.3	8.6	6.8	5.6	5.7	6.8	7.9
Not stated	9.2	14.2	11.8	12.9	11.1	9.0	8.2	8.7	9.9	10.3
White	6.1	10.8	7.9	8.6	7.5	6.1	5.4	5.7	6.8	7.7
Smoker	10.1	14.0	10.3	11.0	9.9	9.2	9.4	10.9	13.3	14.7
Nonsmoker	5.2	10.3	7.1	7.9	6.6	5.2	4.6	4.9	5.9	6.9
Not stated	7.6	(B)	9.7	10.9	9.1	7.8	6.6	7.4	8.2	9.5
Black	13.4	16.1	13.4	13.9	13.0	12.3	13.2	14.8	16.6	17.4
Smoker	22.6	19.6	17.2	17.1	17.3	18.8	23.2	26.3	27.8	30.4
Nonsmoker	12.0	15.9	13.1	13.7	12.6	11.4	11.2	11.8	13.6	14.6
Not stated	16.9	(B)	17.5	17.5	17.4	13.9	16.9	18.4	23.7	22.7
1994: All races \1	7.6	14.3	9.7	10.5	9.1	7.6	6.6	6.9	8.2	9.7
Smoker	12.3	17.1	11.4	12.0	11.1	10.6	11.9	13.9	17.0	19.0
Nonsmoker	6.7	14.1	9.3	10.2	8.7	6.9	5.8	5.9	7.0	8.5
Not stated	9.7	20.2	12.4	13.5	11.7	9.4	9.0	8.4	10.8	13.3
White	6.2	11.6	8.1	8.8	7.7	6.2	5.5	5.8	6.9	8.3
Smoker	10.6	16.3	10.9	11.5	10.6	9.6	9.9	11.2	13.9	16.1
Nonsmoker	5.4	10.8	7.2	8.0	6.8	5.3	4.8	5.0	6.0	7.3
Not stated	8.2	(B)	10.7	11.9	9.9	8.0	7.7	6.9	9.3	11.3
Black	13.3	16.5	13.2	13.7	12.9	12.2	12.9	14.6	16.4	18.0
Smoker	22.8	20.6	16.8	17.3	16.6	18.3	23.1	26.5	29.3	30.6
Nonsmoker	12.1	16.4	13.0	13.5	12.6	11.5	11.1	12.0	13.3	15.4
Not stated	16.8	(B)	17.2	16.8	17.5	15.9	15.6	17.1	19.3	27.7
1995: All races \1	7.6	14.2	9.7	10.6	9.1	7.6	6.6	6.9	8.3	9.8
Smoker	12.2	15.2	11.3	12.0	10.9	10.6	11.6	13.7	16.8	19.6
Nonsmoker	6.8	14.1	9.3	10.3	8.7	7.0	5.9	5.9	7.1	8.7
Not stated	10.2	16.0	13.2	13.3	13.1	10.1	9.0	9.5	11.9	11.2
White	6.4	11.6	8.2	8.9	7.8	6.4	5.6	5.9	7.1	8.5
Smoker	10.6	14.8	10.8	11.3	10.5	9.7	9.9	11.2	13.9	16.5
Nonsmoker	5.6	11.1	7.4	8.2	6.9	5.5	4.9	5.2	6.2	7.6
Not stated	8.7	(B)	12.0	13.1	11.4	9.1	7.4	7.7	9.8	10.1
Black	13.2	16.7	13.2	13.8	12.7	12.1	12.8	14.3	16.4	17.4
Smoker	22.9	18.3	16.9	19.0	15.7	18.2	22.8	26.9	29.5	32.2
Nonsmoker	12.0	16.6	12.9	13.5	12.5	11.5	11.2	11.7	13.4	15.0
Not stated	17.5	(B)	16.8	14.8	18.3	14.8	17.3	19.0	23.8	13.0

Notes:
B Base data too small to meet statistical standards for reliability of a derived figure.
\1 Includes races other than White and Black.

Source: U.S. National Center for Health Statistics, Monthly Vital Statistics Reports.

F2.16. Live Births—Drinking Status of Mother Who Drank during Pregnancy, According to Age and Race of Mother: 1994 to 1996

[In thousands, except percents. Excludes California, New York, and South Dakota, which did not require reporting of alcohol use during pregnancy.]

DRINKING STATUS, DRINKING MEASURE, AND RACE OF MOTHER	All ages	Under 15 years	AGE OF MOTHER							
			15-19 years	15-17 years	18-19 years	20-24 years	25-29 years	30-34 years	35-39 years	40-49 years
1994										
All races \1	3,374,330	11,201	435,964	168,354	267,610	858,177	930,843	773,920	311,080	53,145
Drinker	57,056	70	3,964	1,387	2,577	11,329	14,941	17,100	8,256	1,396
Nondrinker	3,262,567	10,992	425,544	164,523	261,021	833,969	900,859	743,413	297,164	50,626
Not stated	54,707	139	6,456	2,444	4,012	12,879	15,043	13,407	5,660	1,123
White	2,649,508	4,677	290,536	104,365	186,171	643,812	760,370	649,089	257,828	43,196
Drinker	40,163	44	2,809	974	1,835	7,547	9,936	12,596	6,177	1,054
Nondrinker	2,566,617	4,556	283,210	101,771	181,439	626,553	738,483	625,565	247,006	41,244
Not stated	42,728	77	4,517	1,620	2,897	9,712	11,951	10,928	4,645	898
Black	593,508	6,208	133,280	59,446	73,834	185,799	131,707	91,098	38,459	6,957
Drinker	14,808	17	871	290	581	3,186	4,490	4,066	1,881	297
Nondrinker	569,512	6,133	130,784	58,456	72,328	180,096	124,896	85,231	35,867	6,505
Not stated	9,188	58	1,625	700	925	2,517	2,321	1,801	711	155
Percent:										
Drinker \1	1.7	0.6	0.9	0.8	1.0	1.3	1.6	2.2	2.7	2.7
White	1.5	1.0	1.0	0.9	1.0	1.2	1.3	2.0	2.4	2.5
Black	2.5	(Z)	0.7	0.5	0.8	1.7	3.5	4.6	5.0	4.4
PERCENT DISTRIBUTION										
All races: \1										
Drinker	100.0	100.0	100.0	100.0	100.0	100.0	100.0	100.0	100.0	100.0
1 drink or less	52.7	62.9	55.6	57.1	54.9	52.0	51.6	53.9	52.4	49.9
2 drinks	19.4	(Z)	18.4	17.7	18.8	19.3	19.2	19.3	20.3	19.7
3-4 drinks	13.0	(Z)	12.3	11.7	12.6	13.4	13.4	12.7	12.4	15.2
5 drinks or more	14.9	(Z)	13.7	13.6	13.7	15.3	15.8	14.1	14.8	15.2
White										
Drinker	100.0	100.0	100.0	100.0	100.0	100.0	100.0	100.0	100.0	100.0
1 drink or less	59.8	(Z)	57.4	59.0	56.5	57.4	60.3	61.5	59.4	55.8
2 drinks	18.1	(Z)	16.9	16.7	17.0	17.6	17.6	18.2	19.3	18.9
3-4 drinks	11.3	(Z)	12.0	11.5	12.3	12.1	11.1	10.9	11.1	13.4
5 drinks	10.8	(Z)	13.7	12.8	14.1	12.9	10.9	9.4	10.2	12.0
Black										
Drinker	100.0	100.0	100.0	100.0	100.0	100.0	100.0	100.0	100.0	100.0
1 drink or less	33.1	(Z)	48.0	46.3	48.8	39.6	32.4	29.3	27.8	27.2
2 drinks	23.5	(Z)	24.1	25.1	23.6	23.7	23.3	22.9	24.9	22.3
3-4 drinks	17.7	(Z)	14.3	13.1	14.8	16.7	18.5	18.5	16.8	22.8
5 drinks or more	25.6	(Z)	13.7	15.4	12.9	20.0	25.9	29.3	30.6	27.7
1995										
All races \1	3,337,069	10,586	431,930	166,266	265,664	829,905	911,556	774,300	322,225	56,567
Drinker	50,820	61	3,844	1,373	2,471	9,612	12,573	15,303	8,045	1,382
Nondrinker	3,231,681	10,374	421,579	162,431	259,148	807,392	884,616	745,621	308,119	53,980
Not stated	54,568	151	6,507	2,462	4,045	12,901	14,367	13,376	6,061	1,205
White	2,640,303	4,610	293,384	105,572	187,812	629,126	748,670	650,689	267,770	46,054
Drinker	36,464	37	2,833	987	1,846	6,644	8,574	11,216	6,108	1,052
Nondrinker	2,561,196	4,502	285,993	102,910	183,083	612,729	728,701	628,546	256,699	44,026
Not stated	42,643	71	4,558	1,675	2,883	9,753	11,395	10,927	4,963	976
Black	562,779	5,658	126,281	56,113	70,168	172,492	123,656	88,488	38,897	7,307
Drinker	12,578	18	773	297	476	2,493	3,569	3,673	1,754	298
Nondrinker	541,238	5,567	123,907	55,153	68,754	167,543	117,972	83,052	36,350	6,847
Not stated	8,963	73	1,601	663	938	2,456	2,115	1,763	793	162
Percent:										
Drinker \1	1.5	0.6	0.9	0.8	0.9	1.2	1.4	2.0	2.5	2.5
White	1.4	0.8	1.0	0.9	1.0	1.1	1.2	1.8	2.3	2.3
Black	2.3	(B)	0.6	0.5	0.7	1.5	2.9	4.2	4.6	4.2

F2.16. Live Births—Drinking Status of Mother Who Drank during Pregnancy, According to Age and Race of Mother; 1994 to 1996 *(continued)*

DRINKING STATUS, DRINKING MEASURE, AND RACE OF MOTHER	All ages	AGE OF MOTHER								
		Under 15 years	15-19 years	15-17 years	18-19 years	20-24 years	25-29 years	30-34 years	35-39 years	40-49 years
All races: \1										
Drinker	100.0	100.0	100.0	100.0	100.0	100.0	100.0	100.0	100.0	100.0
1 drink or less	54.3	(B)	56.4	59.8	54.7	53.7	53.9	55.1	53.6	51.1
2 drinks	18.6	(B)	19.2	18.4	19.7	18.1	18.5	18.5	19.2	18.7
3-4 drinks	12.4	(B)	10.7	10.0	11.0	12.8	12.4	12.5	12.4	13.7
5 drinks or more	14.7	(B)	13.7	11.9	14.6	15.3	15.2	14.0	14.7	16.4
White										
Drinker	100.0	100.0	100.0	100.0	100.0	100.0	100.0	100.0	100.0	100.0
1 drink or less	60.8	(B)	58.1	60.6	56.9	59.1	61.8	62.5	60.1	56.2
2 drinks	17.2	(B)	18.5	17.1	19.1	16.7	16.4	17.2	18.2	18.0
3-4 drinks	11.0	(B)	10.4	9.8	10.7	11.5	10.6	10.9	11.0	12.8
5 drinks	10.9	(B)	13.0	12.4	13.2	12.7	11.2	9.4	10.7	12.9
Black										
Drinker	100.0	100.0	100.0	100.0	100.0	100.0	100.0	100.0	100.0	100.0
1 drink or less	35.5	(B)	51.7	58.2	48.0	40.6	35.4	31.5	31.7	32.1
2 drinks	22.9	(B)	21.5	21.2	21.7	22.3	23.7	22.8	22.8	21.4
3-4 drinks	16.8	(B)	11.6	(B)	11.8	17.1	16.4	17.4	17.7	17.7
5 drinks or more	24.8	(B)	15.2	(B)	18.4	20.1	24.4	28.3	27.8	28.8

Notes:
B Base data too small to meet statistical standards for reliability of derived figure.
Z Less than 50. NA Not available.
\1 Includes races other than White or Black.

Source: U.S. National Center for Health Statistics, Monthly Vital Statistics Reports.

F2.17. Percent of Singleton Babies Born in 1990–93 Who Were Ever Breastfed, Percent Distribution by Duration of Breastfeeding, and Mean Duration of Breastfeeding in Weeks, According to Selected Characteristics of the Mother: United States, 1995

Characteristic	Percent breastfed at all	Total	Duration of breastfeeding			Mean duration in weeks
			0-2 months	3-4 months	5 or more months	
Percent distribution						
All babies[1]	55.2	100.0	40.3	8.6	51.1	28.7
Race and Hispanic origin						
Hispanic	62.2	100.0	42.7	7.1	50.2	26.7
Non-Hispanic white	59.1	100.0	38.5	8.1	53.3	29.8
Non-Hispanic black	25.1	100.0	45.0	14.0	40.9	22.9

Notes:
[1] Includes babies born to women of other race and origin groups not shown separately.
To compute mean duration for all ever-breastfed babies born 1990-93, babies currently being breastfed at interview were assigned the value 83 weeks, which was the mean duration of breastfeeding for all babies born 1990-93 who were breastfed 12 months or longer. In duration of breastfeeding, 0-2 months equals 0-12 weeks, 3-4 months equals 13-20 weeks, 5 or more months equals 21 weeks or more. Percents may not add to 100 due to rounding.

F3. CONTRACEPTION AND ABORTION

F3.1. Number of Women 15–44 Years of Age Who Have Ever Had Intercourse and Percent Who Used the Specified Contraceptive Method at First Intercourse, According to Race and Hispanic Origin and Year: United States, 1995

Race and Hispanic origin	Number thousands	Used any method	Pill	Condom Percent[1]	Withdrawal	All other methods
All women[2]	53,588	59.0	19.5	29.2	6.8	3.5
Race and Hispanic origin						
Hispanic	5,882	36.2	10.6	19.8	4.1	1.7
Non-Hispanic white	38,090	64.8	21.0	32.0	7.8	4.0
Non-Hispanic black	7,462	60.1	20.5	24.5	2.9	2.2

Notes:
[1]For women reporting use of more than one contraceptive method, the method with highest-use effectiveness was coded.
[2]Includes women of other race and origin groups not shown separately.

Source: National Survey of Family Growth, 1995.

F3.2. Use of Any Method of Birth Control at First Intercourse

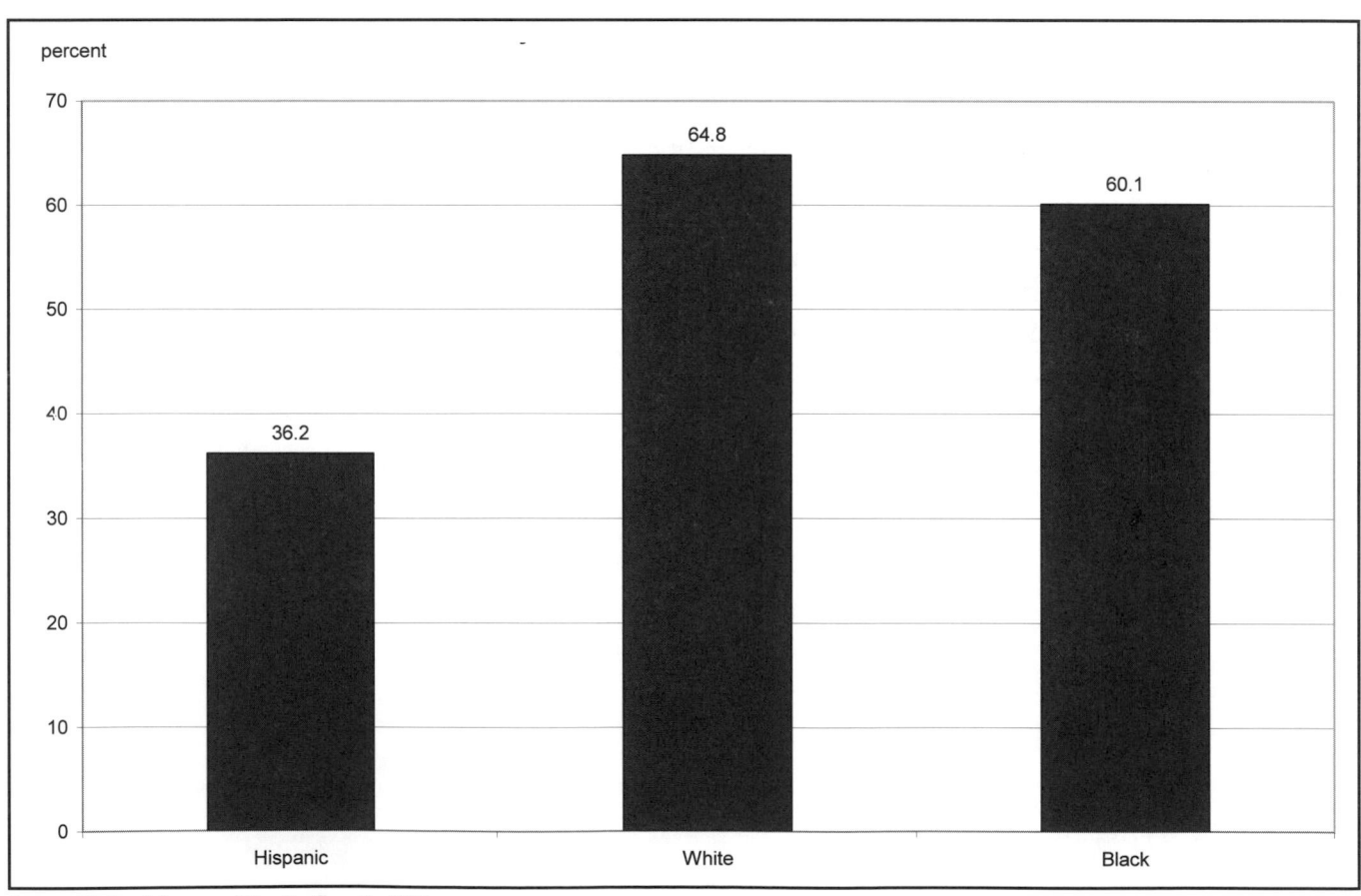

Source: National Survey of Family Growth, 1995.

F3.3. Number of Women 15–44 Years of Age and Percent Distribution by Current Contraceptive Status and Method, According to Race and Hispanic Origin: United States, 1995

| | Race and Hispanic Origin | | |
Contraceptive Method	Hispanic	Non-Hispanic White	Non-Hispanic Black
All women (number in thousands)	6,702	42,522	8,210
Percent Distribution			
Total	100.0	100.0	100.0
Using Contraception	58.9	66.0	62.2
Female Sterilization	21.6	16.3	24.9
Male Sterilization	2.4	9.0	1.1
Pill	13.6	18.8	14.8
Implant	1.2	0.7	1.4
Injectable	2.8	1.6	3.3
Intrauterine Device	0.9	0.5	0.5
Diaphragm	0.4	1.5	0.5
Condom	12.1	13.0	12.5
Female Condom	-	-	-
Periodic Abstinence	1.3	1.6	0.7
Natural Family Planning	0.1	0.3	0.0
Withdrawal	2.0	2.1	0.9
Other Methods	0.6	1.0	1.5
Not Using Contraception 1	41.1	34.0	37.8
Surgically sterile-female	2.3	3.1	3.5
Surgically sterile-male	1.4	1.2	1.7
Pregnant or postpartum	6.4	4.3	4.6
Seeking pregnancy	4.0	3.7	4.6
Other Non-use:			
Never had intercourse 2	12.1	10.4	8.9
No intercourse in 3 months before interview	8.6	5.7	7.2
Had intercourse in 3 months before interview	5.6	5.0	7.0

Notes:

- Quantity zero.

1 Includes other categories not shown separately: "sterile, nonsurgical-male"; "sterile, surgical-male"; "sterile, unknown-male."

2 Never had voluntary intercourse or never had (voluntary) intercourse since first menstrual period.

0.0 Quantity more than zero, but less that 0.05.

NOTE: Percents "using contraception" and "not using contraception" may not add to 100 due to rounding. Due to rounding, percents in specific method categories may not add to total percents using contraception and not using contraception. Also, some methods shown separately.

Source: National Survey of Family Growth, 1995.

F3.4. Number of Unmarried Women 15–44 Years of Age Who Have Had Intercourse in the 12 Months Prior to Interview and Percent Distribution by How Often Their Male Partners Used Condoms for Disease Prevention, According to Selected Characteristics: United States, 1995

Characteristic	Number in thousands	Total	Every time	More than half the time	Half the time	Less than half the time	Not at all
				Percent distribution			
All women[1]	12,708	100.0	31.3	13.9	8.4	13.9	32.5
Race and Hispanic origin of woman and number of male sexual partners in the 12 months prior to interview							
Hispanic	1,077	100.0	30.9	15.4	11.3	13.7	28.7
1 partner	707	100.0	29.8	12.5	9.4	11.5	36.8
2 or more partners	370	100.0	33.1	21.0	14.9	17.8	13.2
Non-Hispanic white	8,202	100.0	27.7	13.0	8.1	14.7	36.5
1 partner	5,341	100.0	28.6	7.7	5.9	10.5	47.4
2 or more partners	2,861	100.0	26.2	23.0	12.1	22.5	16.3
Non-Hispanic black	3,042	100.0	39.2	15.4	9.2	12.8	23.4
1 partner	1,890	100.0	38.4	12.0	6.4	12.3	30.8
2 or more partners	1,153	100.0	40.5	21.0	13.8	13.6	11.2

Notes:
[1]Includes women with missing information on number of partners in the 12 months prior to interview.
NOTES: The frequency of condom use for disease prevention was asked only for a subset of respondents. If she reported ever using condoms for disease prevention in her life AND she had at least 1 sexual partner in the past 12 months, she was asked how often she used condoms in the past 12 months for this purpose. See "Definitions of Terms." Percents may not add to 100 due to rounding.

Source: National Survey of Family Growth, 1995.

F3.5. Adolescent Sexual Relations and Birth Control

Have you ever touched another person's genitals, that is, their private parts, or has another person ever touched your genitals in a sexual way?

	White	Black	Native American	Asian	Hispanic	Total
No	39.4%	34.9%	34.8%	58.0%	44.6%	39.9%
Yes	60.5	65.0	65.2	42.0	55.3	60.0
Invalid response	0.1	0.1	-	-	0.1	0.1

Have you ever had sexual intercourse? When we say sexual intercourse, we mean when a male inserts his penis into a female's vagina.

	White	Black	Native American	Asian	Hispanic	Total
No	61.4%	41.5%	50.4%	74.1%	58.3%	58.1%
Yes	38.6	58.5	49.6	25.9	41.7	41.9

Did you or your partner use any method of birth control the first time you had sexual intercourse?

	White	Black	Native American	Asian	Hispanic	Total
No	26.8%	27.8%	45.2%	50.0%	40.2%	30.1%
Yes	73.2	72.2	54.8	50.0	59.8	69.9

Did you or your partner use any method of birth control when you had sexual intercourse most recently?

	White	Black	Native American	Asian	Hispanic	Total
No	26.1%	24.3%	28.9%	33.7%	34.8%	27.0%
Yes	67.7	71.1	66.7	57.9	61.8	67.5
You only had intercourse once.	6.3	4.6	4.4	8.4	3.4	5.5

Source: The National Longitudinal Study of Adolescent Health, 1996.

F3.6. Adolescent Motivations for Birth Control

In general, birth control is too much of a hassle to use.

	White	Black	Native American	Asian	Hispanic	Total
Strongly agree	5.2%	11.8%	7.3%	3.1%	8.6%	6.8%
Agree	3.7	9.9	5.3	8.1	8.3	5.5
Neither agree nor disagree	13.4	12.9	17.8	24.5	19.4	14.6
Disagree	26.9	28.9	26.4	29.5	26.9	27.2
Strongly disagree	50.8	36.5	43.2	34.7	36.8	45.9

In general, birth control is too expensive to buy.

	White	Black	Native American	Asian	Hispanic	Total
Strongly agree	4.6%	7.7%	3.0%	3.7%	6.0%	5.3%
Agree	6.1	7.6	8.6	6.4	8.3	6.6
Neither agree nor disagree	19.6	18.1	23.8	30.5	26.1	20.7
Disagree	28.5	33.6	25.8	31.3	30.2	29.6
Strongly disagree	41.3	33.0	38.7	28.1	29.3	37.9

It takes too much planning ahead of time to have birth control on hand when you are going to have sex.

	White	Black	Native American	Asian	Hispanic	Total
Strongly agree	3.9%	6.6%	6.6%	4.7%	6.3%	4.6%
Agree	4.0	6.4	6.6	6.3	6.8	5.0
Neither agree nor disagree	20.9	18.3	20.5	30.3	25.9	21.3
Disagree	32.1	34.3	27.8	37.1	33.7	32.7
Strongly disagree	39.4	34.4	38.4	21.7	27.3	36.4

It {is/would be} too hard to get a {girl/boy} to use birth control with you.

	White	Black	Native American	Asian	Hispanic	Total
Strongly agree	3.6%	6.6%	6.6%	4.7%	6.3%	4.6%
Agree	4.0	6.4	6.6	6.3	6.8	5.0
Neither agree nor disagree	20.9	18.3	20.5	30.3	25.9	21.3
Disagree	32.1	34.3	27.8	37.1	33.7	32.7
Strongly disagree	39.4	34.4	38.4	21.7	27.3	36.4

For you, using birth control {interferes/would interfere} with sexual enjoyment.

	White	Black	Native American	Asian	Hispanic	Total
Strongly agree	35.2%	35.8%	33.8%	19.5%	28.2%	33.8%
Agree	27.9	30.1	28.4	27.3	26.9	28.2
Neither agree nor disagree	20.0	17.3	22.4	36.2	24.4	20.7
Disagree	8.2	8.6	7.4	11.5	10.8	8.7
Strongly disagree	8.7	8.1	8.0	5.5	9.8	8.5

It {is/would be} easy for you to get birth control.

	White	Black	Native American	Asian	Hispanic	Total
Strongly agree	35.2%	35.8%	33.8%	19.5%	28.2%	33.8%
Agree	27.9	30.1	28.4	27.3	26.9	28.2
Neither agree nor disagree	20.0	17.3	22.4	36.2	24.4	20.7
Disagree	8.2	8.6	7.4	11.5	10.8	8.7
Strongly disagree	8.7	8.1	8.0	5.5	9.8	8.5

Using birth control is morally wrong.

	White	Black	Native American	Asian	Hispanic	Total
Strongly agree	3.6%	5.8%	3.0%	3.7%	5.7%	4.2%
Agree	2.4	5.5	4.3	7.3	5.9	3.5
Neither agree nor disagree	18.2	17.4	19.9	29.0	21.9	18.9
Disagree	27.2	30.9	24.2	29.2	30.3	28.3
Strongly disagree	48.6	40.5	48.7	30.8	36.3	45.0

If you used birth control, your friends might think you were looking for sex.

	White	Black	Native American	Asian	Hispanic	Total
Strongly agree	5.7%	8.9%	8.3%	6.6%	9.1%	6.8%
Agree	9.8	12.3	5.6	23.2	15.4	11.3
Neither agree nor disagree	27.9	28.8	34.1	39.1	29.8	28.8
Disagree	25.9	26.0	24.5	17.7	25.7	25.4
Strongly disagree	30.8	23.9	27.5	13.5	20.0	27.6

Source: The National Longitudinal Study of Adolescent Health, 1996.

F3.7. Abortions—Number, Rate, and Ratio, by Race: 1972 to 1995

YEAR	ALL RACES Women 15-44 years old (1,000)	ALL RACES Abortions Number (1,000)	ALL RACES Abortions Rate per 1,000 women	ALL RACES Abortions Ratio per 1,000 live births \1	WHITE Women 15-44 years old (1,000)	WHITE Abortions Number (1,000)	WHITE Abortions Rate per 1,000 women	WHITE Abortions Ratio per 1,000 live births \1	BLACK AND OTHER Women 15-44 years old (1,000)	BLACK AND OTHER Abortions Number (1,000)	BLACK AND OTHER Abortions Rate per 1,000 women	BLACK AND OTHER Abortions Ratio per 1,000 live births \1
1972	44,588	587	13.2	184	38,532	455	11.8	175	6,056	132	21.7	223
1975	47,606	1,034	21.7	331	40,857	701	17.2	276	6,749	333	49.3	565
1976	48,721	1,179	24.2	361	41,721	785	18.8	296	7,000	394	56.3	638
1977	49,814	1,317	26.4	400	42,567	889	20.9	333	7,247	428	59.0	679
1978	50,920	1,410	27.7	413	43,427	969	22.3	356	7,493	440	58.7	665
1979	52,016	1,498	28.8	420	44,266	1,062	24.0	373	7,750	435	56.2	625
1980	53,048	1,554	29.3	428	44,942	1,094	24.3	376	8,106	460	56.5	642
1981	53,901	1,577	29.3	430	45,494	1,108	24.3	377	8,407	470	55.9	645
1982	54,679	1,574	28.8	428	46,049	1,095	23.8	373	8,630	479	55.5	646
1983 \2	55,340	1,575	28.5	436	46,506	1,084	23.3	376	8,834	491	55.5	670
1984	56,061	1,577	28.1	423	47,023	1,087	23.1	366	9,038	491	54.3	646
1985	56,754	1,589	28.0	422	47,512	1,076	22.6	360	9,242	513	55.5	659
1986 \2	57,483	1,574	27.4	416	48,010	1,045	21.8	350	9,473	529	55.9	661
1987	57,964	1,559	27.1	405	48,288	1,017	21.1	338	9,676	542	56.0	648
1988	58,192	1,591	27.3	401	48,325	1,026	21.2	333	9,867	565	57.3	638
1989 \2	58,365	1,567	26.8	380	48,104	1,006	20.9	309	10,261	561	54.7	650
1990 \2	58,700	1,609	27.4	389	48,224	1,039	21.5	318	10,476	570	54.4	655
1991	59,080	1,557	26.3	379	48,406	982	20.3	303	10,674	574	53.8	661
1992	59,020	1,529	25.9	380	48161	943	19.6	298	10859	585	53.9	681
1993 \2	59,143	1,500	25.4	378	48,137	911	18.9	291	11,007	589	53.5	700
1994 \2	59,284	1,431	24.1	364	48,121	861	17.9	277	11,163	570	51.1	699
1995	59,442	1,364	22.9	351	48,140	820	17.0	265	11,302	544	48.1	686

Notes:
\1 Live births are those which occurred from July 1 of year shown through June 30 of the following year (to match time of conception with abortions). Births are classified by race of child 1972-1988, and by race of mother after 1988.
\2 Total numbers of abortions in 1983 and 1986 have been estimated by interpolation; 1989, 1990, 1993 and 1994 have been estimated using trends in CDC data.

Source: 1975-1988, S.K. Henshaw and J. Van Vort, eds., Abortion Factbook, 1992 Edition: Readings, Trends, and State and Local Data to 1988, The Alan Guttmacher Institute, New York, NY, 1992 (copyright); 1989-1992, S.K. Henshaw and J. Van Vort, "Abortion Services in the United States, 1991 and 1992," Family Planning Perspectives, 26:100, 1994-95, unpublished data.

F3.8. Abortions, by Selected Characteristics: 1973 to 1995

[Number of abortions from surveys conducted by source; characteristics from the U.S. Centers for Disease Control's (CDC) annual abortion surveillance summaries, with adjustments for changes in States reporting data to the CDC each year]

CHARACTERISTIC	NUMBER (1,000)		
	1973	1980	1981
Total abortions	745	1,554	1,577
Age of woman:			
Less than 15 years old	12	15	15
15 to 19 years old	232	445	433
20 to 24 years old	241	549	555
25 to 29 years old	130	304	316
30 to 34 years old	73	153	167
35 to 39 years old	41	67	70
40 years old and over	17	21	21
Race of woman:			
White	549	1,094	1,108
Black and other	196	460	470
Marital status of woman: \2			
Married	216	320	299
Unmarried	528	1,234	1,279
Number of prior live births:			
None	411	900	912
1	115	305	312
2	104	216	220
3	61	83	85
4 or more	55	51	49
Number of prior induced abortions:			
None	(NA)	1,043	1,023
1	(NA)	373	390
2 or more	(NA)	138	165
Weeks of gestation: \3			
Less than 9 weeks	284	800	810
9 to 10 weeks	222	417	424
11 to 12 weeks	131	202	204
13 weeks or more	108	136	139

See footnotes at end of table.

F3.8. Abortions, by Selected Characteristics: 1973 to 1995 *(continued)*

CHARACTERISTIC	1982	1983	1984	1985	1986	1987
Total abortions	1,574	1,575	1,577	1,589	1,574	1,559
Age of woman:						
Less than 15 years old	15	16	17	17	16	14
15 to 19 years old	419	411	399	399	389	382
20 to 24 years old	552	548	551	548	531	518
25 to 29 years old	326	328	332	336	339	337
30 to 34 years old	168	172	176	181	186	192
35 to 39 years old	73	78	82	87	92	93
40 years old and over	21	21	20	21	21	23
Race of woman:						
White	1,095	1,084	1,087	1,076	1,045	1,017
Black and other	479	491	491	513	529	542
Marital status of woman: \2						
Married	300	295	287	281	279	275
Unmarried	1,274	1,280	1,290	1,307	1,295	1,284
Number of prior live births:						
None	903	890	877	872	854	821
1	321	329	339	349	352	360
2	222	228	234	240	240	248
3	82	83	83	85	86	88
4 or more	46	45	44	43	42	43
Number of prior induced abortions:						
None	994	964	948	944	922	901
1	398	406	414	416	417	416
2 or more	182	205	216	228	236	242
Weeks of gestation: \3						
Less than 9 weeks	806	792	813	779	811	792
9 to 10 weeks	420	424	425	425	416	417
11 to 12 weeks	205	210	201	211	193	194
13 weeks or more	143	149	138	173	154	156

See footnotes at end of table.

F3.8. Abortions, by Selected Characteristics: 1973 to 1995 *(continued)*

CHARACTERISTIC	NUMBER (1,000)					
	1988	**1989**	**1990**	**1991**	**1992**	**1993**
Total abortions	1,591	1,567	1,609	1,557	1,529	1,500
Age of woman:						
Less than 15 years old	14	13	13	12	13	12
15 to 19 years old	393	371	351	314	295	289
20 to 24 years old	520	509	532	533	526	514
25 to 29 years old	347	345	360	348	341	332
30 to 34 years old	197	203	216	213	213	211
35 to 39 years old	96	99	108	107	110	111
40 years old and over	24	26	29	29	31	31
Race of woman:						
White	1,026	1,006	1,039	982	944	911
Black and other	565	561	570	574	585	589
Marital status of woman: \2						
Married	277	270	284	271	257	251
Unmarried	1,314	1,297	1,325	1,285	1272	1,249
Number of prior live births:						
None	814	791	780	724	691	686
1	379	376	396	398	396	391
2	262	261	280	281	281	271
3	93	94	102	105	105	102
4 or more	43	45	50	50	57	50
Number of prior induced abortions:						
None	908	879	891	840	810	791
1	429	429	443	437	431	426
2 or more	254	259	275	279	288	283
Weeks of gestation: \3						
Less than 9 weeks	800	803	817	805	799	778
9 to 10 weeks	424	412	418	399	378	370
11 to 12 weeks	198	192	199	188	182	180
13 weeks or more	168	159	175	164	171	172

See footnotes at end of table.

F3.8. Abortions, by Selected Characteristics: 1973 to 1995 *(continued)*

CHARACTERISTIC	1994	1995	PERCENT DISTRIBUTION			
			1973	1980	1985	1986
Total abortions	1,431	1,364	100	100	100	100
Age of woman:						
Less than 15 years old	12	11	2	1	1	1
15 to 19 years old	276	264	31	29	25	25
20 to 24 years old	478	442	32	35	35	34
25 to 29 years old	316	308	17	20	21	22
30 to 34 years old	205	196	10	10	11	12
35 to 39 years old	111	110	6	4	5	6
40 years old and over	32	32	2	1	1	1
Race of woman:						
White	861	820	74	70	68	66
Black and other	570	544	26	30	32	34
Marital status of woman: \2						
Married	235	221	29	21	18	18
Unmarried	1,196	1,143	71	79	82	82
Number of prior live births:						
None	654	614	55	58	55	54
1	372	359	15	20	22	22
2	258	248	14	14	15	15
3	98	95	8	5	5	5
4 or more	49	48	7	3	3	3
Number of prior induced abortions:						
None	752	721	(NA)	67	60	59
1	404	383	(NA)	24	26	27
2 or more	276	260	(NA)	9	14	15
Weeks of gestation: \3						
Less than 9 weeks	760	728	38	52	49	52
9 to 10 weeks	338	317	30	27	27	26
11 to 12 weeks	161	153	18	13	13	12
13 weeks or more	172	166	15	9	11	10

See footnotes at end of table.

F3.8. Abortions, by Selected Characteristics: 1973 to 1995 *(continued)*

	PERCENT DISTRIBUTION					
CHARACTERISTIC	1987	1988	1989	1990	1991	1992
Total abortions	100	100	100	100	100	100
Age of woman:						
Less than 15 years old	1	1	1	1	1	1
15 to 19 years old	25	25	24	22	20	19
20 to 24 years old	33	33	33	33	34	34
25 to 29 years old	22	22	22	22	22	22
30 to 34 years old	12	12	13	13	14	14
35 to 39 years old	6	6	6	7	7	7
40 years old and over	2	2	2	2	2	2
Race of woman:						
White	65	65	64	65	63	62
Black and other	35	36	36	35	37	38
Marital status of woman: \2						
Married	18	17	17	18	17	17
Unmarried	82	83	83	82	83	83
Number of prior live births:						
None	53	51	51	49	46	45
1	23	24	24	25	26	26
2	16	17	17	17	18	18
3	6	6	6	6	7	7
4 or more	3	3	3	3	3	4
Number of prior induced abortions:						
None	58	57	56	55	54	53
1	27	27	27	28	28	28
2 or more	16	16	17	17	18	19
Weeks of gestation: \3						
Less than 9 weeks	51	50	51	51	52	52
9 to 10 weeks	27	27	26	26	26	25
11 to 12 weeks	13	12	12	12	12	12
13 weeks or more	10	11	10	11	11	11

See footnotes at end of table.

F3.8. Abortions, by Selected Characteristics: 1973 to 1995 *(continued)*

CHARACTERISTIC	1993	1994	1995	ABORTION RATIO \1		
				1973	1980	1985
Total abortions	100	100	100	193	300	297
Age of woman:						
Less than 15 years old	1	1	1	476	607	624
15 to 19 years old	19	19	19	280	451	462
20 to 24 years old	34	33	32	181	310	328
25 to 29 years old	22	22	23	128	213	219
30 to 34 years old	14	14	14	165	213	203
35 to 39 years old	7	8	8	246	317	280
40 years old and over	2	2	2	334	461	409
Race of woman:						
White	61	60	60	178	274	265
Black and other	39	40	40	252	392	397
Marital status of woman: \2						
Married	17	16	16	74	98	88
Unmarried	83	84	84	564	649	605
Number of prior live births:						
None	46	46	45	242	365	358
1	26	26	26	108	208	219
2	18	18	18	190	283	288
3	7	7	7	228	288	281
4 or more	3	3	4	196	251	230
Number of prior induced abortions:						
None	53	53	53	(NA)	(NA)	(NA)
1	28	28	28	(NA)	(NA)	(NA)
2 or more	19	19	19	(NA)	(NA)	(NA)
Weeks of gestation: \3						
Less than 9 weeks	52	53	53	(NA)	(NA)	(NA)
9 to 10 weeks	25	24	23	(NA)	(NA)	(NA)
11 to 12 weeks	12	11	11	(NA)	(NA)	(NA)
13 weeks or more	11	12	12	(NA)	(NA)	(NA)

See footnotes at end of table.

F3.8. Abortions, by Selected Characteristics: 1973 to 1995 *(continued)*

CHARACTERISTIC	ABORTION RATIO \1					
	1986	1987	1988	1989	1990	1991
Total abortions	294	288	286	275	280	275
Age of woman:						
Less than 15 years old	605	578	553	523	515	502
15 to 19 years old	457	449	444	418	403	379
20 to 24 years old	328	327	327	318	328	330
25 to 29 years old	219	216	218	213	224	224
30 to 34 years old	201	197	194	189	196	192
35 to 39 years old	277	265	254	244	249	241
40 years old and over	381	374	361	350	354	339
Race of woman:						
White	259	252	250	236	241	233
Black and other	398	393	389	394	396	398
Marital status of woman: \2						
Married	88	87	87	83	88	86
Unmarried	589	571	556	533	527	512
Number of prior live births:						
None	353	341	333	319	316	303
1	220	222	227	220	230	231
2	285	285	288	279	292	294
3	279	276	276	266	279	285
4 or more	225	224	213	210	223	218
Number of prior induced abortions:						
None	(NA)	(NA)	(NA)	(NA)	(NA)	(NA)
1	(NA)	(NA)	(NA)	(NA)	(NA)	(NA)
2 or more	(NA)	(NA)	(NA)	(NA)	(NA)	(NA)
Weeks of gestation: \3						
Less than 9 weeks	(NA)	(NA)	(NA)	(NA)	(NA)	(NA)
9 to 10 weeks	(NA)	(NA)	(NA)	(NA)	(NA)	(NA)
11 to 12 weeks	(NA)	(NA)	(NA)	(NA)	(NA)	(NA)
13 weeks or more	(NA)	(NA)	(NA)	(NA)	(NA)	(NA)

See footnotes at end of table.

F3.8. Abortions, by Selected Characteristics: 1973 TO 1995 *(continued)*

CHARACTERISTIC	1992	1993	1994	1995
Total abortions	275	274	260	260
Age of woman:				
Less than 15 years old	511	493	489	480
15 to 19 years old	370	365	354	348
20 to 24 years old	333	335	327	317
25 to 29 years old	228	231	228	225
30 to 34 years old	192	189	184	179
35 to 39 years old	239	234	227	220
40 years old and over	338	329	322	310
Race of woman:				
White	229	225	217	210
Black and other	405	412	412	409
Marital status of woman: \2				
Married	84	85	81	77
Unmarried	508	497	485	477
Number of prior live births:				
None	298	297	287	277
1	233	233	227	223
2	299	297	291	285
3	290	289	288	284
4 or more	244	227	229	228
Number of prior induced abortions:				
None	(NA)	(NA)	(NA)	(NA)
1	(NA)	(NA)	(NA)	(NA)
2 or more	(NA)	(NA)	(NA)	(NA)
Weeks of gestation: \3				
Less than 9 weeks	(NA)	(NA)	(NA)	(NA)
9 to 10 weeks	(NA)	(NA)	(NA)	(NA)
11 to 12 weeks	(NA)	(NA)	(NA)	(NA)
13 weeks or more	(NA)	(NA)	(NA)	(NA)

Notes:

NA Not available or not applicable.

\1 Number of abortions per 1,000 abortions and live births. Live births are those which occurred from July 1 of year shown through June 30 of the following year (to match time of conception with abortions).

\2 Separated women included with unmarried.

\3 After 1984, data not exactly comparable with prior years because of a change in the method of calculation.

Source: S.K. Henshaw and J. Van Vort, eds., Abortion Factbook, 1992 Abortion Factbook, 1992 Edition: Readings, Trends, and State and Local Data to 1988, The Alan Guttmacher Institute, New York, NY, 1992 (copyright); S.K. Henshaw and J. Van Vort, Abortion Services in the United States, 1991 and 1992; Family Perspectives, 26:100, 1994; and unpublished data.

F3.9. Attitudes toward Abortion

Please tell me whether or not you think it should be possible for a pregnant woman to obtain a legal abortion?
...If there is a strong chance of serious defect in the baby?

	White	Black	Other
Yes	76.8%	68.7%	71.8%
No	19.3	26.4	22.6
Don't know	4	4.9	5.6
(N)	**1490**	**265**	**124**

...If she is married and does not want any more children?

	White	Black	Other
Yes	41.6%	34.8%	37.1%
No	53.7	60.6	59.7
Don't know	4.7	4.5	3.2
(N)	**1489**	**264**	**124**

...If the woman's own health is seriously endangered by the pregnancy?

	White	Black	Other
Yes	84.5%	80.7%	84.7%
No	11.6	12.5	9.7
Don't know	3.9	6.8	5.6
(N)	**1491**	**264**	**124**

...If the family has a very low income and cannot afford any more children?

	White	Black	Other
Yes	43.3%	35.8%	40.3%
No	52.1	57.4	53.2
Don't know	4.6	6.8	6.5
(N)	**1489**	**265**	**124**

...If she became pregnant as a result of rape?

	White	Black	Other
Yes	77.9%	70.9%	72.6%
No	18	22.6	23.4
Don't know	4.1	6.4	4
(N)	**1490**	**256**	**124**

...If she is not married and does not want to marry the man?

	White	Black	Other
Yes	42.2%	30.8%	37.9%
No	53.2	64.3	58.1
Don't know	4.6	4.9	4
(N)	**1490**	**263**	**124**

...If the woman wants it for any reason?

	White	Black	Other
Yes	40.1%	33.6%	33.9%
No	55	60	58.9
Don't know	4.8	6.4	7.3
(N)	**1487**	**265**	**124**

Source: General Social Survey, 1998.

F3.10. Number of Women 15–24 Years of Age, Percent Who Ever Received Family Planning Services, and Percent Who Received the Specified Services at First Family Planning Visit: United States, 1995

Characteristic	Number in thousands	Ever received family planning services[1]	Services received at first visit[1]		
			Birth control method	Birth control counseling	Birth control checkup or test
			Percent		
All women[2]	18,002	58.6	50.8	39.9	40.2
Ever had intercourse...............	12,464	79.5	69.9	54.4	55.4
Race and Hispanic origin:					
Hispanic	1,644	74.4	60.9	48.5	47.4
Non-Hispanic white	8,269	79.9	71.5	54.1	58.2
Non-Hispanic black	2,074	83.1	73.1	58.7	53.4

Notes:

[1]First family planning visit refers to first receipt of any of the following family planning services from a medical care provider: sterilization operation, birth control method, check up or medical test for birth control, counseling about birth control, or counseling about getting sterilized.

[2]Includes women of other race and origin groups not shown separately.

NOTE: Percents do not add to 100 because women could report more than one service at first visit.

Source: National Survey of Family Growth, 1995.

F3.11. Number of Women 15–44 Years of Age, Percent Who Have Ever Received Any Infertility Services, and Percent Who Have Ever Received the Specified Infertility Services: United States, 1995

Characteristic	Number in thousands	Any services[1]	Advice	Tests on woman or man	Ovulation drugs	Surgery or treatment for blocked tubes	Assisted reproductive technology[2]
					Percent		
All women	60,201	15.4	6.4	4.2	3.0	1.5	1.0
Race and Hispanic origin							
Hispanic	6,702	13.4	4.9	2.4	1.7	0.9	0.6
Non-Hispanic white	42,522	16.3	7.2	4.9	3.5	1.6	1.2
Non-Hispanic black	8,210	13.0	3.8	2.2	1.4	0.9	0.3
Non-Hispanic other	2,767	12.3	5.0	3.9	2.9	1.9	1.4

Notes:

0.0 Quantity more than zero but less than 0.05.

[1]Includes services to help get pregnant as well as to help prevent miscarriage.

[2]Includes artificial insemination, In vitro fertilization, gamete intrafallopian transfer (GIFT), and other techniques not shown separately.

NOTE: Percents do not add to total ever receiving "any services" because some women reported more than one service. Also "any services" includes services to help prevent miscarriage and other infertility services, not shown separately.

Source: National Survey of Family Growth, 1995.

F3.12. Number of Women 18–44 Years of Age and Percent Who Had Formal Instruction about the Specified Sex-education Topics before They Were 18: United States, 1995

| Characteristic | Number in thousands | Received any formal instruction | Topic of formal instruction | | | |
			Birth control methods	Sexually transmitted diseases	Safe sex to prevent HIV[1]	How to say no to sex
All women	54,748	72.8	62.0	62.7	52.0	55.0
Race and Hispanic origin						
Hispanic	6,015	64.8	56.8	55.4	50.2	49.3
Non-Hispanic white	38,987	74.0	62.2	63.6	50.9	55.0
Non-Hispanic black	7,357	76.1	67.1	67.8	59.9	62.5
Non-Hispanic other	2,390	63.1	55.7	51.0	47.4	46.5

Notes:
[1]This question was limited to women 15-29 years of age at interview. HIV is human immunodeficiency virus, the virus that causes acquired immunodeficiency syndrome (AIDS).
NOTE: Percents do not add to 100 because respondents could report more than one type of formal instruction.

Source: National Survey of Family Growth, 1995.

G. Religion and Religiosity

Compared with most other western industrialized societies, the United States is a religious society. Most Americans identify with or claim a religious affiliation. Most attend a religious service at least monthly and believe in God and an afterlife, and most say they pray privately or in religious services. But social scientists have found substantial differences in the rates of religious behavior exhibited by different racial and ethnic groups. Because of classifications in the data sources, however, only Blacks, Whites, and "Others" are considered here. In this case, "Other" is composed of those who identify themselves as neither White nor Black. Data on affiliation, participation, and beliefs are presented.

The views about religion and religiosity presented in this section reflect a variety of factors. As mentioned in the other sections of this book, a number of factors account for these differences. Some of these are social class, culture, history, and social structure. In the case of religion, the Black-White differences are not only large, they likely reflect additional factors. Some of these additional factors include religious affiliation, size and type of church, the theology of their churches, and their personal experiences in life. Thus, the differing views may reflect their social position, life experiences, religious dogma, or some combination of all of these factors.

G1. AFFILIATION AND PARTICIPATION

Blacks are more likely than Whites to be Protestant while other minorities are more likely than Whites to be Catholic (G1.1). This latter difference likely reflects recent immigration patterns. Blacks are generally more religious than Whites and this is shown in a number of ways in this section. As shown in G1.1 through G1.3, Blacks are more likely than Whites to have a religious prefer-

ence, to attend church, and to say religion is important to them (G1.4).

G2. RELIGIOUS BELIEFS

Blacks are also more likely than Whites to hold traditional beliefs about the Bible (G2.2), beliefs about God, belief in life after death, belief in heaven and hell, and belief in miracles (G2.3). They are also more likely than Whites and "Others" to believe that God concerns himself with every human being (G2.5). Blacks are also more likely to believe they are part of a spiritual force, to believe they work with God as a partner, and to look to God for strength, and they are more likely than Whites to rely on God when making decisions (G2.6).

G3. PERSONAL RELIGIOSITY

Personal religiosity is shown in a number of ways. Blacks are more likely than Whites and "Others" to demonstrate this personal religiosity. They, more than Whites and "Others" pray privately, meditate, seek help, and receive comfort from fellow parishioners (G3.1 through G3.3). Blacks are also more likely than Whites and "Others" to say they have had a religious turning point in their lives (G3.4), and are more likely to describe themselves as "extremely or very religious" (G3.5 and G3.6). Blacks are also more likely than Whites and "Others" to say they have felt God's presence, felt strength and comfort in their religion, and felt inner peace or harmony. They are also more likely than Whites and "Others" to say they desire to be closer to God, to feel God's love, to feel spiritually touched by the beauty of creation, and to feel that individuals come closer to God through art and music (G3.7). Further, more Blacks than Whites believe God watches over them (G3.8). While some of these differences are small, other differences are quite large.

G4. CONSEQUENCES OF RELIGION

Pollsters have asked respondents about the consequences of religion, and Blacks are somewhat less likely than Whites and "Others" to be critical of the role religion plays in American society (G4.1). They believe individuals trust too much in science and too little in religion (G4.2). Blacks more than Whites say they carry their religious beliefs over into other aspects of their life, are willing to forgive others, forgive themselves, and know that God forgives them (G4.3). Whites and "Oth-ers" are less likely to believe that religious leaders should try to influence how people vote, or influence the government (G4.4).

G5. IMAGES OF HUMANKIND

Images about whether the world is good or evil, and images about whether people are good or evil are presented in G5. The differences by race are minimal.

G1. AFFILIATION AND PARTICIPATION

G1.1. Religious Preference

What is your religious preference?			
	White	**Black**	**Other**
Protestant	53.2%	76.0%	23.6%
Catholic	26.4	7.3	47.6
Jewish	2.3		
None	14.4	10.9	17.8
Other	3.7	5.8	11.0
(N)	**2215**	**396**	**191**

Source: General Social Survey, 1998.

G1.2. Church Attendance and Strength of Affiliation

How often do you attend religious services?				
	White	**Black**	**Other**	**Total**
Never	20.8%	12.1%	21.2%	19.6%
At least once a year	11.0	8.2	9.5	10.5
Once a year	10.9	9.2	10.1	10.6
Several times a year	11.1	7.7	16.4	11.0
Once a month	7.2	6.4	11.6	7.4
2-3 times a month	7.4	16.7	7.9	8.8
Nearly every week	7.1	6.9	2.1	6.7
Every week	17.1	22.6	12.7	17.5
More than once a week	7.3	10.3	8.5	7.8
(N)	**2209**	**390**	**189**	**2788**

Source: General Social Survey, 1998.

G1.3. Self-Reported Frequency of Attendance at Church of Whites and Blacks

	Weekly	**Almost Weekly**	**Monthly**	**Seldom**	**Never**
Race					
White	29	12	14	33	11
Black	33	13	27	19	7

Source: The Gallup Poll Monthly, February 1995, p. 20.

G1.4. Percentage of Whites and Blacks Who Say Religion is Very Important or Fairly Important in Their Lives

	Very	**Fairly**
Race		
White	56	30
Blacks	80	18

Source: The Gallup Poll Monthly, February 1995, p. 20.

G2. RELIGIOUS BELIEFS

G2.1. How Much Truth in Religion?

Which of the following statements come closest to your own view:	White	Black	Other
Little truth in any religion	3.5%	3.4%	10.3%
Basic truth in many religions	85.9	76.7	75.0
Truth in only one religion	10.6	19.8	14.7
(N)	**878**	**116**	**68**

Source: General Social Survey, 1998.

G2.2. Beliefs about the Bible

The United States Supreme Court has ruled that no state or local government may require the reading of the Lord's Prayer or Bible verses in public schools. What are your views on this? Do you approve or disapprove of the court ruling?

	White	Black	Other	Total
Approve	44.7%	29.8%	43.0%	42.5%
Disapprove	50.9	66.7	48.4	52.9
No opinion	4.4	3.5	8.6	4.6
(N)	**1484**	**255**	**128**	**1867**

Which of these statements comes closest to describing your feelings about the Bible?

	White	Black	Other	Total
The Bible is the actual word of God and is to be taken literally, word for word	27.1%	50.6%	32.5%	30.7%
The Bible is the inspired word of God but not everything in it should be taken literally, word for word	52.2	36.7	43.3	49.4
The Bible is an ancient book of fables, legends, history, and moral precepts recorded by men	17.3	8.7	19.7	16.3
Other	1.1	.6	1.9	1.1
Don't know	2.4	3.3	2.5	2.5
(N)	**1866**	**332**	**157**	**2355**

Source: General Social Survey, 1998.

G2.3. Belief in God and Religious Doctrines

What best describes your beliefs about God?	White	Black	Other
Don't believe now, never have	3.3%	0.0%	5%
Don't believe now, used to	5.8	1.3	6.3
Believe now, didn't used to	6.8	3.3	3.8
Believe now, always have	84.1	95.3	85
(N)	**891**	**150**	**80**
Do you believe in...			
Life after death?			
Yes, definitely	58.7%	61.9%	51.2%
Yes, probably	22.3	16.5	26.8
No, probably not	9.9	8.6	9.8
No, definitely not	9.1	12.9	12.2
(N)	**906**	**139**	**82**
Heaven?			
Yes, definitely	64.7%	79.3%	64.6%
Yes, probably	20	13.8	20.7
No, probably not	8.5	4.8	4.9
No, definitely not	6.9	2.1	9.8
(N)	**931**	**145**	**82**
Hell?			
Yes, definitely	52.9%	74.6%	50%
Yes, probably	19.4	12.7	25.6
No, probably not	14.7	5.6	11.5
No, definitely not	13	7	12.8
(N)	**906**	**142**	**78**
Religious Miracles?			
Yes, definitely	50.3%	58.9%	50.6%
Yes, probably	27.4	27	23.5
No, probably not	13.7	5.7	13.6
No, definitely not	8.6	8.5	12.3
(N)	**900**	**141**	**81**

Source: General Social Survey, 1998.

G2.4. Belief in Afterlife

Do you believe there is a life after death?	White	Black	Other	Total
Yes	72.2%	70.6%	70.4%	71.9%
No	15.9	17.3	16.4	16.1
Undecided	11.8	12.1	13.2	12.0
(N)	**1858**	**330**	**159**	**2347**

Source: General Social Survey, 1998.

G2.5. Belief about God and the Human Condition

There is a God who concerns Himself with every human being personally.

	White	Black	Other
Strongly agree	40.2%	56.6%	34.9%
Agree	30.5	31.5	40.7
Neither	13.1	6.3	10.5
Disagree	9.8	4.9	8.1
Strongly disagree	6.4	0.7	5.8
(N)	**950**	**143**	**86**

To me, life is meaningful only because God exists.

	White	Black	Other
Strongly agree	18.3%	36.1%	20.2%
Agree	23.1	29.9	25.0
Neither	25.5	17.0	25.0
Disagree	22.2	10.2	20.2
Strongly disagree	10.9	6.8	9.5
(N)	**938**	**147**	**84**

Source: General Social Survey, 1998.

G2.6. Religious Beliefs and Coping

Think about how you try to understand and deal with major problems in your life. To what extent is each of the following involved in the way that you cope?

I think about how my life is part of a larger spiritual force.

	White	Black	Other	Total
A great deal	18.0%	28.6%	21.6%	19.7%
Quite a bit	20.0	26.0	23.5	21.1
Somewhat	36.5	29.6	32.4	35.2
Not at all	25.5	15.8	22.5	23.9
(N)	**650**	**150**	**63**	**863**

I work together with God as partners.

	White	Black	Other	Total
A great deal	19.2%	39.4%	24.0%	22.3%
Quite a bit	21.2	27.5	29.0	22.6
Somewhat	38.9	26.9	21.0	35.9
Not at all	20.7	6.2	26.0	19.1
(N)	**1104**	**193**	**100**	**1397**

I look to God for strength, support, and guidance.

	White	Black	Other	Total
A great deal	39.0%	67.7%	46.2%	43.5%
Quite a bit	21.6	16.2	17.3	20.6
Somewhat	25.0	12.1	21.2	22.9
Not at all	14.5	4.0	15.4	13.1
(N)	**1114**	**198**	**104**	**1416**

I feel God is punishing me for my sins or lack of spirituality.

	White	Black	Other	Total
A great deal	1.5%	2.6%	5.9%	2.0%
Quite a bit	3.2	4.6	7.9	3.8
Somewhat	16.5	23.1	16.8	17.4
Not at all	78.8	69.7	69.3	76.8
(N)	**1111**	**195**	**101**	**1407**

I wonder whether God has abandoned me.

	White	Black	Other	Total
A great deal	.9%	1.0%	5.0%	1.2%
Quite a bit	1.6	1.5	3.0	1.7
Somewhat	9.7	9.2	8.0	9.5
Not at all	87.8	88.3	84.0	87.6
(N)	**1111**	**196**	**100**	**1407**

I try to make sense of the situation and decide what to do without relying on God.

	White	Black	Other	Total
A great deal	13.7%	5.6%	18.0%	12.9%
Quite a bit	16.7	8.2	18.0	15.6
Somewhat	35.4	26.2	28.0	33.6
Not at all	34.2	60.0	36.0	37.9
(N)	**1103**	**195**	**100**	**1398**

Source: General Social Survey, 1998.

G3. PERSONAL RELIGIOSITY

G3.1. Frequency of Prayer

About how often do you pray?	White	Black	Other	Total
Several times a day	22.8%	38.9%	19.4%	24.8%
Once a day	28.4	35.9	33.0	29.8
Several times a week	15.0	12.1	8.7	14.1
Less than once a week	8.0	3.0	11.7	7.5
Never	2.1	–	–	1.7
Don't know	0.3	–	–	0.2
(N)	**1130**	**198**	**103**	**1431**

Source: General Social Survey, 1998.

G3.2. Frequency of Private Prayer and Meditation

How often do you pray privately in places other than at church or synagogue?	White	Black	Other
More than once/day	21.8%	41.3%	19.6%
Once a day	25.2	31.1	32.4
A few times/week	15.3	9.2	7.8
Once a week	5.2	3.6	3.9
Few times/month	5.8	4.1	5.9
Once a month	2.4	1.0	3.9
Less than once/month	10.0	3.6	10.8
Never	14.3	6.1	15.7
(N)	**1108**	**196**	**102**
Within your religious or spiritual tradition, how often do you meditate?			
More than once/day	7.4%	18.3%	8.2%
Once a day	13.0	18.8	12.2
A few times/week	8.8	13.6	9.2
Once a week	5.1	2.6	8.2
Few times/month	4.6	4.2	2.0
Once a month	3.4	1.6	6.1
Less than once/month	7.8	3.7	4.1
Never	50.0	37.2	50.0
(N)	**1081**	**191**	**98**

Source: General Social Survey, 1998.

G3.3. Help From and Interaction With Congregation

If you were ill, how much would the people within your congregation help you out?				
	White	**Black**	**Other**	**Total**
A great deal	46.1%	48.3%	40.7%	46.2%
Some	31.5	35.7	33.3	32.4
A little	14.6	9.8	13.0	13.6
None	7.7	6.3	13.0	7.8
(N)	**609**	**143**	**54**	**806**
If you had a problem or were faced with a difficult situation, how much comfort would the people in your congregation be willing to give you?				
A great deal	53.0%	57.6%	56.6%	54.0%
Some	30.3	26.6	32.1	29.8
A little	10.8	10.8	1.9	10.2
None	5.6	5.0	9.4	6.0
(N)	**613**	**139**	**53**	**805**
How often do the people in your congregation make too many demands on you?				
Very often	1.8%	3.3%	9.5%	2.6%
Fairly often	5.7	7.3	12.7	6.5
Once in a while	28.9	32.5	20.6	28.9
Never	63.5	57.0	57.0	61.9
(N)	**661**	**151**	**63**	**875**
How often are the people in your congregation critical of you and the things you do?				
Very often	1.8%	4.0%	7.9%	2.7%
Fairly often	2.0	6.7	6.3	3.1
Once in a while	18.9	19.3	19.0	19.0
Never	77.2	70.0	66.7	75.2
(N)	**650**	**150**	**63**	**863**

Source: General Social Survey, 1998.

G3.4. Religious Turning Point

Has there ever been a turning point in your life when you made a new and personal commitment to religion?			
	White	**Black**	**Other**
Yes	43%	66.7%	45.7%
No	57	33.3	54.3
(N)	**973**	**153**	**92**

Source: General Social Survey, 1998.

G3.5. Are You a Religious Person?

To what extent do you consider yourself to be a religious person? Are you . . .	White	Black	Other
Very religious	16.3%	32.3%	20.2%
Moderately religious	43.4	44.1	29.8
Slightly religious	24.2	14.9	31.7
Not religious	16.1	8.7	18.3
(N)	**1128**	**195**	**104**
To what extent do you consider yourself to be a spiritual person? Are you . . .			
Very spiritual	19.8%	34.5%	23.1%
Moderately spiritual	41.5	38.1	28.8
Slightly spiritual	26.3	19.6	30.8
Not spiritual	12.3	7.7	17.3
(N)	**1124**	**194**	**104**
Did you ever have a religious or spiritual experience that changed your life?			
Yes	36.8%	55.9%	33%
No	63.2	44.1	67
(N)	**1126**	**195**	**103**

Source: General Social Survey, 1998.

G3.6. Personal Religiosity

Would you describe yourself as . . .	White	Black	Other
Extremely religious	6.6%	10.8%	3.6%
Very religious	17.3	33.1	20.5
Somewhat religious	51.4	43.9	47
Neither	10.6	4.7	13.3
Somewhat non-religious	5.3	2	6
Very non-religious	3.8	2.7	6
Extremely non-religious	5	2.7	3.6
(N)	**971**	**148**	**83**

Source: General Social Survey, 1998.

G3.7. Beliefs about God and One's Own Religion

To what extent can you say you experience the following?
I can feel God's presence.

	White	Black	Other
Many times a day	14.5%	30.6%	25.2%
Every day	24.6	34.2	23.3
Most days	14.5	14.5	6.8
Some days	14.2	9.3	18.4
Once in a while	18.5	9.8	13.6
Never/almost never	13.7	1.6	12.6
(N)	**1102**	**193**	**103**

I find strength and comfort in my religion.

	White	Black	Other
Many times a day	14.7%	24.5%	16.5%
Every day	24.2	39.1	20.4
Most days	18.7	14.6	8.7
Some days	13.9	8.3	23.3
Once in a while	13.6	8.3	12.6
Never/almost never	14.9	5.2	18.4
(N)	**1101**	**192**	**103**

I feel deep inner peace or harmony.

	White	Black	Other
Many times a day	10.5%	18.7%	10.7%
Every day	18.4	24.9	17.5
Most days	27.9	26.9	31.1
Some days	20.9	17.6	17.5
Once in a while	15.4	10.4	13.6
Never/almost never	6.9	1.6	9.7
(N)	**1104**	**193**	**103**

I desire to be closer to or in union with God.

	White	Black	Other
Many times a day	14%	27.5%	23.1%
Every day	26.7	37.8	22.1
Most days	16.9	15	13.5
Some days	15.3	13.5	10.6
Once in a while	14.2	5.7	15.4
Never/almost never	12.9	.5	15.4
(N)	**1091**	**193**	**104**

I feel God's love for me, directly or through others.

	White	Black	Other
Many times a day	14.9%	28.1%	18.8%
Every day	25.4	32.8	29.7
Most days	18.6	15.1	12.9
Some days	15.5	14.1	12.9
Once in a while	14	6.3	15.8
Never/almost never	11.5	3.6	9.9
(N)	**1097**	**192**	**101**

I am spiritually touched by the beauty of creation.

	White	Black	Other
Many times a day	25.5%	27.5%	22.1%
Every day	27.4	38.9	23.1
Most days	18.1	13	19.2
Some days	12.5	10.4	17.3
Once in a while	9.7	8.8	10.6
Never/almost never	6.8	1.6	7.7
(N)	**1103**	**193**	**104**

Source: General Social Survey, 1998.

G3.8. Religious Beliefs and Daily Living

I believe in God who watches over me.			
	White	**Black**	**Other**
Strongly agree	55.2%	77%	63.5%
Agree	31.9	19.9	29.8
Disagree	8.7	2	3.8
Strongly disagree	4.1	1	2.9
(N)	**1115**	**196**	**104**

Source: General Social Survey, 1998.

G4. CONSEQUENCES OF RELIGION

G4.1. Consequences of Religion

Looking around the world, religions bring more conflict than peace.			
	White	**Black**	**Other**
Strongly agree	8.4%	7.9%	9.3%
Agree	27.4	20.5	32.6
Neither	22.9	15.9	14
Disagree	33.1	38.4	33.7
Strongly disagree	8.2	17.2	10.5
(N)	**966**	**151**	**86**
People with very strong religious beliefs are often too intolerant of others.			
Strongly agree	13%	9.1%	12.8%
Agree	36.9	26.6	47.7
Neither	22.1	26.6	25.6
Disagree	22.8	28.7	10.5
Strongly disagree	5.2	9.1	3.5
(N)	**960**	**143**	**86**
The U.S. would be a better country if religion had less influence.			
Strongly agree	4.6%	2.1%	4.6%
Agree	10.3	8.9	21.8
Neither	27	22.6	33.3
Disagree	41	39.7	32.2
Strongly disagree	17	26.7	8
(N)	**958**	**146**	**87**

Source: General Social Survey, 1998.

G4.2. Trust in People and Science

We trust too much in science and not enough in religious faith.			
	White	**Black**	**Other**
Strongly agree	7%	18%	12.4%
Agree	20	36.7	23.6
Neither	28.4	22.7	22.5
Disagree	30.5	16	31.5
Strongly disagree	14	6.7	10.1
(N)	**968**	**150**	**89**

Source: General Social Survey, 1998.

G4.3. Religious Beliefs and Daily Living

I try hard to carry my religious beliefs over into all my other dealings in life.	White	Black	Other
Strongly agree	25.1%	41%	30.4%
Agree	45.9	42.1	36.3
Disagree	21.0	14.4	24.5
Strongly disagree	8.0	2.6	8.8
(N)	**1117**	**195**	**102**
I have forgiven myself for things that I have done wrong.			
Always/almost always	41.5%	60.0%	44.2%
Often	39.3	22.6	29.8
Seldom	13.6	11.3	17.3
Never	5.7	6.2	8.7
(N)	**1113**	**195**	**104**
I have forgiven those who hurt me.			
Always/almost always	45.6%	57.9%	44.2%
Often	41.4	28.2	27.9
Seldom	9.7	10.3	12.5
Never	3.3	3.6	15.4
(N)	**1118**	**195**	**104**
I know that God forgives me.			
Always/almost always	72.3%	88.2%	70.6%
Often	18.8	9.2	18.6
Seldom	3.5	1.5	3.9
Never	5.3	1.0	6.9
(N)	**1106**	**195**	**102**

Source: General Social Survey, 1998.

G4.4. Attitudes about Religion and Politics

Religious leaders should not try to influence how people vote in elections.	White	Black	Other
Strongly agree	38.2%	23.7%	37.8%
Agree	28.7	38.2	28.9
Neither	17.3	17.8	13.3
Disagree	11.8	15.8	11.1
Strongly disagree	4.1	4.6	8.9
(N)	**987**	**152**	**90**
Religious leaders should not try to influence government decisions.			
Strongly agree	32%	17.1%	32.6%
Agree	28.4	31.5	34.8
Neither	17.8	25.3	15.7
Disagree	16.2	21.2	9.0
Strongly disagree	5.5	4.8	7.9
(N)	**974**	**146**	**89**
Do you think that churches and religious organizations in this country have too much power or too little power?			
Far too much power	6.3%	4.5%	9.1%
Too much power	18.2	7.6	22.1
About the right amount of power	56.5	50.8	46.8
Too little power	14.8	28.8	19.5
Far too little power	4.2	8.3	2.6
(N)	**873**	**132**	**77**

Source: General Social Survey, 1998.

G5. IMAGES OF HUMANKIND

G5.1. Images of Good and Evil

If you think that the world is basically filled with evil and sin, place yourself at 1. If you think there is much goodness in the world which hints at God's goodness, place yourself at 7. If you think things are somewhere between these two, place yourself at 2, 3, 4, 5, or 6.

	White	Black	Other	Total
The world is evil	4.2%	10.3%	8.9%	5.3%
2	3.8	4.2	5.1	3.9
3	8.4	8.2	8.9	8.4
4	29.1	26.1	39.2	29.4
5	23.8	22.7	17.1	23.2
6	17.5	14.5	7.6	16.4
The world is good	13.0	13.6	13.3	13.1
Don't know	0.3	0.3	–	0.3
(N)	**1852**	**330**	**158**	**2340**

If you think that human nature is basically good, place yourself at 1. If you think that human nature is fundamentally perverse and corrupt, place yourself at 7. If you think things are somewhere between these two, place yourself at 2, 3, 4, 5, or 6.

	White	Black	Other	Total
People are good	15.6%	12.1%	12.6%	14.9%
2	21.7	16.7	16.5	20.6
3	20.3	15.7	18.4	19.5
4	25.0	28.3	28.2	25.7
5	8.0	11.6	10.7	6.4
6	4.0	4.0	3.9	4.0
People are evil	5.0	11.6	10.7	6.4
Don't know	0.4	–	–	0.3
(N)	**1130**	**198**	**103**	**1431**

Source: General Social Survey, 1998.

H. Crime and Delinquency

H1. ARREST RATES FOR ADULTS

Significant differences in rates of criminal and delinquent behaviors appear between racial and ethnic groups. For example, Blacks constitute 13 percent of the population, yet in 1996 they accounted for 35 percent of the persons arrested for serious crimes including murder, rape, robbery, assault, burglary, larceny, motor theft, and arson (see H1.1). Also, Native Americans comprise about 0.6 percent of the general population, yet they accounted for 1.3 percent of those arrested in 1996. On the other hand, Asians are three percent of the population and are underrepresented (one percent) among those arrested. Arrest rates for the different racial and ethnic groups for both serious and non-serious crimes as well as for delinquent activities among those under 18 years of age and among those living in urban, suburban, and rural areas are presented in H1.1 through H1.8.

There are several explanations for these differences in arrest rates which should be considered as the statistics in this section are reviewed. Minority spokespeople argue that prejudice leads citizens to report more minority individuals to the police as potential offenders, and that police officers watch minorities more closely. Recently, the practice of profiling by police and other law enforcement agencies has come under attack as unconstitutional, as police officers have targeted minorities for greater attention, especially along drug trafficking routes. Such practices probably result in higher arrest rates among members of minority groups.

A second possible explanation for these differences between racial and ethnic groups' arrest rates is the intertwining of race and ethnicity with social class. Minorities are overrepresented in the lower classes (see Section C, Economics and Employment) who have higher rates of street offenses. Thus, some of the differences in arrest rates between racial groups may be partially the consequence of poverty.

A third explanation for these racial and ethnic differences in deviant behavior are some differences in family structure and processes. Many of these family differences are reported in Section E, Family. For example, 67 percent of Black children are born to single mothers as compared with 20 percent of White children. These family differences may contribute to differences in arrest rates; youth with greater parental supervision (two parents) will participate in fewer delinquent acts than children of single parents.

A final explanation is that the type of crimes about which statistics are kept and reported disregard criminal behavior of the majority. Most studies and statistical collection efforts focus on serious crimes which tend to be street crimes such as murder, rape, robbery, and so on. White-collar crimes such as tax evasion, stock market fraud, and embezzlement are considered non-serious crimes and are given less attention. These criminal activities are committed more often by individuals in the middle and upper classes since they have more access to tax evasion schemes, stock offerings, and corporate positions from which to embezzle. Driving under the influence of alcohol is defined as a non-serious crime. Whites comprise 67 percent of the population but accounted for 87 percent of the driving-under-the-influence (DUI) arrests in 1996 (see H1.1, H1.2, and H1.3).

These alternative explanations suggest that differences in arrest rates between different racial and ethnic groups may not be entirely the consequence of unique characteristics of the groups, but rather may be partly caused by conditions and forces external to the group.

H2. ARREST RATES FOR JUVENILES

The rates of delinquent behavior by those under 18 years of age by race and ethnicity for 1997 are reported in H2.2. As can be seen, White youth are underrepresented in every type of criminal activity with the exception of burglary, larceny-theft, and arson. On the other hand, Black youth are overrepresented in every category except arson, larceny-theft, and burglary. Blacks comprise 26.5 percent of the population under 18 years and account for 44.2 percent of the violent crime arrests and 26.6 percent of property crime arrests. Native Americans and Asians constitute only a small percentages of the under 18-years population and their rates of delinquent activities tend to be close to their proportion of the general population. Native American youth are arrested more often for liquor law violations than other groups and Asian youth are significantly overrepresented in running away from home (H2.3 to H2.5). The differences in self-reported delinquency between racial and ethnic groups are significantly smaller than those reported in arrest records (see H2.6, H2.7, and H2.8).

H3. INCARCERATION AND SENTENCE

Minority populations are convicted more often than Whites and are given longer sentences. Members of racial and ethnic groups are significantly overrepresented in the prison and jail populations in the United States. As can be seen in H3.2, Blacks represented 43 percent of jail inmates in 1996 although they comprised only 13 percent of the population. Blacks also are greatly overrepresented on death row in American society (see H3.3).

H4. VICTIMS OF CRIMES

The Justice Department regularly surveys a sample of the public about the frequency of being the victim of a crime. The rates per 1,000 individuals in 1996 are presented in H4.1. Blacks clearly have a much higher rate of being victimized for crimes of violence. Whites are at about the national average and "Other" minorities are victims of violent crimes less often. The same pattern appears for property crimes with the exception that "Other" minorities have a rate a little higher than Whites (H4.2). The differences in students reporting they were victims of crimes while in school in 1995 are rather modest (H4.3). Black students have the highest rates, followed by Whites and then "Others." The homicide victimization rate among Black men is appallingly high

(H4.4). As shown in H4.6, in 1995, the rate for Black men per one thousand population was 56.3, as compared with 7.8 for White men.

H5. HATE CRIMES

Hate crimes are motivated by the offender's bias against the victim's race, ethnic group, religion, disability, national origin, or sexual orientation. The numbers of hate crimes by the type of bias reported in 1996 are presented in H5.1. The FBI obtained information about nearly 9,000 incidents, involving nearly 11,000 offenses and more than 11,000 victims. Blacks comprise 13 percent of the population, yet they were the victims in 20 percent of the hate crimes in 1996. The states that reported the incidences of hate crimes and the number that occurred in each state during 1996 are identified in H5.2.

H5.3 presents similar information for 1997. Sixty percent of hate crimes are directed at members of racial groups, followed by attacks against members of various religions (15 percent), against persons with different sexual orientations (14 percent), and against members of ethnic groups (11 percent). (See H5.4.) The types of offenses that are committed as hate crimes are presented in H5.5. Acts of intimidation occurred most often in 1997 followed by acts of vandalism and assault.

H6. ATTITUDES TOWARD CRIME AND POLICE

As can be seen in H6.1 and H6.4, in 1998, Whites were the most comfortable with their home environment during the evening. Forty percent of Whites reported they were afraid to walk alone in their neighborhood as compared with 47 percent of Blacks and 48 percent of "Other" minorities. More Whites than members of "Other" groups are supportive of police officers using force in the performance of their duties (see H6.2). For example, more than 70 percent of Whites approved of a policeman striking an adult male citizen while only 48 percent of Blacks and 46 percent of "Other" minorities approved of this police behavior. Finally, Whites are less likely to report that the courts are "too harsh" on criminals as compared with Blacks and "Other" minorities (see H6.3).

H1. ARREST RATES FOR ADULTS

H1.1. Persons Arrested, by Charge and Race: 1996

[Represents arrests (not charges).]

OFFENSE CHARGED	TOTAL ARRESTS (1,000)					PERCENT DISTRIBUTION				
	Total	White	Black	American Indian or Alaskan Native	Asian or Pacific Islander	Total	White	Black	American Indian or Alaskan Native	Asian or Pacific Islander
Total	11,392.5	7,637.0	3,479.2	144.2	132.2	100.0	67.0	30.5	1.3	1.2
Serious crimes \1	2,109.9	1,311.4	740.7	24.2	33.6	100.0	62.2	35.1	1.1	1.6
Murder and nonnegligent manslaughter	14.7	6.3	8.0	0.2	0.2	100.0	43.0	54.4	1.1	1.5
Forcible rape	24.9	14.0	10.4	0.3	0.3	100.0	56.2	41.5	1.1	1.2
Robbery	124.3	49.4	72.4	0.7	1.8	100.0	39.7	58.3	0.5	1.5
Aggravated assault	395.1	235.9	150.2	4.0	5.0	100.0	59.7	38.0	1.0	1.3
Burglary	271.9	185.3	80.3	2.9	3.5	100.0	68.1	29.5	1.1	1.3
Larceny/theft	1,130.0	734.0	361.7	14.4	19.9	100.0	65.0	32.0	1.3	1.8
Motor vehicle theft	134.7	76.0	54.4	1.6	2.7	100.0	56.4	40.4	1.2	2.0
Arson	14.1	10.5	3.4	0.1	0.1	100.0	74.0	24.0	0.9	1.0
All other nonserious crimes:	9,282.6	6,325.6	2,738.5	120.0	98.6	100.0	68.1	29.5	1.3	1.1
Other assaults	1,001.7	626.0	350.8	13.4	11.5	100.0	62.5	35.0	1.3	1.1
Forgery and counterfeiting	91.5	58.9	30.4	0.7	1.6	100.0	64.3	33.2	0.8	1.7
Fraud	330.7	211.8	114.8	1.6	2.6	100.0	64.0	34.7	0.5	0.8
Embezzlement	11.7	7.5	4.0	0.1	0.2	100.0	63.7	34.3	0.5	1.5
Stolen property—buying, receiving, possessing	116.8	67.8	46.6	0.9	1.5	100.0	58.1	39.9	0.8	1.3
Vandalism	244.0	179.0	58.7	3.3	2.9	100.0	73.4	24.1	1.4	1.2
Weapons; carrying, possessing, etc	164.4	95.5	65.7	1.2	1.9	100.0	58.1	40.0	0.7	1.2
Prostitution and commercialized vice	83.4	49.1	32.0	0.5	1.8	100.0	58.9	38.3	0.6	2.1
Sex offenses (except forcible rape and prostitution)	73.6	54.7	17.2	0.8	0.9	100.0	74.3	23.3	1.1	1.3
Drug abuse violations	1,160.7	701.9	445.8	5.7	7.3	100.0	60.5	38.4	0.5	0.6
Gambling	17.2	7.9	8.7	0.1	0.6	100.0	45.6	50.4	0.4	3.6
Offenses against family and children	106.8	70.8	33.0	1.3	1.7	100.0	66.2	30.9	1.2	1.6
Driving under the influence	1,050.2	911.5	107.1	17.9	13.7	100.0	86.8	10.2	1.7	1.3
Liquor Laws	499.0	403.8	79.2	12.6	3.4	100.0	80.9	15.9	2.5	0.7
Drunkenness	525.4	426.3	84.6	12.5	2.0	100.0	81.1	16.1	2.4	0.4
Disorderly conduct	641.2	401.6	227.1	8.2	4.2	100.0	62.6	35.4	1.3	0.7
Vagrancy	22.7	12.3	9.9	0.4	0.1	100.0	54.2	43.5	1.9	0.4
All other offenses (except traffic)	2,848.6	1,818.6	962.0	35.5	32.5	100.0	63.8	33.8	1.2	1.1
Suspicion	4.9	3.3	1.5	0.1	0.0	100.0	67.8	30.6	1.1	0.5
Curfew and loitering law violations	142.7	103.6	34.9	1.7	2.5	100.0	72.6	24.5	1.2	1.7
Runaways	145.6	113.9	24.4	1.7	5.7	100.0	78.2	16.7	1.2	3.9

Notes:
\1 Includes arson.

Source: U.S. Federal Bureau of Investigation, Crime in the United States, annual.

H1.2. Total Arrests, Distribution by Race: 1997

[9,271 agencies; 1997 estimated population 183,239,000.]

Offense Charged	Total Arrests					Percent Distribution \1				
	Total	White	Black	American Indian or Alaskan Native	Asian or Pacific Islander	Total	White	Black	American Indian or Alaskan Native	Asian or Pacific Islander
TOTAL	10,516,707	7,061,803	3,201,014	132,734	121,156	100	67.1	30.4	1.3	1.2
Murder and nonnegligent manslaughter	12,759	5,345	7,194	94	126	100	41.9	56.4	0.7	1
Forcible rape	22,115	12,867	8,788	237	223	100	58.2	39.7	1.1	1
Robbery	93,979	38,679	53,657	551	1,092	100	41.2	57.1	0.6	1.2
Aggravated Assault	371,768	227,632	136,184	3,809	4,143	100	61.2	36.6	1	0.7
Burglary	245,564	167,100	72,780	2,569	3,115	100	68	29.6	1	1.1
Larceny-theft	1,032,467	667,528	334,046	12,854	18,039	100	64.7	32.4	1.2	1.3
Motor vehicle theft	115,948	67,316	45,203	1,328	2,101	100	58.1	39	1.1	1.8
Arson	13,814	10,114	3,440	108	152	100	73.2	24.9	0.8	1.1
Violent Crime	500,621	284,523	205,823	4,691	5,584	100	56.8	41.1	0.9	1.1
Property Crime	1,407,793	912,058	455,469	16,859	23,407	100	64.8	32.4	1.2	1.7
Crime Index total	1,908,414	1,196,581	661,292	21,550	28,991	100	62.7	34.7	1.1	1.5
Other assaults	963,907	603,008	338,688	12,227	9,984	100	62.6	35.1	1.3	1
Forgery and counterfeiting	82,981	54,738	26,736	485	1,022	100	66	32.2	0.6	1.2
Fraud	274,513	186,880	84,278	1,464	1,891	100	68.1	30.7	0.5	0.7
Embezzlement	12,253	7,742	4,263	61	187	100	63.2	34.8	0.5	1.5
Stolen property; buying receiving, possessing	108,435	61,740	44,596	886	1,213	100	56.9	41.1	0.8	1.1
Vandalism	219,287	160,150	54,119	2,765	2,253	100	73	24.7	1.3	1
Weapons; carrying, possessing, etc	152,251	89,305	60,332	1,073	1,541	100	58.7	39.6	0.7	1
Prostitution and commercialized vice	72,346	41,884	29,199	369	894	100	57.9	40.4	0.5	1.2
Sex offenses (except forcible rape and prostitution)	70,153	51,888	16,552	837	876	100	74	23.6	1.2	1.2
Drug abuse violations	1,101,302	682,568	404,903	6,006	7,825	100	62	36.8	0.5	0.7
Gambling	11,064	3,198	7,420	55	391	100	28.9	67.1	0.5	3.5
Offenses against family and children	104,665	69,119	32,575	1,020	1,951	100	66	31.1	1	1.9
Driving under the influence	971,795	838,693	105,929	14,713	12,460	100	86.3	10.9	1.5	1.3
Liquor laws	430,605	359,721	53,798	13,219	3,867	100	83.5	12.5	3.1	0.9
Drunkenness	508,603	408,537	86,208	11,743	2,115	100	80.3	16.9	2.3	0.4
Disorderly conduct	561,017	348,186	201,169	7,772	3,890	100	62.1	35.9	1.4	0.7
Vagrancy	20,323	10,463	9,418	385	57	100	51.5	46.3	1.9	0.3
All other offenses (except traffic)	2,673,876	1,683,519	924,327	32,863	33,167	100	63	34.6	1.2	1.2
Suspicion	4,408	2,821	1,493	67	27	100	64	33.9	1.5	0.6
Curfew and loitering law violations	128,183	95,829	28,998	1,642	1,714	100	74.8	22.6	1.3	1.3
Runaways	136,326	105,233	24,721	1,532	4,840	100	77.2	18.1	1.1	3.6

Notes:
1 Because of rounding, the percentages may not add to total.

Source: Uniform Crime Reports for the United States, 1997.

H1.3. Arrests, Distribution for Those 18 and Over, by Race: 1997

Offense Charged	Total Arrests					Percent Distribution \1				
	Total	White	Black	American Indian or Alaskan Native	Asian or Pacific Islander	Total	White	Black	American Indian or Alaskan Native	Asian or Pacific Islander
TOTAL	8,549,972	5,673,811	2,680,597	108,141	87,423	100	66.4	31.4	1.3	1
Murder and nonnegligent manslaughter	11,028	4,648	6,197	86	97	100	42.1	56.2	0.8	0.9
Forcible rape	18,324	10,738	7,185	207	194	100	58.6	39.2	1.1	1.1
Robbery	65,928	26,844	38,128	378	578	100	40.7	57.8	0.6	0.9
Aggravated Assault	318,974	196,147	116,117	3,303	3,407	100	61.5	36.4	1	1.1
Burglary	155,218	101,233	50,888	1,474	1,623	100	65.2	32.8	0.9	1
Larceny-theft	686,274	423,794	244,522	7,897	10,061	100	61.8	35.6	1.2	1.5
Motor vehicle theft	69,725	39,968	27,922	616	1,219	100	57.3	40	0.9	1.7
Arson	6,907	4,659	2,111	61	76	100	67.5	30.6	0.9	1.1
Violent Crime	414,254	238,377	167,627	3,974	4,276	100	57.5	40.5	1	1
Property Crime	918,124	569,654	325,443	10,048	12,979	100	62	35.4	1.1	1.4
Crime Index total	1,332,124	808,031	493,070	14,022	17,255	100	60.6	37	1.1	1.3
Other assaults	796,890	497,613	281,171	10,303	7,803	100	62.4	35.3	1.3	1
Forgery and counterfeiting	77,108	50,188	25,558	440	922	100	65.1	33.1	0.6	1.2
Fraud	266,933	181,624	82,116	1,408	1,785	100	68	30.8	0.5	0.7
Embezzlement	11,299	7,141	3,934	55	169	100	63.2	34.8	0.5	1.5
Stolen property; buying receiving, possessing	80,873	45,183	34,354	567	769	100	55.9	42.5	0.7	1
Vandalism	125,299	84,814	37,711	1,689	1,085	100	67.7	30.1	1.3	0.9
Weapons; carrying, possessing, etc	115,935	65,898	48,287	755	995	100	56.8	41.7	0.7	0.9
Prostitution and commercialized vice	71,354	41,290	28,817	360	887	100	57.9	40.4	0.5	1.2
Sex offenses (except forcible rape and prostitution)	57,393	42,902	13,003	734	754	100	74.8	22.7	1.3	1.3
Drug abuse violations	947,899	583,913	352,708	4,878	6,400	100	61.6	37.2	0.5	0.7
Gambling	9,238	3,016	5,793	53	376	100	32.6	62.7	0.6	4.1
Offenses against family and children	97,859	63,922	31,184	965	1,788	100	65.3	31.9	1	1.8
Driving under the influence	958,815	826,867	105,171	14,482	12,295	100	86.2	11	1.5	1.3
Liquor laws	323,304	262,776	48,050	9,720	2,758	100	81.3	14.9	3	0.9
Drunkenness	491,929	393,730	84,736	11,454	2,009	100	80	17.2	2.3	0.4
Disorderly conduct	412,176	253,335	149,949	6,371	2,521	100	61.5	36.4	1.5	0.6
Vagrancy	18,115	8,969	8,728	370	48	100	49.5	48.2	2	0.3
All other offenses (except traffic)	2,351,883	1,450,445	845,204	29,450	26,784	100	61.7	35.9	1.3	1.1
Suspicion	3,292	2,154	1,053	65	20	100	65.4	32	2	0.6
Curfew and loitering law violations	0	0	0	0	0	0	0	0	0	0
Runaways	0	0	0	0	0	0	0	0	0	0

Notes:
1 Because of rounding, the percentages may not add to total.

Source: Uniform Crime Reports for the United States, 1997.

H1.4. City Arrests, Distribution by Race: 1997

[6,626 agencies; 1997 estimated population 136,263,000.]

Offense Charged	Total Arrests					Percent Distribution \1				
	Total	White	Black	American Indian or Alaskan Native	Asian or Pacific Islander	Total	White	Black	American Indian or Alaskan Native	Asian or Pacific Islander
TOTAL	8,070,225	5,200,103	2,675,786	99,128	95,208	100	64.4	33.2	1.2	1.2
Murder and nonnegligent manslaughter	9,868	3,550	6,168	48	102	100	36	62.5	0.5	1
Forcible rape	16,384	8,752	7,311	140	181	100	53.4	44.6	0.9	1.1
Robbery	80,813	32, 415	47,023	420	955	100	40.1	58.2	0.5	1.2
Aggravated Assault	287,088	166,217	114,959	2,392	3,520	100	57.9	40	0.8	1.2
Burglary	178,828	114,377	60,487	1,564	2,400	100	64	33.8	0.9	1.3
Larceny-theft	874,077	558,848	288,400	11,465	15,364	100	63.9	33	1.3	1.8
Motor vehicle theft	91,669	49,826	39,145	942	1,756	100	54.4	42.7	1	1.9
Arson	10,647	7,474	2,978	72	123	100	70.2	28	0.7	1.2
Violent Crime	394,153	210,934	175,461	3,000	4,758	100	53.5	44.5	0.8	1.2
Property Crime	1,155,221	730,525	391,010	14,043	19,643	100	63.2	33.8	1.2	1.7
Crime Index total	1,549,374	941,459	566,471	17,043	24,401	100	60.8	36.6	1.1	1.6
Other assaults	744,574	46,415	287,638	9,010	7,920	100	59.1	38.6	1.2	1.1
Forgery and counterfeiting	63,067	40,595	21,278	350	844	100	64.4	33.7	0.6	1.3
Fraud	142,976	94,397	46,406	759	1,414	100	66	32.5	0.5	1
Embezzlement	9,376	5,674	3,508	50	144	100	60.5	37.4	0.5	1.5
Stolen property; buying receiving, possessing	86,981	46,415	38,876	635	1,055	100	53.4	44.7	0.7	1.2
Vandalism	174,604	122,708	47,891	2,129	1,876	100	70.3	27.4	1.2	1.1
Weapons; carrying, possessing, etc.	122,779	68,220	52,602	709	1,248	100	55.6	42.8	0.6	1
Prostitution and commercialized vice	69,363	39,734	28,463	349	817	100	57.3	41	0.5	1.2
Sex offenses (except forcible rape and prostitution)	52,452	37,092	14,105	549	706	100	70.7	26.9	1	1.3
Drug abuse violations	865,340	504,162	350,886	4,042	6,250	100	58.3	40.5	0.5	0.7
Gambling	9,649	2,398	6,983	41	227	100	24.9	72.4	0.4	2.4
Offenses against family and children	61,250	39,505	19,298	704	1,743	100	64.5	31.5	1.1	2.8
Driving under the influence	594,083	510,198	68,729	8,723	6,433	100	85.9	11.6	1.5	1.1
Liquor laws	341,858	279,639	47,815	11,297	3,107	100	81.8	14	3.3	0.9
Drunkenness	423,328	334, 113	77,403	10,075	1,737	100	78.9	18.3	2.4	0.4
Disorderly conduct	493,405	297,389	186,275	6,325	3,416	100	60.3	37.8	1.3	0.7
Vagrancy	18,647	9,284	8,932	378	53	100	49.8	47.9	2	0.3
All other offenses (except traffic)	2,018,636	1,217,254	751,664	23,426	26,292	100	60.3	37.2	1.2	1.3
Suspicion	3,614	2,236	1,348	8	22	100	61.9	37.3	0.2	0.6
Curfew and loitering law violations	120,313	89,592	27,913	1,357	1,451	100	74.5	23.2	1.1	1.2
Runaways	104,556	78,033	21,302	1,169	4,052	100	74.6	20.4	1.1	3.9

Notes:
1 Because of rounding, the percentages may not add to total.

Source: Uniform Crime Reports for the United States, 1997

H1.5. City Arrests, Distribution for Those 18 and Older, by Race: 1997

Offense Charged	Total Arrests					Percent Distribution \1				
	Total	White	Black	American Indian or Alaskan Native	Asian or Pacific Islander	Total	White	Black	American Indian or Alaskan Native	Asian or Pacific Islander
TOTAL	6,440,939	4,076,139	2,218,186	79,906	66,708	100	63.3	34.4	1.2	1
Murder and nonnegligent manslaughter	8,427	3,010	5,292	45	80	100	35.7	62.8	0.5	0.9
Forcible rape	13,428	7,236	5,912	122	158	100	53.9	44	0.9	1.2
Robbery	56,196	22,178	33,249	284	485	100	39.5	59.2	0.5	0.9
Aggravated Assault	244,930	142,023	97,960	2,061	2,886	100	58	40	0.8	1.2
Burglary	112,767	68,462	42,187	847	1,271	100	60.7	37.4	0.8	1.1
Larceny-theft	573,492	347,853	210,153	6,972	8,514	100	60.7	36.6	1.2	1.5
Motor vehicle theft	54,293	28,957	23,919	387	1,030	100	53.3	44.1	0.7	1.9
Arson	5,157	3,218	1,833	40	66	100	62.4	35.5	0.8	1.3
Violent Crime	322,981	174,447	142,413	2,512	3,609	100	54	44.1	0.8	1.1
Property Crime	745,709	448,490	278,092	8,246	10,881	100	60.1	37.3	1.1	1.5
Crime Index total	1,068,690	622,937	420,505	10,758	14,490	100	58.3	39.3	1	1.4
Other assaults	611,412	358,351	287,638	9,010	6,114	100	58.6	39.1	1.3	1
Forgery and counterfeiting	58,271	36,909	20,280	316	766	100	63.3	34.8	0.5	1.3
Fraud	137,377	90,492	44,846	712	1,327	100	65.9	32.6	0.5	1
Embezzlement	8,555	5,167	3,216	45	127	100	60.4	37.6	0.5	1.5
Stolen property; buying receiving, possessing	63,990	33,235	29,689	388	678	100	51.9	46.4	0.6	1.1
Vandalism	99,488	63,859	33,427	1,316	886	100	64.2	33.6	1.3	0.9
Weapons; carrying, possessing, etc	92,205	48,898	42,058	462	787	100	53	45.6	0.5	0.9
Prostitution and commercialized vice	68,431	39,189	28,091	340	811	100	57.3	41.1	0.5	1.2
Sex offenses (except forcible rape and prostitution)	43,079	30,827	11,149	493	610	100	71.6	25.9	1.1	1.4
Drug abuse violations	737,441	425,376	303,635	3,223	5,207	100	57.7	41.2	0.4	0.7
Gambling	7,901	2,254	5,393	39	215	100	28.5	68.3	0.5	2.7
Offenses against family and children	55,990	35,610	18,110	662	1,608	100	63.6	32.3	1.2	2.9
Driving under the influence	585,442	502,373	68,157	8,567	6,345	100	85.8	11.6	1.5	1.1
Liquor laws	261,394	207,858	42,830	8,483	2,223	100	79.5	16.4	3.2	0.9
Drunkenness	408,978	321,442	76,064	9,831	1,641	100	78.6	18.6	2.4	0.4
Disorderly conduct	360,594	213,516	139,633	5,276	2,169	100	59.2	38.7	1.5	0.6
Vagrancy	16,742	8,048	8,284	366	44	100	48.1	49.5	2.2	0.3
All other offenses (except traffic)	1,752,302	1,028,088	682,612	20,957	20,645	100	58.7	39	1.2	1.2
Suspicion	2,657	1,710	925	7	15	100	64.4	34.8	0.3	0.6
Curfew and loitering law violations	0	0	0	0	0	0	0	0	0	0
Runaways	0	0	0	0	0	0	0	0	0	0

Notes:
1 Because of rounding, the percentages may not add to total.

Source: Uniform Crime Reports for the United States, 1997

H1.6. Suburban County Arrests, Distribution by Race: 1997

[881 agencies; 1997 estimated population 37,263,000].

Offense Charged	Total Arrests					Percent Distribution \1				
	Total	White	Black	American Indian or Alaskan Native	Asian or Pacific Islander	Total	White	Black	American Indian or Alaskan Native	Asian or Pacific Islander
TOTAL	1,591,904	1,181,134	392,355	9,206	9,209	100	74.2	24.6	0.6	0.6
Murder and nonnegligent manslaughter	1,939	1,210	705	10	14	100	62.4	36.4	0.5	0.7
Forcible rape	3,584	2,498	1,038	28	20	100	69.7	29	0.8	0.6
Robbery	10,644	5,034	5,484	60	66	100	47.3	51.5	0.6	0.6
Aggravated Assault	59,845	43,784	15,179	440	442	100	73.2	25.4	0.7	0.7
Burglary	41,593	32,552	8,558	200	283	100	78.3	20.6	0.5	0.7
Larceny-theft	117,279	76,678	38,785	575	1,241	100	65.4	33.1	0.5	1.1
Motor vehicle theft	17,528	12,035	5,265	77	151	100	68.7	30	0.4	0.9
Arson	2,053	1,700	333	2	18	100	82.8	16.2	0.1	0.9
Violent Crime	76,012	52,526	22,406	538	542	100	69.1	29.5	0.7	0.7
Property Crime	178,453	122,965	52,941	854	1,693	100	68.9	29.7	0.5	0.9
Crime Index total	254,465	175,491	75,347	1,392	2,235	100	69	29.6	0.5	0.9
Other assaults	139,672	102,107	35,923	854	788	100	73.1	25.7	0.6	0.6
Forgery and counterfeiting	13,842	9,539	4,179	32	92	100	68.9	30.2	0.2	0.7
Fraud	81,151	54,646	25,984	273	248	100	67.3	32	0.3	0.3
Embezzlement	2,029	1,372	635	3	19	100	67.6	31.3	0.1	0.9
Stolen property; buying receiving, possessing	15,221	10,518	4,467	110	126	100	69.1	29.3	0.7	0.8
Vandalism	28,353	23,636	4,387	165	165	100	83.4	15.5	0.6	0.6
Weapons; carrying, possessing, etc	20,238	14,025	5,965	84	164	100	69.3	29.5	0.4	0.8
Prostitution and commercialized vice	2,811	2,019	714	19	59	100	71.8	25.4	0.7	2.1
Sex offenses (except forcible rape and prostitution)	11,848	9,814	1,879	74	81	100	82.8	15.9	0.6	0.7
Drug abuse violations	165,027	122,351	41,386	664	626	100	74.1	25.1	0.4	0.4
Gambling	968	631	319	6	12	100	65.2	33	0.6	1.2
Offenses against family and children	31,693	20,392	11,159	80	62	100	64.3	35.2	0.3	0.2
Driving under the influence	217,587	195,598	19,547	1,128	1,314	100	89.9	9	0.5	0.6
Liquor laws	48,531	43,241	4,475	454	361	100	89.1	9.2	0.9	0.7
Drunkenness	52,866	45,942	6,160	459	305	100	86.9	11.7	0.9	0.6
Disorderly conduct	40,838	29,611	10,591	395	241	100	72.5	25.9	1	0.6
Vagrancy	1,189	825	358	3	3	100	69.4	30.1	0.3	0.3
All other offenses (except traffic)	434,570	294,763	134,959	2,752	2,096	100	67.8	31.1	0.6	0.5
Suspicion	361	247	53	56	5	100	68.4	14.7	15.5	1.4
Curfew and loitering law violations	6,006	4,964	959	30	53	100	82.7	16	0.5	0.9
Runaways	22,638	19,402	2,909	173	154	100	85.7	12.9	0.8	0.7

Notes:
1 Because of rounding, the percentages may not add to total.

Soutce: Uniform Crime Reports for the United States, 1997

H1.7. Suburban County Arrests for Those 18 and Older, Distribution by Race: 1997

Offense Charged	Total Arrests					Percent Distribution \1				
	Total	White	Black	American Indian or Alaskan Native	Asian or Pacific Islander	Total	White	Black	American Indian or Alaskan Native	Asian or Pacific Islander
TOTAL	1,360,513	1,004,836	340,937	7,609	7,131	100	73.9	25.1	0.6	0.5
Murder and nonnegligent manslaughter	1,717	1,085	617	6	9	100	63.2	35.9	0.3	0.5
Forcible rape	3,036	2,112	885	22	17	100	69.6	29.2	0.7	0.6
Robbery	7,723	3,696	3,944	42	41	100	47.9	51.1	0.5	0.5
Aggravated Assault	52,042	38,483	12,805	389	365	100	73.9	24.6	0.7	0.7
Burglary	26,274	20,101	5,904	127	142	100	76.5	22.5	0.5	0.5
Larceny-theft	83,183	53,401	28,646	380	756	100	64.2	34.4	0.5	0.9
Motor vehicle theft	11,304	7,774	3,410	46	74	100	68.8	30.2	0.4	0.7
Arson	1,034	850	177	2	5	100	82.2	17.1	0.2	0.5
Violent Crime	64, 518	45,376	18,251	459	432	100	70.3	28.3	0.7	0.7
Property Crime	121,795	82,126	38,137	555	977	100	67.4	31.3	0.5	0.8
Crime Index total	186,313	127,502	56,388	1,014	1,409	100	68.4	30.3	0.5	0.8
Other assaults	115,176	85,216	28,683	665	612	100	74	24.9	0.6	0.5
Forgery and counterfeiting	13,155	9,013	4,031	29	82	100	68.5	30.6	0.2	0.6
Fraud	79,792	53,797	25,491	270	234	100	67.4	31.9	0.3	0.3
Embezzlement	1,923	1,301	602	2	18	100	67.7	31.3	0.1	0.9
Stolen property; buying receiving, possessing	11,908	8,161	3,599	70	78	100	68.5	30.2	0.6	0.7
Vandalism	16,073	13,066	2,822	100	85	100	81.3	17.6	0.6	0.5
Weapons; carrying, possessing, etc	15,804	10,938	4,693	68	105	100	69.2	29.7	0.4	0.7
Prostitution and commercialized vice	2,763	1,980	705	19	49	100	71.7	25.5	0.7	2.1
Sex offenses (except forcible rape and prostitution)	9,630	8,083	1,411	64	72	100	83.9	14.7	0.7	0.7
Drug abuse violations	146,571	108,173	37,317	568	513	100	73.8	25.5	0.4	0.4
Gambling	903	598	288	6	11	100	66.2	31.9	0.7	1.2
Offenses against family and children	30,900	19,708	11,057	75	60	100	63.8	35.8	0.2	0.2
Driving under the influence	215,508	193,636	19,451	1,117	1,304	100	89.9	9	0.5	0.6
Liquor laws	33,834	29,419	3,855	314	246	100	87	11.4	0.9	0.7
Drunkenness	51,350	44,532	6,071	450	297	100	86.7	11.8	0.9	0.6
Disorderly conduct	30,573	22,912	7,221	274	166	100	74.9	23.6	0.9	0.5
Vagrancy	961	634	322	2	3	100	66	33.5	0.2	0.3
All other offenses (except traffic)	397,064	265,966	126,879	2,447	1,772	100	67	32	0.6	0.4
Suspicion	312	201	51	55	5	100	64.4	16.3	17.6	1.6
Curfew and loitering law violations	0	0	0	0	0	0	0	0	0	0
Runaways	0	0	0	0	0	0	0	0	0	0

Notes:
1 Because of rounding, the percentages may not add to total.

Source: Uniform Crime Reports for the United States, 1997

H1.8. Rural County Arrest Trends, 1996–1997

[1,610 agencies; 1997 estimated population 18,216,000; 1996 estimated population 18,088,000.]

Number of Persons Arrested

Offense Charged	Total all ages			18 years of age and over		
	1996	1997	Percent Change	1996	1997	Percent Change
TOTAL	797,206	808,466	+1.4	697,759	707,905	+1.5
Murder and nonnegligent manslaughter	948	875	-7.7	861	811	-5.8
Forcible rape	1,937	2,013	+3.9	1,674	1734	+3.6
Robbery	2,184	2,342	+7.2	1,727	1,848	+7.0
Aggravated Assault	22,595	23,375	+3.5	20,076	20,702	+3.1
Burglary	24,862	23,681	-4.8	15,277	15,114	-1.1
Larceny-theft	38,033	38,410	+1.0	27,056	27,367	+1.1
Motor vehicle theft	6,378	6,375	\1	3,741	3,867	+3.4
Arson	1,133	1,058	-6.6	690	674	-2.3
Violent Crime	27,664	28,605	+3.4	24,338	25,095	+3.1
Property Crime	70,406	69,524	-1.3	46,764	47,022	+.6
Crime Index total	98,070	98,129	+.1	71,102	72,117	+1.4
Other assaults	70,736	75,799	+7.2	62,104	66,762	+7.5
Forgery and counterfeiting	5,746	5,567	-3.1	5,417	5,204	-3.9
Fraud	50,408	48,309	-4.2	49,664	47,705	-3.9
Embezzlement	771	800	+3.8	747	775	+3.7
Stolen property; buying receiving, possessing	5,964	5,929	-.6	4,792	4,724	-1.4
Vandalism	16,495	15,610	-5.4	9,958	9,296	-6.6
Weapons; carrying, possessing, etc	8,930	8,851	-.9	7,615	7,615	\1
Prostitution and commercialized vice	199	158	-20.6	184	151	-17.9
Sex offenses (except forcible rape and prostitution)	5,542	5,522	-.4	4,399	4,420	+.5
Drug abuse violations	61,944	66,351	+7.1	55,644	59,693	+7.3
Gambling	332	437	+31.6	317	424	+33.8
Offenses against family and children	10,485	10,354	-1.2	9,976	9,702	-2.7
Driving under the influence	162,080	157,667	-2.7	159,979	155,473	-2.8
Liquor laws	36,829	37,874	+2.8	26,092	26,503	+1.6
Drunkenness	30,011	29,661	-1.2	29,343	28,950	-1.3
Disorderly conduct	24,701	24,908	+.8	19,921	19,450	-2.4
Vagrancy	372	442	+18.8	266	370	+39.1
All other offenses (except traffic)	196,644	205,667	+4.6	180,239	188,571	+4.6
Suspicion	229	249	+8.7	190	160	-15.8
Curfew and loitering law violations	1,828	1,694	-7.3	0	0	0
Runaways	9,119	8,737	-4.2	0	0	0

Source: Uniform Crime Reports for the United States, 1997

H2. ARREST RATES FOR JUVENILES

H2.1. Delinquency Cases and Case Rates, by Sex and Race: 1986 to 1995

SEX, RACE, AND OFFENSE	NUMBER OF CASES			CASE RATE \1		
	1986	**1991**	**1995**	**1986**	**1991**	**1995**
Male, total	955,900	1,146,900	1,338,600	71.9	85.8	92.4
Person	152,900	221,700	285,400	11.5	16.6	19.7
Property	580,100	686,900	676,300	43.6	51.4	46.7
Drugs	60,000	57,200	137,000	4.5	4.3	9.5
Public order	163,000	181,100	239,900	12.3	13.5	16.6
Female, total	224,100	266,300	375,800	17.7	21.0	27.3
Person	37,400	55,900	91,900	3.0	4.4	6.7
Property	129,900	159,800	195,400	10.3	12.6	14.2
Drugs	12,400	7,900	22,200	1.0	0.6	1.6
Public order	44,400	42,700	66,300	3.5	3.4	4.8
White, total	844,300	927,900	1,127,800	40.0	44.4	50.0
Person	109,900	156,700	219,600	5.2	7.5	9.7
Property	524,400	594,600	609,500	24.9	28.4	27.0
Drugs	53,700	32,100	102,100	2.5	1.5	4.5
Public order	156,300	144,600	196,600	7.4	6.9	8.7
Black, total	304,700	439,300	522,900	79.3	112.0	123.7
Person	76,000	112,400	145,000	19.8	28.7	34.3
Property	165,700	223,100	224,900	43.2	56.9	53.2
Drugs	17,100	31,600	53,500	4.4	8.1	12.7
Public order	46,000	72,300	99,600	12.0	18.4	23.6
Other races, total	31,000	46,000	63,600	30.7	37.2	44.0
Person	4,400	8,500	12,700	4.4	6.9	8.8
Property	19,900	29,100	37,300	19.7	23.6	25.8
Drugs	1,600	1,400	3,500	1.6	1.1	2.4
Public order	5,100	7,000	10,100	5.0	5.7	7.0

Notes:
\1 Cases per 1,000 youth at risk.

Source: National Center for Juvenile Justice, Pittsburgh, PA, Juvenile Court Statistics, annual.

H2.2. Total Arrests of Those Under 18, Distribution by Race: 1997

Offense Charged	Total Arrests					Percent Distribution \1				
	Total	White	Black	American Indian or Alaskan Native	Asian or Pacific Islander	Total	White	Black	American Indian or Alaskan Native	Asian or Pacific Islander
TOTAL	1,966,735	1,387,992	520,417	24,593	33,733	100	70.6	26.5	1.3	1.7
Murder and nonnegligent manslaughter	1,731	697	997	8	29	100	40.3	57.6	0.5	1.7
Forcible rape	3,791	2,129	1,603	30	29	100	56.2	42.3	0.8	0.8
Robbery	28,051	11,835	15,529	173	514	100	42.2	55.4	0.6	1.8
Aggravated Assault	52,794	31,485	20,067	506	736	100	59.6	38	1	1.4
Burglary	90,346	65,867	21,892	1,095	1,492	100	72.9	24.2	1.2	1.7
Larceny-theft	346,193	243,734	89,524	4,957	7,978	100	70.4	25.9	1.4	2.3
Motor vehicle theft	46,223	27,348	17,281	712	882	100	59.2	37.4	1.5	1.9
Arson	6,907	5,455	1,329	47	76	100	79	19.2	0.7	1.1
Violent Crime	86,367	46,146	38,196	717	1,308	100	53.4	44.2	0.8	1.5
Property Crime	489,669	342,404	130,026	6,811	10,428	100	69.9	26.6	1.4	2.1
Crime Index total	576,036	388,550	168,222	7,528	11,736	100	67.5	29.2	1.3	2
Other assaults	167,017	105,395	57,517	1,924	2,181	100	63.1	34.4	1.2	1.3
Forgery and counterfeiting	5,873	4,550	1,178	45	100	100	77.5	20.1	0.8	1.7
Fraud	7,580	5,265	2,162	56	106	100	69.3	28.5	0.7	1.4
Embezzlement	954	601	329	6	18	100	63	34.5	0.6	1.9
Stolen property; buying receiving, possessing	27,562	16,557	10,242	319	444	100	60.1	37.2	1.2	1.6
Vandalism	93,988	75,336	16,408	1,076	1,168	100	80.2	17.5	1.1	1.2
Weapons; carrying, possessing, etc	36,316	23,407	12,045	318	546	100	64.5	33.2	0.9	1.5
Prostitution and commercialized vice	992	594	382	9	7	100	59.9	38.5	0.9	0.7
Sex offenses (except forcible rape and prostitution)	12,760	986	3,549	103	122	100	70.4	27.8	0.8	1
Drug abuse violations	153,403	98,655	52,195	1,128	1,425	100	64.3	34	0.7	0.9
Gambling	1,826	182	1,627	2	15	100	10	89.1	0.1	0.8
Offenses against family and children	6,806	5,197	1,391	55	163	100	76.4	20.4	0.8	2.4
Driving under the influence	12,980	11,826	758	231	165	100	91.1	5.8	1.8	1.3
Liquor laws	107,301	96,945	5,748	3,499	1,109	100	90.3	5.4	3.3	1
Drunkenness	16,674	14,807	1,472	289	106	100	88.8	8.8	1.7	0.6
Disorderly conduct	148,841	94,851	51,220	1,401	1,369	100	63.7	34.4	0.9	0.9
Vagrancy	2,208	1,494	690	15	9	100	67.7	31.3	0.7	0.4
All other offenses (except traffic)	321,993	233,074	79,123	3,413	6,383	100	72.4	24.6	1.1	2
Suspicion	1,116	667	440	2	7	100	59.8	39.4	0.2	0.6
Curfew and loitering law violations	128,183	95,829	28,998	1,642	1,714	100	74.8	22.6	1.3	1.3
Runaways	136,326	105,233	24,721	1,532	4,840	100	77.2	18.1	1.1	3.6

Notes:
1 Because of rounding, percentages may not add to total.

Source: Uniform Crime Reports for the United States, 1997

H2.3. City Arrests of Those Under 18, Distribution by Race: 1997

Offense Charged	Total Arrests					Percent Distribution \1				
	Total	White	Black	American Indian or Alaskan Native	Asian or Pacific Islander	Total	White	Black	American Indian or Alaskan Native	Asian or Pacific Islander
TOTAL	1,629,286	1,123,964	457,600	19,222	28,500	100	69	28.1	1.2	1.7
Murder and nonnegligent manslaughter	1,441	540	876	3	22	100	37.5	60.8	0.2	1.5
Forcible rape	2,956	1,516	1,399	18	23	100	51.3	47.3	0.6	0.8
Robbery	24,617	10,237	13,774	136	470	100	41.6	56	0.6	1.9
Aggravated Assault	42,158	24,194	16,999	331	634	100	57.4	40.3	0.8	1.5
Burglary	66,061	45,915	18,300	717	1,129	100	69.5	27.7	1.1	1.7
Larceny-theft	300,585	210,995	78,247	4,493	6,850	100	70.2	26	1.5	2.3
Motor vehicle theft	37,376	20,869	15,226	555	726	100	55.8	40.7	1.5	1.9
Arson	5,490	4,256	1,145	32	57	100	77.5	20.9	0.6	1
Violent Crime	71,172	36,487	33,048	488	1,149	100	51.3	46.4	0.7	1.6
Property Crime	409,512	282,035	112,918	5,797	8,762	100	68.9	27.6	1.4	2.1
Crime Index total	480,684	318,522	145,966	6,285	9,911	100	66.3	30.4	1.3	2.1
Other assaults	133,162	81,655	48,356	1,345	1,806	100	61.3	36.3	1	1.4
Forgery and counterfeiting	4,796	3,686	998	34	78	100	76.9	20.8	0.7	1.6
Fraud	5,599	3,905	1,560	47	87	100	69.7	27.9	0.8	1.6
Embezzlement	821	507	292	5	17	100	61.8	35.6	0.6	2.1
Stolen property; buying receiving, possessing	22,991	13,180	9,187	247	377	100	57.3	40	1.1	1.6
Vandalism	75,116	58,849	14,464	813	990	100	78.3	19.3	1.1	1.3
Weapons; carrying, possessing, etc	30,574	19,322	10,544	247	461	100	63.2	34.5	0.8	1.5
Prostitution and commercialized vice	932	545	372	9	6	100	58.5	39.9	1	0.6
Sex offenses (except forcible rape and prostitution)	9,373	6,265	2,956	56	96	100	66.8	31.5	0.6	1
Drug abuse violations	127,899	78,786	47,251	819	1,043	100	61.6	36.9	0.6	0.8
Gambling	1,748	144	1,590	2	12	100	8.2	91	0.1	0.7
Offenses against family and children	5,260	3,895	1,188	42	135	100	74	22.6	0.8	2.6
Driving under the influence	8,641	7,825	572	156	88	100	90.6	6.6	1.8	1
Liquor laws	80,464	71,781	4,985	2,814	884	100	89.2	6.2	3.5	1.1
Drunkenness	14,350	12,671	1,339	244	96	100	88.3	9.3	1.7	0.7
Disorderly conduct	132,811	83,873	46,642	1,049	1,247	100	63.2	35.1	0.8	0.9
Vagrancy	1,905	1,236	648	12	9	100	64.9	34	0.6	0.5
All other offenses (except traffic)	266,334	189,166	69,052	2,469	5,647	100	71	25.9	0.9	2.1
Suspicion	957	526	423	1	7	100	55	44.2	0.1	0.7
Curfew and loitering law violations	120,313	89,592	27,913	1,357	1,451	100	74.5	23.2	1.1	1.2
Runaways	104,556	78,033	21,302	1,169	4,052	100	74.6	20.4	1.1	3.9

Notes:
1 Because of rounding, percentages may not add to total.

Source: Uniform Crime Reports for the United States, 1997

H2.4. Suburban County Arrests for Those 18 and Under, Distribution by Race: 1997

Offense Charged	Total Arrests					Percent Distribution \1				
	Total	White	Black	American Indian or Alaskan Native	Asian or Pacific Islander	Total	White	Black	American Indian or Alaskan Native	Asian or Pacific Islander
TOTAL	231,391	176,298	51,418	1,597	2,078	100	76.2	22.2	0.7	0.9
Murder and nonnegligent manslaughter	222	125	88	4	5	100	56.3	39.6	1.8	2.3
Forcible rape	548	386	153	6	3	100	70.4	27.9	1.1	0.5
Robbery	2,921	1,338	1,540	18	25	100	45.8	52.7	0.6	0.9
Aggravated Assault	7,803	5,301	2,374	51	77	100	67.9	30.4	0.7	1
Burglary	15,319	12,451	2,654	73	141	100	81.3	17.3	0.5	0.9
Larceny-theft	34,096	23,277	10,139	195	485	100	68.3	29.7	0.6	1.4
Motor vehicle theft	6,224	4,261	1,855	31	77	100	68.5	29.8	0.5	1.2
Arson	1,019	850	156	*	13	100	83.4	15.3	*	1.3
Violent Crime	11,494	7,150	4,155	79	110	100	62.2	36.1	0.7	1
Property Crime	56,658	40,839	14,804	299	716	100	72.1	26.1	0.5	1.3
Crime Index total	68,152	47,989	18,959	378	826	100	70.4	27.8	0.6	1.2
Other assaults	24,496	16,891	7,240	189	176	100	69	29.6	0.8	0.7
Forgery and counterfeiting	687	526	148	3	10	100	76.6	21.5	0.4	1.5
Fraud	1,359	849	493	3	14	100	62.5	36.3	0.2	1
Embezzlement	106	71	33	1	1	100	67	31.1	0.9	0.9
Stolen property; buying receiving, possessing	3,313	2,357	868	40	48	100	71.1	26.2	1.2	1.4
Vandalism	12,280	10,570	1,565	65	80	100	86.1	12.7	0.5	0.7
Weapons; carrying, possessing, etc	4,434	3,087	1,272	16	59	100	69.6	28.7	0.4	1.3
Prostitution and commercialized vice	48	39	9	100	81.3	18.8	*	*	*	*
Sex offenses (except forcible rape and prostitution)	2,218	1,731	468	10	9	100	78	21.1	0.5	0.4
Drug abuse violations	18,456	14,178	4,069	96	113	100	76.8	22	0.5	0.6
Gambling	65	33	31	1		100	50.8		1.5	
Offenses against family and children	793	684	102	5	2	100	86.3	12.9	0.6	0.3
Driving under the influence	2,079	1,962	96	11	10	100	94.4	4.6	0.5	0.5
Liquor laws	14,697	13,822	620	140	115	100	94	4.2	1	0.8
Drunkenness	1,516	1,410	89	9	8	100	93	5.9	0.6	0.5
Disorderly conduct	10,265	6,699	3,370	121	75	100	65.3	32.8	1.2	0.7
Vagrancy	228	191	36	1	*	100	83.8	15.8	0.4	*
All other offenses (except traffic)	37,506	28,797	8,080	305	324	100	76.8	21.5	0.8	0.9
Suspicion	49	46	2	1	*	100	93.9	4.1	2	*
Curfew and loitering law violations	6,006	4,964	959	30	53	100	82.7	16	0.5	0.9
Runaways	22,638	19,402	2,909	173	154	100	85.7	12.9	0.8	0.7

Notes:
*Percentages too small to calculate.

Source: Uniform Crime Reports for the United States, 1997

H2.5. Rural County Arrest Trends, for Those 18 and Under: 1996–1997

[1,610 agencies; 1997 estimated population 18,216,000; 1996 estimated population 18,088,000.]

| | | Number of Persons Arrested | |
Offense Charged	1996	1997	Percent Change
TOTAL	99,447	100,561	+1.1
Murder and nonnegligent manslaughter	87	64	-26.4
Forcible rape	263	279	+6.1
Robbery	457	494	+8.1
Aggravated Assault	2,519	2,673	+6.1
Burglary	9,585	8,567	-10.6
Larceny-theft	10,977	11,043	+.6
Motor vehicle theft	2,637	2,508	-4.9
Arson	443	384	-13.3
Violent Crime	3,326	3,510	+5.5
Property Crime	23,642	22,502	-4.8
Crime Index total	26,968	26,012	-3.5
Other assaults	8,632	9,037	+4.7
Forgery and counterfeiting	329	363	+10.3
Fraud	744	604	-18.8
Embezzlement	24	25	+4.2
Stolen property; buying receiving, possessing	1,172	1,205	+2.8
Vandalism	6,537	6,314	-3.4
Weapons; carrying, possessing, etc	1,315	1,236	-6.0
Prostitution and commercialized vice	15	7	-53.3
Sex offenses (except forcible rape and prostitution)	1,143	1,102	-3.6
Drug abuse violations	6,300	6,658	+5.7
Gambling	15	13	-13.3
Offenses against family and children	509	652	+28.1
Driving under the influence	2,101	2,194	+4.4
Liquor laws	10,737	11,371	+5.9
Drunkenness	668	711	+6.4
Disorderly conduct	4,780	5,458	+14.2
Vagrancy	106	72	-32.1
All other offenses (except traffic)	16,405	17,096	+4.2
Suspicion	39	89	+128.2
Curfew and loitering law violations	1,828	1,694	-7.3
Runaways	9,119	8,737	-4.2

Notes:

Source: Uniform Crime Reports for the United States, 1997

H2.6. Adolescent Risky Behaviors in the Past 12 Months, by Race and Ethnicity: 1995

				RISKY BEHAVIOR		
Race/Ethnicity	Smoke Cigarettes	Drink Alcohol	Get Drunk	Do Something Dangerous Because You Were Dared To	Lie to Parents	Skip School Without Excuse
White	1.38	1.25	0.75	0.96	2.1	0.56
Black	0.68	1.12	0.58	0.62	2.16	0.54
Asian	1.07	1.1	0.7	0.93	2.1	0.79
Chinese	0.74	0.9	0.52	0.81	2.03	0.67
Filipino	1.22	1.23	0.81	0.97	2.35	0.87
Japanese	1.46	1.31	0.88	0.98	1.97	0.78
Asian Indian	1.06	1.04	0.66	1.05	2.12	0.84
Korean	0.99	0.89	0.47	0.69	1.84	0.64
Vietnamese	0.81	0.88	0.63	0.81	1.79	0.67
American Indian	1.53	1.4	0.82	1.27	2.26	0.74
Hispanic	1.11	1.31	0.76	0.89	2.13	0.85
Mexican	1.04	1.33	0.75	0.84	2.09	0.84
Chicano/Chicana	1.51	1.91	1.38	1.24	2.53	1.33
Cuban	1.01	1.41	0.86	1.11	2.1	1.02
Puerto Rican	1.42	1.31	0.75	1.07	2.38	0.99
Central/South America	0.91	1.13	0.61	0.7	2	0.72
Total	**1.2**	**1.21**	**0.7**	**0.88**	**2.1**	**0.58**

Notes:
Scale: 0 = never, 1 = once or twice, 2 = once a month or less, 3 = two or three days a month, 4 = once or twice a week, 5 = three to five times a week, 6 = nearly every day.

Source: The National Longitudinal Study of Adolescent Health, 1995.

H2.7. Self-Reported Delinquent Behavior, by Race and Ethnicity: 1995

In the past 12 months, how often did you . . .
Percent who have done:

	White	Black	Native American	Asian	Hispanic	Total
paint graffiti or signs on someone else's property or in a public place?	6.6	4.7	8.6	9.8	12.8	7.3
deliberately damage property that didn't belong to you?	15.1	10.1	9.7	10.9	8.9	14.8
lie to your parents or guardians about where you had been or whom you were with?	45.8	43.3	47.7	47.4	47.2	45.6
take something from a store without paying for it?	18.4	15.2	25.7	17.4	12.6	18.7
run away from home?	5.9	6.3	6.5	8.6	7.5	6.3
drive a car without its owner's permission?	6.3	8.9	7.5	6.1	10.7	7.9
steal something worth more than $50?	4.4	3.3	5.1	7.4	6.4	4.6
go into a house or building to steal something?	3.9	3.7	4.0	1.3	4.4	3.9
use or threaten to use a weapon to get something from someone?	2.6	5.3	5.1	3.9	4.9	3.5
sell marijuana or other drugs?	7.2	7.8	17.0	5.9	9.4	8.0

H2.7. Self-Reported Delinquent Behavior, by Race and Ethnicity: 1995 *(continued)*

	White	Black	Native American	Asian	Hispanic	Total
steal something worth less than $50?	16.2	10.4	18.3	13.3	18.7	15.6
act loud, rowdy, or unruly in a public place?	42.2	37.7	45.2	44.9	38.7	41.1
take part in a fight where a group of your friends was against another group?	15.9	22.4	33.9	18.0	16.2	18.8
become initiated into a named gang?	3.1	6.8	9.4	3.9	10.2	4.8
pull a knife or gun on someone.	3.2	9.2	7.8	.8	6.9	4.6
shoot or stab someone?	1.1	3.1	3.0	1.2	2.8	1.7
get into a serious physical fight?	18.7	13.5	34.5	16.7	26.5	20.7

Source: The National Longitudinal Study of Adolescent Health, 1998.

H2.8. Self-Reported Smoking and Drinking Behavior, by Race and Ethnicity: 1995.

Have you tried cigarette smoking, even just one or two puffs?
Percent who have done:

White	Black	Native American	Asian	Hispanic	Total
48.9	69.8	45.9	65.0	60.1	54.1

Have you had a drink of beer, wine, or liquor–not just a sip or a taste of someone else's drink–more than two or three times?

48.3	64.0	50.7	63.9	50.5	51.7

Source: The National Longitudinal Study of Adolescent Health, 1998.

H3. INCARCERATION AND SENTENCE

H3.1. U.S. Population Who Had Face-to-Face Contact With Police, by Race and Ethnicity, and Reason for Contact: 1996

[Persons having multiple contacts or more than one reason for any single contact appear in table more than once; therefore may not add to total. Covers persons 12 years and over. Based on the Police-Public Contact Survey of 6,421 persons; data subject to sampling variability.]

REASON FOR CONTACT	NUMBER HAVING CONTACT (1,000)				PERCENT HAVING CONTACT			
	Total	White	Black	Hispanic/1	Total	White	Black	Hispanic /1
Population total	**215,529**	**163,883**	**25,394**	**17,159**	**(X)**	**(X)**	**(X)**	**(X)**
For any reason	44,556	36,262	3,964	2,593	20.7	22.1	15.6	15.1
I reported a crime	12,722	10,640	1,049	634	5.9	6.5	4.1	3.7
I asked police for help	10,087	8,393	744	500	4.7	5.1	2.9	2.9
I reported a problem	7,892	6,449	508	557	3.7	3.9	2.0	3.2
Police ticketed me	10,947	8,988	815	865	5.1	5.5	3.2	5.0
I was in a traffic accident	5,454	4,501	501	241	2.5	2.7	2.0	1.4
I witnessed an accident	2,326	2,007	151	102	1.1	1.2	0.6	0.6
I was the victim of a crime	6,755	5,753	343	360	3.1	3.5	1.4	2.1
I witnessed a crime	3,467	2,776	419	179	1.6	1.7	1.6	1.0
Police suspected me of a crime	2,611	1,945	197	326	1.2	1.2	0.8	1.9
Police asked why I was there	2,690	2,070	361	84	1.2	1.3	1.4	0.5
Police had a warrant for my arrest	492	378	84	30	0.2	0.2	0.3	0.2
I had a casual encounter	8,042	6,901	640	327	3.7	4.2	2.5	1.9
I attended a community meeting	2,437	1,986	285	32	1.1	1.2	1.1	0.2
Some other reason	14,066	11,760	1,075	724	6.5	3.9	2.0	3.2

Notes:
X Not applicable.
\1 Persons of Hispanic origin may be of any race.

Source: U.S. Bureau of Justice Statistics, Police Use of Force, National Collection of Data, issued November 1997, revised January 1998.

H3.2. Jail Inmates, by Race, Sex, and Detention Status: 1986 to 1996

[Data are for midyear. Excludes Federal and State prisons or other correctional institutions; institutions exclusively for juveniles; state-operated jails in Alaska, Connecticut, Delaware, Hawaii, Rhode Island, and Vermont; and other facilities which retain persons for less than 48 hours. As of June 30. Data for 1993 based on National Jail Census; for other years, based on sample survey and subject to sampling variability]

CHARACTERISTIC	1986	1990	1991	1992	1993	1994	1995	1996
Total inmates \1	274,444	405,320	426,479	444,584	459,804	486,474	507,044	518,492
Percent of rated capacity	96	104	101	99	97	96	93	92
Rated capacity	272,830	367,769	389,171	421,237	449,197	475,224	545,763	562,020
Male	251,235	368,002	386,865	403,768	415,576	437,600	455,400	462,400
Female	21,501	37,318	39,614	40,816	44,228	48,800	51,600	56,100
White \2	159,178	186,989	190,333	191,362	180,914	253,500	266,200	288,900
Black \2	112,522	174,335	187,618	195,156	203,463	224,900	232,000	221,000
Other races \2	2,744	5,321	5,391	5,831	6,178	8,100	8,800	8,600
Hispanic \3	38,422	57,449	60,129	62,961	69,200	74,900	74,400	81,000
Non-Hispanic	236,022	347,871	366,350	381,623	390,600	411,600	432,600	437,500
Adult \4	272,736	403,019	424,129	441,781	455,500	479,800	499,300	510,400
Juvenile \5	1,708	2,301	2,350	2,804	4,300	6,700	7,800	8,100

Notes:
\1 1990 to 1993, includes 31,356, 38,675, 43,138, and 52,235 persons, respectively, of unknown race not shown separately.
\2 Beginning 1993, data represent White, Non-Hispanic and Black, Non-Hispanic and rounded to nearest 100.
\3 Hispanic persons may be of any race. Data for 1993 to 1996 are estimated and rounded to nearest 100.
\4 Includes inmates not classified by conviction status.
\5 Juveniles are persons defined by statute as being under a certain age, usually 18, and subject initially to juvenile court authority even if tried as adults in criminal court. In 1994 the definition was changed to include all persons under age 18.

Source: U.S. Bureau of Justice Statistics, through 1994, Jail Inmates, annual; beginning 1995, Prison and Jail Inmates at Midyear, annual.

H3.3. Prisoners under Sentence of Death: 1980 to 1996

[As of December 31. Excludes prisoners under sentence of death who remained within local correctional systems pending exhaustion of appellate process or who had not been committed to prison.]

CHARACTERISTIC	1980	1987	1988	1989	1990	1991	1992	1993	1994	1995	1996
Total \1	688	1,967	2,117	2,243	2,346	2,466	2,575	2,727	2,890	3,064	3,219
White	418	1,128	1,235	1,308	1,368	1,450	1,508	1,575	1,645	1,732	1,820
Black and Other	270	839	882	935	978	1,016	1,067	1,152	1,245	1,332	1,399
Under 20 years	11	10	11	6	8	14	12	13	19	20	16
20-24 years	173	222	195	191	168	179	188	211	231	264	281
25-34 years	334	969	1,048	1,080	1,110	1,087	1,078	1,066	1,088	1,068	1,076
35-54 years	186	744	823	917	1,006	1,129	1,212	1,330	1,449	1,583	1,707
55 years and over	10	39	47	56	64	73	85	96	103	119	139
Years of school completed											
7 years or less	68	181	180	183	178	173	181	185	186	191	196
8 years	74	183	184	178	186	181	180	183	198	195	199
9-11 years	204	650	692	739	775	810	836	885	930	979	1,026
12 years	162	591	657	695	729	783	831	887	939	995	1,034
More than 12 years	43	168	180	192	209	222	232	244	255	272	280
Unknown	163	211	231	263	279	313	315	332	382	422	484
Marital status:											
Never married	268	856	898	956	998	1,071	1,132	1,222	1,320	1,412	1,498
Married	229	571	594	610	632	663	663	671	707	718	731
Divorced \2	217	557	632	684	726	746	780	823	863	924	990
Time elapsed since sentencing											
Less than 12 months	185	295	293	231							
12-47 months	389	804	812	809	231	252	265	262	280	287	285
48-71 months	102	412	409	408	753	718	720	716	755	784	815
72 months and over	38	473	610	802	438	441	444	422	379	423	447
Legal status at arrest:											
Not under sentence	384	1,123	1,207	1,301	1,345	1,415	1,476	1,562	1,662	1,764	1,863
Parole or probation \3	115	480	545	585	578	615	702	754	800	866	892
Prison or escaped	45	91	93	94	128	102	101	102	103	110	111
Unknown	170	290	279	270	305	321	296	298	325	314	353

Notes:

\1 Revisions to the total number of prisoners were not carried to the characteristics except for race.

\2 Includes persons married but separated, widows, widowers, and unknown.

\3 Includes prisoners on mandatory conditional release, work release, leave, AWOL, or bail. Covers 24 prisoners in 1989, 28 in 1990, 29 in 1993 and 1995, and 31 in 1994 and 1996.

Source: U.S. Bureau of Justice Statistics, *Capital Punishment*, annual.

H3.4. Movement of Prisoners under Sentence of Death, by Race: 1980 to 1996

[Prisoners reported under sentence of death by civil authorities. The term "under sentence of death" begins when the court pronounces the first sentence of death for a capital offense.]

STATUS	1980	1985	1986	1987	1988	1989	1990	1991	1992	1993	1994	1995	1996
Under sentence of death, Jan. 1	595	1,420	1,575	1,800	1,967	2,117	2,243	2,346	2,465	2,580	2,727	2,905	3,064
Received death sentence \1 \2	203	281	297	299	296	251	244	266	265	282	306	310	299
White	125	165	164	190	196	133	147	163	147	146	162	168	174
Black	77	114	123	106	91	114	94	101	114	130	136	138	119
Dispositions other than executions	101	108	73	90	128	102	108	116	124	108	112	105	99
Executions	0	18	18	25	11	16	23	14	31	38	31	56	45
Under sentence of death, Dec. 31 \1 \2	688	1,575	1,800	1,967	2,117	2,243	2,346	2,466	2,575	2,727	2,890	3,054	3,219
White	425	896	1,006	1,128	1,238	1,308	1,368	1,450	1,508	1,575	1,645	1,730	1,820
Black	268	664	750	813	853	898	940	1,016	1,029	1,111	1,197	1,275	1,349

Notes:
\1 Includes races other than White or Black.
\2 Revisions to total number of prisoners under death sentence not carried to this category.

Source: U.S. Bureau of Justice Statistics, *Capital Punishment,* annual.

H3.5. Prisoners Executed under Civil Authority: 1930–1996

[Excludes executions by military authorities. The Army (including the Air Force) carried out 160 (148 between 1942 and 1950; 3 each in in 1954, 1955, and 1957; and 1 each in 1958, 1959, and 1961). Of the total, 106 were executed for murder (including 21 involving rape), 53 for rape, and 1 for desertion. The Navy carried out no executions during the period.]

YEAR OR PERIOD	Total \1	White	Black	EXECUTED FOR MURDER Total \1	White	Black	EXECUTED FOR RAPE Total \1	White	Black	EXECUTED, OTHER OFFENSES \2 Total \1	White	Black
All years	4,217	1,971	2,201	3,692	1,884	1,770	455	48	405	70	39	31
1930-1939	1,667	827	816	1,514	803	687	125	10	115	28	14	14
1940-1949	1,284	490	781	1,064	458	595	200	19	179	20	13	7
1950-1959	717	336	376	601	316	280	102	13	89	14	7	7
1960-1967	191	98	93	155	87	68	28	6	22	8	5	3
1968-1976	0	0	0	0	0	0	0	0	0	0	0	0
1977-1984	32	22	10	32	22	15	0	0	0	0	0	0
1985	18	11	7	18	11	7	0	0	0	0	0	0
1986	18	11	7	18	11	7	0	0	0	0	0	0
1987	25	13	12	25	13	12	0	0	0	0	0	0
1988	11	6	5	11	6	5	0	0	0	0	0	0
1989	16	8	8	16	8	8	0	0	0	0	0	0
1990	23	16	7	23	16	7	0	0	0	0	0	0
1991	14	7	7	14	7	7	0	0	0	0	0	0
1992	31	19	11	31	19	11	0	0	0	0	0	0
1993	38	23	14	38	23	14	0	0	0	0	0	0
1994	31	20	11	31	20	11	0	0	0	0	0	0
1995	56	33	22	56	33	22	0	0	0	0	0	0
1996	45	31	14	45	31	14	0	0	0	0	0	0

Notes:
\1 Includes races other than White or Black.
\2 Includes 25 armed robbery, 20 kidnapping, 11 burglary, 8 espionage (6 in 1942 and 2 in 1953), and 6 aggravated assault.

Source: Through 1978, U.S. Law Enforcement Assistance Administration; thereafter, U.S. Bureau of Justice Statistics, *Correctional Populations in the United States, annual.*

H4. VICTIMS OF CRIME

H4.1. Victimization Rates, by Type of Crime, Race, and Ethnicity of the Victim: 1996

[Rate per 1,000 persons age 12 years or older. Based on the National Crime Victimization Survey.]

CHARACTERISTIC	All crimes of violence	CRIMES OF VIOLENCE					Personal theft
		Rape/ sexual assault	Robbery	Assault			
				Total	Aggra-vated	Simple	
Total	42.0	1.4	5.2	35.4	8.8	26.6	1.5
White	40.9	1.3	4.2	35.3	8.2	27.2	1.4
Black	52.3	1.8	11.4	39.1	13.4	25.6	1.9
Other	33.2	2.1	7.4	23.8	7.2	16.6	1.3
Hispanic	44.0	1.2	8.4	34.5	10.6	23.9	2.7
Non-Hispanic	41.6	1.4	4.9	35.3	8.5	26.8	1.3

Source: U.S. Bureau of Justice Statistics, Criminal Victimization 1995, December 1996.

H4.2. Property Victimization Rates, by Race and Ethnicity: 1996

[Victimizations per 1,000 households. Based on National Crime Victimization Survey.]

CHARACTERISTIC	Total	Burglary	Motor vehicle	Theft
Total	266.3	47.2	13.5	205.7
Race:				
White	259.9	44.3	12.1	203.5
Black	310.0	69.3	22.2	218.5
Other	268.4	39.4	16.5	212.5
Ethnicity:				
Hispanic	328.1	56.2	24.6	247.3
Non-Hispanic	261.2	46.4	12.5	202.3

Source: U.S. Bureau of Justice Statistics, Criminal Victimization 1995, December 1996.

H4.3. Reported Criminal Victimization at School, by Race and Ethnicity: 1989 and 1995

[Percent of students ages 12 through 19 reporting. Based on the National Crime Victimization Survey, special School Crime Supplement.]

STUDENT CHARACTERISTICS	1989		1995	
	Number of students (1,000)	Percent reporting any victimization \1	Number of students (1,000)	Percent reporting any victimization \1
Total	21,554	14.5	23,933	14.6
White, non-Hispanic	15,349	14.3	16,351	14.5
Black, non-Hispanic	3,391	14.9	3,752	16.8
Hispanic	2,027	14.7	2,898	12.4
Other, non-Hispanic	787	14.7	932	13.7

Notes:
\1 Includes reported violent and property victimization. If the student reported an incident either he or she is counted as having experienced any victimization.

Source: U.S. Bureau of Justice Statistics, Students' Reports of School Crime: 1989 and 1995.

H4.4. Death Rates for Injury by Firearms, by Sex, Race, and Age: 1995

[Death rate per 100,000 population. Deaths classified according to the ninth revision of the International Classification of Diseases.]

ITEM	5-14 years	15-24 years	25-34 years	35-44 years	45-54 years	55-64 years	65-74 years	75-84 years	85 years and over
MALE									
Firearms:									
White	2.5	31.4	26.1	21.2	19.6	19.9	26.1	39.8	50.8
Black	5.5	140.2	94.4	46.6	32.1	24.3	22.0	20.9	(B)
Accidents:									
White	0.7	1.8	0.8	0.6	0.5	0.4	0.6	0.7	(B)
Black	0.8	4.3	1.5	(B)	(B)	(B)	(B)	(B)	(B)
Suicide:									
White	0.8	15.4	15.1	14.2	14.9	16.6	23.9	38.2	49.5
Black	(B)	13.2	11.9	7.6	6.9	7.5	10.2	13.9	(B)
Homicide:									
White	0.9	13.6	9.8	6.3	4.0	2.8	1.5	0.8	(B)
Black	4.1	121.0	80.7	38.3	24.6	15.9	10.8	(B)	(B)
FEMALE									
Firearms:									
White	0.8	4.6	5.0	4.9	4.4	3.6	3.1	3.0	1.8
Black	1.4	13.5	11.9	7.9	4.4	3.7	3.1	(B)	(B)
Accidents:									
White	0.1	0.2	0.2	0.2	(B)	(B)	(B)	(B)	(B)
Black	(B)	(B)	(B)	(B)	(B)	(B)	(B)	(B)	(B)
Suicide:									
White	0.3	2.0	2.4	2.8	3.0	2.6	2.3	2.0	1.2
Black	(B)	1.5	1.4	0.8	(B)	(B)	(B)	(B)	(B)
Homicide:									
White	0.4	2.2	2.3	1.8	1.2	0.8	0.7	0.8	(B)
Black	1.2	11.8	10.2	6.7	3.4	2.3	(B)	(B)	(B)

Notes:
B Does not meet standard of reliability or precision.

Source: U.S. National Center for Health Statistics, Advance Data from Vital and Health Statistics, No. 231.

H4.5. Homicide Victims, by Race and Sex: 1970 to 1995

[Rates per 100,000 resident population in specified group. Beginning 1970, excludes deaths to nonresidents of U.S. Beginning 1980, deaths classified according to the ninth revision of the International Classification of Diseases; for earlier years, classified according to revision in use at the time.]

| YEAR | Total\1 | HOMICIDE VICTIMS | | | | Total\1 | HOMICIDE RATE \2 | | | |
| | | White | | Black | | | White | | Black | |
		Male	Female	Male	Female		Male	Female	Male	Female
1970	16,848	5,865	1,938	7,265	1,569	8.3	6.8	2.1	67.6	13.3
1980	24,278	10,381	3,177	8,385	1,898	10.7	10.9	3.2	66.6	13.5
1981	23,646	9,941	3,125	8,312	1,825	10.3	10.4	3.1	64.8	12.7
1982	22,358	9,260	3,179	7,730	1,743	9.6	9.6	3.1	59.1	12.0
1983	20,191	8,355	2,880	6,822	1,672	8.6	8.6	2.8	51.4	11.3
1984	19,796	8,171	2,956	6,563	1,677	8.4	8.3	2.9	48.7	11.2
1985	19,893	8,122	3,041	6,616	1,666	8.3	8.2	2.9	48.4	11.0
1986	21,731	8,567	3,123	7,634	1,861	9.0	8.6	3.0	55.0	12.1
1987	21,103	7,979	3,149	7,518	1,969	8.7	7.9	3.0	53.3	12.6
1988	22,032	7,994	3,072	8,314	2,089	9.0	7.9	2.9	58.0	13.2
1989	22,909	8,337	2,971	8,888	2,074	9.2	8.2	2.8	61.1	12.9
1990	24,932	9,147	3,006	9,981	2,163	10.0	9.0	2.8	69.2	13.5
1991	26,513	9,581	3,201	10,628	2,330	10.5	9.3	3.0	72.0	14.2
1992	25,488	9,456	3,012	10,131	2,187	10.0	9.1	2.8	67.5	13.1
1993	26,009	9,054	3,232	10,640	2,297	10.1	8.6	3.0	69.7	13.6
1994	24,926	9,055	2,921	10,083	2,124	9.6	8.5	2.6	65.1	12.4
1995	22,895	8,336	3,028	8,847	1,936	8.7	7.8	2.7	56.3	11.1

Notes:
\1 Includes races not shown separately.
\2 Rate based on enumerated population figures as of April 1 for 1970, 1980 and 1990; July 1 estimates for other years.

Source: U.S. National Center for Health Statistics, Vital Statistics of the United States, annual; and unpublished data.

H4.6. Homicide Rates of Victims, by Race, Sex, and Age: 1990 to 1995

| | WHITE | | | | BLACK | | | |
| | Male | | Female | | Male | | Female | |
AGE	1990	1995	1990	1995	1990	1995	1990	1995
Total \1	9.0	7.8	2.8	2.7	69.2	56.3	13.5	11.1
Under 1 year	6.4	7.1	5.1	5.0	21.4	19.4	22.8	19.2
1-4 yrs	1.8	2.1	1.4	1.8	7.6	8.7	7.2	6.8
5-9 yrs	0.5	0.7	0.7	0.6	2.1	2.1	2.5	1.5
10-14 yrs	1.7	2.0	0.9	1.0	8.1	8.2	4.8	3.0
15-19 yrs	12.5	14.7	3.6	3.9	115.7	110.5	15.6	16.4
20-24 yrs	18.1	18.2	4.5	4.2	162.2	155.5	22.1	17.2
25-29 yrs	16.6	14.3	4.4	4.4	140.0	113.9	26.5	19.6
30-34 yrs	13.6	11.7	4.3	4.1	110.2	83.8	24.0	20.6
35-39 yrs	12.3	9.4	3.4	3.5	92.8	61.1	18.7	17.0
40-44 yrs	10.5	9.0	3.0	3.3	69.0	50.3	11.7	11.8
45-49 yrs	8.9	6.7	2.9	2.6	52.9	44.5	8.2	6.9
50-54 yrs	7.6	5.9	2.3	2.4	41.3	32.1	6.2	6.0
55-59 yrs	5.7	5.4	1.9	2.0	32.8	29.4	6.7	5.5
60-64 yrs	5.3	4.6	1.8	1.4	35.4	24.5	4.5	4.3
65-69 yrs	4.3	3.8	1.5	1.5	24.4	21.4	7.4	5.7
70-74 yrs	3.9	2.4	2.1	2.2	24.1	21.7	6.0	(B)
75-79 yrs	3.8	2.5	2.6	2.0	29.7	19.5	8.9	9.2
80-84 yrs	4.1	2.6	3.1	2.6	28.5	(B)	15.3	(B)
85 yrs and over	4.9	3.5	2.5	2.1	(B)	(B)	19.2	14.4

Notes:

B Base figure to small to meet statistical standards for reliability of a derived figure.

NA Not available.

\1 Includes persons under 15 years old, not shown separately.

\2 Rate based on enumerated population figures as of April 1 for 1990 and July 1 estimates for 1995.

Source: U.S. National Center for Health Statistics, Vital Statistics of the United States.

H4.7. Victim/Offender Relationship, by Race: 1997

[Single Victim/Single Offender]

| | | Race of Offender | | | |
Race of Victim	Total	White	Black	Other	Unknown
White Victims	3,787	3,184	520	45	38
Black Victims	3,646	209	3,388	11	38
Other Race Victims	226	48	35	141	2
Unknown Race	62	13	15	1	33

Source: Uniform Crime Reports for the United States, 1997.

H4.8. Adolescent Victimization of Fighting and Violence, by Race and Ethnicity: 1995

During the past 12 months, how often did each of the following things happen?

	White	Black	Native American	Asian	Hispanic	Total
You saw someone shoot or stab another person	4.9	15.4	13.2	5.9	15.5	8.1
Someone pulled a knife or gun on you	7.9	5.2	16.7	4.5	14.8	10.1
Someone cut or stabbed you	2.8	5.6	4.6	1.4	4.0	3.4
You were jumped	6.7	12.3	17.3	6.5	13.4	8.7

Source: The National Longitudinal Study of Adolescent Health, 1998.

H5. HATE CRIMES

H5.1. Hate Crimes—Number of Incidents, Offenses, Victims, and Offenders, by Bias Motivation: 1996

[The FBI collects statistics on hate crimes from 9,500 law enforcement agencies covering 198 million inhabitants of the U.S. in 1995 and 11,354 agencies and 223 million inhabitants in 1996. Hate crime offenses cover incidents motivated by race, religion, sexual orientation, and ethnicity/national origin.]

BIAS MOTIVATIONS	Incidents	Offenses	Victims	Known offenders
Total bias motivations	**8,759**	**10,706**	**11,039**	**8,935**
Race, total	5,396	6,767	6,994	6,122
Anti-White	1,106	1,384	1,445	1,783
Anti-Black	3,674	4,469	4,600	3,701
Anti-American Indian/Alaskan native	51	69	71	56
Anti-Asian/Pacific Islander	355	527	544	374
Anti-multi-racial group	210	318	334	208
Ethnicity/national origin, total	940	1,163	1,207	1,095
Anti-Hispanic	564	710	728	734
Anti-other ethnicity/national origin	376	453	479	361
Religion, total	1,401	1,500	1,535	523
Anti-Jewish	1,109	1,182	1,209	371
Anti-Catholic	35	37	38	17
Anti-Protestant	75	80	81	44
Anti-Islamic	27	33	33	16
Anti-other religious group	129	139	145	64
Anti-multi-religious group	24	27	27	11
Anti-atheism/agnosticism/etc	2	2	2	0
Sexual orientation, total	1,016	1,256	1,281	1,180
Anti-male homosexual	757	927	940	925
Anti-female homosexual	150	185	192	150
Anti-homosexual	84	94	99	93
Anti-heterosexual	15	38	38	4
Anti-bisexual	10	12	12	8
Multiple bias	6	20	22	15

Source: U.S. Federal Bureau of Investigation <http://WWW.fbi.GOV/ucr/hateinto.htm>.

H5.2. Hate Crimes Reported, by State: 1996

STATE	Number of participating agencies	Population covered	Agencies submitting incidents	Incidents reported
United States	**11,354**	**223,346,702**	**1,834**	**8,759**
Alabama	289	4,167,898	0	0
Alaska	1	254,774	1	9
Arizona	81	4,253,428	19	250
Arkansas	191	2,510,000	1	1
California	718	31,502,681	256	2,052
Colorado	230	3,820,118	27	133
Connecticut	98	2,772,165	44	114
Delaware	50	724,747	9	67
District of Columbia	1	543,000	1	16
Florida	394	14,658,195	51	187
Georgia	2	413,123	2	28
Hawaii	(\1)	(\1)	(\1)	(\1)
Idaho	112	1,202,496	32	72
Illinois	113	5,412,562	113	348
Indiana	179	3,634,883	12	36
Iowa	231	2,841,077	25	43
Kansas	1	312,706	1	28
Kentucky	527	3,848,633	49	109
Louisiana	140	2,697,770	5	6
Maine	131	1,235,309	10	58
Maryland	148	5,071,690	37	387
Massachusetts	405	6,091,117	102	454
Michigan	485	7,958,039	159	486
Minnesota	307	4,648,824	58	268
Mississippi	129	1,716,566	3	3
Missouri	230	4,270,323	25	150
Montana	95	858,174	4	10
Nebraska	10	207,564	2	3
Nevada	4	1,169,351	3	44
New Hampshire	2	81,381	1	1
New Jersey	568	7,995,838	273	839
New Mexico	70	1,298,291	8	44
New York	499	17,645,588	40	903
North Carolina	83	2,888,221	19	34
North Dakota	101	640,486	2	2
Ohio	405	8,873,634	55	234
Oklahoma	293	3,294,345	27	83
Oregon	174	3,155,762	27	172
Pennsylvania	1,137	11,833,651	43	205
Rhode Island	46	990,000	11	40
South Carolina	340	3,677,033	24	42
South Dakota	32	255,844	2	3
Tennessee	191	2,904,931	13	33
Texas	915	19,026,891	88	350
Utah	124	1,988,036	25	59
Vermont	3	35,462	3	4
Virginia	409	6,678,025	32	100
Washington	230	5,466,381	62	198
West Virginia	22	179,467	3	4
Wisconsin	338	5,160,000	21	43
Wyoming	70	480,222	4	4

Notes:
\1 Did not report.

Source: U.S. Federal Bureau of Investigation <http://WWW.fbi.GOV/ucr/hatecm.htm>.

H5.3. Number of Hate Crime Incidents, Offenses, Victims, and Known Offenders, by Bias Motivation: 1997

	Number of			
	Known Incidents	Offenses	Victims\1	Offenders\2
Total	8,049	9,861	10,255	8,474
Single Bias Incidents				
Race:	**4,710**	**5,898**	**6,084**	**5,444**
Anti-White	993	1,267	1,293	1,520
Anti-Black	3,120	3,838	3,951	3,301
Anti-American Indian/Alaskan Native	36	44	46	45
Anti-Asian/Pacific Islander	347	437	466	351
Anti-Multi-Racial Group	214	312	328	227
Religion:	**1,385**	**1,483**	**1,586**	**792**
Anti-Jewish	1,087	1,159	1,247	598
Anti-Catholic	31	32	32	16
Anti-Protestant	53	59	61	19
Anti-Islamic	28	31	32	22
Anti-Other Religious Group	159	173	184	120
Anti-Atheism/Agnosticism, etc	3	3	3	6
Sexual Orientation:	**1,102**	**1,375**	**1,401**	**1,315**
Anti-Male Homosexual	760	912	927	1,032
Anti-Female Homosexual	188	229	236	158
Anti-Homosexual	133	210	214	103
Anti-Heterosexual	12	14	14	14
Anti-Bisexual	9	10	10	8
Ethnicity/National Origin:	**836**	**1,083**	**1,132**	**906**
Anti-Hispanic:	491	636	649	614
Anti-Other Ethnicity/National Origin	345	447	483	292
Disability:	**12**	**12**	**12**	**14**
Anti-Physical	9	9	9	11
Anti-Mental	3	3	3	3
Multiple Bias Incidents\3:	**4**	**10**	**40**	**3**

Notes:
\1 The term "victim" may refer to a person, business institution, or society as a whole.
\2 The term "known offender" does not imply that the identity of the suspect is known, but only that an attribute of the suspect is identified which distinguishes him/her from an unknown offender.
\3 There were 4 multiple-bias incidents. Within these there were 10 offenses, 40 victims, and 3 known offenders.

Source: Uniform Crime Reports for the United States, 1997.

H5.4. Bias-Motivated Offenses, 1997

MOTIVATION	PERCENT DISTRIBUTION\1
Race	59.8
Religion	15.0
Sexual Orientation	13.9
Ethnicity	11.0
Multiple Bias\2	.1
Disability	.1
Total	99.9

Notes:
1 Due to rounding, percentages do not add to 100.
2 This category represents offenses associated with multiple-bias incidents.

Source: Uniform Crime Reports for the United States, 1997.

H5.5. Number of Hate Crimes, Victims, and Known Offenders, by Offense: 1997

| | Number of | | |
	Offenses	Victims \1	Known Offenders \2
Total	9,861	10,255	9,172 \3
Crimes against persons	**6,873**	**6,873**	**7,388**
Murder and nonnegligent manslaughter	8	8	24
Forcible rape	9	9	14
Aggravated assault	1,237	1,237	1,891
Simple assault	1,800	1,800	2,349
Intimidation	3,814	3,814	3,100
Other \4	5	5	10
Crimes against property:	**2,973**	**3,367**	**1,766**
Robbery	144	160	374
Burglary	111	131	84
Theft	95	103	70
Larceny-theft	7	7	7
Arson	60	71	42
Destruction/damage/vandalism	2,549	2,888	1,179
Other \4	7	7	10
Crimes against society \4	**15**	**15**	**18**

Notes:
\1 The term "victim" may refer to a person, business, institution, or society as a whole.
\2 The term "known offender" does not imply that the identity of the suspect is known, but only that an attribute of the suspect is identified which distinguishes him/her from an unknown offender.
\3 The actual number of known offenders is 8,474. Some offenders, however, may be responsible for more than one offense and are, therefore, counted more than once in this table.
\4 Includes offenses other than those listed that are collected in NIBRS.

Source: Uniform Crime Reports for the United States, 1997.

H6. ATTITUDES TOWARD CRIME AND POLICE

H6.1. Afraid to Walk at Night in Neighborhood, by Race: 1998

Is there any area right around here—that is, within a mile—where you would be afraid to walk alone at night?			
	White	**Black**	**Other**
Yes	39.5%	46.6%	48.4%
No	59.1	50.8	51.6
Don't know	1.4	2.7	
(N)	**1491**	**264**	**124**

Source: General Social Survey, 1998.

H6.2. Attitudes toward Police Violence

Are there any situations you can imagine in which you would approve of a policeman striking an adult male citizen?			
	White	**Black**	**Other**
Yes	70.6%	47.5%	45.7%
No	25.6	46.8	47.2
Don't know	3.8	5.7	7.1
(N)	**1495**	**280**	**127**
Would you approve of a policeman striking a citizen who: Had said vulgar and obscene things to the policeman?			
Yes	7.2%	4.3%	3.8%
No	91.1	94.3	94.6
Don't know	1.7	1.4	1.5
(N)	**1497**	**279**	**130**
Was being questioned as a suspect in a murder case?			
Yes	4.7%	6.8%	13.1%
No	93.4	91.8	86.2
Don't know	1.9	1.4	.8
(N)	**1497**	**279**	**130**
Was attempting to escape from custody?			
Yes	72.6%	49.3%	52.3%
No	22.9	43.5	41.5
Don't know	4.5	7.2	6.2
(N)	**1497**	**278**	**130**
Was attacking the policeman with his fists?			
Yes	91.7%	81.4%	86.9%
No	6	16.1	11.5
Don't know	2.3	2.5	1.5
(N)	**1497**	**279**	**130**

Source: General Social Survey, 1998.

H6.3. Courts Dealing with Criminals, by Race of Respondent: Crosstabulation, 1998

		COURTS DEALING WITH CRIMINALS				
Race of Respondent		TOO HARSH	NOT HARSH ENOUGH	ABOUT RIGHT	DON'T KNOW	TOTAL
WHITE	Count	101	1676	298	155	2230
	Percent within RACE of RESPONDENT	4.5%	75.2%	13.4%	7.0%	100.0%
BLACK	Count	58	287	41	14	400
	Percent within RACE of RESPONDENT	14.5%	71.8%	10.3%	3.5%	100.0%
OTHER	Count	16	132	33	10	191
	Percent within RACE of RESPONDENT	8.4%	69.1%	17.3%	5.2%	100.0%
TOTAL	Count	175	2095	372	179	2821
	Percent within RACE of RESPONDENT	6.2%	74.3%	13.2%	6.3%	100.0%

Source: General Social Survey, 1998.

H6.4. Afraid to Walk at Night in Neighborhood, by Race of Respondent: Crosstabulation, 1998

		Afraid to walk at Night in Neighborhood			
Race of Respondent		YES	NO	DON'T KNOW	TOTAL
WHITE	Count	589	881	21	1491
	Percent within RACE of RESPONDENT	39.5%	59.1%	1.4%	100.0%
BLACK	Count	123	134	7	264
	Percent within RACE of RESPONDENT	46.6%	50.8%	2.7%	100.0%
OTHER	Count	60	64	124	
	Percent within RACE of RESPONDENT	48.4%	51.6%	100.0%	
TOTAL	Count	772	1079	28	1879
	Percent within RACE of RESPONDENT	41.1%	57.4%	1.5%	100.0%

Source: General Social Survey, 1998.

I. Political Participation

I1. ELECTED OFFICIALS

Minority populations are generally underrepresented in the political arena. At the national level, few minority candidates have campaigned for the presidency or vice-presidency, and none have been elected. Few senators have been from minority groups. The 104th Congress had two Asian, one Black, and no Hispanic senators. The House of Representatives had 17 members who were Hispanic, four who were Asian, and 40 who were Black. These numbers are all below the percentage of these groups in the population as a whole. The trends in these numbers since 1981 are presented in I1.1. The number of members from various groups in county and local governmental positions is reported in I1.2. And the numbers of Black and Hispanic elected officials by state are reported in I1.3 and I1.4. Both groups are more likely to be represented in states where their population numbers are higher—the South for Blacks, and California, New Mexico, and Texas for Hispanics. The trends over time are also reported in these last two tables.

I2. VOTING AND POLITICAL PARTY IDENTIFICATION

The percentage of minority populations who vote has historically also been lower than among the White population. When they do vote, Blacks and Hispanics, compared with Whites, traditionally vote more for Democratic candidates. This is shown in I2.2. and I2.3. Blacks are more likely than Whites to think of themselves as Democrats, while Whites are more likely to think of themselves as Republicans. "Others" are more likely to characterize themselves as Independents (I2.4). Overall, however, the three groups are not more or less likely to characterize themselves as liberal or conservative (I2.5). But Whites are likely to believe the Republican party will keep the

country prosperous, while Blacks and other minorities tend to rely on the Democratic party (I2.6).

I3. MILITARY PERSONNEL AND PARTICIPATION

Blacks have long been overrepresented in the military services. As the military has down-sized over the past two decades, the number of Blacks in the army has dropped significantly (I3.1). Blacks are overrepresented in the ready reserve, but Asians are underrepresented, and Native Americans are roughly the same proportion in the ready reserve as they are in the population (see I3.2). The percentage of each group by veteran status and by combat era is reported in I3.3. Only a small proportion of any group has had military experience. But minoriites were represented most heavily in the Vietnam era.

I4. POLITICAL ATTITUDES

Minority group members are often more liberal than Whites on political issues, but the particular issue makes a difference. Whites are more likely than Blacks and "Others" to allow an individual who believes that Blacks are "genetically inferior" to speak in public or teach at a university (I4.1). They are also less willing than Blacks to have a book written by such an individual removed from a public library. But few differences appear on attitudes about the legality of abortion (Table I4.2).

On criminal issues, Whites are more likely than Blacks and Hispanics to support the death penalty, (I4.3) and are more likely than Blacks and "Others" to say they have a gun (I4.4). They are also less likely to favor laws requiring a police permit to buy a gun. Whites are also somewhat less likely than Blacks and "Others" to think the courts deal too harshly with criminals, but they are slightly more willing to make marijuana legal (I4.4).

313

Large racial and ethnic differences appear on some attitudes about government spending. Whites and "Others" are more likely than Blacks to support space exploration, but Blacks want more protection for the nation's health and want more money spent to solve the problems of the nation's big cities (I4.5). Blacks, more than Whites and "Others," want more resources devoted to fighting rising crime and drug addiction and improving education and the conditions of Blacks. Whites, on the other hand, want increased spending for military aid (I4.5). Blacks want more money spent on welfare. Blacks, more than Whites, want more money spent on social security, mass transportation, and parks and recreation. Most people, whether Black or White, believe the federal income tax is too high; however, the "Other" group is a little less likely to think this tax is too high (I4.6). Blacks, then "Others," more than Whites, believe the government should reduce income differences (I4.7). Whites are more likely than minorities to believe that workers have received "their share"of the improved economy (I4.8), but minorities are more likely to believe they were better off in 1998 than the past year (I4.9). Finally, Whites are more likely than minorities to have high levels of life satisfaction (I4.10).

I5. SOCIAL ATTITUDES

Confidence in a variety of social institutions also varies by racial and ethnic group. Blacks have more confidence in the U. S. Congress, whereas Whites have more confidence in business. Blacks have more confidence than Whites do in churches and religious organizations, and they have slightly higher confidence in the schools and educational system. They have lower confidence than Whites in the courts and legal system, however (I5.1). Blacks also have somewhat higher confidence than Whites in the executive branch of the federal government, organized labor, the press, and television. Whites, on the other hand, have higher confidence than Blacks in the U. S. Supreme Court, the scientific community, and the military. Blacks and Whites have about the same amount of confidence in congress (I5.2) and social security (I.5.3). They are about equally likely to feel that it is wrong if a taxpayer does not report all his or her income. But Whites, compared to Blacks, are somewhat more likely to think it is acceptable for an individual to give the government incorrect information to get benefits (I5.4).

Blacks, compared with Whites, are a little more likely to feel alienated from life. They are slightly more likely to say that "there is little that people can do to change the course of their lives" and that life does not serve any purpose (I5.5). Blacks and Whites are equally likely, however, to say that one must provide meaning for oneself and that each person makes his or her own fate. But Blacks, more than Whites, believe that people might take advantage of them (I5.6).

I6. RACIAL ATTITUDES

Whites are somewhat more likely than Blacks to say that race relations in the United States are good (I6.1 and I6.2), but the percentages vary over time. Blacks are far less likely than Whites to say that conditions for Black people have improved in the past few years (I6.3). When more specific questions are asked, however, such as perceptions about racial equality (I6.4) or perceptions that the country is moving toward separate societies (I6.5), the differences are huge. A majority of Blacks believe that a new race initiative is needed to improve race relations (I6.6) and a majority also believe that legislation should be passed apologizing for slavery (I6.7). Far fewer Whites, less than a majority, are willing to endorse either of these items. More Whites than Blacks are likely to have negative views of other ameliorative solutions such as affirmative action (Tables I6.8 and I6.9), and Whites are more likely than Blacks to believe that such programs hurt Whites (I6.10).

Blacks are more likely than Whites to favor living in integrated neighborhoods (I6.11), and to marry interracially (I 6.13). As might be expected, both Blacks and Whites feel closest to their own group (I6.14), and both groups characterize both Blacks and Whites as about equally hardworking (I6.15). Table I6.16 also indicates that considerable segregation continues to exist in the workplace.

In recent polls, Whites do not always subscribe to traditional stereotypes of Blacks. For example, they are no more willing than Blacks to attribute poor socioeconomic conditions to "in-born ability," but they are more willing than Blacks to attribute the conditions to lack of motivation. On the other hand, Blacks are much more willing than Whites to attribute poor socioeconomic conditions to discrimination and lack of education (I6.17).

I1. ELECTED OFFICIALS

I1.1 Members of Congress: 1981 to 1995

[As of beginning of first session of each Congress (January 3). Figures for Representatives exclude vacancies.]

MEMBERS OF CONGRESS AND YEAR	Black \1	Asian, Pacific Islander \2	Hispanic \3
REPRESENTATIVES			
97th Cong., 1981	17	3	6
98th Cong., 1983	21	3	8
99th Cong., 1985	20	3	10
100th Cong., 1987	23	4	11
101st Cong., 1989	24	5	10
102d Cong., 1991	25	3	11
103d Cong., 1993 \4	38	4	17
104th Cong., 1995	40	4	17
SENATORS			
97th Cong., 1981	0	3	0
98th Cong., 1983	0	2	0
99th Cong., 1985	0	2	0
100th Cong., 1987	0	2	0
101st Cong., 1989	0	2	0
102d Cong., 1991	0	2	0
103d Cong., 1993 \4	1	2	0
104th Cong., 1995	1	2	0

Notes:
\1 Source: Joint Center for Political and Economic Studies, Washington, DC, Black Elected Officials: A National Roster, annual, (copyright).
\2 Source: Library of Congress, Congressional Research Service, "Asian Pacific Americans in the United States Congress", Report 94-767 GOV.
\3 Source: National Association of Latino Elected and Appointed Officials, Washington, DC, National Roster of Hispanic Elected Officials, annual.
\4 Includes members elected to fill vacant seats through June 14, 1993.

Source: Except as noted, compiled by U.S. Bureau of the Census from data published in Congressional Directory, biennial.

I1.2. Local Elected Officials, by Race, Hispanic Origin, and Type of Government: 1992

RACE, AND HISPANIC ORIGIN	Total	GENERAL PURPOSE			SPECIAL PURPOSE	
		County	Municipal	Town, township	School district	Special district
White	405,905	52,705	114,880	102,676	73,894	61,750
Black	11,542	1,715	4,566	369	4,222	670
American Indian, Eskimo, Aleut	1,800	147	776	86	564	227
Asian, Pacific Islander	514	80	97	16	184	137
Hispanic	5,859	906	1,701	216	2,466	570
Non-Hispanic	413,902	53,741	118,618	102,931	76,398	62,214
Race, Hispanic origin not reported	74,069	4,171	15,212	23,811	9,570	21,305

Source: U.S. Bureau of the Census, 1992 Census of Governments, Popularly Elected Officials (GC92(1)-2).

I1.3. Black Elected Officials, by Office, 1970 to 1993, and by Region and State: 1993

[As of January 1997, no Black elected officials had been identified in Hawaii, Idaho, Montana, North Dakota, or Utah]

STATE	Total	U.S. and State legislatures \1	City and county offices \2	Law enforcement \3	Education \4
1970 (Feb.)	1,469	179	715	213	362
1980 (July)	4,890	326	2,832	526	1,206
1985 (Jan.)	6,016	407	3,517	661	1,431
1990 (Jan.)	7,335	436	4,485	769	1,645
1991 (Jan.)	7,445	473	4,496	847	1,629
1992 (Jan.)	7,517	499	4,557	847	1,614
1993 (Jan.)	**7,984**	**561**	**4,819**	**922**	**1,682**
Alabama	726	63	551	52	88
Alaska	1	-2	1	(NA)	(NA)
Arizona	17	6	3	5	5
Arkansas	484	117	242	73	149
California	255	-18	14	79	90
Colorado	20	4	4	10	2
Connecticut	63	15	36	4	7
Delaware	26	6	16	2	3
District of Columbia	147	-52	139	(NA)	5
Florida	218	41	146	32	15
Georgia	679	82	420	37	105
Illinois	646	106	331	55	134
Indiana	80	21	51	10	6
Iowa	1	1	1	(NA)	(NA)
Kansas	21	7	6	4	4
Kentucky	58	0	42	5	8
Louisiana	846	45	362	113	136
Maine	3	3	2	(NA)	(NA)
Maryland	196	105	115	33	10
Massachusetts	33	10	21	3	2
Michigan	333	19	134	51	129
Minnesota	14	-1	3	7	3
Mississippi	803	98	520	98	140
Missouri	188	19	136	14	22
Nebraska	4	-1	2	(NA)	1
Nevada	16	11	5	4	2
New Hampshire	2	2	(NA)	(NA)	2
New Jersey	222	25	124	(NA)	84
New Mexico	5	4	(NA)	2	1
New York	311	43	75	79	128
North Carolina	506	65	354	29	96
Ohio	231	32	129	30	52
Oklahoma	102	-15	76	1	19
Oregon	7	1	1	2	(NA)
Pennsylvania	162	23	55	58	30
Rhode Island	10	7	1	(NA)	(NA)
South Carolina	542	127	323	13	172
South Dakota	0	-3	(NA)	(NA)	(NA)
Tennessee	174	23	108	26	23
Texas	448	-6	293	45	92
Utah	1	1	(NA)	1	(NA)
Vermont	1	0	(NA)	(NA)	(NA)
Virginia	333	193	137	17	164
Washington	23	6	9	10	2
West Virginia	19	0	14	3	(NA)
Wisconsin	36	14	17	4	8
Wyoming	0	-1	(NA)	(NA)	(NA)

Notes:
\1 Includes elected State administrators.
\2 County commissioners and councilmen, mayors, vice mayors, aldermen, regional officials, and other.
\3 Judges, magistrates, constables, marshals, sheriffs, justices of the peace, and other.
\4 Members of State education agencies, college boards, school boards, and other.
\5 Includes two shadow senators and one shadow representative.

Source: Joint Center for Political and Economic Studies, Washington, D.C., Black Elected Officials: A National Roster, annual. (Copyright.)

I1.4. Hispanic Public Officials, by Office, 1985 to 1994, and by State: 1994

[For States not shown, no Hispanic public officials had been identified]

STATE	Total	State executives and legislators \1	County and municipal officials	Judicial and law enforcement	Education and school boards
1985 (Sept.)	3,147	129	1,316	517	1,185
1986 (Sept.)	3,202	132	1,352	530	1,188
1987 (Sept.)	3,317	138	1,412	568	1,199
1988 (Sept.)	3,360	135	1,425	574	1,226
1989 (Sept.)	3,783	143	1,724	575	1,341
1990 (Sept.)	4,004	144	1,819	583	1,458
1991 (Sept.)	4,202	151	1,867	596	1,588
1992 (Sept.)	4,994	150	1,908	628	2,308
1993 (Sept.)	5,170	182	2,023	633	2,332
1994 (Sept.)	**5,459**	**199**	**2,197**	**651**	**2,412**
Alaska	1	1	0	0	0
Arizona	341	11	144	50	136
Arkansas	2	1	0	0	1
California	796	16	349	50	381
Colorado	201	9	140	10	42
Connecticut	26	12	9	0	5
Delaware	1	0	1	0	0
Dist. of Columbia	1	0	0	1	0
Florida	64	16	33	12	3
Hawaii	2	2	0	0	0
Idaho	2	1	1	0	0
Illinois	881	7	26	3	845
Indiana	8	1	5	1	1
Kansas	7	5	1	0	1
Louisiana	12	3	1	8	0
Maryland	2	0	1	0	1
Massachusetts	1	0	0	0	1
Michigan	8	0	5	1	2
Minnesota	3	2	0	1	0
Missouri	1	0	1	0	0
Montana	2	0	0	1	1
Nebraska	3	0	2	0	1
Nevada	4	1	0	1	2
New Jersey	37	2	17	1	17
New Mexico	716	50	410	105	151
New York	83	12	13	11	47
Ohio	4	0	1	2	1
Oklahoma	1	0	1	0	0
Oregon	5	0	3	1	1
Pennsylvania	8	1	3	1	3
Rhode Island	1	1	0	0	0
Texas	2,215	41	1,022	389	763
Utah	1	1	0	0	0
Washington	14	2	4	2	6
Wisconsin	2	0	2	0	0
Wyoming	3	1	2	0	0

Notes:
\1 Includes U.S. Representatives, not shown separately.
\2 Includes local school council members in the Chicago area.

Source: National Association of Latino Elected and Appointed Officials, Washington, D.C. National Roster of Hispanic Elected Officials, annual.

I2. VOTING AND POLITICAL PARTY IDENTIFICATION

I2.1. Voting in 1996

In 1996, you remember that Clinton ran for President on the Democratic ticket against Dole for the Republicans and Perot for the Reform Party. Do you remember for sure whether or not you voted in that election?

	White	Black	Other
Voted	67.0%	58.1%	35.8%
Did not vote	27.7	33.3	44.2
Ineligible	3.2	4.3	18.4
Refused to answer	.6	0.3	—
Don't know/remember	1.4	4.0	1.6
(N)	**2216**	**396**	**190**

Source: General Social Survey, 1998.

I2.2. Did You Vote for Clinton, Dole, or Perot?

Did you vote for Clinton, Dole, or Perot?

	White	Black	Other
Clinton	45.1%	87.3%	83.8%
Dole	38.3	7.0	10.3
Perot	12.9	2.6	4.4
Other	1.0	.4	
Didn't vote	.3	.4	1.5
Don't know	2.4	2.2	
(N)	**1476**	**229**	**68**

Source: General Social Survey, 1998.

I2.3. Democratic and Republican Percentages of Two-Party Presidential Vote, by Selected Characteristics of Voters: 1988 and 1992

[In percent. Covers citizens of voting age living in private housing units in the contiguous United States. Percentages for Democratic Presidential vote are computed by subtracting the percentage Republican vote from 100 percent; third-party or independent votes are not included as valid data. Data are from the National Election Studies and are based on a sample and subject to sampling variability]

	1988		1992	
CHARACTERISTIC	Democratic	Republican	Democratic	Republican
Total \1	47	53	58	42
Race:				
White	41	59	53	47
Black	92	8	94	6
Education:				
Grade school	61	39	70	30
High school	51	49	63	37
College	42	58	55	45
Union household	59	41	68	32
Non-union household	44	56	56	44

Notes:
\1 Includes other characteristics, not shown separately.

Source: Center for Political Studies, University of Michigan, Ann Arbor, MI, unpublished data. Data for 1984 are published in Warren E. Miller and Santa A. Traugott, *American National Election Studies Data Sourcebook,* 1952-1986, Cambridge, MA: Harvard University Press, 1989 (copyright).

I2.4. Political Party Affiliation

Generally speaking, do you usually think of yourself as a Republican, Democrat, Independent, or what?

	White	Black	Other
Strong Democrat	9.8%	33.0%	9.5%
Not strong Democrat	19.4	30.0	22.8
Independent, near Democrat	11.9	14.3	13.8
Independent	16.5	13.0	29.6
Independent, near Republican	9.8	1.5	10.1
Not strong Republican	20.1	5.5	7.4
Strong Republican	10.3	1.8	1.6
Other party	2.2	1.0	5.3
(N)	**2234**	**400**	**189**

Source: General Social Survey, 1998.

I2.5. Political Views

We hear a lot of talk these days about liberals and conservatives. I'm going to show you a seven-point scale on which the political views that people might hold are arranged from extremely liberal—point 1—to extremely conservative—point 7. Where would you place yourself on this scale?

	White	Black	Other
Extremely liberal	2.3%	1.5%	3.7%
Liberal	12.1	14.3	15.8
Slightly liberal	12.3	12.5	13.7
Moderate	33.8	40.6	35.8
Slightly conservative	16.2	12.5	11.1
Conservative	15.9	11.5	7.4
Extremely conservative	3.4	1.3	2.6
Don't know	4.1	5.8	10.0
(N)	**2235**	**399**	**190**

Source: General Social Survey, 1998.

I2.6. Racial Differences in Beliefs about Which Party Will Keep the Country Prosperous

	Republican	Democratic	No Difference	No Opinion	No. of Interviews
Race					
White	44%	39%	10%	7%	819
Non-white	25%	60%	8%	7%	182
Black	19%	69%	7%	5%	110

Source: The Gallup Poll Monthly, August 1996, p. 5.

I3. MILITARY PERSONNEL AND PARTICIPATION

I3.1. Number of Military Personnel, by Service: 1980–1995

[In thousands. As of end of fiscal year. Includes National Guard, Reserve, and Retired regular personnel on extended or continuous active duty. Excludes Coast Guard.]

		ARMY				NAVY \3				MARINE CORPS				AIR FORCE			
	Total \1 \2	Total \2	White	Black	Other	Total \2	White	Black	Other	Total \2	White	Black	Other	Total \2	White	Black	Other
1980	2,051	777	503	229	32	527	436	55	28	188	142	39	7	558	460	80	15
1981	2,083	781	502	232	36	540	443	58	27	191	145	39	7	570	468	83	16
1982	2,109	780	504	230	37	553	450	62	27	192	149	38	6	583	476	87	16
1983	2,123	780	512	220	38	558	462	66	28	194	152	37	6	592	483	88	17
1984	2,138	780	520	215	40	565	455	67	28	196	153	36	7	597	486	89	18
1985	2,151	781	523	211	41	571	459	70	28	198	152	37	9	602	488	90	19
1986	2,169	781	524	210	43	581	464	75	26	199	151	38	10	608	491	92	21
1987	2,174	781	519	212	45	587	467	81	24	200	150	38	11	607	489	92	22
1988	2,138	772	507	213	47	593	466	85	34	197	147	38	12	576	462	88	21
1989	2,130	770	497	218	49	593	461	91	34	197	146	38	13	571	458	87	22
1990	2,044	732	466	213	49	579	446	93	34	197	145	38	13	535	428	82	21
1991	1,986	711	452	204	49	570	439	92	33	194	144	36	14	510	409	77	20
1992	1,807	610	388	173	45	542	415	88	33	185	138	32	14	470	377	70	19
1993	1,705	572	365	158	45	510	390	84	31	178	134	30	14	444	357	65	18
1994	1,610	541	344	147	45	469	355	78	28	174	131	28	15	426	341	62	19
1995	1,518	509	322	137	45	435	326	75	27	175	130	28	17	400	318	58	19

Notes:
\1 Beginning 1980, excludes Navy Reserve personnel on active duty for Training and Administration of Reserves (TARS). From 1969, the full-time Guard and Reserve.
\2 Includes Cadets.
\3 Prior to 1980, includes Navy Reserve personnel on active duty for Training and Administration of Reserves (TARS).

Source: U.S. Dept. of Defense, Selected Manpopwer Statistics, annual.

I3.2. Ready Reserve Personnel Profile—Race and Sex: 1990 to 1997

YEAR	Total	GROUP White	Black	Asian	American Indian	PERCENT DISTRIBUTION White	Black	Asian	American Indian
1990	1,641,475	1,289,367	271,470	14,616	7,695	78.5	16.5	0.9	0.5
1993	1,840,650	1,425,255	309,699	21,089	9,068	77.4	16.8	1.1	0.5
1994	1,779,436	1,366,387	297,519	22,190	8,870	76.8	16.7	1.2	0.5
1995	1,633,497	1,254,592	273,847	21,792	8,591	76.8	16.8	1.3	0.5
1996	1,522,451	1,166,628	249,114	21,240	8,226	76.6	16.4	1.4	0.5
1997, total	**1,437,722**	**1,102,234**	**229,950**	**21,412**	**8,115**	**76.7**	**16.0**	**1.5**	**0.6**

Source: U.S. Dept. of Defense, *Official Guard and Reserve Manpower Strengths and Statistics,* annual.

I3.3. Veteran Status, by Race: March 1998

VETERAN ERA		NonHispanic Whites	NonHispanic Blacks	American Indians/ Aleuts/Eskimos	Asians and Pacific Islanders	Hispanics	Total
Vietnam Veteran	%	4.3%	2.7%	4.8%	1.5%	1.5%	3.7%
	N	**3141**	**248**	**50**	**52**	**222**	**3713**
Korean Veteran	%	2.1%	1.2%	1.6%	.5%	.4%	1.7%
	N	**1506**	**112**	**17**	**18**	**57**	**1710**
WWII Veteran	%	3.4%	1.7%	1.2%	.7%	.6%	2.7%
	N	**2497**	**150**	**13**	**24**	**82**	**2766**
Other Veteran	%	4.2%	4.3%	5.2%	1.8%	2.0%	3.9%
	N	**3099**	**386**	**55**	**63**	**281**	**3884**
Non Veteran	%	85.9%	90.1%	87.2%	95.4%	95.5%	88.0%
	N	**62478**	**8129**	**926**	**3283**	**13722**	**88528**
	Total	72721	9025	1051	3441	14364	100602

Source: Current Population Surveys, March 1998 [Machine readable data files] conducted by the Bureau of the Census for the Bureau of Labor Statistics. Washington: Bureau of Census [producer and distributor]. Santa Monica, CA: Unicon Research Corporation [producer and distributor of CPS Utilities], 1999.

I4. POLITICAL ATTITUDES

I4.1. Attitudes toward Civil Liberties

	White	Black	Other

Consider a person who believes that Blacks are genetically inferior.
If such a person wanted to make a speech in your community claiming that Blacks are inferior, should he be allowed to speak, or not?

	White	**Black**	**Other**
Allowed	64.7%	54.2%	54.0%
Not allowed	33.4	42.7	45.2
Don't know	1.9	3.1	.8
(N)	**1490**	**262**	**124**

Should such a person be allowed to teach in a college or university, or not?

Allowed	49.2%	34.8%	40.3%
Not allowed	46.7	59.1	57.3
Don't know	4.1	6.1	2.4
(N)	**1490**	**264**	**124**

If some people in your community suggested that a book he wrote which said that Blacks are inferior should be taken out of your public library, would you favor removing this book, or not?

Remove	29.4%	49.2%	40.3%
Not remove	67.2	43.2	54.8
Don't know	3.4	7.6	4.8
(N)	**1490**	**264**	**124**

Source: General Social Survey, 1998.

I4.2. Attitudes about Abortion

	Legal always	Legal under certain circumstances	Illegal always
Race			
White	33%	50%	14%
Non-white	30%	49%	18%

Source: The Gallup Poll Monthly, March 1995, p. 30.

I 4.3. Percent Who Believe in Death Penalty, by Race and Hispanic Origin

	Total %	White %	Black %	Hispanic %
Believe in it	75	80	46	72
Opposed to it	22	17	53	28
Don't know	3	3	1	

Notes:
N=1000

Source: Harris Poll, June 11, 1997.

I4.4. Attitudes toward the Death Penalty, Gun Permits, Courts, and Legalization of Marijuana

Do you favor or oppose the death penalty for persons convicted of murder?			
	White	**Black**	**Other**
Favor	72.4%	45.0%	58.4%
Oppose	20.1	45.2	33.7
Don't know	7.4	9.8	7.9
(N)	**2231**	**398**	**190**
Would you favor or oppose a law which would require a person to obtain a police permit before he or she could buy a gun?			
Favor	80.1%	87.5%	88.7%
Oppose	17.7	10.2	8.9
Don't know	2.2	2.3	2.4
(N)	**1490**	**265**	**124**
In general, do you think the courts in this area deal too harshly or not harshly enough with criminals?			
Too harsh	4.5%	14.5%	8.4%
Not harsh enough	75.2	71.8	69.1
About right	13.4	10.3	17.3
Don't know	7.0	3.5	5.2
(N)	**2230**	**400**	**191**
Some people think the use of marijuana should be made legal. Other people think marijuana use should not be made legal. Which do you favor?			
Legal	28.4%	24.0%	25.6%
Not legal	65.4	70.6	67.4
Don't know	6.2	5.4	7.0
(N)	**1497**	**279**	**129**

Source: General Social Survey, 1998.

I4.5. Attitudes about Government Spending

We are faced with many problems in this country, none of which can be solved easily or inexpensively. I'm going to name some of these problems. For each, are we spending too much money on it, too little money or about the right amount?

		White	Black	Other
Space exploration	Too little	10.9%	5.5%	9.1%
	About right	46.3	29.3	43.4
	Too much	36.5	56.4	40.4
	Don't know	6.3	8.8	7.1
	(N)	**1099**	**181**	**99**
Improving and protecting the environment	Too little	59.4%	59.7%	66.7%
	About right	28.4	26.5	27.3
	Too much	8.3	6.1	4.0
	Don't know	3.9	7.7	2.0
	(N)	**1097**	**181**	**99**
Improving and protecting nation's health	Too little	66.1%	75.8%	58.6%
	About right	25.5	18.7	31.3
	Too much	5.8	3.3	8.1
	Don't know	2.6	2.2	2.0
	(N)	**1098**	**182**	**99**
Solving problems of big cities	Too little	42.8%	61.0%	48.5%
	About right	31.4	20.3	30.3
	Too much	12.7	8.2	13.1
	Don't know	13.0	10.4	8.1
	(N)	**1097**	**182**	**99**
Halting rising crime rate	Too little	58.8%	75.8%	60.6%
	About right	30.1	16.5	32.3
	Too much	7.3	4.9	7.1
	Don't know	3.8	2.7	
	(N)	**1096**	**182**	**99**
Dealing with drug addiction	Too little	56.4%	72.1%	55.6%
	About right	29.3	19.6	29.3
	Too much	10.2	4.5	9.1
	Don't know	4.1	3.9	6.1
	(N)	**1098**	**179**	**99**
Improving nation's education system	Too little	69.2%	74.7%	66.7%
	About right	22.0	21.4	25.3
	Too much	7.2	2.2	4.0
	Don't know	1.6	1.6	4.0
	(N)	**1099**	**182**	**99**
Improving the conditions of blacks	Too little	28.1%	71.4%	32.3%
	About right	42.8	22.5	46.5
	Too much	19.7	1.6	6.1
	Don't know	9.4	4.4	15.2
	(N)	**1094**	**182**	**99**
Military, armaments, and defense	Too little	19.1%	12.8%	9.1%
	About right	47.7	45.0	37.4
	Too much	28.2	35.0	46.5
	Don't know	4.9	7.2	7.1
	(N)	**1094**	**180**	**99**
Foreign aid	Too little	6.4%	7.1%	9.2%
	About right	27.6	22.0	29.6
	Too much	61.0	61.0	53.1
	Don't know	5.0	9.9	8.2
	(N)	**1098**	**182**	**98**
Welfare	Too little	14.5%	23.9%	18.2%
	About right	35.3	38.3	41.4
	Too much	45.9	31.7	36.4
	Don't know	4.3	6.1	4.0
	(N)	**1100**	**180**	**99**

I4.5. Attitudes about Government Spending *(continued)*

		White	Black	Other
Highways and bridges	Too little	39.5%	39.3%	24.1%
	About right	48.4	36.3	57.1
	Too much	8.0	17.3	13.1
	Don't know	4.1	7.0	5.8
	(N)	**2228**	**399**	**191**
Social security	Too little	53.4%	72.0%	52.4%
	About right	34.7	18.8	28.8
	Too much	6.6	3.8	7.3
	Don't know	5.3	5.5	11.5
	(N)	**2228**	**400**	**191**
Mass transportation	Too little	31.2%	37.9%	27.2%
	About right	47.2	45.5	56.5
	Too much	9.9	8.3	6.8
	Don't know	11.7	8.3	9.4
	(N)	**2228**	**398**	**191**
Parks and recreation	Too little	32.3%	42.8%	37.2%
	About right	57.0	46.8	55.0
	Too much	6.4	5.5	4.7
	Don't know	4.4	5.0	3.1
	(N)	**2233**	**400**	**191**

Source: General Social Survey, 1998.

I4.6. Attitudes toward Federal Income Tax

Do you consider the amount of federal income tax which you have to pay as too high, about right, or too low?

	White	Black	Other
Too high	63.2%	63.9%	58.1%
About right	31.8	28.5	30.6
Too low	.9	.8	.8
Don't know	4.1	6.8	10.5
(N)	**1480**	**263**	**124**

Source: General Social Survey, 1998.

I4.7. Should Government Reduce Income Differences?

Here is a scale from 1 to 7. Think of a score of 1 as meaning that the government ought to reduce the income differences between rich and poor, and a score of 7 meaning that the government should not concern itself with reducing income differences. What score between 1 and 7 comes closest to the way you feel?

	White	Black	Other
Government reduce differences	12.8%	24.5%	17.7%
2	8.7	14.4	8.5
3	17.6	15.1	20.0
4	20.9	23.7	18.5
5	11.8	7.2	12.3
6	9.1	4.0	7.7
No government action	17.8	8.3	10.8
Don't know	1.4	2.9	4.6
(N)	**1496**	**278**	**130**

Source: General Social Survey, 1998.

I4.8. Black-White Differences in Perception that American Workers Have Received Their Share of the Improved Economy

Race	Have received	Have not received	No opinion	No. of Interviews
White	32%	62%	6%	432
Non-white	14%	81%	5%	93

Source: The Gallup Poll Monthly, August 1997, p. 20.

I4.9. Percentage of People Who Believe They Were Better Off in 1998 Than 1997, by Race

Race	Better off	Worse off	Same	No Opinion	No. of Interviews
White	53%	20%	26%	1%	1654
Non-white	64%	20%	16%	0%	203

Source: The Gallup Poll Monthly, March 1998, p. 12.

I4.10. Satisfaction with Personal Life, by Race

Race	Very Satisfied	Somewhat Satisfied	Neither Satisfied nor Dissatisfied	Somewhat or Very Dissatisfied	No. of Interviews
White	48%	36%	6%	10%	855
Non-white	26%	48%	5%	20%	141

Source: The Gallup Poll Monthly, June 1995, p. 7.

I5. SOCIAL ATTITUDES

I5.1. Confidence in Social Institutions

How much confidence do you have in . . .

	White	Black	Other
U.S. Congress?			
Complete confidence	2.4%	1.4%	3.5%
A great deal of confidence	11.4	5.4	12.9
Some confidence	53.0	54.1	48.2
Very little confidence	26.1	28.4	27.1
No confidence at all	7.2	10.8	8.2
(N)	**975**	**148**	**85**
Business and industry?			
Complete confidence	3.0%	0.0%	5.9%
A great deal of confidence	24.6	13.9	15.3
Some confidence	54.2	63.2	51.8
Very little confidence	14.7	17.4	22.4
No confidence at all	3.4	5.6	4.7
(N)	**966**	**144**	**85**
Churches and religious organizations?			
Complete confidence	8.7%	16.1%	8.2%
A great deal of confidence	34.2	33.6	31.8
Some confidence	40.0	39.6	41.2
Very little confidence	11.6	7.4	11.8
No confidence at all	5.5	3.4	7.1
(N)	**970**	**149**	**85**
Courts and the legal system?			
Complete confidence	2.6%	4.7%	6.0%
A great deal of confidence	17.8	12	19
Some confidence	47.9	42.7	44
Very little confidence	24	29.3	16.7
No confidence at all	7.6	11.3	14.3
(N)	**983**	**150**	**84**
Schools and the educational system?			
Complete confidence	4.5%	7.2%	11.5%
A great deal of confidence	28.2	30.1	31.0
Some confidence	48.0	44.4	46.0
Very little confidence	15.4	13.7	8.0
No confidence at all	3.9	4.6	3.4
(N)	**985**	**153**	**87**

Source: General Social Survey, 1998.

I5.2. Confidence in People Running Social Institutions

I am going to name some institutions in this country. As far as the people running these institutions are concerned, would you say you have a great deal of confidence, Only some confidence, or hardly any confidence at all in them?
Banks and financial institutions?

	White	Black	Other
A great deal	25.7%	25.7%	25.4%
Only some	57.4	50.4	52.3
Hardly any	15.2	20	17.7
Don't know	1.7	3.9	4.6
(N)	**1497**	**280**	**130**
Major companies?			
A great deal	28.4%	14.3%	26.2%
Only some	55.3	62.1	57.7
Hardly any	12	17.5	10.8
Don't know	4.2	6.1	5.4
(N)	**1498**	**280**	**130**
Organized religion?			
A great deal	27.1%	28%	21.5%
Only some	50.5	51.6	57.7
Hardly any	19.3	17.2	16.2
Don't know	3.1	3.2	4.6
(N)	**1496**	**279**	**130**
Education?			
A great deal	24.2%	38.4%	32.3%
Only some	57.1	45.5	56.9
Hardly any	17.5	15.4	8.5
Don't know	1.2	.7	2.3
(N)	**1495**	**279**	**130**
Executive branch of the federal government?			
A great deal	12.6%	16.1%	23.8%
Only some	46.5	52.5	51.5
Hardly any	38.2	26.8	19.2
Don't know	2.7	4.6	5.4
(N)	**1495**	**280**	**130**
Organized labor?			
A great deal	11.0%	10.0%	13.1%
Only some	50.5	52.1	64.6
Hardly any	30.9	25.7	16.2
Don't know	7.5	12.1	6.2
(N)	**1497**	**280**	**130**
Press?			
A great deal	8.5%	12.5%	10.8%
Only some	46.4	44.6	44.6
Hardly any	42.8	41.1	40.0
Don't know	2.3	1.8	4.6
(N)	**1498**	**280**	**130**
Medicine?			
A great deal	44.5%	43.6%	43.8%
Only some	45.6	44.3	45.4
Hardly any	8.3	10.7	10.0
Don't know	1.7	1.4	0.8
(N)	**1495**	**280**	**130**
Television?			
A great deal	9.3%	12.9%	16.2%
Only some	48.9	50.7	47.7
Hardly any	40.2	34.3	35.4
Don't know	1.6	2.1	0.8
(N)	**1497**	**280**	**130**
U.S. Supreme Court?			
A great deal	32.9%	23.6%	26.2%
Only some	49.9	49.3	50.8
Hardly any	12.8	20.7	13.8
Don't know	4.4	6.4	9.2
(N)	**1495**	**280**	**130**

I5.2. Confidence in People Running Social Institutions *(continued)*

	White	Black	Other
Scientific community?			
A great deal	42.5%	25.0%	38.5%
Only some	43.6	53.2	41.5
Hardly any	6.5	13.2	11.5
Don't know	7.4	8.6	8.5
(N)	**1495**	**280**	**130**
Congress?			
A great deal	10.1%	11.1%	13.8%
Only some	56.3	55.6	56.9
Hardly any	30.7	30.5	20.8
Don't know	2.9	2.9	8.5
(N)	**1495**	**279**	**130**
Military?			
A great deal	36.7%	32.1%	38.5%
Only some	49.2	50.0	39.2
Hardly any	11.7	14.6	16.2
Don't know	2.4	3.2	6.2
(N)	**1496**	**280**	**130**

Source: General Social Survey, 1998.

I5.3. How Serious is the Social Security Problem?

Please tell me which of the following statements comes closest to your opinion about the Social Security program . . .

	White	Black	Other
No problems	3.9%	6.9%	13.9%
Minor problems	22.3	31.4	20.3
Serious problems	57.4	45.1	44.3
Should be replaced	16.4	16.6	21.5
(N)	**1046**	**175**	**79**

Source: General Social Survey, 1998.

I5.4. Cheating the Government

Consider the situations listed below. Do you feel it is wrong or not wrong if...
A taxpayer does not report all of his income in order to pay less income taxes?

	White	Black	Other	Total
Always wrong	4.5%	5.4%	7.1%	4.8%
Almost always wrong	10.1	12.8	13.1	10.7
Wrong only sometimes	52.7	54.4	45.2	52.3
Not wrong at all	32.7	27.5	34.5	32.2
(N)	**959**	**149**	**84**	**1192**
A person gives the government incorrect information about himself to get government benefits that he is not entitled to?				
Always wrong	1.3%	4.0%	3.4%	1.8%
Almost always wrong	2.2	4.0	6.8	2.8
Wrong only sometimes	41.4	47.3	31.8	41.5
Not wrong at all	55.0	44.7	58.0	54.0
(N)	**992**	**150**	**88**	**1230**

Source: General Social Survey, 1998.

I5.5. Attitudes about Life

	White	Black	Other
There is little that people can do to change the course of their lives.			
Strongly agree	2.6%	7.4%	6.8%
Agree	6.1	13.5	13.6
Neither	6.6	10.1	10.2
Disagree	45.9	43.2	31.8
Strongly disagree	38.7	25.7	37.5
(N)	**950**	**148**	**88**
In my opinion, life does not serve any purpose.			
Strongly agree	0.7%	0.7%	1.2%
Agree	2.4	1.4	4.8
Neither	6.0	7.5	8.3
Disagree	35.4	36.1	44.0
Strongly disagree	55.4	54.4	41.7
(N)	**944**	**147**	**84**
Life is only meaningful if you provide meaning yourself.			
Strongly agree	10.0%	12.4%	16.7%
Agree	35.3	35.2	42.9
Neither	18.5	20.7	19.0
Disagree	22.5	16.6	19.0
Strongly disagree	13.7	15.2	2.4
(N)	**936**	**145**	**84**
We each make our own fate.			
Strongly agree	16.0%	17.1%	27.6%
Agree	43.6	42.5	42.5
Neither	20.8	18.5	16.1
Disagree	12.5	15.1	10.3
Strongly disagree	7.0	6.8	3.4
(N)	**942**	**146**	**87**

Source: General Social Surveys, 1998.

I5.6. Trust in People

	White	Black	Other
How often do you think that people would try to take advantage of you if they got the chance and how often would they try to be fair?			
Advantage all time	7.5%	23.3%	18.8%
Advantage most time	23.5	42.7	37.6
Fair most time	54.5	23.3	29.4
Fair all time	14.4	10.7	14.1
(N)	**956**	**150**	**85**
Generally speaking, would you say that people can be trusted or that you can't be too careful in dealing with people?			
Always trusted	5.2%	6.4%	7.0%
Usually trusted	49.9	17.9	27.9
Usually not trusted	37.2	59.6	45.3
Always not trusted	7.7	16.0	19.8
(N)	**974**	**156**	**86**

Source: General Social Surveys, 1998.

I6. RACIAL ATTITUDES

I6.1. Beliefs about the State of Race Relations in the United States, by Race: 1998

Percentage who believe race relations are:	Whites	Blacks
Very good or somewhat good	39%	26%
Neither good nor bad	22%	17%
Somewhat bad or very bad	37%	55%
(N)	**828**	**108**

Source: The Galllup Poll Monthly, May 1998, p.15.

I6.2. Percentage of Blacks and Whites Who Say Race Relations Are Very Good, Somewhat Good, Neither Good nor Bad, Somewhat Bad, or Very Bad, 1998.

	Total	Whites	Blacks
Very good	5%	6%	4%
Somewhat good	34%	35%	27%
Neither good nor bad	23%	24%	17%
Somewhat bad	28%	27%	32%
Very bad	9%	7%	19%
No answer	1%	1%	1%
	100%	100%	100%

Notes:
N=2010, 1654 Whites and 203 Blacks.

Source: The Gallup Poll Monthly, June 1998, p. 28.

I6.3. Have Conditions for Blacks Improved?

In the past few years, do you think conditions for Black people have improved, gotten worse, or stayed about the same?

	White	Black	Other
Improved	67.3%	41.7%	48.8%
Gotten worse	4.1	11.0	3.9
About the same	23.8	44.5	39.4
Don't know	4.8	2.8	7.9
(N)	**1484**	**254**	**127**

Source: General Social Surveys, 1998.

I6.4. Trends in Perception of Racial Equality, by Race: 1963-1995.

In general, do you think Blacks have as good a chance as Whites in your community to get any kind of job for which they are qualified, or don't you think they have as good a chance?

	Yes	No	No Opinion
1995			
Whites	68%	27%	5%
Blacks	36%	62%	2%
1993			
Whites	70%	27%	3%
Blacks	30%	66%	4%
1963			
Whites	46%	44%	10%
Blacks	24%	74%	2%

Source: The Gallup Poll Monthly, March 1995, p. 46.

I6.5. Percentage of Blacks and Whites Who Say Our Nation Is Moving toward Two Societies: One Black, One White—Separate and Unequal, 1968 and 1998.

	Agree	Disagree	No Opinion
Whites			
1998 Jun 5-7	23%	74%	3%
1968	36%	52%	12%
Blacks			
1998 Jun 5-7	45%	47%	8%
1968	31%	49%	20%
Notes:			
N=ca. 1000, 905 Whites, and 95 Blacks.			

Source: The Gallup Poll Monthly, June 1998 p.28

I6.6. Percentage of Blacks and Whites Who Think a New Race Initiative is Needed to Improve Race Relations in This Country

	Needed	Not Needed	No opinion	No. of Interviews
Race				
White	43%	54%	3%	1654
Black	59%	35%	6%	203

Source: The Gallup Poll Monthly, May 1998 p. 14

I6.7. Percentage of Blacks and Whites Who Believe Legislation Should Be Passed That Officially Apologizes to Blacks for Slavery

	Should	Should Not	No Opinion	No. of Interviews
Race				
White	27%	67%	6%	838
Black	66%	31%	3%	109

Source: The Gallup Poll Monthly, July 1997 p. 22

I6.8. Attitudes toward Black-White Relations

Some people say that because of past discrimination, Blacks should be given preference in hiring and promotion. Others say that such preferences in hiring and promotion of Blacks is wrong because it discriminates against Whites. What about your opinion—are you for or against preferential hiring and promotion of Blacks?			
	White	**Black**	**Other**
Strongly support preference	5.2%	21%	9.4%
Support preference	4.8	13.5	9.4
Oppose preference	22.9	21.0	26.8
Strongly oppose preference	60.2	32.1	44.1
Don't know	6.9	12.3	10.2
(N)	**1474**	**252**	**127**

Source: General Social Surveys, 1998.

I6.9. Should Blacks Overcome Prejudice Without Favors?

Do you agree strongly, agree somewhat, neither agree not disagree, disagree somewhat, or disagree strongly with the following statement: the Irish, Italians, Jews, and many other minorities overcame prejudice and worked their way up. Blacks should do the same without special favors.

	White	Black	Other
Agree strongly	45.4%	22.9%	41.7%
Agree somewhat	29.9	23.7	27.6
Neither agree nor disagree	10.9	18.6	13.4
Disagree somewhat	8.0	12.3	7.1
Disagree strongly	4.1	17.4	6.3
Don't know	1.7	5.1	3.9
(N)	**1484**	**253**	**127**

Source: General Social Survey, 1998.

I6.10. Does Affirmative Action Hurt Whites?

What do you think the chances are these days that a White person won't get a job or promotion while an equally or less qualified Black person gets one instead?

	White	Black	Other
Very likely	20.9%	11.1%	18.9%
Somewhat likely	50.7	25.6	39.3
Not very likely	25.9	58.8	34.4
Don't know	2.4	4.6	7.4
(N)	**1470**	**262**	**122**

Source: General Social Survey, 1998.

I6.11. Feelings about Living in an Interracial Neighborhood

Would you please tell me whether you would be very much in favor of it happening, somewhat in favor, neither in favor nor opposed to it happening, somewhat opposed, or very much opposed to it happening. Living in an interracial neighborhood?

	White	Black	Other
Strongly favor	7.0%	35.7%	14.3%
Favor	12.2	17.5	16.7
Neither favor nor oppose	47.0	36.9	41.3
Oppose	22.2	5.2	11.1
Strongly oppose	10.5	3.2	15.1
Don't know	1.2	1.6	1.6
(N)	**1478**	**252**	**126**

Source: General Social Survey, 1998.

I6.12. Attitude toward Relatives Marrying a Black Person

How would you feel about having a close relative or family member marry a Black person?

	White	Black	Other
Strongly favor	7.5%	44.2%	22.8%
Favor	9.6	13.9	15.7
Neither favor nor oppose	40.9	33.1	38.6
Oppose	19.3	4.0	13.4
Strongly oppose	22.0	3.6	7.9
Don't know	0.7	1.2	1.6
(N)	**1482**	**251**	**127**

Source: General Social Survey, 1998.

Table I6.13. Attitudes toward Black-White Marriages

Do you think there should be laws against marriages between (Negroes/Blacks/African-Americans) and Whites?			
	White	**Black**	**Other**
Yes	12.5%	4.2%	4.8%
No	84.6	93.9	93.5
Don't know	2.9	1.9	1.6
(N)	**1491**	**264**	**124**

Source: General Social Survey, 1998

I6.14. Closeness to Blacks and Whites

In general, how close do you feel to Blacks?			
	White	**Black**	**Other**
Not at all close	7.5%	1.2%	4.1%
2	4.6	3.1	7.4
3	5.3	3.5	7.4
4	4.8	0.8	3.3
Neither one nor the other	47.3	18.5	38.0
6	8.1	4.2	5.8
7	11.4	6.6	8.3
8	4.1	10.4	7.4
Very close	5.6	48.6	17.4
Don't know	1.3	3.1	0.8
(N)	**1487**	**259**	**121**
In general, how close do you feel to Whites?			
Not at all close	0.8%	3.4%	2.5%
2	0.8	1.5	1.7
3	0.8	5.7	1.7
4	1.3	4.2	4.2
Neither one nor the other	28.7	39.4	35.8
6	7.1	9.1	10.0
7	15.8	10.6	10.0
8	12.7	9.1	8.3
Very close	30.8	15.5	22.5
Don't know	1.3	1.5	3.3
(N)	**1459**	**264**	**120**

Source: General Social Survey, 1998.

I6.15. Characteristics of Racial Groups

Where would you rate Whites in general on this scale, as to whether people in the group tend to be hard-working or if they tend to be lazy?

Whites	White	Black	Other
Hardworking	4.1%	5.2%	8.6%
2	11.3	6.7	14.1
3	24.0	20.2	28.1
4	46.9	42.1	33.6
5	7.5	13.1	6.3
6	2.6	5.2	2.3
Lazy	0.4	3.6	1.6
Don't know	3.3	4.0	5.5
(N)	**1481**	**252**	**128**
Blacks?			
Hardworking	.7%	8.3%	1.6%
2	4.0	9.5	4.7
3	12.5	15.1	15.6
4	46.3	41.7	37.5
5	20.7	13.9	14.8
6	9.1	5.2	12.5
Lazy	2.6	2.8	7.0
Don't know	4.2	3.6	6.3
(N)	**1480**	**252**	**128**

Do people in these groups tend to be unintelligent or tend to be intelligent?

Whites?	White	Black	Other
Unintelligent	0.3%	1.2%	1.6%
2	2.0	4.0	3.1
3	7.4	8.3	4.7
4	43.5	39.3	36.7
5	21.9	24.2	17.2
6	15.8	9.5	18.0
Intelligent	4.5	9.9	12.5
Don't know	4.6	3.6	6.3
(N)	**1480**	**252**	**128**
Blacks?			
Unintelligent	0.5%	1.6%	0.8%
2	3.9	2.4	6.3
3	11.3	8.3	14.8
4	52.1	42.9	39.8
5	17.1	25.8	20.3
6	8.2	7.1	7.0
Intelligent	2.0	9.1	3.9
Don't know	0.5	2.8	7.0
(N)	**1479**	**252**	**128**

Source: General Social Survey, 1998.

I6.16. Racial Makeup of Workplace

Are people who work where you work all White, mostly White, about half and half, mostly Black, or all Black?			
	White	**Black**	**Other**
All White	32.5%	15.5%	20.5%
Mostly White	49.7	30.5	43.4
Half White-Black	14.0	35.6	27.7
Mostly Black	2.0	12.6	4.8
All Black	0.4	5.2	—
Don't Work	1.3	0.6	3.6
(N)	**990**	**174**	**83**

Source: General Social Survey, 1998

I6.17. Explanations for Racial Differences

On the average (Negroes/Blacks/African-Americans) have worse jobs, income, and housing than White people. Do you think the differences are . . .			
	White	**Black**	**Other**
Mainly due to discrimination?			
Yes	30%	59.1%	47.7%
No	63.8	35.0	43.0
Don't know	6.2	5.9	9.4
(N)	**1482**	**254**	**128**
Because most (Negroes/Blacks/African-Americans) have less in-born ability to learn?			
Yes	9.6%	9.1%	10.2%
No	86.3	89.3	81.3
Don't know	4.2	1.6	8.6
(N)	**1484**	**253**	**128**
Because most (Negroes/Blacks/African-Americans) don't have the chance for education that it takes to rise out of poverty?			
Yes	40.8%	55.5%	42.2%
No	54.4	41.3	50.0
Don't know	4.8	3.1	7.8
(N)	**1484**	**254**	**128**
Because most (Negroes/Blacks/African-Americans) just don't have the motivation or will power to pull themselves up out of poverty?			
Yes	42.7%	36%	52.3%
No	48.5	58.5	37.5
Don't know	8.8	5.5	10.2
(N)	**1481**	**253**	**128**

Source: General Social Survey, 1998.

Index

by Linda Webster

Tim B. Heaton, Ph.D., is professor of sociology, Center for Studies of the Family, Brigham Young University. He has coauthored a number of books and articles on cultural and societal demographics.

Bruce A. Chadwick, Ph.D., is professor of sociology at Brigham Young University in Provo, Utah, where he has served as department chairperson, director of the Family Studies Program, and director of the Center for Studies of the Family. He is a recipient of the Karl G. Maeser Research Award in recognition of his distinguished research career. Chadwick is the author of several books and numerous articles on many sociological topics including the family and race and ethnic relations. Chadwick received his bachelor's, master's, and Ph.D. degrees in sociology from Washington University in St. Louis, Missouri.

Cardell K. Jacobson is professor of sociology at Brigham Young University where he does research and teaches classes on social psychology, race and ethnic relations, and social problems. Recent articles written by him have focused on denominational and racial/ethnic differences in fatalism, religiosity and prejudice, correlates of intergroup marriage, and persistent intentions to be childless. His last book was *American Families: Issues in Race and Ethnicity*. He was recently awarded an Alcuin award for teaching in general education at Brigham Young University.

WITHDRAWAL